International Succession

CW01498037

Edited by
Louis Garb

KLUWER LAW INTERNATIONAL

THE HAGUE / LONDON / NEW YORK

Published by:
Kluwer Law International,
P.O. Box 85889, 2508 CN The Hague, The Netherlands.
sales@kluwerlaw.com
http://www.kluwerlaw.com

Sold and distributed in North, Central and South America by:
Aspen Publishers, Inc.
7201 McKinney Circle
Frederick, MD 21704
USA

Sold and distributed in all other countries by:
Extenza-Turpin Distribution Services
Blackhorse Road
Letchworth
Herts
SG6 1HN
United Kingdom

A C.I.P. Catalogue record for this book is available from the Library of Congress.

Printed on acid-free paper

ISBN 90 411 0781 9

Printed in the Netherlands.

INTERNATIONAL SUCCESSION

Table of Contents

v

Table of Contents

Table of Contents

Preface

In modern times, more and more, people are becoming citizens of the world. Gone are the days of strict separation across national borders. Some of the factors contributing to this new global village phenomenon are positive ones like the development of modern technology. Others are negative, like mass migrations caused by war and persecution. All, however, have significantly broken down the barriers imposed by national borders. One consequence is that it has become common for people to build estates in more than one country. The effect of this right of succession is often complex and one which lawyers, let alone heirs, find bewildering.

This publication provides up-to-date information on succession laws in a substantial number of countries. Each country report will be based on responses to uniform and comprehensive questionnaires. I have no doubt that the work will be of considerable value to legal practitioners in many countries.

This is a useful companion to the editor's work on *Enforcement of Foreign Judgments* and he is to be congratulated on his initiative.

Richard J. Goldstone
Justice of the Constitutional Court of South Africa

Introduction

The advent of the European Economic Community (EEC), now the European Union, in the mid 1950s, enormously accelerated the movement of populations between European nations. In the decade leading up to the new millennium, this has risen to unprecedented levels, fuelled by the internationalization of businesses, the increasing affluence of the Western world, extended periods of peace (in the developed Western countries at any rate), the progressive removal of barriers, reliable transportation and the portability of jobs. Indeed, foreign travel is now within the reach, both from the point of view of time and affordability, of a large proportion of the population of Western Europe.

The problem is not new. In 1907, Dr. Ernest Schuster wrote:

> 'The steady expansion of international commercial dealings, the greater frequency of marriages between members of different nationalities, and the constantly growing number of causes facilitating and widening changes of domicile on the part of persons engaged in mercantile, industrial or scientific pursuits, have largely increased the number of the occasions on which English lawyers have to consult an advocate practising in the country of which the law has to be applied, and in ordinary commercial cases that course, no doubt, has many advantages. But in cases where questions arise as to matters on which the conceptions of English law differ materially from those of continental law (e.g., as to the validity of marriages, the effect of marriage on property, as to settlements and trusts, as to the nature and effects of testamentary dispositions, as to the powers of appointment and similar topics) the communication between English and foreign lawyers, as experience shows, frequently leads to difficulty and misunderstanding. For this reason a knowledge of the main principles of foreign law is of direct practical advantage to any practitioner who is likely to have to deal with international questions.'[1]

If this was true in 1907, it is vitally so today. Demographics in the latter half of the 20th century have led to an explosion in purchases of secondary homes overseas. This will surely lead to a corresponding increase in the number of estates that have a foreign element.

To a certain extent, this has been foreseen. The *Hague Convention of 20 October 1988* was elaborated, after much detailed work, to deal with these very points. Alas,

---

1. E.G. Schuster, *The Principles of German Civil Law.*

1

nearly 10 years later, it is a matter of regret that the Convention has not passed into the internal law of the countries where these problems will arise with ever greater frequency, although there are currently initiatives to bring some or all of its provisions into force in a handful of countries.

This work will be an invaluable tool for practitioners seeking to grapple, often at short notice, with differing, complicated and foreign concepts of law, of practice, and of title.

A majority of countries in the world, and an overwhelming majority of countries in the Western world, have adopted rules and laws based either on the common law of England or on the 'Code Napoléon' promulgated in France on 21 March 1804 (previously the 30th Ventose in the year XII) as their general legal system. The 'Code Napoléon' has been, and is still today, adopted as a system of law by many nations of differing backgrounds and stages of development. The common law of England flourishes, it is generally agreed, only in those countries to which it was taken by conquerors, colonizers or where there was a substantial English sphere of influence. All the countries in Western Continental Europe (with the exception of the Scandinavian countries, the United Kingdom of Great Britain and the Republic of Ireland) have, on the other hand, adopted a codified system of laws, based to a greater or lesser degree on the 'Code Civil' of 1804.

In the words of Professor Neville Brown:

> 'The influence of the French Civil Code has been great in Europe; it has dominated Baden and the Prussian Rhine provinces for nearly a hundred years; the Codes of Belgium and Luxembourg follow it, in many titles, almost literally; its spirit is conspicuous in the Codes of the Netherlands, Italy, Spain and Portugal; and beyond the seas in Egypt, in South America, in Louisiana, in Lower Canada, the lawyer conversant with the formulae and the institutions of French law will find himself at home. Throughout these wide regions it is not too much to say that divergences from the French law, where they are to be found, are deliberate and exceptional, while the resemblances are unconscious and therefore normal and all-pervasive.'[2]

THE COMMON LAW OF ENGLAND

The common law of England is difficult to define in a brief introduction, but can be explained by contrast with statute law, contrast with equity (q.v. below), contrast with local customary law and of course contrast with civil or international law.

The common law was built up year by year, decade on decade, century on century, by custom, by decided cases in the Superior Courts ('precedents') and ultimately a body of Laws decided in the Supreme Court of Appeal, which is the House of Lords, whose decision is final. The whole body of English Law is just a mass of case law. Nevertheless, even in the 19th century, there was an ever

---

2. Neville Brown, *Introduction to French Law*, 3rd edition, p. 5.

increasing volume of statute law dealing with and regulating specific topics. *The Bills of Exchange Act 1882*, the *Sale of Goods Act 1893*, and the *Law of Property Act 1925*, are all examples of statute legislation which still have direct application today.

The development of the common law brought many benefits to England, and to many other countries which adopted it as a basis for their laws. Although they tried to, and often did, change the common law, judges in the common law systems were, and continue to be, wholly independent of the State and have long regarded the common law as supreme and unchangeable by any authority other than themselves. Indeed, in the Middle Ages, it was the judges, rather than Parliament, who legislated in matters of civil rights and criminal liabilities. Until the advent of the European Economic Community, the common law was relatively free from foreign influences and was the embodiment of the English (and American) genius for the practical, as opposed to the theoretical.

'CODE NAPOLÉON – THE CIVIL CODE

Originally called the 'Code Napoléon', renamed 'Code Civil', it was the intention of its authors that it should be interpreted only by reference to itself and its own definitions. The final article of the Law of 39 Ventose An XII consolidated thirty-six already voted Acts into a single Code. The authors of the Code, to generalize, fused many facets of ancient French law and French revolutionary law into a single whole. Of course it had defects and omissions: it did not give personal property the importance it acquired in the course of the 19th century, it did not deal with the rights of employers and employees, it did not deal with insurance. Over the years many revisions were made to it.

France, for at least a century before its revolution, in the view of many, had been the leading nation in the world. The French language was on the verge of succeeding Latin as the common speech of educated men; French literature, arts, culture, splendour, had no equal. Yet pre-revolutionary French law had no admirers nor imitators in other countries. The Civil Code, when it appeared, was, and is, widely copied.

French law, it could be said, is governed and influenced to a far lesser extent by the spirit of history than is the common law of England. Far greater weight is given in a French judgement, as compared to an English one, to *ratio legis*. The common lawyer seeks to interpret a legal principle in the best interests of his client, and will first look to its pedigree. The civil lawyer will look first to its policy.

The Civil Code does not stand alone: the Code of Civil Procedure was promulgated in 1906, the Code of Commerce in 1908, the Code of Criminal Procedure in 1911 and the Criminal Code also in 1911. All have been frequently amended, modified and even replaced. There are the other Codes dealing with agriculture, nationality, companies and many other matters.

Both systems of law are, in Europe, now being influenced to a major degree by the applicability of a third body and source of law: Community law, but this is another subject altogether and beyond the scope of this introduction.

International Succession

The Common Law

Private international law covers broadly four areas:

(a) the nationality of a person or company and problems arising therefrom;
(b) foreigners and foreign entities and their rights in inward and outward transactions;
(c) the conflict of laws, which is to say which law will prevail where there is a conflict and/or a different approach and/or solution to a problem;
(d) conflicts of jurisdiction.

In English private international law the three most important sources are: (1) statutes, (2) decisions of the Court, (3) the opinions of lawyers, in descending order of importance. Statutes are also promulgated to facilitate the enforcement of judgements (the Brussels Convention for example) and deal specifically with various points.

Succession to immovable property is governed by the law of the situs, the formal validity of a marriage is governed by the place of its celebration, and capacity to marry is governed by the law of the antenuptial domicile of each party. Technically speaking this illustrates the categories of private international law where the situs of immovables, the place of celebration of marriage and the domicile of the parties are the connecting factors. In private international law terms the *lex causae* is the expression which denotes the law which covers the matter. A fundamental problem is that it is often difficult to ascertain whether the connecting factor in any private international law problem should be governed by the *lex fori* which is the domestic or internal law of the country in question, or by the *lex causae*, including the private international law rules.

The Civil Law

French private international law has different sources, i.e., '*sources internes*' – the Civil Code, the Code of Civil Procedure and other '*lois*' – and '*sources internationales*' which are, for example, decisions of the International Court in The Hague and international conventions and agreements.

The private international law system of one country usually differs from the private international law of all other countries. Conflicts of law are gradually being harmonized by the various national governments, and internationally by the Commission in Brussels (for European Union members) and The Hague Conference (among others). They continue however to exercise the ingenuity of lawyers and provide much work for the courts. Areas where serious conflicts of law remain include insolvencies, liquidations and bankruptcies, the rights of minor children, succession and property.

International estates cover many subjects: domicile, wills, testamentary freedom, matrimonial regimes, deeds of variation, and trusts. International estates are also subject to different procedural requirements, country by country.

A short introduction to the above concepts may be useful to the reader.

Domicile under Common Law

Civil domicile has been developed by custom and precedent over many years. In English law, everyone must have a domicile, but no-one can have, at any one time, more than one domicile. At birth everyone receives a domicile of origin, which, for a legitimate child, is the domicile of the father at birth. There are other rules for other circumstances. Domicile does not depend on the place where a person is born, nor on the place where the mother and father reside, but on the domicile of the appropriate parent at the time of birth. Thus a domicile of origin may be transmitted through several generations, even though no member of the family has ever resided for any length of time in the country of the domicile of origin. A person can only acquire a domicile of choice by a combination of actual residence in the country of choice and by the intention to reside there indefinitely. Domicile of dependency exists where, as once was the rule, a married woman is obliged to take the domicile of her husband (she can now acquire a separate domicile). For tax and/or inheritance tax purposes, there are other concepts of domicile contained in the various double tax treaties which provide tie-breaker rules destined to resolve conflicts where persons reside in, or own houses in, two or more treaty countries.

Civil Law Domicile

Civil domicile is governed by Article 102 of the French Civil Code which states that 'the domicile of any French person, as to the exercise of his/her civil rights, is the place where he/she is principally established.' Article 103 provides that a change of domicile is made by taking up actual residence in another place, coupled with the intention to make the same his/her principal establishment.

Domicile in the civil law sense should be contrasted with the English concept of domicile.

The Common Law

In English law, a will is a written document in which a testator makes certain provisions which will only take effect on death. Wills in England are almost invariably typewritten, in printed form or produced by computer. By comparison with holograph or authentic wills commonly found in civil law countries, English wills tend to be long and complicated.

The Civil Law

These are generally the holograph will, written out, signed and dated in the hand-writing of the testator but otherwise not usually subject to any particular form, and the authentic will made by public instrument before a notary. Certain countries permit other types of wills. Austria and Switzerland permit oral wills, France permits mystic and privileged wills in certain exceptional circumstances. A number of countries such as Austria, Germany, Greece, Holland, Italy, Portugal and Spain permit conjunctive wills.

INTESTACY

The Common Law

As a general rule, the legal devolution of assets belonging to a person dying intestate, tends under the English system to favour the surviving spouse if there is one. Thus if the deceased leaves one or several children and a surviving spouse, the surviving spouse will take the first £125,000 or equivalent value in the estate, net of inheritance tax, and all the personal assets of the deceased. In addition, a surviving spouse will receive a life interest in one half of the remainder of the estate. The surviving spouse is also favoured from the inheritance tax point of view. In most cases there is no inheritance tax payable between spouses (surviving spouse exemption).

The Civil Law

The order in intestate successions tends to be different from the English, but varies from country to country. Thus civil law countries vary as to who inherits under intestacy and what share (if any) a surviving spouse takes in the presence of children. Generally speaking, the primary beneficiaries under an intestacy in civil law countries are the surviving spouse and children, extending to descendants, collaterals to the fourth degree or further.

TESTAMENTARY FREEDOM AND THE LEGAL RESERVE (*PORTIO LEGITIMA*)

The Common Law

English law, and the various laws deriving from it, do not generally provide for any legal reserve or *portio legitima*. Thus a testator is free, in principle, to leave his or her estate to his/her children, to his/her spouse, to his mistress, to a charity, or if one wishes to be frivolous, to his dog. Inheritance tax is levied on an estate, not on any particular beneficiary. Thus the closeness or relationship by blood or marriage to a deceased is not, and never has been, of relevance in the English system. In the civil law, various categories of heir or beneficiary are liable to pay different rates of inheritance tax depending on their blood or marital relationship with the deceased.

The category of persons who benefit under the English family provision rules is much wider than the typical legal reserve of the Civil Code system. In addition the right has to be claimed; it is not automatic.

The Civil Law

Many countries in the civil law system limit the capacity of a testator to some extent, often in favour of children, and sometimes in favour of surviving spouses, by means of a statutory legal reserve or *portio legitima*. The private international law rules of each country will determine whether the *portio legitima* will apply to foreigners owning properties in that country, and this too varies. France, for example, applies the *lex rei sitae* rule for immovables in its territory, while Spain makes a *renvoi* to the nationality of the property owner.

MATRIMONIAL REGIMES

In English law marriage has no effect on the property or assets belonging to spouses, present or future. In reality English law does not actually apply any regime, but since marriage has no effect on property, the system in England is the equivalent of separation. In civil law countries, spouses are often married under a community system whether absolute or partial, but, as we have seen, testamentary freedom is often curtailed by a legal reserve. Perhaps the rights of the surviving spouse in the common law system mirrors the rights given to spouses under the matrimonial regime imposed by law, but things do not always work as neatly as that, especially where a cross-border transaction is concerned.

In estate planning in England, a will will be a central part of advice given to a client. Typically an estimate will be made of the contents and scope of the wealth that will fall into the estate. Consideration will also be given to how much and what assets should be left to the surviving spouse, what (if anything) is appropriate to pass to a charitable institution (and consequently to avoid or mitigate inheritance tax). The assets which will comprise the estate will be identified, classified, and a preliminary inheritance tax calculation will be done. Crucially, the likely last domicile of the person concerned will have to be determined. By virtue of a document known as a 'deed of variation', the beneficiaries named in a will or the legal beneficiaries in an intestate estate can vary the terms of a will or vary the legal devolution in an intestacy but must do so within two years from the date of death and the new provisions shall be considered as if they were made by the testator in the original will, or were imposed by law in an intestate estate.

Estate planning in civil law countries has in the past been generally held to be less well developed (with some notable exceptions) than in the common law countries, although the subject is now getting the attention in civil law countries that it deserves.

TESTAMENTARY EXECUTORS OF AN ESTATE

The Common Law

One of the great differences between English law and those systems of law based on it, and the laws of countries that have adopted the civil code system is that under the common law, a deceased person is deemed to have, after death, a personal representative who will act in his place and stead. This personal representative will either be the executor if appointed by will, or an administrator if there is no executor appointed in the will or under an intestacy.

In common law systems executors or administrators are *ipso facto* vested in possession of movable and immovable assets of the deceased from the moment of death. For movables and immovables situate outside the jurisdiction of the English Courts, the position is different as movables are vested in the executor/administrator from the moment when they are repatriated. Immovables situate abroad cannot be vested as they are immovable by nature. Thus under the rules of English private international law there is a *renvoi* by English law to the *lex rei sitae* of immovables situate outside of England.

The principal duties of a testamentary executor or administrator are to get in the assets and the liabilities of the estate, to complete and deal with the administration, pay the inheritance tax due, deliver out the legacies, and make any gifts laid down in the will or under the legal devolution. When the administration is complete, the executor or administrator is discharged by the heirs and beneficiaries.

The Civil Law

Executors appointed in the civil law systems tend not to be vested in possession, except in special or unusual circumstances, and tend to have far fewer powers than the English executor. In Germany, for instance, under Article 2205 BGB a testamentary executor administers the estate and disposes of the assets therein. In France the powers of the executors are those expressed by the testator but the powers of executors cannot endure for more than one year from the date of death.

The procedures and formalities for obtaining a Grant of Probate or of Letters of Administration are to be contrasted with the notarial procedures where there is an act of notoriety or a certificate of heirs and no intermediate personal representative, as in the common law system. Assets are vested directly in certain categories of heirs, who have '*saisine*' and who must therefore comply either with the terms of any will and/or apply the mandatory provisions of law.

The Common Law

The person who usually deals with the winding up of estates will be a solicitor. The solicitor will not act in a neutral or official capacity, as will a notary, but has duties and liabilities to the client who may be either the beneficiaries of an estate or its executors and trustees.

The Civil Law

The person who deals with the winding up of estates in civil law countries is generally the notary who is a ministerial officer appointed by the Minister of Justice of the appropriate State and with delegation of some State powers. Notaries are invariably organised in Chambers or Notarial Institutes with either national or regional competence.

Trusts and Fiducie

The concept of a trust is entirely foreign to civil law countries, created as it was through the Courts of Equity, but it is of the utmost importance in international estates and international estate planning.

Trusts developed from the political and social difficulties in England in the 15th and 16th centuries and gradually penetrated the common law to attenuate the formalism and rigidity of the law as it then was. The notion of trust is difficult for a civil lawyer to comprehend. A trust cannot be, and should not be, defined in terms of civil or codified law. A trust, generally, may be defined as the relationship, or legal consequences, which arise when a trustee is bound to hold the legal ownership of one or more assets, on behalf of or for the account of one or several other persons (beneficiaries) in such a manner that the benefit thereof shall be received not by the trustee but by the beneficiaries of the trust. A trust is a relationship and a legal consequence; it is not a legal entity, it is not a company, nor is it a contract.

The proposed French '*loi de fiducie*' is based on a contractual relationship. A trust separates the notion of '*patrimoine*' from that of the legal person. Trust assets are separate both from the personal estate of the trustee and from the personal estate of the beneficiary.

Conclusion

This introduction has attempted to provide the reader with some preparation for the differences of law, standards, language and concepts that are the hallmark of international estates. Even though the laws and procedures between civil and common law countries are vastly different, and solutions to problems are diverse, the problems in international estates are mostly similar and so, surprisingly, are the end results.

International Succession

I am aware that this introduction contains many simplifications and generalizations which in turn can lead to error, but they were in my opinion necessary in the interests of brevity and for ease of understanding by readers in many and varied jurisdictions.

R.A.D. Urquhart
Scrivener Notary of the City of London
Avocat à la Cour de Paris

Questionnaire

Prepared by: Louis GARB

1. Type of System

(a) Civil law, common law or other (specifying closest to which system).

(b) Federal system? If so, indicate important differences in various states (if the differences are too many and significant, a separate chapter will be prepared for each different state or province).

2. Wills

(a) Forms of wills: Brief description of formalities for different types of will – will before witnesses, holographic wills, wills before notary or other authority, secret wills, privileged wills, death bed wills, etc.

(b) Amendment, revocation and revival:
  i. Methods of, including codicils.
  ii. Does marriage automatically revoke or in any other way affect wills made prior to marriage?
  iii. Revival of revoked will.

3. Intestacy

(a) What is the order of succession in cases of intestacy?

(b) Is there any difference in the division of the estate between movables and immovables?

4. Freedom of Testation

(a) Are there compulsory shares (i.e., *réserve héréditaire*, legitimate portions or minimum percentages/amounts (apart from maintenance) for husband/wife/common law wife, children – major/minor – out of wedlock/adopted, or others)?

11

International Succession

(b) *i.* Is a contract of inheritance (made prior to death) binding?

    ii. Do the concepts of partition (*partage*), anticipation (advance distribution), successor or family settlements (*pactes successoraux ou de famille*), exist?

5. Maintenance

Can maintenance be claimed from the estate or the heirs by husband/wife/minor children/parents or others?

6. Community Property Between Husband and Wife

(a) Which part or percentage of the deceased's estate, if any, is recognized as being that share of community property which does *not* form part of the estate and is not taken into account in the division of the estate between heirs?

(b) What is the effect of the matrimonial regime?

7. Gifts (*Inter Vivos*)

(a) Are gifts (to an heir) prior to death set off against the heir's inheritance?

(b) If so, to what limit?

8. Capacity

(a) Capacity of testator? Minimum age/marital status, etc.

(b) Capacity of witnesses? Relationship to deceased/beneficiary, etc.

(c) Capacity of beneficiary? E.g., minor, unborn, company.

9. Authority (Court, Notarial or Other)

Is an order of succession granted through the courts or by any other method, i.e., notary public or other authority?

10. Invalidity of Will

(a) What are the possible grounds for invalidity, e.g., defects in formalities, dispositions under fraud, duress, etc.

(b) Does the invalidity result in the will being void or voidable?

11. Simultaneous Death

(a) Which rules apply in the case of simultaneous death (including a situation where there is forced heirship)?

(b) How is the date of death of two or more potential testators/heirs determined if there is no external evidence? Are there any presumptions?

12. Estate Taxes

(a) Do they exist?

(b) Are they due on all assets worldwide or only on local assets?

(c) Who is taxed (i.e., heirs or estate)?

13. Administration of Estates

(a) Who administers estates? Is it essential to appoint an administrator or can the heirs administer the estate?

(b) Do estate reports have to be submitted and if so, by and to whom?

(c) What external supervision is there on the part of the authorities?

(d) Who has the right to query and object?

(e) How are assets handed over to the heirs?

(f) How do the creditors of the estate receive payment?

(g) How is distribution effected if the testator did not appoint an executor or grant *saisine*?

14. Domicile/Nationality

(a) Does the nationality or domicile of the deceased, either at time of death or at time of execution of a will, affect any of the above answers? (If so, state which answers.)

(b) Would the local court or authority grant an order of probate or succession if the deceased was domiciled and/or executed a will in the jurisdiction but had no assets there whatsoever?

International Succession

1. Jurisdiction

(a) In which circumstances would the local court hold that it had jurisdiction, e.g., local domicile at date of death, assets within the jurisdiction, etc.

(b) Are there different rules for movable and immovable assets?

(c) If local jurisdiction applies, which local court has jurisdiction?

2. Applicable Law

Which *law* does the local court apply – law of domicile at date of death or other?

3. Foreign Succession/Inheritance Orders

(a) Would foreign orders be enforced or recognized in respect of local assets (both movable and immovable)?

(b) Must a local succession/inheritance order be obtained or other local procedures followed in order to give effect to a foreign order as regards the local court, property registration office, bank or any other person in possession of assets of deceased?

(c) What are the formalities for obtaining recognition or enforcement of a foreign succession or inheritance order?

4. Two or More Succession or Probate Orders

In a case where there is an application before either the court or the relevant authority in the local country for an order of succession or inheritance, and a foreign order already exists in one or more foreign countries, what is the order of preference, or which prevails: domicile (as well as its relevant weight), citizenship, nationality or location of assets (movable or immovable).

5. Assets

If there are no assets whatsoever in the jurisdiction but some other connecting factors, e.g., domicile/citizenship/residence, could the local court assume jurisdiction?

6. Expert Evidence

(a) Is there any necessity for a foreign lawyer (or other) to give evidence regarding a foreign will which has been recognized by a foreign court, or regarding the inheritance laws of a foreign country?

(b) If so, can such evidence be by way of affidavit without the necessity of appearance in court?

7. Unity of Succession

Is this accepted in principle?

8. Formalities

Must the formalities of a will executed in a foreign country be the same as those in the local country for such will to be recognized or submitted for a succession order?

9. Legislation

Is the *Hague Convention on the Conflicts of Laws Relating to the Form of Testamentary Dispositions* applicable?

10. Wills

In case of conflicts or foreign factors, which law governs:

(a) Legal requirements for execution of wills, e.g., number of witnesses, execution of codicil.

(b) Construction/interpretation, e.g., of terminology used in the will, such as 'next of kin', etc.

(c) Rights of heirs/beneficiaries, e.g., minimum portion.

(d) Capacity to inherit.

(e) Capacity to make will.

(f) Essential or material validity of will or particular bequests, e.g., public policy/duress/legacy to witness.

15

International Succession

(g) Powers of appointment, i.e., where a person in his will nominates someone else who, in his own will, shall have the power to specify the ultimate recipient of the asset which is the subject matter of the original will.

(h) Amendment, revocation, revival.

(i) Applicability of laws regarding reserve to a non-resident in respect of movable/ immovable property.

11. Domicile/Nationality

(a) If the deceased's domicile or nationality determines any of the above answers, specify whether it is the domicile or nationality at the time of death or the time of making the will.

(b) Is the domicile of the beneficiary at all relevant to any of the answers in Section B?

(c) If domicile/nationality is unclear how is the question resolved?

12. Taxation

If there are estate taxes, would there be any differences between taxation for a non-resident deceased/heir as opposed to that of a local deceased/heir?

Country Reports

Argentina

Prepared by: Alberto D.Q. MOLINARIO
Marval, O'Farell & Mairal, Attorneys at Law

Address: Av. Leandro N. Alem 928
          1001 Buenos Aires
          Argentina
Tel.:   +54 1 310 0100
Fax: +54 1 310 0200
E-mail: adqm@marval.com.ar

SECTION A – BRIEF SURVEY OF THE LOCAL SYSTEM

1. Type of System

(a) Civil law.

(b) Although Argentina is a federal country, the law of successions is uniformly enacted by the National Congress, with the exception of procedural rules which are passed by the provincial legislature in each province and by the National Congress in the Federal District.

2. Wills

(a) The usual forms of testaments are: holographic, by public act and sealed (Section 3622 Civil Code). Military and maritime testaments are considered special forms of testaments with the peculiarity that they lapse if the testator survives certain periods set by the Civil Code.

Holographic Testament: A holographic testament must be entirely written, dated and signed by the testator himself (Section 3639 Civil Code) and must be executed as one or more documents independent from other writings and books which the testator may normally use to record his business (Section 3648 Civil Code).

Testament by Public Act: A testament by public act must be made in the presence of a notary public and three witnesses residing in the place where the testament is executed (Section 3654 Civil Code). The notary public must state the place and date of execution, the witnesses' names, age and residence and whether the notary public drafted the testament himself or received its dispositions in writing (Section 3657 Civil Code). The testament must be read to the testator in the presence of three witnesses, who must see him and must be signed by the testator, by the witnesses and by the notary public (Section 3658 Civil Code). In some special cases, the functions of the notary public may be performed by other persons (Sections 3636, 3655, 3689, 3690 Civil Code, Section 80 Aeronautical Code).

Sealed Testament: A sealed testament must be signed by the testator and delivered to the notary public in a sealed envelope in the presence of five witnesses residing in the place in which the delivery takes place. The notary public must certify the delivery of the testament by the testator, the testator's and witnesses' names, surnames and residence as well as the place and the date on which the act takes place on the envelope (Section 3666 Civil Code). The testator and the witnesses must sign on the envelope.

Military Testament: In time of war, military personnel on a military expedition, or in a besieged garrison, or in a barrack or in a garrison in a foreign country and volunteers, hostages or prisoners, military surgeons, quartermaster corps, chaplains, sutlers, scientists attached to the expedition and other persons accompanying or serving such persons may make a testament before an officer not below the rank of captain, or before an intendant of the army or the judge advocate (*auditor general*) and two witnesses. The testament must state the place and date in which it is made (Section 3672 Civil Code) and must be signed by the testator, by the officer before whom it is made and by the witnesses (Section 3674 Civil Code).

If the person wishing to make a testament is ill or wounded, he may execute it before the chaplain or the physician or the surgeon assisting him. If he is in a detachment, he may execute it before the officer in command thereof, even if he has a rank below that of a captain (Section 3673 Civil Code).

If the person able to make a military testament prefers to make a sealed testament, any of the persons before whom he could have executed an open testament may act as certifying officer (Section 3678 Civil Code). This will lapses 90 days after the state of war ends.

Maritime Testament: Persons on board a man-of-war of the Argentine Republic, whether or not officers or members of the crew, may execute a testament in the presence of the commander of the vessel and three witnesses. The testament must be dated and executed in two copies (Section 3679 Civil Code) and kept with the most important papers of the vessel. Mention thereof must be made in the log-book (Section 3680 Civil Code).

If the person able to make a maritime testament prefers to make a sealed one, the formalities prescribed for testaments of this type of testaments must be observed, the commander of the vessel or his second in command must act as certifying officer, in the presence of three witnesses (Section 3682 Civil Code).

On merchant vessels flying the Argentine flag, testaments may be made in the same form as on men-of-war, before the master, his first mate or the steersman (Section 3683 Civil Code). The maritime testament lapses if the testator survives 90 days after the end of the voyage.

(b) *i.* A testament may be revoked and amended at the will of the testator at any time before his death (Section 3824 Civil Code).

The revocation may be express or tacit (such as a subsequent testament incompatible with the first one) and it may be done either with regard to all or to part of the testament. In any case, the act that revokes or amends a testament must comply with the formalities required for testaments. In consequence, a codicil would not be valid under Argentine law unless it complies with the formalities required to be considered a testament in itself.

A testament is tacitly revoked on several grounds:

– By means of a subsequent testament that annuls the previous testament. The previous testament is only revoked in those provisions that are incompatible with the new testament (Section 3828 Civil Code).
– By the cancellation or destruction of a holographic testament by the testator himself, or by another person by his order, when there is but one original testament. If there are more than one, the testament is not revoked until all the originals have been destroyed or canceled (Section 3833 Civil Code).
– By the testator's breaking the envelope containing a sealed testament, even if the envelope containing the testament remains sound and the testament inside the envelope complies with the formalities required for holographic testaments (Section 3836 Civil Code).
– By the complete destruction of the testament by a fortuitous event or *force majeure* (Section 3837 Civil Code).

As said before, amendments to a testament may be made by means of a new testament, in which case the provisions of the previous testament that are not amended or that are not incompatible with the subsequent testament, remain in full force.

Amendments to a holographic testament may also be introduced in between lines, on the margin, by overwriting new dispositions, by erasing parts of the text, by crossing out sections, by tearing apart parts of the text, etc., as long as the essential parts of the testament are left intact. In these type of amendments, it is essential to ascertain the date in which they are made. If they are simultaneous to the testator's drafting of the testament, amendments do not require further formalities. If the amendments are introduced after the testament is made, they must observe the formalities required for holographic testaments (i.e., they should be signed and dated).

ii. A testament made by a person not married at the time the testament is made is automatically revoked when the person gets married (Section 3826 Civil Code).

iii. In the event a testament is revoked by means of a subsequent one, if the subsequent testament is declared void the previous testament revives (Section 3830 Civil Code), furthermore if the new dispositions contained in the subsequent testament are ineffective on account of the incapacity of the heirs or legatees, the previous testament revives.

A retractation in testamentary form by the maker of the subsequent testament revives his first dispositions without the necessity of an express declaration if the subsequent testament did not contain new dispositions. If the subsequent testament did contain new dispositions, it is disputed whether the testator needs to state his intention to revive the first testament upon executing his retractation of the subsequent testament (Sections 3828 and 3831 Civil Code).

3. Intestacy

(a) Intestate successions belong to the deceased's descendants, ascendants, spouse and relatives within the fourth degree inclusive pursuant to the following rules. If the estate is left vacant, it escheats to the federal or provincial states (Section 3545 Civil Code).

A relative nearer in degree to the deceased person excludes one more remote (Section 3546 Civil Code), without prejudice to the right of representation.

Representation: is the right whereby children in an ulterior degree are placed in the degree which their father or mother held in the family of the deceased person in order to succeed jointly in his or her place to the same share of the estate to which his father or mother would have succeeded (Section 3549 Civil Code). Representation causes the representatives to step in the rights which the person represented would have had in the succession if living, either to participate with the other relatives, or to exclude them (Section 3562 Civil Code). Only deceased persons who would have been called to the succession of the deceased person may be represented (Section 3556 Civil Code).

Representation is allowed without end in the direct descending line (grandparent – parent – grandchildren – great-grandchildren, etc.) (Section 3557 Civil Code) and is not admitted in favour of the ascendants, in which case, the nearest ascendant excludes the more remote (Section 3559 Civil Code). Representation also takes place in the collateral line only in favour of the children and descendants of brothers and sisters with the other coheirs standing in a nearer degree (Section 3560 Civil Code).

In all cases in which representation is allowed, the division of the estate is made *per stirpes*. If it has produced a number of branches, the subdivision is also made in each branch *per stirpes*, among the members of such branch (Section 3563 Civil Code).

The children of the deceased person inherit from him in their own right and share alike (Section 3565 Civil Code) without prejudice to the rights of the surviving spouse. Grandchildren and other descendants inherit from ascendants by right of representation (Section 3566 Civil Code).

Ascendants inherit when there are no descendants (Section 3567 Civil Code); if there is a surviving spouse the latter inherits half of the estate and the other half is inherited by the ascendants. If both father and mother of the deceased live, they inherit from the deceased and share alike (Section 3568 Civil Code). If only one of them lives, he/she inherits the entire estate even if there is another ascendant since representation does not occur in favour of ascendants (Section 3559 Civil Code). If the father and the mother of the deceased are dead, his/her ascendants nearest in degree inherit him and share alike (Section 3569 Civil Code).

These rules change if the deceased is married (please refer to answer 6).

If neither descendants nor ascendants, nor widow/widower survive, the collateral relatives of the deceased who are nearest in degree up to the fourth degree inclusive inherit.

Half brothers or sisters inherit half of what full brothers or sisters inherit (Section 3586 Civil Code).

Widows who have not married after their husband's death and who have not had any children (or if they have, are dead at the time of death of the widows' mother or father-in-law) are entitled to 1/4 of what their husbands would have received from their mother or father's succession (Section 3576bis).

(b) In principle, there is no difference in the division of the estate between movable and immovable property. However, it should be noted that immovable and movable assets permanently situated in Argentina are exclusively governed by Argentine law even if a succession is opened in a foreign country and subject to a foreign law (Section 10 Civil Code).

4. Freedom of Testation

(a) Legitimate portion is a right of succession limited to a specific portion of the deceased's estate. The capacity of the testator to make his testamentary dispositions with respect to his estate extends only to the amount above the legitimate portion which the law recognizes to his forced heirs (Section 3591 Civil Code) and as explained in answer 6 below in cases of married persons.

Forced heirs are the deceased's ascendants, descendants and spouse. They are all entitled to a legitimate portion following the order of succession explained in answer 3 (Section 3592 Civil Code).

The legitimate portion of forced heirs (both minor or major) is 4/5 of all property existing at the time of the death of the deceased and of all the property that the latter may have donated during his life (Section 3593 Civil Code).

Children born in or out of wedlock have the same succession rights (Section 240 Civil Code).

Adopted children have the same rights as natural children (Section 14 Law No. 19,134).

However, children under the simple adoption regime (*adopción simple*) and their descendants are not forced heirs to the succession of the adoptant's ascendants (Section 25 Law No. 19,134). Under the simple adoption regime, neither the adoptant inherits the property that the adopted child may have received for free from his family of blood nor does his family of blood inherit the property that the adopted child may have received for free from the adoptant's family.

The legitimate portion of the ascendants is 2/3 of the property existing at the time of the deceased's death including all the property that the deceased may have donated during his life (Section 3594 Civil Code).

The legitimate portion of the spouse, when there are neither descendants nor ascendants of the deceased is 1/2 of the estate of the deceased spouse even when the estate consists of assets of community property (Section 3595 Civil Code).

Common law spouses do not inherit from each other.

(b) *i.* A future inheritance cannot be the object of a contract, even if it is entered into with the consent of the person whose succession is involved (Section 1175 Civil Code).

ii. The heirs to whom the law grants a legitimate portion of the estate of a deceased person can request a reduction of all donations and/or testamentary dispositions made by the deceased which affect their legitimate portion (Sections 1830/1/2, 3601 Civil Code).

5. Maintenance

The obligation to maintain does not pass on to the obligor's successors or estate upon the obligor's death since maintenance is a strictly personal obligation.

6. Community Property Between Husband and Wife

(a) Upon the death of one spouse, community property of both spouses is divided in halves: the surviving spouse keeps his/her one half of all the community property while the other half forms part of the deceased spouse's estate.

(b) Community property begins from the date of the celebration of the marriage. In principle, the property which each of the spouses or both acquire during their marriage under any title other than inheritance, donation or legacy is community property.

In case of death of a married person, assets which are part of the community property are divided in halves: one half forms part of the deceased's estate whereas the surviving spouse keeps the other half as his share in the community.

As for the widow/widower's right in her/his dead spouse's estate, if the former is called to the succession in participation with descendants, he or she is excluded from participating in that half of the community property which passed on to the dead spouse's estate (Section 3576 Civil Code). Assets that belonged to the deceased person but that were not part of the community property are equally distributed among widow/widower and the deceased's children or descendants (Section 3570 Civil Code).

If ascendants and a widow/widower are left, the latter inherits one half of the deceased spouse's assets and one half of the share of the community property that passed on to the deceased spouse's estate (Section 3571 Civil Code) and ascendants share in the other half of both types of assets.

If neither descendants nor ascendants are left, the spouses inherit each other reciprocally, excluding collateral relatives.

7. Gifts

(a) Except for certain cases, any gift *inter vivos* to a forced heir who participates in the donor's succession must be set off against such heir's inheritance (Section 3476 Civil Code).

(b) Dispensation from such set off may only be granted by the donor by means of a testament in which he expressly states his will to increase the inheritance of a given heir and can only dispense it within the limits set by the forced heirs' legitimate portion (Section 3484 Civil Code).

8. Capacity

(a) The Civil Code establishes that every person legally capable of having a will and of manifesting his intention, has the power to dispose of his property by testament (Section 3606 Civil Code). In principle, persons attain capacity to make a testament at eighteen (Section 3614 Civil Code) (although some authors argue that married women older than sixteen and under eighteen are also capable) except for the following cases:

– Persons who do not have full reason (Section 3615 Civil Code). Insane persons may make a testament during their lucid intervals only when said intervals are sufficiently certain and prolonged to give assurance that the disease has ceased for the time being (Section 3615 Civil Code).
– Deaf-mutes unable to read and write (Section 3617 Civil Code).

Additionally there are some cases of incapacity related to specific forms of testaments:

– Deaf, mutes and deaf-mutes cannot make testaments by public act (Section 3651 Civil Code).
– Persons who cannot use their organs to write may not make holographic or sealed testaments.
– Illiterate persons may not make holographic testaments but they may make sealed testaments if they understand what they read and are able to sign.

(b) Any person may be witness to a testament if it is not forbidden by the law (Section 3696 Civil Code). Witnesses must be fully capable by the time the testament is executed (i.e., over twenty-one years and not affected by any incapacity) (Section 3705 Civil Code and Sections 1 and 9 Law No. 11,357).

Military testaments can be executed in presence of minors over eighteen years. Neither the blind, deaf, dumb, persons deprived of their reason nor the insane can be witnesses to a testament.

Witnesses must be known to the notary. If he is unacquainted with them, he may, before executing the testament, require that two persons vouch for the identity and residence of the witnesses (Section 3699 Civil Code). Witnesses must understand the language of the testator and the language in which the testament is executed (Section 3700 Civil Code) and must reside in the district where the testament is executed (Section 3701 Civil Code).

Neither the testator's ascendants nor his descendants can be witnesses; but his collateral relatives or relatives by affinity may be witnesses, provided the testament does not contain any disposition in their benefit (Section 3702 Civil Code). Similarly, heirs instituted in the testament, the legatees, and those receiving any benefit under the dispositions of the testator cannot be witnesses (Section 3706 Civil Code), nor can relatives of the notary within the fourth degree, his office employees or his servants (Section 3707 Civil Code).

(c) All persons who, having being conceived at the time of the testator's death are not declared by the law to be incapable or unworthy to succeed the testator, can acquire by testament (Section 3733 Civil Code). Unborn children may be beneficiaries of a testament provided they are born alive (Section 70 Civil Code).

A testamentary disposition fails if the person in whose benefit it was made does not survive the testator (Section 3743 Civil Code).

Tutors of minors cannot receive anything under the testaments of minors dying while under their tutorship (Section 3736 Civil Code) except when those tutors are the testator's ascendants (Section 3737 Civil Code), or where the Court had approved the accounts rendered by the tutor (Section 3736 Civil Code).

The confessors of the testator during his last illness, the relatives of such confessors within the fourth degree – if not relatives of the testator –, churches in which they are employed, with the exception of the parish church of the testator, and the communities to which they belong are incapable of succeeding or receiving legacies (Section 3739 Civil Code). A Protestant minister who assisted the testator during his last illness is also subject to the same incapacity (Section 3740 Civil Code).

The notary public and the witnesses to a testament made by public act, their wives and relatives within the fourth degree cannot benefit from the dispositions it contains in their favour (Section 3664 Civil Code); neither can officers of the vessel (unless they are relatives of the testator) receive legacies in maritime testaments (Section 3686 Civil Code).

Legal entities are also capable of being beneficiaries of a testament provided they are incorporated at the time of the testator's death. Nevertheless, corporations which do not yet have the character of legal entities, may receive by testament if the succession or legacy is made for the purpose of founding the corporation and then obtaining the proper government authorizations (Section 3735 Civil Code).

Certain persons may be declared unworthy to succeed by court. Cases of unworthiness are expressly provided for by the Civil Code and are, *inter alia*: persons sentenced for killing or attempting to kill the person whose succession is involved or the latter's spouse or descendants (Section 3291 Civil Code), persons convicted of adultery with the deceased's wife (Section 3294 Civil Code), etc.

9. Authority (Court, Notarial or Other)

When the succession lies between ascendants, descendants or spouses, the heir enters into the possession of the inheritance the day of the death of the person leaving the succession, without any formality or the intervention of the judges (Section 3410 Civil Code). The other relatives called to the succession by law cannot take the possession of the inheritance without a court order (Section 3412 Civil Code).

However, even in the case of ascendants, descendants or spouses, to acquire certain property such as real estate, a registered chattel, etc., heirs need an order of succession to be granted by court. Similarly, in case there are different heirs, they will not acquire any particular property as long as they do not divide the estate, which could also require a court order.

Those heirs instituted in a testament must also apply to the judge for the hereditary possession and submit the testament wherein they are instituted heirs (Section 3413 Civil Code).

10. Invalidity of Will

(a) There are multiple grounds for the invalidity of testaments. The main grounds are: defects in formalities; incapacity of testator; dispositions under fraud; duress; illegality of end pursued by the testator; nonexistence of testator's intention to make a testament; illegality of dispositions; unintelligible dispositions; falseness of cause taken into account by the testator upon making the testament; simulated act; dispositions subject to illegal or impossible conditions or charges or opposed to morality; incapacity of witnesses, etc.

(b) Depending on the type of invalidity affecting the testament, same could be considered void or voidable. If the nullity is apparent (i.e., there is no need to produce evidence to determine its nullity – e.g., a testament by public act which lacks the minimum number of witnesses) the testament is void.

If evidence is to be produced to determine the existence of an invalidity (e.g., the testator had not full reason when he executed the testament), the testament is voidable.

11. Simultaneous Death

(a)–(b) If two or more persons (even if they are forced heirs of each other) die in a common disaster, or under any other circumstance, in such manner as to make it impossible to ascertain which of them died first, the presumption is that they all died at the same time and therefore there is no transmission of rights whatsoever between them (Section 109 Civil Code).

12. Estate Taxes

(a) There is currently no estate tax in Argentina. However, the *Argentine Personal Assets Tax Law 23,966* (the 'Personal Assets Tax') imposes a tax on undistributed estates in respect of their holdings of assets held at 31 December of each year.

The Personal Assets Tax is levied at the rate of 0.5 per cent of the value of the assets, valued as prescribed by the applicable regulation. There is a higher rate levied at 1 per cent, applicable in certain cases, to foreign legal entities holding securities issued by Argentine companies.

The *Personal Assets Tax Law* provides for a non taxable amount of 102 300 US dollars applicable only in respect of undistributed estates located in Argentina.

(b) In the case of undistributed estates located outside Argentina, the tax is due only on their holding of assets located in Argentina while in the case of undistributed estates located in Argentina, the tax is due on their holdings of assets located worldwide.

(c) The tax is imposed on the undistributed estate.

(d) Estate proceedings are subject to a court tax of 1.5 per cent of the value of the assets of the estate.

13. Administration of Estates

(a) All the heirs administer the estate but none of them can administer it by himself; all decisions must be unanimous. All the heirs can appoint an administrator unanimously or can request that a court appoint one, especially if there is no agreement between them (Section 3451 Civil Code).

Procedural rules may require that an administrator be appointed by court.

(b) In case the administrator is appointed in a judicial proceeding, procedural rules in federal jurisdiction determine that he must submit quarterly reports – or whatever other periods may be agreed upon by the heirs – to the court (Section 713 National Civil and Commercial Code of Procedures). He must also file a final report upon vacating his position.

In case one or more heirs administer the estate with or without the other heirs' consent, interested parties may demand that the administrator submit a report of his administration.

(c) Heirs have the right to query and object to the performance of the administrator or its reports. The administrator can also be removed by the court even if there is no petition by the heirs if the administrator is wrongly performing his duties (Section 714 Civil and Commercial Procedural Code of the Nation).

(d) If all the heirs are present and have full capacity, the partition of the estate may be made in the form which they deem appropriate by unanimous consent (Section 3462 Civil Code). This private partition must be executed in a notarial deed or in a private instrument which must then be submitted to the court (Section 1184, 2° Civil Code) for approval (Section 726 National Civil and Commercial Code of Procedure).

Partitions are carried out by court: (i) when there are minors or incapacitated persons with interests in the estate; or absentees whose existence is uncertain; (ii) when third persons, basing their action on a legal interest, object to a private partition; (iii) when the heirs of full age who are present do not agree to a private division (Section 3465 Civil Code); (iv) when there is no unanimous consent among heirs on how to divide the estate.

(e) As a general rule, the debts that form part of the estate are divided among the heirs in proportion to the share which each of them has in the inheritance. Each of the heirs may release himself from all obligations by paying his part of the debt (Section 3491 Civil Code). Thus, creditors may seek payment of the debts from each of the heirs in proportion to his share.

While the estate is not divided, creditors may also request payment of the debts against all the heirs before the court in which the succession is being heard. If they demand payment of ordinary expenses, they could be paid by the appointed administrator, but if they demand payment of extraordinary expenses the court's approval – prior notice to all the heirs – is necessary.

In the partition, whether judicial or extrajudicial, sufficient property must be set aside for the payment of the debts and charges of the succession (Section 3474 Civil Code). Creditors may also demand that the shares be withheld from the heirs until the debts have been paid (Section 3475 Civil Code).

Once the estate is divided, creditors must seek payment from each of the heirs. However, debts may be allotted to one or more heirs irrespective of the share to which each one of them is entitled. Should that be the case, creditors may seek recovery of their debt not only from the heir who was allotted the whole debt but also from the rest of the heirs in proportion to the share to which he was originally entitled (Section 3497 Civil Code).

In cases of testamentary successions, testators may appoint one or more executors (Section 3844 Civil Code).

Despite the appointment of an executor, if there are forced heirs or heirs instituted in the testament, the possession of the inheritance belongs to the heirs, and the latters are the ones who administer the estate or who may decide to appoint an administrator as explained above, but such part thereof must remain in the hands of the executor as may be necessary for the payment of the debts and legacies (Section 3852 Civil Code).

If there are no forced heirs, the testator may determine that the executor administer the estate himself, always with the court's supervision.

(f) As described above, heirs are the ones who administer the estate and who decide its distribution, despite of the appointment of an executor.

If there is no heir (either legitimate or instituted by testament) the executor's role becomes more important since he is to put into effect the dispositions of the testament and to liquidate the estate. If the testator did not appoint an executor, the court – by prior request of an interested party – would appoint the persons who would administer and distribute the estate.

14. Domicile/Nationality

(a) The right of succession to the deceased's estate is governed by Argentine law if the deceased was domiciled in Argentina upon his death (Section 3283 Civil Code). Therefore, in principle, the above rules are only applicable in case the deceased died when domiciled in Argentina.

However, even if a person is not domiciled in Argentina upon his death (and therefore his succession is subject to a foreign law) if his estate comprises immovable or movable assets permanently situated in Argentina, the rights of the parties, the capacity to acquire same, and the modes of transferal and the formalities would be subject to Argentine law (Section 10 Civil Code).

The law of the testator's domicile at the time of making his testament is that which governs his capacity or incapacity to make it (Section 3612 Civil Code). Thus, the testator's domicile would govern his capacity to make the testament, to amend it, to revoke it, etc. (*see* answer 8).

Even if a person domiciled outside Argentina enters into a contract of inheritance valid under the laws that governed such contract, Argentine courts might declare such contract void if the succession is to be governed by Argentine law (*see* answer 4.b.i).

(b) Local courts would give an order of succession if the deceased was domiciled in Argentina upon his death. These circumstances would open the jurisdiction to Argentine judges (Section 3284 Civil Code) and would make Argentine laws applicable (Section 3283 Civil Code).

The place in which a will is executed is not relevant to determine the court competent to give an order of succession.

SECTION B – APPLICABLE LAW/PROCEDURE WHERE FOREIGN ELEMENT/S ARE INVOLVED

1. Jurisdiction

(a) Argentine courts have jurisdiction over the succession of persons domiciled in Argentina upon their death (Section 3284 Civil Code). Even if the deceased was not domiciled in Argentina, Argentine courts have jurisdiction if the deceased left not more than one heir and such heir is domiciled in Argentina (Section 3285 Civil Code). Judicial precedents have also admitted the jurisdiction of Argentine courts when: (i) the succession is governed by Argentine law (*forum causae*); (ii) there are assets in Argentina subject to Argentine law.

International treaties may determine the jurisdiction of Argentine courts in other cases.

(b) Immovable assets (Section 10 Civil Code) and movable assets which are permanently situated in Argentina held without the intention of removing them (Section 11 Civil Code) are governed by Argentine law and judicial precedents have recognized Argentine jurisdictions over such assets, in spite of the foreign domicile of the deceased.

(c) Each province determines in its code of procedures the court that has jurisdiction over successions. As a general rule, civil courts have venue over successions.

2. Applicable Law

In succession cases, Argentine courts apply the law of the deceased's domicile upon his death.

In cases of succession of persons domiciled in a foreign country, the succession of immovable and movable assets permanently situated in Argentina are governed by Argentine law (Sections 10 and 11 Civil Code).

International treaties may establish that other laws be applied.

3. Foreign Succession/Inheritance Order

(a) In principle, foreign orders of succession would be enforced in respect of local assets. However, with respect to immovable assets and movable assets permanently situated in Argentina foreign succession orders may not violate Argentine succession law. There are also some judicial precedents which have decided that with respect to those types of assets Argentine courts have exclusive jurisdiction.

(b) A foreign succession order must be recognized by an Argentine court before it is enforced in Argentina.

(c) If there is an international treaty between Argentina and the state that issues the succession order which governs successions, rules on how to obtain recognition would be determined by such treaty.

Where there is no such treaty, foreign succession orders will be enforceable in Argentina if they comply with the following requisites:

– The succession order must have *res judicata* authority.
– The succession order must have been issued by a competent authority according to the Argentine rules of international jurisdiction.
– Interested parties must have been duly summoned, ensuring their right to defense.
– The succession order must be considered as such in the state in which it was issued.
– The succession order must not affect Argentine public policy principles (Section 14 Civil Code).
– The succession order must not be inconsistent with other granted previously or concurrently by an Argentine court.

A certified and translated copy must be filed with Argentine courts along with evidence that the order is a final one.

4. Two or More Succession or Probate Orders

Where there is an application before an Argentine court for an order of succession and a foreign order already exists, such foreign order would be submitted by the interested parties to the Argentine court hearing in the application for an order of succession. The Argentine court should then decide whether the foreign order could be recognized in Argentina pursuant to the principles set forth in answer B.3.c) above. In the event the foreign order could be recognized, the application for a succession in Argentina should be dismissed; on the other hand, if it cannot be recognized then the application in Argentina would follow its course irrespective of the existence of a foreign order.

An action initiated in Argentina and still pending judicial decision would not constitute an obstacle for the recognition of a foreign order of succession. Only a final judgment issued by Argentine courts might constitute an obstacle if same is contrary to the foreign order of succession the enforcement of which is requested.

5. Assets

Local courts could assume jurisdiction if the deceased was domiciled in Argentina upon his death (Section 3284 Civil Code) or if the only heir who accepts the inheritance is domiciled in Argentina (Section 3285 Civil Code).

6. Expert Evidence

(a) If a succession or some aspect thereof is subject to a foreign law, the provisions of such foreign law governing the succession must be proved to Argentine courts (with the exception of the laws of some countries with which Argentina has signed international treaties). However, certain procedural codes and judicial precedents have admitted the applicability of a foreign law even when the parties had not given evidence of such foreign law.

There is no fixed rule on how foreign laws should be evidenced. In principle, it is necessary to submit the documents evidencing that the foreign succession order complies with the requisites set forth in answer B.3.c). Nevertheless, Argentine courts have admitted the statements of foreign lawyers, reports of the foreign embassies, statements of Argentine experts, etc.

Similarly, to obtain the recognition of a foreign succession order, evidence on aspects of foreign law could also be needed.

(b) There is no rule on how a foreign lawyer should advise Argentine courts on a foreign law. In principle, affidavits could be considered sufficient evidence depending on the circumstances of each case.

7. Unity of Succession

Argentine succession law is based on the principle of unity of succession, although it also contains some other principles which, in practice, may divide an international succession.

8. Formalities

The formalities of a testament are governed by the law of the place in which the testament is executed (Section 3635 Civil Code); if it is executed in a foreign country, Argentine courts require that it complies with the provisions of the laws of the country in which it is executed.

The testament of a person who is outside of his country is valid in Argentina only if made with the formalities prescribed by the law of the place in which he resides, or according to the formalities observed in the Nation to which he belongs, or according to those formalities which the Argentine Civil Code prescribes (Section 3638 Civil Code).

9. Legislation

(a) The Uniform Foreign Probate Act is not applicable in Argentina.

(b) Argentina is not a party to the *Hague Convention on Wills*.

10. Wills

(a) The formalities of a testament are governed by the laws of the state in which the testament is made. The testament of a person who is outside of his country is valid in Argentina only if made with the formalities prescribed by the law of the place in which he resides, or according to the formalities observed in the Nation to which he belongs, or according to formalities which the Argentine Civil Code prescribes (Section 3638 Civil Code).

(b) The terminology of the testament must be studied according to the law that the testator had in mind upon making the testament, which could possibly be the law of his domicile at the time he made the testament. In case this is not possible, the terminology is governed by the law that governs the succession. As regards dispositions on immovable or movable property with a permanent situation in Argentina, they must be governed by Argentine law.

(c) The right of heirs or beneficiaries is governed by the law that governs the succession, therefore, in principle, the law of the testator's domicile at the time of his death in respect of movable property. In respect of immovable property or permanent movable property in Argentina, Argentinean law will apply.

(d) Capacity to inherit is governed by the law of the domicile of the successor at the testator's death (Section 3286 Civil Code).

(e) The capacity to make a testament is governed by the law of the testator's domicile at the time in which the testament is made (Section 3611 Civil Code).

(f) *See* answer a. *above.*

(g) The dispositions of the testator whereby a third person is called to all or part of the residue of the estate upon the death of the instituted heir are void (Section 3732

International Succession

Civil Code). The testator must appoint the heir himself; if he makes reference to one to be appointed by another by his direction, such appointment is not valid (Section 3711 Civil Code).

The testator may subrogate another heir in the place of the heir appointed in the testament in the event of the heir not being willing or able to accept the inheritance. This is the only kind of substitution permitted in testaments (Section 3724 Civil Code).

In principle, powers of appointment would be governed by the law of the testator's last domicile. However, if the succession of immovable or movable assets permanently situated in Argentina is involved, it is likely that Argentine courts will apply Argentine law declaring the appointment of a second successor void in connection with such assets.

(h) The amendment or revocation of a testament made outside Argentina by a person who does not have his domicile in Argentina is valid when it takes place according to the law of the place where the testament is made, or according to the law of the place in which the testator had his domicile at the time. If the testament was made in Argentina, the testament should be revoked according to Argentine law (Section 3825 Civil Code).

(i) Laws regarding reserve also apply to non-residents irrespective of the type of property.

11. Domicile/Nationality

(a)–(b) Aspects related to domicile and nationality have been dealt with in each of the above answers.

The Personal Assets Tax Law regulates an exceptional case where the domicile of the beneficiary is relevant, as follows. Undivided estates are deemed located where the respective judicial proceeding is initiated. However, if no judicial proceeding is started as of 31 December of the relevant tax year, the undivided estate will be deemed located at the last domicile of the deceased, unless there is only one beneficiary and same is domiciled in Argentina, in which case the undistributed estate is deemed located in Argentina until the judicial proceeding is started.

(c) In order for the place of residence to be considered a domicile, the residence must be habitual and not accidental, even if there is no intention of settling in such place permanently (Section 92 Civil Code). In the case of alternative places of residence, the domicile is the place where the family resides or where the principal establishment is located (Section 93 Civil Code). If a person has his family in one place and his business in another, the former is the place of his domicile (Section 94 Civil Code). Involuntary residence on account of banishment, imprisonment, etc., does not change the former domicile, if the family or the principal place of business is maintained there (Section 95 Civil Code). The moment that domicile in a foreign country is abandoned without the intention of returning thereto, the person has the domicile of his birth (Section 96 Civil Code). The last know domicile of a person is that which prevails when the new domicile is unknown (Section 98 Civil Code).

12. Taxation

As mentioned above, the tax is imposed on the undistributed estate.

Austria

Prepared by: Merran LOEWENTHAL, LL.B., Solicitor of the Supreme Court of England & Wales, New South Wales and Australia, and Dr. Friedrich SCHWANK, Austrian attorney

Address: Merran Loewenthal, LL.B.   Law Offices Dr. F. Schwank,
           Stock Exchange Building   Stock Exchange Building
           Wipplingerstrasse 34/108   Wipplingerstrasse 34/101
           A-1010 Vienna   A-1010 Vienna
           Austria   Austria
Tel.:   +43 1 535 63 93   +43 1 533 57 04
Fax: +43 1 535 63 41   +43 1 533 57 06
E-mail: loewenthal@schwank.com   offices@schwank.com
Website: www.schwank.com

SECTION A – BRIEF SURVEY OF THE LOCAL SYSTEM

1. Type of System

(a) Civil law country.

(b) Federal System. The Austrian General Civil Code ('*Allgemeines bürgerliches Gesetzbuch*' hereafter *ABGB*) is federal law providing for uniform inheritance provisions throughout the entire Republic of nine provinces. Provincial law becomes applicable only in unusual cases, usually dealing with the right of inheritance to farms and forests.

2. Wills

(a) Different forms of wills:

(1) Holograph – in the testator's own handwriting – under Article 578, ABGB. Here the entire document must be in the testator's own handwriting and it must be signed. It is advisable also to add the place and date of signature but this is not mandatory.

(2) Allograph – written by a person other than the testator. This can take the form of either:

– a will drawn in another's handwriting, or typed etc. but not prepared as a public document (Article 579, *ABGB*). Such a will must be signed by the testator and by three witnesses, who are at least eighteen years of age and possess legal capacity. They may be neither relatives of the testator nor mentioned as beneficiaries in the will (Articles 591, 594, *ABGB*) OR;
– In the form of a public document, either drawn up by a Notary or by the County Court Officers and the original deposited there. Some testators who are mentally or physically handicapped must draw up their will as a public document in order for it to be valid.

(3) An oral or unwritten will (Articles 585 etc., *ABGB*). Here the testator must declare the provisions of his last will in the presence of three competent witnesses. Although there is no requirement for writing in this case, it is advisable for the witnesses to confirm the provisions in writing. At the death of the testator, at least two of these witnesses must be able to give consistent evidence to the court with regard to the testamentary provisions.

(4) A deed of inheritance (Article 602, *ABGB*). This is only available between spouses and may only deal with three-quarters of the testator's estate. To be valid, this deed must be signed in the presence of a Notary.

(b) Alteration, revocation and revival of a revoked will.

(1) A will may be altered or revoked by any subsequent valid will: persons under any kind of protection must do this by public document. This applies both to wills (where an heir is appointed) and a testamentary disposition where no heir is appointed but only legacies are given (referred to as '*Kodizill*'). Generally any will which has been revoked is no longer valid but the court will look at all the testamentary documents in order to discover the intention of the testator.

(2) A previous will, unless revoked specifically or physically destroyed, will remain valid although the dispositions may be influenced by further developments in the testator's life, e.g., a spouse entitled to a compulsory share on marriage or the subsequent cancellation of a spouse's compulsory share upon divorce. In contrast to Anglo-American legal systems, a subsequent marriage by a testator does not automatically revoke a previous will.

(3) A revoked will will come back into effect only if the testator specifically revives the will by a valid subsequent testamentary document.

3. Intestate Succession

(a) The statutory intestate succession under Articles 731 etc., *ABGB*, is succession *per stirpes*. The deceased's blood relatives are entitled to inherit in the following blood lines (*stirpes*):

i. 1st line: any children, whether legitimate or illegitimate, and their issue;
ii. 2nd line: parents and their issue (siblings, nephews and nieces of the deceased);
iii. 3rd line: grandparents and their issue (uncles, aunts, cousins of the deceased);
iv. 4th line: great-grandparents, but not their issue.

Those in the first blood line are first to inherit. Only where there is no survivor in this line will those in the second line inherit and so on. Within each blood line of inheritance, the closest relationship to the deceased is relevant, e.g., children prevail against grandchildren, parents prevail against siblings etc., in contrast to some Anglo-American legal systems. Any surviving issue will take amongst them the share of any predeceased parent.

Although no relation by blood, the surviving spouse of the deceased has rights upon intestacy such that, where there are heirs in the first blood line, the spouse inherits one third of the entire estate, the first line heirs two thirds amongst themselves. Where there are heirs only in either the second or third blood line, the surviving spouse inherits two thirds of the entire estate. Where there are only heirs in the fourth line, the surviving spouse inherits the entire estate.

(b) There is no difference in inheritance rights between personal and real property.

4. Restrictions on free testamentary disposition

(a) Only the spouse, the relatives of the first blood line, parents and grandparents, are entitled to a compulsory share (Article 762 etc., *ABGB*). The compulsory share for the spouse and the first blood line heirs is half of the portion under the statutory intestacy rules above. For any others entitled to a compulsory share, it is one third of the statutory portion.

The compulsory share is a money claim only and provides a personal right of action against the heirs to the estate. The basis for calculation of the share is the true value of the estate, if necessary to be obtained by way of valuation. However the compulsory share of each entitled person is reduced by any legacies or other gifts made to that person during the deceased's lifetime, although the testator may stipulate that life-time gifts should not be set off against the compulsory share (Articles 784 to 789).

The deceased's spouse is, in addition, entitled under Article 796 to maintenance to the extent that he/she is not able to provide this him/herself, so long as he/she does not marry again. The widow/widower is entitled to the use of the family home, irrespective of his/her needs and may therefore use it even after remarriage. Only entitlement to maintenance ceases upon remarriage.

(b) Generally an expected inheritance cannot be given or assigned or otherwise disposed of, particularly to third parties. However it is possible to renounce any expected right of inheritance or compulsory share but this must be done by way of Notarial Deed and usually during the lifetime of the person from whom the inheritance is expected. An heir under a will or under the statutory intestacy rules or even a person entitled to a compulsory share, may revoke or renounce their rights to such during the estate proceedings; *see below*.

A gift *causa mortis* becomes effective upon death and is a special form of legacy which requires the formality of a Notarial Deed. It is a contract binding upon both the donor, upon whose death it becomes effective, and the donee, the future legatee. This form of legacy is only available for particular objects, not the entire estate.

The estate may be distributed during the owner's life by donations *inter vivos* or *causa mortis*, although in the latter case, the owner remains so until his/her death, upon which ownership passes to the legatee, who must specifically have given his/her consent to the gift.

5. Maintenance

Article 795 provides that maintenance must be paid to those who are entitled to a compulsory share but for some reason do not obtain it (due to disinheritance either under statutory rules or by the testator him/herself) to the extent that they are not otherwise in receipt of maintenance.

6. Community property

(a) The Austrian inheritance laws are based on a separate property system, not a community property system.

However, the spouses may enter into a prenuptial agreement on community property which must be in the form of a Notarial Deed. Such a prenuptial agreement will also include a deed of inheritance which may not be changed, amended or revoked unilaterally without the consent of the other spouse. Irrespective of the existence of a deed of inheritance, each spouse is able to make a will of his/her own covering a quarter of the estate (Article 1253, *ABGB*).

(b) The deed of inheritance does not restrict either spouse from disposing over his/her respective property while alive. The deed of inheritance only becomes operative upon the death of one of the spouses. Compulsory shares may be claimed as against any other will. If no will covering the free quarter has been made beside the deed of inheritance, a quarter of the estate will be considered to be an intestate estate and will go to the statutory heirs.

If there is no prenuptial agreement, each spouse may dispose of his/her entire property freely. Even if the testator is survived by persons with rights to compulsory shares (*Pflichtteilsberechtigte*), there is no strict obligation on the testator to consider these persons in his/her dispositions, although these persons will have rights against the estate/heirs to claim their *Pflichtteile*, (either half or a third of the amount on intestacy, depending upon the relationship) unless the testator has disinherited them (*see below*).

7. Donations *inter vivos*

(a) Donations by a deceased during his/her life may be deducted from the value of the compulsory share of the donee after the death.

(b) Any person entitled to a compulsory share has rights against the heirs to the estate to receive the money value of such share, subject to the above.

8. Personal capacity

(a) Testamentary capacity under Article 566 etc., *ABGB*. In Austria the age of majority is eighteen and it is at this age that anyone may draw up a valid will, provided he/she has the mental capacity to be aware both of the fact that they are making a will and of the contents of such will (Article 569). Minors between the ages of fourteen and eighteen years and those of limited mental capacity may make a will, but only an oral will before a court or in the presence of a Notary.

(b) Witnesses under Article 591 etc., *ABGB*. Nobody under the age of eighteen or disabled persons are able to be witnesses to the signing of a will; close relatives of the testator and persons benefiting under the will should not act as witnesses as they will not be accepted as such under Articles 591, 594. However there is no provision preventing them from witnessing the will, provided that three proper witnesses have acted as *Testamentszeugen*. The witnessing of the will by such close relatives or persons benefiting will not disentitle them, provided three proper witnesses have signed.

(c) Ability to inherit under Article 538 etc., *ABGB*. Generally anyone is entitled to inherit property but Austrian law does recognize that some behaviour is sufficient to disinherit those who would otherwise be entitled to inherit, e.g., anyone who has been convicted of a serious crime against the deceased, or has neglected parental or filial duties unless it can be assumed that the deceased has forgiven him or her. Also anyone who has interfered with the testator's free disposition in making a will, or has tampered with or suppressed a will is unable to inherit. Likewise persons found guilty of adultery or incest are excluded from inheriting under each other's will.

9. Authority

The local county court in the place where the deceased had his/her last residence will have jurisdiction to deal with the estate proceedings. The court will appoint a local Notary to act as Court Commissioner, but any orders in the estate proceedings will be made by the court under Articles 797, *ABGB* and Articles 28 etc., Code on Non-contentious Matters (*Ausserstreitgesetz*).

10. Invalidity of a will

(a) Formal defects, either because it has not been drawn up or signed in the required form, result in the invalidity of the will. On the other hand, there may be defects as to its contents. These may be either unclear or include wrong dispositions by the testator or may be defects influencing the testator's intention at the time he/she drew up the will, e.g., fraud, mistake or undue influence, all of which will invalidate the will. When interpreting the will, the court must have regard to the testator's intention. Any dispositions which are not able to be clearly interpreted cannot take effect, although those parts of the will which are able to be clearly interpreted may take effect (*favor testamenti*).

(b) Formal invalidity of the will results in it being void. However, if a formally valid will is challenged for duress or fraud, the will is voidable on proof.

11. Simultaneous Death

(a) Where two or more persons die simultaneously or in a manner where it is impossible to decide who survived whom, then neither of the persons may inherit from the other.

(b) There is no legal presumption – as in Anglo-American legal systems – that the older of the two died first. The official death certificate is proof as to the date and time of death and in the absence of such, application must be made to the court for an order that the person concerned is no longer alive.

12. Inheritance Tax

(a) Austrian inheritance tax is levied not on the value of the estate, but on the value to any beneficiary of any inheritance (or any gift). The rate of tax depends on

 (i) the relationship between the deceased and the heir, and
 (ii) the amount each heir receives.

Under (i) there are five classes:

 (i) the spouse and any children, including adopted and stepchildren;
 (ii) grandchildren and their issue;
(iii) parents, grandparents, stepparents and brothers and sisters;
(iv) children in law and parents in law and nieces and nephews;
 (v) any other heirs.

International Succession

Nett estate	Inheritance tax in %				
Euro	class of taxation (I–V)				
	I	II	III	IV	V
7,300	2	4	6	8	14
14,600	2.5	5	7.5	10	16
29,200	3	6	9	12	18
43,800	3.5	7	10.5	14	20
58,400	4	8	12	16	22
73,000	5	10	15	20	26
109,500	6	12	18	24	30
146,000	7	14	21	28	34
219,000	8	16	24	32	38
365,000	9	18	27	36	42
730,000	10	20	30	40	46
1,905,000	11	21	32	42	48
1,460,000	12	22	34	44	51
2,920,000	13	23	36	46	54
4,380,000	14	24	38	48	57
and more	15	25	40	50	60
In each tax class an amount is exempt:	2,200	2,200	440	440	110

(b) If at the time of the deceased's death he/she was resident in Austria or at the time of the inheritance the heir is resident in Austria, then the entire estate world-wide is subject to taxation (Article 6, *Inheritance Tax Act*). All Austrian citizens and any foreigners having their usual place of residence in Austria are deemed to be resident in Austria. With companies and other legal entities, the seat or place of management is relevant. Austrian citizens resident abroad remain residents for pur-poses of inheritance tax during the first two years of their relocation from Austria.

(c) Each heir is taxed on the amount of his/her particular inheritance taking into consideration any reductions in the inheritance allowable under the *Inheritance Tax Act*. The inheritance of real property is subject to a further inheritance tax, at a rate of 2 per cent where a spouse, parent or child inherits, otherwise at 3.5 per cent.

(d) Austria has double taxation treaties with a number of countries but only those with France, Germany, Liechtenstein, Sweden, Switzerland, Hungary and the United States deal with inheritance tax.

13. Administration of estates

(a) Whenever a person dies in Austria some form of estate proceedings are obliga-tory, particularly where there is real property to be inherited. Under Articles 797 etc., *ABGB* the heir either under the will or as a result of the statutory intestacy rules is asked to accept his/her inheritance. The estate court will rely upon the court appointed commissioner – a local notary public – to discover whether there are any testamentary dispositions, who are the nearest relatives, the size of the estate, the assets and liabilities, and will complete the so-called *Todfallsaufnahme*. The Austrian estate court will end the proceedings by issuing the certificate of inheritance or *Einantwortungsurkunde*. This proves that the particular heir has been accepted by the court as such and is required for production to the Land Titles Office before the heir can be registered as the new owner of any real property.

(b) It is possible for the heir to apply to the court for the estate to be wound up in writing, either by him/herself or by their lawyer. This is very often done with heirs who live outside Austria. Under Austrian law the heir steps immediately into the shoes of the deceased so that it is unusual for any kind of legal personal representative or executor to be appointed, in contrast to Anglo-American legal systems. Until the Certificate of Inheritance is issued by the court, all assets of the deceased form a legal entity, the 'dormant estate'. If this dormant estate must be represented prior to the issue of the Certificate of Inheritance, or if no heirs are willing to accept their inheritance, the court will appoint a curator for the estate, usually a local notary.

(c) The heirs appointed in the will and/or entitled under the statutory intestacy rules have the option of accepting their inheritance or rejecting it. If they wish to accept it, then they may do so either conditionally or unconditionally. The difference is as follows:

i. By making an unconditional acceptance of inheritance (*Unbedingte Erbserklärung*) the heir accepts that he/she is responsible for meeting the liabilities of the estate, not only to the extent that those liabilities are covered by the estate assets themselves, but also to the extent of using his/her own funds if necessary. The only advantage of such an acceptance is that the assets and liabilities of the estate do not need to be officially valued.

ii. By making a conditional acceptance of inheritance only (*Bedingte Erbserklärung*), the heir accepts the inheritance subject to the liability for any debts and legacies of the deceased only to the value of the assets of the estate. Here an official inventory and valuation of the assets needs to be made.

It is usual in the case of a conditional acceptance that a notice to creditors of the estate is published so that the amount of the liabilities may be valued as well. Should no such notice to creditors be published and the estate assets are used up by payment of the liabilities of which the heir has knowledge, then the heir incurs further liability for any debts of the estate which may turn up later and which the heir may have to pay by using his/her own assets.

iii. In the case of an unconditional acceptance of inheritance the list of assets and liability is based on information from the heirs. In the case of a conditional acceptance, the assets and liabilities must be valued and the notary draws up an inventory. A final accounting with regard to the movements of capital after the date of death is required only in certain circumstances, e.g., if a curator has been appointed or where there are heirs who are minors. In such a case the court of protection will be involved to protect the minors' rights. The final accounting must be presented to the court.

iv. The entire estate proceedings are handled either by the notary as court commissioner or by the heirs or their lawyer if they have applied for the estate to be dealt with in writing. However it is always the court which makes the relevant orders and issues the certificates of inheritance. Any disputes between heirs or between heirs and the commissioner are dealt with by the estate court and any other disputes by the usual civil court.

v. Upon issuing the certificate of inheritance the estate court closes the file, which is sent to the Inheritance Tax Office for an assessment to be made, and the estate is transferred to the heirs. The distribution of the estate itself is usually done by the heirs amongst themselves unless the heirs are minors or wards of court, or a curator has been appointed.

14. Domicile/Nationality

(a) Under the Code on Non-contentious Matters and International Private Law, upon the death of anyone in Austria, some form of legal proceedings will take place. Where the deceased owned real property in Austria, there will be estate proceedings under the Austrian procedural rules. Succession to the deceased's estate, however, will be a matter of the law of the deceased's nationality. Depending on the nationality, the Austrian court may find that succession becomes a matter of Austrian law, despite the fact that the deceased is e.g., a British citizen. This is based on the fact that while Austrian law would refer the question of succession to English law, English law may refer the question of succession to the law of the deceased's last domicile, which may very well be Austria. In these circumstances, under the *Austrian International Private Law*, the Austrian court would accept the *renvoi* back to it and Austrian rules of succession would apply.

(b) If a foreigner dies in Austria leaving only movable property here, then if there is a bilateral agreement between Austria and the particular foreign state which provides for reciprocity in such matters, the Austrian court will hand over the property to the foreign state to be dealt with. Where this is not so – which is in the majority of cases – the Austrian estate proceedings would be 'delivery up' proceedings only or *Ausfolgungsverfahren*. This is a shortened form of estate proceedings in which the Austrian court will order the transfer of the movable property to those entitled under the foreign succession laws or will, upon having evidence of the foreigner's death, the heirs entitled to his/her estate, and the fact that Austria has no agreement as to reciprocity with this foreign state.

(c) The local Austrian court always has jurisdiction over Austrian citizens. For foreign citizens, the Austrian courts only have jurisdiction if the deceased was resident within the jurisdiction of the court or left property within Austria and a court in his/her foreign state would not take appropriate steps.

SECTION B – APPLICABLE PROCEDURE WHERE FOREIGN ELEMENT/S ARE INVOLVED

1. Jurisdiction

(a) *See* Section A, paragraph 14 *above*.

(b) Any changes in the Austrian Land Title records must be carried out in accordance with Austrian procedure, even if questions regarding succession to a deceased foreigner's real property are based on the law of the deceased's nationality.

2. Applicable Law

The county court within which either the deceased was resident or where the real property of the deceased is located is the relevant estate court. According to *Austrian Private International Law* (Article 28) succession to the estate of a deceased person is dependent upon the law of the country of which the deceased was a national at the time of his/her death. If estate proceedings are carried out in Austria, then Austrian procedural law applies with regard to the acceptance or rejection of any inheritance and to the liability of the heirs for the debts of the deceased.

3. Foreign Succession/Inheritance Orders

(a) Foreign decisions regarding succession and other rights in the estate would always be enforceable whereas foreign decisions regarding the deceased's real property in Austria will only be enforceable insofar as they do not violate Austrian law.

(b) In general *see* Section A, paragraph 14 *above*.
   In any estate proceedings in Austria, Austrian procedural law will be applied. If only movable property in Austria is to be handed over, the Austrian court will look first at the rights of any domestic creditors, before granting a release of the property which may very well be carried out under international agreements either to the heirs directly or via diplomatic representation.

(c) For the execution of a foreign decision, the decision together with a certified translation into German should be presented to the Austrian estate court. This will then issue its own decisions and certificates on the basis of the foreign decision.

4. Two or More Succession Orders

See Section A, paragraph 14 *above*.

International Succession

5. Assets

Where there is no property of the deceased located anywhere in Austria, the county court where the deceased was resident will act as the estate court.

6. Expert Evidence

Not necessary.

7. Unity of Succession

Yes; as regards exceptions *see* Section A, paragraph 14 *above*.

8. Formalities

The formal validity of a will may be subject either to the law of the place where the will was signed or the law of the deceased's domicile, or the law of the deceased's domicile at his/her death. Should there be a conflict between any two laws, the law of domicile at death is applicable unless this would lead to the invalidity of the will. As Austrian law is based on the principle of seeking validity, rather than invalidity, the domicile at the time of signing would apply (Article 30, *International Private Law*).

9. Legislation

The Hague Convention applies.

10. Wills

See paragraph 8 *above*. Wills concerning immovable property in Austria are governed by Austrian law as the *lex situs*.

11. Domicile/Nationality

(a) The law of the deceased's domicile at the date of the transaction, alternatively at the date of his/her death is relevant (Article 30, *International Private Law*).

(b) No.

(c) The jurisdiction with which the deceased had the closest connection is relevant.

12. Taxation

See Section A, paragraph 12(c).

If neither the deceased nor the heirs were resident in Austria, the inheritance by such heirs of assets in Austria should not attract Austrian inheritance tax apart from the inheritance of immovables and business assets.

With a non-resident Austrian citizen, Austrian inheritance taxation will apply if two years have not yet passed between the citizen's departure from Austria and the death.

Belgium

Prepared by: MILLER, BOLLE & PARTNERS
LAWYERS

Address: Avenue Louise, 283 box 19
        1050 Bruxelles
        Belgium
Tel.:   +32 2 640 44 00
Fax: +32 2 648 99 95
E-mail: office@millerlaw.be
        bolle@millerlaw.be

SECTION A – BRIEF SURVEY OF THE LOCAL SYSTEM

1. Type of System

(a) Civil law.

(b) The Belgian Civil Code (hereafter BCC) is applicable to the whole of Belgium. It regulates all civil law aspects of a succession; *inter alia* the order of heirs, forced heirship rules, etc.

However, inheritance taxes are now regionalized. Each region of Belgium has adopted particular rules to address specific issues regarding notably tax rates and exemptions. For further details, *see* paragraph 12 of Section A.

2. Wills

(a) A will must be in writing. Verbal wills do not exist under the Belgian Civil Code. There are three forms of wills:

- the holographic will (Article 970 BCC);
- the public will (Article 971 BCC);
- the international will (law of 11th January 1983, completed by the law of February 2nd 1983 which enacts the Treaty of Washington on a uniform law concerning the form of the international wills).

1. The *holographic will* must be written, dated and signed by the testator.

– *Written:*
 The testator must be able to write and understand what he writes. The will must
 be entirely hand-written by the testator: any handwriting by someone other than
 the testator will render the will void. The fact that the holographic will is not
 written on paper but for example on a wall or on a piece of cardboard has no
 effect on the validity of the will.
– *Dated:*
 The will must be entirely dated, specifying the year, month and day in order to
 determine the capacity of the testator when the will was executed and, in case of
 several wills, to give priority to the last one selected by the date of the will.
– *Signed:*
 The will must be signed with the testator's usual and recognized signature.

2. The *public will* is enacted by a notary in the presence of two witnesses, or by two
notaries. The witnesses must be adult, physically and intellectually capable, able to
sign and having no link with the testator and/or the beneficiaries.
 The public will must respect all conditions applicable to any notarial deed act
and also satisfy the following specific additional formalities:

– The testator must dictate his wishes to the notary in the presence of two adult
 witnesses physically and intellectually capable of attesting, and able to sign.
– The will must be hand-written by the notary and must be read over to the
 testator.
– The testator, the two witnesses and the notary must sign the will.

In practice, notaries provide the assistance of witnesses upon demand.

3. The *international will* consists of a private document and of a notarial deed. The
will (hand-written and signed by the testator) is presented by the testator to a notary
and two witnesses, and then joined to a notarial act, which give proofs of the
validity of the will.

(b) *i.* In accordance with Article 1035 BCC, wills may only be revoked by a
 posterior will or by a notarial act evidencing the change of will by the
 testator.
  It is possible to add a codicil to a will, provided that the rules regarding
 the form thereof are respected, *see* point 2(a) *above.*
 ii. A testator's subsequent marriage does not affect the validity of a previous
 will. Nevertheless a problem may arise with respect to the limit of legacies
 benefiting a third person when the testator leaves a spouse or descendants,
 see point 4(a).
 iii. A posterior will may revive a revoked will if the first will still exists and if
 the second will specifies expressly which disposition has been revived.

International Succession

3. Intestacy

(a) Where there is no will, the heirs of the deceased are only the persons who are entitled by the BCC to inherit, i.e., the children, the parents, the collateral relations and the surviving spouse.

The beneficiaries are divided into three lines:

- the descending line (children and grandchildren);
- the ascending line (privileged and ordinary: the parents);
- the collateral line (privileged and ordinary: the brothers and sisters, uncles and aunts).

In order to determine the persons who shall inherit, it is necessary to establish the category (i.e., the group of beneficiaries) and then the degree of heirship in the category. The method to calculate the degree in the category is determined by Articles 737 and 738 BCC.

A difference has to be made whether there is a surviving spouse or not.

Intestacy in the Absence of Surviving Spouse

First category: the descending line
- First degree: if the deceased has two children, each of them inherits half of the estate of the deceased.
- Second degree: if one of those children predeceased the deceased and left one child, the latter inherits of the part of his father/mother, i.e., half of the estate.

Second category: the ascending line
First case: the deceased has two brothers/sisters and his parents. Half of the estate will be shared by the parents and the other half by the brothers/sisters. Consequently, the estate will be shared out as follows:

- Mother: $^{1}/_{4}$
- Father: $^{1}/_{4}$
- Brother/sister 1: $^{1}/_{4}$
- Brother/sister 2: $^{1}/_{4}$

Second case: the deceased has no brother/sister. Each parent receives half of the estate. If one of them predeceases the survivor receives all of the estate.

Third category: the collateral line
Brothers are of the second degree, uncle and niece are of the third degree and cousins are of the fourth degree. The collateral line is stopped at the fourth degree.

If the brother/sister or the uncle/aunt of the deceased, predeceased the deceased and leaves children, the latter may represent their father/mother. However, the representation does not apply at the fourth degree, i.e., between cousins.

Intestacy in the Presence of Surviving Spouse

The marriage property law applies before that of inheritance (*see* hereafter paragraph 6).

Two types of marriage property contracts exist under Belgian law; the community contract and the separation of contract. In the community contract, each spouse owns a private patrimony and half of the common patrimony. In the separation of property contract each spouse owns his own patrimony and there is no common patrimony.

Upon death of one spouse the marriage contract must be dissolved and liquidated. After liquidation, the intestacy rules shall apply.

In accordance with Article 745bis BCC if the deceased has children or grandchildren the surviving spouse inherits the *usufructus* on all the estate.

If the deceased has other successors, the surviving spouse inherits the property of the common patrimony and the *usufructus* on the patrimony of the deceased if the marriage contract is of the community type.

In case of a separation property contract, the surviving spouse inherits the *usufructus* on all the estate of the deceased.

If the deceased has no successor, the surviving spouse inherits the entire estate.

(b) There is no difference between movables and immovables in the principle of inheritance. Nevertheless, some particularities exist, for example the concrete reserve of the surviving spouse (*see* hereafter point 4).

4. Freedom of Testation

(a) The freedom of testation is limited under Belgian law by the mechanism of the 'forced heirship rules', i.e., the reserved compulsory share.

The forced heirship rules protect three types of heirs:

Descending line
In accordance with Article 913 BCC the deceased may dispose of a portion which varies as follows:

Number of children	Compulsory share	Available share
1	$^1/_2$	$^1/_2$
2	$^2/_3$	$^1/_3$
3	$^3/_4$	$^1/_4$
More than 3	$^3/_4$	$^1/_4$

In accordance with Article 914 BCC, the grandchildren represent their parents and therefore benefit from his compulsory reserved share.

International Succession

Ascending line

If the deceased has no child but has two living parents the available share of the deceased corresponds to half of the estate.

If the deceased has no ascendant in his father's line or in his mother's line the available share corresponds to 3/4 of the estate.

Nevertheless, in accordance with Article 915, al. 2 BCC, the share of the ascendants does not apply if the will has been made in favour of the surviving spouse.

Surviving spouse

In accordance with Article 915bis BCC, the surviving spouse may choose between an abstract or a concrete reserved share. The so-called abstract reserved share of the surviving spouse is the right to *usufruct* on half the property of the estate of the deceased. The so-called concrete reserved share of the surviving spouse is the *usufruct* on the real estate property serving on the day of opening of the succession as principal family dwelling and the included furniture.

However, both rights must be considered as a minimum. On the one hand the concrete reserve on the principal family dwelling and furniture will stand if these preferential assets represents more than 50 per cent of the total estate of the deceased. On the other hand, if these assets would be valued at less than 50 per cent of the estate, *usufruct* rights over other assets will be added in order to reach the abstract reserve portion which is the *usufruct* in one half of the estate.

If the deceased had children and a surviving spouse, the reserved share of the latter is deducted proportionally from the available share of the deceased and the reserved share of the children.

(b) *i*. In accordance with Article 893 BCC, donations and wills are the only ways for a person to dispose of his assets gratuitously. Contracts of inheritance (*pactes sur succession future*) are strictly forbidden under Belgian law.

    ii. The attention should be drawn to the fact that a person has the possibility of giving some assets to an heir but the latter has the obligation to declare them at the opening of the succession (return clause) if the donor has not expressly relieved him of the obligation to return the assets.

5. Maintenance

According to BCC, the only cases in which maintenance can only be claimed from the heirs arise out of the marriage of the deceased. Therefore, the persons who could benefit from allowance are:

(A) *The surviving spouses or the surviving ex-spouse.*

According to Article 205 bis §1 of the BCC, the heirs of the deceased spouse owe the surviving spouse a maintenance allowance if the surviving spouse was in need when his/her spouse dies (even in case of legal separation of husband and wife resulting *ipso jure* from separation of bed and board). This allowance must be claimed before Judicial Court (*Tribunal de Première Instance*) not later than one year from date of death. The court will investigate the status of need of the surviving spouse and evaluate the allowance.

If the spouses were divorced at the time of death, the answer will depend on the type of divorce.

1. If the ex-spouses have divorced by mutual consent, they would have decided by themselves the amount of a potential maintenance allowance. The court will investigate if the provisions of the agreement of divorce by mutual consent respect the rights of the parties in particular concerning the potential allowance, and will pronounce the divorce if all conditions are fulfilled.

   Because the goal of the allowance in this type of divorce is the maintenance of a spouse who is in need, the BCC provides that this allowance will also be payable by the heirs of the debtor's ex-spouse after his/her death.

   However, the heirs will be discharged from this obligation if the spouses have specially stipulated in their divorce agreement that no allowance is due after the death of the debtor's ex-spouse.
2. If the spouses were divorced after a full judicial procedure, the judge has to estimate the amount of the allowance. The goal of this allowance is not only maintenance but also compensation for a spouse who is considered as the victim of the divorce. Therefore, the BCC provides that no allowance will be due by the heirs of the debtor's ex-spouse.

(B) *The parents of the deceased spouse.*
According to Article 205bis §2 of the BCC, a parent of the spouse who died without descendants can claim maintenance from any heir if two conditions are fulfilled:

1. the parent must be in a state of need;
2. the parent must have been deprived of a part of his/her inheritance as a result of gifts (*inter vivos* and *post mortem*) made by the deceased to his/her spouse.

The maintenance allowance must not exceed the amount of the part of inheritance of which the parent is deprived as a result of those gifts.

(C) *Children of the deceased spouse who are not the children of the surviving spouse.*
Such children can claim a maintenance allowance, education and adequate upbringing from the surviving spouse (Article 203 §2 of the BCC). The surviving spouse must meet those legal obligations up to the total inheritance he/she received in the estate (*see* paragraph 4) and the additional gifts (*inter vivos* and *post mortem*) he/she was granted by the deceased spouse.

6. Community Property Between Husband and Wife

(a) As explained in paragraph 3 above there are two types of marriage contracts under BCC; the community contract and the separation of property contract.

International Succession

Community contract

Each spouse owns the totality of his own patrimony and the half of the common patrimony. The goods owned before marriage and the goods received by donation or succession are excluded from the common patrimony.

Separation property contract

In the separation property settlement, there are only two patrimonies. Consequently, each spouse owns his own patrimony which is constituted of the assets owned before marriage and all the goods received or purchased during the marriage with his own income.

7. Gifts (*Inter Vivos*)

As explained in paragraph 4, freedom of testacy is limited under Belgian law by the mechanism of the 'forced heirship rules', i.e., the reserved compulsory share. These rules provide the portion of the estate that the deceased may dispose and the portion that is reserved for his heirs according to his familial situation.

To apply those rules, it is first necessary to determine on what basis the reserved portion must be calculated. This is not done on the basis of the assets existing at the time of death, but on the basis of a fictive hereditary mass in which all gifts *inter vivos* made by the deceased are added to the existing assets. This mechanism is called restitution (*mécanisme de rapport*).

Once the compulsory share is calculated on this basis, the remaining part of the succession is disposable. The gifts that have been made and secondly testamentary dispositions are imputed to that disposable part. If the total figure exceeds the disposable portion, it must be reduced. The heirs with a reserved portion may then file a claim for reduction of testamentary dispositions or gifts *inter vivos* (*mécanisme de reduction*).

However, the donor may expressly exempt an heir from the obligation to make return. This exemption will be set off against the available part of the succession but will not deprive a reserved heir of his reserved portion.

8. Capacity

(a) A person must be at least eighteen years old to make a gift or to write a will and must be physically and intellectually capable and able to sign.

(b) The same conditions apply to the witnesses. The following persons are not valid witnesses:

– members of the family of the notary;
– members of the family of the witnesses;

– employees of the notary;
– a spouse of another witness;
– beneficiaries of the will and members of their families;
– persons who have been punished in accordance with Articles 31 to 34 of the penal code.

(c) A beneficiary can also be a foundation or a charitable institution. A person who has not been conceived at the date of the will is excluded.

9. Authority (Court, Notarial or Other)

The order of succession applicable in case of intestacy is determined by the BCC (*see* paragraph 3). Each heir may collect his assets in the estate by virtue of the system of direct factual possession (*saisine*) in terms of those rules.

The BCC does not delegate special authority to any court, notary or other special body to establish the order of succession in a particular case. Transmission of the inheritance operates directly and is not administered by a separate body (such as executors or administrators in common law countries).

However, in case of dispute between the heirs, any of them could claim the application of the BCC's rules before the Court (*Tribunal de Première Instance*).

10. Invalidity of Will

(a) There are three kinds of defect that may affect the validity of a will: defects in the substance of the will, defects in the form of the will and defects in the legal capacity of the testator and the heirs.

Defects in the substance
 i. The consent of the testator.

On the basis of Article 901 BCC, the case law has developed a special theory concerning consent of the testator: the theory of the reinforced consent (*consentement renforcé*).

In matters concerning the contracts and legal documents, defects of consent are of restrictive interpretation. On the other hand, as regards liberalities and wills, the case law requires that the consent must be more certain and complete. A will could therefore be invalidated if an heir could prove that the consent of the testator had lessened when he wrote the will.

The Court could therefore invalidate a will written by a testator being of sound mind but affected by a weakness of mind that subjected him more easily than another person to the influence of those who surrounded him.
 ii. Contract of succession (*pactes sur succession future*).

As explained under paragraph 4, *i.*, contracts on succession are strictly forbidden in Belgium. A will providing such contract will therefore be invalidated.

International Succession

iii. The will must be clear.

The will must be clear and coherent. If the will is so illogical that it is not possible to determine what the wishes of the testator were, it will be invalidated.

Defect in the form
A will is considered as a very formal legal act. As explained under paragraph 2, the formalities must therefore be respected.

(b) The invalidity of a will is pronounced by a Judicial Court (*Tribunal de Première Instance*). Since a will is a formal legal act, the defects that affect it cannot be cured. Each condition or formality is considered as 'public order' (*ordre public*) and subjected to automatic invalidity if confirmed before the judge.

11. Simultaneous Death

In case of simultaneous death both persons are deemed to die at the same time. Consequently, neither of them may inherit from the other.

12. Estate Taxes

(a) One should note that the matter of estate taxes is no longer under federal responsibility, but has been regionalized. Consequently, the region of Brussels (from 2003), the region of Wallonia (from 2001), and the Flemish region (from 2000) are taxed at different rates. These rates are summarized in the tables below.

Region of Brussels

– Direct line or between spouse or cohabitants:

Bracket in euro	%
0,01 to 50.000	3
50.000,01 to 100.000	8
100.000,01 to 175.000	9
175.000,01 to 250.000	18
250.000,01 to 500.000	24
More than 500.000	30

56

– Brothers/sisters:

Bracket in euro	%
0.01 to 12.500	20
12.500,01 to 25.000	25
25.000,01 to 50.000	30
50.000,01 to 100.000	40
100.000,01 to 175.000	55
175.000,01 to 250.000	60
More than 250.000	65

– Uncle/aunt and nephew/niece:

Bracket in euro	%
0,01 to 50.000	35
50.000,01 to 100.000	50
100.000,01 to 175.000	60
More than 175.000	70

– Others:

Bracket in euro	%
0,01 to 50.000	40
50.000,01 to 75.000	55
75.000,01 to 175.000	65
More than 175.000	80

International Succession

Wallonia Region

– Direct line or between spouse or legal cohabitants:

Bracket in euro	%
0,01 to 12.500	3
12.500,01 to 25.000	4
25.000,01 to 50.000	5
50.000,01 to 100.000	7
100.000,01 to 150.000	10
150.000,01 to 200.000	14
200.000,01 to 250.000	18
250.000,01 to 500.000	24
More than 500.000	30

– Others:

Bracket in euro	Brothers/sisters in %	Uncle/aunt and nephew/niece in %	Others in %
0,01 to 12.500	20	25	30
12.500,01 to 25.000	25	30	35
25.000,01 to 75.000	35	40	50
75.000,01 to 175.000	50	55	65
More than 175.000	65	70	80

Flemish Region

In the Flemish region there are two different estates for tax purposes. The first consists of the seal estate and the second of the movables of the deceased. The hereafter mentioned rates of inheritance tax are calculated separately on each of those two estates, instead of the entire estate.

– Direct line or between spouse and legal cohabitant[1]:

Bracket in euro	%
0,01 to 50.000	3
50.000,01 to 250.000	9
More than 250.000	27

– Others:

Bracket in euro	Brothers/sisters %	All the others %
0,01 to 75.000	30	45
75.000,01 to 125.000	55	55
More than 125.000	65	65

(b) In the absence of a double tax treaty, taxes apply on worldwide assets.

Note that Belgium has adopted the rule that if the deceased was domiciled or had the center of his economic interests in Belgium, his succession will be dealt with in Belgium and Belgian rules will apply on his worldwide assets.

If a person was not domiciled in Belgium at the time of death, inheritance tax only applies to real estate located in Belgium.

(c) The taxes are due by the heirs.

13. Administration of Estates

(a) In accordance with Article 724 BCC, Belgian law deals with the transmission of assets in the estate by the system of direct factual possession of all assets, rights and actions of the deceased. Transmission of the inheritance operates directly.

Nevertheless, certain categories of heirs do not derive their rights upon death but must seek an order for possession from the court. This applies where the deceased's estate passes to the State or to a universal legatee not faced with reserved shares and whose title derives from either a holograph will or a will in an international form.

---

1. Two persons may have the legal status of cohabitant if they make a cohabitation declaration according to the new procedure allowed for by the BCC.

International Succession

(b) In accordance with Article 1025 BCC the testator may, by will, appoint at least one person (the testamentory executor) to supervise the implementation of his wishes.

The deceased may instruct the testamentory executor to take possession of movables in the estate for a period not exceeding one year and one day. In such a case, he has the power to sell the assets where there are sufficient funds to discharge all the legacies for which he is responsible. Once this is done, he must render an account of his management of the estate to the heirs.

(c) In case of conflict between the heirs and the testamentory executor the courts will resolve the dispute.

(d) The State may raise queries or object in the case of fraud concerning the death duties.

(e) The creditors of the estate receive payment from the heirs if the latter have accepted the succession.

If all the heirs refuse the succession or if the latter is vacant, a receiver (*curateur à succession vacante*) shall be appointed by the Court (*Tribunal de Première Instance*). The curator shall pay the creditors with the assets of the succession.

(f) As explained in (a) *above*, the heirs take possession of the estate.

14. Domicile/Nationality

(a) Under Belgian law a distinction is made between succession law governing the movable property and the immovable property.

– The law of the last domicile of the deceased governs succession to the worldwide movable property.
– The law of the place where the real estate is located governs succession to immovable property.

Nationality is immaterial from a Belgian estate tax duty point of view. The significant factor is the domicile of the deceased at the time he passed away.

For inheritance tax purposes, the domicile is deemed to be the place where the deceased lived with his family or managed his fortune. In this respect the most significant presumption results from the deceased's name appearing on the list of the inhabitants of the municipality of the particular territory.

Since 2002 there is an additional rule to determine the region which shall be competent to apply the inheritance tax. For a period of five years prior to the death, the deceased shall be deemed to have his domicile in the region of which he has been an inhabitant for the longest period during those five years.

The above rule plays a role if the deceased was domiciled in Belgium and the estate is composed of both movable assets and real estate (the so-called world-wide assets basis).

When the estate of the deceased is composed only of real estate in Belgium, Belgian inheritance tax is always applicable regardless of whether or not the deceased was domiciled in Belgium. If the deceased was not domiciled in Belgium, the competent region to apply the inheritance taxes shall be the one in which the highest cadastral value (the income generated by the real estate has estimated by tax authorities) is located.

(b) In our opinion, no court or authority will grant an order of probate or succession if there is no asset.

SECTION B – APPLICABLE LAW/PROCEDURE WHERE FOREIGN ELEMENT/S ARE INVOLVED

1. Jurisdiction

(a) In terms of Article 635, 4° of the Judicial Code (hereafter BJC) a Belgian court would also have jurisdiction over an interested non-Belgian party if the proceedings were commenced in Belgium. This is subject to the Belgian court having jurisdiction because of the last domicile of the deceased being in Belgium, immovable assets being situated in Belgium or by virtue of the Belgian domicile of an heir.

(b) Belgian private international law makes a distinction between succession law applicable to movable assets and succession law applicable to immovable assets: the law of the domicile at the time of death applies to all movable assets. The *lex rei sitae* applies to immovable assets.

(c) The competent court is the First degree (*Tribunal de Première Instance*) of the place of last domicile in Belgium or of the place where the immovable property is situated in Belgium or where the plaintiff was domiciled.

2. Applicable Law

The court shall apply the law of the domicile at the time of death to all movable assets and the *lex rei sitae* to immovable assets.

There are two derogations to the applicable law:

– The mechanism of the *renvoi* i.e., where the foreign conflict rules referred to by the Belgian conflict rules lead back to Belgian law, the latter shall apply.
– *Droit de prélèvement*: in case of division of an estate comprising assets situated in a foreign country, co-heirs who are not nationals of such country may levy in a proportion of the foreign property from which they would be excluded by virtue of local laws or customs against the assets situated in Belgium (Article 912 BCC).

International Succession

3. Foreign Succession/Inheritance Orders

Foreign orders rendered by foreign courts cannot be enforced until an executor has been granted by the Belgian judge. The Belgian Court (*Tribunal de Première Instance*) shall verify if the foreign decision complies with the conditions of Article 570 BJC, i.e., whether the decision rendered contains anything that might be contrary to Belgian public order or public policy, whether the rights of defense have been complied with, whether the foreign judge was merely competent on basis of the nationality of the plaintiff, whether there is no national recourse of action left (*with regard to the law of the country in which the decision is rendered*) and whether the judgment issued complies with the fixed conditions of authenticity, (*also with regard to the law of the country in which the decision is rendered*).

4. Two or More Succession or Probate Orders

An international estate may be subject to several different legal systems so that there can be a plurality of order of successions. Theoretically each order of succession will apply to the part of the estate that corresponds to such order. Therefore, the *lex rei sitae* will govern the order of succession for the immovable part of the succession, and the law of the domicile at the time of death will govern this order for all movable assets.

However, the parallel application of several different rules could lead to many difficulties and the Belgian judge will therefore try to find a single *lex sucessionis* applicable to all the assets by the mechanism of the *renvoi* (paragraph 2 *above*). The nationality of the deceased is generally the most used coordinating factor to determine the *lex successionis* is such cases.

5. Assets

Even if there are no assets whatsoever in the jurisdiction, if the deceased had his last domicile in the said jurisdiction, the local court will assume jurisdiction. This, however, only concerns movable assets (*mobilia sequuntur personam*).

6. Expert Evidence

There is no necessity to give additional evidence regarding a foreign will if it has been recognized by a foreign court.

There is also no necessity to give evidence of the foreign inheritance laws to the Belgian Court. In Belgium, the judge is presumed to have knowledge of the law and that principle applies also for foreign law.

In practice, the lawyer who wants to implement a foreign inheritance law in Belgium will provide evidence of this law to be sure that the judge will apply it. However, it is in principle the judge's task to check the existence of the foreign law.

7. Unity of Succession

The principle of unity of succession exists under Belgian internal law. However, as mentioned above, in Belgian private international law, the laws applicable to movable and immovable assets are different.

8. Formalities

Belgium has contracted the *Hague Convention of 5 October 1961 on the Conflicts of Laws relating to the Form of Testamentary Dispositions*. According to Article 1 of this Convention, a will

'*shall be valid as regards form if its form complies with the internal law:*

a) of the place where the testator made it, or

b) of a nationality possessed by the testator, either at the time when he made the disposition, or at the time of his death, or

c) of a place in which the testator had his domicile either at the time when he made the disposition, or at the time of his death, or

d) of the place in which the testator had his habitual residence either at the time when he made the disposition, or at the time of his death, or

e) so far as immovables are concerned, of the place where they are situated.'

Since this Convention concerns the form of the will, Belgian Courts consider that the formalities of a will executed in a foreign country need not be the same as those applicable in Belgium, but must respect the law that governs the situation according to the Convention.

This rule applies to all cases: Article 6 of the Convention provides that its application shall be independent of any requirement of reciprocity and even if the nationality of the persons involved or the law to be applied is not that of a Contracting State.

Belgium has, however, made a single reservation to this convention: a will made orally, save in exceptional circumstances, by a Belgian without other nationality, may not be recognized in Belgium.

9. Legislation

As explained under paragraph 8, the *Hague Convention on the Conflicts of Laws of 5 October 1961 Relating to the Form of Testamentary Dispositions* is applicable in Belgium since 19 December 1971 (law of 29 July 1971).

International Succession

10. Wills

(a) As explained under paragraph 8, Belgium ratified the *Hague Convention on the Conflicts of Laws of 5 October 1961*. The law that will govern the execution of a will as regards to its form will therefore follow this convention.

The interpretation of the concept of 'form' in this Convention is quite broad since it includes the age, nationality or other personal conditions of the testator and witnesses required for the validity of a testamentary disposition.

(b) The testator cannot choose the *lex successionnis* but he may choose the law that must be used for the interpretation of his will. Indeed, even if the *lex successionis* is the Belgian Law, the testator could chose a foreign law for the interpretation of legal concepts such as 'next of kin' or 'trust' that do not exist in Belgian Law.

If the deceased has not chosen a special law, the law of his last domicile will apply.

(c) The rights of the heirs, e.g., the minimum portion, is governed by the *lex successionis*, which is, as explained under paragraph 1, the law of the last domicile of the deceased for the movable assets and the *lex rei sitae* for immovable assets.

(d) According to Article 3 al. 3 of the BCC, the law that governs the legal status and the capacity of a person is the national law of this person. Therefore the nationality determines the law applicable concerning the capacity to inherit.

(e) As explained under point (d), the nationality determines the law applicable concerning the capacity to make a will.

If the testator changed nationality after having made his will, the applicable law remains his national law at the time he made his will.

(f) In general it is accepted in Belgium that the exception of international public policy can be an obstacle to the normal application of the foreign law when the latter is in contradiction with the international public policy of Belgium. The international public policy of Belgium can be defined as the most essential principles of established moral, political or economic order.

Since the international public policy is a concept that varies in time and space, it is impossible to determine which foreign law is considered incompatible with the Belgian legislation. In any case, before the exception of international public policy can be invoked, the effects claimed in Belgium by the application of the foreign law must be 'aggressive' from the point of view of the *lex fori*.

Although there is virtually no jurisprudence on the field of succession/international public policy, we can imagine that an essential principle in Belgium such as the free consent of the testator could be considered as a rule of international public policy.

(g) A distinction must be made between the law applicable to the relation between the *donor* and the *appointor* and the *lex successionis* applicable in this case.

Relation between the donor *and the* appointor
The *appointor* is not bequeathing his *own* property but rather is acting as agent for the *donor* in disposing of the *donor*'s property. This would suggest that we should look to the law governing the instrument creating the power of appointment.

In Belgium, the law governing this kind of relation, (*mandat ou représentation*) is the national law of the person who is represented by the other. The national law of the *donor* will therefore apply to determine the validity of the power of appointment.

Lex successionis
The general principle will apply even if the estate of the *donor* is bequeathed by the *appointor* in his own will. That estate remains the estate of the *donor* and therefore, at the death of the *appointor*, the law of the last domicile of the *donor* will apply to the movable part of his estate and the *lex rei sitae* to the immovable part of this estate.

(h) According to Article 2 of the *Hague Convention of 5 October 1961 on the Conflicts of Laws Relating to the Form of Testamentary Dispositions*, Article 1 shall apply to testamentary dispositions revoking an earlier testamentary disposition.

The revocation, amendment or revival would be subject to the general *lex successionis* determined as explained under point 1.

(i) The applicability of a potential reserve must be determined within the scope of the *lex successionis*. That potential reserve will be applicable to any heirs, even if they are non-resident or not entitled to such reserve by their national succession law.

If the movable and immovable part of the succession cannot be submitted to the same *lex successionis* by the mechanism of the *renvoi* (*see* point 2 & 4), two or more separate reserves could apply to each part of the succession.

11. Domicile/Nationality

(a) The place of the last domicile of the deceased, i.e., principal establishment at the time of death is the domicile to be taken into consideration.

(b) The domicile of the beneficiary is irrelevant to the applicable law.

(c) The domicile is, according to Article 102 BCC, the place where the person has, at the same time, situated his residence, the centre of his affairs, the seat of his wealth and the affection of his family. It is not necessarily the place where the deceased lived at the time of death.

12. Taxation

According to Article 1 §1 of the *Code des droits de succession* the tax is due on 'the value, debts deducted, of everything that is collected in the succession of an inhabitant of the Kingdom'. Article 1 §2 defines an inhabitant of the Kingdom as the person who, at the time of death, had established his domicile or the centre of his fortune in Belgium.

The concept of 'centre of fortune' has been defined by the Supreme Court of Belgium as '*the place of the fortune of the taxpayer, it being understood that this expression does not envisage the place where the goods which constitute fortune are located, but the place where the owner, who manages or controls them, has the seat of his business or his occupation*'.

Furthermore, Article 1, §1, 2° of the *Code des droits de succession* makes (the *droit de mutation par décès*) the value of the immovable assets situated in Belgium and accumulated in a succession of a non-inhabitant in Belgium, liable to a tax.

Bermuda

Prepared by: Monica JONES (partner)*
Appleby Spurling & Kempe

Address: Cedar House
         41 Cedar Avenue
         Hamilton, Bermuda
Tel.:   441 295 2244
Fax: 441 295 8666

SECTION A – BRIEF SURVEY OF THE LOCAL SYSTEM

1. Type of System

(a) The legal system of Bermuda is a common law system.

(b) Not applicable.

2. Wills

(a) Under Bermuda law, a will must be in writing and signed by the testator in the presence of two witnesses (who should sign in the presence of each other and the testator) in order to be valid. A will need not be dated though it is prudent to do so in order to establish which is the last will, if more than one exists. A holograph will is valid under Bermuda law if it is entirely in the handwriting of the testator and signed at the foot or end thereof by the testator (to be proved by the oath of two or more persons acquainted with the testator's handwriting).

Furthermore, under Bermuda law, for a will to be valid the testator must be eighteen years or over and must be of sound disposing mind. There is a statutory exception allowing any member of Her Majesty's Forces currently in actual naval, military or air force service or any mariner or seaman being at sea to dispose of his personal estate by means of a 'Privileged will' (for which no formalities are required).

(b) *i.* A codicil, executed in the same manner as a will (*see* 2(a) *above*), may amend a will.

---

* Ms. Jones would like to thank Ms. Karen Corless, Mark Cave and Ms. Jane Sheere for their hard work and effort in bringing this document to fruition.

67

A will, or any part thereof, is revocable by codicil, by another will, or, by the testator, or some person in his presence and by the testator's direction, burning, tearing or otherwise destroying the will, with the intention of revoking it.

Re-execution of a revoked will or the execution of a codicil showing an intention to revive the revoked will revives a revoked will. In the case of a will, which has been partly revoked and later wholly revoked, when revived the revival does not extend to the part which was revoked before revocation of the whole will unless an intention to revive that part is shown.

Generally, there is a presumption that any interlineations, obliterations or alterations to a will are made after the execution of the will unless the attestation clause is altered to show that they were made before signing the will. Therefore, the testator and the witnesses should sign any interlineations, obliterations or alterations to a will.

ii. Marriage generally revokes a will. However, a testator may make a will in contemplation of marriage, which will be valid after the marriage, provided it is clear that the will (or specific gifts in the will) are clearly intended not to be revoked by the marriage.[1]

Furthermore, a disposition in a will in exercise of a power of appointment shall take effect notwithstanding the testator's subsequent marriage unless the real or personal estate so appointed would in default of appointment pass to the testator's estate representatives.

iii. Either the re-execution of the revoked will or a codicil showing an intention to revive the revoked will revives a revoked will. In the case where a will has been, first, partly revoked, and later wholly, a revival does not extend to the part that was revoked before the revocation of the whole will unless an intention to revive that part is shown.

3. Intestacy

(a) The *Succession Act 1974* governs intestate succession.

1974 Act Section 5	Surviving Spouse	Issue	Other Relatives	Entitlement to Intestate's Estate
CASE 1	Yes	No	No	In trust for surviving spouse absolutely
CASE 2	Yes	Yes	–	• Personal chattels to spouse • Greater of 1/2 residuary estate or USD 100,000 to spouse • Remainder to issue on intestacy trusts

---

1. *Wills Act*, s. 14.

1974 Act Section 5	Surviving Spouse	Issue	Other Relatives	Entitlement to Intestate's Estate
CASE 3	Yes	No	Parent(s) and/or brothers and sisters of the whole blood and/or their issue	• Personal chattels to spouse • Greater of 66²/₃ residuary estate or USD 150,000 to spouse • Remainder in trust for parent(s) but if none to brothers and sisters of the whole blood or their issue on intestacy trusts.
CASE 4	No	Yes	–	To issue on intestacy trusts
CASE 5	No	No	Both Parents	In trust for parents equally
CASE 6	No	No	One Parent	In trust for one parent
CASE 7(1)	No	No	Brothers and sisters of whole blood	Brothers and sisters of whole blood on intestacy trusts
CASE 7(2)	No	No	Brothers and sisters of half blood	Brothers and sisters of half blood on intestacy trusts
CASE 7(3)	No	No	Grandparent(s)	Grandparent(s) if more than one in equal shares
CASE 7(4)	No	No	Uncles and aunts of whole blood	Uncles and aunts of whole blood on intestacy trusts
CASE 7(5)	No	No	Uncles and aunts of half blood	Uncles and aunts of half blood on intestacy trusts
CASE 8	No	No	No	Bermuda Government as *bona vacantia*

Note: Issue includes all children regardless of whether they are born in or out of wedlock. Illegitimate or adulterine children are treated the same as legitimate children.

International Succession

(b) Under Bermuda law, there is no difference in the application of conflict law rules or foreign factors to the devolution of movable or immovable property whether or not a will exists (*see* 1(b) of Section B).

4. Freedom of Testation

(a) Under Bermuda law, no person is entitled to a compulsory share. However, under the *Succession Act 1974*, the spouse of the deceased; a former spouse who has not remarried; a child of the deceased; or, a grandchild of the deceased, who immediately before the death of the deceased was being maintained either wholly or partly by the deceased, may apply to the Court for an order for reasonable financial provision out of the deceased's estate if by reason of the deceased's will or the law relating to intestacy or a combination of both he or she does not receive reasonable financial provision. In the case of a spouse, reasonable financial provision means such financial provision as it would be reasonable, given all the circumstances of the case, for the person to receive, whether or not that provision in required for his or her maintenance. In the case of any other applicant, reasonable financial provision means such financial provision, as it would be reasonable in all the circumstances of the case for the applicant to receive for his or her maintenance.

(b) *i.* A contract of inheritance is binding upon the deceased if full valuable consideration is given.

ii. No. However, the testator may insert a hotchpot clause directing past advances or other sums or property to be brought into account when determining the individual shares of each member of a class of beneficiaries. Additionally, under Bermuda law it is possible for a deed of family arrangement to be entered into by the family members for redirecting the division of the estate of a deceased person.

5. Maintenance

See 4(a) *above.*

6. Community Property Between Husband and Wife

(a) Under Bermuda law, there is no concept of community of property.

(b) Under Bermuda law, there is no concept of a matrimonial regime.

Property may be held jointly, either as tenants-in-common or joint tenants. 'Tenancy-in-common' describes the situation where two or more persons hold property in equal or unequal undivided shares, each person having an equal right to possess the whole property but no right of survivorship. 'Joint tenancy' describes the situation where two or more co-owners take identical interests simultaneously by the same instrument and have the same right of possession. A joint tenancy differs from a tenancy in common in that each joint tenant has a right of survivorship to the other's shares. Where property is held jointly as tenants-in-common the deceased's share forms part of his free estate rather than passing to the surviving joint owner on his demise. Household and personal effects in the matrimonial home are normally regarded as jointly owned and pass to the surviving spouse by survivorship unless there is evidence to the contrary.

Inter vivos gifts of Bermuda assets, as defined in the *Stamp Duties Act 1976*, between spouses are subject to stamp duty; testamentary gifts between spouses are not. Rates payable on *inter vivos* gifts of Bermuda assets are as follows:

First USD 100,000	2.5%
Next USD 400,000	3%
Next USD 500,000	4%
Next USD 500,000	5%
Over USD 1,500,000	6%

Inter vivos gifts of non-Bermuda assets are assessed a duty of 0.1 per cent of the value of the assets.

Under Section 33(1) of the *Wills Act 1988*, there is a presumption, except where a contrary intention is shown, that if a testator devises or bequeaths real or personal estate to his spouse in terms which in themselves give an absolute interest to the spouse, but by the same instrument purports to give his issue an interest in the same estate, the gift to the spouse is absolute notwithstanding the purported gift to the issue.

7. Gifts (*Inter Vivos*)

(a) No. Gifts to an heir prior to death are not set-off against the heir's inheritance unless expressly provided for in the deceased's will (*see* 4(b) 2 *above*). Furthermore, prior gifts are not set-off against an heir's inheritance on intestacy.

(b) Not applicable.

8. Capacity

(a) As indicated *above* in 2(a), a testator must be either aged twenty-one years or over or have been married and aged eighteen years or over, except in the case of privileged wills. The testator must also be of sound disposing mind, which is generally understood as meaning the person has the legal capacity to make a will. Capacity in relation to wills means that the testator understands that he is giving the property away, the nature and extent of his property and the nature and extent of any claims by persons whom he may reasonably be expected to make provision for.

International Succession

If a testator does not speak or read English, then one must translate and interpret the will for the testator, who must confirm his approval of the contents of the will before signing the will. If the testator is blind or cannot read, one should follow the same procedures as above. If a testator cannot write or is too ill to write such a testator may direct someone else to sign the will on his behalf in his presence.

(b) There is no express statutory provision requiring witnesses to be of a particular age however it is prudent for witnesses to be aged eighteen years or older, if possible, so they may give a valid attestation before the Bermuda Court to the execution of the will. Furthermore, a gift to a witness or the spouse of a witness will be void unless there are sufficient other witnesses to the execution of the will to validate the gift.

(c) There are no restrictions on the capacity of a beneficiary, however, if a beneficiary is under eighteen years of age or of unsound mind, unless there is express provision contained in the will, the beneficiary will be unable to give a valid receipt for a legacy or share of residue left to him. Therefore, the legacy or share of residue will have to be retained by the executors/administrators (or other trustees appointed) until the beneficiary attains eighteen years of age and is deemed to be of sound mind and is therefore able to give a receipt.

A beneficiary or the spouse of a beneficiary may witness a will; however, any gift, appointment or disposition to such a beneficiary will be void.

9. Authority (Court, Notarial or Other)

A grant of probate (if there is a will appointing executors); letters of administration with the will annexed (if there is a will but no executors appointed who are able and willing to act); re-seal of a foreign grant or letters of administration (in the case of intestacy) (hereinafter 'Grant') must be obtained from the Registrar of the Supreme Court (the 'Registrar') in the name of the Court and under the seal of the Court. In the case of estates worth USD 50,000 and under the Court will grant a certificate.

The Registrar reviews an application for the Grant that is in the prescribed form. The Registrar shall not make a Grant in any case where the will is contested until the contention is disposed of or where it appears to the Registrar that a Grant ought not to be made without the direction of the court.

10. Invalidity of Will

(a) A will is invalid if it is formally defective or the testator lacks testamentary capacity. The testator must also know and approve of the contents of a will; thus, if a testator executes a will in ignorance of its contents, the will is invalid. Undue influence, duress or fraud will also invalidate a will.

(b) A will that is invalid is void.

11. Simultaneous Death

(a) Where two or more persons die in circumstances that render it uncertain who survived whom, the presumption is that the deaths occurred in order of seniority with the youngest deceased having survived the others. However, between spouses who die in circumstances that render it uncertain who survived whom, if the elder spouse dies intestate, Bermuda law deems that the elder intestate spouse survived the younger spouse so that the younger spouse takes no interest under the estate of his or her elder intestate spouse. If such spouses died either both intestate or both testate then the younger spouse will be deemed to have survived the older.

(b) There is a statutory presumption that the deaths occurred in order of seniority, the youngest having survived the others.

12. Estate Taxes

(a) In Bermuda, the *Stamp Duties Act 1976* imposes stamp duty on the affidavit of value filed with the application for a Grant.

(b) No, duty is not payable on all assets worldwide; it is essentially only payable on Bermuda assets as defined in the *Stamp Duties Act 1976*. Stamp duty is payable on the net value of a person's Bermuda property as set out in the affidavit of value. The net value of a person's Bermuda property is the total value of the deceased's Bermuda property less certain deductions authorized by the *Stamp Duties Act 1976*. These deductions include certain debts incurred solely by the deceased prior to death, the costs of the funeral, the cost of any valuation of the deceased's property for the purposes of the application for a Grant, the value of all benefits passing to the surviving spouse and the value of all gifts to qualifying charities.
   The following rates apply:

Net Value of Deceased's Bermuda Property	Stamp Duty Payable
First 50,000	Nil
The next 150,000	5%
The next 800,000	10%
Balance over 1,000,000	15%

Non-Bermuda property passing under a will or on intestacy is exempt from stamp duty on death. The *Stamp Duties Act 1976*, also provides that any Bermuda securities or money in a Bermudian bank or deposit company denominated in a currency other than Bermuda area currency do not fall within the definition of 'property' which must be listed in the affidavit of value. Furthermore, shares in a local company having no more than five shareholders and of which at least 75 per cent of the assets are foreign and 85 per cent of the net income is foreign derived also do not fall within the definition of Bermuda 'property', in the *Stamp Duties Act 1976*, for the purposes of assessing the stamp duty payable.

(c) The estate is primarily liable for the payment of stamp duty.

13. Administration of Estates

(a) Estates are administered by estate representatives who are either executors, original or by representation, appointed by the will or, if there is no will or where there is no executor appointed in the will or the executor is unwilling to act, administrators appointed by the court. The order of persons entitled to apply for a Grant of administration is established by the *Non-Contentious Probate Rules 1974*. Heirs per se cannot administer the estate, however, where no executor is appointed by will or the executor is unwilling to serve, heirs may apply to the court for a Grant of letters of administration.

If the person appointed executor is a minor then the person will not be able to act as executor until the person attains the age of majority. Therefore, an adult, usually the minor's parent or guardian, holds the Grant for the minor's use and benefit. The minor can take the Grant on attaining majority. Moreover, if one of several executors appointed by a will is a minor, the adult executors may take out a general Grant immediately, which provides for the reservation of the power of the minor to take a Grant of double probate when he attains the age of majority. A person, on behalf of an infant executor, may not at any time renounce such an infant executor's right to probate on attaining age of majority. Similar rules apply in the case of mentally or physically incapacitated person appointed executors by a will.

(b) In most circumstances, a Grant will be necessary in order to administer an estate. The probate division of the Supreme Court requires that in order to obtain a Grant, the applicant must file the following documents:

1. An application for a Grant, which lists the various documents being submitted with the application;
2. If there is a will, it must be submitted together with any codicils and any testamentary paper incorporated by reference;
3. If there is a renunciation, it will usually accompany any subsequent application for a Grant;
4. An oath of executor or administrator stating:

   (i) Whether the deceased had property in Bermuda at the time of his/her death or was resident or domiciled in Bermuda at the time of his or her death;
   (ii) The gross value of the estate to be covered by the Grant (this would only include Bermuda property as defined in the *Stamp Duties Act 1976*) calculated as at the deceased's death.

5. An affidavit of value confirming the particulars or description of the Bermuda property as defined in the *Stamp Duties Act 1976*, owned by the deceased at the date of death and its value at that date. The affidavit will contain a statement as to the net value of the estate (i.e., the gross value less allowable deductions) and the amount of stamp duty payable.
6. Additionally any valuations prepared for the affidavit of value will accompany the application.

Small estates will not require an affidavit of value to be submitted.

(c) An Estate representative is under a statutory duty when required to do so by the Court to exhibit on oath in the Court, a full inventory of the estate, and when so required, to render an account of the administration of the estate to the Court.

(d) A beneficiary may challenge the manner in which the executors or administrators administer the estate. Where a charity is a beneficiary, the Attorney General will represent the interests of the charity.

(e) Once the administration of the estate has been completed (i.e., all debts and liabilities paid, etc.), the executors or administrators transfer the assets to the heirs. The form of the transfer depends upon the asset in question. Furthermore, interim distributions to the heirs are possible if the executors or administrators believe that the remaining assets in the estate will be sufficient to pay all the remaining debts and liabilities.

(f) The payment of creditors is dependent on whether the estate is solvent or not. If the estate is solvent, the order of application of the assets of the estate to satisfy creditor claims is established in Part II of Schedule 1 of the *Administration of Estates Act 1974*. If the Estate is insolvent, funeral, testamentary and administration expenses have priority. All other creditors are subject to the same rules and respective rights of secured and unsecured creditors as found under the law of bankruptcy. The executors or administrators pay the unsecured creditors out of the residuary of the estate. In the case of a solvent estate, a will may vary the order of application of assets of the estate to satisfy creditor claims. Under Bermuda law, the presumption is that the executors or administrator reduces the entire residuary estate to cash, and, then any debts, funeral and testamentary expenses are paid from that cash pool. In practise, the executor or administrator will only make sufficient cash to meet the deceased's expenses available.

(g) Where there is a will but no executor, one must file an application for a Grant of letters of administration with the will annexed with the Court. Rule 18 of the *Non-Contentious Probate Rules 1974*, sets out the order of persons who may be appointed administrators of the estate. Priority will be given to the person with the most immediate interest in the estate.

On intestacy, one must file an application for a Grant of letters of administration with the Court. Rule 20 of the *Non-Contentious Probate Rules 1974* sets out the order of persons entitled to act as administrator in those circumstances which closely mirror the order of entitlement to the estate on intestacy.

14. Domicile/Nationality

(a) In addition to the express formalities required under Bermuda law (*see* Part I, Section 2(a)), a will shall be treated as properly executed if its execution conformed to the internal law in force in the territory where it was executed, or in the territory where, at the time of its execution or of the testator's death, the testator was domiciled or had his habitual residence, or in states of which at either of those times he was a national.[2] Furthermore, a will shall be treated as properly executed if it was executed on board a vessel or aircraft of any description provided that the execution of the will conformed with the internal law in force in the territory with which the vessel or aircraft may be taken to be most closely connected.[3] Moreover, as far as a will disposes of immovable property, the will is valid if its execution conformed to the internal law in force in the territory where the immovable property is situated.[4]

(b) A Bermuda Grant may be issued even if there are no assets in Bermuda if the testator was either domiciled in Bermuda or ordinarily resident in Bermuda at the time of death but not if the testator only executed a will in Bermuda. The affidavit of value in such cases is submitted at a nil value. The 'ordinary residence' of the testator in Bermuda or having assets in Bermuda are conclusive for establishing that the Court has jurisdiction.

Section B – Applicable Law/Procedure where Foreign Element/s are involved

1. Jurisdiction

(a) If an affidavit is made in support of an application to the court for a Grant in which the deponent states that the deceased person at the time of death was ordinarily resident in Bermuda or that some property of the deceased was then in Bermuda the affidavit shall be conclusive for the purpose of establishing the jurisdiction of the Bermuda Court.

(b) Under Bermuda law, irrespective of whether there is a will or not, movable property passes in accordance with the law of the deceased's domicile at the date of death and immovable property situate in Bermuda passes in accordance with Bermuda law. Immovable property situate elsewhere passes in accordance with the law of the jurisdiction in which it is situated.

---

2. *Wills Act*, s. 37.
3. *Wills Act*, s. 38(1)(a).
4. *Wills Act*, s. 38(1)(b).

(c) The Supreme Court of Bermuda including a judge whether sitting in Court or in Chambers or where expressly provided by the *Supreme Court Act 1905*, or the *Rules of the Supreme Court 1985*, the Registrar, has jurisdiction where local jurisdiction applies.

2. Applicable Law

Under Bermuda law, a will is to be interpreted in accordance with the law intended by the testator. In the absence of indications to the contrary, this is presumed to be the law of the testator's domicile when the will was executed. Under Section 40 of the *Wills Act 1988*, the construction of a will does not alter as a result of any change in the testator's domicile after execution of the will. However, as stated in 1(b) *above* immovable property passes in accordance with *Lex situs*.

3. Foreign Succession/Inheritance Orders

(a) Under Bermuda law, foreign Grants are not automatically recognized or enforced in respect of local assets, both movable and immovable. Furthermore, in order to seek recognition of a foreign grant it must be a Grant of probate or administration or other document purporting to be of the same nature granted by a court in the United Kingdom or any British possession, colony or dependency; a member nation of the commonwealth; or any state of the United States or the District of Columbia. If a foreign Grant is from a country, territory or state other than those listed above a new Grant must be applied for.

(b) Yes, in order to give effect to a foreign Grant, as defined in (a) *above*, one must apply to the Court for 'resealing' the foreign Grant under seal of the Bermuda Court.

(c) A Grant from a country listed in 3(a) may be resealed on production of a copy of the will and Grant, certified under seal or authority of the original court. Before resealing, in the case of letters of administration, one must satisfy the Court that sufficient security has been given to cover property in Bermuda. The court may also require evidence as to the domicile of the deceased and adequate security in respect of the debts due to creditors in Bermuda. Upon resealing, stamp duty is payable on the portion of the estate that consists of Bermuda property as defined in the *Stamp Duties Act 1976*.

4. Two or More Succession or Probate Orders

A foreign succession order, per se, will not be valid under Bermuda law. However, the executor or administrator under the foreign succession order may apply to the Bermuda court for re-sealing of the foreign order as described in 3 above. In the case of two or more foreign succession orders, where they purport to deal with the same asset, then the one arising from the will most recent in time will prevail.

International Succession

If two or more foreign succession orders apply to different assets, then the respective executor or administrator under each of the foreign succession orders may apply to the Bermuda court for re-sealing of the foreign Grant as described in 3(c) above.

5. Assets

Yes, *see* Section A14(b) *above*.

6. Expert Evidence

(a) Where evidence of the law of a country outside of Bermuda is required upon the application for a Grant, an affidavit of any person who practises, or has practised as a lawyer in that country and is conversant with its law may be accepted by the Registrar. Furthermore, the Registrar in special circumstances may accept the affidavit of any other person if the Registrar is satisfied that due to the person's official position they are able to give valid evidence regarding the law of such a country.

(b) Yes, *see* (a) *above*.

7. Unity of Succession

No.

8. Formalities

Bermuda law will treat a will as properly executed if its execution conformed to the internal law in force in the territory where it was executed, or in the territory where, at the time of its execution or of the testator's death, he was domiciled or had his habitual residence, or in a state of which, at either of those times he was a national. Furthermore, a will shall be treated as properly executed if it was executed on board a vessel or aircraft of any description if the execution of the will conformed with the internal law in force in the territory with which the vessel or aircraft may be taken to be most closely connected.[5] Moreover, as far as a will disposes immovable property, provided the execution of such will conformed to the internal law in force in the territory where the property was situated the will is properly executed.

9. Legislation

No.

---

5. *Wills Act*, s. 38(1)(a).

10. Wills

(a) *See* Section A14(a).

(b) Under Section 32 of the *Wills Act 1988*, the Court will endeavour to find the testator's true meaning when construing a will. In the absence of indications to the contrary, the presumption will be that the testator intended his will to be construed in accordance with the law of the jurisdiction of his domicile at the time of execution of the will, however, if it is clear from the express words of the will, or must necessarily be implied, that the will be construed in accordance with the law of another jurisdiction, the Bermuda Court will require evidence of the appropriate rules of construction.

(c) The rights of beneficiaries or heirs will depend upon the law that governs the devolution of the assets in question. There are no rules of forced heirship under Bermuda law.

(d) The law that governs the devolution of the asset in question determines the capacity to inherit.

(e) The law of the jurisdiction where execution of the will occurred determines the capacity to make a will.

(f) The law applicable to the asset will govern the essential or material validity of the will in question.

(g) A testator has capacity to exercise by a will a power of appointment over movables provided the testator has testamentary capacity under the law of the jurisdiction the testator was domiciled in at the time of execution of the will.

(h) The law of the jurisdiction where the testator executes the will governs the amendment, revocation and revival of a will.

(i) The laws regarding reserve to a non-resident apply with respect to movable property but not immovable property.

11. Domicile/Nationality

(a) The deceased's domicile at time of death will determine the administration of the estate; the nationality of the deceased is not relevant.

(b) The domicile of the beneficiary is generally not relevant under Bermuda law. However, where the issue is the capacity to inherit immovables nationality is relevant to the inheritance of Bermuda immovable property. Under the *Bermuda Immigration and Protection Act 1956*, beneficiaries of Bermuda real and leasehold property, who do not have Bermudian status, are required to obtain a licence to have such property transferred to them.

International Succession

(c) Under Bermuda law, a deceased can only have one domicile. A person acquires a 'domicile of origin' at birth, which if the person is legitimate is the domicile of his father, or if the person is illegitimate is the domicile of his mother. Until the age of sixteen, a person's domicile will change with the domicile of the relevant parent and is termed the 'domicile of dependency'. At the age of sixteen, a person acquires a 'domicile of choice' determined by the person's physical presence in a jurisdiction with the intention of remaining in that jurisdiction permanently or indefinitely. If either physical presence or the necessary intention cease without the person acquiring a new domicile of choice, the domicile of origin is revived.

A person's domicile of origin will revive where there is no domicile of dependence or choice. Therefore, it is not possible for a person either to have no domicile or more that one domicile under Bermuda law.

12. Taxation

Stamp duty is assessed on the estate, not the heirs.

Brazil

Prepared by: Adriana CAMARGO RODRIGUES and Geraldo Luiz DOS SANTOS LIMA, lawyers in São Paulo, Brazil, members of the firm of Suchodolski Advogados Associados S/C

Address: Suchodolski Advogados Associados S/C
          Rua Augusta, 1819 – 24th floor
          São Paulo, SP – Brazil
          CEP: 01413-000
Tel.:   +55 11 3372 1300
Fax: +55 11 3372 1301

SECTION A – BRIEF SURVEY OF THE LOCAL SYSTEM

1. Type of System

(a) Brazil has a civil law system.

(b) The Brazilian Civil Code, which governs succession, is in force throughout the country. Differences regarding estate tax apply on a state-by-state basis. The new Brazilian Civil Code entered into force in January 2003.

2. Wills

(a) There are ordinary and special forms of will. Ordinary forms of will are:

- Public (Articles 1864–1867 of the Civil Code): this type of will is made by means of a public instrument signed by the testator. The notary public writes and registers the will in the register, as dictated by the testator before two witnesses.
- Sealed (Articles 1868–1875 of the Civil Code): this type of will is executed with the certification by a notary public of its authenticity, but its contents are confidential. It is written and signed by the testator and brought to the notary public for certification and formal approval before two witnesses. The notary public only registers that the will exists, as well as the date of certification.
- Private (Articles 1876–1880 of the Civil Code): the private will is written and signed by the testator before three witnesses, who also sign it. After the decease of the testator, the witnesses are called to court to confirm the will.

81

International Succession

Special forms of will are:

– Maritime and aeronautical wills (Articles 1888–1892 of the Civil Code): the maritime and the aeronautical wills can be made on board of Brazilian ships or aircrafts, as the case may be. The captain or the scrivener writes the will, as dictated by the testator before two witnesses. It is also possible that the testator writes the will and the captain or the scrivener only certifies it. The will expires ninety days after the disembarkation of the testator in a place where he could prepare an ordinary will.
– Military will (Articles 1893–1896 of the Civil Code): the military will is used by military personnel as well as civilians working for the army, within the country or abroad, in a place under siege, or where communication has been severed, where there is no notary public available. It must be made before two witnesses, or three, in case the testator cannot sign. This will expires if the testator survives the war or illness.

    Brazilian law does not allow joint wills.

(b) *i.* A will may be revoked by another instrument of the same form. The revocation may be either total or partial. The sealed will is considered revoked if opened or torn up by the testator or someone having his/her consent. If a new descendant is born or known after the will is made, the will is deemed revoked if such descendant survives the testator. The will is also revoked if made in ignorance of other necessary heirs (descendants or ancestors).
  ii. In principle, a will made prior to marriage is not affected by this latter event. However, in case of marriage under the regime of universal community of property after the will is made, one-half of the assets formerly belonging to the testator is transferred to the spouse. There is, therefore, an impact on the will previously executed.
  iii. A will cannot be revived after it has been revoked by a subsequent one, unless the latter will is held void.

3. Intestacy

(a) The order of succession is set forth in Article 1829 of the Civil Code as follows:

– descendants;
– ancestors;
– surviving spouse;
– collateral relations up to the fourth degree;
– Municipality, Federal District or Federation.

Brazilian law does not allow for any kind of discrimination concerning children. Therefore, legitimate, adopted, illegitimate and adulterine children have the same succession rights.
    The heirs in each of the classes are preferred in the order appearing above, except where representation is permitted. Representation occurs whenever a relative of the original heir is appointed by law to replace him in the succession line.

There is equal division among heirs in the same class. However, it is important to note that in the classes of ancestors and collaterals, closest degrees exclude farther relations.

(b) The law provides for unity of succession.

4. Freedom of Testation

(a) According to Article 1846 of the Civil Code, a testator who has any descendants or, in the absence of descendants, a testator who has any ancestors or a spouse, cannot dispose of more than 50 per cent of the estate.

(b) *i.* Brazilian law does not recognize the binding effect of contracts of inheritance.
    ii. These instruments are considered contracts of inheritance and, thus, in principle, Brazilian law does not recognize them.

The exception to this general principle is provided under Article 2018 of the Brazilian Civil Code, according to which ancestors may establish partages, provided that the rights of other compulsory heirs (paragraph 4(a) *above*) cannot be affected. Also, certain provisions on succession matters may be included in antenuptial agreements.

5. Maintenance

Maintenance is provided to the surviving spouse, irrespective of the marriage regime, by means of the right to live in the house destined to be the home of the family, if it is the only property of that type in the estate.

6. Community Property Between Husband and Wife

(a) In case of marriage under the regime of universal community of property, one-half of the properties of a couple belongs to each of the spouses. Therefore, this part of the property is not comprised in the estate of the deceased spouse.

Moreover, if a spouse inherits an asset in severalty, such asset does not become part of the common property of the couple.

In case of marriage under the regime of partial community of property, only assets acquired after the spouses got married are deemed to belong to the couple, in equal shares of 50 per cent. Thus, the share of properties belonging to one spouse will not be comprised in the estate of the other spouse.

(b) The matrimonial regime defines what part of the property of a couple belongs to each of the spouses. Only the part of the property belonging to a spouse will constitute the estate of this spouse.

7. Gifts (*Inter Vivos*)

(a) Gifts to a descendant prior to death are considered anticipes and, therefore, set off against such heir's inheritance. However, the donor may establish either in the instrument of donation as well as in the will that specific gifts not be set off against an heir's inheritance. Ordinary expenses of an ancestor for a descendant, while minor, for the purposes of education, general maintenance, marriage and defense in criminal lawsuits are not set off against the heir's inheritance.

(b) The objective of setting off gifts against inheritance is to assure equality of inheritances between compulsory heirs. Because the law deems gifts to descendants an advance of such heirs' inheritances, there is no pre-established limit for the set-off.

8. Capacity

(a) According to Article 1860 of the Civil Code, everyone has the capacity to testate, except for the following persons:

– those younger than sixteen years of age;
– those who are unable to understand the meaning of will declarations at the time of testate.

The subsequent incapacity of a person who has made a will does not have any effects upon the will. Moreover, even if the incapacity of a person who lacks capacity is overcome, a will made during the phase of incapacity still remains invalid.

(b) The law (Article 228 of the Civil Code) prevents the following persons from being witnesses:

– those younger than sixteen years of age;
– persons suffering from mental disorders;
– deaf-mute persons, as well as blind persons;
– those with any kind interest in the will (heirs and legatees);
– ancestors and descendants up to the third level and the spouse.

(c) As per Articles 1801, 1802 and 1814 of the Civil Code, the following persons cannot be beneficiaries:

– the unborn, unless the will mentions a child to be had on occasion by persons designated in the will who existed at the time of the decease;
– the person who wrote the will at the request of the deceased, or said person's spouse, ancestors, descendants, brothers and sisters;
– the witnesses to the will;
– the mistress of a married testator, unless the testator is not living with the spouse for more than five years;

- notary public, civilian or military server, captain or scrivener, before whom the will is made or approved;
- a person who committed voluntary homicide against the deceased testator, as well as those who assisted;
- those who slanderously accused the deceased testator in court or who committed libel or slander against the testator, and,
- those who by means of violence or fraud, prevented the testator from freely disposing of his estate in a will or codicil, as well as those who contravened instructions of the will.

9. Authority

An order of succession is granted through the courts. The administrator submits a list of assets and heirs to court, for the purpose of recognition of the heirs. After heirs are recognized in court, the division of assets is determined and the order of succession is granted. In case of wills, the executor appointed by the testator requests recognition of the will in court. After this procedure, a list of assets and heirs is submitted and the procedures above are followed.

10. Invalidity of Will

(a) Defects in the required formalities result in the invalidity of the will (Article 145 of the Civil Code). Duress, fraud, malice and error are also causes for the invalidity of the will (Article 171 of the Civil Code).

(b) Invalidity of the will arising out of defects in the requisite formalities result in the will being void. In all other cases, the will is voidable.

11. Simultaneous Death

(a) In case of simultaneous death, there is no succession between the deceased parties.

(b) If two or more people die on the same occasion and it is not possible to determine the order of deaths, it is assumed that they died at the same time (Article 8 of the Civil Code).

12. Estate Taxes

(a) Estate taxes exist in Brazil. Article 155 of the Brazilian Federal Constitution establishes that states may impose taxes on the transfer of assets and rights arising out of the decease of a person.

International Succession

(b) In the state of São Paulo, the relevant tax, *Imposto sobre Transmissão Causa Mortis e Doação* (ITCMD), is regulated by State Law No. 10705/2000 and State Law No. 10992/2001. According to this legislation, ITCMD is applicable on the transmission of movable and immovable assets and related rights. For this reason, the tax will only be applied upon the transfer of assets located within its jurisdiction. The ITCMD is rated between 2.5 per cent and 4 per cent and must be collected until the 180th day after the decease of a party. If ITCMD is not collected in due time, a fine of 20 per cent on the amount originally due is applicable, unless a court order declares differently. In such case, collection must take place within 30 days from the court order.

The assessment of this tax varies from state to state, but in the average it corresponds to 4 per cent, which is the case of the State of Rio de Janeiro.

(c) Heirs or legatees are taxed for ITCMD, which rate is applicable on the value of the asset being transferred.

13. Administration of Estates

(a) The estate is administered by a provisional administrator until the designation of the estate administrator (Article 985 of the Brazilian Code of Civil Procedure). The estate administrator is designated by the court among certain persons involved in the succession, namely (Article 990 of the Brazilian Code of Civil Procedure):

- the surviving spouse, married under the universal community of property regime, if living with the deceased party at the time of the death of the latter;
- the heir in possession and administration of the estate, in case there is no surviving spouse or if the surviving spouse cannot be appointed administrator;
- any heir, if there are no heirs in possession and administration of the estate;
- the executor, if the administration of the estate was assigned to him, or if the heritage is fully shared in legacies;
- the court-appointed administrator, if any;
- in case there is no court appointed administrator, a third party with good reputation.

(b) Firstly, the estate administrator must submit a report describing all assets comprised in the estate, as well as defining the heirs and specifying who the surviving spouse is (Article 993 of the Brazilian Code of Civil Procedure). The estate administrator remains obligated to render account of the administration to the court and to the heirs (Article 991 of the Brazilian Code of Civil Procedure).

(c) In case of an incompetent heir, the Public Prosecution Office represents the interests of such heir.

(d) The following persons have the right to query and object:

- surviving spouse;
- heirs;
- legatees;

– Public Treasury;
– Public Prosecution Office, in some cases;
– executor;
– any other persons understanding that they have rights in the succession.

(e) After the partage is made and ratified by the court, the heirs receive the assets, as specified for each of them in the partage.

(f) Payment to creditors with whom the deceased party had a debt which is due and outstanding is effected before the partage is made. In case of clearly legal debts which are not due yet, payment to creditors is effected by including them in the partage.

(g) *See* paragraph 13(a) *above*.

14. Domicile/Nationality

(a) Succession obeys the law of the domicile of the deceased, irrespective of the nature and location of the assets comprising the estate.

Regarding assets located in Brazil belonging to foreigners, the order of succession shall obey the Brazilian law for the benefit of the Brazilian spouse and the couple's children, when the law of the domicile of the deceased is not more favourable to them.

The law of the domicile of the beneficiary governs the capacity to be a beneficiary.

Moreover, Brazilian law applies to immovable assets located in Brazil.

In all cases, foreign law will not be applied in the matters where it is contrary to Brazilian national sovereignty, *ordre public* or morality.

(b) The jurisdiction of the last domicile prevails. However, in connection with immovable assets located within the Brazilian jurisdiction, any other foreign jurisdiction is excluded. A local court may only give an order of probate or succession if the deceased was domiciled in Brazil and/or executed a will in the jurisdiction and had assets (movable or immovable) in Brazil.

Section B – Applicable Law/Procedure Where Foreign Element/s are Involved

1. Jurisdiction

(a) The local court holds that it has jurisdiction if Brazil was the last domicile of the deceased party, or where there are any assets located in Brazil, even if the deceased was not a Brazilian.

(b) In principle the same rules apply to both movable and immovable assets.

(c) The civil court for family law and succession matters has jurisdiction.

International Succession

2. Applicable Law

The local court must apply the law of the domicile of the deceased, regardless of the nature and location of the assets. However, in case of assets located in Brazil belonging to a non-Brazilian deceased party, Brazilian law will be applicable in favour of the Brazilian spouse and children unless the law of the domicile of the deceased party is more favourable to them. Brazilian Law applies to immovable property in Brazil unless the law of the domicile is more favourable to the Brazilian spouse or childen.

3. Foreign Inheritance/Succession Orders

(a, b) According to Article 89, II, of the Brazilian Code of Civil Procedure, only Brazilian authorities have standing to grant succession orders regarding assets located in Brazil, whether movable or immovable, even if the deceased party holds another nationality and did not reside within the Brazilian territory.

(c) A foreign succession or inheritance order will only be recognized in Brazil if it does not fall in one of the cases where Brazilian courts are exclusively competent (e.g., movable and/or immovable assets located in Brazil). For the recognition and enforcement of such an order, it must be previously confirmed by the Federal Supreme Court of Brazil. Such confirmation only is given if the order:

- fulfils all formalities required for its enforcement under the laws of the country where it was issued;
- was issued by a competent court with proper venue after service of process upon the parties, or after sufficient evidence of a party's absence has been given, as required under applicable law;
- is not subject to any kind of appeal;
- is legalized by the competent Brazilian consul and accompanied of a sworn translation into Portuguese and;
- is not contrary to Brazilian national sovereignty, ordre public or morality.

4. Two or More Succession or Probate Orders

The first order for which confirmation by the Federal Supreme Court was requested shall prevail, provided that there is no order granted or to be granted in Brazil. *See* also paragraph 3 *above*.

5. Assets

According to Article 96 of the Brazilian Code of Civil Procedure, the authorities of the domicile in Brazil of a Brazilian deceased party must assume jurisdiction, even if the decease does not take place within the Brazilian territory.

The local court could also claim jurisdiction in case the deceased party was domiciled in Brazil, even if there were no assets in this jurisdiction.

6. Expert Evidence

(a) A party alleging foreign law in court must submit evidence of such law. For this purpose, the said party may use different means, such as, by way of example only, submission of (i) law texts with an affidavit from the relevant consulate, (ii) literature written by recognized competent legal authors and/or (iii) a legal opinion from a recognized competent legal counsel from the relevant jurisdiction.

(b) In case evidence from a foreign lawyer is submitted, this procedure can be made by way of legal opinion, together with proof that the subscriber of the legal opinion is a lawyer in his/her jurisdiction.

7. Unity of Succession

Unity of succession is accepted under Brazilian law.

8. Formalities

According to Article 9 of the Introduction Law to the Brazilian Civil Code, both the formalities required in Brazil and the formalities of the foreign country where the will was executed must be observed for such will to be recognized or submitted for a succession order.

9. Legislation

The *1961 Hague Convention on the Conflicts of Laws Relating to the Form of Testamentary Dispositions* is not applicable.

10. Wills

(a) *See* paragraph 8 *above*.

(b) The interpretation of the terminology in a will shall be made according to the meaning of such terminology in the country where the will was made, if not against Brazilian national sovereignty, ordre public, or morality.

(c) *See* paragraph 2 *above*.

(d) Regarding the capacity to inherit, the law of the domicile of the heir or legatee is applicable.

(e) Regarding the capacity to make a will, the law of the domicile of the party making a will is in principle applicable.

International Succession

(f) The will is governed by the law of the jurisdiction where it was made. For the formalities, *see* paragraph 8 *above*. For the law applicable to the succession as a whole, *see* paragraph 2 *above*.

(g) Brazilian law determines that succession is commenced simultaneously with the death of deceased party. Thus, a power of appointment is not permitted.

(h) Amendments, revocation and revival, when permitted, are submitted to the law of the place where they are first made (*lex loci celebrationis*).

(i) *See* paragraph 2 *above*.

11. Domicile/Nationality

(a) Regarding the capacity to make wills, the domicile at the time of making the will is applicable. In regard to the capacity to inherit, the domicile at the time when succession procedures are to be commenced is determinative.

(b) The law of the domicile of the beneficiary is applicable for the purpose of assessing his/her capacity to inherit.

(c) When the domicile of a party is unclear, such party's residence or the place where such party is located is deemed his/her domicile. If a party has more than one domicile, the last one is deemed such party's domicile (in case of the deceased) or any of such places is considered the domicile of said party (in all other cases).

12. Taxation

As mentioned under paragraph 12(b) of Section A *above*, estate tax is applicable solely on the grounds of the location of the assets and, thus, irrespective of the residence of the deceased, heirs or legatees.

British Virgin Islands

Prepared by: Christopher J. MCKENZIE
Harney Westwood & Riegels

Address: Craigmuir Chambers
PO Box 71, Road Town
Tortola
British Virgin Islands
Tel.: +1 284 494 2233
Fax: +1 284 494 3547/4885

SECTION A – BRIEF SURVEY OF LOCAL SYSTEM

The following principles will apply subject to the application (if any) of the conflict of laws issues referred to in Section B.

1. Type of System

The legal system of the British Virgin Islands (BVI) is the English common law system. The principles of English common law apply in the Territory by virtue of the *1705 Common Law (Declaration of Application) Act* (Cap 13) and those of English equity apply by virtue of the *West Indies Associated States Supreme Court (Virgin Islands) Act* (Cap 80).

2. Wills

(a) In order to be valid under the internal law of the BVI, unless privileged or made pursuant to the terms of the *Mental Health Act* (Cap 191), a will must comply with the requirements of Section 7 of the *Wills Act* (Cap 81) (*Wills Act*). These prescribe that the will must be in writing and that it must be signed at the foot or end by the testator or by some other person in his presence and by his direction; the testator's signature must be made or acknowledged by him in the presence of at least two witnesses who must be present at the same time and such witnesses must also attest and subscribe the will in the presence of the testator.

The English doctrine of incorporation by reference applies in the BVI, so that a testator may incorporate in his will a document which has not been executed in accordance with the requirements of the *Wills Act*, but the document may nevertheless be made part of his will, provided that (1) the document must be adequately described in the will to enable such document to be identified, (2) the document is already in existence when the will is executed, and (3) it is referred to in the will as being already in existence. Rule 22 of the Supreme Court (Non-Contentious) Probate Rules (Probate Rules) effectively prescribes, moreover, that such a document must be admitted to probate as part of the will: if the testator wishes the document to remain confidential, he must employ a secret trust.

Section 11 of the *Wills Act* enables privileged wills to be made by providing that any soldier being in actual military service, or any mariner or seaman being at sea, may dispose of his personal estate as he might have done by the law of England before the making of the Act. The *Wills Act* came into effect on 1 January 1873 and at that time the law of England permitted privileged testators to dispose of their personal property (but not, at that stage, their real property); they could do this by way of an informal will which need not satisfy any formal requirements: such a privileged remains valid, unless revoked, even if the testator ceases to be privileged prior to his death; furthermore, a will of this nature may be in writing, but, if so, it need not be signed or witnessed, and can even be made orally.

The *Mental Health Act* contains provisions enabling the court to make orders and to give directions and authorizations for the execution of wills on behalf of those who are incapable, by reason of mental disorder, of managing and administering their property and affairs.

(b) *i.* Section 20 of the *Wills Act* makes it clear that, unless revoked on marriage by Section 18 (*see below*), a will can only be revoked by another will or codicil which is executed in accordance with the formal requirements of Section 7 of the Act or by 'burning, tearing or otherwise destroying the same by the testator, or by some person in his presence and by his direction, with the intention of revoking the same'.

Section 21 provides, *inter alia*, that no alteration to a will is valid or effective, except so far as the words or effect of the will before such altera-tion shall not be apparent, unless the alteration is made in accordance with the requirements of Section 7 of the *Wills Act*.

ii. Section 18 of the *Wills Act* provides that (subject to two exceptions) a will is automatically revoked on the marriage of the testator. The two exceptions relate to certain wills made in exercise of a power of appointment and to 'clinical marriage[s] solemnized in the Territory agreeably to the provisions of any Marriage Ordinance then in force'. Provisions relating to clinical marriages of those believed to be *in articulo mortis* are contained in Section 55 of the Marriage Ordinance (Cap 272).

iii. Section 22 of the *Wills Act* deals with the revival of revoked wills. It pro-vides that wills and codicils which have been revoked may only be revived by re-execution or by a codicil which is executed in accordance with the formalities prescribed by Section 7 of the Act. Section 22 provides further that when a will or codicil which is partly revoked, and subsequently wholly revoked, is revived, such revival shall not extend to that part of the docu-ment as has been revoked before the revocation of the whole, unless a contrary intention is shown.

3. Intestacy

(a) The BVI's rules of intestacy are set out in the *Intestates Estates Act* (Cap 34). The terms of this Act may be summarized, broadly, as follows:

(1) If the deceased leaves a surviving spouse, the surviving spouse will take the personal chattels (as defined in the Act) and the residuary estate will stand charged with the payment to such spouse of a sum equal to 10 per cent of the net value of the estate (or USD 240 if greater) with interest thereon at 5 per cent per annum.

(2) Subject to (1), the balance of the residuary estate will be held in trust for the surviving spouse for life if the deceased leaves no issue.

(3) Subject to (1), if the deceased leaves a surviving spouse and issue, one-half of the balance of the residuary estate will be held in trust for the surviving spouse for life, with remainder to the deceased's issue on 'statutory trusts' (*see below*). The other half of the balance of the residuary estate will be held on statutory trusts for the deceased's issue (but if those statutory trusts fail during the lifetime of the spouse then this property will be held in trust for the spouse for the remainder of his or her lifetime).

(4) If the deceased leaves issue, but no surviving spouse, then the residuary estate will be held on statutory trusts for such issue.

(5) If the deceased leaves no issue, but one or both parents, then, subject to the interest of any surviving spouse, the residuary estate will be held in trust for the deceased's parents equally, or for the surviving parent.

(6) If the deceased leaves no issue or parent, then, subject to the interests of any surviving spouse, the residuary estate will be held in trust for the following surviving relatives (in the following order of priority and manner): (i) on statutory trusts for the deceased's brothers and sisters of the whole blood or, if none, (ii) on statutory trusts for the deceased's half-brothers and half-sisters or, if none, (iii) for the deceased's surviving grandparent or grandparents equally or, if none, (iv) on statutory trusts for the deceased's uncles and aunts of the whole blood or, if none, (v) on statutory trusts for the deceased's uncles and aunts of the half blood.

(7) If the deceased leaves neither issue nor parents, nor any relatives within the categories described in paragraph (6)(i) to (v) above, the entire estate will pass to the surviving spouse or, if there is no surviving spouse, the estate will pass to the Crown *bona vacantia* (and the Crown may make provision for any dependants of the deceased or any person for whom the deceased 'might reasonably have been expected to make provision').

(8) Where this term is used in the *Intestates Estates Act*, 'statutory trusts' may be summarized as meaning that (i) the property in question is to be held upon trust for sale for all those within the relevant class of relatives of the intestate and their children and remoter issue in equal shares *per stirpes* on attaining the age of eighteen years, (ii) the statutory provisions which relate to maintenance and accumulation apply to these trusts, (iii) the provisions relating to *hotchpot* referred to in Section A7 below may apply to the entitlement of issue

of the deceased and (iv), if these trusts fail, such property shall pass under the provisions of the Act as if those concerned had died before the deceased. It follows from this that the entitlements of a child, sibling, uncle or aunt who has predeceased the intestate will pass to his or her own children (or remoter issue) on attaining eighteen.

(9) The Act also contains provisions, *inter alia*, enabling the life interest of a spouse to be purchased or redeemed by paying its capitalized value to the spouse and enabling the residuary estate to be disposed of free from such life interest.

(10) Subject to three exceptions, references in the *Intestates Estates Act* to 'children' and 'issue' only extend to legitimate children and issue and references to other relatives only extend to those related through legitimate unions. As a result of the *Legitimacy Act* (Cap 271), however, legitimated children are generally treated for such purposes as if they were born legitimate. The second exception relates to the death intestate of the mother of an illegitimate child without legitimate issue: pursuant to Section 11(1) of the *Legitimacy Act*, her illegitimate children, including adulterine children, (or their issue) can inherit under the intestacy rules as if such children had been born legitimate. Thirdly, Section 11(2) of the same Act provides that on the death intestate of an illegitimate child, his mother will be entitled to take the interest in that child's estate to which she would have been entitled had the child been born legitimate and had she been the only surviving parent. Similar considerations apply generally to the interpretation of references to relatives in wills: these will be construed as references to legitimate relatives only unless a contrary intention is apparent.

(b) The rules relating to intestacy do not distinguish between movable and immovable property.

4. Freedom of Testation

(a) Section 3 of the *Wills Act* makes it clear that there is full freedom of testamentary disposition in the BVI and the laws of the Territory do not include provisions specifying that particular relatives, such as spouses, issue or others are entitled to fixed shares of the deceased's estate.

This freedom of testamentary disposition is reinforced, in the context of gifts to trustees, by the provisions of Section 83 of the Trustee Ordinance (Cap 303) which was added to the original Trustee Ordinance by the *Trustee (Amendment) Act, 1993* (No. 7 of 1993) and which applies to transfers or dispositions made after 1 November 1993. This provides that '(1) If a person transfers or disposes of personal property to the trustee of a trust (a) he shall be deemed to have had capacity to do so if he is at the time of such transfer or disposition of full age and of sound mind under the law of his domicile; and (b) no rule relating to inheritance or succession of the law of his domicile shall affect any such transfer or disposition or otherwise affect the validity of such trust (. . .)'. It is thought that the provisions of Section

83(1)(b) apply to testamentary transfers or dispositions, in addition to *inter vivos* transfers or dispositions.

(b) *i.–ii.* Since the principles of English common law and equity apply in the Territory, legally valid contracts to leave property by will, or not to revoke a will, will generally be valid to the same extent as they are under English law. These principles are somewhat complex, but, generally, a contract complying with the requirements of BVI law will be binding on the deceased's personal representatives and those claiming through the deceased as volunteers. In the context of contracts relating to land, it should be noted that Section 4 of the *Conveyancing and Law of Property Act* (Cap 220) provides that no action may be brought upon any contract for the sale or other disposition of land or any interest in land, unless the agreement upon which such action is brought, or some memorandum or note thereof, is in writing, and signed by the party to be charged or by some person authorized by him.

Section 70 of the *International Business Companies Act* (Cap 291) includes various provisions concerning, *inter alia*, the validity of contracts entered into by companies incorporated under that Act which relate to the transfer of property on death, but little use is made of the provisions of this section in practice.

5. Maintenance

There is full freedom of testamentary disposition in the BVI. If a legally valid will has been made, disappointed relatives and dependants have no recourse to the courts, since there is no statutory provision equivalent to the UK *Inheritance (Provision for Family and Dependants) Act 1975* in force in the Territory, although there are (fairly limited) provisions in the *Matrimonial Proceedings and Property Act 1995* (No. 6 of 1995) which, *inter alia*, enable various orders for financial provision on divorce, nullity or judicial separation to be varied, revoked or (but only in relation to the matrimonial home) made following the death of one of the parties to a marriage who is domiciled and/or resident in the BVI.

6. Community Property Between Husband and Wife

(a–b) There is, as such, no community of property regime forming part of the internal laws of the BVI. It is however relevant that pursuant to the Territory's rules of private international law, in the absence of a contract or settlement, the rights obtained by parties to a marriage in each other's movable property, including after acquired property, as a result of the marriage will be determined by the law of the matrimonial domicile. Furthermore, property held by the deceased as a beneficial joint tenant (cf. a tenant in common) will pass outside his will (or the intestacy rules) to the surviving joint tenant (or joint tenants) by virtue of the doctrine of survivorship.

International Succession

7. Gifts (*Inter Vivos*)

(a–b) In the case of wills, the English rules relating to 'satisfaction' (where an obligation created by a will to pay a legacy is regarded as having been separately discharged) and 'ademption' (where an asset bequeathed or devised by will ceases to be subject to the testator's power of disposition or ceases to conform to the description given in the will) apply in the BVI.

Hotchpot provisions are to be found in Section 5(1)(c) of the *Intestate Estates Act*, which provides that where any part of the residuary estate of a person dying intestate which is directed to be held on 'statutory trusts' for the deceased's issue (*see* Section A3(a) *above*) is divisible into shares, then, subject to any contrary intention expressed or appearing from the circumstances of the case, any money or property which has been paid to a child of the deceased, by way of 'advancement' or on marriage, by the intestate or settled by the intestate for the benefit of such child, is to be taken as being paid or settled in or towards the satisfaction of the child's share (or the share which such child would have taken if living at the intestate's death) and shall be brought into account at its value at the intestate's death. This provision only applies to the shares of the deceased's issue and not to those of other relatives such as siblings, uncles and aunts.

8. Capacity

(a) Section 6 of the *Wills Act* prescribes that no one under eighteen years old may make a valid will. In order to have testamentary capacity, a testator must also understand the effect of his wishes being carried out at his death, the extent of the property of which he is disposing and the nature of the claims on him. The courts of the BVI will have regard to English case law in applying these principles. As mentioned in Section A2(a) *above*, the procedure enabling wills to be executed on behalf of those who are incapable, by reason of mental disorder, of managing their property and affairs is set out in the *Mental Health Act*.

(b) A blind person is incapable of witnessing a will and, pursuant to English case law principles, a witness must be both mentally and physically present in order to satisfy the requirements of Section 7 of the *Wills Act*. Section 13 provides, however, that the competency of an attesting witness to be admitted as a witness to prove the execution of the will shall not, on that account, cause the will to be invalid.

Section 14 of the *Wills Act* effectively provides that if one of the witnesses to the will's execution is a beneficiary or the spouse of a beneficiary, the interest of that beneficiary or beneficiary's spouse shall be forfeit, although the other terms of the will will remain valid, but there is in the BVI no equivalent to those of the provisions of the English *Wills Act 1968* (which enable gifts to attesting witnesses and their spouses to take effect if the will would nevertheless have been properly executed without that attestation). Sections 15 and 16 of the *Wills Act* specifically provide, however, that creditors and their spouses and executors may act as witnesses.

(c) The *Wills Act* and *Intestates Estates Act* contain no provisions, as such, relating to the capacity of beneficiaries, minors (subject to the application of the rule relating to the remoteness of vesting) unborn persons and (provided they are capable of holding property) companies can, in principle, be beneficiaries. A minor can hold land in the BVI, but cannot give a valid receipt for a legacy and wills often therefore provide that personal representatives can accept a receipt from the minor's parent or guardian or from the minor himself. Since the *Age of Majority Act* (No. 21 of 1994) came into force on 3 January 1995, the age of majority in the BVI has been eighteen.

9. Authority (Court, Notarial or Other)

In order to obtain title to the deceased's estate in the BVI, his personal representative (i.e., his executor or his administrator) will require a grant of representation from the High Court. If the deceased left a will including a valid appointment of an executor, the application will be one for a grant of probate; if the deceased did not leave a valid will, the application will be one for a grant of letters of administration by his administrator; if he left a valid will, but the will did not contain a valid appointment of executors (or the executors are all unable or unwilling to act), an application by his administrator for a grant of letters of administration with the will annexed will be necessary. An administrator derives his authority to act from the grant, but an executor will derive his authority to act from the will (and the grant of probate will be authentication of his authority), although the grant will be necessary where he is required to prove his title. In each case, the application is made to the Probate Registry.

An application for probate must be in the prescribed form and must be accompanied by the deceased's original will and various other documents prescribed by the Probate Rules.

A grant of probate may only be issued to a corporate executor if it is a 'trust corporation' as defined by the *Trust Corporation (Probate and Administration) Act* (Cap 75). If a corporate executor does not fall within this definition, it may nevertheless be possible for letters of administration with the will annexed to be granted to its nominee.

An application for letters of administration must be in the prescribed form and must be accompanied by the documents which are prescribed by the Probate Rules. In all cases in which the application is one for a grant of letters of administration (with or without the will annexed), an administrator's bond, in twice the value of the personal estate and twice the annual value of the realty to be placed in possession of the administrator, is required. One surety to the bond (being either a 'trust corporation' as defined in the *Trust Corporation (Probate and Administration) Act* or an individual resident in the Territory) is needed, but there have been occasions on which the requirement for a surety has been dispensed with by the judge.

On applying for a grant of probate or letters of administration, a declaration on oath of the value of the deceased's estate (setting out in it details of the assets forming part of the deceased's real and personal estate in the Territory and their approximate values) must be filed, together with the order and the grant for which the application is being sought.

Although not specifically required by the Probate Rules, an affidavit of foreign law, sworn before an appropriately qualified lawyer from the jurisdiction in which the deceased died domiciled, is likely to be required by the Registrar if the deceased died domiciled outside the Territory and the grant does not merely give the personal representatives title to immovable property situated in the BVI. *See* Section B *below*.

The *Probates (Resealing) Act* (Cap 60) enables grants of probate and letters of administration (and documents of like effect) which have been issued by the courts of the United Kingdom or of any 'British protectorate or protected state and any territory in respect of which a mandate or trusteeship is being exercised by Her Majesty's Government or any part of Her Majesty's Dominions' to be resealed in the Territory. It is not the case, therefore, that all Commonwealth grants can be resealed in the BVI (*see* for instance *Re TC Pagarani deceased*) and Hong Kong grants issued after 30 June 1997 cannot be resealed in the Territory. Once a grant has been resealed pursuant to the provisions of the *Probates (Resealing) Act*, it will have the same force and effect in the BVI as if it had been granted by the High Court. The procedure for applying for the resealing of a grant of probate or letters of administration is set out in the Probate Rules which specify the documents which must be filed at the Probate Registry. If the application is one for the resealing of letters of administration, the provisions referred to above relating to administrators' bonds and sureties will be applicable.

Although the Probate Rules contain specific requirements relating to the identity of the persons before whom affidavits sworn outside the Territory may be sworn, in practice, the Probate Registry will accept affidavits which have been sworn before a notary public.

For further information relating to the requirements for applying for or for the resealing of grants of probate and letters of administration, reference should be made to the Probate Rules and, where the provisions of these Rules are silent, to the English probate rules (since Section 11 of the *West Indies Associated States Supreme Court (Virgin Islands) Act* (Cap 80) provides that where there is no special provision in the BVI's probate rules, the court's jurisdiction shall be exercised as nearly as may be in conformity with the law and practice administered for the time being in the High Court of Justice in England).

Only very limited use is now made of the simplified procedure for obtaining grants in relation to small estates which is set out in the *Administration of Small Estates Act* (Cap 4), since this only applies to estates valued at no more than USD 240.

10. Invalidity of Will

(a)–(b) A will will be invalid (i.e., void) if it has not been executed in accordance with the provisions of Section 7 of the *Wills Act*, if it has been effectively revoked or if the testator was a minor or lacked testamentary capacity when executing the will. A will made by a testator as a result of undue influence (i.e., coercion) or fraud (i.e., deception) of another person (or that part of the will which was so made) is similarly invalid.

11. Simultaneous Death

(a–b) There are no rules or presumptions which apply in the case of simultaneous deaths, either where a valid will has been made or on intestacy. Accordingly, the common law position applies: where persons who are in immediate succession to each other die in circumstances in which it cannot be established which of them died first, each is deemed to have predeceased the other. It is therefore essential to include an appropriately worded survivorship provision in a will if a disposition is to be dependent upon an individual predeceasing the testator.

12. Estate Taxes

(a–c) There are no estate taxes in the BVI and the Probate Registry's fees for processing applications for grants of representation are merely nominal.

13. Administration of Estates

(a) The administration of estates is carried out by the deceased's personal representative who will either be the executor appointed by his will or his administrator if the deceased did not leave a will or left a will which did not contain a valid appointment of an executor.

(b) As mentioned in Section A9 above, on applying for probate or letters of administration, a declaration on oath, setting out details of all the assets comprised in the deceased's BVI situs real and personal estate and their values must be filed with the Probate Registry. Since the purpose of this declaration is merely to determine whether the value of the estate exceeds USD 5,000 in value (because a fee of USD 20 is payable in relation to such estate), given that today the values of most estates will exceed this figure, in practice only very approximate values are generally provided.

The law also requires personal representatives to account to beneficiaries for their administration of the estate and this will generally involve providing them with full and accurate estate accounts unless this requirement is dispensed with by the beneficiaries.

Although the affidavit which must be sworn by the deceased's personal representative and filed at the Probate Registry must state that such personal representative will, within twelve months of the grant, file at the Registry a statement and account (verified by affidavit) of such personal representative's administration of the estate, this is in practice seldom done and, as matters currently stand, it is unlikely that this requirement will be enforced by the Probate Registry in the absence of any allegation or evidence of misfeasance.

International Succession

(c) *See* (b) *above*.

(d) Any beneficiary who wishes to challenge the administration of the estate by the personal representative may apply to the court to object.

(e) Personal property is transferred to the beneficiaries in accordance with the usual legal requirements for transferring such property to them. Thus, money is paid over to them; chattels are transferred by delivery; shares are transferred by completing the relevant transfer form and marking up the books of the company. The transfer of real property will generally require an 'assent' to the beneficiaries.

(f) Creditors are paid by the personal representatives from the deceased's estate. It is generally considered prudent to advertise for creditors pursuant to the provisions of Section 28 of the Trustee Ordinance and to wait for the relevant time limit referred to in the advertisement to expire before making distributions. Section 28 provides that if notices in the Gazette and in a local newspaper and 'such other like notices, including notices elsewhere than in the Territory, as would, in any special case, have been directed by the Court in an action for administration' are given of the personal representatives' intention to make conveyances or distributions to those entitled, if such notices require any person interested to send to the personal representatives particulars of his claim within the time (not being less than twenty-eight days) fixed in the last notice given and if, following the expiration of the notice period, a conveyance or distribution of the property referred to in the notice is made to those entitled, having regard only to the claims of those of whom the personal representatives then had no notice, the personal representatives will not (in relation to the property so conveyed or distributed) be liable to any person of whose claim such personal representatives had no notice at the time of the conveyance or distribution. The provisions of this section apply without prejudice to the right of any person to trace the property (or any property representing it) into the hands of any person who may have received it.

(g) If no executor is appointed, the estate will be administered and distributions will be effected by the administrator. Since the Probate Rules do not fix an order of priority for the entitlement to apply for letters of administration, it is considered that, subject to the provisions of Rule 26 of the Probate Rules, the order of priority will be determined in accordance with the prevailing rules of English law. Rule 26 provides, *inter alia*, that where administration is applied for by one or some of the next-of-kin only and there is another next-of-kin equally entitled, the Registrar may require proof by affidavit that notice of the application has been given to such other next-of-kin.

14. Domicile/Nationality

(a) According to the common law principles of private international law which apply in the BVI, most issues relating to the succession to the deceased's movable property will (subject to the application, if any, of the doctrine of *renvoi*) be determined by the law of the deceased's domicile at the relevant time (*see* Section B11(a) *below*). The formal and essential validity of a will of a foreign domiciliary and his or her capacity to execute such a will, in so far as it disposes of movables, will (subject to *renvoi* considerations) therefore be determined by the law of his domicile and not in accordance with the provisions of the internal law of the BVI which are set out above. Should such a person die intestate, the succession to his movable property will be determined (subject to *renvoi* considerations) by the law of the jurisdiction in which he dies domiciled. For further details, *see* generally Section B *below*.

A BVI grant of probate or letters of administration will, however, be needed in order to give the personal representatives title to BVI-situs assets (*see* Section B1 *below*), no matter where the deceased died domiciled (although a BVI grant will only provide title to the assets situated in the Territory). Furthermore, since the administration of a deceased person's assets is governed wholly by the law from which the personal representatives derive their authority to collect them, if a person dies leaving BVI situs assets, not only will the procedure set out in Section A9 above apply in relation to the application for a grant, but the estate must be administered in accordance with BVI law, with the result that the rules set out in Section A13 *above* will be applicable and assets in the hands of the BVI personal representative will be liable for the worldwide debts of the deceased and foreign creditors will rank equally with BVI creditors; the order of priority of debts prescribed by BVI law and BVI issues concerning whether or not such debts are time-barred will apply. The only exception to this relates to foreign taxes and penalties: pursuant to the rule in the *Government of India* v. *Taylor* case, these will not be enforced in the BVI (although they may be recognized if relevant to the issue and not contrary to public policy).

(b) As a result of Section 11 of the *West Indies Associated States Supreme Court (Virgin Islands) Act* (Cap 80), it is possible that the court may have jurisdiction to make a grant of representation notwithstanding that the deceased leaves no estate within the Territory on the basis of the provisions of Section 2(1) of the *Administration of Justice Act 1932* of England and Wales (which, though repealed, are still relevant as a result of Section 25 of the *Supreme Court Act 1987* of England and Wales). It is similarly possible that such a grant could be issued pursuant to the court's inherent jurisdiction, but there have been no decided cases on these issues. To be admissible to proof in the BVI, following English principles, it will however generally be necessary that the will of a non-domiciliary should dispose of property in the BVI, since, following the decision in *Aldrich* v. *AG*, it would be contrary to principle for the court to make a grant of representation in the estate of a person who dies out of the jurisdiction leaving no assets within it.

In any event, the affidavit in support of the application for a grant which is being sought in relation to an estate where there are no assets situated in the Territory must include in it a statement of the purpose for which the grant is required and it is unlikely that the grant will issue unless the Registrar (or the court) is satisfied that there exists good reason to grant representation in the BVI.

International Succession

Section B – Applicable Law/Procedure Where Foreign Element/s are Involved

The following principles will apply subject to the application (where relevant) of the doctrine of *renvoi*. For further information concerning *renvoi, see Dicey and Morris – The Conflict of Laws* (1999, 13th edn.) and *Cheshire and North's Private International Law* (1992, 12th edn.).

1. Jurisdiction

The courts of the Territory would have jurisdiction in relation to assets situated within the Territory.

The situs of assets will generally fall to be determined in accordance with the English common law principles of private international law, although it is noteworthy in this context that Section 116 of the *International Business Companies Act* provides that 'For purposes of determining matters relating to title and jurisdiction but not for purposes of taxation, the *situs* of the ownership of shares, debt obligations or other securities of a company incorporated under [that Act] is in the [BVI]'.

Pursuant to the English common law principles of private international law which apply in the BVI, the *situs* of a specialty debt (i.e., a debt due on a deed) is where the deed is kept at the particular time and this rule is increasingly taken advantage of in the BVI by foreign domiciliaries.

As far as trusts are concerned, Section 82 of the Trustee Ordinance provides that the BVI courts will have jurisdiction in the following circumstances:

(a) where the proper law of a trust or a particular aspect of a trust is the law of the Territory;
(b) where the trustee of any trust is resident in the Territory;
(c) where, in the case of a corporate trustee of any trust, it is incorporated or registered to do business in the Territory;
(d) where any trust property is situate in the Territory but only in respect of property so situate;
(e) where the administration of any trust is carried on in the Territory; and
(f) where the court thinks it appropriate.

Since the principles of English common law apply in the BVI, the BVI court will also have jurisdiction to entertain an action in similar circumstances to those in which the English courts would have such jurisdiction pursuant to English common law conflict of laws principles. Order 11, rule 1 of the Rules of the Supreme Court 1970 sets out the circumstances in which service out of the jurisdiction of a writ, or notice of a writ, is permissible with the leave of the court.

The grounds on which leave can be granted include:

(a) if an act, deed, will, contract, obligation or liability affecting land situate within the jurisdiction is sought to be construed;

(b) if the action begun by writ is for the administration of the estate of a person who died domiciled within the jurisdiction;

(c) if the action is for the execution, as to property situate within the jurisdiction, of the trusts of a written instrument, being trusts that ought to be executed according to the laws of the BVI; and

(d) if the action begun is brought against a defendant not domiciled or ordinarily resident in the BVI to enforce, rescind, dissolve, annul or otherwise effect a contract which was made within the jurisdiction or was made by or through an agent trading or residing in the jurisdiction on behalf of a principal trading or residing out of the jurisdiction or by its terms or implication are governed by the laws of the BVI.

2. Applicable Law

See Section A14(a) *above* and Section B10 *below*.

3. Foreign Succession/Inheritance Orders

A foreign judgment will be capable of recognition and (by suing on the judgment itself) enforcement in the BVI at common law in similar circumstances to those in which such a judgment might be recognized and enforced by the UK courts as a result of the application of the common law principles of English private international law (but disregarding any limitations imposed on those principles by UK statutes).

Furthermore, statutory provisions relating to the registration, recognition and enforcement of foreign judgments substantially the same as those contained in Part II of the UK *Administration of Justice Act 1920* are incorporated in the BVI's *Reciprocal Enforcement of Judgments Act* (Cap 65) which enables judgments obtained in the High Court of England or Northern Ireland or in the Court of Session in Scotland to be registered, recognized and enforced in the BVI pursuant to provisions which are the same in substance as those contained in the UK Act of 1920. Section 6(1) of the *Reciprocal Enforcement of Judgments Act* incorporates terms similar to those set out in Section 14 of the 1920 Act and enables the Governor in Council by Order to declare that the Act shall extend to judgments obtained in a superior court of any part of her Majesty's dominions outside the UK where reciprocal arrangements have been made. Orders under Section 6(1) have been made extending the *Reciprocal Enforcement of Judgments Act* to judgments obtained in the superior courts of the Bahamas, Barbados, Bermuda, Belize, Trinidad and Tobago, Guyana, St. Lucia, St. Vincent, Grenada, Jamaica, New South Wales (Australia) and certain High Courts of Nigeria.

Although statutory provisions substantially the same as those set forth in the UK *Foreign Judgments (Reciprocal Enforcement) Act 1933* are to be found in the BVI's *Foreign Judgments (Reciprocal Enforcement) Act* (Cap 27) which would enable judgments given in the superior courts of the foreign jurisdictions to which the Act extends to be registered, recognized and enforced in the BVI pursuant to provisions equivalent to those contained in the UK Act of 1933 and an Order has been made under Section 9(1) of the Act directing that the Act's provisions are to apply to the judgments of the superior courts (as defined in the Order) of a number of specified jurisdictions, because no further Order has been made under Section 3(1) of the Act extending the Act to the jurisdictions in question, the Act's provisions are currently in practice ineffective.

The *Reciprocal Enforcement of Judgments Act* provides that where a judgment to which the Act applies has been obtained, the judgment creditor may apply to the courts of the BVI at any time within twelve months after the date of the judgment (or longer at the court's discretion) to have the judgment registered in the court, and on any such application the court may, if it thinks it just and convenient to do so in all the circumstances, order the judgment to be registered, and once registered the judgment will be of the same force and effect, and proceedings may be taken upon it, as if it were a judgment of the court of the Territory.

For the purposes of the *Reciprocal Enforcement of Judgments Act*, a judgment is defined as any judgment or order given or made in civil proceedings whereby any sum of money is payable. The provisions of the Act provide, however, that no such judgment shall be ordered to be registered if:

(1) the original court acted without jurisdiction;
(2) the judgment debtor, being a person who was neither carrying on business nor ordinarily resident within the jurisdiction of the original court, did not voluntarily appear or agree to submit to the jurisdiction of that court;
(3) the judgment debtor, being the defendant in the proceedings, was not duly served with the process of the original court and did not appear, notwithstanding that he was ordinarily resident or carrying on a business within the jurisdiction of that court, or agree to submit to the jurisdiction of that court;
(4) judgment was obtained by fraud;
(5) the judgment debtor satisfies the registering court either that an application is pending or that he is entitled and intends to appeal against the judgment; or
(6) the judgment was in respect of a cause of action which for reasons of public policy or for some other similar reason could not have been entertained by the registering court.

It is considered that in view of policy considerations and the court's discretion, the Territory's courts would not recognize, enforce or register a judgment relating to a forced heirship claim with respect to movable property, unless the deceased died domiciled in the jurisdiction the forced heirship rules of which the judgment is applying and the provisions of Section 83 of the Trustee Ordinance (*see* Section A4(a) *above*) are inapplicable, or one relating to immovable property in the Territory.

4. Two or More Succession or Probate Orders

The succession to immovables will generally be determined in accordance with the rules of the *lex situs* and that to movables will generally be determined in accordance with those of the law of domicile at death.

5. Assets

A grant of representation issued by the BVI court will only give the personal representatives title to the deceased's BVI situs assets and, subject to Sections A14(b) and B1 above, the BVI court will only have jurisdiction in relation to assets situated in the Territory.

6. Expert Evidence

The rules as to expert evidence are set out in Order 38 of the Rules of the Supreme Court. The court has a general power to conduct a trial in a manner which it deems necessary. The rules provide that the court can order expert evidence to be given by affidavit only, but in most disputes the court will require experts to attend, give evidence and be available for cross examination. The extent of expert evidence will be decided by the judge, normally in interlocutory proceedings during the course of the case, and each case will be dealt with on its own facts.

7. Unity of Succession

Unity of succession does not apply in the BVI: BVI law adopts the doctrine of schism, with the succession to immovables generally being determined by the *lex situs* and the succession to movables generally being determined by the law of the deceased's domicile at death.

8. Formalities

See Section B10(a) *below*.

9. Legislation

The *Hague Convention on the Conflict of Laws Relating to the Form of Testamentary Dispositions* is inapplicable in the BVI and BVI law contains no equivalent to the English *Wills Act 1963* (nor indeed to the English *Wills Act 1861*). The formal validity of a will insofar as it disposes of immovables will be determined in accordance with the law of the situs and the formal validity of a will insofar as it disposes of movables will be determined pursuant to the law of the deceased's last domicile.

10. Wills

(a) The legal requirements for the execution of wills will be determined by the *lex situs* insofar as immovable property is concerned and by the law of the deceased's domicile at death insofar as movable property is concerned.

International Succession

(b) The construction of a will will be governed by the law intended by the testator. If the will contains a statement to the effect that it is to be construed in accordance with the law of a particular jurisdiction, this will be conclusive. In the absence of such a statement, there is a rebuttable presumption that the law intended by the testator will be that of his domicile at the time when the will was made. This is the case whether the will disposes of movables or immovables.

(c) Similarly, issues relating to a will's essential or material validity will generally be determined by the law of the situs insofar as immovable property is concerned and by the law of the deceased's last domicile in relation to movable property.

The issue of whether a beneficiary is able to take under a will disposing of immovable property will be determined by the law of the situs and whether he is able to take under a will disposing of movable property will usually be determined by the law of the deceased's domicile at death if the issue turns on a rule of substantive law, rather than one of procedure.

(d) A legatee under a will has capacity to receive a legacy of movables if he has capacity either under the law of his domicile or under the law of the testator's domicile. In the case of a will disposing of immovable property, this issue will be determined by the law of the situs.

(e) Although there is no decided case on this issue, it is thought that a testator's capacity to execute a will disposing of immovables will be determined by the *lex situs* and, on the basis of English authority (such as the decision *in bonis Maraver*), it is considered that the capacity of a testator to execute a will disposing of movables will be determined by the law of his domicile: it is not however clear whether the relevant law will be that of his domicile when making the will or that of his domicile at death (*see* Section B11(a) *below*).

(f) Issues relating to the essential or material validity of a will or particular bequests, such as the presumption relating to survivorship and questions relating to whether a gift to a witness is valid, whether the testator acted under duress or undue influence or whether the court can make provision for relatives, will be determined by the law of domicile at death in the case of a will disposing of movables since these are issues of substantive law rather than procedure. Such issues will be determined by the *lex situs* in the case of immovable property.

(g) There is no equivalent in BVI law to those of the provisions of the English *Wills Act 1963* which relate to powers of appointment and the systems of law applicable to the various conflict of laws issues concerning powers of appointment will therefore be determined by applying the relevant English common law principles of private international law relating to powers of appointment.

(h) In the case of movable property, a later will or codicil which purports to revoke an earlier will in whole or in part will be effective if the later instrument is valid under BVI principles of private international law; if an issue arises as to the effect of a revocation clause, however, the issue will be one of construction and will be determined in accordance with the law governing this issue. The rule that a will is revoked by marriage, on the other hand, is thought by many to be one which is correctly classified as one of matrimonial law rather than a rule of succession; on this basis, the question of whether or not a will disposing of movables is revoked on marriage will depend on whether there is a similar rule forming part of the law of the testator's domicile at the time of his or her marriage. In the case of other methods of revocation, the issue of whether a will disposing of movables has been revoked will be determined in accordance with the law of the testator's domicile, although it is not clear whether it is the law of domicile when making the will or the law of domicile at death which governs the issue (*see* Section B11(b) *below*).

All issues relating to the revocation of a will disposing of immovables will be determined by the *lex situs*, save that the question of whether or not such a will is revoked on marriage will be determined by the law of the testator's domicile on marriage if (as is thought) this is a rule of matrimonial law rather than one of succession.

(i) Substantive issues relating to the essential validity of a disposition will be determined by the law of the deceased's domicile in the case of movable property and all issues relating to the material validity of a disposition of immovables will be determined by the *lex situs*.

11. Domicile/Nationality

(a) Other than in relation to (1) the construction issue referred to in Section B10(b) *above*, (2) a person's capacity to execute a will disposing of movables and (3) whether a will disposing of movables is revoked by methods other than by later will or codicil or marriage, where an issue falls to be determined in accordance with the law of the deceased's domicile, it will be his domicile at death which will be relevant.

It is not clear whether a testator's capacity to execute a will disposing of movables will be determined by the law of his domicile when making the will or that at his death, although it is considered that, on principle, the issue should be determined by the law of the testator's domicile when making the will.

Similarly, it is submitted that it should be the law of the testator's domicile when the alleged act of revocation took place, rather than his domicile at death, which should determine whether a will disposing of movables is revoked (other than by a later will or codicil or marriage), but the issue has yet to be determined by the courts.

A person's domicile will be determined in accordance with the English common law principles applicable to this issue, save that pursuant to Section 59 of the *Matrimonial Proceedings and Property Act 1995* (No. 6 of 1995), which came into effect on 13 February 1996, the domicile of a married woman is no longer to be that of her husband and a married woman may change her domicile independently. Accordingly, a married woman's domicile will be determined in precisely the same way as a man's whether or not the marriage took place after 13 February 1996 (cf. Section 1 of the UK's *Domicile and Matrimonial Proceedings Act 1973*, which specifies that a woman who was already married when that statutory provision came into effect would retain the domicile of her husband until losing it either by the acquisition of a new domicile of choice or by the revival of her domicile of origin). Furthermore, there is, in the BVI, no equivalent to Section 3(1) of the UK's *Domicile and Matrimonial Proceedings Act 1973*, so that a child is incapable of acquiring an independent domicile until he reaches full age: under Section 3(1) of the UK statute, a child is capable of obtaining an independent domicile at the age of sixteen.

(b) The domicile of a beneficiary will only be material to the extent that this is relevant under the system of law which determines the issue, on applying the principles set out above.

(c) Under the internal law of the BVI, a person may only have one domicile and nationality is not a relevant consideration. These factors could however be relevant as a matter of foreign law if, on applying the Territory's principles of private international law, that law determines the issue.

12. Taxation

There are no estate taxes in the BVI.

Canada – Ontario

Prepared by: Archie RABINOWITZ, B.A., LL.B[1]
Goodman and Carr LLP, Barristers and Solicitors

Address: 2300-200 King Street West
 Toronto, Ontario
 Canada, M5H 3W5
Tel.: +1 416 595 2449
Fax: +1 416 595 0567
E-mail: arabinowitz@goodmancarr.com

SECTION A – BRIEF SURVEY OF THE LOCAL SYSTEM

1. Type of System

(a) The federal government of Canada and all Canadian provinces and territories, save for Quebec, function under a common law system. Quebec's legal system is a civil law system.

(b) Canada operates under a federal system of government which divides the responsibility for various government powers between the federal and provincial governments. Each province in Canada has the power to legislate its own laws in relation to property and civil rights within the province. The principles embodied within these various pieces of legislation in each common law province share essential common principles with the other common law provinces; however, the laws of each province may vary in substance. The analysis contained within this paper will focus only on the estate laws of the Province of Ontario.

2. Wills

(a) Ontario law provides for four different types of wills.

– *The Formal or Attested Will*

---

1. The author acknowledges the contributions of Michelle Cass, LL.B C.F.P. and Chris Foulon, Student-at-Law.

International Succession

The formal or attested will is a document made in writing which must be signed at the end thereof by the testator or by some other person in his or her presence by his or her direction. The will must also be signed by two witnesses to the testator's signature or to the testator's acknowledgement of his or his agent's signature, who must sign in the presence of the testator. There is no standard format required of an attested will. The essential requirement is that the wishes of the testator are recorded or represented in some form of print and that the testator confirms those wishes through a witnessed signature. There is no requirement for wills to be executed before a notary or before other legal authority. The *Succession Law Reform Act R.S.O. 1990*, c. S.26 (*SLRA*), which governs the law of succession in Ontario, recognizes that minor defects in execution ought not invalidate a will.

– The Holographic Will

The holographic will must be in the testator's own handwriting and it must be signed by the testator in order to be valid. Such a will does not require the presence, attestation or signature of a witness. A will that is typewritten or in a handwriting other than the testator's does not constitute a valid holographic will. A holographic document is only considered to be a testamentary document if it contains a deliberate and final expression of intention regarding the disposal of property upon death.

– The Privileged Will

A person who is a member of the Canadian Armed Forces, while on active service, may make a will in writing signed by him or by someone else in his presence and by his direction without any further formality, without the requirement of attestation, and without the requirement of a signature by a witness. Such a will remains in force until it is revoked by the testator, even if the person has ceased active military service.

– The International Will

The international will is prescribed by the *Convention Providing a Uniform Law on the Form of an International Will*. In Ontario, a will made in the form of an international will as prescribed by the Annex to the Convention, is valid irrespective of the place where the will is made, of the location of the assets or of the nationality, domicile or residence of the testator. The formalities required of these wills are those as set out in the Convention.

Oral wills or wills on videotape are not valid in Ontario. There is no concept of a death-bed will; however, Ontario does recognize gifts *mortis causa*.

(b) *i.* Amendments to wills must be made in accordance with the same formalities as set out for a will which includes amendments by codicil. In addition, a will may be revoked in whole or in part by a codicil. A formal will is normally changed by a codicil executed with the same formalities, although this is not necessary. A holographic codicil can be used to amend a formal or holographic will. For a holographic codicil to amend a formal will, however, the codicil must express a present intention to change the will. As a general rule, the terms of a codicil will be construed so as to interfere with a will as little as possible.

ii. Marriage automatically revokes the will of a testator. The *SLRA* allows for three exceptions to this general rule: (1) a will made prior to marriage, that has been made in contemplation of the upcoming marriage is allowed to stand if there is a declaration in the will that the will has been made in contemplation of the upcoming marriage and the testator's intention is clear that the will is to continue to be valid after the marriage; (2) a will made prior to marriage is also allowed to stand if the surviving spouse elects in writing within one year of the death of the testator to take under the will; or (3) the will is made in exercise of a power of appointment of property which would not in default of the appointment pass to the heir, executor or administrator of the testator or to the persons who would otherwise be entitled to share or an intestacy.

iii. A previously revoked will can only be revived in accordance with Section 19 of the *SLRA*. The Act provides that a will or any part of a will that has been revoked, can be revived only by a properly executed will or codicil that shows an intention to give effect to the revoked will; or by re-execution of the will with the required formalities. A letter by a testator may revive a revoked holographic will. When a will is revived it is deemed to have been made at the time at which it was revived.

3. Intestacy

(a) Intestate succession is governed by Part II of the *SLRA*. The *SLRA* provides that where a person dies intestate and is survived by a spouse and not survived by issue, then the spouse is entitled to the property absolutely. If the deceased is survived by both a spouse and issue, then the surviving spouse is entitled to receive the payment of the preferential share before the estate is distributed. In Ontario the preferential share is CAD 200,000. The surviving spouse is also entitled to a distributive share. Under the *SLRA*, where a person dies intestate and leaves a spouse and one child, the spouse and child are each entitled to one-half of the residue of the property that remains after payment of the preferential share. If a person dies leaving a spouse and more than one child, then the spouse is entitled to one-third of the residue of the property that remains after payment of the preferential share and the children of the deceased equally share the remaining two-thirds. If a child has predeceased the intestate, leaving surviving issue at the date of the intestate's death, the spouse's share is the same as if the child had been living at the date of the intestate's death and the deceased child's share would then be divided among his or her issue equally. If all of the intestate's children have predeceased him or her, after the surviving spouse's share has been paid, the intestate's issue who are in the nearest degree in which there are issue surviving him or her are entitled to the remainder of the estate.

International Succession

If a person dies intestate and leaves no spouse or issue, then the property is distributed between the parents of the deceased equally or where only one parent survives to that surviving parent absolutely. If no spouse, issue or parent survives then the property is distributed among the deceased's siblings equally. If any sibling predeceases the intestate the deceased sibling's share will be distributed among the deceased sibling's children equally. If no spouse, issue, parent, or sibling survives the intestate, then the property is to be distributed among the nephews and nieces of the intestate equally. If none of the above survive the intestate, the estate will be distributed among the highest level/degree of next-of-kin equally. Where a person dies intestate and there is no surviving spouse, issue, parent, sibling, nephew or niece, or next-of-kin, the property becomes the property of the provincial Crown.

'Issue' refers to any lineal descendant of a person whether born within or outside of marriage and includes issue conceived before and born after the death of the person. Adopted children are to be regarded as the children of the adoptive parents, as if they were natural parents. Therefore, illegitimate (including adulterine children), adopted and unborn children share the same rights as do natural children born within marriage.

(b) There is no difference under Ontario law in the manner in which movable and immovable estate devolves on an intestacy.

4. Freedom of Testation

(a) While there are no compulsory shares that must be left to a spouse under Ontario law, the *Family Law Act R.S.O. 1990*, c. F.3 (FLA) provides for a deferred equalization scheme that applies to all assets acquired by legally married spouses during marriage. The equalization scheme is triggered by marriage breakdown or death. The FLA ensures that if the surviving spouse so elects, a certain minimum share in the estate is available to him or her. Section 5(2) of the *FLA* provides that if, when a spouse dies, the 'net family property' of the deceased spouse exceeds the 'net family property' of the surviving spouse, the surviving spouse is entitled to one-half the difference between these values. Therefore, if all of the couple's assets were in the name of the deceased spouse and the deceased's will did not provide for the surviving spouse, the surviving spouse could elect to take his or her entitlement under the *FLA* and receive a payment equal to one-half of the value of the assets. The *FLA* provides that the surviving spouse may take either under the will or under the terms of the *FLA* but he or she may not take under both.

To take his or her entitlement under the *FLA*, the surviving spouse must file his or her election and bring an application against the estate to claim an equalizing payment. The claimant's rights under the will cease once the application succeeds and the will is then read as if the surviving spouse had predeceased the testator. The surviving spouse also loses the right to share on an intestacy once he or she is successful in an equalization application. The *FLA* awards to the surviving spouse a right of payment and not a right to property. A successful claimant therefore becomes a creditor of the estate rather than a property owner.

The traditional common law rights of dower and curtesy no longer exist in Ontario.

Freedom of testation is also restricted by dependants' relief provisions as contained within Part V of the *SLRA* and in the *inter vivos* support provisions in the *FLA*. A person seeking support must make an application to the Ontario Court. The court may suspend the administration of an estate pending the application of a dependant. 'Dependants' include a spouse, child, parent or sibling of the deceased who the deceased was providing support or was under a legal obligation to provide support immediately before or after his or her death. Dependants include common law spouses, adopted children and illegitimate children. The courts have a wide discretion to provide relief to a testator's dependants if the court is satisfied that adequate provision for the proper support of the dependants has not been made by the testator. In fact, the *SLRA* even provides the court with a discretion to make an order for support, even in the case where the dependant has entered into a contract waiving his or her right to support.

(b) So long as a contract of inheritance meets the regular rules of contracts, a contract of inheritance will be binding on the estate of the deceased and the disappointed party can sue the estate for the usual contractual remedies. A plaintiff in these cases will usually be entitled to damages, but if specific property was promised in the contract, the plaintiff may be entitled to specific performance. If the contract is deemed to be unenforceable, a plaintiff may still have a claim in *quantum meruit* if the unenforcability would result in an unjust enrichment.

5. Maintenance

See 4(a) *above*.

6. Community Property Between Husband and Wife

(a) *See* 3(a) and 4(a) *above*.

(b) Both spouses in Ontario have an equal right of possession of the 'matrimonial home'. However, this right ceases when the parties cease to be spouses via marriage breakdown or death. This right of possession may be allowed to continue, however, by court order in which the court grants the surviving spouse continuing possessory rights to the matrimonial home. If the deceased and his or her spouse held the matrimonial property as beneficial joint tenants, then clearly the property would pass by right of survivorship to the surviving spouse.

7. Gifts (*Inter Vivos*)

(a) An *inter vivos* gift is a gratuitous transfer of property from the owner to another person. The owner of the property must intend that the transfer of title have present effect, the gift must be delivered and the property must be accepted as a gift in order for the gift to be valid. A valid gift to an heir, given prior to death, is not set off against the heir's inheritance under a will, unless the will specifies to the contrary.

(b) Not applicable.

8. Capacity

(a) An individual under the age of majority (presently the age of eighteen) ordinarily cannot make a valid will. There are two statutory exceptions. An individual under the age of majority who is married or is contemplating marriage can make a valid will but in the case of contemplating marriage, the will does not become valid unless and until the marriage takes place. Secondly, a member of the regular or active component of the Canadian Armed Forces or a sailor at sea, who is under the age of majority, may make a valid will. Other than in regard to the statutory exception above, marital status does not effect the capacity of a testator. The testator must also be of sound mind. This requires that the testator understand the nature of the act of making a will and of its effect and understand the extent of the property involved. The test for mental capacity is whether the testator was capable, at the time of giving instructions regarding the will, of having such knowledge and appreciation of facts, and control of his intentions, and free from delusions, as would enable him to have a will of his own in the distribution of property and to be able to act on that distribution.

(b) A witness must be of legal age and have mental capacity at the time of signing. If a beneficiary or his or her spouse witnesses a will, such attestation does not invalidate the will, although a court will invalidate a gift made to these witnesses as beneficiaries under the will unless the court is convinced that no undue influence occurred.

(c) The *Children's Law Reform Act R.S.O. 1990*, c. C.12 abolished any distinction made between the status of children born within and children born out of wedlock. All natural children are therefore entitled to inherit from their parents, unless the wills provide otherwise. A child who is adopted, gains the right to inherit from the adoptive parents and their kindred, and loses the right to inherit from his or her natural parents and their kindred unless a will provides otherwise.

There are certain restrictions on the rights of minors and of the unborn. Unless the will directs the executor to establish a trust for a minor, or to pay the minors share to the minors parent or guardian, the minor's share must be paid into court to the minor's credit. These same rules apply to mentally incompetent beneficiaries.

A beneficiary under a will loses his or her rights of payment if s/he criminally caused the death of the deceased. An individual may also become ineligible to receive a gift under a will if s/he or his/her spouse acts as a witness to the will. The Ontario legislation states that such gifts will be invalidated unless the court is satisfied that the witness did not exercise any improper or undue influence.

9. Authority (Court, Notarial or Other)

In Ontario, the Ontario Court (General Division) has jurisdiction over both probate and interpretation of wills. The court grants Certificates of Appointment of Estate Trustee with a will (formerly 'letters probate') or Certificates of Appointment of Estate Trustee without a will (formerly 'letters of administration'). The court also rules on the formal validity of wills, appoints administrators and executors and performs passing of accounts.

Depending on the nature and value of the assets that an estate is comprised of, it may not be necessary to obtain certificates of appointment in all cases. However, when dealing with assets such as real property (except property held as a joint tenancy), registered securities, bank accounts, or choses in action, a grant of a Certificate will be required.

10. Invalidity of Will

(a) A will may be held to be invalid if it fails to meet the formality criteria set out in paragraph 2 *above*. In addition, for a will to be valid, the testator must have knowledge of and approve of the contents of the will and the testator must have the capacity to execute the will. An otherwise valid will may also be set aside due to undue influence that amounts to force or coercion. Fraudulent misrepresentations made by a named beneficiary to the testator, that induced the disposition of property, may be grounds to set aside the provisions of the will. The court may also set aside a will or specific provisions of a will on the ground of mistake. Dispositions may be set aside due to mistakes of fact, mistakes in drafting of the will, or due to a mistake in signing the wrong testamentary instrument.

(b) A will which is invalid is void. In a case where the individual lacks testamentary capacity the entire will is void. In cases of fraud, undue influence or mistake the will is usually only voidable to the extent of disallowing the unethical or inadvertent action. The remainder of the will which benefits innocent parties remains valid.

11. Simultaneous Death

(a)–(b) Prior to 31 March 1978, where two or more persons died in circumstances where it was uncertain who survived the others, the deaths were presumed to have occurred in the order of seniority with the youngest person deemed to have survived the older persons. After 31 March 1978, where two or more persons die in circumstances where it is uncertain which person survived the others, then the estate of each person is to be disposed of as if each person survived the others.

12. Estate Taxes

(a) Canada imposes no estate taxes or succession duties. However, the province of Ontario levies probate fees of approximately 5 per cent on the first CAD 50,000.00

and 1.5 per cent on the balance of the gross value (not including real property located outside of Ontario) of the estate. In addition, the federal *Income Tax Act R.S.C. 1985*, c. 1, s. 70(5) (*ITA*) deems that all of an individual's capital assets are disposed of on his or her death and the *ITA* imposes a tax on three-quarters of the value of any capital gains made on these assets.

(b) The capital gain taxes apply to any taxable capital properties owned by the deceased. The probate fees are levied as a percentage of the sum of the gross value of the world-wide movable assets and the immovable assets within the jurisdiction.

(c) Unless the will makes an express provision stating otherwise, the estate must pay the taxes that arise from the deemed capital gains. The estate is also liable to pay the probate fees assessed. Taxes and other debts of the estate have first priority in the order of application of the assets of the estate.

13. Administration of Estates

(a) Estates are administered by an Estate Trustee named in the will whose appointment is often validated by the court upon the granting of a certificate of Appointment of Estate Trustee with a will. Alternatively, the court will appoint an Estate Trustee in the case where an executor has not been named, where a named executor cannot or will not perform his duties, or due to a deceased dying intestate. Although the heirs do not have a right to administer the estate in their capacity as heirs, they may have priority to apply to be named Estate Trustee of the estate in the absence of a named Estate Trustee.

A person may be disqualified as Estate Trustee in special circumstances, particularly where the chosen executor is of unsound mind, criminally responsible for the deceased's death, a bankrupt, serving a lengthy prison sentence or adverse in interest to a beneficiary. In the case where a deceased dies intestate or testate without naming an Estate Trustee, the court will appoint one. Once the Estate Trustee has assumed control of the assets, paid off creditors and if necessary obtained the grant of a Certificate of Appointment of Estate Trustee, the Estate Trustee must distribute the estate among the beneficiaries.

(b) In an application for Certificate of Appointment, the applicant must file with the local registrar an application that gives details about the deceased's background, details about the will or about people entitled to share in an intestacy and information regarding the value of the estate. A valuation of the deceased's property must be delivered upon application. If the court is alerted that there may be something wrong with the will, then the will must be proved in solemn form in open court.

(c) Estate Trustees have a duty to keep proper records of account and to be ready to account to the court when requested to do so. The accounts are passed by a judge who has authority to make a full inquiry of all of the estate, its administration and its disbursement. These proceedings ordinarily will occur only if the accounts are challenged or voluntarily by the administrator in order to establish a basis for obtaining compensation for his or her efforts as administrator.

(d) A beneficiary or his or her representative may object to an Estate Trustee's handling of the estate, as may a creditor who possesses an outstanding claim.

(e) All real and personal property from the estate is vested in the personal representative in trust for a period of up to three years from the death of the deceased in order to pay the debts and distribute the assets of the estate. After this period, the real property vests in the beneficiaries entitled to the property unless the personal representative registers a caution in the land registry office to delay the vesting of the property. These cautions may be necessary if the personal representative determines that the property needs to be sold in order to meet the obligations or to properly distribute the proceeds of the estate.

(f) Creditors of the estate are paid before any distribution of the assets. These debts must be paid as soon as possible. Secured debts incurred during the deceased's lifetime have first priority, followed by funeral expenses, testamentary expenses and the costs of administration of the estate. Unless a contrary provision appears in the will, all real and personal property is applied rateably to the payment of debts. The order in which classes of property will be used to pay debts is as follows: non-bequeathed property; residuary bequests; property in trust to pay debts; general legacies; and specific legacies. If the deceased specifically devises real property that is subject to a mortgage, then unless the will directs otherwise, the property is primarily responsible for the payment of the mortgage debt.

(g) If no Estate Trustee is appointed in the will or no Estate Trustee is able or willing to act, then the court will appoint an Estate Trustee of the estate. In Ontario, a person residing outside of the province may not be granted a Certificate of Appointment of Estate Trustee unless a bond is given to the Accountant of the Ontario Court in the amount of a penalty of double the value of the estate. Such a bond is not required of government agents, trust companies, or surviving spouses in certain cases and the court may reduce or dispense with the requirement of the bond in certain circumstances.

14. Domicile/Nationality

(a) Sections 36(1) and 36(2) of the *SLRA* deal with the intrinsic validity of wills. Intrinsic validity deals with the essential validity of wills and is concerned with the effects and meaning of a will. Section 36(1) states that the manner and formalities of making a will, and its essential validity and effect, so far as it relates to an interest in land, are governed by the internal law of the place where the land is situated. This section actually applies to all immovables including land and all permanent attachments to land. In contrast, Section 36(2) of the *SLRA* states that the manner and formalities of making a will, and its essential validity and effect as it relates to an interest in movables, are governed by the internal law of the place where the testator was domiciled at the time of his or her death. Section 37(1) of the *SLRA* deals with the formal validity of wills. Formal validity is concerned with matters such as the capacity of the testator, the manner of execution of the will, and the number of witnesses required. Section 37(1) states that in regard to the manner and formalities of making a will, and its essential validity and effect in relation to an interest in movables or immovables, a will is valid and admissible to the courts if at the time of its making it complied with the internal law of the place where the will was made; the testator was then domiciled; the testator then had his or her habitual residence; or the testator then was a national. Section 38 further provides that a change of domicile by a testator after making a will does not render it invalid with regard to the manner or formalities of its making. Finally, Section 35 of the *SLRA* states that the provisions listed above apply to wills made either in or out of Ontario.

(b) The foundation of jurisdiction is the presence of property of the deceased within the jurisdiction. The existence of a foreign domicile by the deceased does not necessarily take the matter out of the jurisdiction of the Ontario courts. Section 12 of the *Estates Act R.S.O. 1990*, c. E.21 (EA) provides the court with a discretion in deciding whether to grant probate of the will or grant letters of administration even where the deceased has no fixed place of abode within the jurisdiction or resided out of Ontario at the time of death and where the deceased died leaving no property in Ontario. However, in most cases the court will not give an order of probate or succession in such a situation, since the foundation of jurisdiction is the existence of property within the jurisdiction at the time of death.

SECTION B – APPLICABLE LAW/PROCEDURE WHERE FOREIGN ELEMENT/S ARE INVOLVED

1. Jurisdiction

(a) Generally, the key factors in a court determining jurisdiction is the fixed place of residence of the deceased and the presence of assets within the jurisdiction. Even if the deceased had a foreign domicile or had no fixed residence within Ontario, the court may grant administration or ancillary administration within the province if the deceased left property within Ontario. Practically speaking, a court would not be asked to assume jurisdiction over a deceased's estate who was domiciled within Ontario at the time of death if the deceased had no assets situate in Ontario, unless by doing so, the estate would be subject to lower probate fees in the jurisdiction in which the estate does have assets.

(b) In cases dealing with immovables within the province, the Ontario court has held it has exclusive jurisdiction regarding the administration of such assets. The court also has jurisdiction to deal with personal property within the province and outside the jurisdiction. However, the court would not view its jurisdiction over such property as exclusive.

(c) The Ontario Court (General Division) has jurisdiction. Section 26 of the EA provides that the application for administration should be filed in the office of the court for the county or district in which the deceased had at the time of death a fixed place of abode, failing which, administration should be filed in the office of the court of the county or district in which the deceased owned property at the time of death, or failing that, it should be filed in any office of the Ontario Court (General Division).

2. Applicable Law

As mentioned above, the court will apply different law depending on whether the assets in question are movables or immovables and depending on whether the question of law at issue is one of formal or intrinsic validity. Sections 36(1) and 36(2) of the *SLRA* deal with the intrinsic validity of wills. Intrinsic validity deals with the essential validity of wills and is concerned with the effects and meaning of a will. Section 36(1) states that the manner and formalities of making a will, and its essential validity and effect, so far as it relates to an interest in land, are governed by the internal law of the place where the land is situated. In contrast, Section 36(2) of the *SLRA* states that the manner and formalities of making a will, and its essential validity and effect as it relates to an interest in movables, are governed by the internal law of the place where the testator was domiciled at the time of his or her death. Section 37(1) of the *SLRA* deals with the formal validity of wills. Formal validity is concerned with matters such as the capacity of the testator, the manner of execution of the will, and the number of witnesses required. Section 37(1) states that in regard to the manner and formalities of making a will, and its essential validity and effect in relation to an interest in movables or immovables, a will is valid and admissible to the courts if at the time of its making it complied with the internal law of the place where the will was made; the testator was then domiciled; the testator then had his or her habitual residence; or the testator then was a national.

3. Foreign Succession/Inheritance Orders

(a) A personal representative who is appointed by a foreign order is not recognized as having the authority to administer the movable or immovable estate of the deceased located in Ontario unless the Ontario court reseals the original grant of authority when dealing with a foreign Commonwealth nation or unless ancillary letters of administration are granted when dealing with a foreign non-Common-wealth nation. The same essential procedures are followed in resealing an original grant of authority or in granting ancillary letters of administration.

(b) A local succession/inheritance order can be obtained to give effect to a foreign order through a foreign applicant applying for a Certificate of Appointment of Estate Trustee with a will. The foreign applicant must also file a certified copy of the grant that has been issued in the original jurisdiction. In some cases, a foreign applicant may be required to post security before a local succession order will be provided.

International Succession

(c) In order to obtain recognition of a foreign succession order, the foreign applicant must apply to have the grant originally made to him or her resealed. A reciprocity agreement between the Commonwealth countries enables a foreigner who has obtained a grant of probate in his or her own jurisdiction to produce the probate to the court in the local jurisdiction, to be sealed there, without obliging the foreigner to provide all of the proofs that would normally be necessary had the original application been made in the local country. A foreign applicant from a non-Commonwealth jurisdiction may apply for an ancillary appointment of estate trustee on the same terms and following the same procedures as for resealing. The application for resealing or for an ancillary appointment of estate trustee should be made in the district where the deceased had his fixed place of residence, or if there was no fixed residence, then the application should be made in the district where the deceased owned property.

4. Two or More Succession or Probate Orders

If there is an application before the court in Ontario for an order of succession or inheritance and a foreign order already exists in a foreign country, the Ontario court has a discretion in deciding whether or not to grant the order by considering the particular circumstances of the case before it. Generally, the courts will give the consideration of the deceased's fixed place of residence the highest relevance in determining which jurisdiction should grant probate. The court will also consider, however, within which jurisdiction the deceased owned property. In the case where a deceased dies resident in one jurisdiction, leaving the bulk of his or her property there and leaving a smaller amount of property in another jurisdiction, then ancillary grants of administration may be issued. The court also exercises the discretion to appoint the same person as appointed in the other jurisdiction or to appoint someone else within the court's jurisdiction. In the case of land that is located within Ontario, the Ontario courts have held that they exercise exclusive jurisdiction with respect to a question dealing with an interest in that land.

5. Assets

The foundation of jurisdiction is the presence of property of the deceased within the jurisdiction. The existence of a foreign domicile by the deceased does not take the matter out of the jurisdiction of the Ontario courts. Section 12 of the EA provides the court with a discretion in deciding whether to grant a Certificate of Appointment of Estate Trustee even where the deceased has no fixed place of abode within the jurisdiction or resided out of Ontario at the time of death and where the deceased died leaving no property in Ontario. However, in most cases the court will not give an order of probate or succession in such a situation, since the foundation of jurisdiction is the existence of property within the jurisdiction at the time of death.

6. Expert Evidence

(a) Probate may be granted regarding the will of a person domiciled abroad upon proof that it is a valid will according to the law of the domicile and that there are assets within the jurisdiction. The will need not first be proved in the courts of the foreign jurisdiction. This proof need not be supplied by a foreign lawyer.

(b) In the regular course, affidavit evidence is sufficient. If the will is contested, however, evidence regarding the inheritance laws of a foreign country may have to be provided in open court, in which case the deponent of the affidavit would likely be required to give oral evidence, subject to the discretion of the court.

7. Unity of Succession

The concept of unity of succession is not accepted in Ontario. Ontario law provides that immovable assets devolve in accordance with the law of the jurisdiction where the land is situated and movable assets in accordance with the law of the place where the deceased was domiciled at the time of death.

8. Formalities

In Ontario, a will is considered valid and is admissible to probate for both movables and immovables if at the time that it was made it complied with the law of the jurisdiction where the will was made; the testator was domiciled at the date of making the will; the testator then had a habitual residence; or the testator was a national at the time of making a will. It is not therefore necessary for the formalities of a will executed in a foreign country to be the same as those of Ontario for a will to be submitted and recognized for a succession order.

9. Legislation

The *1961 Hague Convention on the Conflicts of Laws Relating to the Form of Testamentary Dispositions* is not applicable in Canada. However, in 1966 Canada approved a new Part II of the *Uniform Act* that arose out of the Conference on Uniformity of Legislation in Canada. The new legislation in Ontario (Sections 34–41 of the *SLRA*) implemented the changes made by the report of the Private International Law Committee and the *Hague Convention*, save for one important exception. The *Canadian Uniform Act* recognized that the national law of a State could not be used as a determinant in respect to assessing the formal validity of wills in a federal State. The Canadian Conference held that in cases of federal States where there is no one body of laws covering the wills of nationals, regard should be had to the laws of the province in which the testator was most closely connected.

International Succession

10. Wills

(a) Legal requirements for execution of wills, such as the number of witnesses required or the execution of a codicil, are matters of procedure or formality. Matters of formality are governed by s. 37(1) of the *SLRA* (*see* Section B, paragraph 2 *above*). As regards the manner and formalities of a will, a will is valid in Ontario and admissible to the courts in relation to both immovables and movables if at the time it was made it complied with the law of the jurisdiction where: the will was made; the testator was domiciled; the testator had a habitual residence; or the testator was a national.

(b) The courts will resort to the terminology of the place where the testator was domiciled at the time of making a will in aid of the will's construction or interpretation (whether the words relate to movables or immovables) in the absence of an express or implied acknowledgement that Canadian law will apply.

(c) Matters regarding the rights of heirs or beneficiaries to minimum portions are matters of intrinsic validity. Matters of intrinsic validity are governed by Sections 36(1) and 36(2) of the *SLRA* (*see* Section B, paragraph 2 *above*). The formal requirements of making a will and the issues of the validity and effect of a will in relation to an interest in immovables is governed by the law of the jurisdiction where the land is situated. The formal requirements of making a will and the issues of the validity and effect of a will in relation to an interest in movables is governed by the place where the testator was domiciled at the time of death. However, any estate making a bequest to a beneficiary would be subject to a court award of support provisions for spouses or dependants as described in Section A, paragraph 4(a) *above*.

(d) Capacity to inherit will depend on the law which governs the asset being devolved. If the asset is immovable property, the capacity to inherit will be governed by the internal law of the place where the asset is located. If the asset conveyed is movable, then the capacity to inherit will be governed by the internal law of the place where the testator was domiciled at the time of his or her death.

(e) Capacity to make a will depends on the law which governs the assets being transferred. If the asset is immovable property, the capacity of an individual to make a will transferring this property will be governed by the internal law of the place where the asset is located. If the asset conveyed by the will is movable, then the capacity of the individual to make a will transferring the property will be governed by the internal law of the place where the testator was domiciled at the time of his or her death.

(f) Matters regarding the essential or material validity of a will or of particular bequests are matters of intrinsic validity. Matters of intrinsic validity are governed by Sections 36(1) and 36(2) of the *SLRA* as outlined in (c) *above*.

(g) Powers of appointment or the rule against perpetuities are matters of intrinsic validity and therefore the rule governing this issue is the same as the rule in (c) *above*. Further, Section 37(2)(c) of the *SLRA* states that 'as regards the manner and formalities of making a will of an interest in moveables or in land, the following are properly made, (c) a will so far as it exercises a power of appointment, if the making of the will conforms to the law governing the essential validity of the power.'

(h) Amendment, revocation and revival are matters of procedure or formality, which are governed by Section 37(1) of the *SLRA* as outlined in (a) above. Further, Section 37(2)(b) of the *SLRA* states that 'as regards the manner and formalities of making a will of an interest in movables or in land, the following are properly made, (b) a will so far as it revokes a will which under Sections 34 to 42 [the Conflict of Laws sections] would be treated as properly made or revokes a provision which under those sections would be treated as comprised in a properly made will, if the making of the later will conformed to any law by reference to which the revoked will or provision would be treated as properly made.'

(i) Any estate administered in Ontario would be subject to a claim for a minimum share or support order by a spouse or dependent as outlined in Section A, paragraph 4(a) *above*. Such an order would apply to all assets administered by the Ontario court. An Ontario court would recognize an automatic reserve or minimum share provision laid down in foreign law in certain cases. In dealing with immovables, the Ontario court will apply the internal law of the place where the land is situated. If the land is in Ontario, then the Ontario minimum share or support provisions would be applicable to this asset. If the land is in a foreign jurisdiction, then the automatic reserve provisions of that jurisdiction would be applicable to the immovable assets. In dealing with movables, the Ontario court will apply the Ontario law relating to reserve, or the foreign law relating to reserve, depending on where the testator was domiciled at the time of his or her death. If the testator is domiciled in Ontario at the time of death, then the law governing minimum share in Ontario will govern as it relates to movables. If the testator is domiciled in a foreign jurisdiction at the time of death, then the foreign law as it relates to reserve portions will be applied as it relates to movables.

11. Domicile/Nationality

(a) In cases dealing with the intrinsic validity of a disposition of movables, the domicile of the deceased at the time of death is the relevant factor. Section 36(2) of the SLRA states that the manner and formalities of making a will, and its essential validity and effect, so far as it relates to an interest in movables, are governed by the internal law of the place where the testator was domiciled at the time of his or her death. In cases dealing with the formal validity of wills dealing with moveables or immoveables, the domicile of the deceased at the time of making the will is the relevant factor. Section 37(1) of the *SLRA* states as regards the manner and formalities of making a will of an interest in moveables or in land, a will is valid and admissible in probate if at the time of making the will it complied with the internal law of the place where: the will was made; the testator was then domiciled; the testator then had his or her habitual residence; or the testator then was a national.

International Succession

(b) The domicile of a beneficiary is irrelevant in Canadian law.

(c) If the domicile of the deceased is unclear or if the deceased had more than one domicile, the Ontario court would likely inquire regarding in which jurisdiction the deceased held property prior to death. If the deceased held immovable property in both jurisdictions, then it is likely that both jurisdictions would grant letters of administration or letters probate or that a primary and ancillary granting of administration would be granted.

12. Taxation

Canada does not impose any estate taxes or duties. However, the province of Ontario levies probate fees of approximately 1.5 per cent of the gross value (not including immovables outside of Ontario) of all estates that are wound up in Ontario. Therefore, the non-residency of a deceased or heir would not effect the payment of these fees so long as the estate is administered in Ontario. The deemed disposition of capital gains that occurs upon the death of a deceased under the federal *ITA* imposes a tax on three-quarters of the value of any capital gains made on the assets held by the deceased prior to death. These taxes are paid out of the estate. The capital gain taxes apply to any taxable capital properties owned by the deceased and the status of non-residency of the deceased or heirs does not effect the liability for these taxes if the estate possesses such properties which have appreciated in value.

Canada – Quebec

Prepared by: Didier FRÉCHETTE, Frank ZYLBERBERG and Martin RAYMOND

Mendelsohn
1000 Sherbrooke St. West, 27th Floor
Montreal, Quebec H3A 3G4

Tel.:   514 987 5000
Fax: 514 987 1213
E-mail: dfrechette@mendelsohn.ca; fzylberberg@mendelsohn.ca

SECTION A – BRIEF REVIEW OF THE LEGAL SYSTEM

1. Type of System

Canada is a federation which comprises ten provinces and three territories. Pursuant to a constitutional division of powers, the federal Parliament and the provincial Legislature have either exclusive or concurrent legislative jurisdiction in specified areas of activities. Most areas of private law (including succession law), which are referred to in the Canadian Constitution as 'Property and Civil Rights', are under the exclusive jurisdiction of the provincial Legislatures.

The Province of Quebec is the only Canadian province which has a civil law system derived from the French Civil Code. All of the other provinces have a common law legal system directly related to common law of England. However, the Quebec civil law system has evolved over the years and has incorporated some important traditional features of common law jurisdictions. One of the most important of these is the concept of trust which, although historically a common law institution, is now fully integrated in the civil law of Quebec.

The private law rules of succession are found in the Civil Code of Quebec, which underwent a major reform in 1994. While Quebec succession law has many similarities to French law, it is fully autonomous and there are many significant distinctions.

While the private law rules of succession are exclusively within provincial jurisdiction, both the provincial Legislatures and the federal Parliament have concurrent jurisdiction in matters of taxation. In practice, however, most provinces adapt the federal tax legislation, which is administered on their behalf by the federal government. The Province of Quebec has its own taxation legislation, although it generally tracks the rules found in the federal *Income Tax Act*.

2. Wills

(a) A will must be in writing to be valid. The Civil Code of Quebec provides for three different types of wills. The formalities governing the various kinds of wills must be observed on pain of nullity. However, if a will made in one form does not meet the requirements of that form, it can nevertheless be valid as a will made in another form if it meets the requirement for validity of that other form.

The only forms of will that may be made are the notarial will, the holograph will and the will made in the presence of witnesses.

Notarial Will

A notarial will is made before a notary, *en minute*, in the presence of a witness or two witnesses. The date and place of the making of the will must be noted on the will. The notary has an obligation to verify the identity of the testator and to read the will to the testator before it is signed. As will be seen below, this form of will is particularly popular since it does not have to be probated by the court after the death of the testator.

Holograph Will

A holograph will is a will written entirely by the testator and signed by him without the use of any mechanical process. It is subject to no other formal requirement.

Wills Made in the Presence of Witnesses

A will made in the presence of witnesses is written by the testator or by a third person. After signing the will, the testator declares in the presence of two witnesses of full age that the document that he is signing is his will. He need not divulge its content. He signs it at the end or, if he has already signed it, acknowledges his signature. He may also cause a third person to sign it for him in his presence and according to his instructions. The two witnesses thereupon sign the will in the presence of the testator. If the will has been prepared by a third person or by a mechanical process, the testator and the witnesses must initial or sign each page which does not bear their signature.

(b) *i.* A will can be amended or clarified by a codicil (for example, to change the appointment of executor or to add a particular legacy). The codicil must be in one of the three forms described above, but does not have to be in the same form as the will. For example, it is possible to modify a notarial will by a holograph codicil. In such case, the will itself will not have to be probated by the court, but the codicil will.

ii. Marriage does not automatically result in the revocation of a will. However, it results in the creation of a family patrimony (which may give rise to a monetary claim in favour of (or against) the surviving spouse upon the death of a spouse. It may also give rise to a *post-mortem* maintenance obligation in favour of the spouse. For further details, please consult question 4 of Section A.

However, a legacy made to a spouse before divorce is revoked by law, unless the will or codicil clearly indicates the testator's intention of benefiting the spouse despite that possibility. Revocation of the legacy also entails revocation of the appointment of the spouse as liquidator (i.e., executor) of the estate.

iii. A will can be revoked either expressly or tacitly. Express revocation results from a subsequent will explicitly declaring the change of intention. A will that revokes another will can be made in a form different from that of the revoked will.

Subsequent testamentary provisions entail revocation of previous provisions to the extent they are inconsistent. Also, the disposition by the testator of the bequeathed property (even if the property is involuntarily destroyed) entails the revocation of a legacy of that particular property.

The Civil Code of Quebec specifically provides that the revocation of a previous revocation does not revive the original will, unless the testator manifested a contrary intention or unless such intention is apparent from the circumstances.

3. Intestacy

(a) If no will has been made by the deceased, or if all the legatees named in the will have predeceased the testator, the Civil Code of Quebec provides for the order of devolution of succession.

– If the deceased is survived by a spouse as well as descendants, the estate will devolve one-third to the surviving spouse and two-thirds to the descendants. As will be seen below in question 12, this is detrimental from a taxation perspective with respect to appreciated assets, since the favourable tax treatment is only available in respect of property transferred to the surviving spouse.
– In the event that no spouse survives the deceased, the entire succession devolves to the descendants. The first degree of descendants is composed of the children of the deceased. Among them, descendants of the same degree share the estate in equal portions. The descendants in the closest degree take the shares of the descendants, to the exclusion of all others. If a child predeceases the testator, there is representation *per stirpes*. Illegitimate, adulterine and adopted children are not treated differently.

In the absence of descendants, the estate will devolve to privileged ascendants (father and mother) as well as privileged collaterals (brothers and sisters) of the deceased and their descendants in the first degree.

– Two-thirds of the estate devolves to the surviving spouse and one-third to the privileged ascendants.

International Succession

– If there are neither descendants, privileged ascendants nor privileged collaterals, the entire estate devolves to the surviving spouse.
– If there are no descendants and no privileged descendants, two-thirds devolves to the surviving spouse and one-third to the privileged collaterals.
– Without any descendants and surviving spouse, the estate is partitioned equally between the privileged ascendants and the privileged collaterals.

Throughout these dispositions, we can see two different orders of succession. The first includes the descendants and the surviving spouse; the second order includes the surviving spouse, the privileged ascendants and the privileged collaterals.

The third order of succession is relevant only if there are no spouse, no descendants and privileged ascendants or collaterals. This third order comprises ordinary ascendants and collaterals and include ascendants other than the mother and father, and collaterals other than brothers, sisters, nephews and nieces of the first degree.

If there is no one in the three orders of succession or if all potential successors have renounced the succession, the estate devolves to the State in respect of property situated in Quebec. This rule is derived from the *Hague Convention on the Law Applicable to Successions* and allows property left outside Quebec to be taken by that foreign State.

(b) There are no differences between movables and immovables. The law considers neither the origin nor the nature of the property; all the property as a whole constitutes one patrimony. However, if there are immovables outside of Quebec, the law of *situs* will apply, as discussed further in Section B.

4. Freedom of Testation

(a) In Quebec civil law, the right to dispose of property fully and freely, either *inter vivos* or by will, is an essential attribute of the right of ownership. Therefore, as a general rule, the principle of freedom of testation applies. However there are two exceptions if the deceased leaves a spouse and/or dependants.

Family Patrimony

First, the death of a spouse entails the dissolution of the 'family patrimony'. The family patrimony is a pool of assets consisting of family residences, furniture, motor vehicles of the family and rights under pension plans which have accrued during the marriage.

Upon death, the surviving spouse has a monetary claim equal to 50 per cent of the value of the family patrimony assets which belonged to the deceased spouse. The heirs of the deceased have a corresponding claim against the surviving spouse equal to 50 per cent of the family patrimony assets owned by him or her. Each claim is then offset against the other and only the difference is paid to the surviving spouse or the residual heirs of the deceased, as the case may be. This claim must be satisfied out of the residue of the estate – it will not affect particular legacies, even if they pertain to family patrimony assets. Of course, this has little relevance when the spouse is the sole heir of the estate.

The claim resulting from the dissolution of the family patrimony (which occurs only upon death or divorce) is an asset which may be seized by the creditors of the deceased (if for example the estate is insolvent) or by the creditors of the surviving spouse.

Post-Mortem *Maintenance Obligation*

Second, all alimentary creditors of the deceased can claim a financial contribution from the estate as maintenance. These include the surviving spouse, the former spouse, the children (including major children) and, in certain cases, the parents of the deceased. The claim must be asserted within six months of death.

This right exists even when the claimant is an heir of the deceased and even if the right of support was not exercised before the date of death. The contribution is made in the form of a lump sum payable in cash or by instalments.

With respect to a former spouse (i.e., divorced or separated), the contribution is statutorily fixed at an amount equal to the value of twelve months' support. The contribution for the parents of the deceased is statutorily fixed at the value of six months' support. However, in neither case may the contribution exceed 10 per cent of the value of the estate.

The contribution to a surviving spouse or to a child (including majors) must be calculated based on an assessment of all the relevant factors, including the needs and means of the dependant spouse or child, the autonomy of the dependant, the assets of the estate and the benefits otherwise derived from the estate. The contribution granted to a spouse or to a child may not exceed the difference between one-half of the share that he could have claimed had the entire succession devolved according to law (*ab intestate*) and what he actually received from the estate.

A clause in a will whereby the legacies are made conditional upon the legatees renouncing their rights to claim *post-mortem* maintenance has been held to be void by reason of being against public order.

(b) *i.–ii.* Section 631 of the Civil Code of Quebec provides that no person may exercise his option (to accept or renounce) with respect to an estate not yet opened or make any stipulation with respect to such an estate, even with the consent of the person whose estate it is. This provision generally prohibits what is referred to as a *pacte sur successions futures*. The case law has recognized a key exception in the case of closely held corporations for properly drafted buy-sell arrangements in shareholders' agreements.

It is possible to make a donation *mortis causa*, i.e., a gift conditional and effective upon the death of the donor. However, such gifts are generally valid only if they are made between spouses in a marriage contract also known as a pre-nuptial agreement.

5. Maintenance

Post-mortem maintenance can be claimed by an ex-spouse (i.e., separated or divorced) a surviving spouse, dependent children (including major children whose needs justify it), and in certain cases, by the parents of the deceased. The modalities of the obligation to pay maintenance were discussed in paragraph 4(a) *above*.

6. Community of Property Between Husband and Wife

(a) As mentioned *above* in paragraph 4(a), the death of a spouse entails the dissolution of the 'family patrimony'. The family patrimony is a pool of assets consisting of the residences of the family, the movable property with which they are furnished or decorated, the motor vehicles used for family travel and the benefits accrued during the marriage under a retirement plan.

Upon dissolution of the family patrimony (which occurs as a result of death or divorce), each spouse has a monetary claim against the other equal to 50 per cent of the value of the family patrimony assets owned by the surviving spouse. The claims are then offset against each other and only the difference is paid to the surviving spouse or the residual heirs, depending on the relative value of the family patrimony assets owned by each spouse at the time of death.

(b) If the deceased had opted to be married under the regime of partnership of acquests, the death of a spouse entails the dissolution of the partnership and each spouse will have a claim equal to 50 per cent of the other spouse's acquests. The 'acquests' represent a larger pool of assets than the family patrimony (described *above*) and include, in particular, the proceeds of the spouse's work during the marriage and the fruits and income generated from all of the spouse's property during the marriage. However, the acquests do not include property owned at the time of the marriage and property acquired by gift or inheritance.

The claims resulting from the dissolution of the partnership of acquests can be made by the surviving spouse. The residual heirs of the deceased can assert a claim only if the surviving spouse has not renounced the right to make a claim. Therefore, the surviving spouse will generally renounce rights in the partnership of acquests if it is felt that the claim of the estate against the surviving spouse will exceed the latter's claim against the estate.

7. Gifts (*Inter Vivos*)

(a) As a general rule, gifts made prior to death are not set off against an heir's inheritance.

However, gifts made with a view to avoid the obligation of the estate to provide *post-mortem* maintenance (as explained in question 5) can be annulled by the court. Further, gifts made within three years of death will be included in the value of the estate for the purposes of calculating the maximum amount of the maintenance obligation.

Also, a gift made during the deemed mortal illness of the donor is void, unless circumstances tend to render it valid.

8. Capacity

(a) The testator's capacity is considered as at the time the will was made. The fact that the testator may have subsequently become incapable has no relevance.

A will made by a minor is void, except with respect to items of little value, even if the testator dies after the age of majority. Since the legal representatives of the minor (i.e., the parents) may not make a valid will on his behalf, his estate will devolve according to law (*ab intestate*). An exception may be available if the minor is legally married.

With respect to persons of full age (eighteen years old) whose mental capacities are diminished, the validity of the will depends on the severity of the impairment. More specifically, a person in respect of who a simple 'adviser' was appointed may make a valid will without assistance. A will made by a person under tutorship may be confirmed by the court if the circumstances in which it was drawn up allow it. Finally, a person under curatorship may not make a will. As with the minor, the curator or the legal representative of the major who is incapable may not make a will on his behalf; his estate will devolve according to law (*ab intestate*), unless a valid will was made before the incapacity.

(b) A witness must be of full age (eighteen years old). In the case of notarial wills, the employees of the attesting notary may not act as witness.

A legacy made to a witness (even a supernumerary) is null, but the validity of the will is not otherwise affected.

(c) In order to be a beneficiary the person must exist at the time the succession opens (which includes children conceived but yet unborn, if they are born alive and viable).

An absentee is presumed alive (and therefore can receive property by will) for seven years following his disappearance. His legal representative will receive the property on his behalf if he is called to inherit during the seven years of absence.

A declaratory judgement of death may be pronounced after seven years and the property will then devolve to the heirs of the absentee.

The capacity to receive by will of corporations is determined based on the laws of the jurisdiction of incorporation. In the case of Canadian corporations, whether federally or provincially incorporated, there are no significant restrictions to the capacity to receive by gift or by will.

Finally, persons 'unworthy' of inheriting (and thus incapable of receiving property by will or *ab intestate*) include persons convicted of homicide or attempted homicide on the life of the deceased and persons deprived by law of parental authority over their children. Other persons may be declared unworthy by the courts in certain circumstances.

International Succession

9. Authority (Court, Notarial or Other)

Holograph wills and wills made in the presence of witnesses must be probated by an order of the court before assets can be distributed. Notarial wills do not have to be probated by the court.

All of the universal legatees must be summoned to the probate hearing unless an exemption is granted by the court. A probate order does not prevent an eventual challenge of the validity of the will; it only certifies that the will is valid as to its form and that certified copies can be issued to interested persons.

If there are legatees outside the Province of Quebec, there is no specific formality to summon them to the probate hearing; it is generally sufficient to notify them by way of registered mail.

10. Invalidity of Will

(a) Some of the possible grounds to invalidate a will are fear of serious injury to the person or property when induced by violence, threats, error and fraud.

The invalidity can also be caused by defects in formalities, such as the necessity to initial each page of a will made in presence of witnesses.

(b) When threat, error or fraud has been shown to vitiate the consent of the testator, the entire will is null *ab initio*.

If a will intended to be made in a particular form does not meet the requirements of that form, it is valid as a will made in another form if it meets the requirements for validity of that other form.

Defects in consent are generally considered to give rise to relative nullity (i.e., voidable). Defects in form result in absolute nullity (i.e., void).

While there are several rules governing the extinctive prescription (i.e., limitation period) in Quebec, Section 626 of the Civil Code of Quebec provides that a successor is entitled to have his heirship recognized within 10 years of the opening of the succession (generally the date of the testator's death).

11. Simultaneous Death

(a)–(b) Section 616 of the Civil Code of Quebec provides that, where two persons die and it is impossible to determine which survived the other, they are deemed to have died at the same time if at least one of them is called to the succession of the other. The succession of each of the deceased then devolves to the persons who would have been called to take it in his or her place. This rule applies to both testamentary and *ab intestate* successions.

In other words, each spouse is presumed to have predeceased the other. Therefore, the respective estate of each spouse cannot receive any property from the other spouse's estate. Each estate will be settled as if the spouse had predeceased the testator.

12. Estate Taxes

(a) There are no estate taxes *per se* in the Province of Quebec. Unlike most of the common law provinces, only a nominal fee is exigible when a will is probated by the court (the amount of the fee does not depend on the gross value of the estate).

However, a deceased is deemed for income tax purposes to have disposed of all of his property at fair market value immediately before his death. Therefore, the estate is liable for a tax on any accrued gain realized as a result of this deemed disposition. The current combined maximum federal and provincial tax rate on capital gains is approximately 24.1 per cent. Further, if the deceased owned depreciable property on which depreciation had been deducted by the deceased (e.g., a building), the deemed disposition may result in recapture of previously claimed depreciation if the fair market value on death exceeds the undepreciated capital cost of the property. The combined maximum federal and provincial tax rate applicable to recapture of depreciation is approximately 48 per cent.

The deceased is also deemed to have reacquired the property immediately after the deemed disposition for a cost equal to the deemed proceeds. Therefore, the heirs will eventually acquire these assets with a high tax cost and will not be taxed again on the same gain.

There is a notable exception when property is transferred to the deceased's spouse or to a trust under which the spouse is entitled to receive all the income and no person except the spouse may receive the income or capital before the spouse's death. In such case, the accrued gain will only be taxed when the surviving spouse dies.

The 1995 Protocol of the *Canada-United States Tax Treaty* extends the benefit of this tax-deferred spousal rollover to transfers between US residents in respect of taxable Canadian property (e.g., Canadian real estate) owned by a US resident prior to his death and transferred to his US resident spouse.

(b) With respect to taxpayers who are resident in Canada for income tax purposes, the deemed disposition on death applies to their worldwide assets. However, Canada has a wide network of income tax treaties and some of these treaties include provisions to better coordinate the operation of the death tax regimes of the two Contracting States. Therefore, to the extent taxes are paid as a result of the taxpayer's death in a foreign country in respect of a foreign property (e.g., real estate situated outside Canada) a foreign tax credit may be available against Canadian tax.

For example, under the 1995 Protocol to the *Canada-United States Tax Treaty,* the Canadian government undertakes to grant a foreign tax credit in respect of US estate or inheritance taxes payable in the US in respect of property situated in the US owned by a Canadian resident prior to his death.

A non-resident who dies abroad will be subject to Canadian death tax only if he owns taxable Canadian property which has appreciated in value. This includes real estate situated in Canada and also shares of Canadian private corporations. However, if the deceased was resident of a country with which Canada has an income tax treaty, he will generally be subject to Canadian tax only in respect of real estate situated in Canada. No foreign tax credit would be granted by the

Canadian government (the country of residence would be expected to grant a foreign tax credit in respect of Canadian tax so paid).

(c) The tax applies only to the estate and is paid when the terminal return is filed on behalf of the deceased. No taxes are imposed directly on the beneficiaries – they receive the assets free of tax.

During the period of administration, the estate is treated as a separate trust and will be taxed on any investment income generated during that period. To the extent the property appreciates in value while held by the estate, the assets can generally flow out of the estate to the beneficiaries (i.e., the heirs) on a rollover basis; that is, the accrued gain will not be recognized on the final distribution of the assets to the heirs, but the will be recognized when the heirs eventually dispose of the property.

There is an important exception to this principle when property is distributed to non-resident heirs. In this case, the distribution of the property will be deemed to occur at fair market value, which will trigger a taxable gain if the property has appreciated in value during the period of administration of the estate. In order to avoid double taxation, a retroactive foreign tax credit can be claimed by the Canadian estate against this tax in respect of foreign taxes paid by the non-resident heir when he or she eventually disposes of the property. Thus, it will be possible to re-file the estate's return for the year of distribution to claim a foreign tax credit for taxes paid by the heir when he sells the property. Note that this special credit is only available if the heir is resident in a country with which Canada has an income tax treaty for the elimination of double taxation.

13. Administration of Estates

(a) In the Province of Quebec, the persons who are responsible for the administration of an estate are referred to as the 'liquidators' of the estate.

The role of the liquidators consists of identifying and calling in the heirs, determining the contents of the estate, recovering the claims, paying the debts of the estate (including the debts resulting from the maintenance obligation and the dissolution of the family patrimony described in question 4 *above*), paying the particular legacies, rendering an account and delivering the property to the residual heirs.

Any capable person may hold the office of liquidator. Trust companies authorized by law may also act as liquidator. No person is bound to accept the office of liquidator, unless he is the sole heir. The liquidators are generally appointed by the testator in his will. The testator may designate one or several liquidators and may also provide for the mode of replacement.

(b) The liquidator is bound to make an inventory of the property of the estate. He may be exempted from this obligation, but only with the consent of all the heirs. If they give their consent, the heirs become liable for the debts of the estate beyond the value of the property received. The inventory of the estate is critical because it provides a basis for the heirs to determine whether to accept the estate or renounce it (if it is insolvent). Any interested person may apply to the court to have an inventory made if the liquidator is negligent in doing so.

The inventory must be published in a public register with a notice identifying the deceased and indicating the place where the inventory may be consulted by interested persons. The notice is also published in a newspaper circulated in the locality where the deceased had his last known address.

The inventory can be made either by a notarial act or by a private writing before two witnesses. In the latter case, the author and the witnesses sign it, indicating the place and date of execution.

If the liquidation of the estate takes longer than one year, the liquidator must, at the end of the first year and at least once a year thereafter render an annual account of management to the heirs, creditors and particular legatees which have not yet been paid.

(c) Every interested person may query and object. The basis of each case must be examined. A holograph will and a will made in the presence of witnesses can be probated on the demand of any interested person, but only the known heirs and successors are required to be summoned to the probate of the will. Once probated, it becomes public and a certified copy can be obtained by anyone who requests it and who intends to object in any way.

In the case of a notarial will, no probate is required because it is an authentic act that makes proof against all persons of the declarations it contains. Therefore, a notarial will keeps its private nature but an interested person may apply to the court to have the content of the will divulged.

(d) There is no direct external supervision from governmental authorities. The courts will only take action when requested to do so by the parties.

In the case of uncertainty as to appropriate course of action, the liquidator can file a motion for direction with the court.

A limited supervision is exercised by the tax authorities to ensure that all applicable taxes have been paid by the estate before it is wound up. Therefore, the liquidators are required to request clearance certificates before property can be distributed to the heirs. Failure to obtain the clearance certificates will result in the liquidator's personal liability, up to the value of the assets transferred.

(e) The liquidation is completed when the creditors and the particular legatees have been paid. A final account must be prepared by the liquidators indicating the debts and legacies left unpaid, those guaranteed by security or assumed by the heirs and specifying the mode of payment for each.

Once the final account has been rendered, the liquidator is discharged of his office and makes the final delivery of the property to the heirs. The closure of the account must also be published in a public register.

As a general principle, all the residual heirs become undivided co-owners of all the property of the estate. It is then possible to effect partition of the property either in cash or in kind.

In partitioning the assets among the residual heirs, the surviving spouse may, in preference to any other heirs, require that the family residence together with the movable property serving for the use of the household be placed in her share. Similarly, the assets of a family business or the capital shares connected with a family business are allotted by preference to the heirs who were actively participating in the operation of the business.

The will can also provide for the creation of separate testamentary trusts for the benefit of certain beneficiaries (e.g., minors, spendthrift, persons in precarious financial situation).

(f) Outside creditors are paid first, before the particular legacies are satisfied and before the claim of the spouse resulting from the dissolution of the family patrimony and the claims of the dependants resulting from the maintenance obligation are satisfied.

(g) If no designation has been made in the will or if the deceased dies *ab intestate*, the office of liquidator devolves as of right to the heirs. The heirs may then, by majority vote, designate a liquidator and provide for the mode of his replacement.

14. Domicile/Nationality

(a) The formalities of validity of a will are determined based on the law of domicile of the testator at the time the will was made.

The rules pertaining to the family patrimony and the obligation to provide maintenance are of public order and will apply if the deceased was domiciled in Quebec.

The extent of the tax liability (whether on worldwide assets or only on taxable Canadian property) depends on the residence of the deceased at the time of death.

Succession in respect of movable property is governed by the laws of the jurisdiction in which the deceased was domiciled. Succession as to immovable property depends on the rules of the jurisdiction in which the property is situated.

(b) Yes they would. The court will issue letters of probate to the foreign authorities of the jurisdiction in which the assets are located. Every interested person may obtain from the clerk of the court of the last domicile of the deceased or from a notary letters of probate for use outside Quebec, to prove his quality of heir, legatee or liquidator of the estate. The letters of probate will also certify that the estate has opened and that the will is the latest will of the deceased.

SECTION B – APPLICABLE LAW/PROCEDURES WHERE FOREIGN ELEMENT/S ARE INVOLVED

1. Jurisdiction

(a) Pursuant to Section 3153 of the Civil Code of Quebec, the Quebec court will have jurisdiction if the succession opens (i.e., place of death of the testator) in Quebec, if the deceased was domiciled in Quebec or if the deceased had elected that Quebec law should govern his succession.

(b) Not specifically. However, in addition to the grounds of jurisdiction explained above, the courts will also exercise jurisdiction if any property of the deceased is situated in Quebec and a ruling is required as to the devolution of the property.

(c) The Quebec Superior Court will have jurisdiction, as indicated in Section 31 of the Code of Civil Procedure. It is the court of original general jurisdiction that hears in the first instance every proceeding not assigned exclusively to another court by a specific provision of law.

2. Applicable Law

(a) Pursuant to Section 3098 of the Civil Code of Quebec, the local court will apply different law depending on whether the succession involves movable property (law of the last domicile of the deceased) or immovable property (law of the place where the property is situated). The Superior Court may also apply a foreign law if the deceased made such a designation in his will. In cases of emergency or serious inconvenience, the laws of Quebec may be applied provisionally to ensure the protection of property.

An exception may apply to the testator's freedom to designate an applicable law if the designation deprives the spouse or a child of a right of succession (such as the *post-mortem* maintenance obligation discussed in question 5 of Section A) to which, but for such designation, he would have been entitled. Such designation will be without effect. In addition, the designation has no effect to the extent that it affects special rules of inheritance to which certain categories of property are subject, under the law of the country in which they are situated, because of their economic, family or social destination.

3. Foreign Succession/Inheritance Orders

(a) Section 3155 of the Civil Code of Quebec indicates that a Quebec authority will generally recognize and declare enforceable decisions rendered outside Quebec, without entering into any examination of the merits of the decision.

However, some exceptions may apply. For example, if the foreign authority had no jurisdiction under the Quebec rules of private international law or if the foreign decision is not final or enforceable. Further, subject to specific mutual assistance agreements in certain income tax treaties (most notably, the *Canada-United States Income Tax Treaty*), the Quebec courts will not recognize and enforce decisions aimed at enforcing the taxation laws of a foreign country.

(b) Section 785 of the Code of Civil Procedure indicates that an application for recognition and enforcement of a decision rendered outside Quebec is made by means of a motion (which is the most straightforward and expedient procedure). As soon as such motion is granted, the foreign order will become enforceable. In its review of the foreign order, the local court will only verify whether the foreign court was competent under the Quebec rules of private international law and whether the foreign decision was final and enforceable in the foreign jurisdiction. The merits of the foreign decision will not be examined.

International Succession

(c) The party that requests the enforceability of the foreign order must present a copy of the order as well as an attestation emanating from a competent foreign public officer stating that the decision is no longer subject to ordinary remedy in the state in which it was rendered and that it is final or enforceable. If a document is drafted in a language other than French or English, it must be accompanied with a translation authenticated in Quebec.

4. Two or More Succession or Probate Orders

To the extent that the object of the foreign decision was substantially connected with the country where it was rendered and the foreign court had jurisdiction under the Quebec rules of private international law, the doctrine of *lis pendens* will apply and the Quebec court should decline to exercise its jurisdiction.

The foreign court will be considered to have validly exercised its jurisdiction if the succession opened in the foreign State, if the deceased was domiciled in that State or if he elected that the law of that foreign State govern his succession.

5. Assets

The last domicile of the deceased will determine the jurisdiction applicable to the succession to movable property. The Quebec Courts will assume jurisdiction if the deceased was domiciled in Quebec prior to his death, even if there are no assets in the province. Section 615 of the Civil Code of Quebec provides that when a person dies leaving property situated outside Quebec or claims against persons not residing in Quebec, letters of probate may be issued by the court.

6. Expert Evidence

(a) What will be needed is an attestation emanating from a competent foreign public officer stating that the decision is no longer subject to ordinary remedy and that it is final or enforceable.

(b) Only the attestation from the foreign public officer will be necessary. Because it makes proof of its content against all persons, no testimony will generally be necessary. However, if the attestation is contested, the person invoking the act will be required to prove its authenticity. In that case an affidavit may be useful.

7. Unity of Succession

Because there are different rules applicable depending on the nature of the property involved (i.e., movable or immovable), the unity of succession is not accepted in Quebec's private international law rules.

8. Formalities

In addition to the forms of will allowed under Quebec law (*see* paragraph 2(a) of Section A), a testamentary disposition may also be made in the form prescribed by the Law of the domicile or nationality of the testator either at the time of the disposition or at the time of his death.

9. Legislation

The *Hague Convention on the Conflicts of Laws Relating to the Form of Testamentary Dispositions* is not applicable in Quebec. However, it has inspired several provisions of the Civil Code of Quebec. For instance, Section 3109 of the Civil Code of Quebec concerning the form of juridical acts is based upon Section 1 of the Convention.

10. Wills

In case of conflicts or foreign factors, which law governs:

(a) The form of a juridical act is governed by the law of the place where it is made (Section 3109 of the Civil Code of Quebec). Other factors may also be examined to salvage the formal validity of the will under certain circumstances. Thus, the form of a will can also be valid if it complies with the law of the *situs* of the property or the law of the domicile or nationality of the deceased when he drafted the will or even when he died.

(b) Without an express designation of applicable law, the courts will apply the law of the country with which the act is most closely connected, in view of its nature and the attendant circumstances. If a law was designated in the will, it will generally be applied.

(c) The obligation to provide *post-mortem* maintenance (as described in question 5 of Section A) is governed by the Law of the last domicile of the deceased.

(d) The capacity to inherit will be governed by the law of the domicile of the heir at the time the succession opens.

(e) This will be determined based on the law of the domicile of the testator at the time the will was drawn up.

(f) The laws applicable to the requirements as to form of the will are explained in question 8. With respect to other issues, the law of the last domicile of the deceased will generally apply.

International Succession

(g) If the power of appointment pertained to movable property, it will be subject to the law of the last domicile of the deceased. Note that it is not possible to grant a general (unrestricted) power of appointment in Quebec. If it pertains to immovable property, it will be governed by the law of the *situs*.

(h) Since it is a question about the form of the will, the answer in paragraph 10(a) is applicable.

(i) The answer to paragraph 2(a) is applicable here.

11. Domicile/Nationality

(a) The domicile and the nationality are key factors in examining the formal validity of the will (Section 3109(3)). The nationality and the domicile will be examined at the time of the disposition or at the time of death, as long as it can be considered valid at one period in time.

If there is a conflict between domicile and nationality, the place of domicile would generally prevail.

(b) The domicile is relevant in order to ascertain the beneficiary's capacity to inherit.

(c) The court will establish one domicile based on an evaluation of all the relevant facts. When it is not possible to establish it with certainty, the person will be presumed domiciled where he is resident. The court will examine the physical aspects (e.g., frequent physical presence), but also the intentional aspect (e.g., family, employment, social relationships, etc.).

12. Taxation

As explained thoroughly in question 12 of Section A, there is no estate tax *per se* in the Province of Quebec. However, Canadian residents are deemed to dispose of their property at fair market value immediately before they die, thus triggering taxable capital gains and recapture of previously claimed capital cost allowance (i.e., depreciation).

A non-resident who owned taxable Canadian property (and in the case of Quebec, taxable Quebec property) prior to his death will be considered to have disposed of that property at fair market value and will be subject to Canadian tax in respect of this deemed disposition if the property had appreciated in value. These include in particular real estate situated in Canada and shares of Canadian private corporations.

Cayman Islands

Prepared by: Ian LAMBERT, Tony PURSALL, Anna PECCARINO
Maples and Calder, attorneys at law

Address: PO Box 309 GT, Ugland House
         South Church Street
         Grand Cayman, Cayman Islands
Tel.:   +1 345 949 8066
Fax: +1 345 949 8080

Section A – Brief Survey of the Local System

1. Type of System

(a) The laws of the Cayman Islands are based on English common law and rules of equity, supplemented by local legislation. The principles and procedure for succession and the administration of estates are found in *The Wills Law (1997 Revision), The Succession Law (1995 Revision)* and *The Probate and Administration Rules*.

(b) The Cayman Islands do not have a federal system.

2. Wills

(a) Forms of wills. In order for a will to be validly executed under Cayman Islands law, it must comply with Section 6 of the *Wills Law*. This requires that the will must be in writing and signed at the foot or end by the testator, or by some other person in the testator's presence and at his direction. The signature must be made or acknowledged by the testator in the presence of two or more witnesses present at the same time, and the witnesses must attest and subscribe the will in the presence of the testator. A will executed in accordance with the *Wills Law* does not require any other publication in order to be valid. Section 6 also includes specific requirements as to the position of the signature of the testator. Section 7 extends these principles to any appointment made by will in exercise of any power.

A testator may refer in his will to the terms of some extrinsic document or documents in existence at the time the will is executed, and incorporate the terms of those documents by reference. In this regard, the principles of English law would also be applicable under Cayman Islands law and the extrinsic document or documents would therefore need to be clearly identified.

International Succession

There is no special provision under the *Wills Law* for the execution of a will before a notary or other authority.

In certain cases, evidence may be admissible to prove that a gift under a will which appears on the face of the will to be an absolute gift to the donee is held on a fully or partly secret trust, the terms of which are binding on the donee. The principles of English law in this area would also apply under Cayman Islands law.

Under the proviso to Section 7, the requirements of Sections 6 and 7 do not apply to wills made by soldiers in actual military service or by any mariner at sea, but it is considered that this exception is only applicable if the testator dies while in military service or at sea.

(b) Amendment, revocation and revival.

i. Section 16 of the *Wills Law* provides that alterations made to a will after its execution shall not be valid or have any effect, except so far as the words or effect of the will before such alteration shall not be apparent, unless the alteration is executed in the manner required under the Law for the execution of a will.

   Section 15 provides that no will or codicil, or any part thereof, shall be revoked otherwise than:
   – by marriage;
   – by another will or codicil executed in the manner required by the Law;
   – by some writing declaring an intention to revoke the same and executed in the manner which a will is required to be executed under the Law;
   – by the burning, tearing or otherwise destroying of the same by the testator (or by some person in his presence and at his direction) with the intention of revoking the same.

   Section 14 confirms that no will shall be revoked by any presumption of an intention on the ground of an alteration in circumstances.

ii. Under Section 13, marriage automatically revokes a prior will, except a will made in exercise of a power of appointment when the real or personal estate thereby appointed would not in default of such appointment pass to the testator's heir, customary heir, executor or administrator, or the person entitled as the testator's next-of-kin under the *Succession Law*.[1]

---

1. A power of appointment is a power vested in someone allowing them to 'appoint' the relevant property that the power of appointment relates to in favour of some person or persons, and whether outright (absolutely) or subject to terms, conditions or trusts. A power of appointment is called a 'general' power if the holder can appoint in favour of himself. A power of appointment under which the holder can only appoint in favour of a specified class of persons not including the holder is called 'special'. A power of appointment exercisable in favour of anyone except a certain class of persons (including the holder) is called an 'intermediate' power. A power of appointment is typically conferred on the holder under the terms of a will or a trust (the instrument that confers the power), which may specify whether the power is exercisable only by deed, by written instrument and/or by will. It is important conceptually to distinguish the instrument conferring the power and any instrument exercising the power. Section 13 refers to the latter.

iii. Section 17 provides that no will or codicil, or any part thereof, which is revoked shall be revived otherwise than by re-execution or by a codicil executed
in the manner required under the *Wills Law*, and showing an intention to revive
the same. Where a will or codicil is partly revoked, and afterwards is wholly
revoked, a revival does not extend to the part which was revoked before the
revocation of the whole, unless an intention to the contrary is shown.

3. Intestacy

(a) The order of succession to real and personal estate on intestacy is provided in
Section 29 of the *Succession Law*, which may be summarized as follows:

  i. If the intestate leaves a surviving spouse and issue:
  – the surviving spouse takes the personal chattels[2] absolutely;
  – the residuary estate (other than personal chattels) is charged with a payment
     of a net sum of KYD20,000 (approximately USD24,000) or a sum equal to
     50 per cent of the net value of the estate (whichever is the greater) to the
     surviving spouse, with interest thereon at 5 per cent *per annum* until paid or
     appropriated; and
  – subject to providing for such sum, and the interest thereon, the residuary
     estate (other than personal chattels) is held on the statutory trusts (provided
     in Section 30)[3] for the issue of the intestate, but if those trusts fail or deter-
     mine in the lifetime of the surviving spouse, then such residuary estate is
     held on trust for the surviving spouse for the residue of his or her life.

  ii. If the intestate leaves a surviving spouse but no issue:
  – the surviving spouse takes the personal chattels absolutely;
  – if the intestate leaves one or both parents, the surviving parent or parents
     share 25 per cent of the residuary estate and 75 per cent is held for the
     surviving spouse absolutely; and
  – if the intestate leaves no surviving parent, the residuary estate is held for the
     surviving spouse absolutely.

  iii. If the intestate leaves issue but no husband or wife, the residuary estate is held
  on the statutory trusts for the issue of the intestate.

---

2. 'Personal chattels' is defined in Section 2 of the Succession Law as: 'vehicles, animals and
   accessories (not kept or used for business purposes), garden tools and furniture, plate, linen,
   china, glass, books, pictures, prints, furniture, jewellery, articles of household or personal use or
   ornament, musical and scientific instruments and apparatus, wines, liquors and consumable
   stores, but does not include any chattels used at the death of the intestate for business purposes,
   nor money nor securities for money'.
3. The statutory trusts set out in Section 30 are quite extensive. In essence, they provide a trust for
   the issue (descendants) or the intestate in equal shares, with a precondition that the beneficiary
   in each case (the relevant issue) either attains the age of eighteen years or marries before that
   age. The distribution is *per stirpes*, so that any grandchildren of the intestate may take (collectively
   in equal shares among themselves) the share of any child who has predeceased the intestate (and
   likewise for great grandchildren where the relevant child and grandchild have both predeceased
   the intestate).

iv. If the intestate leaves no issue but one parent then, subject to the interest of the surviving spouse, the residuary estate is held on trust for such parent absolutely.

v. If the intestate leaves no issue but both parents then, subject to the interest of the surviving spouse, the residuary estate is held on trust for the parents in equal shares absolutely.

vi. If the intestate leaves no issue or parent then, subject to the interest of the surviving spouse, the residuary estate is held on trust for the following persons in the following order: (1) on the statutory trusts, for the intestate's brothers and sisters of the whole blood, or if none then (2) on the statutory trusts, for the intestate's brothers and sisters of the half blood, or if none then (3) for the intestate's grandparents (in equal shares if both survive the intestate), or if none then (4) on the statutory trusts, for the intestate's uncles and aunts of the whole blood, or if none then (5) on the statutory trusts, for the intestate's uncles and aunts of the half blood, or if none then (6) for the surviving spouse absolutely.

vii. In default of any person taking an absolute interest under the above provisions, the residuary estate passes to the Crown as *bona vacantia* (but the Crown may make provision for any dependants of the intestate or any other persons for whom the intestate might reasonably have been expected to make provision).

(b) The intestacy rules do not distinguish between movables and immovables.

4. Freedom of Testation

(a) There are no compulsory shares of inheritance. There are no restrictions under Cayman Islands law on the freedom of testation, and no provisions requiring that a testator must leave to any specified relatives any fixed proportions of his estate.

(b) *i.* In order to be binding, a disposition made (prior to death) of assets to take effect on death, or otherwise bind the estate of a deceased person on death, must comply with the formalities necessary for a valid will. These are based on the traditional English rules and are to be found in the *Wills Law*. In general a will can always be revoked, whether or not declared to be irrevocable, although (as in England) the doctrine of 'mutual wills' may prevent the second to die of two people making mutual wills from revoking his or her will. Cayman Islands law does not have or recognize a concept of 'contract of inheritance' as such.

ii. The concepts of partition (*partege*), anticipation (advance distribution), successor or family settlements (*pactes successoraux ou de famille*) do not exist in Cayman Islands law.

5. Maintenance

There are no provisions under Cayman Islands law to enable any person to claim maintenance from a deceased's estate. There is no equivalent under Cayman

Islands law of the (English) *Inheritance (Provision for Family and Dependants) Act 1975.*

6. Community Property Between Husband and Wife

(a) There are no principles of community of property under Cayman Islands law. It should, however, be noted that where husband and wife hold property as joint tenants (rather than as tenants in common), such property will pass on the first death to the survivor and does not form part of the estate of the deceased, under the principle of survivorship.

(b) Not applicable.

7. Gifts (*Inter Vivos*)

(a) The English common law rules relating to satisfaction of a legacy (where a gift under a will is regarded as having been separately discharged) and ademption (where the relevant asset ceases to be owned by the testator, or ceases to conform to the description given in the will) similarly apply under Cayman Islands law.

Where a deceased is intestate, there is a *hotchpot* rule in Section 30 of the Succession Law, which will apply where any part of the residuary estate of an intestate is held on the statutory trusts for his issue (not for other relatives), and is divided into shares. Under this rule, any money or property which has been paid or settled on a child of the intestate by way of advancement or on that child's marriage must be brought into account in determining the value of that child's share (or the value of the shares of that child's issue, if the child has predeceased the intestate).

(b) *See* (a) *above.*

8. Capacity

(a) Under Section 5 of the *Wills Law*, the minimum age for a testator now making a will is eighteen, in order for the will to be valid. There is no requirement that a testator needs to be married. In order for the will to be valid, a testator must have sufficient mental capacity to understand the effect of the will being carried out on his death, the extent of the property within his estate and the nature of any claims against him.

(b) Section 10 of the *Wills Law* provides that any gift (or beneficial devise, legacy, estate, interest or appointment) to an attesting witness or his or her spouse shall, as regards such person and person claiming through such person, be null and void (although this would not affect the validity of any other provisions of the will). Section 11 confirms that a creditor attesting a will may be a witness to prove its execution. *See* also 2(a) *above*, concerning the need for both witnesses to be present at the same time to see the testator make or acknowledge his signature.

(c) A minor (meaning, as a matter of the internal laws of the Cayman Islands, a person who has not attained the age of eighteen), is not capable of owning property in his own right. However, it is possible for a valid gift to be made under a will to a minor but the personal representatives will not be able to obtain a valid receipt until the beneficiary attains the age of majority. For this reason, a will should usually include a receipt clause enabling the personal representatives to obtain a valid receipt in respect of a payment to a parent or guardian of the beneficiary. A gift may be made to a class including unborn persons, subject to the requirement under the *Perpetuities Law (1999 Revision)* that the interests must vest within the maximum permitted period. A gift may be made to a company.

9. Authority (Court, Notarial or Other)

The authority to grant probate or issue letters of administration in respect of an estate of a deceased person is vested in the Grand Court of the Cayman Islands, except where the estate is a 'small estate' (meaning an estate of a value of KYD2,000 (approximately USD2,400) or less), where certain functions of a Judge in Chambers in relation to the procedure may be performed by a magistrate in chambers.

10. Invalidity of Will

(a)–(b) A will will be void if it has not been executed in compliance with the requirements of the *Wills Law*. (A will will also be invalid, in the sense of ineffective, if it has been revoked in accordance with the formalities prescribed by the *Wills Law*.) The English common law principles relating to lack of testamentary capacity, undue influence and fraud are similarly applicable under Cayman Islands law, and in these cases the will would be void.

11. Simultaneous Death

(a) There are no statutory provisions under Cayman Islands law specifically concerning simultaneous death, and under the common law there is no presumption as to the order of deaths in cases where it is not clear which of two persons predeceased the other. An express provision may be included in a will if it is intended that a disposition is only to take effect if a beneficiary survives the testator, and a provision may also be included to introduce a presumption as to order of deaths for the purposes of a gift under the will.

(b) *See* (a) *above*.

12. Estate Taxes

(a) The Cayman Islands do not have any system of direct taxation, and in particular do not have any taxes in the nature of estate or inheritance taxes.

(b) Not applicable.

(c) Not applicable.

13. Administration of Estates

(a) Section 3 of the Succession Law provides that no person acting otherwise than as an agent of necessity shall take possession of or in any manner administer any part of the estate of a deceased person unless he has first obtained from the Court a grant of probate of the will or letters of administration of the estate of such a deceased person. A grant of probate is made where a valid will exists and an executor is named therein, otherwise the grant is of letters of administration. No grant of probate or letters of administration can be made to any person who has not attained the age of eighteen, nor may a grant be made to more than four persons jointly. A grant of probate is deemed to take effect from the time of death of the deceased, but a grant of letters of administration takes effect from the time of the grant. Under Section 6, personal representatives are entitled to commission for their services, based on the net value of the estate.

(b) Every personal representative must file estate accounts within one year after grant of probate or letters of administration (Section 7). The accounts must be supported by affidavit and are open to inspection of persons beneficially interested. In practice, personal representatives may ask for an extension of time.

(c) There is no proactive supervision of personal representatives by the Court, but *see* (d) *below*. Under Section 43, any person acting as executor or administrator who commits an offence under the Law may be ordered by the Court to forfeit his commission and to pay a fine of KYD1,000 (approximately USD1,200) and to make restoration to the estate.

(d) Any beneficially interested person may apply to the Court for removal of any personal representative, on grounds of neglect or misconduct in the administration of the estate (Section 8). The Court may appoint another suitable person in place of the personal representative removed. It should also be noted that, under Section 19 and Rule 40 of the Probate and Administration Rules, every person to whom any grant of letters of administration is made must give a bond in respect of duly collecting, getting in and administering the estate (no bond is required in an application for probate). The bond must, unless the Court thinks fit to reduce the same, be in a penalty of double the amount of the sworn value of the estate, and must be given with one or more surety or sureties. Under Rule 41, no surety is required where an application for administration is made by a trust corporation authorized to conduct trusteeship business.

(e) Under Section 5, personal representatives have one year within which to realize and administer an estate. Personal representatives derive from the grant of probate or the letters of administration of the estate their authority to call in the assets. Where the estate includes real estate (which was not held by the deceased on a joint tenancy basis), it devolves to and becomes vested in the personal representatives by Section 25, in the same manner as personalty. The assets of the estate are then distributed to the beneficiaries by the personal representatives.

(f) Creditors may claim against the personal representatives, for payment out of the estate. However, under Section 44 of the *Trusts Law (2001 Revision)* personal representatives may give notice by advertisement in a local newspaper or, where appropriate, notices outside the Cayman Islands, requiring any person interested to send to them within a fixed period (not less than twenty-eight days) particulars of his claim. At the expiration of the period, the personal representatives may distribute the property having regard only to claims of which they had notice, without liability to any other creditors. However, this does not preclude the rights of a creditor to trace against assets[4] distributed to a beneficiary.

(g) Where a deceased person has left a will in which no executor is named, Section 3(8) provides for the court to make a grant of letters of administration with the will annexed. Where the deceased dies wholly intestate, Rule 33 of the Probate and Administration Rules sets out the order of priority of persons who may apply for letters of administration, and this list commences with the surviving spouse.

14. Domicile/Nationality

(a) Where the deceased dies domiciled outside the Cayman Islands, account needs to be taken of the Cayman Islands rules of private international law, which are based on the (English) common law rules.

In relation to immovable property in the deceased's estate at the date of death, succession will be determined according to the *lex situs* (including its own conflicts of laws rules). So far as movable property comprised in the deceased's estate is concerned, issues relating to the formal and essential validity of a will and testamentary capacity will be determined according to the principles applicable in the jurisdiction of the deceased's domicile at the date of death (subject to any application of the principle of *renvoi* under the conflict of laws rules of that jurisdiction). Similarly, if the deceased dies intestate, then under the common law conflict of laws rules applicable in the Cayman Islands, succession to movable property comprised in his estate would be determined according to the law of the jurisdiction of domicile (again, subject to any application of *renvoi*).

It should be noted that so far as assets having Cayman Islands *situs* are concerned (including real estate situated in the Cayman Islands and the shares of companies incorporated under Cayman Islands law whose minute books are maintained in the Cayman Islands), a Cayman Islands grant of probate or letters of administration is

---

4. The Cayman Islands rules on 'tracing' and 'following' assets are essentially the English law rules. They do permit the same asset to be 'followed' through various hands and the 'proceeds' of any asset to be 'traced' into the hands of the holder of an asset who has disposed of it, although there are various limitations and defences, most notably the defence of 'change of position' by the recipient against whom a claim is being brought.

required in order for the personal representatives to obtain title to the Cayman Islands assets. This could be either (1) an original grant of probate or letters of administration in the Cayman Islands, or (2) a foreign grant of probate or letters of administration resealed in the Cayman Islands, under Section 23 of the *Succession Law*. It should also be noted that the personal representatives of the Cayman Islands estate may be liable for foreign debts of the deceased, which would rank equally with the claims of Cayman Islands creditors. For further details, *see* Section B *below*.

(b) In practice, the Grand Court would probably decline to issue a grant of probate or letters of administration if there are no assets of the deceased in the Cayman Islands, unless perhaps the issue of a grant of probate could be shown to be a necessary preliminary to the personal representatives being able to call in assets situated outside the Cayman Islands.

SECTION B – APPLICABLE LAW/PROCEDURE WHERE FOREIGN ELEMENT/S ARE INVOLVED

Where foreign elements are involved in a Cayman Islands succession matter, the Cayman Islands conflict of laws rules will be relevant in determining the extent to which issues will be resolved according to the principles of Cayman Islands law, or alternatively the extent to which the courts of the Cayman Islands would apply the foreign law, or the law of another jurisdiction under the principle of *renvoi*. The Cayman Islands rules of conflict of laws are based on the English common law.

1. Jurisdiction

(a) The courts of the Cayman Islands will have jurisdiction in relation to assets of a deceased person situated within the jurisdiction. The rules of Cayman Islands law relating to the determination of the *situs* of an asset are similar to the English common law rules, therefore the following are regarded, as a matter of Cayman Islands law, as having Cayman Islands *situs*:

– land in the Cayman Islands;
– a chose in action which is properly recoverable in the Cayman Islands, or can be enforced in the Cayman Islands; and
– chattels located in the Cayman Islands.

It should be noted that under Cayman Islands law a debt due on a deed (a specialty debt) is regarded as being situated in the jurisdiction where the deed is situated from time to time, and not in the jurisdiction where the debtor resides.

Shares in a company incorporated under Cayman Islands law, where the register of members is maintained at the company's registered office in the Cayman Islands, have Cayman Islands *situs*. Bearer shares are situated where the share certificates themselves are situated. However, since 26 April 2002, bearer shares must be deposited with a custodian.

International Succession

There are no death, estate or inheritance taxes in the Cayman Islands. This is important insofar as the fact that estate taxes are due on overseas assets of a deceased person may in some overseas jurisdictions give the local courts jurisdiction over the deceased person's estate. No such issue arises in the Cayman Islands.

(b) *See* (a) *above*. The Cayman Islands court will have jurisdiction over immovable property in the jurisdiction. In respect of movable property, it will have jurisdiction over the relevant chose if it is physically situate in the Cayman Islands or (in the case of a chose in action) if the relevant obligor is situate in the jurisdiction.

(c) The Grand Court of the Cayman Islands.

2. Applicable Law

As a matter of Cayman Islands law, succession to movables is generally governed by the law of domicile of the deceased at his death (the *lex domicilii*), and succession of immovables is generally governed by the law of the place they are situate (the *lex situs*).

3. Foreign Succession/Inheritance Orders

(a) Foreign judgements are strictly only 'enforced' where they are final money judgments. In respect of assets of a deceased person situate in the Cayman Islands, such assets cannot effectively be dealt with until a grant of probate or letters of administration is first obtained from the Cayman Islands Grand Court. A foreign judgment or order may be relevant, and may therefore be formally 'recognized' by the Cayman Islands Grand Court, in determining to whom a grant should be made.

The legal position is therefore different, for example, from the position relating to a trustee-in-bankruptcy's succession to title to assets of a bankrupt person. A foreign trustee-in-bankruptcy may be recognized as succeeding to a bankrupt's assets in the Cayman Islands without the need for any form of Cayman Islands court order, provided certain requirements for recognition of the foreign bankruptcy are met.[5]

(b) In order for the personal representatives of the deceased to call in assets situate in the Cayman Islands, a grant of probate or letters of administration must be obtained in the Cayman Islands. Section 23 of the *Succession Law* provides a

---

5. A Cayman Islands court will recognize that the courts of a foreign country have jurisdiction over a debtor if the debtor was domiciled in that country at the time of the presentation of the petition or if the debtor submitted to the jurisdiction of its courts, whether by himself presenting the petition or by appearing in the proceedings. There is case authority indicating that if the only (or substantially the only) creditor in the bankruptcy is a foreign revenue authority then the court will not assist the trustee-in-bankruptcy on traditional principles of English common law and public policy. However, given the recent international trends towards inter-jurisdictional co-operation in tax matters, it is uncertain whether such principles would be applied by the court in quite the same way today.

procedure for a foreign grant of probate or letters of administration to be resealed by the Grand Court of the Cayman Islands, in which case the personal representatives would (as regards property situated in the Cayman Islands) derive their authority from the resealed grant.

(c) *i.* Section 23 of the *Succession Law*, 1975, as amended, provides:

'Where a Court of Probate in any part of her Majesty's Dominions, or in any foreign country, or a British Court in a foreign country, has granted probate or letters of administration in respect of the estate of a deceased person, the probate or letters so granted may, on being produced to and a copy thereof deposited with the Court, be sealed with the seal of the Court, and thereupon shall be of like force and effect[6] and have the same operation in the Islands as if granted by the Court. For the purposes of this Law, a duplicate of any probate or letters of administration sealed with the seal of the Court granting the same, or a copy thereof certified as correct by or under the authority of the Court granting the same, shall have the same effect as the original.'

ii. Rule 42 of the Probate and Administration Rules provides:

'An application under Section 23 of the Law for the resealing of probate or administration granted in a country to which that Section applies shall be made by the person to whom the grant was made or by any person authorised in writing to apply on his behalf and on any such application:

(1) the Judge may require that the application be advertised in such manner as he may direct and be supported by an oath sworn by the person making the application. The Judge may also require that an inventory of the estate be filed, although normally this may be limited to Cayman Islands assets;

(2) where the grant is one of letters of administration a bond in the prescribed form shall be given by the applicant unless the Judge decides to dispense therewith;

(3) there shall be lodged a copy of the will, if any, to which the application relates certified as correct by or under the authority of the Court which made the grant;

(4) upon resealing of the grant the Clerk shall send notice thereof to the Court which made the grant.'

iii. The following must be submitted:

(1) authorization in writing to make application on behalf of the executor or administrator for resealing by the Grand Court of the Cayman Islands of the grant of probate or letters of administration;

---

6. The phrase 'of like force and effect' in this context simply means that an overseas grant can be resealed in the Cayman Islands court and if it is resealed it is treated as if were the same as an original grant made by the Cayman Islands court. The grant determines who has title to the deceased's assets within the jurisdiction. It does not determine the validity or invalidity of any dispositions made by will.

    (2) a copy of the will certified by or under the authority of the Court which made the grant of probate or letters of administration;

    (3) two certified copies of the grant of probate or letters of administration, sealed with the seal of the Court issuing the same;

    (4) application to the Grand Court; and

    (5) affidavit in support.[7]

4. Two or More Succession or Probate Orders

Under Cayman Islands law, there is a distinction between movable and immovable property. The question of succession to movables would, as a matter of the conflict of laws rules of the Cayman Islands, be determined according to the law of the deceased's domicile at death. (Domicile would be determined according to Cayman Islands rules, which are basically the same as the traditional English common law rules i.e., consisting of domicile of origin, domicile of dependency and domicile of choice.)[8] For immovables, succession would be governed by the *lex situs*.

5. Assets

See Sections A14(b) and B1 *above*. The courts of the Cayman Islands will generally only have jurisdiction in relation to assets situate within the Cayman Islands. There are no death, estate or inheritance taxes which might necessitate the Cayman Islands court or government asserting jurisdiction over the estate of a deceased person with no assets in the Cayman Islands.

6. Expert Evidence

(a) In general there is no necessity for a foreign lawyer (or other) to give evidence regarding a foreign will which has been recognized by a foreign court, or regarding the inheritance laws of a foreign country. If a foreign will has been admitted to probate, generally the procedure for resealing grants of probate (*see above*) should be followed. Normally evidence from a foreign lawyer is not needed.

---

7. This may be sworn in the same manner as for any court proceeding in the Cayman Islands. If it is sworn overseas, it may be sworn in any manner permitted by the local law. Often it will be sworn before a British Consulate or Embassy official.

8. If two different jurisdictions each maintained that the deceased was domiciled in their jurisdiction, there is potential for conflict. So far as Cayman Islands law is concerned, however, the Cayman Islands court is not concerned with foreign rules of domicile. It will determine according to its own rules where the deceased was domiciled. Having determined the identity of that jurisdiction, it will then look to its rules of succession to determine the entitlement to movables located in the Cayman Islands. In relation to any immovables (i.e., land) in the Cayman Islands, the court will always apply Cayman Islands law.

(b) Any evidence given by affidavit[9] in Cayman proceedings is subject to a rule entitling the other parties in the action to cross-examine the affidavit. If an application for cross-examination is made, the maker of the affidavit would have to appear in court. Affidavit evidence on which a party intends to rely at trial will only be admissible if the maker of the affidavit is present at trial and can be cross-examined on it.

7. Unity of Succession

The principle of unity of succession does apply in the Cayman Islands. This means that in general conceptual terms a deceased is considered to have one worldwide estate and in particular that the worldwide assets are available to satisfy the claims of worldwide creditors. This in turn means that the estate of a deceased person in a particular jurisdiction (e.g., the Cayman Islands) cannot be wound up and administered locally, in isolation from the rest of the deceased's worldwide estate. Specifically, it is possible that a person might die with a surplus of debts over assets in a foreign jurisdiction but with assets in the Cayman Islands, which on the principle of unity of succession should be made available to his creditors in the foreign jurisdiction. Under the principle of unity of succession, the basic intention is that the same persons should be entrusted with the administration of a deceased person's estate in all jurisdictions. The Cayman Islands rules of succession (for example the rules concerning the resealing of foreign grants of probate) are grounded in this principle.

8. Formalities

See Section 10(a) *below*.

9. Legislation

The *Hague Convention on the Conflicts of Laws Relating to the Form of Testamentary Dispositions* was extended to the Cayman Islands by Order in Council dated 16 December 1964, which came into force on 14 February 1965.

10. Wills

(a) A will of immovables must comply with the formalities prescribed by the *lex situs*, and a will of movables must comply with the formalities prescribed by the law of the testator's last domicile.

---

9. *See* footnote 7 *above* for the formalities of execution for an affidavit.

(b) As under English common law, a will is to be interpreted in accordance with the law intended by the testator. There is a rebuttable presumption that the testator intended this to be the law of his domicile as at the date of making the will.

(c) *See* (f) *below.*

(d) A legatee has the capacity to receive a legacy of movables if he has the capacity either by the law of his domicile or by the law of the testator's domicile. As regards immovables, the capacity to inherit will generally be governed by the *lex situs*. (By capacity to inherit is meant capacity to take legal title and give a receipt. A person lacking the capacity, such as a minor, may nevertheless be entitled beneficially to the legacy or assets although it may need to be paid, transferred to, or registered in the name of a trustee or guardian for his/her benefit.)

(e) The law of the jurisdiction of the testator's domicile governs whether or not he has the personal capacity to make a will of movables. Difficulties may arise where the domicile changes between the time of making the will and the testator's death. It is not settled whether the issue of capacity will be determined according to the law of domicile at the date of making the will, or the law of domicile at the date of death. In this context, personal capacity includes issues such as whether, and if so to what extent, a minor, married woman or a person suffering from physical or mental illness, can make a valid will. It does not cover matters such as the extent to which rules of forced heirship may be applicable (*see* (c) *above*).

As regards the personal capacity of a testator to make a will disposing of immovables, it is thought that the *lex situs* would govern the question of capacity, although there is no authority on this point.

(f) The material or essential validity of a will insofar as it relates to movable property is generally governed by the laws of the testator's domicile at the time of his death. For immovables, essential validity is generally determined according to the *lex situs*.

(g) The exercise of a power of appointment conferred by will may involve questions connected with several jurisdictions. For example, the testator, the donee of the power, and the appointee may be personally subject to the laws of different jurisdictions. Issues such as: (1) the capacity of a donee to exercise a power of appointment by will, (2) the law governing the formal validity of the exercise of the power, (3) the law governing the interpretation of the power, (4) the law governing the material or essential validity of the exercise of the power, and (5) the law governing whether the exercise of a power has been revoked, will be determined according to the English common law principles.

(h) Questions relating to the effectiveness of an amendment to a will are matters relating to the formal validity of the will, therefore *see* (a) *above*.

The Cayman Islands conflict of laws rules relating to revocation would follow those of the English common law. It is therefore necessary to distinguish between the modes of revocation:

   i. Where the alleged act of revocation is the execution of a later will or codicil, the question of whether the later instrument revokes the first depends on whether the second instrument is itself valid, which will involve a consideration of the Cayman Islands conflict of laws rules relating to capacity and formal validity (*see* (a) and (e) *above*). The position may be complicated where there are separate wills confined to property in separate jurisdictions. The question of whether one will revokes the other would be determined in accordance with the English common law principles of conflict of laws.

   ii. Where the alleged act of revocation is the burning, tearing or destroying of the will, the question of the effectiveness of the revocation would, as a matter of the conflict of laws rules of the Cayman Islands, be determined according to the law of the testator's domicile at the date of the alleged act of revocation. This rule applies to movables, and is also thought to apply to immovables (although there may be an argument that the *lex situs* may apply to immovables).

   iii. Where it is necessary to consider whether a will has been revoked by subsequent marriage, the question of whether or not the revocation is effective will, following the English conflict of laws rules, be determined according to the law of the testator's domicile immediately after the marriage. This rule should apply to both movable and immovable property.

(i) *See* (c) *above*.

11. Domicile/Nationality

(a) *See* Section 10 *above*. The domicile of the deceased will be determined in accordance with English common law principles. It should be noted that the common law rule that the domicile of a married woman is that of her husband continues to apply under Cayman Islands law, so that a wife may not acquire a separate domicile.

(b) The domicile of a beneficiary will only be relevant to the extent that, under the Cayman Islands conflict of law rules, a foreign law is to determine an issue and that foreign law regards the domicile of the beneficiary as a relevant consideration in relation to the issue.

(c) Under Cayman Islands law, a person may only have a single domicile at any one time. Nationality is not regarded under Cayman Islands law as a relevant consideration in succession matters, unless under the Cayman Islands conflict of law rules a foreign law is to determine an issue and that foreign law regards nationality as a relevant consideration.

12. Taxation

Not applicable – *see* Section A12(a) *above*.

China

Prepared by: Richard XIAOYUN WANG
Richard Wang & Co.

Address: Suite 1804–1806, Union Building
100 Yanan Road East
Shanghai 200002
P.R. China
Tel.: +86 21 6323 6800 / 6326 5800
Fax: +86 21 6323 8906
E-mail: rw@guomai.sh.cn

Section A – Brief Survey of the Local System

1. Type of System

(a) The legal system of the People's Republic of China (PR China) is a civil law system.

(b) PR China (excluding Taiwan, Hong Kong and Macao) has a uniform system of basic laws and regulations.

2. Wills

(a) There are five types of will under the *Law of Succession of the People's Republic of China (Succession Law)*:

- Notarial will: A will made by the testator to a notarial agency, which cannot be altered or revoked by other types of will.
- Holographic will: A will made in the testator's own handwriting and signed by him, specifying the date of its making.
- Allographic will: A will written on behalf of the testator in the presence of no less than two witnesses, of whom one writes the will, dates it and signs it along with the other witness or witnesses and with the testator.
- Sound-recording will: A will made in the form of the sound-recording in the presence of no less than two witnesses. There is no necessity to prove the identity of the witnesses. Any person with the exception of those described in paragraph 8(b) *below* can be the witness of the sound-recording will. The sound-recording

will shall be valid provided that at least two witnesses prove their presence at the time of making the sound-recording will and the truth of such will.

– Nuncupative will: A will made by the testator orally in the presence of no less than two witnesses only in an emergency situation. When the emergency situation is over and if the testator is able to make a will in writing or in the form of a sound-recording, the nuncupative will made before shall be invalidated after a reasonable short period after the emergency situation during which the testator should be able to make a will in other proper forms in order to replace the nuncupative will.

(b) *i*. A testator may revoke or alter a will he/she previously made at his/her sole discretion before his/her death. The revocation of the will may therefore be made without observing any particular form or procedure. When several wills conflict with one another in contents, the last one shall prevail. A notarial will may not be revoked or altered by other types of will.

ii. A will made prior to marriage shall not be revoked automatically by the marriage unless such will is revoked in the testator's sole discretion during the marriage. The property acquired by the spouses in the course of their matrimonial life shall, unless otherwise agreed upon, be deemed as the community property of the spouses. If such property is partitioned, half of it shall be allotted first to the surviving spouse as his/her own property, and the remainder shall constitute the deceased's estate. Any disposition involving the surviving spouse's own property in a will made previously shall be invalid.

iii. The revival of a revoked will manifesting the genuine intention of the testator shall be valid. The testator must show his/her revival of a revoked will in writing unless special circumstances prevent him/her from doing so, in which case he/she may use a sound-recording form or other forms as described in paragraph 2 *above*, except that a notarial revoked will can only be revived in the form of a notarial will.

3. Intestacy

(a) In case of intestacy the estate of the deceased shall be inherited in the following order:

– first: spouse, children, parents;
– second: brothers and sisters, paternal grandparents, maternal grandparents.

When succession opens, the successor(s) first in order shall inherit to the exclusion of the successor(s) second in order. The successor(s) second in order shall inherit in default of any successor first in order.

In general, the estate shall be shared equally among successors of the same order. For example, if there were a spouse, four children and two parents, the estate shall be shared equally among the seven successors, i.e., one-seventh for each.

Successors may take unequal shares if an agreement to that effect is reached among them.

The 'children' referred to in this text include legitimate children, illegitimate children, and adopted children, as well as stepchildren who supported or were supported by the deceased. The 'parents' referred to in this text include natural parents and adoptive parents, as well as step-parents who supported or were supported by the deceased. The 'brothers and sisters' referred to in this text include blood brothers and sisters, brothers and sisters of half blood, adopted brothers and sisters, as well as step-brothers and step-sisters who supported or were supported by the deceased. Children born out of adultery shall have the same right of succession as the children born out of marriage.

Inheritance in subrogation only takes place where a deceased survived his/her child. Where a deceased survived his/her child, the direct lineal descendants of the predeceased child inherit in subrogation. Descendants who inherit in subrogation generally shall take only the share of the estate their father or mother was entitled to.

Widowed daughters-in-law or sons-in-law who have made the predominant contributions in maintaining their parents-in-law, are regarded as successors first in order.

At the time of the partitioning of the estate, reservation shall be made for the share of an unborn child. The share reserved shall, if the baby is stillborn, be dealt with in accordance with statutory succession.

At the time of distributing the estate, due consideration shall be given to successors who are unable to work and have special financial difficulties; successors who have made the predominant contributions in maintaining the deceased or have lived with the deceased may be given a larger share; successors who had the ability and were in a position to maintain the deceased but failed to fulfil their duties shall be given no share or a smaller share of the estate. The court decides how much consideration should be given to successors who are unable to work or who have made predominant contribution to maintaining the deceased.

An estate which is left with neither a successor nor a legatee shall belong to the State or, where the deceased was a member of an organization of collective ownership before his/her death, to such an organization.

(b) There is no difference in the division of the estate on intestacy between movables and immovables.

4. Freedom of Testation

(a) The testator is free to dispose of his/her assets, with the following exceptions:

- the testator shall not dispose of the part of the matrimonial community property belonging to the surviving spouse;
- the testator shall not dispose of the part of the family community property belonging to the other member of the family. Land cannot be considered as part of

the family community property because no ownership of the land by a citizen or a family is possible under the present law of PR China;
– the testator shall leave a necessary portion of an estate in his/her will for a successor who neither has working capacity nor has a source of income.

(b) There is no conception of contract of inheritance under the *Succession Law* in PR China. However, a legacy-support agreement entered into by and between a testator and a citizen or an organization of collective ownership in accordance with relevant laws and regulations is permissible and binding.

A successor who, after the death of the deceased, disclaims inheritance should make his decision known before the disposition of the estate. In the absence of such an indication, he/she is deemed to have accepted the inheritance.

A legatee should, within two months from the time he/she learns of the legacy, make known whether he/she accepts it or disclaims it. In the absence of such an indication within the specified period, he/she is deemed to have disclaimed the legacy.

5. Maintenance

Reservation of a necessary portion of an estate shall be made in a will for a successor who neither has working capacity nor has a source of income.

An appropriate share of the estate may be given to a person, other than a successor, who depended on the support of the deceased and who neither has working capacity nor has a source of income, or to a person, other than a successor, who was largely responsible for supporting the deceased.

6. Community Property Between Husband and Wife

(a) There is a concept of community property between husband and wife under *The Marriage Law of The People's Republic of China*, i.e., the property acquired by the spouses in the course of their matrimonial life with the exceptions as agreed. The surviving spouse is entitled to claim for 50 per cent of the total assets of the spouses. The other 50 per cent constitutes the deceased's estate which is to be distributed according to a will or the rules governing succession on intestacy.

(b) If there is a marriage agreement made in writing by the spouses in accordance with the relevant laws and regulations, covering the division of the property, such agreement shall be binding.

7. Gifts (*Inter Vivos*)

(a)–(b) Gifts to an heir prior to death are not set off against the heir's inheritance unless a contract of inheritance has been made. Such gifts do not prevent the heir from acquiring his/her portion of estate or legacy.

International Succession

8. Capacity

(a) Wills made by persons with no capacity or with limited capacity shall be void. The testator shall be no less than eighteen years of age, and must be mentally fit.

(b) None of the following persons shall act as a witness of a will:

- persons with no capacity or with limited capacity;
- successors and legatees; or
- persons whose interests are related to those of the successors and legatees, including the creditors of the successors or legatees, the debtors of the successors or legatees, the business partners of the successors or legatees, and the relatives of the successors or legatees other than the statutory successors.

(c) There is no limit on the capacity of beneficiaries. Even an unborn child has the right to a reservation of its share at the time of partitioning the estate. However, the share reserved shall, if the baby is stillborn, be dealt with in accordance with statutory succession. Only natural persons can be successors. The State or a collective can only be legatees.

A successor shall be disinherited upon his/her commission of any one of the following acts:

- intentional killing of the deceased;
- killing any other successor in fighting over the estate;
- a serious act of abandoning or maltreating the deceased;
- a serious act of forging, tampering with or destroying the will.

It is not statutorily required to go through court proceedings or notarial proceedings in order for the successors or executors to carry out the will.

9. Authority (Court, Notarial or Other)

The time and mode for partitioning and distributing the estate shall be decided by the successors through consultation. If no agreement is reached through consultation, they may institute legal proceedings to have the case decided by the court.

A lawsuit brought on a dispute over succession shall be under the jurisdiction of a court of the place where the deceased has his/her domicile upon his/her death, or where the principal part of his/her estate is located. A successor shall be entitled to institute a lawsuit in the court at his/her sole discretion against the other successors who encroached on his/her share of the estate.

10. Invalidity of Will

(a) Wills made by persons with no capacity or with limited capacity shall be void. Wills shall manifest the genuine intention of the testators; therefore those made under duress or as a result of fraud shall be void. Forged wills shall be void. If a will has been tampered with, the affected parts of it shall be void.

(b) All defects shall result in a will being void in its entirety except that unaffected part of a will that may remain binding if it has been tampered with in part only.

11. Simultaneous Death

If more than one person, who are entitled to an inheritance relationship with each other, died in the same accident in which it is impossible to establish the sequence of death, it is deemed that the person without any successor(s) predeceased.

If these persons can establish their own successor(s) respectively, it is deemed that persons of elder generation predeceased persons of younger generation.

If these persons are of the same generation, it is deemed that they deceased simultaneously, and no inheritance relationship shall be established among them.

12. Estate Taxes

There are no estate taxes under the existing relevant laws and regulations of PR China.

13. Administration of Estates

(a) Estates are administered by the heirs themselves or by an administrator appointed either in the will or by the court. The heirs may themselves administer the estate if all the heirs agree to this and it is not prohibited by the will. The estates will be administered by an administrator if it is so stated in a will. If the testator did not appoint an administrator, the court may appoint a competent administrator.

(b) There are no strict statutory requirements for the reporting on administration of the estate submitted by the administrator. However, the administrator shall not take any action detrimental to the interest of the heirs.

(c) The court will not execute any external supervision unless the case of succession has been filed with the court. However, each of the successors or legatees can file a case of succession with a court if in his/her opinion his/her right to succession has been violated. The court will examine the validity of the will, capacity of the successors or legatees, the time and mode for partitioning the estate in accordance with relevant laws or regulations.

(d) Anyone who has interest in the estate may settle the dispute of succession through consultation with the successors. If no agreement is reached through consultation, he/she may institute legal proceedings in the court.

International Succession

(e) The assets are formally transferred to the heirs who themselves distribute the estate in a way they agreed previously. If no agreement of the partitioning of the estate is reached, the assets will be handed over to the heirs in accordance with the judgment made by the court.

(f) The successor to an estate shall pay all debts payable by the deceased, up to the actual value of such estate, unless the successor pays voluntarily in excess of the limit.

The successor who disclaims inheritance assumes no responsibility for the payment of debts payable by the deceased according to law.

The implementation of a legacy shall not affect the payment of debts payable by the deceased.

(g) *See* (a) *above*.

14. Domicile/Nationality

(a) The domicile of the deceased at the time of his/her death will affect the governing law of succession. For inheritance by a Chinese citizen of an estate outside PR China or of an estate of a foreigner within PR China, the law of the deceased's domicile shall apply in the case of movable property; in the case of immovable property, the law of the place where the property is located shall apply. For inheritance by a foreigner of an estate within PR China or of an estate of a Chinese citizen outside PR China, the law of the deceased's domicile shall apply in the case of movable property; in the case of immovable property, the law of the place where the property is located shall apply. Where treaties or agreements exist between PR China and foreign countries, matters of inheritance shall be handled in accordance with such treaties or agreements.

(b) If the deceased was a resident in PR China, the local court will give an order of succession in accordance with relevant laws and regulations even if the deceased has no assets in PR China.

SECTION B – APPLICABLE LAW/PROCEDURE WHERE FOREIGN ELEMENT/S ARE INVOLVED

1. Jurisdiction

(a) According to the stipulation of *The Civil Procedure Law of PR China*, a lawsuit with regard to a dispute over succession shall be under the jurisdiction of the court of the place where the deceased had his/her domicile at his/her death, or where the principal part of his/her estate is located.

(b) The jurisdiction as mentioned in (a) above will not be affected by the difference between movables and immovables.

(c) Local courts of different levels shall have jurisdiction as court of first instance over different succession cases, depending on the difference in claim amount and/or foreign interests.

The district/county courts shall have jurisdiction as courts of first instance over most succession cases. The intermediate courts shall have jurisdiction as courts of first instance over the following succession cases:

– major cases involving foreign elements;
– cases that have a major impact on the area under their jurisdiction; and
– cases determined by the Supreme Court to be under the jurisdiction of the intermediate courts.

The high courts shall have jurisdiction over the following cases:

– cases that have a major impact on the area under their jurisdiction; and
– cases as determined by the Supreme Court to be under the jurisdiction of the high
  courts.

2. Applicable Law

See paragraph 14(a) of Section A *above*.

3. Foreign Succession/Inheritance Orders

(a) Foreign orders would be recognized, subject to compliance with relevant procedural requirements.

(b) An order or judgment from the local intermediate courts must be obtained to give the foreign authority/administrator possession of assets of the deceased and to give a foreign succession effect.

(c) An application to the court must be filed together with the following required documentation:
    If applied for by a foreign court:

– an application for judicial assistance;
– the original of the legally effective judgment or order;
– a Chinese translation of the judgment or order.

If applied for by an applicant other than a foreign court:

– an application for execution prepared by a local attorney;
– evidence of the fact that the judgment or order has become effective (such as
  certificate of service). The judgment would only be regarded as 'effective' from
  the point of view of Chinese law if it had been served on the parties concerned.

International Succession

Signatures of the parties concerned (including its agent *ad litem* or legal representative) on the certificate of service are accepted as a proof of service;
- the original of the legally effective judgment or order from a foreign court which has been authenticated by the Chinese Consulate in that foreign country;
- a certificate of identity notarized and authenticated by the Chinese Consulate as above;
- a power of attorney notarized and authenticated by the Chinese Consulate as above.

4. Two or More Succession or Probate Orders

It depends on what governing law is applied. In the case of movable property, the law of the place of the domicile of the deceased shall be applied, so the order therein shall prevail. In the case of immovable property, the law of the place where the property is located shall apply, so the order therein shall prevail. If there is a conflict between two foreign or succession or probate orders and such conflict cannot be resolved by the above rule, the Chinese law shall be applied.

5. Assets

The local court may assume jurisdiction over the succession case on the grounds of the domicile of the testator at the time of death.

6. Expert Evidence

(a) There is no necessity for a foreign lawyer to give evidence regarding a foreign will or regarding the inheritance laws of a foreign country. It is, however, at the sole discretion of the local court to decide whether a foreign lawyer shall be permitted to give expert evidence.

From the statutory point of view, the applicable foreign law may be provided by:

- the plaintiff or the defendant;
- a central authority of that foreign country which has concluded a Judicial Assistance Treaty with PR China;
- a Chinese embassy or consulate accredited to that country;
- a foreign embassy or consulate accredited to PR China;
- Chinese or foreign experts on foreign law.

From the practical point of view, in most cases an expert witness is asked to provide evidence of foreign law.

(b) Expert evidence is normally provided in the form of an affidavit without necessity of appearance in court.

164

7. Unity of Succession

This is accepted in principle in China.

8. Formalities

Wills executed outside PR China are deemed valid if they meet the legal require-ment either according to the law of PR China in the event that the law of PR China shall apply or according to the foreign law in the event that the foreign law shall apply.

9. Legislation

The *1961 Hague Convention on the Conflicts of Laws Relating to the Form of Testamentary Dispositions* is not applicable.

10. Wills

(a–i) The legal requirements for execution of wills must be met according to the rules as follows:

– the law of the testator's domicile at the time of death in case of movable property;
– the law of the place where the property is located in case of immovable property.

11. Domicile/Nationality

(a)–(b) *See* paragraph 10 *above.*

(c) As can be seen from the above, nationality is not relevant to the question of testamentary capacity, succession, etc. Where a deceased has more than one domi-cile, the relevant one is the last domicile before his/her demise. If it is not clear, the court may apply the laws of the respective jurisdictions according to the nature of the assets in question (movable or immovable).

12. Taxation

There is no estate tax under the existing taxation law of PR China.

Czech Republic

Prepared by: Jírí SVOBODA
Notary Public

Address: Dlouhá c. 16
11000 Praha – 1
Czech Republic
Tel./Fax: +420 2 232 6420
E-mail: svobodanot@mbox.vol.cz

SECTION A – BRIEF SURVEY OF THE LOCAL SYSTEM

1. Type of System

(a) The juridical system in the Czech Republic is founded on that of continental Europe: that of written law.

The current Civil Code (Law No. 40/1964 of the Compendium) is a disordered agglomeration of texts from the 1960s and later amendments that were adopted particularly after November 1989. The Ministry of Justice has already begun work on the recodification of the Civil Code.

(b) As regards constitutional law, the Czech Republic is a unitary state.

2. Wills

(a) Inheritance by way of will is regulated by Chapter 3, Articles 476 to 480 of the Civil Code.

  i. The *holographic will*: The testator can draw up a holographic will as regards his assets. The testator must write the will out in his own handwriting, note the day, month and year on which he draws it up and sign it by his own hand, otherwise the will is entirely void. This form of will is the one most in use. The Civil Code strictly excludes the possibility of joint wills (including those made by spouses).

    A will that is not in the testator's handwriting must at least be signed by the testator himself and he must declare, in the presence of two witnesses, that the instrument in question contains his last wishes. The witnesses must also sign the will in their own hand. (This form of will is used less often.)

A testator who is unable to read or write must express his last wishes in an instrument written and read out in the presence of three witnesses, who attend together, and the instrument must be read and signed by the witnesses. The testator must also confirm that the instrument in question contains his last wishes in the presence of the witnesses. The law also stipulates that the person who has written or read out the will can act as witness but that that person cannot have both written and read it out. In addition, the law requires that the will must state the testator's incapacity to read or write, the person who has written out the will, the person who has read it out and the manner in which the testator has confirmed that the instrument contained his last wishes. The witnesses must also sign the will themselves.

ii. The *public will* (*authentique*): This will is drawn up by a notary; in certain cases this is done in the presence of witnesses. The notarial instrument is the only other form of will allowed for by law. The law prescribes three instances in which it is necessary to draw up a will in this form. The need arises when the following persons wish to draw up a will:
   – minors over the age of fifteen;
   – blind and deaf persons who are unable to read;
   – mute persons who are unable to read.

The law, however, allows for certain exceptions to the above-mentioned obligations. For instance, deaf persons who are unable to read or write can express their last wishes by way of the notarial instrument to which reference has just been made or, in the presence of three witnesses, who attend together and are able to communicate in sign language, by way of a notarial instrument, that must be translated into sign language.

The formalities required in relation to the drawing up of a notarial instrument are set out in the *Law of Notarial Procedure* (Law No. 358/1992 of the Compendium), Articles 62 to 71. The law requires that such an instrument contain the following:
   – the location, day, month and year the instrument was drawn up;
   – the first and last names of the notary and his principal place of business;
   – the first and last names, the address and the number of the birth certificate (of the Social Security), or, should such number not exist, the date of birth, of all parties to the instrument and their representatives, the witnesses, agents and interpreters;
   – a declaration by the parties to the instrument of their juridical capacity;
   – information on the verification of the identity of the parties to the instrument, witnesses, agents and interpreters;
   – the contents of the instrument, for example, that of the will itself;
   – information as to the approval of the instrument by the parties to it after its reading;
   – the signatures of the parties to the instrument or of their representatives as well as those of the witnesses, agents and interpreters;
   – the imprint of the notary's official seal and his signature.

The law also regulates those cases where the person in question is unable to read or write. If the testator is unable to read or write, the notary must draw up the instrument in the presence of two witnesses. According to the law, these witnesses must be present when the person concerned, that is, in whose interest they are in attendance, is declaring what is to be contained in the notarial instrument, upon the reading of the instrument and upon its approval by the person concerned. This procedure does not apply if the person concerned is able to understand the legal instrument with the help of special equipment or aids and can sign in his own hand.

The law also prescribes that witnesses to the instrument have juridical capacity, be able to read and write and are not closely related to the persons concerned or those interested in the matter, nor can they be the notary's clerks.

The law also regulates the procedure to be used in the drawing up of a notarial instrument in relation to persons who are deaf or mute.

If the person concerned is not familiar with the language in which the notarial instrument is drawn up, the presence of a sworn interpreter is required and that person cannot have any interest in the matter. But if the notary knows the language of the person concerned or of the witness, the presence of the interpreter is not required.

If the notary has drawn up a will by way of notarial instrument, he gives notice of this fact to the Central Register of Wills created in 2001 in the electronic version and administered by Chamber of Notaries of the Czech Republic. The Central Register is a register of public wills as well as those deposited with notaries. It does not contain any content of the wills, only the personal data of the testator.

The Civil Code does not recognize death-bed wills. Joint wills drawn up by several testators are not recognized as mentioned earlier, nor are oral wills.

(b) *i.* A will is revoked by a subsequent will which is valid, if the later will cannot subsist with the former, or by way of express revocation. The law requires that, in general, revocation must be by way of one of the forms stipulated for wills. The revocation of a will, however, need not be done in the same form as that of the will itself. For example, a public will can be revoked by a holographic will and *vice versa*. The testator can revoke the will (with the exception of that drawn up by notarial instrument as these are held by the notary) by destroying the paper on which it is written up.

ii. Marriage and divorce as such do not affect the validity of prior wills. The will can therefore even relate to the patrimony that the deceased acquired jointly with his spouse since the time of the marriage.

iii. If the will was validly revoked, no account is taken of it or of the heirs mentioned within it. The testamentary heirs of a revoked will have the right to make known their view as to such revocation or to object to the nullity of such will by way of court proceedings.

3. Intestacy

(a) Succession upon intestacy is covered by Chapter 2, Articles 473 to 475(a) of the Civil Code and although such provisions precede those relating to testamentary succession, succession upon intestacy will only take effect if the deceased has not left a will, if the will was invalid or if the will only dealt with some of the deceased's assets. The Civil Code sets out four categories of succession, whereby the heirs in one category will prevent those in the next category from succeeding (e.g., the heirs in the first category preventing those in the second category, etc.).

The heirs of *the first category* are the children and the surviving spouse of the deceased who will take in equal measure. If one of the deceased's children does not inherit, his share is taken in equal measure by his children (i.e., the grandchildren of the deceased). If such grandchildren, or one of them, do not inherit, their share is taken in equal measure by their descendants (i.e., the great-grandchildren, the great-great-grandchildren, etc.). In these instances, the share passes by way of 'representation.' The legal concept here of 'not inheriting' includes the following cases:

– the child dying before his brothers and sisters;
– the child having validly renounced his inheritance;
– the location at which the child is residing remaining unknown;
– the child being incapable of inheriting;
– the child being validly disinherited.

In order that the first category of heirs succeed, the deceased must have left at least one descendant. It is not possible therefore that the surviving spouse could be the sole heir of the first category. The law makes no distinction as between legitimate, illegitimate or adopted children, with all such children having the same rights and obligations.

A share is deemed not to be taken and only passes to the others in the same category if there are no 'substitutable heirs' who would take that share by way of representation (e.g., a child who has predeceased not leaving any children of his own). In certain cases where the parents have died, their children can represent them in the succession and take their share of the inheritance; representation is applicable in relation to the descendants and the brothers and sisters of the deceased (the latter, however, only belonging to the third category).

If that share of the predeceased heir is not taken by way of representation, it is added to that to be inherited by the others in the same category. If the surviving spouse does not inherit, his share is passed immediately to others in the same category; it is not possible within the first category for the surviving spouse's children to inherit unless they are also the children of the deceased.

The deceased's surviving spouse who inherits is in the same position as the deceased's children although there is a distinction to be drawn in that the death of the deceased results in the dissolution of the community of property between the spouses, upon which the surviving spouse has the right to half of the property deemed to have been held as community property. The rest of the property formerly held in community and the deceased's sole property then passes to the estate. As regards community of property, *see infra*.

If the deceased's descendants do not inherit, the inheritance passes to *the second category*, that of the surviving spouse, the deceased's parents and those who lived in the deceased's household for at least a year prior to the deceased's death having thereby shared the same household as the deceased or been maintained by him (the latter being referred to as co-habitants). The heirs of the second category inherit in equal measure subject to the surviving spouse acquiring at least half of the assets. As regards community of property, *see infra*.

The second category inherits when the deceased's descendants (i.e., the children and grandchildren of the deceased) do not inherit (as to the meaning of such legal concept, *see above*). The parents, as well as adoptive parents, will have a right to the inheritance.

The second category of those to inherit also includes a special group of persons, namely the co-habitants, that is those who have lived in the household with the deceased for at least one year before his death and who thereby shared the same household or were maintained by the deceased. The co-habitants need not be related to the deceased in any way and their potential number is unlimited.

The law does not preclude the possibility that the co-habitants are of the same sex as the deceased (e.g., as regards a homosexual relationship).

If neither the surviving spouse nor the parents inherit, the co-habitants alone cannot inherit within the second category and will in such cases only inherit as members of the third category.

If neither the surviving spouse nor the parents inherit, the deceased's brothers and sisters and the co-habitants will inherit as members of *the third category*. As for the co-habitants, *see above*. The law makes no distinction between brothers and sisters of the full blood and those of the half blood on the father's or mother's side. The persons to inherit in the third category take in equal measure. If one of the deceased's brothers or sisters does not inherit, that share of the inheritance reverts to his or her children, that is, the deceased's nephews and nieces. As the law refers to 'the children' and not 'the descendants,' this part of the inheritance will revert only to the nephews and nieces and not to the children of the nephews and nieces (i.e., great-nephews and great-nieces).

If no heir in the third category inherits, the inheritance will pass to those in *the fourth category*, that is, the grandparents of the deceased in equal measure; and if all of them do not inherit, the inheritance reverts to their children in equal measure (i.e., the deceased's uncles and aunts).

Cousins and other relations cannot inherit by way of legal succession but can of course inherit by way of testamentary succession.

Should there be only one heir, the court confirms his acquisition of the inheritance by way of a decision. If there are several heirs, they conclude a contract on the administration of the inheritance before the court notary which the court will approve if it is not contrary to the law or public morals. If the heirs do not arrive at an agreement or if the agreement is not approved, the court confirms the acquisition of the inheritance in accordance with each heir's share of it. If no heir takes the inheritance, the court confirms that it passes to the state in default of heirs.

(b) The Civil Code does not make any distinction between the succession of immovables and movables. There is, however, one difference in relation to the court's powers in respect of the succession of a foreigner's estate. Where a foreigner (i.e., a national of another state) owns immovables in the Czech Republic, and if international agreements to which the Czech Republic is party do not stipulate otherwise,

Czech courts will always have jurisdiction in relation to these, in accordance with the law on private international law and procedure.

The Czech court will deal with the succession of a foreigner's assets which is to take place in the Czech Republic in the following instances:

– when the state of which the deceased was a national does not confer jurisdiction over the succession of the estates of Czech nationals to the Czech courts, when it does not give legal force to the decisions of such courts or when it refuses to deal with the above-mentioned succession relating to its national or makes no pronouncement upon it;
– when the deceased had his domicile in the Czech Republic and the heir who resides there requests it;
– in all cases involving immovables located in the Czech Republic.

4. Freedom of Testation

(a) The Civil Code provides for a part of the estate to be subject to compulsory shares and that the deceased's descendants are the heirs entitled to such shares. In accordance with the Civil Code, descendants who are minors must receive at least as much as that to which they would have been legally entitled upon intestacy. The descendants who are of age must receive at least half as much as that to which they would have been legally entitled upon intestacy. If the will contravenes such stipulations, it is deemed voidable to this extent unless the descendants in question were legitimately disinherited. The law then limits testamentary freedom in this way in favour of those entitled to a compulsory share of the estate.

For example, if the deceased is a widower with two sons, one a minor and one having reached full age, the minor will receive his entire entitlement upon intestacy – that is, one-half of the estate – and the one having reached full age will obtain half of his entitlement upon intestacy – that is, one-quarter of the estate. The testator can only dispose freely then of one-quarter of his estate.

Voidability here means that the descendants have to invoke such nullity, or rather they must bring it up within the context of the procedure upon succession, otherwise the court will not take such nullity into consideration.

The surviving spouse can be left out of the inheritance altogether such that he inherits nothing. His rights are protected by the institution of community of property – which will be examined below. The heirs with a right to a compulsory share are only the deceased's descendants (without any distinction being made as to whether they are legitimate, illegitimate or adopted); the other heirs can be left out of the inheritance.

(b) *i.* The Civil Code does not allow for contracts on succession when the property has not passed to the heirs.
ii. Likewise, it is not possible to conclude agreements on the succession of a living person or pacts on succession nor can advance division be undertaken.

5. Maintenance

The Civil Code does not make any provision for maintenance. In general no legal right of maintenance for the benefit of one or other of the heirs or the surviving spouse exists. The law pertaining to the family (the Family Code) does provide for maintenance but such an obligation does not relate directly to succession.

6. Community Property Between Husband and Wife

(a) Community of property relates to all that can be held as property, and therefore essentially to property which the spouses acquire, have acquired or will acquire for consideration during their married life, with the exception of that property mentioned below. When establishing community of property between spouses, the first principle to be applied is that the share of each is equal; that is to say, that the surviving spouse will have the right to half of the property held in community with only the other half of such property and all that owned solely by the deceased spouse forming part of his inheritance.

In the Czech Republic, the institution of community of property does exist. In accordance with Article 143 of the Civil Code, the community of property as between spouses covers all that can be held as property (essentially therefore only property) and acquired by one of the spouses during the course of the marriage, with the exception of those assets acquired by way of inheritance or as gifts, those assets which by their nature serve exclusively to meet the personal needs of one of the spouses and that property recovered by one of the spouses within the context of settlements for the restitution of property. Community of property also covers obligations arisen to one of the spouses or to both of them together during the course of the marriage. Community of property arises upon the day of the marriage, without regard to other circumstances such as whether the spouses live together or not. As well as community property, each of the spouses can possess his own property exclusively, for example in relation to property that was in his possession before contracting the marriage. Community property, however, will also include those gains, returns and increases in value made on property held exclusively by one of the spouses. Community of property subsists for the duration of the marriage and is deemed therefore no longer to exist once the marriage has ended (by way of divorce or the death of one of the spouses). The law also provides for certain cases where community of property is deemed no longer to exist during the marriage (e.g., in relation to the confiscation of property under the Penal Code or upon a declaration of bankruptcy).

The form of community property set out *above* is not obligatory. The spouses can agree, by way of a notarial instrument (the recourse to such instrument here being compulsory), to increase or diminish the share of property to be held in community from that which is stipulated by law. Likewise, they can also conclude an agreement on the administration of the property to be held in community. The spouses can also agree to, upon the end of the marriage, the subsistence of community of property. Such an agreement must also be made by way of notarial instrument.

(b) The spouses share the use of the assets that are held in community of property and must also share the expenses arising from the use and the maintenance of such assets.

Each of the spouses has the right to administer and dispose of the assets held in community of property alone during his lifetime, though such right does not extend to those assets which are deemed important, in relation to which the spouses must act jointly.

After the death of her spouse, the widow has the right to retain the use of her deceased husband's name.

7. Gifts (*Inter Vivos*)

(a) In the case of intestate succession, gifts for no consideration from the deceased while he was alive (with the exception of those donations deemed to be 'ordinary') to an heir entitled to a share are taken into account.

In the case of succession by will, it will be necessary to have recourse to refunding (*le rapport*) if the testator so requests it.

(b) Refunding (*le rapport*) may only be imposed upon an heir and his co-heirs. Therefore an heir who renounces his inheritance will not be subject to this.

8. Capacity

(a) The essential requirement for drawing up a will is that the testator has juridical capacity. Such capacity is acquired on the day that the testator attains his majority, that is, on his eighteenth birthday. Minors over the age of fifteen can draw up their last wishes only by way of notarial instrument.

Minors over the age of sixteen, who are deemed emancipated, have full capacity in relation to the disposition of their property by way of will. According to Article 8 of the Civil Code, a minor is deemed emancipated upon marriage, such that a minor who is over sixteen and married has full juridical capacity, including the capacity to draw up a will.

(b) Only those persons having full juridical capacity can be witnesses to a will. Those persons who cannot act as witnesses are the blind, the deaf, the mute, those who do not understand the language in which the will is drawn up and those who will inherit under the will.

Those persons taking under the will, those taking by law, and relations and close friends of the heirs cannot act as public officials, witnesses, interpreters or persons who write or read out the will in connection with the drawing up of the will.

(c) The Civil Code does not recognize the concept of legatee. According to the Civil Code, persons not yet conceived, persons whose identity is uncertain as well as those having committed an offence against the deceased and the members of his family cannot take as beneficiaries. A child who is yet to be born can, however, take as long as he is born alive.

9. Authority (Court, Notarial or Other)

Devolution upon succession is one of those juridical procedures deemed incontestable in the Czech Republic. The authority having jurisdiction over devolution upon succession, on the basis of the deceased's domicile or residence, is the Regional Court (*Tribunal de Grandes Instances*). The court, however, does not actually undertake, barring a few exceptions, the measures relating to the devolution upon succession. The law provides that the court must (it is obligatory) appoint a specific notary from a previously compiled list, the latter having to undertake, as a paid agent of the court, all the necessary measures relating to the devolution upon succession, with the exception of that relating to the actual court decision and juridical assistance carried out abroad. The notary himself then as agent of the court carries out the devolution upon succession, draws up the necessary reports, hears the participants, produces the necessary proofs, writes up the contracts between the heirs and prepares the drafts of all the court decisions and all other documents relating to the devolution. The court only approves the draft decisions drawn up by the notary. If the file on the matter presented by the notary is incomplete, the court can refer the matter back to the notary and request him to get the file in order.

The list from which the notaries are chosen to undertake the measures relating to the devolution upon succession is composed by the President of the respective Appeal Court on the basis of that proposed by the regional Chamber of Notaries each year.

The court can only retract a matter from an appointed notary for one reason, that being for unnecessary delays, despite warnings having been given, in undertaking the necessary juridical procedure. The court will then appoint another notary to carry out the devolution upon succession. The retraction of a matter is not deemed to amount to a judicial decision and the notary cannot challenge it.

10. Invalidity of Will

(a) Defects in form (*see* paragraph 2 *above*) will result in the nullity of the will.

Conditions set out in a will do not have any juridical effect with the exception of those relating to refunding. If the will contains a condition (with the exception of that relating to refunding), the will as such, if it complies with the necessary formalities, is valid and the condition is simply not taken into account.

A will drawn up by a person not having juridical capacity is invalid. A juridical instrument drawn up by a person suffering from a psychiatric disorder such that he is deemed incapable of drawing up such an instrument is also invalid. Those instruments which, either by virtue of their content or their objectives, are contrary to the law, exceed those rights given by law or are contrary to public morality are deemed to be invalid.

(b) The law distinguishes between two kinds of nullity in relation to juridical instruments:

– that of voidability (as explained above, the participants must invoke such nullity otherwise the instrument is deemed valid), which the court is not legally obliged to consider;
– that of absolute nullity, which has a direct effect and which the court is legally obliged to take into consideration.

An example of voidability would involve a will in which the testator disinherits his descendants (who are entitled to a compulsory share). Such a will would be considered valid if the descendants do not invoke the will's nullity. The descendants are free to choose whether to invoke its invalidity or not. The court will only take such nullity into consideration if it has been invoked or if a minor aged between fifteen and eighteen disposed of assets which he had received in another will.

The will is deemed absolutely null and void if, for example:

– the will is not in written form (say, in the case of an oral will);
– the testator did not have juridical capacity;
– the formalities set out under 2(a) *above* have not been complied with;
– the will is a joint will of two spouses or was partially written by someone else.

11. Simultaneous Death

(a) The Civil Code does not have any specific provisions for those cases involving the simultaneous death of persons who are to inherit from each other. Civil law proceeds on the basis that if it is not possible to determine the chronology of the deaths, it would be deemed that all such persons died at the same time and that these persons will not inherit one from the other even if, in other circumstances, they would inherit one from the other (e.g., in the case of a father and son).

(b) The date of death is established in the first instance by the doctor who examines the deceased and draws up the death certificate. The city officials then draw up a further document. If the cause of death is unknown or if there may be foul play involved, an autopsy is carried out. In this case, the determination of the date of death will depend solely on the degree to which the medical causes are established.

The date of death can also be established by the court following its consideration of the matter. If the deceased's death cannot be established by ordinary means and if it is improbable that the deceased was alive up until a certain date, the court can then proceed, upon the request of a person legally interested in the matter, to issue a declaration on the death of the deceased. In its decision, the court will establish either the date of death or the date after which the deceased was no longer alive.

12. Estate Taxes

(a) Yes, with Law No. 357/1992 of the Compendium, as later amended, on inheritance taxes, taxes on donations and taxes on the transfer of immovables applying. Tax applying to inheritances is progressive. It will depend upon the family tie between the heir and the deceased and the value of the property. Those who are in direct line as well as the surviving spouse are not subject to any payment of inheritance tax.

The rate of tax on inheritances applying to those who are related in direct line and the surviving spouse is between 0.5 per cent and 2.5 per cent.

The rate of tax on inheritances applying to those who are collateral relations (e.g., brothers and sisters, nephews and nieces) is between 1.5 per cent to 6 per cent.

For other persons the rate is between 3.5 per cent to 20 per cent.

(b) The basis of assessment according to the law is on the value of the asset acquired by the individual heir with deductions made for the deceased's debts transferred to this heir, the value of those assets which are exonerated from tax, the remuneration of the solicitor as well as inheritance taxes paid abroad. The system relating to the imposition of inheritance tax is founded both upon the nature of the assets inherited and the nationality of the deceased at the time of his death.

If the inheritance consists of immovables located in the Czech Republic, inheritance taxes are imposed and levied in all cases without taking the nationality of the deceased into account, but if the immovables are located abroad, taxes are not imposed or levied on a foreigner. If the deceased was, at the time of his death, a national of the Czech Republic and had his permanent residence there, taxes are imposed on all of his estate located in the Czech Republic and abroad. If the deceased was, at the time of his death, a national of the Czech Republic, but did not have his permanent residence there, inheritance taxes will be imposed only on that part of his estate located in the Czech Republic.

The above stipulations will apply only if an international agreement to which the Czech Republic is a party does not provide otherwise.

(c) The taxes are always paid by the heir benefiting from all or a part of the inheritance.

13. Administration of Estates

(a)–(c) Up until the devolution upon succession has been concluded, all the heirs who have not renounced their inheritance are deemed co-owners of all of the assets forming part of the estate. All the heirs decide upon the administration of the estate. In the course of the devolution upon succession, however, the heirs cannot freely dispose of the assets. According to the Civil Code, the heirs can only sell the assets forming part of the inheritance or take measures other than those falling within the framework of an ordinary administration with the consent of the court.

The heirs can decide that only one of the heirs will administer the assets comprising the inheritance within the framework of an ordinary administration. The heirs can conclude such an agreement at any time, despite the devolution upon succession.

If the public interest or that of one of the participants requires it, the court can, even of its own motion, appoint an administrator of the estate or of a part of it within the framework of what are referred to as urgent measures. The appointment of an administrator would be deemed particularly appropriate where the deceased was a businessman, if the business is to be devolved and the heirs have no experience in managing a business.

The administrator of the succession will undertake, in the course of the devolution upon succession, those acts necessary to maintain the value of the assets comprising the estate within the time-period specified by the court. According to the Civil Code, the administrator must carry out his role in a professional manner and is accountable for losses caused by his non-observance of those obligations laid down by the law or established by the court. The court has the right to demand that the administrator provide it with current reports on his activities.

Upon the conclusion of the devolution upon succession, the administrator will provide the heirs, by way of the court, with a final report on his activities, upon which basis the court will determine his remuneration. The activities of the administrator come within the jurisdiction of the court, which has the right, on grounds of sufficient importance, to remove him from his post.

(d) The Civil Code proceeds from the principle that the estate is acquired on the death of the deceased – the concept of *hereditas iacens* is unknown. At the time of the deceased's death, the heirs are unknown in effect and are only deemed known once the devolution upon succession has been concluded. Until the devolution upon succession has been validly concluded, the estate is represented by all the heirs apart from those who have renounced their inheritance.

(e) The heirs are the owners of the deceased's assets from the instant he dies with retroactive effect. If there is a sole heir, he will acquire all the assets. Where there is more than one heir, they can come to an agreement on the succession themselves. If the agreement is not contrary to the law or public morals, the court will give its approval to it. If the heirs do not come to any agreement or if the agreement is not approved by the court, the court will confirm the acquisition of the inheritance in accordance with each heir's share of it. The heirs' title to the assets is established by way of the decision by the court having jurisdiction, with such decision relating either to its approval of the agreement on the succession or the acquisition of the inheritance.

The Civil Code does not deal with acceptance of the inheritance upon the limitation of the heir's liability for the debts of the estate to the amount of the net assets he actually receives (*acceptation sous bénéfice d'inventaire*).

(f) The creditors are parties to the devolution upon succession only to the extent that their debts remain unsettled. The creditor claims that owed to him and the heirs will make a pronouncement as to whether they recognize this or not. If they do recognize the creditor's claim, it is included in the liabilities of the estate and in general the principle by which the heirs are liable for the estate's liabilities in proportion to the assets they inherit is adhered to. If the heirs do not recognize the claim, the creditor has the possibility of having his right vindicated by way of independent legal procedure.

(g) The Civil Code does not recognize the notion of testamentary executor. The heirs take possession of the deceased's assets on the basis of the appropriate court decision.

14. Domicile/Nationality

(a) The nationality of the deceased is important as regards the devolution upon succession. If at the time of his death the deceased was a Czech national, it will necessarily be the Czech court that has jurisdiction. If the deceased was a national of another State, the court having jurisdiction is determined on the basis of private international law. According to Czech law, jurisdiction is established foremost on the basis of an international agreement, should such exist. If such an agreement does not exist, reliance is had on the law on private international law and procedure.

(b) Local jurisdiction is established on the basis of the domicile or the residence of the deceased at the time of his death and not that at the time the will was drawn up.

Where the deceased has not left any assets, devolution upon succession as such will not proceed, the procedure being suspended due to the lack of such assets. However, if the matter concerns assets located abroad, the Czech court will only proceed as regards the devolution upon succession if the assets are delivered up to the Czech authorities or if the foreign State recognizes the juridical effects of decisions rendered by the Czech juridical authorities.

SECTION B – APPLICABLE PROCEDURE WHERE FOREIGN ELEMENT/S ARE INVOLVED

1. Jurisdiction

(a) Jurisdiction over devolution upon succession rests with the Regional Court (*Tribunal de Grandes Instances*) in whose jurisdiction the deceased had his last domicile and if he did not have domicile, or such domicile cannot be established, the court in whose jurisdiction the deceased had his last temporary residence. If such a court cannot be determined, jurisdiction rests with the court in whose jurisdiction the deceased's property is located. If there are several courts having local jurisdiction, the court having taken the first measure in relation to the devolution upon succession will be deemed that with which jurisdiction rests.

(b) Where the deceased was a national of another State at the time of his death and the succession takes place in the Czech Republic, jurisdiction as regards the devolution upon succession will rest with the Czech court (if international agreements to which the Czech Republic is a party do not provide otherwise) when:

- the State of which the deceased was a national does not confer jurisdiction over the succession of the estates of Czech nationals to the Czech courts or it does not give legal force to the decisions of such courts or it refuses to deal with the above-mentioned succession relating to its national or makes no pronouncement upon it;
- if the deceased had his domicile in the Czech Republic and the heir who resides there requests it;
- in all cases, immovables are located in the Czech Republic (*lex rei sitae*).

(c) *See* paragraph 1(a) *above.*

2. Applicable Law

The Czech court always has jurisdiction for the devolution upon succession when the deceased was a Czech national at the time of his death. The Czech court will apply Czech law (i.e., the law of the State of which the deceased was a national at the time of his death is applied). However, if the matter concerns assets located abroad, the Czech court will only proceed as regards the devolution upon succession if the assets are delivered up to the Czech authorities or if the foreign State recognizes the juridical effects of decisions rendered by the Czech juridical authorities.

Where the deceased at the time of his death was the national of another State and the Czech court has jurisdiction, the Czech court will apply the substantive law of the State of which the deceased was a national at the time of his death and the local procedural law (that is to say, the Civil Code in force in the State of which the deceased was a national at the time of his death and the Code of Civil Procedure in force in the Czech Republic). Renvoi would be accepted if it is in line with a reasonable settlement of the issue.

3. Foreign Succession/Inheritance Orders

(a)–(c) Issues relating to the validation of foreign decisions are regulated by the law on private international law and procedure. Article 63 of this law provides that decisions of judicial authorities in foreign States, as well as foreign juridical settlements and foreign notarial instruments, are enforceable in the Czech Republic if they have, according to the attestation of the respective foreign authority, taken effect and have been validated by the Czech authorities. The law also provides that the validation of foreign decisions in matters concerning property does not require a special decision. A foreign decision is deemed validated by the fact that a Czech authority takes it into account in the same way as it would a decision emanating from the Czech authority.

Upon the conditions set out in the above-mentioned law, it is even possible to execute a foreign decision on rights of property in the Czech Republic if the execution order has been issued by a Czech court.

International Succession

(b) Taking the above into consideration, the foreign heir must present the respective document to the bank, with an authorized translation into Czech, proving that he has acquired the assets (bank account, etc.).

4. Two or More Succession or Probate Orders

See 3(a) & (b) *above.*

5. Assets

The local court can assume jurisdiction if there are no assets in the jurisdiction (*see* 14(b) *supra*).

6. Expert Evidence

(a)–(b) If the Czech court is to apply the substantive law of another State, it will request, by way of the Ministry of Justice of the Czech Republic, the relevant legislative provisions, which will also deal with issues relating to the validity of a will drawn up in another State. There is no obligation to obtain any particular form of evidence from a foreign legal expert.

7. Unity of Succession

The legislation of the Czech Republic is based on the principle of the unity of succession. At the time of death the heir takes on all the rights and obligations of the deceased. At the time of death, all the rights and obligations attaching to the patrimony pass from the deceased to the heir.

8. Formalities

The formalities concerning the execution of a will drawn up abroad are the same as those relating to the execution of a will drawn up locally. As regards formalities relating to wills drawn up abroad, *see* 10(a) *below.*

9. Legislation

The Czech Republic has only ratified the *1973 Hague Convention on the International Administration of Successions.* The Convention was published under Law No. 218/1995 of the Compendium.

10. Wills

If the international agreements to which the Czech Republic is a party do not stipulate otherwise (and if the foreign law is not contrary to Czech public policy), the following stipulations are applicable:

(a) The formalities of a will must comply with the law of the State of which the testator was a national at the time it was drawn up; it is sufficient, however, that a will complies with the law of the State in which it was drawn up. The same also applies as regards the formalities concerning the revocation of a will.

(b) This is governed by the legislation on private international law and the procedural law of the State of which the deceased was a national at the time he manifested his intent.

(c)–(d) The law of succession is that of the State of which the deceased was a national at the time of his death.

(e) Capacity as regards drawing up or revoking a will as well as the effects arising from lack of intent and its manifestations are governed by the legislation on private international law and the procedural law of the State of which the deceased was a national at the time he manifested his intent. The same law is decisive in determining what other legal provisions apply in the event of death.

(f) *See* (a) and (b) *above*.

(g) The Civil Code of the Czech Republic does not recognize the concept of 'legatee' and therefore this question is not applicable.

(h) As for the amendment and revocation of wills, the above applies.

(i) The protection of that part of the inheritance subject to compulsory shares comes under the substantive law on succession and the answer given at (c) therefore applies.

11. Domicile/Nationality

(a) The domicile or the residence of the deceased at the time of his death will determine the competence of the Regional Court for the regulation of the succession, that is to say which of the Regional Courts has jurisdiction. What is important for determining the jurisdiction of the Czech court is the nationality (the citizenship) of the deceased at the time of his death. As regards the issues relating to the will, *see above*.

(b) The domicile of the beneficiary is irrelevant.

International Succession

(c) *See* Section A3(b) and *above* at 1(a). If the deceased at the time of his death was a national of, for example, the Czech Republic and Germany, the Czech courts will always have jurisdiction provided that the deceased left assets in the Czech Republic. If the deceased only left assets in Germany, *see* paragraph 2 *above*. If the deceased had several nationalities but none of these was that of the Czech Republic, *see* paragraph 1(b) above. If these conditions are not fulfilled, the Czech court does not have jurisdiction as regards the devolution upon succession.

12. Taxation

The nationals of the Czech Republic and those of other States have taxes imposed in the same manner.

Denmark

Prepared by: Hans Henrik SKJØDT
Advokaterne Amagertorv 11

      11 Amagertorv
      DK-1160
      Copenhagen K
      Denmark
Tel.:   + 45 33 12 60 40
Fax: + 45 33 14 19 33
E-mail: hhs@amagertorv11.dk
WWW: www.amagertorv11.dk

SECTION A – BRIEF SURVEY OF THE LOCAL SYSTEM

1. Type of System

(a) The legal system of Denmark is a civil law system.

(b) The law of Denmark only covers Denmark as such and not the Faroer Islands or Greenland.

2. Wills

(a) In general, wills must be in writing and either signed or acknowledged before a notary public or in the presence of two witnesses. The testator will usually sign the will but this is not a requirement.

In the case of wills executed in the presence of witnesses, the two witnesses must be present at the time of execution. The witnesses must immediately endorse the will in writing stating their position, private address, the time and place and whether they were present at the execution or acknowledgement of the will according to the testator's wishes. The witnesses must also state whether the testator was capable of acting sensibly and whether there are other circumstances which may be of importance for the validity of the will.

The *Inheritance Act* also includes rules regarding extraordinary forms of wills. In certain situations, an oral or a holographic will is acknowledged. Oral wills are acknowledged if illness or an emergency prevents the execution of a will before a notary or before witnesses and in this case, wills can be communicated orally in the presence of two witnesses. The witnesses must as soon as possible record the will in writing and sign the document. A holographic will is acknowledged in the same circumstances, i.e., if it is established in this way due to illness or an emergency. The holographic will must be written by the testator in his own hand and cannot be typewritten.

Extraordinary wills will lapse if, within a three month period, there have been no circumstances preventing the execution of the will in accordance with the ordinary rules for making ordinary wills.

No special rules apply in respect of wills executed by military servicemen or seamen.

(b) *i.* A will may be revoked in its entirety by execution of a new will or by the testator otherwise clearly indicating that the will shall no longer be valid. Revocation of the will may therefore be made without observing any particular form or procedure.

A revocation in part of a will is commonly made by the execution of a codicil in which it is clearly stated one or more provisions of the main will are terminated. Revocation in part can also be effected in a more formless manner, e.g., by the testator deleting one or more provisions in the will and at the same time make a written certification in the margin that the provision has been deleted by him. If the testator wishes to combine the revocation with a new provision, this, however, will require a codicil to the will which must be executed before a notary or in the presence of two witnesses.

If the testator executes a new will without indicating that a previous will is revoked, the rule of presumption is that the previous will has been terminated. If a codicil includes provisions which clearly conflict with provisions of the main will, the provision of the codicil will take precedence to the will.

ii. There is no rule of presumption or other rule applying in the event of a testator getting married subsequent to making a will. However, the surviving spouse would have a good chance of claiming full or partial revocation if it is obvious from the will and other circumstances show that a marriage was not foreseen. There is, however, no case law on this.

If a spouse during the marriage has executed a will with the other spouse as beneficiary, the will will in general be considered as having been revoked in the event of separation or divorce. The same rule applies if a will has been made with a fiancé(e) as beneficiary and the engagement is subsequently terminated.

iii. It is assumed that the revocation of a will may itself be revoked in a formless manner with the effect that the revoked provision applies once again. The solution in this case is not absolutely clear in the absence of case law. The testator is in this event best advised to execute a new will.

3. Intestacy

(a) Intestate succession is governed by the *Inheritance Act*. If the intestate leaves a spouse (or a registered partner), one-third of the deceased's estate will go to the spouse (or a registered partner) whereas the remaining two-thirds will be distributed equally between the children of the deceased ('heirs of the body'). Heirs of the body also include adopted children. If the deceased leaves no heirs of the body, the entire estate will be left to the surviving spouse.

If the deceased does not leave a surviving spouse (or a registered partner), his children, i.e., heirs of the body, will receive the entire estate in equal shares. This means that if one of such children has predeceased the testator, his children will succeed to the share of the predeceased child.

If the intestate leaves no spouse (or a registered partner) or heirs of the body, the entire estate will go to the parents. If one of the parents have predeceased the intestate, the deceased parent's (other) children succeed in that share. If the predeceased parent leaves no (other) children, the other parent (or his other children) will succeed into the entire estate.

If there are no surviving relatives in the line of parents/their heirs of the body, the estate will go to the grandparents or their heirs of the body. If there are no such heirs, the estate will go to the state.

(b) There is no difference in the division of the estate on intestacy between movables and immovables.

4. Freedom of Testation

(a) The testator is free to dispose of his assets unless he leaves a surviving spouse (or a registered partner) and/or children. If the testator leaves such heirs, he may freely dispose of only 50 per cent of his estate.

(b) Contracts of inheritance are acknowledged only in two forms:
– an heir may contract with the testator (with or without compensation/advance distribution) to renounce his right of inheritance, and
– a testator may undertake not to revoke a will or to write a will.

5. Maintenance

There are no specific rules relating to maintenance, but the surviving spouse has a right of priority to succeed to the estate of the deceased if the estate is of 'insignificant value'. The surviving spouse may claim ordinary furniture, working utilities and other chattels for the maintenance of the home or his occupation even if the value exceeds the inheritance and a claim to communal property due to the spouse (within certain limits).

6. Community Property Between Husband and Wife

(a) The statutory rule applying in Denmark is that there exists absolute community of property between spouses. Spouses may, however, execute a marriage contract stating that another division of property shall apply between them.

International Succession

If full community of property applies in a marriage, the surviving spouse has a claim for 50 per cent of the total assets of the spouses. The other 50 per cent constitute the deceased's estate which is distributed according to a will or the rules governing succession on intestacy.

(b) If the spouses have executed a marriage contract establishing a different division of property, this contract will be of decisive importance for the amount in the estate left by the deceased.

If the marriage contract states that the spouses shall have separate properties (no community of property), all of the deceased's assets will constitute the estate.

A marriage contract may also state that the deceased's assets are subject to full community of property whereas the surviving spouse's assets shall be his separate property. In this event, the surviving spouse keeps his separate property and has a claim for 50 per cent of the deceased's assets by virtue of the marriage. In this case only 50 per cent of the deceased's assets will constitute the estate.

7. Gifts (*Inter Vivos*)

(a) Gifts to an heir prior to death are not set off against the heir's inheritance unless a contract of inheritance has been made. It should be noted that this requires that the gift had not been given on the death bed as such gifts must be made by way of a will.

(b) Not applicable.

8. Capacity

(a) A testator must be of full age (eighteen) or be married. The latter is only relevant for females as dispensation for marriage is never given to males below the age of eighteen.

(b) Individuals witnessing a will must be no less than eighteen years of age and be of a sound mind and be impartial. If a witness has been included in the will as beneficiary or the witness is a close relative of the testator, he is considered impartial unless the inclusion of the witness as a beneficiary is insignificant and has been made on reasonable grounds that is, that they are being objective and not biased because of the fact that they are beneficiaries or relatives.

(c) There are no restrictions on the capacity of beneficiaries.

9. Authority (Court, Notarial or Other)

A grant of probate from the court is always the first step regardless of whether the estate is administered by the heirs or by an administrator. A petition must in any case be filed to the Probate Court and the court will examine if all formalities are fulfilled. The grant of probate is necessary to give the heirs or the administrator authority to dispose in all aspects.

10. Invalidity of Will

(a) A number of defects may cause a will to be invalid. These defects can relate to both form and procedure, lack of capacity, deficiencies relating to the declaration of the testator's intent, or defects in content or authority. A testator must at the execution be of a sound mind. A will may furthermore be considered void if it is established that it has been produced by duress, improper influence or certain forms of abuse.

(b) Most defects cause the will to be declared voidable. A few deficiencies may even lead to the will being considered non-existent (conflict with statute, etc.).

11. Simultaneous Death

If two individuals who are each entitled to inherit from the other have died without it being possible to establish which of the two predeceased the other, neither of them will succeed to the estate of the other.

12. Estate Taxes

(a) The *Inheritance Tax Act 1995* with later changes governs the taxation of estates passing on death and *inter vivos* gifts.

(b) In the case of a deceased domiciled in Denmark, the deceased's worldwide estate is liable to Danish inheritance tax. Where the deceased was neither domiciled nor deemed to be domiciled in Denmark for inheritance tax purposes, only Danish real property or Danish assets as such (if covered by Danish probate jurisdiction) are liable to inheritance tax.

(c) Inheritance tax is charged by reference to the estate. In general inheritance tax is charged at 15 per cent of the net assets less an allowance of 224,600 DKK (2003, indexed) and less the inheritance to a surviving spouse. However, if the deceased leaves non-related or distantly related beneficiaries, a surcharge of 25 per cent applies on those beneficiaries' part of the estate less a proportion of the 15 per cent tax, which gives a total charge of 36.25 per cent on this part of the estate.

13. Administration of Estates

(a) Estates are administered by the heirs or by an administrator appointed either in the will or by the court. The heirs may themselves administer the estate if all the heirs agree to this and it is not prohibited by the will. In all other cases, the estate will have to be administered by an administrator. If the will has not appointed an administrator, the administrator is appointed by the Probate Court.

It must be noted that certain estates are not subject to administration. A surviving spouse in a marriage subject to full community of property is entitled to succeed to the deceased's property without administration if the spouses leave children of the marriage. At the time of death of the longest living spouse or if the spouse remarries, the total joint estate of the two spouses will be subject to administration and distributed between the heirs.

(b) Reports on the administration of the estate have to be submitted by the heirs or by the administrator to the Probate Court and the local tax authorities for inheritance tax purposes and income tax purposes.

(c) All estates are subject to supervision but this supervision is more detailed for estates which are handled by an administrator. In relation to these estates the Probate Court will make sample checks of documents, correspondence, etc.

(d) If the heirs administer the estate themselves, they must in principle agree on all transactions. If no such agreement can be reached, the administration of the estate must be passed to an administrator.

In relation to estates handled by an administrator, all heirs have a right to take part in a decision as to dispositions made by the estate. This does not, however, apply to beneficiaries who are subject to a fixed sum or a certain specific chattel from the estate; such beneficiaries have no right of voting in the estate.

(e) The assets are formally transferred to the heirs who themselves administer the estate according to a court order. It is then left to the heirs to distribute the assets between themselves as they see fit.

In relation to other estates, assets are transferred to the beneficiaries once the administrator no longer requires them for the purpose of the administration of the estate. A transfer deed is required in respect of real property; other assets may be transferred by whatever normal manner of transfer applies to each particular asset.

(f) All estates must immediately publish a notification in the public gazette (*Statstidende*) whereby the creditors are notified to register their claim with the estate within eight weeks of the date of publication of the notification. At the same time, the estate must make a separate written notification to all known creditors domiciled outside Denmark advising them of the time limit for registration of a claim.

All creditors who have registered a claim are then paid by the heirs/the administrator provided the claim can be recognized by the administrator. If the estate is handled by the heirs themselves and in the event of the heirs having already depleted the assets, the heirs are personally, directly and jointly liable for payment of the creditors.

(g) *See* 13(a) *above.*

14. Domicile/Nationality

(a) Under Danish law, the law of the deceased's domicile at the time of death is considered to govern the distribution of all assets. However, it is recognized that the heirs (all of them) are entitled to decide that Danish law is applicable.

(b) If the deceased was resident in Denmark, the local court will give an order of probate even if the deceased had no assets in Denmark.

SECTION B – APPLICABLE LAW/PROCEDURE WHERE FOREIGN ELEMENT/S ARE INVOLVED

1. Jurisdiction

(a) The local court will hold that it has jurisdiction if the deceased at the time of death was resident in Denmark. A Danish Probate Court may also become competent following a resolution from the Ministry of Justice if the deceased did not have residence in Denmark and subject to the requirement either that:

– the deceased was a Danish citizen or had another 'special connection' to Denmark and leaves assets which are not included under probate outside Denmark; or
– if the deceased leaves assets in Denmark which are not included under probate outside Denmark.

(b) The sole fact that a person who dies abroad leaves assets in Denmark does not make Danish courts competent. It is without relevance whether such assets are constituted by real property or chattels.

As mentioned in 1(a) *above*, the Danish courts may be made competent with respect to assets left in Denmark but only if these assets are not included under probate outside Denmark.

(c) If local jurisdiction applies, the local court covering the area where the deceased was resident has jurisdiction. The Probate Court may refer the matter to another Danish Probate Court if it is found to be more appropriate.

2. Applicable Law

The Probate Court will apply the Danish rules relating to administration whereas the rules governing succession are decided according to the place where the deceased was domiciled at the time of death. There is no difference between movable and immovable assets in this respect. *Lex situs* does not apply, but the foreign court will have to request the assistance of the Danish Court to effect transfer.

189

International Succession

3. Foreign Succession/Inheritance Orders

(a) Foreign orders are usually acknowledged in Denmark. The foreign administrator who can establish his authority to dispose of the assets of the estate according to his home state rules will be able to ask the Danish Probate Court to release the assets to him. The Probate Court will require a banker's guarantee for any estate tax which may apply in respect of real property.

(b) An order from the local Danish Probate Court must be obtained to give a foreign authority/administrator possession of assets of the deceased and to give a foreign succession effect.

(c) A petition to the Probate Court must be filed by the foreign authority or administrator. There are no special formalities concerning documentation of the foreign succession or inheritance order and the petition is just prepared as a normal letter explaining the circumstances.

4. Two or More Succession or Probate Orders

In the event of there being an application before either the court or the relevant authority in the local country for an order of succession or inheritance, and a foreign order already exists in one or more foreign countries, the order of the country of domicile prevails.

5. Assets

See 1(a) *above*.

6. Expert Evidence

(a) If administration of the estate is to be made in Denmark according to foreign inheritance law (*see* 2 *above*), it might be necessary to obtain evidence from a foreign lawyer regarding a foreign will or regarding the inheritance laws of a foreign state.

(b) Such evidence can be by way of affidavit without the necessity of appearance in court.

7. Unity of Succession

This is recognized as the basic principle in Denmark.

8. Formalities

A will executed outside Denmark is acknowledged if it meets the formality requirements either of the laws at the place of execution (*locus regit actum*) or the laws at
the place of the testator's domicile at the time of execution or the laws at the place
of domicile at the time of death. It is therefore without relevance whether the
formality requirements in the testator's last country of domicile are met.

9. Legislation

*The 1961 Hague Convention on the Conflicts of Laws Relating to the Form of
Testamentary Dispositions* is applicable.

10. Wills

(a) Validity requirements must be established according to the rules in the country
where the will was executed or according to the law of the testator's domicile at the
time of execution or the law in the country of domicile at the time of death. This
means that if a person executed a will with only one witness in a place where two
witnesses are required, the will would be valid if he died in a country where only
one witness was required.

(b) As a main rule, a will will be interpreted according to the rules of the country of
domicile at the time of execution of the will.

(c) The law of the country of domicile at the time of death.

(d) The law of the country of domicile at the time of death.

(e) The law of the country of domicile at the time of death.

(f) The law of the country of domicile at the time of execution of the will.

(g) The law of the country of domicile at the time of execution of the will.

(h) The law of the state of domicile at the time of any amendment, revocation or
revival.

(i) This is applicable both for movable and immovable property.

11. Domicile/Nationality

(a) *See* 10 *above*.

International Succession

(b) Not relevant.

(c) The Danish rules of competence (extended concept of domicile) usually apply. Otherwise, it may be examined whether the deceased had any particular connection in respect of the domicile to any particular country.

12. Taxation

There is no difference between estate taxes for a non-resident deceased/heir and those for a local deceased/heir.

England and Wales

Revised by: John WOOD (partner) Herbert SMITH
Based on a previous version by John WOOD and Clive CUTBILL

Address: Exchange House
         Primrose Street
         London EC2A 2HS
Tel.:   +44 171 374 8000
Fax: +44 171 496 0043

Section A – Brief Survey of the Local System

1. Type of System

(a) The legal system of England and Wales is a common law system.

(b) It should be appreciated that the law of England and Wales is distinct from the law of Scotland and the law of Northern Ireland. There is no general concept of 'the law of the United Kingdom'.

2. Wills

(a) In general, wills must be in writing and signed by the testator in the presence of two witnesses who should sign in the presence of each other and in the presence of the testator. The will need not be dated but, to avoid difficulties in proving the date upon which it was executed (in order to establish which is the last will), it is desirable that it should be dated. Witnesses must be of full age (at least eighteen years old) and capacity. If the will is witnessed by a beneficiary or the spouse of a beneficiary, the will is valid but the gift to the beneficiary is ineffective.

The law of England and Wales does not draw any distinction between holographic and typewritten wills. Holographic wills must, therefore, be executed in the normal fashion. There is no requirement for wills to be executed before a notary or other legal authority; so long as the witnesses are of legal capacity and full age, that is sufficient. There is no concept of a 'death-bed will'. The law of England and Wales does, however, recognize the concept of *donationes mortis causa*.

Wills may generally only be made by persons of full age (eighteen years or over).

Despite the above, by statute, soldiers in actual military service (including members of the Air Force) at the time they make their will, mariners or seamen at sea, whether in the military or merchant marine and 'any member of Her Majesty's naval or marine forces so circumstanced that if he were a soldier he would be in actual military service', even though not at sea, may make what is known as a 'privileged will' (for which there are no formalities required).

In addition to the formalities expressly required by English law, a will is treated under English law as properly executed if its execution conforms to the internal law in force in the territory where it was executed, or in the territory where, at the time of its execution or of the testator's death, he was domiciled or had his habitual residence, or in a state of which at either of those times he was a national.

(b) *i.* Wills may be amended by codicil. A codicil should be executed in the same manner as a will. A will may be revoked in whole or in part in any manner which would be sufficient to amend the will. Thus, the deletion of a part of a will (but not all of it) which is signed by the testator and two witnesses, each in the presence of the other, will be sufficient to revoke the part of the will deleted but leave the remainder standing. Similarly, a codicil may revoke a part of a will whilst leaving the remainder standing. A will may also be revoked by destruction by the testator or by another person acting at his direction and in his presence.

A subsequent validly executed will revokes a prior will to the extent that it is inconsistent with it. However, unless the subsequent will contains general words of revocation (such as 'I hereby revoke all former testamentary dispositions made by me'), it will not revoke a prior will to the extent that any part of that prior will is not superseded by the subsequent will.

ii. Marriage automatically revokes a will made prior to marriage unless the will is expressed to be made in contemplation of marriage to a particular person. It is not a pre-requisite that that marriage is solemnized, either within a particular period or at all, for a will made in contemplation of marriage to be valid. It is, however, sometimes the case that wills made in contemplation of marriage are expressed to be effective only if the marriage takes place either at all or within a specified period.

Following a divorce any appointment of the former spouse as an executor or as a beneficiary takes effect as though the former spouse had died on the date of the final dissolution of the marriage (decree absolute). This will not be the case if the will clearly expresses a contrary intention.

iii. A will which has been revoked may be revived by a properly executed codicil clearly indicating an intention to revive that will.

(c) Generally where a testamentary gift is made to a legatee who has died at the time of the testator's death the gift fails (the 'doctrine of lapse').

There is, however, a statutory exception from this doctrine with regard to gifts to children, who predecease the testator. Section 33 of the *Wills Act 1837* (as amended) operates to automatically add a substitutionary gift in favour of the child's issue, where the child predeceases the testator. The gift of real or personal property to a child, or other issue of the testator does not lapse if any issue of the devisee or legatee are living at the death of the testator. The gift takes effect as if the death of the beneficiary under the will happened immediately after the death of the testator.

The statutory rule deals with both 'single gifts' and 'class gifts'.

i. Single Gifts – If the will makes a gift to a child or remoter descendant of the testator, and the donee dies before the testator leaving issue at the testator's death, such issue takes the gift in the manner described below.

ii. Class Gifts – If the will makes a gift to a class consisting of the children or remoter descendants of the testator, and a member of the class dies before the testator leaving issue living at the testator's death, those issues are included in the class and taken in the manner described below.

If the issue becomes entitled by virtue of the above provisions they take 'through all degrees, according to their stock, in equal shares if more than one, any gift or share which their parent would have taken and so that no issue shall take whose parent is living at the testator's death and so capable of taking'. A person conceived before the testator's death and born living thereafter is to be taken to have been living at the testator's death.

The section is not dependent upon the issue coming of age – their interests vest immediately, however young they may be and however great the value of the property.

The section does not apply if contrary intention appears in the will. Practitioners will normally include express substitutional provisions in wills both for clarity and to provide a suitable vesting age for minor children.

3. Intestacy

(a) Intestate succession is governed by the *Administration of Estates Act 1925* as amended.

– If the intestate leaves a spouse who survives him by a period of twenty-eight days, the spouse will take:
  – the deceased's personal chattels (which are defined as: 'carriages, horses, stable furniture and effects (not used for business purposes), motor cars and accessories (not used for business purposes), garden effects, domestic animals, plate, plated articles, linen, china, glass, books, pictures, prints, furniture, jewellery, articles of household or personal use or ornament, musical and scientific instruments and apparatus, wines, liquors and consumable stores, but not any chattels used at the death of the intestate for business purposes nor money or securities for money';
  – a 'fixed net sum' with interest from the date of death; and
  – an interest in the residuary estate of the deceased.

The size of the fixed net sum and the interest in the residuary estate will vary depending upon the other relatives who survive the intestate.

– If the intestate leaves issue (i.e., children, grandchildren or remoter descendants) who attain the age of eighteen years or marry under that age, the surviving spouse's fixed net sum is presently £125,000 although the sum is increased periodically by statutory instrument. The spouse's interest in the balance of the residuary estate will be a life interest in one-half.

- If the intestate leaves no issue but, in addition to the spouse, there is: a parent, a brother or sister of the whole blood who attains eighteen or marries under that age; or issue of a brother or sister of the whole blood who attain eighteen or marry under that age, the fixed net sum will be greater. It is presently £200,000. Instead of a life interest in one-half of the residue of the estate, the surviving spouse will take one-half of the residue absolutely (i.e., both capital and income).
- If the intestate leaves no issue who attain the age of eighteen years or marry under that age and no relatives of the type referred to in the immediately preceding paragraph, the surviving spouse will take the entire residuary estate.

The extent of the surviving spouse's eventual interest cannot necessarily be quantified at the death of the intestate as it may not then be apparent whether issue or other relatives will survive to attain eighteen or marry under that age.

A surviving spouse who has a life interest only in part of the residuary estate may make a formal election to receive a capital value calculated in accordance with a detailed statutory formula instead.

- Where there is no surviving spouse or the surviving spouse dies within the twenty-eight day survivorship period, the entire residuary estate of the intestate is distributed between the relatives who would have taken subject to the surviving spouse's interest, had there been a surviving spouse.
- If there is no surviving spouse at the deceased's death (or the spouse survives the deceased but dies within twenty-eight days of the deceased) and there are no other relatives of the categories referred to above, the property 'escheats' to the state as *bona vacantia*. There is a procedure for more distant relatives and other persons who were dependent upon the intestate (whether or not related to him) and other persons for whom the intestate might reasonably have been expected to make provision to obtain discretionary payments from the state out of an estate which has escheated as *bona vacantia*.

Under English law an adopted child is the child of his adoptive parents and not of his natural parents. A legitimated child (and any other person taking by virtue of their relationship to a legitimated child) is entitled to take an interest on intestacy as if the legitimated person had been born legitimate. Illegitimate children are regarded as the children of both of their parents solely for the purposes of their inheritance (or the inheritance of their issue) from their parents or for the inheritance of both of their parents from them under the intestacy rules.

Property which passes to children or remoter issue under an intestacy is held on what are known as 'the statutory trusts'. These provide for the property to be held in trust in equal shares for the children of the deceased who were living at his death and who attain eighteen or marry under that age. If a child of the deceased predeceases him but leaves issue who attain eighteen or marry under that age, those issue take, in equal shares *per stirpes*, the property which the deceased child would have taken. This distribution works through all degrees of issue on the basis that no issue can take if his parent was alive at the date of the deceased's death. Thus:

- where the deceased (D) dies intestate leaving two adult children (A and B) and grandchildren (E and F) (who attain eighteen or marry under that age and who are the children of his deceased child (C), who had attained eighteen or married under that age) that part of the estate destined for D's children and issue would be divided:

one-third to A; one-third to B; one-sixth to E; and one-sixth to F.

Note that if C had not attained eighteen or married under that age, his children, E and F, would have had no entitlement to share in D's estate and the portion passing to the issue would have been taken equally by A and B alone.

(b) There is no difference under English law in the manner in which movable and immovable estate devolves on an intestacy (*see* 14(a) *below*).

4. Freedom of Testation

(a) There are no compulsory shares which must be left to any person under English law. Under the *Inheritance (Provision for Family and Dependants) Act 1975*, as amended, the wife or husband of the deceased; a person who was living in the same household as the deceased 'as the husband or wife' of the deceased at the date of the deceased's death and had been doing so for a period of at least two years ending with the death; a former wife or former husband of the deceased who has not remarried; a child of the deceased; any person (not being a child of the deceased) who, in the case of any marriage to which the deceased was at any time a party, was treated by the deceased as a child of the family in relation to that marriage; and any person (not being a person mentioned above) who immediately before the death of the deceased was being maintained, either wholly or partly, by the deceased may apply to the court for an order for 'reasonable financial provision' out of the deceased's estate if, by reason of the deceased's will or intestacy, he or she does not receive reasonable financial provision.

In the case of a spouse only, reasonable financial provisions means such financial provision as it would be reasonable in all the circumstances of the case for the person to receive, whether or not the provision is required for his or her maintenance; in the case of any other applicant, including a cohabitant, it means such financial provision as it would be reasonable in all the circumstances of the case for the applicant to receive for his or her maintenance.

(b) *i.* A contract of inheritance is contractually binding on the deceased and a disappointed party may sue the estate to receive that which the deceased contracted to leave. However, a contract of inheritance confers no rights *in rem* and the only remedy available to the disappointed party will be a claim in damages. To the extent that the estate is insufficient to meet such a claim, for example, because the deceased dissipated his assets at any time prior to death, the disappointed party will have no further remedy.

   ii. *See* 4(b)(i) *above.*

   iii. English law recognizes the concept of a 'mutual will'. If two individuals agree that they will each leave their property to the other on the first death and that on the second death their joint estates (including what the survivor has inherited from the other) will pass in a particular way; or if they both agree that they will each leave their separate estates to the same beneficiaries, the wills may be regarded as 'mutual wills'. If wills are mutual wills, after the death of the first person to die the other is unable validly to change his will. If he purports to do so, the recipient under the revised will takes the property as trustee for the recipient under the initial will.

In order to establish that wills are 'mutual' it is necessary to show that the two testators intended that the survivor of them should be unable to change his will after the first death. Such evidence would normally be found either in the wills themselves or in a separate agreement entered into between the testators at the time of their execution. In the absence of evidence of an intention that the wills should be 'mutual' the mere fact that they are in identical form (e.g., leaving everything to the surviving spouse and, on the second death, to their children) will not be sufficient to establish mutuality.

5. Maintenance

See 4(a) *above*.

6. Community of Property between Husband and Wife

(a) English law has no concept of community of property. However, if the matrimonial domicile of the deceased recognizes community of property, English law will only treat that part of the deceased's estate which the matrimonial domicile regarded as his or hers to dispose as forming part of his or her estate.

(b) Property may be held jointly, either as 'tenants in common' or 'beneficial joint tenants'. This is a trust relationship and the co-owner need not be the spouse. Where property is held as tenants in common, the deceased's share of the jointly owned property will form part of his or her estate and pass accordingly; where property is held as joint tenants, the deceased's share will accrue automatically to the survivor(s) on death.

7. Gifts (*Inter Vivos*)

(a) Gifts to an heir prior to death are not set off against the heir's inheritance under a will, unless the will specifies to the contrary. The intestacy rules have been changed so that it is no longer necessary to bring prior gifts into account on an intestacy.

(b) Not applicable.

8. Capacity

(a) As indicated in 2(a) *above*, except in the case of privileged wills, a testator must be of full age (eighteen); marital status is irrelevant. Clearly the testator must be of sound mind. This is generally interpreted to mean that he understands both the nature of his assets and those whom he may reasonably be expected to have in contemplation as recipients of his estate. The fact that a testator may suffer from an insane delusion which does not affect his ability to comprehend these matters will not preclude him from making a will. It is also accepted that a person who may generally be suffering from insane delusions may have 'lucid intervals' and if a will is made during such a lucid interval, it will be valid.

If a person is of unsound mind, a 'statutory will' may be made on his behalf by a person authorized to do so, and in terms approved by the Court of Protection (which has responsibility for the oversight of the affairs of persons of unsound mind).

(b) *See* 2(a) *above*. Witnesses must be of full age and have mental capacity. No specific qualification is either required to validate the will or sufficient to invalidate it. Note, however, that a gift to a witness or the spouse of a witness will be invalid (unless there are sufficient other witnesses to validate the gift).

(c) There are no restrictions on the identity of beneficiaries. Where a beneficiary is under age (younger than eighteen), unless there is a specific direction contained in the will, he will be unable to give a valid receipt for a legacy or share of residue left to him and it will therefore have to be retained by the executors/administrators (or other trustees appointed) until he attains full age and is able to give a receipt.

9. Authority (Court, Notarial or Other)

A Grant of Probate (if there is a will appointing executors); Letters of Administration with the will annexed (if there is a will but no executors appointed who are able and willing to act); or Letters of Administration (in the case of an intestacy) must be obtained from the High Court of Justice in order to obtain legal title to assets which do not pass by delivery.

In order to apply for a Grant of Probate or Letters of Administration, the executor or intending administrator must swear an oath, exhibiting the will (if any) and any codicils thereto and setting out the basis upon which he applies for the Grant and the extent of the testator's estate in England and Wales which will pass under the Grant. The application is made to a Registry of the Family Division of the High Court; the Principal Registry is in London and there are other District Registries, to which applications may also be made, in certain other towns in England and Wales. Where there is a dispute as to the validity of a will, it may be necessary to make an application 'in solemn form'. In that case, the validity of the will will be tested in formal court proceedings.

Before a Grant of Probate or Letters of Administration may be issued, save where the estate falls below a specified value, an account of the assets and liabilities of the deceased as at his death must be delivered to the Inland Revenue and any inheritance tax assessed as payable must be discharged.

The authority of an executor is derived from the will; the authority of an administrator (either on an intestacy or where there is a will but no executor able and willing to act) derives from the Grant. However, an executor will still require a Grant of Probate in order to make title to assets which do not pass by delivery.

10. Invalidity of Will

(a) A will will be invalid if it is formally defective or if the testator lacks testamentary capacity. The testator must also know and approve of the contents of a will. Thus if he agrees to execute any will which another person draws up for him, and executes it in ignorance of its contents, the will is invalid. Undue influence, duress or fraud will also invalidate a will. It is important that the testator both understood and voluntarily wished to make the dispositions included in the will.

(b) A will which is invalid is void but may possibly be relevant as evidence in a succession claim, for example, under the *Inheritance (Provision for Family and Dependants) Act 1975* (*see* 4(a) *above*).

11. Simultaneous Death

(a)–(b) In the event that two or more persons die in circumstances rendering it uncertain which of them survived the other or others, the deaths are (unless the court orders otherwise) presumed to have occurred in the order of seniority and the youngest is deemed to have survived the others. The only exception to this rule is that it does not apply between spouses if the elder spouse dies intestate. In those circumstances, the elder intestate is deemed to have survived his or her younger spouse so that the deceased spouse takes no interest under the estate of his or her elder intestate spouse.

12. Estate Taxes

(a) The *Inheritance Tax Act 1984* (and ancillary legislation) governs the taxation of estates passing on death and *inter vivos* gifts.

(b) In the case of a deceased domiciled in the United Kingdom (there is a special definition of domicile solely for the purposes of inheritance tax) the deceased's worldwide estate is liable to UK inheritance tax. Where the deceased is neither domiciled nor deemed to be domiciled in the United Kingdom for inheritance tax purposes, only assets situated in the United Kingdom are liable to inheritance tax.

(c) Inheritance tax is charged by reference to the value of the estate. There are, however, exemptions for property passing to certain categories of beneficiary (e.g., spouses or charities). It should be noted that property passing to a spouse will not be entirely exempt from UK inheritance tax if the deceased was domiciled in the United Kingdom and the recipient spouse was not. The principles governing UK inheritance tax are too detailed to be included in this chapter.

13. Administration of Estates

(a) Estates are administered by the executors appointed by the will or the administrators appointed by the court. Heirs cannot administer the estate as such, although where no executor is appointed by a will, the heirs will generally be the persons entitled to apply for a Grant of Letters of Administration.

(b) As indicated above, an inventory of the estate must generally be supplied to the Inland Revenue for inheritance tax purposes and the gross and net values of the estate must be specified when an application for Probate or Letters of Administration is made to the High Court. Otherwise than for the purposes of determining a final inheritance tax liability, however, estate reports do not have to be submitted as a matter of routine.

As indicated in 9 *above*, where inheritance tax is payable on an estate, any tax due must be discharged before the Probate or Letters of Administration are issued. Because a Grant of Probate or Letters of Administration will generally be required before the executors or administrators are able to obtain possession of the deceased's assets, and they cannot obtain the Grant of Probate or Letters of Administration without having paid the inheritance tax, it may be necessary for them to borrow to meet the inheritance tax liability. In most cases, building societies with which the deceased held money will release part of the deceased's deposit by way of a cheque drawn in favour of the Inland Revenue specifically for the purpose of enabling the executors or intending administrators to discharge the inheritance tax liability.

(c) Executors or administrators undertake to the court that they will, if so required, give a full account of their administration to the court. Executors or administrators will not ordinarily be required to give such an account unless a beneficiary challenges the manner in which they have administered the estate. Executors or administrators are, however, under a general legal duty to account to the beneficiaries for their administration.

(d) A beneficiary may challenge the manner in which the executors or administrators administer the estate. Where property is held on trust for charitable purposes, the Attorney General represents the interests of charity.

(e) Assets are transferred to the beneficiaries once the executors or administrators no longer require them for the purposes of the administration of the estate. A written assent made by the executors or administrators is required in the case of land; other assets may be transferred by whatever normal manner of transfer applies to the asset, so long as it is clear that the executors or administrators no longer require them for the purposes of the administration.

(f) The creditors of the estate are paid by the executors or administrators out of the residuary assets of the deceased. The law presumes the entire residuary estate (i.e., everything other than assets specifically bequeathed) to be reduced to cash and the debts, funeral and testamentary expenses paid from that cash pool. In practice, assets are, of course, only realized to the extent that it is necessary to make available sufficient cash to pay debts, funeral and testamentary expenses (including pecuniary legacies administrative expenses and borrowing costs incurred, e.g., those relating to bridging finance in respect of inheritance tax).

(g) If no executor is appointed or there is no executor who is able and willing to act, a Grant of Letters of Administration must be obtained from the High Court. There are specific rules which specify the persons who are entitled to apply for such a Grant and in which order.

International Succession

14. Domicile/Nationality

(a) *See* 2(a) *above* as to formal validity. As indicated in 7 *below*, under English law, the law of the *situs* is taken to govern the devolution of the deceased's immovable property and the law of the deceased's domicile at death is taken to govern the devolution of his movable property.

(b) Since 1932 the High Court has had jurisdiction to issue Grants of Probate or Letters of Administration notwithstanding that the deceased left no assets in England and Wales. However, the court is generally unwilling to make a Grant in those circumstances, particularly where the deceased died domiciled elsewhere on the basis that:

'such a Grant (. . .) would be nothing more than a piece of paper.'

(*Per* Ormrod J. – *Aldrich -v- Attorney General* [1968] P281 at 295).

SECTION B – APPLICABLE LAW/PROCEDURE WHERE FOREIGN ELEMENT/S ARE INVOLVED

1. Jurisdiction

(a) Please *see* Section A14(b) *above*.

(b) A Grant of Probate or Letters of Administration is required to make title to both movable and immovable assets in England and Wales. Although the law governing the devolution of movable and immovable assets may vary (*see* Section A *above*) the formalities for obtaining a Grant of Probate or Letters of Administration remain the same.

(c) Save where there is a dispute as to the validity of the will (in which case it may be necessary for proceedings to be issued out of the Chancery Chamber or a Chancery District Registry applications for Grants of Probate or Letters of Administration are made to a Registry of the Family Division of the High Court. The Principal Registry is in London and there are other District Registries in certain other towns in England and Wales.

2. Applicable Law

Under English law, movable property passes in accordance with the law of the deceased's domicile at the date of his death and immovable property passes in accordance with the law of its *situs*.

3. Foreign Succession/Inheritance Orders

(a) 'Confirmations' issued by the Scottish courts and Grants of Representation issued by the Northern Irish courts are formally recognized in England and Wales if the deceased died domiciled in Scotland or Northern Ireland respectively. Otherwise, the order of a foreign court will not normally be recognized in England and Wales without further steps being taken. This is the case both in respect of movable and immovable assets.

(b) Save in respect of Scottish confirmations or Northern Irish Grants of Representation in the circumstances referred to in (a) *above*, or where it is possible to 're-seal' a Grant (*see below*), a Grant of Probate or Letters of Administration must be obtained in England and Wales before title can be made to any assets (movable or immovable) comprised in the estate of any deceased, wherever resident or domiciled.

Grants of Representation made in countries to which the *Colonial Probates Act 1892* applies may be 're-sealed' with the seal of the Family Division of the High Court and thereafter they are of the same effect as though they had been made by an English court. Broadly, the countries to which the Act applies are those within the Commonwealth.

(c) Where the deceased died domiciled outside England and Wales and there is no Scottish Confirmation or Northern Irish Grant, an English Grant of Probate or Letters of Administration will have to be obtained in order to make title to assets within England and Wales. Where the procedure for re-sealing a Colonial Grant is not applicable, applications for a Grant of Probate or Letters of Administration are governed by Rule 30 of the *Non-Contentious Probate Rules 1987*. This Rule provides as follows:

'(1) Subject to paragraph (3) *below*, where the deceased died domiciled outside England and Wales, a district judge or registrar may order that a grant, limited in such way as the district judge or registrar may direct, do issue to any of the following persons:

(a) to the person entrusted with the administration of the estate by the court having jurisdiction at the place where the deceased died domiciled; or

(b) where there is no person so entrusted, to the person beneficially entitled to the estate by the law of the place where the deceased died domiciled or, if there is more than one person so entitled, to such of them as the district judge or registrar may direct; or

(c) if in the opinion of the district judge or registrar the circumstances so require, to such person as the district judge or registrar may direct.

(2) A grant made under paragraph (1)(a) or (b) *above* may be issued jointly with such person as the district judge or registrar may direct if the grant is required to be made to not less than two administrators.

(3) Without any order made under paragraph (1) *above* –

(a) probate of any will which is admissible to proof may be granted:

> *i.* if the will is in the English or Welsh language, to the executor named therein, or
>
> *ii.* if the will describes the duties of a named person in terms sufficient to constitute him executor according to the tenor of the will, to that person; and
>
> (b) where the whole or substantially the whole of the estate in England and Wales consists of immovable property, a grant in respect of the whole estate may be made in accordance with the law which would have been applicable if the deceased had died domiciled in England and Wales.'

Where a will is written in a language other than English or Welsh, the Probate Registry will normally require a notarially certified translation. Where the deceased died domiciled outside England and Wales, an affidavit of law is normally required from a lawyer qualified in the jurisdiction of the deceased's domicile which addresses the validity of the will and sets out the manner in which that law provides for an estate to be administered which may, where a Grant is being sought on the basis of Rule 30(1)(b), necessitate including details of the manner in which the deceased's estate would devolve in accordance with that law.

Rule 39 of the *Non-Contentious Probate Rules 1987* governs the re-sealing of Grants of Representation. Except with the leave of a district judge or a registrar, no Grant is to be re-sealed unless it was made to a person mentioned in sub-paragraph (a) or (b) of paragraph (1) of Rule 30 or to a person to whom a Grant could have been made under sub-paragraph (a) of paragraph (3) of that Rule.

Where the re-sealing procedure is available, it is not necessary for an affidavit of law or an executor or administrator's oath to be provided. The court will, however, require evidence as to the deceased's domicile. Before the Grant can be issued, an Inland Revenue Account, which has been 'controlled' by the Inland Revenue, must also be lodged with the court. The Inland Revenue Account will contain a Statement of Domicile and, although more evidence than the Statement itself may be required by the Inland Revenue for them to accept that the deceased was not domiciled in the United Kingdom, a Statement of Domicile which has been accepted by the Inland Revenue will generally be accepted by the court.

The Grant which is lodged for re-sealing must include a copy of any will to which it relates or be accompanied by a copy which has been certified as correct by the court making the Grant or under its authority. In addition to the Grant and the controlled Inland Revenue Account, a further copy of the Grant and any will must be provided for deposit at the Probate Registry.

It is the practice of the Probate Registry not to re-seal a Grant unless the original is in English.

4. Two or more Succession or Probate Orders

As indicated in 3(a) *above*, a foreign succession order is generally of no validity in England and Wales. However, as will be noted from 3(c) *above*, under Rule 30 of the *Non-Contentious Probate Rules 1987* a Grant of Representation may be issued to a person entrusted with the administration of the deceased's estate by the courts of the deceased's domicile. The foreign order entrusting the administration of the deceased's estate to that person merely gives him a standing to apply for a Grant in England and Wales.

5. Assets

Please *see* Section A14(b) *above*.

6. Expert Evidence

(a) As indicated in 3(c) *above*, an affidavit of law will normally be required from a lawyer qualified in the jurisdiction of the deceased's domicile before a Grant of Representation may be issued to the estate of a person who died domiciled outside England and Wales. That affidavit must cover the manner of administration of the estate as prescribed by the law of the deceased's domicile, identify the persons entitled to apply for a Grant to the deceased's estate in England and Wales and, if relevant, state the manner in which the estate devolves. The affidavit must be sworn or affirmed before a person authorized under English law to administer oaths. This includes a practising English solicitor, notary public or barrister, who may administer oaths both in England and elsewhere. Outside England an oath may be administered by any person who is authorized by the local law of the relevant place to administer oaths. It will, however, be necessary for the capacity of a foreign authorized person to be established by means of the 'Apostille' procedure. British diplomatic and consular officers are also empowered to administer oaths in the country in which they are appointed; their official seals will be recognized by the English court without the need for further evidence of their authority to be provided.

(b) Save where an application is being made 'in solemn form', where an application is contested, affidavit evidence is sufficient and a foreign lawyer will not be required to appear in court to give evidence. Obviously if it is necessary for the application for the Grant to be determined by proceedings in court, it may be necessary for a lawyer qualified in the jurisdiction of the deceased's domicile to give evidence.

7. Unity of Succession

English law provides that immovable assets devolve in accordance with the law of their *situs* and movable assets in accordance with the law of the deceased's domicile. Difficult issues of conflicts of laws may arise, particularly where questions of *renvoi* are concerned.

8. Formalities

English law will treat a will as properly executed if its execution conforms to the internal law in force at the relevant time in the territory where it was executed, or in the territory where, at the time of its execution or of the testator's death, the testator was domiciled or had his habitual residence, or in a state of which at either of those times the testator was a national (*see* Section A2(a) *above*). It is not, therefore, essential that the will is formally valid in accordance with the normal rules of English law: Section 2 of the *Wills Act 1963* provides additional rules under which certain other wills may be regarded as validly executed.

9. Legislation

The *Wills Act 1963* was enacted to give broad effect to The *1961 Hague Convention on the Conflicts of Laws Relating to the Form of Testamentary Dispositions.*

10. Wills

The underlying rule of English law is that immovable property passes in accordance with the law of its *situs* and movable property passes in accordance with the law of the deceased's domicile as at the date of his death. The rules relating to conflicts of laws are complicated and the following should only be regarded as a synopsis of the position. Detailed advice may be required in particular circumstances.

(a) In order to effect a disposition of immovable property situated in England and Wales, a will must be recognized as valid under English law on the basis of the principles enunciated above. To effect a disposition of movable property situated in England and Wales, it must satisfy the requirements of the law of the deceased's domicile as at his date of death.

(b) The English courts will endeavour to find the testator's true meaning when construing a will. If it is clear that the testator meant his will to be construed in accordance with the principles of another legal system, the court will give effect to that intention. Domicile or nationality will not necessarily be the governing factor in this case, although in the absence of evidence to the contrary, it is presumed that the testator intended his will to be construed in accordance with the law of his domicile at the time the will was made. If English is the language of the will, the court may conclude that English constructions should be applied to terms used. If it is clear from the express words of the will, or it must necessarily be implied, that it is to be construed in accordance with a non-English law, evidence of the appropriate rules of construction will be required.

(c) The rights of beneficiaries or heirs (e.g., to minimum portions) will, similarly, depend upon the law which governs the devolution of the asset in question: if movable, the law of the deceased's domicile at the date of his death; and, if immovable, the law of its *situs*.

(d) Capacity to inherit will, again, depend upon the law which governs the devolution of the asset in question: capacity to inherit immovable assets will depend upon the law of the assets' *situs*; capacity to inherit movable assets will depend upon the more liberal of the law of the deceased's domicile and the law governing the beneficiary.

(e) There is no English authority on what law governs the capacity to make a will of immovable property. The view is, however, that because immovable property passes in accordance with the law of the *situs* it is the law of the *situs* which is relevant. Capacity to make a will of movable property is tested in accordance with the law of the deceased's domicile; the deceased may therefore be regarded as capable of making a will of movable assets but not of immovable assets (or vice versa) depending upon his capacity under the law governing the relevant disposition.

(f) Similarly, essential or material validity of a will will be judged by the law applicable to the asset in question. A will may, therefore, be formally or materially valid in respect of immovables but not movables, or vice versa.

(g) Where a power of appointment is created by an instrument governed by English law, a testator's capacity to exercise the power over movables, by will, is determined by the law of his domicile at the time the will was made. It is believed that where the subject matter of the power is immovable property, capacity to exercise the power will depend upon the law of the *situs*. The material or essential validity of an exercise by will of a power of appointment generally depends upon the law governing the instrument creating the power, not the will, in the case of movable property; and upon the law of the *situs* in the case of immovable property.

(h) The legal requirements concerning revocation of wills, except where revocation is by the execution of a new will, are governed in all cases, it is considered, by the law of the testator's domicile at the date of the purported revocation. The law is, however, far from clear on this question. Amendment, revocation as a result of the execution of a new will and revival of wills will depend upon the law which governs the making of the will.

(i) The *Inheritance (Provision for Family and Dependants) Act 1975* (*see* Section A4(a) *above*) applies only where the deceased died domiciled in England and Wales. Residence is irrelevant for the purposes of this Act.

11. Domicile/Nationality

(a) Generally, it is the domicile of the deceased at the date of his death which is relevant to the devolution of his estate. It should be noted that under the *Wills Act 1963* a will may be formally valid if it is executed in accordance with the formalities required by the law of the deceased's domicile either at the date of his death or at the date of its execution. However, the view is generally taken that where capacity to make a will or exercise a power by his will depends upon the testator's domicile, it is his domicile at the date of the will which is relevant. Similarly, where the validity of a purported revocation depends upon the deceased's domicile, it will be the domicile at the date of the relevant act which will be important.

(b) The domicile of a beneficiary is generally irrelevant in English law; where it is relevant in the case of capacity to inherit movables, it would seem to be the domicile at the date of the testator's death which will count.

(c) Under English law a deceased can have only one domicile. At birth, a person acquires a 'domicile of origin'. That domicile is: where the person is born legitimate, the domicile of his father; and, where he is born illegitimate, the domicile of his mother.

Until the age of sixteen, a person's domicile may change with the domicile of the relevant parent. Any such altered domicile is referred to as a 'domicile of dependency'.

At the age of sixteen, a person may acquire a 'domicile of choice'. In order to acquire a domicile of choice, it is necessary to be physically present in a jurisdiction with the intention of remaining there permanently or indefinitely. If either the physical presence or the necessary intention ceases without a new domicile of choice being acquired, the domicile of origin will revive.

For example, if a person is born, legitimate, at a time when his father is domiciled in England and Wales, English law will regard his domicile of origin as English. If his father subsequently acquires a domicile of choice in France, prior to the child attaining sixteen, English law will regard the child as acquiring a domicile of dependency in France. At the age of sixteen, if the child is still physically present in France, and intends to remain there permanently or indefinitely, he will acquire a domicile of choice in France. If he does not intend to remain permanently or indefinitely in France his domicile of origin in England will revive (irrespective of whether or not he intends to return to England). If, having acquired a domicile of choice in France, he moves to Italy his domicile of choice would be lost. If he intends to remain permanently or indefinitely in Italy, he will acquire a domicile of choice in Italy. If not, his domicile of origin in England will revive.

It is not possible either to have no domicile (a domicile of origin will revive where there is no domicile of dependence or choice) or to have more than one domicile under English law.

12. Taxation

UK inheritance tax is payable in respect of transfers made, rather than property received. Accordingly, it is the domicile of the deceased, rather than the beneficiaries, which is relevant in determining UK inheritance tax liabilities. Residence is, of itself, irrelevant. Note, however, that there is a special definition of 'domicile' for UK inheritance tax purposes only, *see* Section A12(b) *above*. Thus, where a person is not actually domiciled in the United Kingdom but has been resident for a substantial period of time he may be deemed to be domiciled in the United Kingdom for inheritance tax purposes only. (The UK government is currently reviewing the application of the domicile rules for tax purposes and it is possible that changes may be made in the near future).

Finland

Prepared by: Barbara ENGBLOM-LINDGREN and Thomas REINIUS
Lindgren & Mitts
Asianajotoimisto-Advokatbyrå-Law Office

Address: Pohjoisesplanadi 33 A
         FIN-00100 Helsinki
         Finland
Tel.:   +358 (0)9 669 895
Fax: +358 (0)9 669 576
E-mail: office@lindgrenlaw.fi

SECTION A – BRIEF SURVEY OF THE LOCAL SYSTEM

1. Type of System

(a) The Finnish legal system is a civil law system.

(b) The system in Finland is not federal.

2. Wills

(a) An ordinary will shall be drafted in writing and signed in presence of two impartial witnesses. The witnesses must acknowledge that the document they witness is a will, but they do not need to have knowledge of the specific content of the will. The witnesses shall state in the will that the testator is of sound mind and that the testator is acting on his own free discretion. The witnesses shall also state that the testator has personally signed the will.

    Holographic wills are allowed, if they are handwritten by the testator.

    A deathbed will shall be dictated in the presence of two witnesses.

    Holographic and deathbed wills may be deemed invalid as mentioned in Section 10 *below*, if the testator has been able to draft an ordinary will within three months prior to his death.

(b) *i.* Amendments to a will must be made following similar procedure as to the actual drafting of the will. There are no distinct formalities required for revoking a will. Thus, a will may be revoked by dispersing the actual document, or by stating in writing that the will is invalid or by drafting a new

209

will. Such provisions of a previous will that are not superseded by a latter shall remain valid.

ii. Marriage does not as such revoke or affect a will made prior to marriage. The intent of the deceased shall nevertheless be taken into consideration in the interpretation of a will.

iii. Revival of a revoked will may be made through a new statement where the will has been originally revoked through a statement.

3. Intestacy

(a) The children of the deceased inherit the estate. If the deceased has no children or grandchildren, the spouse shall inherit the estate.

If the deceased was unmarried, the parents inherit, if they are not alive; the brothers and sisters; if they are not alive; their children. If the spouse inherits, the parents/brothers and sisters/their children will inherit the estate after the death of the spouse. The succession is *per stirpes*.

If the deceased does not have any heirs mentioned above and he has not drafted a will, the estate devolves to the State.

The spouse inherits the estate only if the deceased has no lineal descendants. Lineal descendants are children born in or out of wedlock or adopted.

(b) There is no difference in the division of the estate between movables and immovables.

4. Freedom of Testation

(a) Only the children of the deceased are entitled to a compulsory share. The compulsory share constitutes half of the estate.

(b) A person cannot make decisions concerning the distribution of his estate in any other way than by a will. A contract regarding the distribution of the estate between the heirs or between the heirs and any third party that has been made prior to death is not valid.

5. Maintenance

The children and the spouse may claim maintenance assuming that certain requirements regarding the need for such maintenance are met. In general the granting of such maintenance is somewhat uncommon.

6. Community Property Between Husband and Wife

(a) Half of the total community property does not form part of the estate and shall be distributed to the surviving spouse prior to the distribution of the estate.

The spouses may decide otherwise by a marriage settlement.

It is also possible in a will or deed of donation to stipulate that assets received through such will or gift shall not constitute community property.

(b) The spouses are entitled to define community property by marriage settlement. A marriage settlement stipulates how to distribute the property in case of divorce or death and may therefore effect the distribution of the estate.

7. Gifts (*Inter Vivos*)

(a) Gifts to lineal descendants of the donor are presumed to be inheritance in advance unless otherwise stipulated. Gifts to heirs of the donor are not presumed to be inheritance in advance unless otherwise stipulated.

(b) In case gifts are included in the inheritance, the value of the gift is added to the estate.

8. Capacity

(a) A person over eighteen years of age is entitled to draft a will. A person over fifteen years of age is entitled to draft a will in regard to property pursuant to earnings from his employment. Moreover anyone being or having been married is entitled to draft a will. The testator must be of sound mind.

(b) The following persons are not entitled to witness a will:

– children who are under fifteen years of age;
– mentally disturbed people;
– beneficiaries of the will;
– any person married to the testator;
– parents, grandparents, children, grandchildren; brothers, sisters, brothers and sisters in-law; parents in-law; adoptive parents or children of the testator or beneficiary.

(c) Anyone who is alive, conceived but unborn or child to such a person may be a beneficiary, as well as a company, a foundation, etc.

9. Authority (Court, Notarial or Other)

The heirs must receive a copy of the will. They may approve the will in writing. The will comes into force immediately, if all of the heirs have approved it in writing. If a person wishes to contest the will, he must file an action within six months from the service of the will. If no such action is filed, the will comes into force after a period of six months.

There are no special courts for inheritance matters.

10. Invalidity of Will

(a) A will has a defect of form if the testator or the witnesses have lacked capacity to make a will, or if both witnesses were not simultaneously present upon signing of the will. Furthermore, a will has a defect of form if the formalities regarding making a holographic or a deathbed will have not been followed as mentioned in answer 2(a) *above*. Also dispositions under fraud and duress make a will voidable.

If an heir wishes to contest the will he must take action within six months from being informed of the contents of the will. Each heir may contest the will. Each heir may also approve the will in writing prior to the end of the above mentioned period. If all of the heirs approve the will in such a manner, the will becomes immediately valid.

(b) It is necessary to contest the will in court, otherwise, irrespective of the defect, it becames valid.

11. Simultaneous Death

(a)–(b) In case of simultaneous death the presumption is that the heir died before the person whose estate is in question. In case of simultaneous death of the heirs there is no presumption.

12. Estate taxes

(a) There is a tax on inheritance in Finland and it is imposed on the individual share of each beneficiary. The inheritance tax is based on the market value of the property inherited on the date of death. Insurance payments due to death to a beneficiary or to the estate are partly subject to inheritance tax, unless the payment is subject to income taxation.

(b) Taxes are due on assets worldwide provided that the deceased was domiciled in Finland at the time of death.

(c) The heirs are taxed. The level of tax depends on kinship between deceased and the heir. Recipients are divided into three categories, the tax being twice and correspondingly three times the amount in the first category.

The first category includes the spouse, the children, the grandchildren and the parents.

The second category includes the siblings of the deceased and their descendants. Other recipients fall under the third category.

The tax rates in the first category in EUR are as follows:

Taxable Amount	Tax at lower limit	Tax on the excess
3.400–17.000	85	10%
17.000–50.000	1.445	13%
50.000 or more	5.735	16%

13. Administration of Estates

(a) The estate is administered by the parties of the estate. These include the widow, the heirs and the general testamentaries – but not legatees. The parties of the estate may privately administer the estate in order to settle it.

The court may appoint an estate administrator on petition of a party to the estate or the creditor of the estate. A testator may also appoint an executor to administer the estate in the will.

If the debts of the estate exceed the assets, the heirs should apply for the order for an administrator. Otherwise the parties to the estate may be held personally liable for the debts.

(b) The estate administrator should submit an annual report once a year to the parties of the estate. This is not required by law but it is a common practice. A party to the estate may also upon demand require the estate administrator to submit a report.

Furthermore, having settled the estate the estate administrator shall submit the parties of the estate a final report on the administration.

(c) The court may on demand of the party to the estate appoint an independent person to review the administration of the estate.

(d) The parties of the estate have the right to query and object.

(e) After the estate has been settled, each party to the estate may demand distribution of the estate. The parties to the estate may jointly agree on the distribution of the assets as they see fit.

A party to the estate may, nevertheless, request the court to appoint a distributor of the estate. A distributor shall also be appointed in case a party to the estate is legally incompetent, or a share of a party has been seized. The distributor of the estate effects the distribution by giving each party a share of all types of property, unless the parties jointly agree otherwise.

(f) The creditors of the estate are entitled to receive payment before the heirs. The debts of the estate are usually paid during the settling of the estate.

If the parties to the estate distribute the property before all the debts have been paid, all the parties that have taken part in the distribution incur liability for all known debts at the time of the distribution.

A party may, however, prohibit the distribution until all known debts of the estate have been fully paid or funds required for their payment have been placed into escrow.

(g) The distribution may be effected by the parties of the estate. The deed of distribution shall then be signed by the parties of the estate in presence of two witnesses.

International Succession

14. Domicile/Nationality

(a) As long as the Finnish law is applicable the nationality or domicile of the deceased should not affect the information above.

(b) If the deceased was domiciled in Finland the local court may give an order of probate or succession even if the deceased had no assets in the jurisdiction.

SECTION B – APPLICABLE LAW/PROCEDURE WHERE FOREIGN ELEMENT/S ARE INVOLVED

1. Jurisdiction

(a) The rules regarding jurisdiction are based on the principle of domicile. A local court may under certain circumstances hold that it has jurisdiction also in case of Finnish nationality or assets within the jurisdiction.

(b) A local court does not claim jurisdiction over immovable property situated abroad, if it is evident that the court's measures would not have any effect abroad.

(c) The local court, in which the deceased had domicile, would ordinarily have the jurisdiction. The District Court in Helsinki has jurisdiction, if the deceased was not domiciled in Finland.

2. Applicable Law

The applicable law is based on the principle of domicile of the deceased at the time of death. The applicable law embraces the whole estate of the deceased with the exception of immovable property situated abroad.

In case the applicable law cannot reasonably be determined based on the principle of domicile, it is possible to take the nationality of the deceased and also other aspects into consideration.

Furthermore, following the formal requirements set forth in respect of a will it is possible to determine the applicable law. The applicable law should in this case have some reasonable connection with the deceased.

A local court would not under any circumstances apply norms that are contrary to the Finnish *ordre public*.

3. Foreign Succession/Inheritance Orders

(a)–(b) Whether foreign succession orders given outside the Nordic countries are recognized or enforceable in Finland is somewhat unclear. It would, nevertheless, be well-founded to expect the local court to recognize a foreign order, if the connection to the country where the order has been given is sufficient.

(c) There are no general rules on obtaining recognition or enforcement of a foreign succession or inheritance order.

4. Two or More Succession or Probate Orders

The domicile of the deceased should primarily prevail in case of two or more succession or probate orders.

5. Assets

The local court may assume jurisdiction in case of local domicile or Finnish citizenship, even if there were no assets in the jurisdiction.

6. Expert Evidence

(a) There is no necessity as such for a foreign lawyer to give further evidence regarding a foreign will that has been recognized by a foreign court. The court might, however, ask a party to present evidence regarding the will.

(b) It is possible to submit evidence to the court without the necessity of appearance in court.

7. Unity of Succession

The question is not applicable in Finland.

8. Formalities

As a general rule the formalities of a will executed in a foreign country need not be the same as those in Finland for such will to be recognized.

9. Legislation

Finland has signed The *Hague convention on the Conflicts of Laws Relating to the Form of Testamentary Dispositions*.

10. Wills

(a) With regard to the legal requirements for execution of wills the local court may, according to the principle of *favor testamenti*, apply either *lex loci actus, lex patriae,*

International Succession

lex domicili or the habitual residence of the deceased. In case of immovable property *lex rei sitae* may also be applied.

(b) In principle the law applicable to the will is also the law governing the construction and interpretation of the will. The intent of the deceased including the assumption on the applicable law shall, however, also be taken into consideration.

(c)–(d) The applicable law to inheritance as provided in Section 2 *above* governs also the legal rights and capacity to receive inheritance on grounds of will and the legal order of heirs and their minimum portions.

(e) In regard to the legal requirements for the capacity to make a will the local court may according to *favor testamenti* principle apply different options as provided in answer (a) *above*.

(f) The essential or material validity of the will should primarily be based on *favor testamenti* as provided in answer (a) *above*.

(g) The law applicable to the will should also govern the powers of appointment, i.e., where a person in his will nominates someone else who in his own will, shall have the power to specify the ultimate recipient.

(h) The law applicable to making a will as provided in answer (a) *above* is also applicable to revoking or amending the will.

(i) The laws regarding reserve should apply to a non-resident in respect of both movable and immovable property.

11. Domicile/Nationality

(a) *See* the answers *above*.

(b) *See* the answers *above*.

(c) If the domicile of the deceased were unclear, the local court would determine domicile *in casu*. In order for a person to have domicile in a particular country it is required that the person in question has permanent residence and an intention to continue residing in that country. If residence in another country is only temporary and it may be assumed that the person in question had the intention to return to his domicile, the domicile remains unchanged.

12. Taxation

Liability to inheritance tax covers any property, if the deceased person or the heir is a resident of Finland. If both the deceased and the heir are non-residents, tax liability covers only real property, which is situated in Finland, and shares in a corporate body in which more than 50 per cent of the assets consist of Finnish real property.

If inheritance tax has already been paid abroad, the tax will be credited against Finnish tax, unless the foreign tax was imposed on real property situated in Finland.

Finland has concluded treaties to avoid double taxation on inheritance with the following states: the Scandinavian countries, the Netherlands, USA, France and Switzerland.

Tax treaties take precedence over national rules for property subject to tax and over rules for avoiding double taxation.

France

Prepared by: Joseph ROUBACHE
Avocat au Barreau de Paris

Address: 105, rue Jouffroy d'Abbans – 75017 PARIS
Tel.:   +33 01 56 33 30 30
Fax: +33 01 46 22 64 40
email: JRoubache.avocat@giepolaris.com

SECTION A – BRIEF SURVEY OF THE LOCAL SYSTEM

1. Type of System

(a) Civil Law.

(b) The French Civil Code governs family law: inheritance, marriage, gifts, for the whole of the country, including for the overseas territories.

2. Wills

(a) There must be a written document.
   The Civil Code recognizes *three main forms of wills*:

– *Holographic*: This comprises a written will, dated and signed by the testator in accordance with Article 970 of the Civil Code; the will stands alone. This is the most common type of will. Upon the death of the testator, certain formalities relating to the deposit of the will at a notary are required. In addition, if there are beneficiaries who are 'non-seised' *non-saisis* (*see* paragraph 13(1)), the verification by a judge of the will's validity is required (in terms of its form).
– *Public* (*authentique*): This refers to a will drawn up by two notaries, or by a notary and two witnesses, in accordance with the testator's instructions (Articles 971 and those which follow of the Civil Code). As to its form, this will must comply with very stringent rules but, because it reflects an act of a public nature, the rules relating to its execution after the death of the testator are less onerous (e.g., there is no requirement for a judge to verify its validity). This is the only type of will that can be used by a testator who does not or cannot write and sign the will (usually following illness).

– *Secret* (Article 976 of the Civil Code): A secret will can be drawn up by the testator, who then gives it sealed to a notary in the presence of two witnesses. The notary must then write a statement on the envelope enclosing the will which asserts that, upon declaration by the testator, the contents comprise the testator's signed will which he or another drew up and which specifies the form of writing used (whether handwritten or typed). Given the complex rules relating to the wills validity, this form of will is very rarely used.

– *International will*: The *Act of 29 April 1994* allows notaries on French territory to draw up wills in accordance with the *1973 Washington Convention on International Wills*, which regulates the form that international wills must take. French Diplomatic and Consular Agents are allowed to draw up such wills for French citizens abroad.

(b) *i.* All wills can be altered by the testator subject to the above-mentioned rules on form. The will can be revoked in its entirety or in part in accordance with the rules set out in Article 1035, and those which follow, of the Civil Code, in particular by a subsequent will.

In accordance with the relevant jurisprudence, a holographic will can be revoked by a public will, but the destruction of a will will not be presumed to have revoked the will, the judge in such a case having to determine the intention of the testator.

A bequest can be revoked by the sale of the object of the bequest.

A will may be nullified should the legatee die before the testator.

Codicils are subject to the same rules that apply to the will itself.

ii. A testator's subsequent marriage does not affect the validity of a previous will.

iii. By way of a subsequent will, a testator can 'revive' legacies which have been revoked in an intervening will, provided that the first will has not been destroyed.

3. Intestacy

(a) The heirs in this instance are ascertained in accordance with their relationship with the deceased, keeping three fundamental principles in mind:

The Concept of Order

This principle specifies certain categories based upon particular ties of kinship.

The following categories are thus distinguished:

– Descendants, which category excludes those belonging to the categories set out below, with the exception of the surviving spouse. There is no distinction with illegitimate (including adulterine) or adopted children.

International Succession

– Ancestors, which category comprises the deceased's forbearers.
– Collateral Relations, which category includes persons sharing a common ancestor with the deceased.

The last two categories, each subdivide into two further sub-categories: that of 'privileged ancestors' which comprises the father and mother, as opposed to 'ordinary ancestors' (grandparents, great-grandparents) and that of 'privileged collateral relations', i.e., brothers and sisters of the deceased and their offspring, as opposed to 'ordinary collateral relations' (uncles, aunts, cousins . . . , up to the sixth degree – cousins from relations of the full blood).

In the absence of those categories as specified above (which group can be enlarged to include family up to the twelfth degree if the deceased was unable to draw up a will) the estate devolves upon the state.

Since the Law of 3 December 2001, greater rights are granted to the surviving spouse following the death of the other spouse.

Conjugal Home

If the conjugal home is included within the estate in succession:

(a) The surviving spouse may use the conjugal home (including the furniture) until his/her death (Article 764 of the Civil Code).

(b) The spouse may reside *gratuitously* in it (including the furniture) for one year (Article 763 of the Civil Code). After one year, the surviving spouse has to pay rental to the owner of the home.

Right of Property

The new law also allocates a larger share in the estate to the surviving spouse (Article 757 of the Civil Code).

Where there are children, the surviving spouse may now choose between one-quarter of the estate in full ownership or the entire estate in usufruct. Where there are children born of another union, the surviving spouse is entitled to receive one-quarter of the estate in full ownership.

Share

The surviving spouse will have a share in the inheritance which, in the absence of a will or donation between spouses, depends on the nature of the other heirs to the succession.

	Share to the spouse for successions opened before 1 July 2002	Share to the spouse for successions opened after 1 July 2002
With one or more children, all being born of the two spouses	One-quarter in usufruct	At the surviving spouse's choice, either: – one-quarter of the estate in full ownership – or the entire estate in usufruct
With children, where one or more were born of a previous union	One-quarter in usufruct	One-quarter in full ownership
With no children, where the deceased's father and mother are alive	One-half in usufruct	One-half in full ownership
With no children and no brothers, where only one parent is alive	One-half in full ownership	Three-quarters in full ownership
With no children and neither parent, where there are brothers and sisters	One-half in usufruct	All of the estate in full ownership, excluding one-half of the family estate*

These rules may always be amended through a will or by executing a donation between spouses.

However, where there are no children or surviving parents, the spouse is entitled to a minimum of one-quarter of the estate in full ownership: a person is not entitled to deprive his spouse of this.

_____

* *Protection of family estate*

The spouse now takes precedence over ordinary ascendants and privileged collaterals.

Concerning the latter, worries were expressed as to keeping property inherited from the deceased spouse's parents in the family. To limit the consequences of this drawback, the legislator, after discussion, has decided that half of the property received by the deceased through donation or inheritance from his or her parents, is inherited in turn by the brothers and sisters or nephews and nieces, provided that they themselves are descendants of the parent from whom the property was originally inherited.

International Succession

Degree

In relation to each particular category, those with the closest blood ties to the deceased will determine those who will inherit to the exclusion of others.

Those within a category who are more closely related will inherit to the exclusion of others within that category (allowing for exceptions which arise because of 'representation'), whereas those who are as closely related within a particular category will share the assets of the estate in equal measures.

To ascertain the number of degrees as between the deceased and a relation, one calculates, in relation to ancestors or descendants, the number of generations between them, whereas in relation to collateral relatives, the degree in question is equal to the sum total of generations by which they are removed from their common ancestor.

Subdivision (la fente)

In all cases of succession which devolves upon ancestors and collateral relations, the succession will subdivide into two parts. One-half will devolve upon beneficiaries who are related to the father of the deceased (the paternal strand) and the other half will devolve upon those related to the deceased's mother (the maternal strand).

Mention must be made of 'representation' which allows for the devolution of succession upon the descendants of a deceased heir (solely in relation to descendants and privileged collateral relations), with regard given to heirs with closer blood ties (e.g., where a child predeceases his father, his children will take the share that their father would have received from his father if he had been alive to inherit, with their aunts and uncles, that is, the deceased's surviving children, receiving their respective shares).

(b) The principle of unity in regard to successions, which does not allow for any such distinction, is enshrined in Article 732 of the Civil Code.

4. Freedom of Testation

(a) The legal right to an inheritance is one of the cornerstones of French law on succession. Such rights are of a public nature and the principle and its applications are upheld by the courts.

(b) The protective measures which are accorded under this principle, particularly those which protect the deceased's heirs in respect of gifts he could have consented to during his lifetime, will also be examined.

That part of the estate which is subject to 'compulsory shares (*la reserve*) may be defined as the fraction of a person's estate which cannot be disposed of by a testator and that is thus earmarked solely for the benefit of specific heirs who enjoy the protection of the law. This part of the estate subject to compulsory shares provides for equality as between the heirs who are so protected, by giving them each an equal part of the succession. Only the direct descendants, or the ancestors in the absence of descendants, have the right to such compulsory shares, as provided for in Articles 913 and 914 of the Civil Code respectively.

On the other hand the term 'disposable share of the estate' is used to designate the share of the estate which the testator can dispose of to whomever he wishes.

That part of the estate subject to compulsory shares benefits all descendants, or in particular cases the ancestors, whatever the degree to which they are related to the deceased (children, grandchildren, great grandchildren, . . .) and whatever the nature of their parental filiation with the deceased (legitimate, natural or adoptive). The fraction corresponding to each share is related to the number of heirs who are so protected (one-half if the deceased has left one child, two-thirds if he has left two children and three-quarters if he has left three or more children).

Collateral relations cannot assert a claim to that part of the estate which is subject to compulsory shares so in principle they could be completely disinherited.

The existence of a surviving spouse will affect that part of the estate which is subject to compulsory shares; that is, that part of the estate will be reduced because the deceased may have made a disposition in favour of his spouse of the disposable share of his estate in accordance with Article 1094-1 of the Civil Code, as well as one-quarter of the estate absolutely and the surplus (three-quarters) for life in usufruct or the whole estate for life in usufruct.

Pursuant to the Law of 3 December 2001 (Article 914.1 of the Civil Code), where the deceased did not have relatives in the descending or ascending line, the surviving spouse is entitled to receive a compulsory share of one quarter of the estate in full ownership.

(c) *i*. Article 1130(2) of the Civil Code lays down a general principle that all waivers of rights or other agreements relating to a succession which has not yet taken effect, even with the consent of the future deceased, are not permitted.

This prohibition, which is subject, however, to some exceptions, harks back to Roman Law and is founded on numerous grounds, particularly those relating to the protection of compulsory shares of inheritance and the safeguarding of testamentary freedom.

ii. Notwithstanding the prohibition on covenants on future succession, certain dispositions are allowed for by law.

This is the case in respect to:

– Marriage contracts or contracts made during the course of marriage (Articles 1082 and 1093 of the Civil Code); this is the most common exception, in particular during the course of the marriage in favour of the surviving spouse; it is permitted because it can be revoked.

– Certain clauses of a financial nature within the marriage contract or in other contracts containing provisions concerning rights or interests in company shares and securities predetermining to whom such rights or interest would revert upon the death of the testator.

> – Certain devolutions by trustees; stipulations requiring a legatee to keep and then transfer property to another, limited to those gifts made to children and grandchildren or, in the absence of descendants, to brothers and sisters and their children.

Mention must also be made in respect of certain provisions (Articles 918 and 930(2)) of the Civil Code which allow for heirs who have the right to a compulsory share of an inheritance to waive their rights in advance, by requesting a reduction of their share so that they are then able to receive a gift consented to by the future deceased, in cases which are foreseen by these provisions.

Given the significance of these exceptions, these provisions require that such agreements are to be made by deed.

Mention should also be made in respect of other agreements, which, although not gifts in themselves, nevertheless have a significant bearing on future succession: clauses concerning the unequal division of joint estates, tontinary agreements and, of particular importance, life insurance policies.

Advance division is permitted by the Civil Code (Article 1075), either by way of donation or by will. Its numerous tax advantages account for its popularity (such as the lowering of the renewable tax base every ten years, specific reductions on duties.

Pursuant to the *Loi de Finance* (general budget/finance law) in force in 2003, inheritance tax is reduced as follows:

– 50 per cent if the donor is under sixty-five;
– 30 per cent if the donor is between sixty-five and seventy-five;
– 0 per cent if the donor is over seventy-five.

But most importantly this form of division allows the parents, or one of them, to allocate their property in advance whilst they can then continue to enjoy it or the revenues which accrue from it during the remainder of their lifetime.

These types of donations must also conform to the rules as to form which apply to ordinary donations: a deed and express approval to be given by the donees in the agreement or by way of a separate agreement.

5. Maintenance

Under the terms of the new Article 767, which replaces and completes the former Article 207-1 of the French Civil Code, the heirs of the deceased spouse must pay a pension to a needy surviving spouse.

To claim this type of pension, the spouse concerned has a period of one year as from the date of death or the date when the heirs stopped paying the pension that they paid the spouse previously.

This period can also be extended until the inheritance has been divided up.

The alimony is paid by all the heirs, and, in the event of insufficiency, by all the specific legatees in proportion to their emoluments.

6. Community Property Between Husband and Wife

i. Under the law governing community property (limited to transfers made by couples married after 1 February 1966), in the absence of any provisions on disposal in the marriage contract, the surviving spouse is entitled to half of such property.

It is possible to stipulate, either in the marriage contract, during the course of the marriage itself or by modification of any previous arrangements (requiring a deed subject to judicial approval), that should one of the spouses, as joint owner, die, the surviving spouse will be entitled to all of the community property or all the revenue which accrues from the property, or any other percentage, or certain specific goods or real estate. Community property could comprise all the spouse's property, even that which was not obtained for money or considerations.

If one of the spouses has a child from a previous marriage, however, Article 1527 of the Civil Code limits the effects of such stipulations to a special share as set out in Article 1904-1 of the Civil Code (*see also* 4(a) *supra*).

ii. After the death of a spouse, the surviving spouse is entitled to the continued use of the name of the deceased.

7. Gifts (*Inter Vivos*)

i. Refunding (*rapport*) requires an heir to return property, either in kind or in value, that he has received free of charge from the deceased during the latter's lifetime, to the estate of the deceased so that the heirs can be treated equally. This mechanism allows for the restoration of the estate, as though no gift has been made. The donor may have intended, however, that the heirs be treated differently; he may have intended to pass anticipatory title (*libéralités préciputaires*): in this case the donee is exempted from having to bring the gift into account, except for that part of the donation which would exceed the disposable share of the estate.

Set-off (*reduction*) also requires the making good of any transfers from that part of the estate which is subject to compulsory shares. In order to calculate this, the liquidator of the estate will determine, upon the death, the overall amount of that part of the estate which is to be subject to compulsory shares by adding both existing property, after the deduction of debts, and gifts made by the deceased, accounting for certain advancements.

This exercise first allows for the calculation of that part of the estate subject to compulsory shares and the disposable share of the estate and then for the 'charging' of the gifts, starting with those made the longest time ago, in order to reduce those that exceed the disposable share of the estate. Gifts made by way of an advance will first be deducted from the donee's compulsory share and then from the disposable share of the estate. In contrast, anticipatory gifts are first deducted from the disposable share of the estate.

(The rules pertaining to refunding and set-off, as regards the protection of compulsory shares and the restoration of equality as between the heirs are of a

complex nature and would entail elaboration going beyond the scope of this
text.)
ii. Refunding is only operative by an heir in relation to other heirs: therefore an
heir who renounces his claim is not subject to refunding and an heir does not
have to bring gifts into account in relation to legatees who are not heirs.

Anticipatory donations are not subject to refunding in principle but they may
be reduced if they lessen the amount to be set aside for the compulsory shares.

8. Capacity

i. The basic principle is that a minor under the age of sixteen is incapable of
making a will. A minor between the ages of sixteen and eighteen can make a
will to dispose of half of the property that he would have been entitled to
dispose of had he been of full age.

A minor over the age of sixteen who is 'emancipated' is fully capable of
disposing of his property by will. In accordance with Article 476 of the Civil
Code, such a minor is deemed emancipated upon marriage.
ii. The witnesses to an authentic will must be French nationals, of full age and
entitled to exercise their civil rights, in accordance with Article 980 of the Civil
Code. A husband and wife cannot witness the same will. In addition, the provisions stipulate that witnesses must also be able to sign.

Article 975 of the Civil Code stipulates that neither the legatees nor their
parents or relations up to the fourth degree, nor notary clerks who assist in the
execution of the will, can be witnesses.
iii. Article 906, and those that follow, of the Civil Code set out those who cannot
be beneficiaries; such persons are numerous:
– a person who has not yet been conceived (Article 906 of the Civil Code);
– a person whose identity cannot be established (in cases where the information given by the testator is insufficient to identity the person in question);
– persons in certain professions: doctors, chemists (who treated the person
during his illness), religious ministers (with the exception of those who are
related to the deceased);
– the guardian, until the guardianship has ended;
– etc.

9. Authority (Court, Notarial or Other)

Death is confirmed by way of an official certificate drawn up by a registrar. In cases
in which the person is missing and presumed dead, a judicial pronouncement is
made. The effect of which is to allow for the succession of the missing person's
estate.

The Civil Code does not yet provide for the means by which devolution upon
succession is established.

Notaries have instituted a procedure which involves the production of an attested
affidavit.

This document is authenticated by a notary upon the attestation of two witnesses or, less commonly, by the Magistrate (where the succession involved is not very significant and in the absence of a will or a marriage contract).

The attested affidavit allows the heirs to satisfy third parties as to the devolution of the estate.

Certain property belonging to the deceased will require that particular formalities be observed so that it can devolve upon the heirs: real estate, for instance, requires a particular kind of attestation which can only be drawn up by a notary.

This instrument must be published in an official publication, such publication serving to inform third parties. Another example: registered securities documenting the deceased's interests in particular companies require the drawing up of a certificate which serves to record their transfer to the heirs in the registers of the companies in question.

10. Invalidity of Will

(a) Testamentary defects can be numerous, with such defects contravening rules as to form, or demonstrating an absence of consent on the part of the testator (duress, improper or undue influence).

Particular mention must be made of the nullity of the 'joint will' (a will which is drawn up by two or more persons at a time whether for the benefit of the third party or for the mutual and reciprocal benefit of the persons in question) as set out in Article 968 of the Civil Code.

(b) The most common consequence is the nullity of the will in question, although confirmation given by the testator's heirs may be able to override this. If they are in agreement, the heirs can deliver up a 'verbal legacy', representing the intention of the deceased as attested, although not by way of a formal will.

Certain defects can be overlooked by the courts: for example, an incomplete dating of a holographic will.

11. Simultaneous Death

The provisions of Articles 720 to 722 of the Civil Code which governed the devolution of successions in the event of simultaneous death 'according to circumstances, age and sex' were repealed by the Law of 3 December 2001.

Today, in the event of simultaneous death, the devolution of each spouse is made in favour of his or her heirs, pursuant to the general rules of the Civil Code.

12. Estate Taxes

i. Inheritance has been liable to taxation in France for several centuries: it is proportionate and progressive. It depends upon the blood tie between the heir and the deceased.

International Succession

    The level of taxation for those who are directly related to the deceased and as between spouses is from 5 to 40 per cent.

    Tax can reach up to 60 per cent of the share received by each heir or legatee.

ii. They are payable in France upon the transfer, not for money or consideration, of all property owned by the deceased wherever located, except on property subject to international conventions aiming to avoid double-taxation, if the deceased was domiciled in France on the date of his death.

iii. Inheritance tax attaches to the net share received by each heir or legatee and not the estate itself. Certain heirs benefits from certain deductions in relation to their share: 46,000 euros for each child, 76,000 euros for the surviving spouse, 1,500 euros for all other heirs or legatees.

    Tax reductions (305 euros or 610 euros per child as from the third), benefit heirs with three or more children.

13. Administration of Estates

i. French law confers the power to administer the estate on the heirs.

    Nevertheless it is necessary to differentiate between:

    – Successors who are 'empowered' (*saisis*), i.e., those who are legally entitled to exercise the powers formerly held by the deceased over the deceased's estate;

    – Successors who are not 'empowered' (*non-saisis*), that do not benefit from such an entitlement.

    The latter must first validate their hereditary entitlement (transfer of possession if it is a holographic will) before they can administer the estate themselves.

    In certain exceptional circumstances, the administration of the estate can be conferred upon a third party, as specified by the court where the heirs are in disagreement or upon demand of the heirs creditors should the heirs be insolvent.

    In addition, if there are no known heirs, the *Administration Française des Domaines* will be called upon by the judge to administer the estate.

    Should the estate devolve upon a person lacking capacity, during the period of incapacity, the property that he will inherit will be administered by this trustee or his guardian or will be under judicial control until such time as he is of full capacity.

ii. A statement concerning the administration of the estate is necessary only in the above-mentioned exception, that is, when the estate is not administered by the heirs.

    This statement must be given to the heirs and is subject to judicial approval.

    An executor (*see infra*) who has been 'empowered' must also draw up a statement as to his activities upon completion.

iii. No such control is exercised by the public authorities with the above-mentioned exception involving, the administration of the estate by the *Administration Française des Domaines*.

iv. The heirs or their legal representatives when the heir is incapacitated, administer the estate in accordance with the principles laid down in the Civil Code in respect of joint ownership when there are many heirs.

Note must be made of the fact that in most cases the joint ownership of the heirs necessitates unanimity, such that one heir on his own cannot take legal action on behalf of the joint ownership without authorization from the other heirs.

v. The heirs become the owners of the deceased's estate from the moment of his death. They take possession as soon as they have established the devolution upon succession, which allows them to show good title to third parties, or, in the case of 'non-empowered' heirs (*non-saisis*), after they have had their titles validated.

Taking possession of the deceased's estate in this way is not without consequence in respect of the duty owed by the heirs to the creditors of the estate, a duty deemed to be *ultra vires* (*see infra*). A distinction must be made as regards those legatees who are not heirs and who therefore have to have their legacy transferred to them by the heirs.

It should also be noted that if the heirs are entitled to take possession of the deceased's property, they may wish to renounce the succession (by way of a declaration made to the *Greffe du Tribunal* in the area where the deceased was domiciled) if the liabilities are much greater than the assets, provided that they have not yet taken possession (*tacit acceptance*).

They can also accept possession on the basis of a 'stock-taking' of the estate's assets (also by way of a declaration made to the *Greffe du Tribunal*), if they are uncertain as to the solvency of the deceased: in these circumstances, they will not be held liable to the creditors of the deceased over and above the value of estate's assets, provided that limits on the powers of administration and realization of the deceased's estate have been complied with.

vi. In principle once the heirs have accepted the administration of the succession, they can levy amounts due either on the deceased's assets or on the heir's own property. Their acceptance does result in some uncertainty as to the deceased's estate and that of each of the heirs.

To avoid such confusion, which could enable the heir's creditors to be paid out of the deceased's estate, the latter's creditors can request registration of a claim allowing for the separation of the estate. These creditors can also serve a formal notice upon the heirs to do so (*see supra*), three months after the death, if the heirs do not undertake the registration. The heirs have a period of forty days in which to draw up an inventory of the assets and the liabilities of the estate. The creditor can also seize estate property as they could have done during the lifetime of the deceased.

vii. The heir is invested with the powers of the deceased from the time of his death, but can he exercise them immediately? Contrary to the common law, which requires a third party to check the heir's titles and to administer the estate for the period required to establish succession, the legal empowerment or the 'seisin' (*saisine*) of the heir in the French jurisdiction allows him to exercise those powers previously exercised by the deceased immediately.

The seisin allows the heir to which it applies to take possession of the estate's assets, to collect its income and to represent the estate.

International Succession

*Some Characteristics of the 'Seisin' (*saisine*)*

- it is of a public nature and the deceased cannot withdraw it from the heirs in his will unless he disinherits them (*see infra* on the limitations of the executor's powers);
- it applies to all heirs designated by the law (new Article 724 of the Civil Code);
- it is a joint power: conferred to each of the heirs in relation to all of the estate;
- a person can be 'seised' and not inherit: therefore a nephew, the closest relation to a deceased uncle may be disinherited by the will in favour of a third party, who may himself have to ask the nephew for the delivery of his legacy.

The Distribution as Between the Heirs (division)

Division is the act which ends the joint ownership of the estate as between the heirs and substitutes the individual rights in respect of specific property.

In accordance with Article 815 of the Civil Code, nothing remains jointly owned and each heir can bring about division. The heirs can nevertheless agree to remain joint owners for a further specified period. The heir's creditors can also bring about division or oppose any action undertaken without their knowledge.

The most common form of 'amicable division', which is what happens in most cases, is undertaken by way of deed (obligatory when the estate consists of real estate), in which the following terms are specified: the property to be divided, the rights of each of the heirs in relation to the whole of the property (i.e., refunding and set-off in respect of donations made), the allocation of property upon division, having regard to the principle of equality as between them, at least in terms of its value, and should the circumstances be such, in respect of the amounts due as between the heirs, and the method by which such amounts will be paid.

The division may only be partial and may only affect certain property belonging to the estate.

If there is an heir who lacks capacity (whether of full age or a minor), *amicable division* is still possible, but will be subject to the approval of the court.

Judicial division is the exception: once division is directed by the judge (upon the request of one of the heirs) a notary is commissioned, as well as experts to assists in evaluations should the need arise; the notary draws up a liquidation statement which he presents to the heirs, then draws up a memorandum recording their agreement or any dissent and lodges this with the court for its approval.

The court can direct the following: the sale of property, the devolution of the shares upon each of the heirs as determined by the notary.

The Powers of the Executor

These powers are constrained by the public nature of the seisin conferred upon the heirs, and also by the existence of heirs who have rights to a compulsory share.

Though the notion of executor is not entirely absent from the Civil Code, its practical implications are limited.

An executor may be any person capable of obligating himself. He will possibly be a notary.

The rule (Article 1026 of the Civil Code) is that he does not have 'seisin', but that the testator can confer this upon him in relation to personal property, enabling him to sell it, keep the proceeds, deliver the legacies or pay the debts.

This partial seisin is limited in time to one year of the date of death.

The testator can also confer upon the executor the power to sell his real estate and to distribute the proceeds to those with entitlements, but only if the testator, once deceased, does not leave any heir with a right to a compulsory share.

14. Domicile/Nationality

i. The above answers apply even if the deceased was not a French national provided that he was domiciled in France at the time of his death and that there is property located within France.

Certain answers may be affected if the deceased was domiciled outside of France leaving real estate in France.

In these circumstances, French law applies the principle of *lex rei sitae* (law relating to the location of real estate), in particular as regards the rules meant to protect the compulsory shares, and as such, public order.

ii. From the time that the deceased was domiciled in the jurisdiction of the court, he will have owned at least certain assets, personal property such as clothing, enabling the local court to validate an holographic will or deal with disputes relating to the estate.

SECTION B – APPLICABLE LAW/PROCEDURE WHERE FOREIGN ELEMENT/S ARE INVOLVED

1. Jurisdiction

i. French court would be competent to deal with a succession in two instances:
  – if the deceased domiciled in France upon his death, and
  – if real estate was located in France where the deceased was not domiciled in France.

ii. Under French domestic law, inheritance law is uniform.

Under French private international law, the following applies:
  – *personal property of an estate* is governed by *the law of the jurisdiction in which the deceased was last domiciled*;
  – *real estate of an estate* is governed by *the law of the jurisdiction in which that property is located*.

International Succession

The designation or personal property or real estate is governed by French law, *lege fori.*

But *renvoi* is recognized by French courts if the law of conflicts as applied abroad so allows. Likewise if the law of a foreign jurisdiction is contrary to French public policy (right of primogeniture, sexual, racial or religious discrimination . . .). French law would prevail in respect of the property located in France.

iii. The competent court in relation to the estate is the *Tribunal de Grande Instance* (similar to a County Court) of the deceased's domicile or the place at which the real estate is located, or failing this the *TGI* in Paris. Finally, the French courts will judge themselves competent should no foreign court deem itself competent.

2. Applicable Law

A French court could apply the law of a foreign jurisdiction in accordance with the principle which allows for independence as between judicial and legislative powers as to the law applicable, *see* 1*ii. above.*

3. Foreign Succession/Inheritance Orders

i. A judicial decision handed down by a court in another legal jurisdiction cannot in principle be enforced in France until an exequatur judgement is handed down by a French court; the role of the court in this instance is to ensure that the decision of the foreign court was handed down in compliance with due process, and that it conforms to the requirements of French public policy.

By virtue of Articles 14 and 15 of the Civil Code, French citizens benefit from privileged jurisdiction; that is, a French citizen party to a decision handed down by a foreign court, who is able to show that the foreign court in question was not competent to make that decision (because he did not submit to its jurisdiction), can resist the enforcement of this decision in France.

ii. In general inheritance law will govern the way in which assets are transferred from the estate.

The heirs can only take possession of certain assets located in France, after having validated their title or having their claims recognized in accordance with French domestic law, in particular in relation to personal property, an attestation in the form of a deed which is executed and authenticated by a notary (with French law remaining applicable), and in relation to company stocks and shares, a certificate also by way of deed.

For other assets, such as those held by banks, the heirs have to prove the competence of the foreign jurisdiction and title which is recognized there. In practice, they will frequently have recourse to French tax law; the institutions holding the deceased's capital cannot, in effect, hand over the funds to the heirs until they receive a certificate from the French taxation authorities confirming the inheritance taxes have been paid.

iii. A 'certificate of customary usage', though not absolutely necessary, is preferable.
Usually a certificate drawn up by a notary or other legal expert having knowledge of foreign law and authenticated documentation (foreign deeds, judgements, . . .) and accompanied by a certified translation will be enough; their deposit with the protocol of a French notary will ensure their safe-keeping.

4. Two or More Succession or Probate Orders

In the case there are two contradictory succession orders from abroad, French law would recognize the succession order which conferred movables according to the national law of the testator and immovables according to the situation of the immovable property.

5. Assets

Yes (*see supra* 1).

6. Expert Evidence

i. No, *see supra* 3(c), although it is preferable.
ii. In principle, the contents of the law in a foreign jurisdiction is a legal fact, the proof of which the parties should establish should they so wish. Judicial approval is not required.

7. Unity of Succession

Yes in relation to French domestic law, but not in relation to private international law, *see supra* 1.

8. Formalities

The formalities prescribed by Article 1007 of the Civil Code are only required for wills which have been discovered in France. Nevertheless a will originating from a foreign jurisdiction must be registered (a requirement for taxation purposes) in France. (*Recette des Impots* of the deceased domiciled in France and of the location of the real estate, if the will includes dispositions which would affect these, or *Recette des impots de Non-Residents* in Paris for non-residents).

9. Legislation

i. Not applicable.
ii. It has been in force since 19 November 1967.

International Succession

10. Wills

    i. *Locus regit actum*: the law of the jurisdiction in which the will was drawn up will apply as to these formalities, e.g., a joint will, which is prohibited in France by Article 968 of the Civil Code, may be recognized if the local law allows for it.

    ii. The inheritance law in question applies.

    iii. The inheritance law in question applies but regard must be had to the right to levy:

Article 2 of the *Act of 14 July 1819*:

'when an inheritance is to be shared between heirs abroad and heirs in France, the latter can levy a charge on the assets which are located in France, equal to that of the value of the assets located abroad, which would not be put at their disposal, regardless of entitlement, by virtue of local laws and customs'.

    iv. The law which would be applicable to the heir in question.

    v. As per Article 5 of the *1961 Hague Convention on the Conflicts of Laws Relating to the Form of Testamentary Dispositions* the law which relates to the formalities of a will.

    vi. *See* (a) *supra*.

    vii. The basic rule is that inheritance law applies.

    viii. The law which relates to the formalities of a will.

    ix. In accordance with the applicable inheritance law, with the exception of the application of the right to levy.

11. Domicile/Nationality

    i. The applicable law as to its construction would depend upon the applicable inheritance law, whereas the law applicable to the formalities of the will would depend on where it had been drawn up.

    ii. The overriding criterion is that of domicile, the location at which the deceased had his principal residence (material criterion) and his intention to remain there with a certain degree of permanence (criterion of intent). In case of doubt, the criterion of intent is held to be of greater weight. In such cases the matter would be decided by a *judge of fact*.

12. Taxation

Heirs who are not domiciled cannot take possession of the deceased's assets which are located in France until they can prove to those who hold these assets that they have paid the inheritance tax due to the French authorities. They cannot receive the proceeds of sale of the deceased's real estate until they have also provided the notary with the same information.

The domicile of the deceased in France renders the whole of his estate, whether located in France or abroad, liable to payment of inheritance tax, although this will not be the case if the provisions of international conventions aimed to avoid double taxation apply.

Article 784A of the *CGI* allows for tax which is paid outside France to be set against tax that is owed within France in accordance with the following formulation.

Imputed tax:

$$\frac{\text{'tax paid outside of France} \times \text{the gross value of the property outside of France'}}{\text{gross value of the entire estate.}}$$

Germany

Prepared by: Dr. Heinz L. BAUER
Bauer Gronen Kiesgen

Address: Hamburger Allee 1
          60486 Frankfurt am Main
          Germany
Tel.:   +49 69 505032 200
Fax: +49 69 505032 299
E-mail: Bauer@BGK.de

SECTION A – BRIEF SURVEY OF THE LOCAL SYSTEM

1. Type of System

(a) Civil Law.

(b) Although Germany is a federation, the German Civil Code (BGB) applies throughout the country.

2. Wills

(a) There must be a written document.

The BGB recognizes two standard forms of will:

- *Holographic will*: which must be wholly in written form, dated and signed by the testator (Article 2247 BGB); this form is not permitted for the use of minors (those under the age of eighteen) (Article 2247(IV) BGB).
- *Will made by way of public instrument* (*authenticated will*) (Article 2232 BGB):
    - a declaration made by the testator of his final intentions to a notary; or
    - a written document which the testator then orally asserts to represent his final intentions; the testator can provide this document either sealed or unsealed and it can be written up by the testator himself or by someone else.

Spouses and partners of a 'lifetime partnership' between two persons of the same sex (*Lebenspartnerschaft*) can draw up a will, whether holographic (written by one of them and signed by both) or by way of public instrument (Article 2265 BGB, Article 10IV Part G (*Lebenspartnerschaftgesetz*).

The two standard forms of will do not require the involvement of witnesses.

Extraordinary wills, foreseen for exceptional circumstances and emergency situations, do not necessitate the involvement of a notary but do require the involvement of witnesses. Such wills must be reconfirmed by the testator within three months after which his situation has been normalized (Articles 2249 to 2252 BGB).

Germany is not a signatory of the *1973 Washington Convention on International Wills*.

(b) *i.* All wills can be changed by the testator in accordance with the rules applicable to the above-mentioned wills.

A will can be revoked in whole or in part at any time (Article 2254 BGB) by another will, an express disposition or a tacit disposition (Articles 2255 & 2258 BGB); the same applies for a codicil.

More specifically, the revocation of a will (holographic or other) may be effected by a subsequent will (Article 2254 BGB). The will which serves to revoke a prior will does not have to be in the same form as the latter. For example, a will made by way of public instrument can be revoked by a holographic will and vice versa.

The recovery of a will by way of public instrument previously lodged at the Probate Court (*Nachlassgericht*) amounts to its revocation (Article 2256 BGB). This is not the case for the recovery of a holographic will (Article 2256(III) BGB).

ii. Marriage does not affect the validity of a previous will.

Marriage, however, does confer the right to challenge the validity of a will if the testator did not made provision for his spouse and the latter's existence was unknown to the testator at the time he drew up the will (Article 2079 BGB).

Divorce results in the nullity of a will in favour of the divorced spouse (2077 BGB). A similar regime is applied to 'lifetime partnership' (Article 10V Part G).

iii. A revocation can in its turn be revoked. Such revocation would result in the validity of the previous will (Article 2257 BGB).

3. Intestacy

(a) Succession devolves in accordance with the order of succession. The order is determined in accordance with the heirs' blood ties with the deceased:

- *The heirs of the first order* comprise the descendants of the deceased. A descendant who is living when the succession occurs will exclude from the succession those descendants who are related to the deceased through him. If this descendant is no longer living at the time that the succession takes place, those descendants who are related to the deceased through him will take in his place (succession *per stirpes*). Children will take in equal measures.
- *The heirs of the second order* comprise the ancestors of the deceased (father and mother) and their descendants (brothers and sisters, nephews and nieces and their children). If the ancestors are alive when succession takes place, they alone will

succeed in equal measures. If the father or the mother is no longer alive when the succession takes place, his or her descendants will take in his or her place in accordance with the provisions applicable to the succession of heirs of the first order. If the deceased parent does not leave any descendants, the surviving parent alone will succeed.

– *The heirs of the third order* comprise the grandparents of the deceased and their descendants (uncles and aunts, cousins, etc.). If the grandparents are alive when the succession occurs, they alone will take in equal shares. If at the time the succession takes place, the grandfather or the grandmother, paternal or maternal, is no longer alive, his or her descendants will take in his or her place. If no such descendants exist, the remaining grandparent alone will succeed and if the latter is deceased as well, his or her descendants will succeed. If at the time of succession the paternal or maternal grandparents are no longer alive and if they leave no descendants, the other grandparents or their descendants will alone succeed. In all instances where descendants take their parent's or grandparent's share, the provisions applicable to the succession of heirs of the first order will also apply.

– *The heirs of the fourth order* comprise the great grandparents of the deceased and their descendants;

– *The heirs of the fifth order and of subsequent orders* comprise more distant ancestors and their descendants.

As regards heirs of the above orders, a closer relative will prevent a more distant relative from succeeding (Article 1930 BGB).

An *illegitimate child* (*nichteheliches Kind*) born after 1 July 1949 will inherit, as regards succession after from 1 April 1998 as a legitimate child. Adopted children also inherit equally. Adopted Adults also inherit but the effects of such Adoption, however, are not extended to the relations of the adopted parent or spouse of the adopted adult.

The surviving spouse or the partner of a (homosexual) lifetime partnership is entitled to one-quarter of the inheritance if there are heirs of the first order living and to one-half of it if there are heirs of the second order or grandparents living. Furthermore, when descendants of a grandparent would take a share in accordance with the provisions of Article 1926 BGB, the surviving spouse will take that share. In the absence of heirs of the first or second order or the grandparents, the surviving spouse takes the entire inheritance (Article 1931 BGB).

It is also important to remember the impact of *the matrimonial regime* and especially of the legal regime as regards the community of after-acquired property (*Zugewinngemeinschaft*). When one of the spouses dies, the principle of equal division of property acquired after the marriage will serve to increase that to which the surviving spouse is entitled by one-quarter of the inheritance; it is immaterial whether in any particular case the spouses did acquire property or not ('fixed equalisation' Article 1371 BGB). If the surviving spouse was disinherited or was in the process of obtaining a divorce, however, he can only claim that property which was actually acquired after the marriage.

If the matrimonial regime was based upon the separation of property, the surviving spouse will inherit with one or two children respectively in equal shares (Article 1931(IV) BGB); if there are more than two children, the general rule

(Article 1931(I) BGB) applies, i.e., that the surviving spouse shall receive one-quarter of the estate with the balance being divided between the children. A similar regime is applied to 'lifetime partnerships' (Article 10I, II Part G).

If the heirs of a German national cannot be determined by the Probate Court within a reasonable period of time, the German tax authorities become the successors (Articles 1964 & 1936 BGB).

(b) German law does not allow for a distinction to be made between the succession of movables and that of immovables. It should be noted that from the moment of death, the deceased's property passes wholly and immediately to his heirs (successors), without the need for official intervention or for any particular form of consent or seisin; this is the case even if the heirs do not realize that the deceased's property has been passed on to them (Articles 1922 & 1942 BGB). The definitive acquisition of the inheritance, however, will only occur after the expiry of the period within which the heirs are allowed to renounce the succession.

4. Freedom of Testation

(a) Freedom of testation is guaranteed by the German constitution. There are, however, certain safeguards to protect members of the deceased's family.

German law does not recognize an heir's entitlement to a compulsory share as such but does ensure that the testator's close relations will take some part of the inheritance by way of a monetary payment. If the descendants (or in their absence the parents) or the spouse or a 'lifetime (homosexual) partner' of the deceased is disinherited by a testamentary disposition, they have a legal right to a monetary payment (*Pflichtteil*, Article 2303 BGB). Unmarried couples, however, do not benefit from this right.

This monetary payment will be equal to half of the value of the legal hereditary entitlement upon intestacy. A claim for such payment must be made within a period of three years from the time the person with the right became aware of the deceased's property having passed and of the disposition which has encroached upon his rights in this regard; in any case within thirty years after the deceased's death (Article 2332 BGB, Article 10VI Part G).

The right essentially allows for a pecuniary claim to be made as against the legatees.

The deceased can deprive a descendant of his 'compulsory share' in his will if he has been badly mistreated by the descendant in question (Articles 2333 ff. BGB).

(b) *i*. The deceased can appoint an heir by way of contract (*Erbvertrag*, Articles 2274 ff. BGB). The contract can designate as heir a party to the contract as well as a third party. Like all contracts, a contract of inheritance binds the parties as soon as it is concluded by deed; the obligations under the contract do not come into force, however, until the succession takes place. To avoid this contractual agreement having to take effect, the person whose property is to pass should reserve for himself the power to cancel the contract (Article 2293 BGB). Otherwise the law only allows for the contract to be contested (Article 2281 BGB) or terminated (Article 2290 BGB) by way of a contract concluded by the parties having entered into the initial contract. Once one of the parties to the inheritance contract has died, it is no longer possible to terminate the contract.

A person whose property is to pass can cancel all dispositions in relation to which inheritance contracts have been concluded and in which provision has been made for a legacy or a charge by making a will; in this instance the consent of the other contracting party is required (Article 2291). All contracts of inheritance made between spouses or 'lifetime partners' can also be cancelled by a joint will (Article 2292 BGB).

The law also allows for a negative form of inheritance contract, that is to say, a contract renouncing the succession, such that the spouse or a 'lifetime partner' or relations renounce their legal hereditary entitlement upon intestacy; the contract can, however, be limited to the renunciation of the right to a 'compulsory share'.

ii. Whereas German law prohibits contracts by which a testator is forced to make or revoke a testamentary disposition (Article 2302 BGB), German jurisprudence allows for contracts in which succession is renounced to be entered into with the person whose property is to pass.

German law allows for advance division (e.g., Article 593(a) BGB); this entails the drawing up of *inter vivos* agreements, and often concerns the donation of agricultural property; it enables parents to divide their property in advance whilst retaining the use of such property for the remainder of their lives. Agreements relating to such donations must conform to provisions laid down in respect of ordinary donations, i.e., they must be by deed.

5. Maintenance

German law stipulates that during the thirty days following the succession, the heirs must provide maintenance to those family members (including 'lifetime partners', Article 11I Part G) of the deceased who, around the time of death, were members of the deceased's household and maintained by him, commensurate with the maintenance previously paid by the deceased. They must also allow them the continued use of the family home as well as property used in connection with it (Article 1969 BGB).

When succession takes place and there is an heir about to be born, the mother can, if she is not able to provide for her own needs, ask to receive from the heirs that which is deemed generally necessary for her upkeep until the child is born (Article 1963 BGB). Otherwise, the surviving spouse and the children have the right to demand payment of the 'compulsory share' to which they are entitled (*see* 4(a) *above*).

As for maintenance paid after a divorce, the right to such maintenance subsists until the death of the payee; upon the death of the payer, the obligation becomes the liability of the heirs (Article 1586(b) BGB).

6. Community Property Between Husband and Wife

(a) The share of community property which does not pass upon succession is one-quarter ('fixed rate of division of after-acquired property' Article 1371 BGB); *see* 3(a) *above*.

(b) The law does not allow for a person to contract to dispose of all of his property without the consent of his spouse.

In cases of divorce, after marriage acquired property is calculated by subtracting the value of the goods at the start of the marriage from the value of the goods at the end of the marriage. A former spouse has the right to compensation on this basis (Article 1378 BGB), which right lapses after three years.

7. Gifts (*Inter Vivos*)

(a) Upon the division of the inheritance, the descendants who inherit are obliged to bring into account the gifts they received from the deceased during the latter's lifetime, unless the deceased had decided otherwise when the gift was made (Articles 2050 & 1934(b)(III) BGB).

As regards those entitled to a 'compulsory share', if the deceased made a donation to a third party, those having such an entitlement can demand the amount by which their 'compulsory share' would increase upon the addition of the gift to the inheritance. Regard will not be had of gifts where more than ten years have elapsed since they were made. If a gift was made to the spouse of the deceased, the time-limit only begins to run after the marriage is dissolved (Article 2325 BGB). This time limit may also be applicable to 'lifetime partners' (Article 10VI 2 Part G).

As regards inheritance contracts, the contractual heir can, if the deceased made a donation with a view to adversely affecting that contractual party's interests, demand the restitution of that gift by the recipient in accordance with the provisions on restitution upon unjust enrichment (Article 2287 BGB).

When there is a remainder involved (Article 2100 BGB), a disposition by an heir, who takes subject to a legacy or as tenant for life, of part of the inheritance at undervalue is null and void to the extent that it encroaches upon or is contrary to the interests of those who will take afterwards (Article 2113 BGB).

(b) When assessing the amount to be brought into account (*rapport*) (Article 2050 BGB), the value of the gift is deemed to be its value at the time it was made.

When assessing the amount which a person having a right to a compulsory share can require to be added to the inheritance (Article 2325 BGB), a consumable good is valued as at the time the gift was made; all other goods are valued as at the time succession takes place (Article 2325 II BGB).

8. Capacity

(a) A minor is only able to make a will if he is at least sixteen years of age (Article 2229 BGB). Such a minor does not require the consent of his legal guardian to make a will; his capacity, however, is limited to disposition by a will by way of public instrument, an oral declaration or an unsealed written statement (Articles 2247(IV) & 2233(I) BGB).

Persons incapacitated by mental illness, mental deficiency or derangement such that they cannot appreciate the significance of any declaration they may make or act in a discerning manner are not able to make a will (Article 2229(III) BGB).

As regards contracts of inheritance, a person can enter into such contract with his spouse even though the latter's capacity to exercise his rights may be limited. In this case, he requires the consent of his legal representative; if such representative is a guardian, the approval of the Guardianship Court is required also (Article 2275 BGB).

(b) The law (Article 26 *Beurkundungsgesetz-BeurkG* (*BeurkG*), Law on authentication) prevents certain people from participating in the drawing up of a will as witnesses, such as, for example, the spouse or close relations of the notary, a minor or a beneficiary in the will. But as the participation of witnesses is not obligatory in Germany, non-compliance with this rule does not result in the invalidity of the will (Article 26(II)(6) *BeurkG*).

The nationality of a witness has no bearing on the matter; he must, however, understand the language in which the will is drawn up.

(c) To inherit, an heir must be alive at the time the succession takes place (Article 1923 BGB). By way of a legal fiction (Article 1923(II) BGB), a person who has not yet been born but has already been conceived (*nasciturus*) is deemed to have been born before the succession takes place.

When there is a remainder involved and a person not yet conceived at the time of the devolution (*nondum conceptus*) has been appointed as heir, in cases of doubt, the person must be assumed to have been appointed as remainderman. It is likewise with the appointment of a legal entity which has not been formed until after succession has taken place (Article 2101 BGB).

A will which contains a gift in favour of a nursing home or other type of home in which the deceased had lived may be null and void if the management of such a home was aware of such a gift being made (Article 14(I) *Heimgesetz*, Law pertaining to the management of such homes).

9. Authority (Court, Notarial or Other)

Death is established by way of a certificate drawn up by a registrar or, when a person has gone missing, a court judgment allowing for the devolution of a missing person's assets.

The German Civil Code provides for the issuing of an official certificate referred to as the *Erbschein* which includes information as to the identity of the heirs but none as to the size of the inheritance (Article 2353 BGB). This certificate is issued by the Probate Court and allows third parties to obtain property from the heirs in good faith. It does not, however, carry the weight of a final judgment. To obtain an order having such an effect, an ordinary civil action must be brought by the interested parties (e.g., an action to contest the right to an inheritance).

In specific cases, it may be sufficient to present the will by way of public instrument or the inheritance contract after its opening by the probate court to establish an heir's status; this may be possible, for example, as regards the land registry index, banks and insurance companies.

10. Invalidity of Will

(a) The reasons for the invalidity of a testamentary disposition are numerous.

A disposition may be void, either wholly or partially, *ex nunc*, when it contravenes laws meant to uphold public decency or morality (Article 138 BGB), or when it does not conform to legal requirements (i.e., as to formalities or capacity), including those which relate to the authentication of the will (Articles 7 & 27 BeurkG: invalidity on the grounds that the notary or his spouse or certain of his relations or those connected to him will benefit from the will).

A disposition may be voidable *ex tunc* by revocation (Articles 2253 ff. BGB), by a request to have it set aside (*Anfechtung*), by dissolution of a marriage, an engagement or a 'lifetime partnership' (Articles 2077, 2268 & 2279 BGB, Article 10V Part G), by a renunciation of the succession (Article 2352 BGB), by a beneficiary predeceasing the testator (Article 1923(I) BGB), by a repudiation of the succession (Article 1944 BGB), by a declaration as to the unworthiness of the right to inherit (Articles 2344 & 2342(II) BGB), or by the expiry of time (Articles 2109, 2162, 2210 & 2252 BGB).

(b) The consequences arising from invalidity and voidability are different and will depend on the specific facts involved. In certain cases, the possibility of conversion (Article 140 BGB) can be considered. Article 140 BGB reads: 'If a judicial instrument meets conditions applying to another judicial instrument, the latter is deemed valid if it can be presumed that the applicability of its provisions would have been intended if the nullity of the first had been known.'

On this basis, jurisprudence recognizes the following:

– the conversion of a contract of inheritance (*Erbvertrag*) into a will or joint will;
– the conversion of a joint will as between persons who are not married into two separate wills;
– the conversion of a promise to make a donation into a will.

11. Simultaneous Death

(a) German law does not recognize any presumptions as to survival in cases involving simultaneous death. On the contrary, according to the law (Article 11 *Verschollenheitsgesetz*, Law relating to missing persons) the deaths of those involved are considered to be simultaneous if the survival of the deceased persons in relation to each other cannot be established.

(b) The dates are determined either by the death certificate drawn up by the registry or by the Probate Court. If the court applies Article 11 of the Law relating to missing persons, the persons having died in the same incident cannot inherit one from the other.

12. Estate Taxes

(a) Inheritance tax does exist and is governed by the same law as that relating to *inter vivos* transfers. It is proportional and progressive and is dependant on the blood tie between the heir and the deceased. The rates of tax for direct relations and as between spouses are from 7 to 40 per cent. They can reach up to 50 per cent of that received by the heir or the legatee.

(b) In Germany, the tax liability is deemed 'unlimited', that is to say, in respect of the entire inheritance wherever its location, and attaches to the deceased's domicile for tax purposes as well as to that of the heir. Even if only one of these has their domicile in Germany for tax purposes, unlimited tax liability will be established.

By way of legal fiction, the law also confers domicile in Germany for tax purposes upon certain German subjects, such as state employees carrying out their duties or assigned duties abroad.

To prevent tax evasion, the law also establishes unlimited tax liability upon German nationals not domiciled in Germany if they have spent less than five years permanent residence abroad.

As for assets located in Germany belonging to a deceased or heirs who are domiciled abroad, tax to be paid to the German tax authorities is limited to these assets only.

(c) German law does not recognize one legal entity like that of the 'estate' recognized in common law. On the contrary, the whole of the deceased's property passes immediately to the heirs. It is therefore not the 'estate' which is taxed (*Nachlass-Steuer*) but each heir in relation to his share of the succession (*Erbanfall-Steuer*).

Certain heirs benefit from the tax deductions on their shares: i.e., up to 307,000 euro for the spouse (who may also benefit from a special marital exemption up to 256,000), 205,000 euro for each child. In tax law 'lifetime partners' are not privileged.

13. Administration of Estates

(a) Given the fact that in accordance with German law the deceased's property passes immediately and directly at the time of death to the heirs without the intervention of state authorities, there is normally no need for an administrator.

If there are several heirs, the administration of the succession is carried out by all of them. Each joint heir is bound as regards the others to comply with measures which will allow for an orderly and lawful administration; each heir can also take measures deemed necessary to protect and preserve the property that has devolved without having to obtain the agreement of the others (Article 2038 BGB).

Otherwise each of the joint heirs can ask for the division of the property which has devolved except in special cases (Article 2042 BGB).

The deceased can, however, in his will appoint an administrator (*Testamentsvollstrecke* Articles 2197 ff. BGB). His functions and rights are broader than those of an executor under French law and are similar to those of an executor under American law.

In certain cases, e.g., where the succession may be overindebted, the administration of the succession may be conferred upon a third party by the court (*Nachlass-Verwalter*, Article 1975 BGB). Where there is a vacant succession, a fiduciary administrator, *Nachlass-Pfleger*, can be nominated by the court (Article 1960 BGB).

(b) An account of the administration is not necessary except in the above-mentioned cases, when the succession is not directly administered by the heirs.

The above-mentioned administrators appointed by the court (Articles 1840 ff., 1915(I) BGB) must report to the judge whereas the testamentary administrator will report to the heirs.

In order to limit their liabilities, the heirs can, or upon a demand made by a creditor must, draw up an inventory (Article 1993 BGB) and present it to the court. In addition, a prior heir must provide a statement of the property belonging to the inheritance upon the request of a reversionary heir (Article 2121 BGB).

(c) There is no state control over the administration of the devolution of the deceased's property. As for the control exercised by the court, *see* supra.

(d) The heirs, or their legal representatives in cases of incapacity, have such a right, in accordance with the principles laid down by the BGB, as regards the co-ownership of the succession. When a testamentary administrator is appointed, he represents the succession. All rights given to him in connection with the administration of the devolution of the deceased's property can only be invoked at law by him (Article 2212 BGB).

(e) The heirs are the owners of the property of the deceased as soon as he dies and they take possession directly, though they must establish their rights to the satisfaction of certain third parties. A distinction must be made as regards persons entitled only to a particular legacy (*Vermaechtnisnehmer*), who must obtain their legacy from the heirs.

Heirs can only renounce the succession if they have not previously accepted it, not even tacitly. The right of renunciation (*Ausschlagung*) can only be exercised within a six week period. This period is extended to six months if the deceased was last domiciled abroad or if the heir himself was residing abroad once the time period had started to run (Article 1944 BGB).

(f) In principle the creditors are paid by the heirs, by way of a charge upon the property of the deceased which has passed or the heirs' own property if they have accepted the succession. If the creditors had begun proceedings to recover a debt from the deceased whilst the latter had been alive, such proceedings will be suspended until such time as the heirs can be substituted (if they have accepted the succession) (Article 239 ZPO, the Code relating to civil proceedings). The heirs can request that judgement be made against them subject to the limitation of their liabilities (Article 305 ZPO).

Article 305 ZPO reads as follows: 'Recourse had by heirs to those exceptions set out in Articles 2014 and 2015 of the Civil Code does not preclude a judgement being made against them, subject to the limitation of their liabilities.' Following on from this, Articles 2014 and 2015 BGB read: 'The heir has the right to refuse to discharge an obligation relating to the succession up until three months following the acceptance of the succession but not after the inventory has been drawn up.' and 'Once an heir has made a request to be allowed to summons the creditors of the estate publicly, such request being made within a time period of one year following the acceptance of the succession, and such request is granted, the heir can then refuse to discharge an obligation relating to the succession until the procedure involving the summons has been completed.'

Article 305 ZPO means therefore that the above exceptions will not prevent an unconditional judgement being made against the heirs but allows them to limit their liabilities as regards the operative provisions of such a judgement (*le dispositif du jugement*), without the merits as to the recourse to the said exceptions having been considered.

The creditors to the succession can be called upon to produce their claims by way of a formal notice (Article 1970 BGB).

(g) Until the inheritance has been divided, each of the heirs can dispose of his share in it but is not allowed to dispose of specific property forming part of it (Article 2033 BGB). The heirs can only dispose of specific property when acting jointly. Similarly, a debtor cannot settle his account as regards the succession with the repayment of a debt owed only to one of the heirs (Article 2040 BGB).

Division cannot be carried out as long as the share of each of the heirs remains uncertain due to the expected birth of an heir (Article 2043 BGB).

The deceased can, by way of testamentary disposition, prohibit division of the inheritance or that relating to certain property forming part of it; this stipulation becomes ineffective after a period of thirty years has elapsed from the time the deceased's property was to pass.

The obligations relating to the succession must be dealt with first. In order to discharge those obligations, the property which is to pass should be converted into cash insofar as this is necessary (Article 2046 BGB). The excess remaining after the discharge of such obligations will go to the heirs in accordance with the share each is to take. Writings concerning relations between the deceased, his family or the succession in its entirety remain common property (Article 2047 BGB).

The person whose property is to pass can regulate the way in which it is to be divided upon his death. He can prescribe that the division is to follow an equitable assessment made by a third party. The decision of that third party is not binding on the heirs if it is manifestly unjust; should that be the case, the court will hand down a judgment on the matter (Article 2048 BGB).

If, as often happens, a testamentary administrator has been appointed by the deceased, he is entrusted with the division upon succession as between the heirs if there is more than one heir. He must, however, solicit the views of the heirs as to his proposals before dividing the property (Article 2204 BGB).

14. Domicile/Nationality

(a) The nationality of the deceased and his domicile are only significant in relation to the application of provisions on the conflict of laws, which will be examined below.

(b) Even given this improbable scenario, where the deceased has no assets the court would have jurisdiction if the deceased was a German national.

SECTION B – APPLICABLE LAW/PROCEDURE WHERE FOREIGN ELEMENT/S ARE INVOLVED

1. Jurisdiction

(a) The court would deem itself to have jurisdiction if:
– German inheritance law is applicable (even only partially);
– there are assets (movables or immovables) on German territory;
– an international convention confers such jurisdiction (e.g., *Establishment Convention* between Iran and Germany; *Consular Treaty* between Turkey and Germany).

(b) German domestic law and private international law on succession admits the unity of succession. A distinction between movable and immovable property can be made under private international law, as in Article 3 *EGBGB* (Law on German private international law) which states as follows: 'To the extent that such provisions result in a person's patrimony being subjected to the law of a particular state, the related provisions in Sections 3 and 4 do not apply to property not located in the state whose law would apply, when the law deriving from their location results in the application of special measures.'

(c) The territorial jurisdiction of the Probate Court is based upon the deceased's domicile or, for want of domicile, by the temporary residence of the deceased at the time of his death; in cases involving German nationals without domicile or temporary residence in Germany, jurisdiction rests with the Berlin-Schoeneberg Court. In cases involving a foreigner without domicile or temporary residence in Germany, jurisdiction rests with the court in whose territory the assets of the succession are located (Article 73 *FGG*, Law pertaining to non-contentious jurisdiction).

2. Applicable Law

The answer depends upon the facts before the court.

In general the court will apply those provisions applicable under private international law. This may result in the application of German law or the law of another state. As regards the succession, the connecting factor is generally that of the nationality of the deceased at the time of his death. If the court has to rule upon the

247

validity of the will as regards its form, it may also apply the law in force in the domicile of the deceased at the time he made the disposition. *Lex situs* applies to immovable property in Germany.

3. Foreign Succession/Inheritance Orders

(a) A foreign judicial decision is not usually directly enforceable in Germany until a German execution order has been obtained (Articles 722, 723 & 328 ZPO, the Code relating to civil proceedings). The recognition of a judicial act in non-contentious proceedings follows the same rules applicable to foreign judgements. Proof of entitlement to inheritance from a foreign country does not automatically bind a German court but may be recognized by it (Article 16(a) *FGG*).

The Council Regulation (EC) No. 44/2001 of December 2000 on jurisdiction and the recognition and enforcement of judgments in civil and commercial matters expressly excludes wills and successions from its ambit.

(b) To take possession of property located in Germany which has devolved upon the heirs and is governed by foreign law, a special heir's certificate (*Fremdrechtserbschein*) can be obtained from a German court. Article 2369 of the BGB states that: 'When property located in Germany makes up part of an inheritance in relation to which no German Probate Court is competent to issue the general heir's certificate, a request can be made to obtain the issue of a special heir's certificate for such property.'

A request can also be made for an execution order for a foreign judgment. *See supra.*

(c) It is necessary to submit an officially recorded copy or an execution copy of the foreign order with certified translations; in certain cases it is also necessary to prove delivery of the foreign order.

4. Two or More Succession or Probate Orders

Normally, when acting within the sphere of its international jurisdiction (when German law applies or when the assets of the deceased are located in Germany), a German court will itself hand down an order confirming the right of the heir (*Erbschein*) without taking account of the existence of a corresponding foreign decision.

If there are foreign orders, the German court will look into them.

A foreign order corresponding to that issued in Germany confirming the right of an heir can be taken into consideration by a German court, for example to render unnecessary the taking of evidence as to facts that would otherwise have to be established by way of German legal procedure. However, the German court is not bound by the foreign order itself. The court, as regards non-contentious matters, is not prevented from delivering a new order confirming the right of heir if the foreign order is deemed to be ineffective according to German law, say, for example, because its content does not conform to German provisions as to private international law (regard being had, however, to those facts ascertained in the foreign order).

The German legal doctrine relating to this matter is, however, contentious.

5. Assets

Yes, *see supra.*

6. Expert Evidence

(a) The German court must, of its own motion, apply, and thus examine, the foreign law at issue. Often it calls upon an expert or an academic institute specializing in international law, or it requests information within the framework of the *1968 European Convention on Information Pertaining to Foreign Law.*

The parties are allowed, however, and even encouraged, to pass on information they have been able to obtain.

German law does not recognize a 'certificate of foreign law', but the judge is not prevented from referring to such a document if it is filed by the parties in order to establish the contents of foreign law.

(b) An affidavit with or without judicial confirmation is not excluded as a source of information to be used by the judge as to the contents of foreign law.

7. Unity of Succession

German law admits the unity of succession, whether in domestic law or private international law. However attention must be paid to Article 3 III *EGBGB* (German private international law), *see supra* 1(b), and the rules of *renvoi* (Article 4 *EGBGB*).

8. Formalities

Also for a will drawn up abroad, each person in possession of such a will not held on official deposit must hand this over to the court as soon as he is aware of the testator's death (Article 2259 BGB). The court will examine the will of a German national drawn up abroad as well as that of a foreigner, because only knowledge of the will's contents will enable the court to decide whether it has jurisdiction.

9. Legislation

The *1961 Hague Convention on the Conflicts of Laws Relating to the Form of Testamentary Dispositions* entered into force in Germany on 1 January 1966. Germany is not party to the *1973 Washington Convention on International Wills.*

International Succession

10. Wills

(a) The formalities of the will are governed, in accordance with the *1961 Hague Convention on the Conflicts of Laws Relating to the Form of Testamentary Dispositions* which has been incorporated into German domestic law (Article 26 EGBGB), by the following:
- the law of the nationality of the deceased at the time the will was drawn up or at the time of his death;
- the law of the location the will was drawn up;
- the law of the domicile of the deceased or his habitual residence at the time the will was drawn up or at the time of his death;
- for immovables, the law of their location;
- the law applicable to the succession.

In matters relating to succession, German law allows for the application of *professio juris*; the testator can therefore choose for German law to apply to his immovables located in Germany (Article 25 *EGBGB*).

(b) The inheritance law is to be applied (which according to German private international law is the law of the nationality of the deceased).

(c) The inheritance law is to be applied.

(d) The inheritance law is to be applied; if this law requires the civil capacity of the heir be established, this should be done in accordance with the law of the nationality of the heir (though legal opinion is divided on this matter).

(e) The inheritance law at the time the will was drawn up is to be applied (though legal opinion is also divided on this matter).

(f) As to the validity of its form, *see* (a) immediately *above*. As to the validity of its content, German private international law provides the following (Article 26V *EGBGB*): 'Other than as regards form, the validity of a testamentary disposition, and its resulting irrevocability, is subject to the law governing the succession at the time the disposition was made. The acquisition or loss of German nationality does not affect the capacity to make a will which a person previously had.'

(g) The inheritance law is to be applied.

(h) The rules relating to the formalities of the will are to be applied.

(i) Yes.

11. Domicile/Nationality

(a) The law which applies as to its content depends upon the inheritance law to be applied (German law: the nationality at the time of death); as to the formalities, this can be the nationality or the domicile, either when the will was drawn up or when the testator died.

(b) No.

(c) When the law of the state of which a person is a national is applicable and that person has several nationalities, reference must be made to the law of the state with which that person was most closely linked, that is, by his habitual residence or in relation to the main events in his life. If the person has German nationality also, that nationality will prevail.

When a person is stateless or his nationality cannot be established, the law of the state in which he is habitually resident, or, failing this, the law of his residence will be applied (Article 5 *EGBGB*).

12. Taxation

If neither the deceased nor the heir is domiciled in Germany, there may be a limited tax liability. To prevent tax evasion, the law (*Aussensteuergesetz*) has extended limited tax liability in cases where the deceased was, in a ten year period before his unlimited tax liability as a German national ended, for at least five years subject to unlimited tax liability (*see supra*) and had transferred his domicile to a state with lower taxation (less than 30 per cent) than that in Germany.

If an inheritance is subject to tax in Germany and abroad, there is the possibility of set-off under certain conditions and when German inheritance tax liability is unlimited. German law provides for a reduction limited to that part of the domestic tax which corresponds to the value of the overseas assets ('ordinary set-off'). All such provisions apply in the absence of international agreements designed to avoid double taxation.

Greece

Prepared by: Mme Aspassia MARTINI-VARDAKA, Notary

Address: 86–88 Rue Kolokotroni
        GR18535 Piree
        Greece
Tel.:   +30 210 417 4294
Fax: +30 210 417 2830

Section A – Brief Survey of the Local System

1. Type of System

(a) Civil law is that which governs inheritance law.

(b) There are no important differences between the provinces.

2. Wills

In accordance with Article 1712 of the Civil Code, the deceased can appoint an heir by way of a unilateral testamentary disposition.

(a) The different forms of wills are those which follow:

  i. Holographic (Articles 1721 and 1722 of the Civil Code): In accordance with Article 1721 of the Civil Code, this form of will must be entirely in written form in the testator's own handwriting and dated and signed by him. The day, month and the year must be evident from the date included in the will. The holographic will is not subject to any other formality. The inclusion of the wrong date does not in itself result in the nullity of the will. If there are other defects in the will, the court can, following consideration of the matter, nullify the will in whole or in part. Additions to the will made in the margin or at the bottom of the will must be signed by the testator otherwise they are deemed not to have been written. Deletions, insertions, scratchings out and other similar defects, which are ascertained by the court first examining the will upon the death of the testator, may, following the court's consideration of the matter, result in the nullity of the will, either in whole or in part.

Article 1722 of the Civil Code provides that the holographic will can be deposited by the testator with a notary in accordance with those provisions ordinarily applying to the deposit of documents.

ii. *Public* (*authentique*) (Articles 1724 and 1730–1737 of the Civil Code): In accordance with Article 1724 of the Civil Code, this form of will is drawn up by a notary in the presence of three witnesses, or by two notaries with one witness present, upon the testator's declaration of his last wishes and in accordance also with the provisions of Articles 1725 to 1737.

Article 1730 of the Civil Code provides that the testator must make his declaration orally to the notary and the other persons who are party to the instrument. The testator can dictate his last wishes from memory or notes.

In accordance with Article 1731 of the Civil Code, the witnesses swear before the notary and the testator to keep the testamentary dispositions secret until the estate passes to the heirs. Non-compliance with this provision does not nullify the will.

Article 1732 of the Civil Code provides that such a will must comprise the following:

– the day, month, year and location the will was drawn up;
– the designation of the testator, such that there is no doubt as to his identity;
– the first and last names of the notary and the other persons who are party to the instrument and, although the omission of this information would not result in the nullity of the will, the principal office of the notary and the professions and addresses of those other persons who are party to the instrument;
– a declaration of the testator's last wishes and a statement to the effect that the stipulations in Article 1730 were observed.

Mention must also be made in the instrument that the stipulations in Articles 1729 and 1731 of the Civil Code were observed; the omission of this formality, however, will not result in the nullity of the will.

In terms of Article 1729, if the notary did not know the testator personally, the witnesses have to certify that they knew him, unless his identity was proved by a second notary.

Article 1731 requires the witnesses to declare before the notary that they will not disclose the contents of the will if these became known to them, prior to the decease of the testator.

As already mentioned, failure to observe the provisions of these articles does not result in the nullity of the will.

In accordance with Article 1733 of the Civil Code, the instrument must be read out to the testator in the presence of the persons who are party to it and it must be certified that this has been done.

The instrument must also be signed by the testator and the persons who are party to it. If the instrument consists of several pages, the signatures must also be placed at the bottom of each page. If the testator declares that he is unable to sign his name, his signature is replaced by the incorporation of this declaration in the instrument.

In accordance with Article 1734 of the Civil Code, those provisions which apply to notarial instruments generally will also apply to this form of will, except if provision is made to the contrary.

Article 1735 of the Civil Code provides that if the testator declares that he is deaf, the instrument must be given to him to read and it must be certified in the instrument that this has been done.

Article 1736 of the Civil Code specifies that if the testator declares that he is deaf and unable to read, the will must be drawn up in the presence of five witnesses or a second notary and three witnesses.

In accordance with Article 1737 of the Civil Code, if the testator, in the notary's view, is not familiar with Greek or declares himself unfamiliar with the language, he is to be assisted by an interpreter. As regards the latter, the provisions of Articles 1725 to 1728 of the Civil Code apply in an analogous manner.

The interpreter must also swear to translate the testator's last wishes faithfully and to translate the instrument, before it is to be signed, so that it is comprehensible in the language in which the testator expresses himself.

The interpreter must be chosen by the testator and must swear to keep the testamentary dispositions secret until the estate passes to the heirs; non-observance of this formality, however, does not result in the nullity of the will.

The instrument must also include, in addition to that stipulated in Articles 1732 and 1733 of the Civil Code, the first and last name of the interpreter, confirmation that the stipulations in Article 1732(1) and (2) have been observed and the signature of the interpreter. The instrument must also state that the prescriptions in Article 1732(3) were complied with although the non-observance of this formality does not result in the nullity of the will.

iii. *Secret*: According to Article 1738 of the Civil Code, the secret will is executed by the testator depositing a written document with a notary in the presence of three witnesses or two notaries and one witness, with the testator making an oral declaration that the written document contains his last wishes.

Article 1740 of the Civil Code provides that the document deposited with the notary, whether written by the testator or another person, must, with the exception of that case set out in Article 1744, bear the signature of the testator. If the document was written wholly or partially by another person, it must also bear the signature of the testator every half page. The provisions of Article 1721(4) are also applicable in this instance.

In accordance with Article 1741 of the Civil Code, if the document which is being deposited, or the envelope in which it is inserted, is not sealed such that the seal would be broken or damaged upon being opened, it must be sealed in such manner in the presence of the testator and those who are party to the instrument.

Article 1742 of the Civil Code provides that the notary should inscribe on the sealed document or the document to be sealed in the manner stipulated above, or on the envelope in which the document is inserted, the first and last name of the testator and the date of deposit; this endorsement will be undersigned by the testator and those who are party to the instrument. If the testator declares that he is unable to sign, his signature is replaced by an attestation relating to the endorsement. The provisions of Article 1730(2) of the Civil Code are also applicable in this instance.

In accordance with Article 1743 of the Civil Code, an instrument must be drawn up concerning the preparation of the secret will.

The provisions in Articles 1732(1)–(3), 1733, 1734 and 1735 of the Civil Code are applicable to this instrument in an analogous manner. The instrument must also provide confirmation that the stipulations in Articles 1730(2), 1738, 1741 and 1742 have been observed.

The notary must also note down on the document that is deposited with him, or the envelope in which such document is inserted, the number of the instrument and annex the number to the instrument; non-compliance with this provision, however, does not result in the nullity of the will.

In accordance with Article 1744 of the Civil Code, if the testator declares that he can read but cannot write, or that he is unable to sign the document containing his last wishes, he must declare in the presence of the notary and the persons who are party to the instrument that he has read the document and must specify the reason for which he is unable to sign it. All of this must be attested to in the instrument.

According to Article 1745 of the Civil Code, a person who is, in the notary's view, mute or is deaf and mute or is otherwise prevented from speaking can draw up a secret will. To do so, the person must in his own handwriting on the document he is depositing, or the envelope in which such document is inserted, declare that the document is his will and, where the document was written up by another person, was read by him. This declaration must be written out by the testator in the presence of the notary and the other persons who are party to the instrument and attested to in it.

Article 1746 of the Civil Code provides that if the testator, in the notary's view, is not familiar with Greek or declares himself unfamiliar with the language, the provisions of Article 1737 are applicable to the secret will in an analogous manner.

iv. *Special (extraordinaire)*: Such wills are examined in cursory form only. It should be noted therefore that more detailed formalities may also be applicable in certain cases.

The forms of such wills and their corresponding formalities then are as follows:

– wills aboard ship: in accordance with Article 1749 of the Civil Code, a person who is on a Greek ship on a voyage at sea can make an oral will, provided such will complies with the requisite formalities as set out in Articles 1749–1751 and those analogous to the provisions set out in Articles 1725–1735;

– wills by military personnel: in accordance with Article 1753 of the Civil Code, those serving with the military can when on expedition or in times of blockade, siege or captivity make an oral declaration as to their last wishes before an officer in the presence of another officer or two witnesses. As to those who are party to the instrument, the provisions of Articles 1725–1728 apply in an analogous manner;

– wills drawn up in isolated locations: these wills can be made before certain specified persons by those residing in isolated areas following an epidemic or other extraordinary situations such that the drawing up of a public or secret will in the ordinary manner is impossible or very difficult. Such wills must comply with the provisions set out in Article 1757 and those relating to wills aboard ship of the Civil Code. The person who draws up such a will reminds the testator that it is valid for three months and then deposits it with a notary in Greece or a Greek consular authority abroad.

(b) *i.* In accordance with Article 1763 of the Civil Code, all wills can be revoked in the following ways:

- by declaration to this effect in a later will; if this later will is revoked, the earlier will produces those effects which would have arisen had it not been revoked;
- by declaration made before a notary in the presence of three witnesses and in accordance with those other formalities applying to notarial instruments. If this declaration is revoked in the same manner, the earlier will produces those effects which would have arisen had it not been revoked.

Article 1764 of the Civil Code provides that a later will revokes an earlier will only to the extent that its provisions are incompatible with the latter.

If the later will is revoked, the earlier will produces those effects which would have arisen had it not been revoked.

Revocation of an holographic will: In accordance with Article 1765 of the Civil Code, this form of will can also be revoked if the testator destroys the instrument with the intention of revoking it or if he makes changes to it that clearly express his intention to revoke it in the manner of a written declaration.

If the testator has destroyed the will or if he has changed it in the above-mentioned manner, he is presumed to have had the intention to revoke the will.

The recovery of an holographic will deposited with a notary for its safe-keeping is not deemed to amount to the revocation of the will.

ii. Marriage does not automatically affect a previously made will.

iii. According to Article 1763(2) of the Civil Code, all wills can be revoked by a declaration made before a notary in the presence of three witnesses and in accordance with those formalities applying to notarial instruments. If this declaration is revoked in the same manner, the will produces those effects which would have arisen had it not been revoked.

3. Intestacy

(a) According to Article 1813 of the Civil Code, those in *the first category* who will first take upon intestacy are the descendants of the deceased. Those descendants most closely related to the deceased will exclude those more distantly related from taking. If a descendant who would have taken at the time the estate passes has predeceased, his descendants will take in his place (succession *per stirpes*). Children will take in equal measure. There is no difference for illegitimate, adulterine or adopted children.

Article 1814 of the Civil Code provides that those in *the second category* who will take jointly are the father and mother of the deceased, his brothers and sisters as well as the children and grandchildren of those brothers and sisters who have predeceased. The father and mother, as well as the brothers and sisters, inherit in equal measure; the children and grandchildren of those brothers and sisters who have predeceased will inherit *per stirpes*. The children of predeceased brothers and sisters will exclude the grandchildren of that same person from taking.

In accordance with Article 1815 of the Civil Code, half brothers and sisters who take concurrently with the father and mother or with whole brothers and sisters, or with the children or grandchildren of the latter, will take half of the share that passes to the whole brothers and sisters. Likewise, the children or grandchildren of half brothers and sisters who have predeceased will take a half share.

According to Article 1816 of the Civil Code, those who will take in *the third category* are the grandparents of the deceased and, amongst their descendants, their children and grandchildren.

If, at the time the estate passes to the heirs, both strands of grandparents are living, they alone will inherit in equal measure. If, at that time, the grandfather or grandmother of the paternal or maternal strand is deceased, the children and grandchildren of the predeceased will take in his or her place. In the absence of such children or grandchildren, the share that the predeceased would have taken will revert instead to the grandfather or grandmother of the same strand or, in his or her absence, to his or her children and grandchildren.

If at the time the estate passes to the heirs, the grandfather and grandmother of either strand are deceased and they leave no children or grandchildren, the grandfather and the grandmother (or one of them) of the other strand, or their children or grandchildren, will alone inherit.

The surviving children of the predeceased grandparent will take in equal measure and will exclude the grandchildren of that predeceased. The grandchildren who take will take *per stirpes*.

According to Article 1817 of the Civil Code, those in *the fourth category* who will take are the great-grandparents of the deceased. The great-grandparents who are living at the time the estate passes to the heirs will inherit in equal measure without distinction as to the strand to which they belong.

Article 1821 of the Civil Code provides that in the absence of relations in the first, second, third and fourth categories, the surviving spouse will take the entire inheritance upon intestacy.

According to Article 1824 of the Civil Code, if at the time the estate passes to the heirs there is no relation to whom it would revert by law nor a surviving spouse, the state will take as heir upon intestacy.

In accordance with Article 1818 of the Civil Code, where inheritance is *per stirpes*, those persons who are descended from several persons within one category will take that share reverting to them from each of the descendants to whom they are related. Each one of these shares is deemed to be a distinct hereditary share to be added up together.

Article 1819 of the Civil Code provides that no relation will take under intestacy if there is a person in a previous category who takes.

Article 1820 of the Civil Code provides that the surviving spouse will take one-quarter of the estate upon intestacy if taking concurrently with relations in the first category and one-half of the estate if taking concurrently with relations in any of the remaining categories.

If the surviving spouse takes concurrently upon intestacy with the relations of the second, third or fourth categories, he will receive in addition to his hereditary share upon intestacy the furnishings, implements, clothing and other similar household objects which were used either by him alone or the couple.

(b) No distinction between movables and immovables is made.

4. Freedom of Testation

(a) Yes, in accordance with Article 1825 of the Civil Code, the descendants and the father and mother of the deceased, as well as the surviving spouse, who would have taken upon intestacy are entitled to a compulsory share of the estate (subject to exclusion of remoter relations as in intestacy). This share amounts to half of that share that would have been received upon intestacy.

A person who takes by way of compulsory share is deemed to take such share as heir.

According to Article 1827 of the Civil Code, if an heir entitled to a compulsory share is left a share of the estate which is less than that which he would take by way of the compulsory share, he has a right to the difference.

Article 1828 provides that if a legacy is made to an heir entitled to a compulsory share, that heir can exercise his right to the compulsory share by renouncing the legacy. If the heir does not renounce the legacy, he exercises his right as to that share of the compulsory share which remains outstanding. The person obliged to pass on the legacy can fix a reasonable period of time within which such an heir can exercise his right to renounce the legacy. After this time has expired, the right to renounce the legacy lapses.

(b) *i.* A contract of inheritance is not binding.

    ii. No. According to Article 368 of the Civil Code, an agreement made in relation to the succession of the property of a living person is void whether it is concluded with that person or a third party, and whether it concerns the whole or part of that property to be passed upon death. This is also the case in relation to an agreement made which limits testamentary freedom.

In accordance with Article 366 of the Civil Code, an agreement relating to the transfer of a patrimony to be received, or part of or a life interest in such a patrimony, is void.

Successoral pacts are void. But according to Article 1929 of the Civil Code, if the testator, having appointed an heir, has prescribed that the inheritance, or some part of it, be retained in his own family, those who will take, in cases of uncertainty, after the death of the appointed heir and subject to the provisions of Article 1923, are those who would have inherited upon intestacy had the testator died at the same time as the appointed heir. In terms of Article 1923, the testator may make a bequest in terms of which the beneficiary has to pass on all or part of his bequest to a third party. However, a provision that the third party must in turn pass on a portion of his bequest to a fourth party is invalid.

This family trust would not be applicable to other more distant relations of the testator.

According to Article 2010 of the Civil Code, if the testator has expressed the wish that the object of the legacy must be retained within the family in perpetuity, those to whom the legacy will pass in their capacity as reversionary legatees, are those family members referred to in the previous Article who would have inherited upon intestacy had the testator died at the same time as the first encumbered legatee.

Article 1891 of the Civil Code provides that an ascendant can whilst he is still alive divide his patrimony between his descendants (*partage d'ascendant*). The division is undertaken by way of contract and can only relate to the patrimony as it is constituted at the time the contract is drawn up. The ascendant, however, is not bound by such division as regards his testamentary dispositions.

5. Maintenance

According to Article 1820 of the Civil Code, the surviving spouse is deemed heir upon intestacy to one-quarter of the estate if he takes concurrently with the relations belonging to the first category and to one-half if he takes concurrently with the relations belonging to the following categories. He also receives, despite any relations who are to take concurrently with him, the furnishings, implements, clothing and other similar household objects which he alone or the couple used. If the deceased spouse has left children, however, their needs are also taken into account if this is deemed to be so required by special circumstances arising from considerations of equity.

The court can take into account the requirements of needy parents or needy children and make adjustments with regard to the shares that they are to receive in respect of household items. For example, if a parent was left a fridge and one of the children does not have one, then the said appliance would go to the child (if the parent already had a fridge). Similarly, if a car had been left to the parents and they were too elderly or infirm to drive the car, it would pass to the children. If, on the other hand, the parents are living in poverty, the children's share has to be adjusted in order to provide a minimum living standard for the parents.

6. Community Property Between Husband and Wife

(a)–(b) The provisions of Article 1403 and those which follow of the Civil Code and which allow the possibility of a pre-nuptial contract excluding community of property do not apply because the special 'public register' in which the contracts between the parties have to be entered in order to be deemed valid does not yet exist.

7. Gifts (*Inter Vivos*)

(a)–(b) Yes. In accordance with Article 1831 of the Civil Code, the calculation of that part of the inheritance to be subject to compulsory shares is done on the basis of the composition and value of the estate, after the deduction of debts, funeral expenses and expenses relating to the inventory, at the time of death of the deceased. Added to the estate are those dispositions for which no compensation was received, that the deceased made during his lifetime, on the basis of their value and benefit resulting at the time they were made, to an heir entitled to a compulsory share, whether by way of donation or in some other manner, as well as all other donations that the deceased made in the ten-year period preceding his death, unless such donation was necessary owing to some particular moral duty or for reasons of propriety.

Article 1835 of the Civil Code provides that all donations that the deceased made in his lifetime and that are to be taken into consideration when calculating the inheritance in accordance with the terms of Article 1831 are subject to rescission, to the extent that the deceased's estate does not cover the compulsory shares which are due.

As regards successive donations, the earlier donation will be subject to rescission to the extent that the later donation is insufficient.

In accordance with Article 1895 of the Civil Code, the descendants, when they inherit upon intestacy, are held to bring into account as between themselves all donations or gifts received from the deceased during his lifetime as well as all monies received for their education if such sums exceeded that which would have been commensurate with the deceased's financial position. There is no obligation to bring into account if the deceased had stipulated that this was to be the case at the time the donation was made or the expenses incurred.

8. Capacity

(a) According to Article 1719 of the Civil Code, the following persons are deemed incapable of making a will:

– minors (the age of majority in Greece being eighteen years old);
– those who are forbidden by court order;
– those who have been appointed with a judicial guardian for reasons of prodigality;
– those who at the time of making their will are not capable of discernment or are deprived of their mental faculties due to mental illness.

Incapacity due to a court order or the appointment of a judicial guardian for prodigality runs from the date that the application on the basis of which the court order or the appointment of the judicial guardian was made was filed.

According to Article 1723 of the Civil Code, a person who is unable to read a written text is not capable of making a holographic will.

According to Article 1748 of the Civil Code, a person who is unable to read is not capable of making a secret will.

(b) In accordance with Article 1725 of the Civil Code, those who cannot act as notary or witness in the drawing up of the will are the following:

– the spouse or ex-spouse of the testator;
– those persons to whom the testator is related by blood or marriage directly or collaterally up to the third degree inclusive.

Article 1726 of the Civil Code provides that those who also cannot act as notary or witness in the drawing up of the will are the following:

– those who benefit from the will;
– those who are appointed as executors in the will;
– those who are related to either of the two above in same manner as specified under Article 1725.

If any of the persons specified in the paragraph above acts as notary or witness to the will, it is only the disposition or appointment made in relation to such person that is void.

According to Article 1727 of the Civil Code, those who cannot act as second notary or witness in the drawing up of the will are those who are related to the notary in the same manner as specified under Article 1725.

The second notary and the witnesses must not be related as between themselves in the same manner as specified under Article 1725. However, the non-observance of this provision does not result in the nullity of the will.

Article 1728 of the Civil Code provides that those who cannot act as witness in the drawing up of the will are the following:

– those who are completely blind or deaf;
– clerks or employees of the notary;
– minors (the age of majority in Greece being eighteen years old).

In addition, those who cannot act as witnesses in the drawing up of the will are foreigners and persons who have been deprived of their capacity to act as witnesses of contracts, for as long as such incapacity lasts; the non-observance of this provision, however, does not result in the nullity of the will.

In accordance with Article 1731 of the Civil Code, witnesses will swear before a notary to keep the provisions of the will secret until the estate is to pass to the heirs. The non-observance of this provision, however, does not result in the nullity of the will.

(c) A person can only be heir if he was living or at least conceived at the time the estate passes to the heirs. The time at which the estate is deemed to pass is at the death of the testator.

9. Authority (Court, Notarial or Other)

See paragraph 13(a) *below.*

International Succession

10. Invalidity of Will

(a)–(b) There are a number of reasons for which a will may be invalid. Such reasons should be the subject of separate study; however, many of the relevant articles will now be examined in brief.

In accordance with Article 1719 of the Civil Code, subject to contrary legal provisions, a will is deemed invalid as regards its drawing up if the provisions of Articles 1719–1757 have not been observed.

As regards its content, Article 1781 of the Civil Code provides that a testamentary disposition in relation to which the person who is to be beneficiary is uncertain such that he is impossible to identify is void.

According to Article 1782 of the Civil Code, a testamentary disposition which results from threats made contrary to the law or immorally is deemed void. Likewise, a disposition resulting from fraud, in the absence of which the testator would not have made, is voidable.

Article 1783 of the Civil Code provides that a testamentary disposition is voidable if the testator was mistaken as to the identity of the person whom he intended to benefit or the object which he intended a person to inherit. Any error relating to the designation or description of such a person or object does not invalidate the disposition.

In accordance with Article 1784 of the Civil Code, a testamentary disposition based on erroneous grounds, which are mentioned in the will and relate to the past, present or the future, in the absence of which the testator would not have made such a disposition, is also voidable.

Article 1785 of the Civil Code provides that, in cases of uncertainty, a testamentary disposition made in favour of the surviving spouse is voidable if the marriage was nullified or dissolved during the lifetime of the testator or if the testator, having grounds upon which to do so, had commenced divorce proceedings against his spouse.

According to Article 1786 of the Civil Code, the will is voidable if the testator omitted to include an heir entitled to a compulsory share of the estate, who was living at the time of the testator's death but whose existence was not known to the testator at the time the testator drew up his will or who was born or became an heir entitled to a compulsory share of the estate after the will was drawn up. The will cannot be voided, however, if it can be shown that the testator would have made the same will even if he had known of the true situation which existed or came about in future.

As regards testamentary dispositions, Article 1794 of the Civil Code provides that incomprehensible conditions attached to such a disposition will be deemed not to have been written.

In accordance with Article 1795 of the Civil Code, a condition of celibacy attached to a testamentary disposition is deemed not to have been written. However, a condition of widowhood is valid when it concerns a disposition made by one spouse in favour of the other.

Article 1796 of the Civil Code provides that testamentary dispositions made on the basis of a reciprocal testamentary gift from the heir or legatee are void.

According to Article 1798 of the Civil Code, a testamentary disposition which is conditional upon the beneficiary abstaining from some action or undertaking some action for an indeterminate period of time is, in cases of uncertainty, deemed to have been made without the condition.

It should be noted that in addition to the cases to which the Civil Code refers, there is a great deal of jurisprudence concerning itself with related matters.

11. Simultaneous Death

(a) In accordance with Article 38 of the Civil Code, if several persons have died and it cannot be established which of them survived the others, it is presumed that all such persons died at the same time.

Article 39 of the Civil Code provides that the death of a person whose body has not been found is deemed established where that person has gone missing in circumstances rendering his death certain.

(b) There are no relevant provisions.

12. Estate Taxes

(a) Estate taxes do exist.

(b) Such taxes are due on local assets and on movables located abroad if the deceased was a Greek national who resided abroad less than ten years or had his domicile in Greece.

(c) Each heir is taxed according to the value of the inheritance at the time of the deceased's death and the order of succession.

13. Administration of Estates

(a) Greek law confers the duty of administration of the estate on the heirs but the following cases must be distinguished:

– In accordance with Article 1865 of the Civil Code, if the heir is unknown, or if it is uncertain as to whether he has accepted succession, the Inheritance Court can, upon the request of any person having a legitimate interest or even of its own motion, appoint an administrator to the estate. In cases of urgency, the State Prosecutor appoints a provisional administrator. The latter has to ensure that the court appoints a permanent administrator as quickly as possible.
– The Inheritance Court can, upon the request of any creditor of the estate, prescribe the liquidation of such estate. Liquidation is prescribed even if the succession is vacant or if the heir has accepted the inheritance subject to the limitation of his liability for the debts of the estate to the amount of assets that he actually

receives (*bénéfice d'inventaire*). The court can refuse the request, however, if the heir furnishes security in respect of the creditor having made the request.

According to Article 1918 of the Civil Code, the liquidator will manage the estate; he will be accountable for any negligence and has to render accounts. Until the inventory has been concluded, he will attend to the verification of the estate's obligations, the recovery of debts and the alienation of movables and immovables which form part of the estate. All monies received must be deposited in an interest-bearing account at a reputable bank. As regards the alienation of immovables, public securities, or shares or debentures in public limited companies, the provisions of Article 1908 of the Civil Code apply.

– The testator can appoint as executor one or more individuals or legal entities. He can also leave it to the executor to appoint co-executors or successors.

(b) Estate reports must be submitted by the liquidator if appointed.

(c) There is no external supervision.

(d) The heirs or their legal representatives have the right to query and object.

(e) According to Article 1846 of the Civil Code, the heir acquires the estate as of right upon its devolution subject to the provisions of Article 1198.

Article 1199 of the Civil Code provides that, by way of registration referred to in Article 1193, the rights of property and all other rights *in rem* over the immovables are deemed acquired by the heir or legatee from the time of death of the deceased, subject to the provisions on conditions precedent.

However, Article 1847 of the Civil Code provides that the heir can renounce the inheritance within a time period of four months from the day he became aware of the devolution and the basis upon which this has occurred. In instances where devolution results from a will, the time period only begins to run after the will has been examined after the death of the testator. If the deceased was last domiciled abroad or if the heir became aware of the devolution whilst residing abroad, the time period is one year. This time period is suspended upon the same grounds as those applying to the prescription.

In accordance with Article 1848 of the Civil Code, renunciation is carried out by way of declaration before the Registrar of the Inheritance Court. If such renunciation is carried out by a representative, a special mandate by way of notarial instrument is required.

(f) Article 1916 of the Civil Code provides that within one month from the date he has been notified of the judgment, the liquidator must publish a summary of such judgment in the press with a request that the estate's creditors produce their claims and the necessary information to substantiate these. The judgment in which the liquidation is ordered will set out the details of publication. In all cases, the summary with the request to the creditors is advertised in a newspaper circulating in the last domicile or residence of the deceased.

In accordance with Article 1917 of the Civil Code, within a time period of four months from the date upon which the last advertisements as referred to in the above paragraph were placed, whoever makes themselves out to be a creditor of the estate must make his claim known to the liquidator and provide the latter with the necessary information to substantiate this.

On the basis of claims which come forward, the liquidator is required to conclude the inventory of the estate within three months from the end of the time period in which such claims were to be produced. This time period can be extended by the Inheritance Court in special circumstances.

According to Article 1920 of the Civil Code, if the inventory reveals that the estate's assets are insufficient to cover its debts, the liquidator must, before satisfying any creditor, have the court stipulate the way in which the creditors will be paid *pro rata*, whilst upholding those privileges acquired by law as well as those mortgages registered and sureties entered into before the death of the deceased. Conditional creditors are also taken into account.

In accordance with Article 1921 of the Civil Code, the creditors who have not come forward within the requisite time period in accordance with the provisions of Article 1917 are not paid unless estate assets remain after the claims of those creditors having come forward in such manner have been met.

(g) According to Article 2017 of the Civil Code, the testator can appoint one or more individuals or legal entities as executors in his will. He can also leave it up to the executor to appoint co-executors or successors.

In accordance with Article 2018 of the Civil Code, the appointment of a testamentary executor is deemed void if at the time he accepts his position he is not capable of carrying out legal transactions or only has limited capacity.

Article 2019 of the Civil Code provides that the powers of the executor are deemed to arise from the time that he accepts his position. Acceptance or refusal is undertaken by way of declaration before the Registrar of the Inheritance Court and an official record of this is drawn up. A declaration made before the estate passes to the heirs, or that is conditional or limited to a certain time period, is deemed void. Upon the request of any person interested in the matter, the President of the Inheritance Court determines a period within which the executor must make his declaration; after this period has expired, the latter is deemed to have refused to take up his position as executor.

According to Article 2020 of the Civil Code, the executor's role is to execute the testamentary dispositions. He can carry out any act which is either expressly permitted by the testator or necessary in order to carry out the wishes of the latter. He also has the right, on the same basis, to administer the estate in whole or in part.

Article 2021 of the Civil Code provides that if, in those circumstances set out in the *previous* Article, it is necessary to alienate immovables from the estate, public securities, or shares or debentures of public limited companies, to contract for a loan, or to approve an expenditure or to spend over 100,000 drachmas, and the heir does not agree to this, the executor has the right to carry out such acts upon authorization of the Inheritance Court. The court must first hear from the heir when this is possible or not excessively difficult.

According to Article 2022 of the Civil Code, the testator can, by way of formal declaration set out in the will, relieve the executor of the restrictions set out in the *above* Article.

International Succession

According to Article 2023 of the Civil Code, in the carrying out of his functions the executor is accountable to the heir, in accordance with the rules set out in the mandate, for all loss or injury sustained to the estate for which he is responsible. When carrying out the administration of the estate, he is required to provide reports. If there are several executors, they are jointly responsible for acts in relation to which they are collectively at fault. In addition, the testator can stipulate the way in which the patrimony is to be divided or the heirs can themselves effect the division.

14. Domicile/Nationality

(a) Article 28 of the Civil Code provides that matters relating to succession are regulated by the law of the nationality of the deceased at the time of his death.

(b) Whether the deceased had assets in the jurisdiction is not relevant.

SECTION B – APPLICABLE LAW/PROCEDURE WHERE FOREIGN ELEMENT/S ARE INVOLVED

1. Jurisdiction

(a) A Greek court will have jurisdiction in relation to an inheritance only when the last domicile of the deceased was in Greece (Article 30 of the Code of Civil Procedure) or the deceased left assets in Greece.

(b) No; Greek law accepts the principle of unity of succession and does not have different rules for movables and immovables. (However, *see* paragraph 10(c) *infra*.)

(c) According to Articles 30 and 810 of the Code of Civil Procedure, the court having jurisdiction in matters relating to succession is the Court of First Instance of the last domicile of the deceased.

2. Applicable Law

The law to be applied is that of the last nationality of the deceased (Article 28 of the Civil Code). In the absence of a nationality, the law to be applied is that of the last domicile of the deceased (Article 30 of the Civil Code). Where several nationalities are involved, the law to be applied is that of Greek nationality (Article 31 of the Civil Code). Immovable property is governed by *lex rei sitae*.

3. Foreign Succession/Inheritance Orders

(a) A foreign decision can be executed in Greece after a certain specified procedure is followed. In accordance with Article 905(2) of the Code of Civil Procedure, a decision is delivered by the Court of First Instance and execution is authorized if the foreign decision is not contrary to public morals or public policy.

(b) After having validated their titles (*see* (a) *above*), the heirs must pay tax on the inheritance if such is due under Greek law. In addition, if immovables are involved, they must have registered at the Mortgage Registry having jurisdiction a public instrument in which they declare to have accepted the inheritance.

(c) *See* (a) *above*.

4. Two or More Succession or Probate Orders

Though legal doctrine and jurisprudence are divided on the matter, the prevailing opinion would seem to be that as regards the civil law to be applied, it would be that of the nationality of the deceased at the time of his death (Article 28 of the Civil Code) whilst as regards the procedural law to be applied, it would be that of the *lex fori*.

5. Assets

The local court can assume jurisdiction despite an absence of assets in the jurisdiction (*see* paragraph 1 *above*).

6. Expert Evidence

(a)–(b) The court having jurisdiction can request proof of the foreign law. Often the opinion of the Institute of International Law (based in Athens) is sought and their views are in principle upheld.

As regards wills which are found abroad, the procedure relating to the recognition of foreign public instruments is applicable.

7. Unity of Succession

Yes. The principle of *successio in universum jus de fun dis* is embodied in the law and provides that as regards matters relating to inheritance it is the law of the nationality of the deceased at the time of his death which applies, subject to paragraph 10(c) *below*.

8. Formalities

The formalities stipulated in Greek law are required only in relation to wills which are found in Greece (Article 1776 of the Civil Code).

International Succession

9. Legislation

The *1961 Hague Convention on the Conflicts of Laws on the Form of Testamentary Dispositions* has been in force in Greece since 27 November 1983 by virtue of Law 1325/1983.

10. Wills

(a) Article 1 of the *1961 Hague Convention on the Conflicts of Laws on the Form of Testamentary Dispositions* applies.

(b) As to construction and interpretation, *lex hereditatis* applies (i.e., the law of the nationality of the deceased) (Article 28 of the Civil Code).

(c) As to rights of heirs, *lex hereditatis* applies (Article 28 of the Civil Code); but if immovables are involved, the rights of those entitled to a compulsory share in the estate are subject to the principle of *lex rei sitae*.

(d) As to capacity to inherit, *lex hereditatis* applies (Article 28 of the Civil Code).

(e) Article 5 of the *1961 Hague Convention on the Conflicts of Laws on the Form of Testamentary Dispositions* provides that the applicable law regarding capacity to make a will is that relating to the form of the will.

(f) As to validity, the law of the domicile of the deceased applies.

(g) This is not possible under Greek law and would be invalid.

(h) As to amendment and revocation, Article 2 of the *1961 Hague Convention on the Conflicts of Laws on the Form of Testamentary Dispositions* applies.

(i) The laws relating to the protection of that part of the estate subject to compulsory shares are applicable to non-residents in accordance with the inheritance law which applies.

11. Domicile/Nationality

(a) The law to be applied to the content is that of the inheritance law at the time of death whereas the law to be applied to the form is that of Article 1 of the *1961 Hague Convention on the Conflicts of Laws on the Form of Testamentary Dispositions*.

(b) The domicile of the beneficiary is irrelevant.

(c) The concept of domicile embodies two elements:

- the material, i.e., the location of principal residence; and
- the intentional, i.e., the intention to stay at a location with a certain degree of permanence.

In contested cases, the determination of the domicile is a matter for the sovereign power of the courts who consider the facts of the particular case (*lex fori*).

More specifically, the matter will be considered by the Court of First Instance or the Court of Appeal, both of which consider the subject-matter of a case (as opposed to the Court of Cassation which only deals with form and compliance with procedure).

12. Taxation

Taken in the light of international conventions which have been entered into in order to avoid double taxation, Greek law embodies the following principles:

- territoriality: inheritance taxes are due in Greece if the deceased's movables or immovables are located in Greece, regardless of the nationality of the deceased or his domicile;
- nationality: inheritance taxes are due in Greece on movables located abroad if the deceased was a Greek national and resided abroad less than ten years;
- domicile: inheritance taxes are due in Greece on movables located abroad if the deceased had his domicile in Greece.

Guernsey

Prepared by: St John A. ROBILLIARD (Partner), Ozannes

Address: 1 Le Marchant Street
St Peter Port, Guernsey
GY1 4HP United Kingdom
Tel.:   +44(0)1481 723466
Fax: +44(0)1481 710487
E-mail: S.Robilliard@Ozannes.com

SECTION A – BRIEF SURVEY OF THE LOCAL SYSTEM

1. Type of System

(a) The legal system of Guernsey is a customary law system. With regard to matters such as succession and land law, the law has developed from the common law of Normandy and France prior to 1789. In other matters such as tort and certain aspects of contract law, English common law is now followed.

(b) The Bailiwick of Guernsey is that part of the Channel Islands which is subject to the jurisdiction of the Bailiff of Guernsey who presides in the Royal Court of Guernsey. The Bailiwick consists of the Island of Guernsey (together with the Islands of Herm and Jethou), the Island of Alderney (which has a separate system of inheritance), and the Island of Sark (which also has a separate system of inheritance) off which the Island of Brecqhou lies.

Subject to statutory exceptions, the law of Guernsey is applicable through the Bailiwick.

2. Wills

(a) The law distinguishes between wills made inside the Island of Guernsey and those made outside. Where a will is made within the Island of Guernsey it is necessary that there are two wills, one for real property and one for personal property. The will of real property must be signed by the testator before two jurats (a permanent judge of fact – the Royal Court has twelve jurats) of the Royal Court of Guernsey and countersigned by an advocate of the Royal Court. A will of personal property may be signed by the testator with two independent witnesses who are aged at least fourteen.

A will of both realty and personalty can be made outside the Bailiwick of Guernsey provided that it is validly made in accordance with the requirements for wills of personalty.

In Alderney a will must be signed before two jurats of the Court of Alderney, and in Sark a will must be witnessed by the Seneschal (judge of the court) and Greffier (clerk of the court). Alternatively it may be made in Guernsey under the rules applicable there.

Guernsey law does recognize a holographic will made in respect of personal property.

(b) A will can be amended by a codicil and a codicil will be executed in accordance with the same rules that are applicable to the making of the will.

(c) Marriage does not automatically revoke a will under Guernsey law (although marriage will affect a will if the spouse's legal rights are not recognized in it to the extent that it will be modified by the imposition of those legal rights). Guernsey does not have any special rules about wills that were made shortly before death.

3. Intestacy

Guernsey

It is first of all necessary to distinguish between personal property (*meubles*) and real property (*immeubles*).

It is secondly important to distinguish between *immeubles* which are *propres* and which are *acquets*.

A *propre* is real property which the deceased has himself inherited (although not taken under a will). *Propres* are divided between *propres paternal*, that is to say a *propre* inherited on the paternal side, and *propres maternal*, that is to say a *propre* inherited on the maternal side.

An *acquet* is real property acquired by the deceased during his lifetime by gift, by purchase or by taking under a will.

The principle of the law is that the rules for *meubles* and *acquets* are the same, namely to find the person or class of persons to whom the deceased is most closely related. In succession to *propres* the aim of the law is to find the person or persons most closely related to the deceased in the blood family line through which the *propre* was inherited.

The rules (*Loi sur les Successions (1840)* as amended) basically are:

1. Direct succession, that is where the deceased has left legitimate children or other issue: the heirs are the children of the deceased who will take equal shares, although if one or more of those children have pre-deceased the deceased, their children take the share that would have gone to their parent *par representation* with the possibility of there being *representation* to all living generations where applicable.

2. Indirect succession: the principle of Guernsey law is that property only ascends where it can neither descend nor, in effect, go sideways. Therefore in the absence of ascendants, the heirs of a deceased are firstly his brothers and sisters. Secondly the applicable descendants of his brothers and sisters. Thirdly, his ascendants. Fourthly, his other collaterals.

The following particular rules apply:

- Where on the application of the above rules a class has been identified, representation is permitted *a l'infini* where the property is a *propre*.
- *Meubles* and *acquets* pass to the next in line, whether in the paternal or maternal line, in parity of degree where the succession is collateral rather than ascendant. In the case of *acquets* and *meubles* representation is only permitted where a brother or sister comes to the succession. Where the brothers and sisters are all dead their children will take per capita.
- Where ascendants come to inherit, the paternal line prefers the maternal line in the case of parity of degree.
- *Propres* may only be inherited by the closest relative or class of relatives under the above rules in the line of inheritance; thus paternal *propres* go to the paternal family and maternal *propres* to the maternal family. Where there is more than one person in parity of degree then all of those persons will take equally.
- In collateral successions relatives of the half-blood may succeed in common with relatives of the whole-blood, and on the father's side brothers and sisters of the half-blood succeed in common with brothers and sisters of the whole-blood. Brothers and sisters of the half-blood on the mother's side will only succeed in the absence of brothers and sisters of the whole blood.
- Succession applies up to and including the sixth degree. Where there is a collateral succession one finds the common ancestor and counts the number of degrees on the longest line for this purpose. In the absence of anyone who can succeed in the sixth degree, in Guernsey and Alderney the property would pass to the Crown. However, in Sark property would pass to the Seigneur of Sark.

Alderney

As regards personal property (*meubles*), similar principles apply as in Guernsey.

As regards real property (*immeubles*), Alderney has abolished the distinction between *propres* and *acquets*. In intestacy where there is more than one heir, there is a presumption of sale unless all the relevant heirs apply for the property to be vested in them. The heirs who will take the property or the proceeds of sale of the property, as the case may be, are as follows (Alderney Land and Property law 1949, Part IX):

- surviving spouse, but only where there is no other heir in the specified categories;
- descendants: the same rules as Guernsey apply;
- the deceased's parents who will take in equal shares;
- the deceased's brothers and sisters of the whole-blood and their issue representing them *per stirpes*;

– brothers and sisters of the half-blood and their issue representing them *per stirpes*;
– surviving grandparents in equal shares; failing them the great grandparents will inherit;
– surviving uncles and aunts of the whole-blood only and to each stock of descent from such uncle or aunt;
– uncles and aunts of the half-blood with stocks of descent.

As stated above, a spouse is only an heir in the absence of any of the above classes. If there is no spouse and no person in any of the above classes, the property goes to the Crown.

Sark

As regards personal property (*meubles*), broadly similar principles apply to those in Guernsey, but with certain variations in more remote instances.

The Real Property (Succession) (Sark) Law 1999 came into force in 2000. In order to understand the rules it is necessary to know that Sark is divided into approximately forty units known as tenament and some other twenty units colloquially called free-holds (defined as property in the law). These land holdings are indivisible and therefore on inheritance only one person may take, although there are limited rights to make wills of real property. The rules of intestate succession are set out in the schedule to the law and are:

– Inheritance is up to but not including the seventh degree of relationship computed by the canonical mode. In the absence of anyone entitled to inherit the property escheats to the Seigneur (feudal lord of Sark).
– In the application of the rules there is no discrimination by sex or by reason of illegitimacy (although succession to the property of an illegitimate child is only through the maternal line) or adoption.
– Representation is allowed infinitely.

The classes of persons who may inherit are:

i. descendants;
ii. brothers and sisters and their descendants;
iii. ascendants;
iv. other collaterals descending from a common ancestor.

A member of one class may only take in the absence of any person in the preceding class. Thus the nearest in degree inherits. In parity of degree, the eldest in that class inherits.

A distinction is made between property that has been acquired by the deceased (*acquets*) and property that is inherited (*propre*). A *propre* includes not only inherited property but that acquired by the *retrait lignager* (the right of a family member to preemption on sale). Where property is a *propre*, it may only be inherited by someone in the family from which the property descended.

273

International Succession

The fundamental in applying these principles is that they identify one person who takes the entire property or where there is more than one property, all of the properties.

Note: for the purposes of intestate succession in Guernsey and Alderney, only lines through legitimate (including adopted) persons are recognized.

4. Freedom of Testation

Guernsey – Real Property

A person who does not have any legitimate descendants is free, subject to the rights of the surviving spouse, to leave his real property to whom he wishes. If he has legitimate descendants his real property may only be left to one or more of (Inheritance (Guernsey) Law 1954, as amended):

   i. his spouse;
  ii. his descendants;
 iii. his illegitimate descendants and their descendants;
 iv. his step-children and their descendants;
  v. the illegitimate children of his descendants, or the illegitimate children of his step-children, but no other person or persons.

Where there is a surviving spouse, whether or not there are descendants, she/he will be entitled to a life interest (*usufruit*) over 50 per cent of the deceased's real property up to an upper limit based on its annual rental value (£200). She retains this unto death or re-marriage.

Guernsey – Personal Property

In a case where a person has no spouse or descendants, he is free to leave his personal property to whom he pleases. If there are surviving descendants (*Loi Relative a la Portion Disponible des Biens Meubles des Peres et Meres (1930); Law of Inheritance (Guernsey) Law, 1979*), his children, or those who represent them if one or more of them have pre-deceased him, are entitled to one-half of the personal estate if there is no surviving spouse, or one-third of the personal estate if there is. In each case the children, or those representing them, take equally. It should be noted that step-children, illegitimate children or illegitimate grandchildren may be recognized by will as being included for these purposes to *legitime*. If there is no will or the will does not recognize them they will not share in the *legitime* with the legitimate children. In a case decided in 2000 the Royal Court held that where a parent made gifts of personalty to one child during her/his (the parent's) life time it was presumed to be in advance of what the child would have inherited amongst her *legitime*. Guernsey law recognizes the principle of a person being *indigné* which means that by a person's act towards the deceased he can show himself as being unworthy of succeeding (this principle was applied in 1998 in a case involving a manslaughter in Spain). It should also be noted that by will *legitime* can be put into a simple will trust for one generation (*Loi Supplémentaire a la loi des Successions (1889)*) under which the children of the deceased may only be entitled to income, but on their death their children must be entitled to the share that their parent would have inherited.

A surviving spouse has a right to one-half of the personal property where there are no descendants, and one-third of the personal property where there are descendants. This right is known as the *Droit de Conjoint*. It would be possible to challenge this right where the parties had become estranged and were living apart at the time of the deceased's death. Where the *Droit de Conjoint* exists it is not possible to put it into trust. Guernsey law does not recognize any rights to maintenance or support from an estate outside the above rules which are in any case automatic and do not depend on the relative individual showing that he or she was dependant on the deceased. Persons who live together who are unmarried have no rights on the property of the other.

Where a person is validly adopted he will, from the date of the adoption, be treated as a natural legitimate child of the person or persons who adopted him.

It is possible for any person who would be entitled to automatic rights of inheritance to renounce them by a contract registered at the Royal Court.

Where a number of people inherit a number of different pieces of land, it is possible to divide that between them by a *Partage*. Under a *Partage* the different pieces of property that were owned by the deceased, are divided between a number of his heirs. The *Partage* may also involve monetary payments to certain heirs to compensate them for getting smaller or no pieces of land.

Under the customary law, an advance on a succession of either real or personal property would be taken into account on ascertaining a person's entitlement on an inheritance.

The customary law also recognized a principle known as *la reserve* whereby gifts of real property made during the deceased's lifetime could be set aside where they exceeded the portion of the property which he could give on death. This principle has not been referred to in any recent statute and therefore it remains to be seen how much if any of it now survives.

Alderney – Personal Property

Similar rules apply as in Guernsey, but with one major exception, namely that whilst a widow has the right to the *Droit de Conjoint*, a widower does not.

Alderney – Real Property

A surviving widow has the right to *Douaire*. This is the right of a life interest *usufruit* over one-third of the real property, or the proceeds of sale of the real property. *Douaire* is earned by the consummation of the marriage.

International Succession

A surviving widower has the right of *franc veuvage*. This is the right to a life interest over all of the property (or proceeds of sale), but a widower is only entitled to this if a living child has been born of the marriage.

Both of these rights continue unto death or re-marriage.

Sark – Personal Property

Rules are the same as for Guernsey.

Sark – Real Property

Under the *Real Property (Succession) (Sark) Law 1999*, which came into force in 2000, where a person has descendants he may make a will and leave a property in its entirety to one of those descendants. If he has more than one property, he can leave each property to different descendants. The fundamental principle remains, however, that the property cannot be divided. The Chief Pleas (Sark Parliament) may by ordinance extend the definition of 'descendant' which currently means any legitimate or illegitimate or adopted descendant of any sex or age to include a surviving spouse.

Where a person has no descendants, he may leave his property to any one person and if he has more than one property he may leave each to separate people, but again a single property may not be divided between separate owners. As an alternative he may set up a trust for sale and the trustee has a power to reasonably postpone the sale. The beneficiaries may be any one or more natural persons or charities. This may only be done when a person does not have descendants.

The *Droits du Douaire* and *Franc Veuvage* have been abolished from the date of the coming into force of the law, but existing rights are not affected. Under any succession opening after the coming into force of the law, a surviving spouse is to have life enjoyment over one-third and may reasonably select the property or part of the property over which this is to be exercised (this amount can by increased by ordinance of the Chief Pleas).

5. Maintenance

Under Guernsey law the legitimate interests of surviving spouses and children are protected by their vested rights which have been outlined above. No other persons, e.g., unmarried partners or parents, are included within these classes and there exists no principle under which claims for maintenance can be brought.

6. Community Property Between Husband and Wife

Guernsey is not a community of property regime. On the death of a husband, household 'paraphernalia' will belong to the surviving spouse in addition to the *Droit du Conjoint*.

276

7. Gifts (*Inter Vivos*)

There is a particular rule whereby if a person dies leaving no descendants, but collaterals and ascendants, and if that person's parent made an advance to him acknowledged in writing as being an advance of succession, then on that person's death the parent is entitled to be reimbursed by the estate for the advance.

With regard to personal property, where a gift is so great as to reduce the *legitime* to which the other heirs are entitled, that proportion may well be taken into account thereby reducing that beneficiary's entitlement to *legitime*, which applies on a presumption rather than on a rule of law. It is, however, clear that during his lifetime a person could make gifts to a trust and the trust could prefer some heirs rather than others (*Trusts (Guernsey) Law 1989* as amended).

With regard to real property, the question remains unresolved as to how far the customary law would still set aside a gift which preferred one heir rather than another. Under the customary law the principle was that parents could not make any donation of real property to a person who would not be entitled to inherit it. If, however, there was a grandparent whose children had died, but there were other descendants, up to one-third of the real property could be given provided it was given to a person who would not be entitled to succeed to it on death. These principles have not been tested in court for many years and therefore it is open to question today as to how far they survive.

8. Capacity

(a) The testator must be of the age of majority, which is eighteen in Guernsey, Sark and Alderney. His marital status is not relevant.

(b) In the case of a will of real property made by a person in Guernsey, the witnesses must be two jurats of the Royal Court of Guernsey or, if made in Alderney, two jurats of the Court of Alderney or, if in Sark, *inter alia*, the Seneschal of the Court of Sark. With regards to wills of personalty, or wills of realty and personalty or realty made outside the Bailiwick of Guernsey, wills may be witnessed by any persons who are fourteen or over, other than the spouse or descendants of the testator, or any person benefiting under the will or their spouse. If this is infringed the legacy or bequest to them becomes invalid, although the will otherwise remains valid. An executor may witness a will provided that neither the executor nor his spouse is a beneficiary.

(c) As regards natural persons, they must be living at the time of the decease in order to inherit. A minor may inherit property, but will be subject to restrictions as to the disposal of that property. There is no reason why a company should not be a beneficiary, although a company could only be a beneficiary where a natural person, not being a spouse or descendant, could inherit.

9. Authority (Court, Notarial or Other)

It is necessary to distinguish wills of realty and wills of personalty.

International Succession

A will of realty is potentially a conveyancing document and it appoints no executors. Therefore it is informally registered in the Guernsey Greffe (for property situate in Guernsey), with the Alderney Court (for property situate in Alderney), and the Sark Greffe (for property situate in Sark).

With regard to personal property situated anywhere in the Bailiwick of Guernsey (i.e., Guernsey, Alderney and Sark), it is necessary to seek a Grant of Probate or a Grant of Letters of Administration from the Guernsey Ecclesiastical Court.

Where there is a valid will, application is made by an executor or the executors with a valuation of the estate and an oath is administered. In the case of an intestacy, a prospective administrator will apply producing the death certificate, a valuation of the personalty, his details and a bond for twice the value of the assets. He then swears an appropriate oath.

10. Invalidity of Will

Where a will has not formally been executed, e.g., with less than the required number of witnesses or the wrong witnesses (in the case of a will of real property), it will be invalid. The document is not a will and therefore an intestacy would automatically apply.

A will may be contested on the grounds that the testator lacked testamentary capacity. The burden of proof is on the person seeking to disprove testamentary capacity. Clearly, one may lack testamentary capacity by reason of mental incapacity, but also where one did not truly exercise one's will, whether by reason of fraud, duress or some other factor. The will is presumed valid, but where it has been successfully contested on one of these grounds it is voidable.

SECTION B – APPLICABLE PROCEDURE WHERE FOREIGN ELEMENT/S ARE INVOLVED

1. Jurisdiction

Guernsey law will apply to real property situated within the jurisdiction, and to personal property situated anywhere owned by a person dying domiciled in Guernsey. The relevant court with regard to movable property is the Ecclesiastical Court of Guernsey (for property in the Bailiwick of Guernsey, i.e., Guernsey, Alderney and Sark), although where any caveat is entered the matter must be referred to the Royal Court of Guernsey. In the case of a dispute involving immovable property, the courts are the Royal Court of Guernsey in the case of immovable property situated in Guernsey, the Court of Alderney in the case of immovable property situated in Alderney, and the Court of Sark where the immovable property is situated in Sark.

2. Applicable Law

In the case of real property, the law of the relevant part of the Bailiwick of Guernsey where the real property is situated applies. In the case of personal property, the law of domicile at the time of death applies.

3. Foreign Succession/Inheritance Orders

(a) No foreign order would be recognized to the extent that it conflicted with the local law relating to locally situated real property. With regard to personal property, it is necessary to make a separate application, but in the case of grants coming from the United Kingdom, a Guernsey grant is basically issued on the submission of a court-sealed and certified copy of the original grant. For other jurisdictions a lawyer from that jurisdiction, certified by the British Consulate in that country, must attest to the law of inheritance of the country and the validity of the order (a court-sealed copy of which must be produced).

(b) In the case of personal property situate in the Bailiwick of Guernsey, the person holding it will only release it on the basis of a valid Guernsey grant. Occasionally, with regard to small amounts, releases may be made without a formal Grant of Guernsey Probate or Letters of Administration, but this is entirely at the discretion of the relevant body.

4. Two or More Succession or Probate Orders

In the case of real property, the court will apply local law and therefore not recognize any order which is inconsistent with that law.

With regard to movable property, the court will only have regard to the law of the deceased's domicile on death.

5. Assets

Where a person dies domiciled in Guernsey, but without any movable assets in Guernsey, there is no reason why the court should not grant a declaration in an appropriate form. There is a procedure whereby British courts can make a request of other British courts, and therefore if a person has died domiciled in Guernsey and had assets in another British jurisdiction, that jurisdiction could, if it wished, apply to the Guernsey court to answer questions on the Guernsey law of succession.

6. Expert Evidence

(a) Where there is personal property in Guernsey, and a person has died domiciled other than in the United Kingdom, it is necessary to have a certificate as to the applicable foreign law from an appropriate lawyer certified by the British Consulate in that country.

(b) It is not normal for the lawyer to have to appear in court. If, however, the matter is contested, it would be referred by the Ecclesiastical Court to the Guernsey Royal Court. In such a case it is likely that affidavits as to foreign law would be put in by all of the relevant parties. Where they disagree the other parties would be entitled to insist that the deponents be called as witnesses in order to be questioned.

International Succession

7. Unity of Succession

It is accepted that with regard to movable property, the law of the deceased's last domicile should govern the disposition of that property wherever situate.

8. Formalities

A will would be recognized under Guernsey law even though it does not comply with the Guernsey rules, if it is formally valid (*The Execution of Wills (Bailiwick of Guernsey) Law, 1994*) in:

– the territory where it is executed;
– the territory where the testator died was domiciled or had his habitual residence;
– the territory where the testator was either a national at the time of execution or his death; or
– in the case of real property, the territory where the real property was situated.

9. Legislation

Guernsey is not a party to any applicable Hague Convention.

10. Wills

(a) The legal requirement for execution of wills is a matter of formal validity and therefore any will formally valid under Guernsey law, or under the *Wills (Bailiwick of Guernsey) Law, 1994*, would be recognized.

(b) The construction of a will will be interpreted by the law of the testator's domicile at the time that he made it.

(c) The rights of heirs and beneficiaries is a matter for the substantive law. Therefore, if it is real property, the Guernsey law as to who can succeed will apply. If it is personal property, then the Guernsey law will apply if the individual dies domiciled in Guernsey. If he dies domiciled elsewhere, it will be the law of that jurisdiction.

(d) The capacity to inherit will be decided by the law governing essential validity.

(e) The capacity to make a will is a matter of the law of the applicable domicile at the time the will was made.

(f) Guernsey law will apply public policy where it perceives a foreign will overriding that public policy. Where something has vitiated the intention of the person making the will, that would be perceived as a matter of the law of the applicable domicile, although if that law was radically different, Guernsey public policy may override it. A legacy to a witness would be regarded as a matter of formal validity, unless there were other grounds (e.g., fraud or duress) to override this.

(g) Execution of the will must conform with the law governing the essential validity of the power. A will exercising a power of appointment is not improperly executed by reason only that the execution is not in accordance with formalities applicable to the instrument creating the power.

(h) The instrument amending or revoking a will must be properly executed under the normal rules, i.e., the same rules under which the will may be executed.

(i) In the case of a Guernsey trust, Guernsey law will not recognize a reserve in respect of a non-domiciled Guernsey person so as to overturn the trust. With regard to other cases, Guernsey law will recognize reserves, as it is a concept known to Guernsey law and it will have regard to the law of the domicile, in the case of movable property, and the law of the place where the property is situated, in the case of immovable property.

11. Domicile/Nationality

(a) Domicile or nationality can be a determinate when it saves an otherwise invalid will under the *Execution of Wills (Bailiwick of Guernsey) Law, 1994* and this can be either at the time of making the will or at the time of death in the case of formal validity. In the case of substantive matters it is only the domicile at the time of death which matters.

(b) The domicile of a beneficiary is irrelevant for the purposes of Guernsey law, although if a beneficiary is domiciled in Guernsey and is under age, he will not be fully free to deal with his property, and in particular any real property that he owns can only be sold with the confirmation of the Royal Court.

(c) Where there is more than one nationality, this is not a problem as nationality is only relevant as a saving factor for the formal validity of wills. With regard to domicile, Guernsey law will only recognize one domicile at a time. Thus the starting point would be the individual's domicile at birth which would be determined by the domicile of his father. The domicile which one takes at birth can alter, but may only alter to one other domicile. If through the person's habits, for example living in a number of different countries, there is no clearly identifiable domicile to replace the birth domicile, this would remain through life.

12. Taxation

There is no applicable taxation with regard to immovable property in Guernsey, Alderney or Sark, although from the death of the deceased the new owners automatically become owners of it without the necessity of any judicial act and they would be liable to property rates from the moment of death.

International Succession

With regard to probate for movable property, a small duty of approximately one-third of a per cent is payable to the Ecclesiastical Court. No distinction is made between residents and non-residents.

Other than the above, there are no applicable estate duties in the Bailiwick of Guernsey on either immovable or movable property.

Hungary

Prepared by: Vera VARKONYI

Address: 1027 Budapest
         Csalogany u. 21 1.emelet 3
         1536 Budapest Pf. 280
         Hungary
Tel.:   +36 1 213 94 33
Fax: +36 1 202 42 76

Section A – Brief Survey Of The Local System

1. Type of System

(a) The law of succession in Hungary is essentially that of a system of law based upon civil (continental) law and is governed by Articles 598 to 684 of the Civil Code.

The general rules on the law of succession are those contained in the following provisions:

- Article 598 of the Civil Code, which reads: 'The estate of a person who has died is transferred in its entirety to the heirs (i.e., referred to as succession).'
- Article 599(1), which reads: 'A person inherits in accordance with the law or a will.'
- Article 599(2), which reads: 'If the deceased has made a will, the order of succession is determined in accordance with it. In the absence of such a will, the order of succession is determined in accordance with the law.'
- Article 599(3), which reads: 'In the absence of heirs, the estate devolves upon the state.'

The law of succession also deals with the following areas:

- incapacity to inherit;
- unworthiness to inherit;
- the renunciation of the succession;
- the legal order of succession;
- the rules of succession as regards subdivision into lineages (*la fente*);
- the life interest of the surviving spouse and the redemption of such interest;
- the rights of succession as regards adoption;

International Succession

- refunding (*rapport*);
- the rules relating to testamentary dispositions including that providing for the principle of freedom of testation;
- the different forms of will;
- the contents of a will;
- the nullity and voidability of wills;
- agreements on future succession;
- that part of the estate subject to compulsory shares by law;
- the acquisition of succession;
- the debts of the estate and the liability for such debts; and
- the division of the estate and its legal effects.

(b) Hungary is not a federal state.

2. Wills

In accordance with Hungarian law, wills can be executed in three forms:

- *Public*: This will must be executed in the presence of a notary in accordance with those formalities applying to deeds. In certain cases of physical or mental incapacity (i.e., limited capacity), recourse may be had only to a public will; therefore this form of will is that which must be used by the blind, those unable to sign their names or to read, as well as illiterate persons. In these cases specified, the attendance of two witnesses not having any interest in the matter is also required at the time the will is being drawn up. The latter provision also applies to persons subject to a guardianship limiting their capacity.
- *Holographic* (i.e., 'private'): This form of will is subdivided into three kinds:
  - the will which is written up and signed by the testator in his own hand;
  - the will which is typewritten, signed by another person and requires the signature of two witnesses not having any interest in the matter;
  - the will in the form of private document which is deposited with a notary, whether unsealed or sealed (secret). Such a will must be written up in a language which the testator understands and can read and write. (Article 627 of the Civil Code) It must also include the place and time at which it was drawn up (Article 629(1) of the Civil Code) and be deposited in person with the notary. For a secret will which is typewritten or written in the hand of another person, the attendance of two witnesses is not deemed to be a precondition as to its validity. For a will in the form of private document which consists of several separate sheets, a precondition as regards its validity is that the pagination must follow on from one page to the next and each such page must be signed by the testator and the witnesses.
- *Oral*: In order to be valid, this form of will can only be executed in extraordinary circumstances and under certain specific conditions. The conditions are that the testator finds himself in a situation which endangers his life and is unable to draw up a written will. The testator must also make, in the presence of two

witnesses, an oral declaration as to his last wishes, with these having to be very detailed. The oral will is only valid upon compliance with these three conditions.

(b) *i.* The forms to be used for the revocation and amendment of a will, as well for additions to it, are the same as those applying to the will itself. By way of example, there is no problem amending a public will by way of a written will in the form of a private document or adding to a written will by way of a public will, as long, of course, as the correct formalities are observed as regards each form used. As regards oral wills, given the special conditions attaching to the use of this form of will, recourse to it is not possible in every case. For example, an oral will cannot be added to by a written will as the fact that the testator is able to use the written form excludes the possibility of him making an oral will.

  ii. Marriage does not affect in any way the validity of the content or the form of a will having been made prior to such marriage.

  iii. In general, the revival of a will which has been revoked is not possible; the only exception to this is where the revocation itself was invalid.

3. Intestacy

(a) Hungarian law groups those persons inheriting upon intestacy into three categories (*les parentèles*) according to the degree to which they are related to the deceased. There is no overlapping possible as between each of the three categories. That is, if one person belonging to one category is alive, those persons in the following category will not take as heirs unless as heirs of a predeceased descendant.

The three categories are as follows:

– The *descendants* of the deceased, who will take in equal shares. If one of the descendants has predeceased the deceased, the descendants of the predeceased will take in his place in equal shares. Hungarian law does not make a distinction between legitimate, illegitimate or adopted children.

  In the absence of descendants, the surviving spouse will take the inheritance.
– In the absence of descendants and the surviving spouse, the lawful heirs will be the *father and mother* in equal shares. In the event that either the father or mother has predeceased, the father or mother who is still alive does not take her or his share; that share reverts to the descendants of the parent having predeceased, i.e., the *brothers and sisters* of the deceased and their descendants who will inherit in the manner set out in the *above* paragraph.
– In the absence of the father and mother and their descendants, the heirs will be the two sets of *grandparents* and, should they have predeceased, their descendants in the manner set out *above*. In practice then, it is the *cousins* who will be the heirs.

The *above* sets out those relations, and only those relations, who are lawfully entitled to the inheritance upon intestacy. There is, however, another rule, according to which, in the event that those relations most closely related are ancestors more distant than the grandparents of the deceased, they will take in equal shares. Obviously this rule is referred to and applied very rarely.

There are special rules relating to the inheritance by spouses and by way of subdivision by lineage (*la fente*).

The *surviving spouse*, as has already been mentioned, will only have a right to property in the estate if there are no descendants (*see above*).

If there are one or more descendants, the spouse receives a life interest in all that he has not inherited. Only the descendants can request that conditions be attached to the life interest and such request must be made by way of court proceedings. The spouse will have rights of property, however, if an agreement is made with the descendants. In the absence of such an agreement, either the surviving spouse or the descendants can request the redemption of the surviving spouse's life interest in the course of court proceedings. If the life interest is to be redeemed, the surviving spouse is entitled to a share of estate property equal to that of a child. However, the redemption of the surviving spouse's right to live in the family residence and to the movables belonging to such residence cannot be requested.

As regards succession by way of *subdivision by lineage (la fente)*, this is a factor only if there are no descendants who survive the deceased. The ancestors of the deceased and their descendants will inherit the right of property in that which had reverted free of charge to the deceased, them and those sharing common ancestors with the deceased. For example, that which was received by the above-mentioned persons in the form of a gift or property that had been inherited is deemed to originate from subdivision. In this case, the surviving spouse will still have a life interest although, as regards its redemption, he will obtain a right of property in one-third of the deceased spouse's estate.

Succession follows the principle of *ipso jure*, which means that in law the estate passes to the heirs immediately upon death of the deceased, without the need for recourse to any particular judicial process. There is therefore no part of the estate which is unclaimed. As a result of this, in many cases, there is no need for recourse to the procedure upon succession. If such procedure has to be carried out, essentially the function of the notary in this instance is not to divide and distribute the estate but to note the fact that the property has devolved to the heirs.

(b) There is no difference between the succession of movables and immovables.

4. Freedom of Testation

(a) Hungarian inheritance law ensures that a part of the deceased's estate is subject to compulsory shares for the benefit of his descendants, the surviving spouse and, should they be lawful heirs, his father and mother. The part of the estate which is subject to compulsory shares is equal to half of the share that the heir, who has been left out of or does not take under the will, would have received upon intestacy. If the surviving spouse would have inherited a life interest in accordance with the order of succession upon intestacy, the life interest he is to receive in the form of a compulsory share is to be determined on the basis of his needs.

There is no difference made between legitimate, illegitimate and adopted children as regards the value of the compulsory share to be received from the estate. (Hungarian law does not make any distinction to the prejudice of illegitimate children).

(b) *i.* The answer is in the affirmative; that is, such a contract can bind the parties.

   ii. The Hungarian Civil Code regulates different types of contracts that can be concluded by persons still living which concern future succession. The relevant provisions are those which follow:

– By virtue of Articles 603 to 605 of the Civil Code, a contract concerning the renunciation of succession can be concluded between the person whose property is to pass and his future heirs. In this instance the heirs renounce their rights to future inheritance, either not having received anything in return or having received satisfaction out of that part of the estate which will be subject to compulsory shares, and either wholly or partially. Several scenarios are possible; for example, the contract can relate to the estate property in its entirety or only to certain specific property. In general, renunciation will also bind the descendants of the person having so renounced.

   Such a contract may be deemed invalid in only one specific case: if, in the period between the conclusion of the contract and the death of the father or the mother, the property comprising either estate is increased in such measure that had not been possible to foresee at the time the contract of renunciation was concluded.

– By virtue of Article 660 of the Civil Code, a disposition relating to an inheritance which is expected or foreseen can be made. However, only the descendants as between themselves are able to conclude a contract on their future inheritance. Such a contract would be concerned with the division of the future inheritance expected from their father and mother. The contract could govern all aspects of the future inheritance as between the children, with account taken also of the various *inter vivos* gifts which had been received up until that time from the father and the mother, in accordance with those agreements concluded by living persons.

As regards these above contracts, the formalities which apply to them are those general rules applying to contracts concluded between living persons. However, the consequences arising from defects in the consent of the parties in contracts of renunciation are the same as those relating to wills.

5. Maintenance

Hungarian inheritance law ensures a legal right of maintenance to those persons close to the deceased by way of an entitlement to a compulsory share in the estate of the deceased for their benefit.

6. Community Property Between Husband and Wife

(a) Hungarian family law upholds the principle of the unity of property. That is, that property acquired during the course of marriage is jointly and indivisibly held by way of community of after-acquired property. By virtue of the law, there is a derogation to this rule: that property acquired free of charge or inherited by one of the spouses during the course of the marriage will remain the separate (i.e., exclusive) property of the spouse having so acquired it. Likewise, property acquired before marriage will remain the separate property of the spouse having so acquired it. If the parties have entered into a marriage contract by which the property is divided up differently, it is those contractual provisions which will prevail.

This presumption of the community of property results in the surviving spouse being able to demand half of all property acquired jointly with the deceased during the course of the marriage.

(b) Given the presumption of the community of property, in the event of dispute, the descendants will have to prove that the contested property does not form part of that property subject to it. The conditions upon which the presumption will apply are that the couple lived conjugally during the marriage and the property was acquired for consideration during the course of such marriage.

7. Gifts (*Inter Vivos*)

(a) Donations as between living persons can only be taken into account as regards those heirs who are entitled to a compulsory share of the estate and only after the death of the person whose property is to pass. All those gifts made to third persons by the deceased during a period of fifteen years prior to his death will have to be added to that part of the estate that will be subject to compulsory shares. The person having a right to a compulsory share can take action against the beneficiary of a gift if such gift encroaches upon that part of the estate which is to be lawfully subject to such shares and could require the beneficiary to pay in cash a sum up to the amount of that part of the estate that will be subject to compulsory shares.

When adding that amount corresponding to the value of the donation to that part of the estate to be subject to the compulsory shares, the value of such donation is deemed to be that at the time it was made. The Civil Code clearly sets out those gifts which will not be taken into account when establishing that part of the estate to be subject to compulsory shares and these are as follows:

– donations made by the deceased before there were persons having a right to a compulsory share;
– donations not surpassing a customary amount;
– maintenance benefiting the surviving spouse and descendants;
– maintenance, for which nothing was given in return, necessary for the survival of other living persons who are otherwise destitute;
– donations which the deceased had specified would not be taken into account will not be added to that part of the estate subject to the compulsory share of the

person having been granted this dispensation. However, such donations will be taken into account as regards that part of the estate subject to the compulsory shares of others.

As between persons having a right to a compulsory share, the 'bringing into account' of donations received during the lifetime of the deceased and of hereditary property will take place within the context of the division and distribution of the estate. If there are several persons who are heirs, each of them must add to the estate the value of the donations which he received during the deceased's lifetime.

(b) As regards the 'bringing into account' of gifts, if a descendant received a donation whose value exceeds that of the share he is to receive upon intestacy from the deceased during the latter's lifetime, that heir cannot receive anything further from the estate but will not have to take any further measures.

In contrast, where the descendant received more by way of donation from the deceased during the latter's lifetime than that to which he is entitled by way of compulsory share, those rules relating to set-off will apply. Such heirs will also have to 'bring into account' such donations.

8. Capacity

(a) A will can be drawn up by persons having the requisite capacity and by those having a limited capacity. The minimum age at which a person can execute such a document is fourteen years of age as this is when the minor acquires limited capacity. As has already been mentioned *above* at 2, those persons having limited capacity, that is, those who are blind, illiterate, unable to sign their names or read, are only able to draw up a public will.

It is not necessary to have the consent of the spouse or, in the case of those persons having limited capacity, the consent of their legal representative, judicial administrator or guardian in order to be able to draw up a will.

(b) More onerous provisions apply to the witnesses of a will than to the testator. As well as requiring the requisite capacity, having to be of full age and being able to read and write, the witnesses must be able to attest to the identity of the testator. The relationship, that of kinship or other, as between the testator and the witnesses is not of importance but in contrast, the will will be invalid if a witness is related to a beneficiary in the will or is himself a beneficiary. As specified in the Civil Code, relationships between witnesses and beneficiaries which will result in the invalidity of a will are those which follow: the spouse, direct relations, adopted children, illegitimate children, adoptive parents, parents-in-law, brothers and sisters, a person who is co-habitee, the spouse of a direct relation, the fiancé(e), direct relations of the spouse, the brothers and sisters of the spouse as· well as the spouses of the brothers and sisters. In certain instances, however, the testator may be able to override this.

(c) The beneficiary of a will must be an individual or a legal entity (*personne morale*) or else the state given it has juridical capacity. Juridical capacity is conferred upon a living person from the time he is conceived. That is, the embryo is deemed a person having the capacity to take or inherit as long as he is born alive. If the deceased wishes to give a legacy to an organization without juridical capacity, he hás to do it through a person with such capacity and specify this.

9. Authority (Court, Notarial or Other)

For the procedure upon succession, the involvement of a notary will always be required from the outset.

If there are immovables included in the estate, or certain movables, shares in a business or cash deposits figuring on a register, recourse must be had to the procedure upon succession. The notary, as well as attesting to the fact of devolution of the estate, also takes measures at the same time to deal with the registrations in the land register and those necessary in relation to other authorities.

The procedure is different if a dispute of some sort arises during the course of the procedure upon succession being carried out by a notary. The notary will try to get the parties to agree to an amicable division, but if this is not possible, he can only take measures under a provisional mandate or may be unable to take any at all. In the latter cases, the notary will ask the heirs to make their submissions as to their claims and demands in the framework of civil proceedings. When there is a dispute relating to the succession, he can make a provisional order authorizing certain heirs to enter into possession of estate property, such possession being of a provisional nature, whereas when there is a dispute as to the deceased's ownership of estate property, he should not, in general, attest to the devolution of the contested property.

Decree No. 6/1958 IM of the Minister of Justice regulating procedure upon succession specifies the person or persons to whom provisional title over the estate property is given when there is a dispute. That is, there is a certain order of precedence established as to whom will acquire rights of succession. In the first instance, those taking by way of a will which is valid as regards formalities precede those who would have taken upon intestacy whereas a will which is invalid due to defects in formality enables the lawful heirs to take the estate property. Furthermore, as regards the acquisition of legal title by way of will and other related dispositions, rights arising by way of contracts on succession precede those arising by way of will and, as regards rights arising as between wills, those rights which arise from a later will will prevail over those arising from earlier wills, whereas rights arising from a holographic will, when valid, will always prevail over those arising from an oral will.

Naturally, within the context of the issue brought before it, the court can in its decision arrive at a conclusion which differs from the devolution of the estate which had been made provisionally. After a final decision has been reached by the court, the notary will make an order concerning the devolution of the estate in accordance with the judgement.

If proceedings have not been initiated within a period of thirty days from the date the notary requested the parties to make their submissions, the notary's provisional order will have become definitive. However, as regards those claims relating to the succession not submitted within that time limit, persons with such claims have the right, even if the procedure upon succession has been completed, to bring proceedings. With the passing of time, however, such proceedings will encounter numerous obstacles as regards proof, as well as obstacles relating to the legal protection afforded to those having acquired property in good faith. These obstacles are likely to result in the limited success of bringing the law into operation at a later date.

During the course of the procedure upon succession, the heirs have the right to uphold the content of wills which are defective or invalid as regards their formalities. They can also enter into various contracts as between themselves or with the creditors of the estate. Upon the adoption of an order, the notary must respect those declarations which are unambiguous and can be judicially interpreted. The declarations may also be different such that, in effect, each heir disposes of his own share of the estate. The limitations applying to such declarations will be further examined later; such limitations serve to protect the rights and interests of minors, heirs lacking capacity and heirs who have not yet been located.

10. Invalidity of Will

(a) The causes of invalidity as to form and the resulting effects have already been examined. Furthermore, a single will made by two or more persons does not take effect as the will is deemed to be a personal act (Article 623(2) of the Civil Code).

The causes of invalidity as regards the contents of a will are as follows:

- an appointment of one or more 'substitutable heirs' (that is, an heir or heirs who, after a certain date, are replaced by another or others);
- a request as to the fulfilment of conditions which are incomprehensible, impossible and/or contradictory;
- defects as to consent, which encompass the following:
  - the deceased having been mistaken as to the content of his testamentary disposition or not having intended to have made a testamentary disposition having such content;
  - the deceased having been incited to have made his testamentary disposition on the basis of a false premise or in the expectation of something which later fails to materialize; and
  - the deceased having been persuaded by way of illegal threats or undue influence to have made a testamentary disposition.
- the incapacity of the testator.

(b) Nullity arising from defects in form and from defects in the content of the will will have the same effects. The will is invalid and it will not be possible to inherit on that basis. On the other hand, as regards the way in which rights are to be realized, there is an essential difference as between defects arising in relation to one or the other. In the event of dispute, nullity on the grounds of defects as to form is recorded by the notary during the course of the procedure upon succession and the person wishing to inherit on the basis of that will has to begin proceedings in order to establish its validity. The notary has no right to record defects as to the content of the will; he can only inform those persons having an interest in the matter of the established fact or the doubt as to the existence of such nullity and will pass on the legacy to the legatee appointed in the will, with such legatee having provisional title in relation to it. The nullity will then be established by the court.

The legal consequences of nullity or validity only apply to those persons party to the proceedings. The will can only be deemed to be invalid, as to its form as well as its content, as regards those persons having challenged it.

11. Simultaneous Death

(a) There are no special rules in Hungarian law dealing with persons who die together during the course of the same incident. If such persons take from one another and it is not possible to establish who died earlier or later, neither will take from the other.

If it is possible to establish the time of death of the various persons, the order in which those persons died will establish who is to inherit from the other. That is, the right of inheritance of the person having died the latest will prevail.

(b) A determination as to the times of death is based upon the report on the medical and legal investigation into the causes of death, with such determination having been made by a doctor. Where persons have died at the same time in an incident, say a car accident, murder or asphyxiation, it may not be possible to establish the exact time of death and therefore the doctor will indicate that the persons died at the same time. If the heirs do not wish to accept this finding, they can ask the court for the modification of the dates in accordance with those rules of evidence to be applied during the course of the proceedings (experts, witnesses).

12. Estate Taxes

(a) Such taxes exist. The amount of taxes to be paid depends upon the degree to which the beneficiary is related to the deceased.

(b) These taxes are only due on property which is the subject of procedure upon succession being carried out in Hungary.

(c) The payment of such taxes is not an obligation for which the heirs are jointly liable. Each of the heirs will pay tax on the property he has inherited and will not be responsible for the payment of taxes owed by other heirs. An heir who is a minor can defer payment of these taxes, without incurring any interest, up until two years from the date he will have attained full age.

13. Administration of Estates

(a) Regard being had to the principle of succession *ipso jure*, the heirs automatically take possession of the estate. If a dispute arises or there is reason to fear the appropriation of or a risk to property, or yet again if there is an heir whose rights are protected by law *ex officio* (e.g., a minor not having a legal representative), the question as to how to protect estate property arises.

The protection of estate property can involve taking the following measures:
- the deposit of cash, titles or other objects of value forming part of the estate with the court;
- the placing of movables forming part of the estate under seal;
- the sequestration or seizure of immovables and movables forming part of the estate, which also involves the appointment of an administrator, who is respons-ible for the safekeeping of the sealed property, to manage the estate;
- the appointment of a judicial administrator (*ad hoc* administrator) for the collec-tion of debts; and
- the ordering of the sale of property in order to protect the heir's material interests.

In the absence of those circumstances set out *above*, the heirs jointly have the right, obligation and responsibility to keep, manage and take care of the property forming part of the estate before it is distributed.

(b) An estate report will have to be drawn up. An administrator who is appointed must always draw up a report to submit to the entity having appointed him. His duty is to be carried out as long as the reason for his appointment subsists. For example, if a legal representative is acting for an heir who is a minor or there is an heir yet to be located who appears, it will be deemed sufficient that the *ad hoc* administrator renders his account to such persons. This is another matter for which the legal representative will have to account in all cases and each year to the supervisory authority having control of that part of the estate.

(c) Public authorities only exercise external control over the management of the succession if the heir is represented by a judicial administrator because the said heir has not yet been located. The legal representative of a minor or another person lacking the requisite capacity will be held to account for the estate property handed over to him, together with the other property owned by the person whom he repre-sents. As regards these matters, it is the local supervisory authority which will have jurisdiction.

(d) The heirs, or the legal representatives acting on their behalf, or the judicial administrator (who is entrusted to represent a person who has not yet been located or who cannot be identified, or who represents a minor or a person lacking the requisite capacity where there is a conflict of interests as between such heirs and their representatives), have the right to deal with such matters relating to the suc-cession. Naturally, such matters could also be dealt with by a legal representative and, if there are no conflicts of interest, by heirs with power of attorney from other heirs.

(e) As the heirs are the legal owners of the deceased's estate at the time of his death, there is no need for a particular legal process or instrument to allow for the handing over of the estate's assets to the heirs. Entering into possession and disposing of estate property is also deemed to amount to a renunciation of the right to repudiate the succession.

If there is a dispute involving the succession, it is the court that will establish the lawful heir. In such cases, another person may already have entered into possession of the estate. Such a person will be held to account to the heirs in accordance with the general rules on responsibility set out in the Civil Code.

(f) In general the heirs are jointly responsible for the estate's debts. This is not the case if they were not aware of the existence of such debts until after the distribution of estate property. The heirs are responsible for the estate's expenses up to the value of the estate property. In addition, the creditors of the estate have the right to request the drawing up of an inventory of the estate property without having to obtain the heirs' consent.

The order in which the estate's debts are settled is set out in Article 677 of the Civil Code. By virtue of this provision, the deceased's property must be allocated to pay off the debts in the following order of preference:
– expenses relating to the funeral deemed fitting for the deceased;
– expenses incurred in connection with the acquisition, the insurance and the management of the estate property (expenses relating to the succession itself);
– the debts of the deceased;
– the obligations arising in connection with the compulsory shares; and
– the obligations arising from legacies and hereditary liabilities.

As concerns those categories set out *above*, when paying off the creditors, the debts relating to one of the former categories will prevail over those in the categories which follow. Within one particular category, where it will not be possible to pay off all the creditors, each must be paid proportionately. If the heirs disregard such creditors, and therefore one or several creditors are not paid off, the heirs will have to meet such liabilities from their own property. During the course of the procedure upon succession carried out by the notary, the creditors are able to make a declaration as to their claims to the notary and the latter can, after receiving the necessary authority from the heirs, pay off those debts.

(g) Before the estate is divided, the heirs have joint possession; that is, those claims relating to the succession must be made on behalf of all the heirs. The debtor wanting to pay off a debt must pay the money over to all the heirs and in the event of a dispute, he should pay the money over to the judge. This joint possession of property ends upon the division of the estate property. If recourse was had to the procedure upon succession, the notary will determine, in accordance with the division as directed by the heirs, the devolution of the estate. A limit will be fixed as against the heirs if any of them are minors, lack the requisite capacity or have not yet been located. In such cases, these persons will obtain upon division less than that to which they would have been lawfully entitled.

The Hungarian Civil Code does not regulate the institution of the testamentary executor as such. If the deceased had appointed such a person in his will, that

person, on the basis of the mandate conferred upon him by the will and in accordance with the general rules concerning the law of succession, may have the following powers:
- to manage the property belonging to the estate before its division;
- to ensure that the division proceeds in accordance with the will;
- to sell estate property and to account to the heirs for the sale proceeds; and
- to carry out certain duties and tasks (such as the funeral of the deceased, taking care of animals, etc.).

14. Domicile/Nationality

(a) Those provisions relating to Hungarian inheritance law set out *above* concern deceased persons having had Hungarian nationality and those procedures upon succession which are carried out in Hungary. In this regard, the domicile of the deceased is not of importance. As for a deceased person having a nationality other than Hungarian, it will be his own personal law (i.e., that of the nationality of the deceased) which will be applied in relation to the succession. Certain international agreements may allow for other possibilities. During the course of the procedure upon succession, the procedural rules to be applied are those of Hungary.

(b) The general rules relating to contentious procedure are those to be applied as regards the jurisdiction of the local court. In the event of judicial proceedings, jurisdiction will be determined upon the basis of the domicile of the defendant or, at the plaintiff's request, the location at which the immovables subject to the proceedings are found. If the plaintiff resides abroad or the matter concerns a person who has not yet been located, the court having jurisdiction is that of the domicile of the plaintiff or, at the plaintiff's request, that of the location of the property (even if this concerns movables). As to the procedure to be carried out by the notary, jurisdiction will be determined on the basis of the last domicile of the deceased in Hungary. If the deceased never had his domicile in Hungary, it will be on the basis of the location where each part of the estate is situated.

Section B – Applicable Law/Procedure Where Foreign Element/s are Involved

1. Jurisdiction

(a) By virtue of *Decree No. 13 of 1979* on private international law, a Hungarian court or another Hungarian authority shall have exclusive jurisdiction in relation to the following:

- all procedures involving immovables located in Hungary; and
- all procedures involving an estate in Hungary of a deceased Hungarian national.

International Succession

(b) Different rules exist for movables and immovables. As for the latter which are located in Hungary, only the Hungarian authorities have jurisdiction. If the estate includes movables located in Hungary and abroad, the requisite jurisdiction as regards procedure will depend on the nature of the agreement concluded between the two countries concerned. When there is no such agreement, the Hungarian court and the Hungarian notary have jurisdiction in relation to those movables located within the country.

(c) The law to be applied and the territorial jurisdiction of the court do not follow on from one another, as has already been mentioned in the preceding paragraph. The rules relating to general territorial jurisdiction of the courts are those to be applied.

2. Applicable Law

The rules governing executory procedure in Hungary are those to be applied. The local court having jurisdiction on the basis of the domicile of the person whose estate is to pass or the location at which that property subject to the executory measures is found will have the authority to deal with the execution of foreign decisions.

3. Foreign Succession/Inheritance Orders

(a) Only the Hungarian authorities will be able to make decisions relating to the succession of immovables. As regards movables, if a foreign decision is to be executed, this can occur within the framework of the executory procedure governed by Hungarian law. A Hungarian court will deal with such executory procedure within the context of the foreign decision made. The rules relating to this matter do not set out any specific provisions.

(b) By virtue of the *Decree on Private International Law* (Article 73), those decisions made by foreign courts or other authorities in relation to those matters over which the Hungarian courts or other authorities do not have exclusive jurisdiction must be recognized.

However, a foreign inheritance order cannot be recognized if:

- its recognition would be contrary to Hungarian public policy:
- the foreign court proceeded on the basis of some form of territorial jurisdiction that could not be applied to its own nationals (or other legal entities);
- the person to whom the decision relates did not have the possibility of participating in the procedure due to some procedural irregularity;
- a Hungarian court has already handed down a final judgement in relation to the same matter and the same parties.

(c) The foreign decision will be executory as regards claims relating to succession when there is an international or bilateral agreement.

4. Two or More Succession or Probate Orders

In principle this is not possible. Where there is no international agreement on the matter, the Hungarian authorities can only ascertain the devolution upon succession in relation to property which is located in Hungary. If the foreign authority had taken a decision in disregard of the jurisdiction of the Hungarian authorities, it will also be necessary to initiate the procedure upon succession in Hungary.

5. Assets

In the absence of an international agreement to the contrary, if the deceased has not left any assets in Hungary, no procedure can be carried out within the country. On the other hand, upon request, the Hungarian notary can issue a certificate on succession that could be used during the course of a procedure carried out abroad which relates to the succession of a Hungarian national. In this certificate, the notary will attest that the order of succession is in accordance with that of the personal law (i.e., that of Hungary) of the deceased.

6. Expert Evidence

(a)–(b) There is no need to obtain evidence from a foreign legal expert in relation to a foreign will which has already been approved by a foreign jurisdiction or by foreign legislation on inheritance. The foreign law may be established before a Hungarian court by way of a procedure allowing for the presentation of a wide range of evidence. In cases of uncertainty, the Hungarian Ministry of Justice will be authorized to render an expert opinion. If the application of foreign law is not possible, Hungarian law will apply.

One way in which foreign law can be ascertained is by recourse to those provisions of the *European Convention on the Provision of Evidence on Foreign Law* signed by Hungary on 7 June 1968 in London as well as the *Protocol* to the Convention signed on 15 March 1977 in Strasbourg, these two documents having been in force in Hungary since 20 October 1992.

7. Unity of Succession

This does exist as regards domestic law but not in relation to private international law.

8. Formalities

Those formalities relating to a will having been drawn up in a foreign country do not have to be identical to those of Hungary for that will to be executory in Hungary. The Hungarian rules of private international law provide that in the

International Succession

absence of a bilateral agreement, a will drawn up in another country and subject to examination by Hungarian authorities will be recognized if it satisfies those conditions as to validity which apply in the country in which it was drawn up. An examination as to its validity in the country in which it was drawn up will not be carried out unless the will does not comply with the formalities of the personal law of the deceased because the main rule is that the law which was the personal law of the deceased at the time of his death applies. It should be noted, however, that if the formalities comply with either the law of the domicile or habitual residence of the testator either at the time of drawing up his will or of his death, or the law of the location at which immovables are situated, the will may also be deemed valid.

9. Legislation

The *1961 Hague Convention on the Conflicts of Laws Relating to the Form of Testamentary Dispositions* has been in force in Hungary since 1966.

10. Wills

(a) As regards wills which have been drawn up abroad, it is those rules set out in 8 *above* which will apply.

(b) There are no specific provisions concerning the content of a will or the terminology used. A minimum requirement, however, is that the document is characteristic of a will and the wishes of the deceased have been expressed unambiguously; this must be evident upon interpretation of the will itself. *See* also the information provided at Section A10. In the event of dispute, the court cannot decline to interpret the will.

(c) This information has been provided in Section A. In the event of a dispute, the person having a right to a compulsory share is the one who has to initiate proceedings in relation to a will which is, in terms of its form, valid.

(d) Coinciding with juridical capacity, it is the personal law of the deceased that should be applied.

(e) The personal law of the deceased is to be applied.

(f) As regards the validity of the content of the will, Hungarian private international law provides that the law to be applied is that of the personal law of the testator at time of his death.

(g) The answer is in the affirmative only in relation to the movables which are the subject of legacies. Insofar as this is the main rule, here the inheritance law relating to the personal law of the deceased is that which will apply.

(h) The law to be applied is that relating to the form of the will.

(i) Special judicial protection (a judicial administrator to deal with the realization of that part of the estate subject to compulsory shares and a supervisory authority to safeguard estate property) is accorded to a non-resident only if he cannot be summoned according to the ordinary rules or if he has not yet been located.

11. Domicile/Nationality

(a) The law of inheritance to be applied depends upon, as has been mentioned previously, the personal law of the deceased; that is to say, the law of the nationality of the deceased having been in force at the time of the deceased's death will apply. As to the validity of the will, insofar as this is a supplementary rule, this will depend upon the law having been in force at the time and the location the will was drawn up.

(b) The domicile or the nationality of the heir is of no importance in relation to inheritance law and the law to be applied. The rights and obligations are the same for heirs having different nationalities or domiciles.

(c) The permanent domicile is that which prevails. Such domicile could be defined on the basis of the register of addresses in relation to which a declaration of domicile is made. If the domicile cannot be established, the ground upon which authority can be exercised is that of the location at which the succession is carried out. Determination of the nationality will be *ex officio*. If the nationality cannot be established, that nationality considered to be the deceased's last will prevail as regards the personal law to be applied to the deceased's estate.

12. Taxation

There is no difference in this regard. Inheritance tax has only to be paid in relation to that property which is handed over or devolves in Hungary, in accordance with the conditions and procedures which would apply if all the persons involved in the succession (the deceased and the heirs) were residents.

India

Prepared by: Lalit BHASIN
Bhasin & Co., Advocates
Supreme Court of India

Address: 10, Hailey Road, 10th Floor
　　　　 New Delhi 110-001
　　　　 India
Tel.: 　　+91 11 3322601/6968/9878
Fax: 　　+91 11 3329273

SECTION A – BRIEF SURVEY OF THE LOCAL SYSTEM

1. Type of System

India is a multi-racial and multi-religious country. The population consists mainly of Hindus, Mohammedans, Christians and Sikhs. Even in these major religious divisions, there are sects and sub-sects; for instance the Mohammedans are divided into two sects, namely, Shias and Sunnis, both of whom are again divided into sub-sects. There are slight differences as to the law of succession to be applied in relation to them. Mohammedans as a whole are governed by the personal law applicable to their sect or sub-sect. There are also a relatively small number of Parsis, a very small number of Jews, and some other local communities. The persons professing these faiths were largely governed by personal laws applicable to them, but now the law of succession has been codified to a large extent.

The Hindus who form the largest majority of Indians are governed by the *Hindu Succession Act 1956* insofar as intestate succession is concerned. The term 'Hindu' in this Act includes a Buddhist, Jain or Sikh by religion so far as intestate succession is concerned.

The *Indian Succession Act 1925* sets out, *inter alia*, the rules for intestate succession. These rules are not applicable to Hindus, Buddhists, Sikhs, Jain or Mohammedans since the Hindus are governed by the *Hindu Succession Act* and the Mohammedans by the Muslim Personal Law. The *Indian Succession Act* contains a separate chapter for Parsi intestates. This Act also contains the rules for testamentary succession which are, with a few exceptions, applicable to all except the Mohammedans.

Such rules apply to:

– Europeans by birth or descent domiciled in India;
– persons of mixed European and Native Blood and East Indians;

– Jews (although some courts have applied Jewish religious law);
– Parsis (for testamentary succession only);
– Hindus (for testamentary succession only); and
– persons marrying under the *Special Marriage Act 1954*.

2. Wills

(a) There are two types of wills: privileged wills and unprivileged wills. A soldier employed in an expedition or engaged in actual warfare or an airman so employed or engaged or a mariner being at sea may dispose of his property by a will. Such wills are referred to as *privileged wills*. A privileged will may be made in writing or by word of mouth. It may be written wholly by the testator or it may be written by another person and signed by the testator. In such case it need not be attested. An oral will becomes null and void at the expiration of one month after the testator, being still alive, has ceased to be entitled to make a privileged will. The provisions relating to privileged wills are not, however, applicable to Hindus.

The other type of will is an *unprivileged will*. Any person can execute his will for the disposition of his property after his death. The will in this instance has to be signed by the testator, or by some other person in his presence and by his direction, and it has to be attested by two witnesses, each of whom has seen the testator (or the other person) signing it (except in the case of Mohammedans). Each of the witnesses should sign the will in the presence of the testator, but it is not necessary that both witnesses be present at the same time. No particular form of attestation is necessary under the Act but the following is the usual form:

> 'Signed by the said *A.B.* the testator above named as his last will and testament in the presence of us present at the same time who at his request in his presence have hereunto subscribed our names as witnesses.
> *C.D.*
> *E.F.*'

A will may be written in any language without the need for technical wording but the wording should be such that the intention of the testator can be known therefrom. It is also not necessary that the testator himself should write the will; it may be written by anyone. However, if it is written by a person who himself benefits by it, the court will be more vigilant and zealous in examining the evidence in support of the instrument in order to be able to satisfy itself that it does express the true will of the deceased. Once it is proven that the will has been made by a person of competent understanding and acting apparently as a free agent, the burden of proving that it was executed under undue influence rests upon the person making such an allegation.

Illness which impairs the mind of a person in such a manner as to deprive him of the power of understanding the nature of the instrument or the effect of its provisions will vitiate the will. But mere debility unaccompanied by mental incapacity will not deprive a person from making a will.

International Succession

Wills and codicils are exempted from stamp duty. It is also unnecessary for a will to be registered. However, the *Registration Act* provides that a will may be presented for registration by the testator or, after his death, by any person claiming as executor or otherwise under a will. There is no time limit for presentation of a will for registration. In any case, mere registration of the will does not serve as proof of the testamentary capacity of the testator; this must be established in the ordinary way. However, if the will bequeaths any property to religious or charitable causes, it should have been executed not less than twelve months before the testator's death, and deposited with the Registrar within six months of its execution.

In the case of a *Mohammedan*, a will may be made either verbally or in writing. A Mohammedan will, though in writing, does not require any signature or attestation. However, the burden of establishing an oral will is always a very heavy one.

(b) *i.* If the testator wishes to make any amendment in the will, he can either write a fresh will or execute a codicil.

The same principles are applied by the courts in construing a codicil as in the case of a will.

ii. A will may be revoked or altered by the testator at any time when he is competent to dispose of his property by will. A will is revocable so long as the testator is living. The only instance in which a will cannot be revoked is in the case of mutual or joint wills which become irrevocable after the death of one of the testators, if the survivor takes advantage of the provisions made by the deceased. Revocation can be effected by making another will or codicil, by a written document declaring an intention to revoke the will and executed in the same manner as such will or by destroying the will.

A will is not always automatically revoked upon the marriage of the testator. Although Section 69 of the *Indian Succession Act* provides for revocation of a will upon the testator's marriage, this Section is not applicable to Hindus or Mohammedans.

iii. A will or codicil which has been revoked in any manner cannot be revived other than by the re-execution thereof, or by a codicil executed in the usual manner showing an intention to revive the same.

3. Intestacy

A person is considered to have died intestate in respect of all property in relation to which:

– he has not made a testamentary disposition, e.g., when he has left no will; or
– he has made a will but that will is not capable of taking effect, e.g., when he has bequeathed his property for an illegal purpose or if the subject of the bequest is non-existent.

Intestacy is of two kinds: total or partial. A person may die partially testate and partially intestate, e.g., where the will contains several bequests to several legatees but there is no disposition of the residue, he dies intestate as regards the residue.

302

(a) The rules pertaining to the order of succession are different for Europeans and Indian Christians, Hindus, Parsis and Mohammedans.

In the case of *Europeans and Indian Christians* the property of an intestate devolves upon the wife or husband, or upon those who are the relations of the deceased, in the order and according to the detailed rules contained in the *Indian Succession Act.*

Where a European or Indian Christian intestate has left a widow:

– if he has also left any lineal descendants, one-third of his property shall belong to his widow, and the remaining two-thirds shall go to his lineal descendants;
– if he has left no lineal descendant but has left persons who are of kindred to him, one-half of his property shall belong to his widow, and the other half shall go to those who are of kindred to him;
– if he has left none who are of kindred to him, the whole of his property shall devolve to his widow.

A widow is not entitled if, by a valid contract made before her marriage, she has been excluded from her lawful share of her husband's estate.

A husband surviving his wife has the same rights in respect of her property if she dies intestate as a widow has in respect of her husband's property if he dies intestate.

In so far as *Parsi* intestates are concerned, there are special rules. The property of a male Parsi is divided as follows:

– where he dies leaving a widow and children, as between them, the share of each son and of the widow shall be double that of each daughter; or
– where he dies leaving children but no widow, as between the children, the share of each son shall be double that of each daughter.

Where a male Parsi dies leaving one or both parents in addition to children or a widow and children, the property in relation to which he dies intestate shall be divided so that the father shall receive a share equal to half that of a son and the mother shall receive a share equal to half that of a daughter.

In case of a Parsi female dying intestate:

– if she dies leaving a widower and children, the widower and each child shall receive equal shares;
– if she dies leaving children but no widower, the property is divided among the children in equal shares.

So far as *Hindus* are concerned, intestate succession is governed by the *Hindu Succession Act 1956* which is applicable also to Buddhists, Jains or Sikhs.

The property of a male Hindu dying intestate shall devolve:

– firstly, upon the heirs, being the relatives specified in class 1 of the Schedule to the Act;
– secondly, if there are no heirs of class 1, then upon the heirs, being the relatives specified in class 2 of the Schedule;

- thirdly, if there are no heirs of the above two classes, then upon the agnates of the deceased; and
- lastly, if there are no agnates, then upon the cognates of the deceased.

(It is perhaps useful to note that an agnate is a person related to another by blood or adoption wholly through the male line of descent whilst a cognate is a person related to another by blood or adoption but not wholly through the male line of descent).

The heirs in class 1 and class 2 are listed in the Schedule to the Act and include as follows:

- Class 1: Son; daughter; widow, mother; son of a predeceased son, daughter of a predeceased son; son of a predeceased daughter; daughter of a predeceased daughter; widow of a predeceased son; son of a predeceased son of a predeceased son; daughter of a predeceased son of a predeceased son; and widow of a predeceased son of a predeceased son.
- Class 2: – Father.
            He excludes all others in this class. The rest take equally.
            – Son's daughter's son; son's daughter's daughter; brother; sister;
            – Daughter's son's son; daughter's son's daughter; daughter's daughter's son; daughter's daughter's daughter;
            – Brother's son; sister's son; brother's daughter; sister's daughter;
            – Father's father; father's mother;
            – Father's widow; brother's widow;
            – Father's brother; father's sister;
            – Mother's father; mother's mother;
            – Mother's brother; mother's sister.

(N.B. In this Schedule, references to brothers or sisters do not include references to brothers or sisters by uterine blood).

Insofar as *Mohammedans* are concerned, the estate of a deceased Mohammedan is to be applied successively in payment of:

- his funeral expenses and death-bed charges;
- expenses of obtaining probate, letters of administration or succession certificate;
- wages due for service rendered to the deceased within three months preceding his death by any person;
- other debts of the deceased;
- legacies not exceeding one-third of what remains after all the above payments have been made.

Residual assets are to be distributed among the heirs of the deceased according to the sect to which the deceased belonged at the moment of his death. A deceased Mohammedan is presumed to have been Sunni and the onus is on the person alleging him to have been a Shia to prove this.

The Hanafi Law (which is applicable to *Sunni Mohammedans*) classifies heirs in three classes.

Class 1 includes the surviving spouse and mother and these heirs are unconditional heirs. Class 1 also includes others who become heirs subject to certain conditions. These include the maternal/paternal grandmother, uterine brothers and/or sisters, daughters, sons' daughters, the father, the father's father, full sisters and consanguine sisters.

Class 2 comprises sons, daughters, sons' sons, sons' daughters, the father, the true grandfather, full brothers, full sisters, consanguine brothers, consanguine sisters, sons of brothers, full paternal uncles, consanguine paternal uncles and sons of paternal uncles.

Class 3 heirs in Hanafi Law are daughters' children or their descendants and sons' daughters' children or their descendants.

The heirs of Class 1 & 2 inherit together, however, among these the claims of all entitled heirs in Class 1 are to be satisfied first; then if there is a residue it will go to Class 2 heirs. There are other rules for inheritance by persons in classes 2 & 3.

Among the *Shia Mohammedans*, there are two groups of heirs: firstly, heirs by consanguinity, i.e., blood relations; and secondly, heirs by marriage, i.e., husband and wife. Heirs by consanguinity are again divided into three classes, all of which are further subdivided into two groups. These classes are respectively composed as follows:

– Class 1: Parents; Children and other descendants.
– Class 2: Grand parents; Brothers and sisters and their descendants.
– Class 3: Paternal; Maternal; i.e., uncles and aunts of the deceased and his parents and grand parents and their descendants.

Of these three classes of heirs, the first excludes the second from inheritance and the second excludes the third. The husband or wife is never excluded from succession but inherits together with the heirs most closely related by consanguinity, with the husband taking one-quarter or one-half, and the wife taking one-eighth or one-quarter depending upon the number of other heirs who are to take.

For example, a Shia Mohammedan dies leaving a daughter's son, a father's mother, and a full brother. In accordance with Shia Law, the daughter's son, being an heir of the first class, will succeed to the whole inheritance thereby excluding the father's mother and the full brother, both of whom belong to the second class of heirs. In Hanafi law, the father's mother will take one-sixth, the full brother will take five-sixth as a residuary; and the daughter's son, being a distant kinsman, will be entirely excluded from inheritance.

(b) The above rules apply to all property (movable or immovable) of which the deceased has not made a testamentary disposition (*see* 14 *below*).

4. Freedom of Testation

(a) Any person of sound mind not being a minor is entitled to dispose of his property by will. Generally speaking, all persons who have sufficient discretion and free will are capable of disposing of their property by will. A married woman, however, may, by will, dispose only of any property which she herself could alienate during her lifetime. Those restrictions applicable to Mohammedans have been discussed earlier.

There are no compulsory or minimum percentages or amounts to be devolved upon the husband, the wife or common law wife or children of the deceased. Inheritance is either by law of succession, in cases of intestacy, or in accordance with a person's will.

As a result of a recent judgment of the Supreme Court of India striking down Section 118 of *Indian Succession Act* on the grounds that it was violative of constitutional right of equality before law, the sights of Indian Christians to make a bequest for religions or charitable purposes are now the same as that of other citizens.

(b) A contract of inheritance is not envisaged in the Indian law of contract.

5. Maintenance

Maintenance can be claimed under the Code of Criminal Procedure, which is applicable to all Indian citizens.

Sections 21 and 22 of the *Hindu Adoptions & Maintenance Act 1950* create rights in favour of certain persons, referred to as dependants. Dependants are relations of a deceased Hindu and can claim maintenance as against the property of the deceased in the hands of the heirs.

This right of dependants exists as against the property and not as against the heirs personally. The obligation is limited to the extent to which the heir has the estate of the deceased in his or her hands. Further, the dependant will be entitled to claim maintenance only if he has not obtained any share in the estate of a Hindu by testamentary or intestate succession. The dependants include, subject to certain conditions, the parents, the widow, minor legitimate or illegitimate sons/unmarried daughters, etc.

In the case of *Mohammedans*, children who are affluent are bound to maintain their poor parents. In addition, a son in straitened circumstances is bound to maintain his mother if she is poor even though not infirm. In the event a Mohammedan divorces his wife, the wife is entitled to maintenance during the period of *iddat* (i.e., the period during which it is incumbent upon the woman whose marriage has been dissolved by divorce or death to remain in seclusion, and to abstain from taking another husband), but a widow is not entitled to maintenance during the period of *iddat* consequent upon her husband's death.

6. Community Property between Husband and Wife

(a) A person can give by will only such property as belongs to him. A property which is jointly owned by husband and wife cannot be bequeathed by either in their respective wills. However, it is possible for two *Hindus* to make a joint will.

By recent amendment a Christian widow is entitled to succeed to her distributable share in the property of her deceased husband.

(b) The concept of 'matrimonial regime' is not applicable in India.

7. Gifts (*Inter Vivos*)

(a)–(b) If a person (who is not a minor) has made a valid gift to another, including his heir, the act is complete upon the donee accepting the gift. A valid gift to an heir prior to death is not set off against the heir's share in the property of the deceased under the law of succession.

In the case of a *Mohammedan*, a gift, as distinguished from that passing by will, may be made, even to an heir, of the whole of the donor's property.

8. Capacity

(a) Any person of sound mind not being a minor may dispose of his property by will, except a Mohammedan (*see* 2 and 4 *above*).

As has been stated above, a married woman may, by will, dispose only of any property which she herself could alienate during her lifetime.

(b) There are no stipulations as to the capacity of witnesses. A relation of the deceased can be a witness to his will. It is not necessary that the witnesses should know the contents of the will which they are attesting. The executor named in the will is able to attest as is a beneficiary. But any legacy or bequest made over to a person who attests the will, or to his wife or her husband, or to any person claiming under either of them, shall be null and void. This provision, however, does not apply to Hindus. Hence, a witness attesting to a *Hindu*'s will does not lose the legacy given to him by the will.

(c) The beneficiary may be anyone including a minor. If a bequest is made in favour of an unborn child, the will is deemed contingent, i.e., should the event not happen, the will has no effect. In the case of a *Mohammedan*, a bequest to an unborn child is void, but a bequest may be made to a child in the womb, provided the child is born within six months from the date of the execution of the will.

A Mohammedan cannot by will dispose of more than a third of the surplus of his estate after payment of funeral expenses and debts. Bequests in excess of this share of the estate cannot take effect unless the heirs consent thereto after the death of the testator. For example, if a testator had three heirs and left the 'surplus' to one only, he can only receive the property if the other two agreed and if only one of them agreed, he will receive the latter's share.

9. Authority (Court, Notarial or Others)

An order of succession ('succession certificate') is granted by a court of competent jurisdiction. It cannot be granted by a notary public or other authority.

307

10. Invalidity of Will

(a)–(b) The requirements of a valid will have been discussed at 2 *above*. A will which does not conform to such requirements would be defective and probate may be refused. A will or any part of a will, the making of which was induced by fraud, coercion or such importunity as takes away the free agency of the testator, is void (Section 61 of the *Indian Succession Act*). Other cases where a bequest is void are as follows:

– a bequest to a person who does not exist at the testator's death;
– a life interest to an unborn child;
– a bequest the vesting of which is delayed for more than eighteen years beyond the life of an existing person; and
– a bequest to a charity by a testator having a nephew or niece or closer relation unless the will is executed twelve months before his death and deposited with the Registrar within six months of its execution.

11. Simultaneous Death

(a) In the case of persons other than Hindus, there is no specific rule as to who, among two or more persons dying simultaneously in the same disaster or calamity (i.e., *commorientes*), died later. It has been held that it is a matter of evidence with the burden of proof on the person who asserts a fact. If the legatee does not survive the testator, the legacy cannot take effect but shall lapse and form part of the testator's residuary property unless it appears from the will that the testator had intended that it should go to some other person. For example, where the testator and the legatee perished in the same shipwreck and there is no evidence to show who died first, the legacy would lapse.

Section 21 of *Hindu Succession Act 1946* specifically deals with the presumption applying in the case of simultaneous deaths and states that where two persons have died in circumstances rendering it uncertain whether either, and if so, who, survived the other, then, for all purposes affecting succession of property, it shall be presumed, unless the contrary is proven, that the younger person survived the elder. Consequently in the case of *commorientes*, it is for the party wishing to rebut this statutory presumption to prove that the elder survived the younger. The said Section 21 applies both to testamentary and intestate succession.

(b) When there is a question as to whether a person is alive or not, and it is proven that he has not been heard of for seven years by those who would normally have heard of him if he had been alive, there is a presumption of death. The burden of proof as to this person's continued existence rests with the person who affirms this. However, there is no presumption as to the time of death, which is a matter of evidence.

12. Estate Taxes

India had an *Estate Duty Act* which has since been repealed.

13. Administration of Estates

(a) When the deceased has left a will, the executor named in that will will administer the estate till the bequests in the will have been carried out.

In case of intestacy, the heir of a *deceased Hindu* succeeds to his share of the estate without it being necessary to appoint an administrator. In the case of a *Mohammedan*, the person entitled to administer the estate would be the person to whom letters of administration are granted. In the absence of an executor or administrator, the persons entitled to administer the estate are the heirs of the deceased.

(b) After probate or letters of administration are granted, there are no reports to be submitted.

(c)–(d) Probate and letters of administration are granted by courts of competent jurisdiction on application of the executor or the legal representatives. A notice of application is published. Any person who has any objection to a particular person being granted probate or letters of administration can file his objections with the court. The person contesting the will or grant of letters of administration, known as the 'caveator', must, however, show that he has some interest in the estate in order for him to establish his *locus standi* in the Probate Court.

The *Indian Succession Act* provides for the removal of an executor or administrator by means of a petition presented to the High Court. The petition can be made by any person claiming to be aggrieved.

(e) In the case of heirs who inherit property by succession, no special procedure is laid down if there is no dispute among such heirs. In the event of a dispute, a succession certificate becomes necessary and this is granted by the court upon petition by the heirs, who have given prior notice to all concerned. Any person claiming a right of succession may make an application to the court for relief.

(f) No creditor has a right of priority over another. The executor or administrator shall pay all such debts that he knows of, including his own, equally and proportionally, as far as the assets of the deceased will allow.

(g) Under Section 218 of the *Indian Succession Act* administration of an estate may be granted to any person who, according to the rules on the distribution of estates, would be entitled to the whole or any part of such an estate. In cases of intestacy, a creditor can claim from the heirs an amount up to the value of the latter's shares in the estate. Usually the heirs apply for the grant of the letters of administration. However, if no person entitled applies, the grant may be made to a creditor of the deceased (Section 218(3) of *Indian Succession Act*).

Under *Hindu law*, every heir takes the property subject to the debts and liabilities of the deceased.

14. Domicile/Nationality

(a) In the case of *Hindus domiciled outside India*, as regards immovable property in India, succession is governed by the *Indian Succession Act*; but as regards movable property, succession is governed by the law of the country of his domicile.

International Succession

In the case of *Hindus domiciled in India*, as regards immovable property outside India, succession is governed by the law of the country in which that property is situated, unless otherwise permitted by the law of that country. As regards movable property outside India, succession is governed by Indian law or by the law of that country in which such property is situated, according to the principles of private international law accepted by that country.

In the case of *Hindus domiciled outside India*, succession to immovable or movable property outside India would not be governed by Indian law but by the law of the country in which the Hindu is domiciled.

In the case of *other persons*, Section 5 of the *Indian Succession Act* provides that succession to immovable property in India shall be regulated by Indian law wherever the deceased may have had his domicile at the time of his death. So far as movable property is concerned, succession is regulated by the law of the country in which the deceased had his domicile at the time of his death.

(b) No probate can be granted in India in the case of a will executed in India by a non-resident which only disposes of property outside India.

Section B – Applicable Law/Procedure Where Foreign Element/s are Involved

1. Jurisdiction

(a) A District Court in India will have jurisdiction if the deceased was domiciled within the territorial jurisdiction of that court at the date of his death. Although domicile has been classed under three heads, by birth, by choice, and by operation of the law, a person can have only one domicile at a time so far as the *Indian Succession Act* is concerned.

(b) There are different rules for movable and immovable assets. *See* Section A14 *above*.

Succession to immovable property in India is regulated by the law of India; succession to movable property is regulated by the law of the country in which the deceased had his domicile at the time of his death.

(c) The local court in India would be that where the deceased had his domicile at the time of his death. The particular local court having jurisdiction in the matter would depend upon the value of the assets. Usually it is the principal judge (District Court) which has jurisdiction. However, certain High Courts which have ordinary original civil jurisdiction will also have jurisdiction in specified areas under their territorial jurisdiction.

2. Applicable Law

The applicable law will depend upon not only the domicile of the deceased at the time of death but also upon the nature of the property. Succession to immovable property in India shall be regulated by the law of India whereas succession to movable property would be regulated by the law of the country in which the deceased had his domicile at the time of his death. However, though the right to succession of movable property is to be regulated by the law of domicile, if a person whose domicile is not in India dies leaving movable property in India, the administration of his property and its application for the payment of his debts is to be regulated by the law of India.

The distinguishing features of the law applicable to persons professing different religions (e.g., Hindus, Mohammedans, Parsis, etc.) have been mentioned earlier.

3. Foreign Succession/Inheritance Orders

(a) A foreign judgment given by a competent court is enforceable in India under Section 13 of the Indian Code of Civil Procedure (CPC) unless it falls under the exceptions mentioned therein, e.g., when it is proven that it has been obtained by fraud, or without notice having been given to the defendant, or where it sustains a claim founded on breach of any law in force in India.

(b) Execution of decrees passed by courts in reciprocating countries is permitted by Indian Courts under Section 44-A of the CPC on the prescribed form. Details of the suit, decree, amounts due and prayer for attachment and sale of property (if desired) are to be given in the application. For this purpose, a certified copy of the decree must be attached to the application for execution. It is not necessary that a succession/inheritance order be obtained from a local court. However, insofar as immovable property situated in India is concerned, the Indian court alone will have the right to investigate the title of the applicant of such property and the court within whose jurisdiction the property is situated will decide upon all matters relating to the property.

4. Two or More Succession or Probate Orders

An application for an order of succession or inheritance, insofar as it relates to immovable property, will have to be filed and decided by the court in India, notwithstanding any order of a foreign court. In respect of movable property the governing law is that of the domicile of the deceased and, therefore, if there is an order of a competent foreign court in respect of movable property of a deceased person domiciled within the jurisdiction of that foreign court, it will have priority. Also refer to Section A14 *above*.

The Supreme Court of India has held that decisions of the Probate Court are judgments *in rem* and as long as an order granting probate remains in force, i.e., until it has been revoked, it is conclusive as to the execution and validity of a will. If, therefore, there are two competing foreign probate orders, it would be necessary for the aggrieved party to move the Probate Court concerned for revocation of the grant of probate.

311

International Succession

5. Assets

The local court will not have jurisdiction in respect of immovable property in a foreign jurisdiction, even if the applicant is a citizen of India or resides in India. But if the deceased was domiciled in India and has left movable property in a foreign country, the local court will have jurisdiction to deal with an application for inheritance of that property.

6. Expert Evidence

(a)–(b) It is not always necessary for a foreign lawyer to give evidence regarding a foreign will which has been recognized by a foreign court or regarding an inheritance in a foreign country. Section 45 of *Indian Evidence Act* provides that foreign law may be proven by:
– evidence given by a person specially skilled in it; and
– direct reference to books printed or published under the authority of the foreign government.

Where foreign law is laid down in an elaborate manner in a foreign code, the court should interpret it without any reference to any additional legal opinion (AIR 1930 Madras, 146). Expert evidence, however, is admissible when the court has to form an opinion upon a point of foreign law and, in such case, a practising lawyer may be produced to give evidence.

7. Unity of Succession

There is no principle of unity of succession in India.

8. Formalities

Wills made by persons who are not domiciled in India which concern immovable property situated within India must be executed in accordance with the rules applicable in India. A will made by such a person which concerns movable property, whether in India or elsewhere, must be executed in accordance with the law of his domicile at the time of his death, wherever the will may have been executed. Accordingly, where a will concerning movable property of a foreigner is brought to India for probate, the court would deal with the instrument exactly as would the court of the testator's domicile.

9. Legislation

The *1961 Hague Convention on Conflicts of Laws Relating to the Form of Testamentary Dispositions* is not binding in India.

10. Wills

(a)–(f) The legal requirements for the execution of wills in India are as mentioned in Section A2 *above*.

Under the *Indian Contract Act*, any agreement which is against public policy is void, though the expression 'public policy' has not been defined. An act would be deemed to be against public policy if it was so unfair and unreasonable that it would shock the court's conscience, as well as if it was forbidden or discouraged by law. Wills which are against public policy in India will be unenforceable to that extent.

In the case of conflict on account of foreign factors, the will will be construed by the general principle that for movable property the law of the country where the testator was domiciled would apply whereas in case of immovable property, the law of the country where the property is situated would prevail.

(g) Under Indian law, an executor or administrator is not the absolute owner of the property of the deceased, in the sense of him being the beneficial owner thereof, as the property only vests in him for the purpose of representation. He cannot therefore nominate someone else as administrator or executor of such property in his own will.

(h) *See* (a)–(f) *above*.

(i) *See* (a)–(f) *above*.

11. Domicile/Nationality

(a) This subject has been dealt with in detail in the reply to Section A 14 *above*.

So far as India itself is concerned, a person domiciled in India is deemed to have only one domicile, i.e., that of India, in which only one legal system prevails. The question of a person having more than one domicile therefore does not arise.

(b) There are no restrictions relating to the domicile of beneficiaries under the *Indian Succession Act*.

(c) In the case of a person domiciled in a country where there are compulsory shares in the deceased's estate (e.g., France), succession of movable property will be governed by the law of the deceased's domicile at the time of death and Indian law will recognize such succession.

12. Taxation

The *Estate Duty Act 1953* which imposed a duty, referred to as 'estate duty', on the principal value of all property has been repealed, and there are no estate taxes as such.

Ireland

Prepared by: Walter BEATTY
Vincent and Beatty

Address: 67/68 Fitzwilliam Square
Dublin 2
Ireland
Tel.: +353 1 634 00 00
Fax: +353 1 634 00 01

SECTION A – BRIEF SURVEY OF THE LOCAL SYSTEM

1. Type of System

(a) Ireland is a Common Law system. Statute law regulates wills. Examples of statutes are the *Wills Act 1837* and the *Succession Act 1965*.

Conflicts in relation to wills are litigated in the Probate Court. Jurisdiction in the Circuit Court is limited to assets of £30,000.00 and land with a rateable valuation not exceeding £200.00. The High Court has unlimited jurisdiction.

All Statute Law is subject to the written Irish Constitution enacted in the year 1937 so if any provision in the *Succession Act* was considered repugnant to the Constitution then the High Court would be the court of first instance in deciding this with a right of appeal to the Supreme Court.

(b) No.

2. Wills

(a) A will must be in permanent form (typescript or handwritten).

It must be signed by the testator in the presence of two witnesses.

Each of these witnesses must witness the signature of the testator in the testator's presence.

There is no requirement for a will to be made in front of a lawyer or other officer of the public. Doing so adds nothing to the will.

A will made on deathbed must comply with the foregoing requirements the same as any other will.

(b) *i*. A will can be amended or revoked by a subsequent will or codicil properly witnessed, and by a declaration to revoke which is witnessed in the manner prescribed for witnessing wills, or by the burning, tearing or destruction of the will or codicil by the testator, or by some person in his presence and by his direction, with the intention of revoking it (Section 85(2) *Succession Act 1965*).

ii. Marriage does result in the revocation of prior wills except in the case of a will made in contemplation of that marriage whether so expressed in the will or not (Section 85(1) *Succession Act 1965*).

iii. A will can only be revived by its re-execution in the presence of two witnesses or by a codicil similarly witnessed which shows an intention to revive the will (*Section 87 Succession Act 1965*).

3. Intestacy

(a) Sections 67, 68, 69, 70, 71, 72 and 73 of the *Succession Act 1965* deal with the right to succeed.

Per stirpes: The meaning of *per stripes* when used in relation to intestate succession, for example, in the case of issue, is that any issue more remote than a child of the deceased shall take through all degrees in equal shares if more than one, the share which the parent or such issue would have taken if living at the death of the deceased. No issue of the deceased shall take if the parent of such issue is living at the death of the deceased and so capable of taking.

Section 67(1) to (4) of the *Succession Act 1965* enacts the following:

- if an intestate dies leaving a spouse and no issue, the spouse shall take the whole estate;
- if an intestate dies leaving a spouse and issue:
  - the spouse shall take two thirds of the estate, and
  - the remainder shall be distributed among the issue in accordance with the final provision below.
- if an intestate dies leaving issue and no spouse, his estate shall be distributed among the issue in accordance with the provision that follows;
- if all the issue are in equal degree of relationship to the deceased, the distribution shall be in equal shares among them; if they are not, it shall be *per stirpes*. Illegitimate and adopted children have the same status as legitimate children.

Section 70(3)(1) of the *Succession Act 1965* provides that in default of any person taking the estate of an intestate, whether under this part or otherwise, the state shall take the estate as ultimate intestate successor.

The provisions of Sections 67 to 72 inclusive of the *Succession Act 1965* are illustrated in the following table:

RELATIVE SURVIVING	DISTRIBUTION OF ESTATE
Husband and issue	Husband takes two-thirds and issue the remainder.
Wife and issue	Wife takes two-thirds and issue take the remainder.
Husband and no issue	Husband takes whole estate.
Wife and no issue	Wife takes whole estate.
Issue and no spouse	Issue take whole estate.
Father, mother, brothers and sisters	Each parent takes one-half.
Father, brothers and sisters	Father takes whole estate.
Mother, brothers and sisters	Mother takes whole estate.
Brothers and sisters	All take in equal shares. Children of a deceased brother or sister take their parent's share.
Nephews and nieces	All take in equal shares.

(b) No, there is no difference.

4. Freedom of Testation

(a) Yes, certain persons have the right to a share in the deceased's estate.

Surviving Spouse: One-half of the estate will devolve to the surviving spouse if there is no issue and one-third to the surviving spouse if there is issue (Section 111(1) & (2) of the *Succession Act 1965*).

The surviving spouse also benefits from the right of election. Where the estate of a deceased person includes a dwelling in which, at the time of the deceased's death, the surviving spouse was ordinarily resident, the surviving spouse may, subject to certain time limits, require the personal representatives (executors) in writing to appropriate the dwelling in or towards satisfaction of any share of the surviving spouse (Section 56(1) *Succession Act 1965*).

Where an estate is bequeathed to the spouse, which is not expressed to be in addition to the legal right share, the spouse has then the right to elect between the legal right share and the portion of the estate bequeathed to the spouse. If the spouse fails to elect then the spouse receives the amount of the estate bequeathed under the will and loses the right to the legal right share (Section 115(1) of the *Succession Act 1965*).

In both cases of election the right can be exercised by the surviving spouse within six months from the date of the receipt of the notice from the personal representative (the executor) or one year from the date of the grant of probate (whichever is the later).

Children: Where, on application by or on behalf of a child of a testator, the court is of opinion that the testator has failed in his moral duty to make proper provision for the child in accordance with his means, whether by his will or otherwise, the court may order that such provision shall be made for the child out of the estate as the court thinks just (Section 117 sub-section (1) of the *Succession Act 1965*). The children have no other automatic right of inheritance.

Some case law has now been built up in relation to this provision. A claim can be defeated by demonstrating that the child has been given a good start in life, e.g., established in business. If it can be shown that the child has been advanced gifts or substantial assets, this will have a significant bearing on any such claim.

Reference to a child in this Section does not mean infant, juvenile or young adult. A child is literally interpreted and could mean somebody aged over fifty years.

Lawfully adopted children are treated in the same way as the natural children of the parents.

No provision exists for any legal right in respect of *brothers or sisters* of a deceased.

(b) *i.* Yes.
Section 113 of the *Succession Act 1965* provides:

'The legal right of a spouse may be renounced in an anti-nuptial contract made in writing between the parties to an intended marriage or may be renounced in writing by the spouse after marriage and during the lifetime of the testator.'

ii. Settlements may be lawfully entered into:

– during the lifetime of the testator; or
– upon the Testator's death in accordance with the settlement instructions in the testator's will.

Such settlements may be fixed or discretionary.

Fixed settlements are for specific persons who are so named. The property being settled is held by trustees for the beneficiaries under the settlement in accordance with the terms of the settlement, i.e., for life or until the beneficiary attains a certain age, marries or does not marry and so forth.

Discretionary trusts are used to nominate a class of persons who may benefit, usually the testator's spouse, children, their spouses and/or grandchildren. The trustees are given absolute discretion as to who is to benefit out of the class of beneficiaries, the extent of such benefit and when it is to take effect.

In a settlement established during the lifetime of the person making the settlement ('the settlor'), the trustees will abide by the settlor's wishes and when the settlor dies, will act in accordance with a 'letter of wishes'.

In a settlement established by will, a letter of wishes will accompany the will and the trustees will again abide by the settlor's wishes as to the regulation of the future disposition of the settlor's estate.

5. Maintenance

The legal right that exists is that already described in 4(a) *above*.

6. Community Property Between Husband and Wife

(a) If the will does not expressly state that additional benefits are intended to take effect then the surviving spouse must elect between the benefit under the will and the legal right share as set out in 4(a) *above*. Unless such benefit is expressed to be in addition to the legal right share, it is deemed to be in satisfaction or in part satisfaction of it. The surviving spouse's right to acquire ownership is limited to a legal right share.

(b) None.

7. Gifts (*Inter Vivos*)

(a) Yes, but only insofar as the individual beneficiary is concerned.

(b) *Children*: Section 63 of the *Succession Act 1965* provides that advancements to children, unless a contrary intention has been expressed, shall be taken into account either to diminish (depending upon the value of the advancement) or to satisfy the share of the child.

The obligation of proving that a child has been made an advancement rests upon the person so asserting, unless the advancement has been expressed in writing by the deceased.

Spouses: Section 116 of the *Succession Act 1965* provides that where a testator has made permanent provision for the spouse, whether under contract or otherwise, the property which is the subject of such provision shall be taken as having been given in or towards the satisfaction of the legal right share of the surviving spouse.

If the value of the property is equal to or greater than the share that could have been obtained by the spouse as a legal right, the spouse shall not be entitled to take any share as a legal right. Otherwise the spouse shall be entitled to take in addition to the provision the shortfall in the spouse's legal right share.

8. Capacity

(a) The testator must be of sound mind and eighteen years of age, except in respect of persons on active military service or mariners, both of whom only having to be sixteen years of age.

(b) A will is not rendered invalid because:

– a witness was incompetent at the time or became incompetent later. *See* Section 81 of the *Succession Act 1965*;
– a witness or witnesses or their spouses were expressed to benefit under the will. *See* Section 82 of the *Succession Act 1965*;
– a witness or witnesses or their spouses were creditors of the testator and the testator's assets were charged with payment of money or debts due to them as creditors. *See* Section 83 of the *Succession Act 1965*.

However, any benefit bequeathed in the will (other than charges and directions for the payment of any debt or debts) to a witness or that witness' spouse is utterly null and void. *See* Section 82 of the *Succession Act 1965*.

(c) A charitable legacy will lose its charitable status if the object of such charity is contrary to public policy. Otherwise the capacity of the beneficiary is not material.

9. Authority (Court, Notarial or Other)

Wills: A will must be proved either in a District Probate Registry or the Principal Probate Registry. Both registries are under the control of the court and the High Court will ensure (when necessary) that a grant of probate issues and that the terms of the will are implemented.

Intestacy: Persons who have the right to succeed are stipulated in the *Succession Act 1965*. *See* reply to 3(a) *above*.

The grant of administration intestate or with the will annexed (where the executor or executors have predeceased the deceased or are incompetent to act or renounce) issues from a District Probate Registry or the Principal Probate Registry. Both registries are under the control of the court.

The grant issues to the personal representative of the deceased and the court will regulate the distribution of the deceased's estate in the event that the personal representative does not act properly in so doing.

10. Invalidity of Will

(a) A mistake in the formalities, such as failure to execute the will in accordance with the *Wills Act 1837*, will render the will ineffective.

International Succession

A will executed not in accordance with the *Wills Act*, by fraud, such as the forgery of the signature of the testator or the testator's signature on a document which did not contain his wishes, would make the entire will invalid.

A will made under duress or when the testator is of unsound mind is also invalid.

(b) There may be circumstances which would render the will only voidable.

11. Simultaneous Death

(a) In the case of a will, the estate is distributed without regard to the person named as beneficiary, who is regarded as having predeceased the testator.

Where there is no will, the estate vests in the next of kin of the deceased.

(b) Section 5 of the *Succession Act 1965* provides:

> 'Where (...) two or more persons have died in circumstances rendering it uncertain which of them survived the other or others, then, for the purpose of the distribution of the estate of any of them, they shall all be deemed to have died simultaneously.'

That is, each is regarded as having predeceased the other with regard to inheritance.

12. Estate Taxes

(a) Yes.

(b) If the deceased is domiciled in Ireland then inheritance taxes are imposed on all the deceased's capital throughout the world.

(c) Inheritance tax is index linked.

(d) A recent codification of the tax laws in relation to inheritances has occurred with the implementation of the *Capital Acquisitions Tax Consolidation Act, 2003*.

Capital Acquisitions Tax (CAT) is a tax on inheritances taken under a will or on intestacy. Liability for CAT depends on a number of factors and depends on whether:

- the disponer is resident in Ireland;
- the beneficiary is resident in Ireland;
- the asset comprising the inheritance is situated in Ireland.

The amount of tax payable on an inheritance is assessed on a beneficiary's relationship to a disponer. Account is also taken of the value of previous benefits (including gifts) taken from a disponer from the same class threshold. There are tax tree thresholds (which increase in line with inflation each year) and if an inheritance is less than a threshold then no tax is payable.

Europe

The spouse of the deceased does not pay inheritance tax.

All prior gifts and prior inheritances are aggregated and, subject to this rule of aggregation, the thresholds in round figures in respect of those who are related to the deceased are as follows:

Child/foster, child/minor, child of a deceased child of disponer – euro 441,198.00.
Lineal ancestor or lineal descendant of disponer i.e., brother/sister/nephew/niece –
    euro 44,120.00.
Strangers in law to disponer – euro 22,060.00.

13. Administration of Estates

(a) The succession is administered by the executor. The number of executors may be unlimited. If all the executors have predeceased the deceased then the administration is usually dealt with by a relative who takes on the obligation and enters into a bond to lawfully administer the estate. The position is the same if there is no will.

The bond is for double the gross assets of the estate and the surety for the bond is usually an insurance company. In the event of any maladministration, the insurance company has to pay up on the bond; this guarantees that there is no loss to the estate.

(b) No, but the insurance company, in the case of a bond, may request a report from time to time.

(c) No. In the event of maladministration, the Probate Division of the High Court will step in to manage the succession.

Where charities are concerned, the Commissioners of Charitable Donations and Bequests can step in to ensure that the charitable legacies are safeguarded.

(d) The executor or, if there is none, the personal representative.

(e) The assets are handed over to the heirs by the executor or the personal representative. In the case of stocks or shares, these may be transferred by the executor or personal representative or they may be sold by the executor or personal representative and the cash proceeds distributed. In the case of property (meaning land and the buildings on it), if this is to be transferred, the executor or personal representative will execute a deed of assent in favour of the party entitled.

(f) The creditors of the estate receive payment from the executor or personal representative out of the proceeds of the estate. The order of payment is as follows:

– funeral expenses;
– testamentary expenses;
– creditors;

International Succession

– specific legatees; and
– universal or residuary legatees.

Apart from monies due by the deceased, the order for payment can of course be changed by the testator who may prefer a legatee by way of first charge on the assets of the testator's estate.

(g) *See* 13(a) *above*. If there is a will, the personal representative will carry out its provisions. If there is no will, the personal representative will administer the estate to ensure that all debts are paid and the residue of the estate is then paid to the next of kin.

The powers of the executor are absolute and providing an executor acts in accordance with his responsibility and within the law, his actions cannot be questioned.

If an executor acts improperly or unlawfully, the court has the power to remove him.

14. Domicile/Nationality

(a) As we have seen at 12(b) *above*, the domicile of the deceased will establish where accountability lies for the payment of inheritance taxes. Where a double taxation agreement exists, then any taxes paid on the Irish estate will be refundable in accordance with that Double Taxation Treaty.

Domicile of origin, which is the country where one is born or brought to as a young person or the country in which one becomes a naturalized citizen, is presumed to be the domicile at the date of death. This presumption can be successfully rebutted to avail of a more favourable tax climate by the undertaking of certain far-reaching actions, such as, changing one's nationality.

Changing one's nationality could involve severing all residential ties with the domicile of origin and leaving instructions in one's will that one is to be buried in the country of adoption. The Irish Revenue Commissioners are very reluctant to accept an alleged change from the domicile of origin and a mere statement as to such a decision having been made will not be sufficient to establish this. The actions of the testator and the steps he has taken to sever connections with his domicile of origin will serve to establish the testator's true intention.

(b) Yes, the court would.

Section B – Applicable Law/Procedure Where Foreign Element/s are Involved

1. Jurisdiction

(a) The court would have jurisdiction on the basis of residency at the time of death if the deceased was domiciled in Ireland. If the deceased was not domiciled in

Ireland but was resident there, then unless the executor or the personal representative of the deceased decided to bring the worldwide estate into Ireland, the Irish court would not be involved. If the deceased had assets in Ireland, the local court would be involved.

(b) No. However, under Section 102(1)(e) of the *Succession Act 1965* a non Irish will so far as immovables are concerned shall be valid as regards form if such form complies with the domestic law of the place where the immovables are situated.

(c) The Probate Division of the High Court.

2. Applicable Law

Section 102 of the *Succession Act 1965* provides *inter alia*:

(1) a testamentary disposition shall be valid as regards form if its form complies with the domestic law:
– of the place where the testator made it, or
– of a nationality possessed by the testator, either at the time when he made the disposition, or at the time of his death, or
– of the place in which the testator had his domicile either at the time when he made the disposition, or at the time of his death, or
– of the place in which the testator had its habitual residence either at the time he made the disposition, or at the time of his death, or
– so far as immovables are concerned, of the place where they are situated.

(2) Without prejudice to subsection 1, a testamentary disposition revoking an earlier testamentary disposition shall also be valid as regards form if it complies with any one of the laws according to the terms of which, under that sub-section, the testamentary disposition that has been revoked was valid.

(3) The determination of whether or not the testator had his domicile in a particular place shall be governed by the law of that place. Irish law should apply to immovables situated in Ireland.

3. Foreign Succession/Inheritance Orders

(a) Yes, providing they do not conflict with local law.

(b) The executor or personal representative must take out either a grant of probate or a grant of administration. The will, however, would be regarded as valid (*see* 2).

(c) *See* reply to 3(b).

4. Two or More Succession or Probate Orders

If a grant of probate has already been obtained from the country of domicile or the place where the deceased died, the Probate Act of that country or, in the absence of a Probate Act, the death certificate of the deceased, together with an Affidavit of Laws, is used to obtain a grant of probate or administration in Ireland. If the deceased left a will, it must be exhibited in the Affidavit of Laws and translated into English.

5. Assets

If there are factors of connection such as residency, nationality or citizenship, the local court can claim to have jurisdiction.

6. Expert Evidence

(a) *See* reply to 6(b) *below*.

(b) It is necessary to have an Affidavit of Laws from a lawyer in the other jurisdiction. The Affidavit should be completed before a notary public in that jurisdiction. As well as dealing with the law in that jurisdiction, the Affidavit would exhibit the death certificate, the will and Probate Act (if any) of the deceased.

7. Unity of Succession

No.

8. Formalities

See reply to 2 (and Section 102 of the *Succession Act 1965*).

9. Legislation

Section 102 of Part viii of the *Succession Act 1965*, which has been quoted in full, as at 2 *above*, enables Ireland to adhere to the *1961 Hague Convention on the Conflicts of Laws Relating to the Form of Testamentary Dispositions*.

10. Wills

(a) *See* reply to 2 (and Section 102 of the *Succession Act 1965*).

(b) As for (a).

(c) As for (a).

(d) As for (a).

(e) As for (a).

(f) Unascertained beneficiaries in Ireland would have to be dealt with by eliminating their whereabouts conclusively by way of Affidavit and, if this is not possible, it is for the High Court to do this.

(g) Yes, if the form of the will complies with the domestic law. *See* Section 102 of the *Succession Act 1965*.

(h) As for (a).

(i) The legal right share of a spouse who is non resident could be established if the testator was resident and his worldwide estate was being administered in Ireland. They apply equally to realty and personalty.

11. Domicile/Nationality

(a) The will takes effect from the testator's date of death. *See* Section 89 of the *Succession Act 1965* which provides:

> 'Every Will shall, with reference to all estate comprised in the Will and every divisible bequest contained in it, be construed to speak and take effect as if it had been executed immediately before the death of the testator, unless a contrary intention appears from the Will.'

However, insofar as the form of the will is concerned, as was seen under the provisions of Section 102 of the *Succession Act 1965*, a will shall be valid as regards form if it complies with the domestic law.

(b) No.

(c) In the event of conflict, the court would have jurisdiction where an estate in Ireland is concerned. However, Section 103 of the *Succession Act 1965* provides:

> '(. . .) a testamentary disposition made on board a vessel or aircraft shall also be valid as regards form if its form complies with the internal law of the place with which having regard to its registration (if any) and any other relevant circumstances, the vessel or aircraft may be taken to have had the most real connection.'

International Succession

12. Taxation

Where the deceased or an heir of the deceased is non resident, if a double taxation agreement exists, any tax paid by the deceased's estate or by the heir in Ireland may be reclaimable against tax paid by the deceased's estate or by the heir in their country of residence.

Isle of Man

Prepared by: John RIMMER (Partner)
Dickinson, Cruickshank & Co

Address: PO Box 33
        33–37 Athol Street
        Douglas
        Isle of Man
        IM1 1BP
        British Isles
Tel.:   +44 1624 647647
Fax: +44 1624 618448

SECTION A – BRIEF SURVEY OF THE LOCAL SYSTEM

1. Type of System

(a) The Isle of Man is a common law jurisdiction, but its law has developed in a unique way.

The Island's legislature, Tynwald, is believed to be the oldest continuous legislative assembly in the world. Legislation has been passed for the Island by that body and, on occasion, by the Imperial Parliament at Westminster. The power of the Imperial Parliament to legislate for the Island is now exercised only in restricted circumstances, and generally with the participation of the Manx government. The Island retains exclusive competence to regulate its internal taxation measures.

The Island has also had its own common or customary law, which still endures. As this has developed, and as the relationship with the United Kingdom has developed, except where Manx custom differs from English law or where statute law applies, Manx common law principles generally follow those applied in English law. This includes the principles of equity (and therefore trust law) and the laws concerning succession to property. Manx land law differs markedly in its origin from English land law: it is largely udal in origin, although it now closely resembles English freehold/leasehold law.

(b) The Island is a British Crown possession, and forms part of the non-metropolitan territories of the United Kingdom. It is not part of the United Kingdom itself or the EU (although special arrangements exist to facilitate free trade between the Island and the EU). The United Kingdom is responsible for good government in the Island and for its defence and international relations. It is not truly a sovereign state, therefore, but it is a separate jurisdiction from those of the United Kingdom.

2. Wills

(a) Manx wills are governed by the *Wills Act 1985*. Generally, under Manx law, only a person over eighteen years old may make a will. As in English law:

1. the will must be in writing (no distinction is drawn between hand-written, i.e., holographic, and printed or typed writing), signed by the testator or by another person in his presence and at his direction;
2. it must appear that the testator intended, by his signature, to give effect to the will;
3. the signature must be made or acknowledged in the presence of two or more witnesses at the same time; and
4. the witnesses must sign the will in the presence of the testator (although not necessarily one another).

The formalities for a codicil, which is generally a shorter document than a will, is made by reference to a particular will and amends it only in certain particulars, are the same as for a will.

Domestic Manx law recognizes wills otherwise only in very limited circumstances (essentially, where the testator is a soldier or airman on active service or a sailor or mariner at sea). Manx law recognizes death-bed gifts made in contemplation of death (*donationes mortis causa*), although, strictly, this is independent of the law concerning wills.

See Section B *below* for cases involving a foreign element.

(b) *i.* Wills may subsequently be revoked or amended in whole or part, expressly or impliedly, by subsequent will, codicil or other testamentary writing made according to the same formalities. They may also be revoked by being burnt, torn or otherwise destroyed by or at the direction of the testator.

Individual specific gifts may be 'adeemed' by disposal of the subject matter of the gift during the lifetime of the testator.

Corrections may be made at the time of execution by manual correction that also observes the same formalities as execution of the will. If corrections are not signed and witnessed, therefore, they will not be valid.

The court has a discretion to 'rectify' a will where it fails to carry into effect the testator's instructions because of a clerical error or a failure to understand his instructions. The applicant for rectification of the will must apply to court within six months of the grant of representation, or apply to the court for leave to make a later application.

ii. Marriage automatically revokes all wills and codicils made previously, with two exceptions:

1. individual dispositions or entire wills made in contemplation of marriage to a particular person; and
2. dispositions in exercise of testamentary powers of appointment. Subject to contrary intention shown in the will, a will is also affected by the divorce of the testator, or if his marriage is annulled: (1) gifts to the spouse of the testator, (2) the conferral on the spouse of a power of appointment, and (3) appointment of the spouse as executor are all treated as if the spouse had died on the date of the dissolution or annulment of the marriage.

iii. Only testamentary writing that observes the same formalities may revive a revoked will: in other words, by codicil or by re-execution. Revival of a will that was partially revoked before being totally revoked will not, subject to contrary intention, extend to the part already revoked at the date of revocation of the whole.

3. Intestacy

(a) To a great extent, Manx law resembles English law. The order of entitlement on intestacy under Manx law, as determined by the *Administration of Estates Act 1990*, however, differs significantly from that in England. In the following, members of a class of beneficiary take in equal shares with those in the same class and exclusively of those in classes below them. It may be summarized briefly as follows.

If the deceased leaves a spouse who survives him for at least fourteen days, the spouse receives the personal chattels of the deceased, GBP 125,000 and half of the residue of the estate. The spouse has a right to redeem the cash legacy against the deceased's interest in the matrimonial home. The issue then inherit the balance on the statutory trusts (*see below*).

If the deceased leaves no spouse, the order of classes of beneficiary entitled to inherit (*see above*) is:

1. issue on statutory trusts;
2. parents;
3. brothers and sisters of the whole blood on the statutory trusts;
4. brothers and sisters of the half-blood on the statutory trusts;
5. grandparents;
6. uncles and aunts of the whole blood on the statutory trusts;
7. uncles and aunts of the half-blood on the statutory trusts;
8. great-uncles and aunts of the whole blood on the statutory trusts;
9. great-uncles and aunts of the half-blood on the statutory trusts;
10. *bona vacantia* to the Treasury of the Isle of Man.

The terms of the statutory trusts are that a beneficiary's interest is dependent upon his attaining the age of eighteen years. If he does not or has predeceased the intestate leaving issue, they take *per stirpes* in his place (also dependent on their attaining eighteen years of age).

(b) Where the intestate dies domiciled in the Isle of Man, movable and immovable assets are treated the same. *See* 14(a) and Section B *below*, however, as regards the rules where the deceased dies domiciled outside the Isle of Man.

4. Freedom of Testation

(a) There is no compulsory sharing of the estate under Manx law, and testators generally have unlimited testamentary freedom, according to the extent of their interest in the assets concerned. *See* 5 *below*, however, for the power of the court to intervene where insufficient provision has been made and for a person entitled to apply for relief.

(b) *i.* A contract of inheritance is not binding upon a testator, although his estate may be liable in damages to a disappointed party entitled to the benefit of a contract to make specific provision for him.

Where two (or more) parties make wills ('mutual wills'), on agreed terms, which they agree not to change, however, and where it would be unconscionable on the death of one for the others subsequently to amend their wills, the court may impose a trust in favour of concerned beneficiaries. This effectively prevents the surviving testator from amending his will (at least as regards those provisions that were the subject of the agreement). A couple merely making reciprocal or 'mirror' wills will not be assumed to be making such an agreement without further evidence that the terms were intended to be based on an agreement that the other would not change theirs.

ii. In Manx law, lifetime advances settled on issue of a deceased intestate person for advancement or on marriage are brought into account in determining their entitlement under the rules of intestacy (*see* 3 *above*). Similarly, a surviving spouse must bring into account, against the fixed cash legacy, gifts made in any part of an effective will left by the deceased. Such gifts and advances are said, in these circumstances, to have been brought into 'hotchpot'.

In addition, where gifts are made to a child of the deceased (including someone in relation to whom the deceased stands in *loco parentis*), or for his benefit, during the testator's lifetime to establish the child in life, they may be brought into account in determining the division of the deceased's estate under his earlier will. The result may be that the donee cannot receive the whole of his entitlement to the estate under the will on its face, because the lifetime gift has 'adeemed' the gift by will (in whole or part). This is the 'rule against double-portions'. It is based on a presumption that the later gift was intended to give effect to the earlier, but it is subject to the contrary intention of the testator.

Similarly, if a gift is made by will for a particular purpose and a lifetime disposition is later made by the testator for that same purpose, it may be presumed that the gift by will is adeemed. Again, this is subject to the testator's contrary intention.

Being a common law jurisdiction, settlements are in general enforceable in the Isle of Man. There is no need for a separate category therefore of special arrangements for succession.

See Section B *below* for cases involving a foreign element, and *see* 5 *below* regarding cases of disappointed parties who claim that insufficient provision is made for them under a will or on intestacy.

5. Maintenance

Manx law makes no automatic provision for relatives of the testator, or anyone else (*see* 4(a) *above*). Instead, the *Inheritance (Provision for Family and Dependants) Act 1982* applies. This allows the court to address what, irrespective of the testator's wishes, ought to have been left to particular persons where a will or the rules of intestacy have made insufficient financial provision. The court is given a power to make orders for specified provision ('family provision orders') varying the devolution of the estate. Provision is not limited to regular, periodic payments (*see below*).

The power conferred on Manx courts by this statute applies only where the deceased dies domiciled in the Isle of Man at his death. It enables application to be made:

(1) for such *reasonable financial provision* as it would in all the circumstances be reasonable to receive by the surviving spouse of the deceased (unless judicially separated from the deceased) or, where it thinks just, by a former spouse of the deceased or a spouse judicially separated from the deceased, where the decree of nullity, dissolution of marriage or separation was made within the twelve months before death, who had applied for financial provision in those proceedings, and where that application was not determined; or
(2) for such *maintenance* as would be reasonable in all the circumstances, by a *former* spouse of the deceased, a child (of whatever age) of the deceased, a person (other than a child of the deceased) treated at some time as a child of any marriage to which the deceased was a party or a person maintained by the deceased at the date of death.

The law details those matters to be taken into consideration when deciding what would be reasonable. They differ depending upon the particular kind of applicant, but always include 'any (. . .) matter (. . .) which in the circumstances of the case the court may consider relevant'.

In favour of the applicant, the court can order:

(1) regular (periodic) payments to be made from the estate of the deceased;
(2) payment of a lump sum from the estate of the deceased;
(3) the transfer of particular assets from the estate of the deceased;
(4) the settlement of assets comprised in the estate of the deceased;
(5) the acquisition of assets, using funds or assets comprised in the estate, for transfer or settlement; and
(6) the variation of settlements ('nuptial settlements') made in contemplation of provision for a marriage of the deceased.

Allowance is also made for interim (temporary) application to be made for urgent maintenance. The application must be made within six months of the date of grant of representation in the Isle of Man, or later with the permission of the court. Gifts made within six years of death to defeat claims under the statute, gifts made by nomination, *donationes mortis causa* (*see* 2(a) *above*) and assets passing by survivorship of co-owners can all be affected by an order. Dispositions under contracts to leave assets in a particular way, entered into other than on arm's length terms and with a view to defeating claims under the statute, can be reversed.

6. Community Property Between Husband and Wife

(a) Community of property does not exist under Manx law. *See* Section B, however, for cases where there is a foreign element.

(b) In line with freedom of testation (*see* 4 and 5 *above*), marriage has no substantive effect on its own on the ownership of property during marriage or on death.

7. Gifts (*Inter Vivos*)

(a) Lifetime gifts to any beneficiary are not as a rule discounted against any gift by will. See 4(b)*ii. above*, however, regarding the rule against double-portions, ademption and the rules of hotchpot.

(b) Where an *inter vivos* gift is made, and it is brought into account in determining the entitlement of the beneficiary, the limit will be the total amount of the testamentary gift.

8. Capacity

(a) *Capacity of testator*: To make a will, the testator must have mental capacity and legal capacity.

He will have mental capacity if he is of sound disposing mind: he must, when he executes the will, understand the nature and extent of his assets, appreciate the fitting objects of his will and know and approve the contents of the will. It will generally suffice if, having given instructions at a time when he can be taken to have had sufficient understanding, the testator at least knows that the will carries his wishes into effect and appreciates the nature of what he is doing when he executes it.

Where an individual lacks mental capacity, a will may nevertheless be made for him under the auspices of the court.

To have legal capacity, a testator must (subject to the special provisions for soldiers, airmen, sailors and mariners – *see* 2(a)) be at least eighteen years of age.

(b) *Capacity of witnesses*: Witnesses need not be of any particular age, although their ability to understand events and, if necessary, to give evidence are crucial. They must therefore at least have mental capacity.

While still capable of witnessing the will, where a gift is made to a witness under the will, or to his or her spouse, that gift is generally void unless there would otherwise be sufficient witnesses for the will to be valid anyway. In principle, this included the benefit of a charging clause in favour of a professional executor or trustee until the law was changed with effect from September 2001.

(c) Not surprisingly, a beneficiary must generally be alive to receive his gift, although a gift can be expressed to take effect in favour of his personal representatives. The beneficiary must also be ascertained within the period allowed by the rule against remoteness of vesting, although he need not actually have come into existence at the date of execution of the will.

Gifts cannot be made to those forbidden by the general law (not merely, for example, by religious custom or law) from receiving gifts (e.g., officials, bodies lacking capacity to receive gifts). Gifts to unincorporated associations (such as clubs and societies) are subject to restrictions, depending on their construction.

9. Authority (Court, Notarial or Other)

As in English law, the assets of a deceased person (except joint property that passes by survivorship) do not vest automatically in 'heirs', but form his 'estate'. The estate is administered by personal representatives (*see* 13 *below*). They may be 'executors', where they are appointed by will, or 'administrators', where they are appointed by the court. In either case, and even though, in the case of executors, their authority derives from the will, application must be made to the court (the Common Law Division (Testamentary Jurisdiction) of the High Court of the Isle of Man) for a grant of representation. In the case of a will 'proved' to the court by executors, this will be a 'grant of probate'. Where there is a will, but executors appointed in the will do not prove it, it will be a 'grant of letters of administration with the will annexed'. Where there is no will, it is a 'grant of letters of administration'. Certain subtypes of grant apply in particular, uncommon, circumstances.

Application is made by a person having the right to make it, in a statutory form, which includes an oath (also in statutory form). Any will and codicils are referred to in the application and accompany the application, together with the fee and a death certificate.

The court retains the original grant of representation, but court-certified copies may be obtained for production to third parties to prove title to assets.

10. Invalidity of Will

(a) A will is invalid if it is defective at law. It will be defective if the formalities for its execution are not met (*see* 2(a) *above*), if the will is executed under duress, if it is forged or if the testator lacks legal or mental capacity to execute the will. It will generally be presumed that a will has been properly executed by a person having

333

capacity if the appropriate formalities appear to have been complied with and the will appears reasonable on its face.

A will may also be challenged because it was prepared, or a particular provision was included in it, because of undue influence, fraud or mistake.

A will that fails to make sufficient provision for a person making an application for a family provision order (*see* 5 *above*) is not void or voidable: the court merely has a discretion to vary it.

(b) A will, or a particular provision of a will, that is defective at law is wholly void. A will, or a provision in a will, may also be set aside by the court if it was included or executed as a result of undue influence, fraud or mistake. In some cases of mistake, rectification of the will may be more appropriate than setting aside (*see* 2(b)i *above*), but an application must generally, in that case, be made within six months of the grant of representation.

11. Simultaneous Death

(a) If the order in which persons die will determine entitlements under a will or the rules of intestacy, admissible evidence of the order in which they die will be heard. The common law position is then that no person dying in circumstances where it cannot be determined whether they survived another is deemed to have survived that other. By statute, this position is largely preserved, but subject to any order of the court and the terms of any instrument. In addition, it is provided that:

1. any land or other asset held jointly is deemed to have been held in equal shares (so that their beneficiaries inherit their respective part shares); and
2. if a will containing a gift by one to the other provides for a gift over to other beneficiaries if the beneficiary predeceases the testator, the gift over takes effect as if the deceased beneficiary died in the testator's lifetime.

(b) There are no presumptions under Manx law that, for example, the younger survives the elder. Instead, subject to contrary evidence and to contrary intention in the will, no relevant person is presumed to have survived the other(s) (*see* (a) *above*).

12. Estate Taxes

(a)–(c): There are no gift, inheritance, wealth, estate, capital gains or death taxes or duties in the Isle of Man, on or as a result of death. Manx-source income will be subject to tax (except interest from approved institutions). The rate is currently 18 per cent, and the Treasury has announced a program of reform under which this will be reduced over the course of the next few years. In practice, the Assessor of Tax will generally not seek to tax personal representatives, but only beneficiaries, who will be taxed in respect of income received.

13. Administration of Estates

(a) The administration of estates is largely governed by the *Administration of Estates Act 1990* and the Probate Rules 1998.

The personal representatives of the deceased administer the estate. They must obtain a grant of representation from the court to give them, or confirm their, authority. Where they are appointed under a valid will, they obtain a grant of probate from the court (*see* 9 *above*), and are 'executors'. Where there is a will, but the personal representatives were not validly appointed as executors, or where there is no will, they must apply for a grant of letters of administration from the court, and are 'administrators'. The beneficiaries of the estate resident in the Isle of Man (if any) generally have a right to apply for letters of administration, but the court will consider an application by any suitable person. The court has discretion as to whether to refuse a grant to a particular person, to appoint others and to pass over others who may apply.

(b) In principle, a Manx court will not issue a grant of representation where there are no assets in the Isle of Man. It might be expected that the absence of any Manx assets would never come to light. After all (in the Isle of Man) there are no estate taxes on capital, there is no return to make on death to any revenue authority and there is no need to make a detailed report to the court when applying for a grant of representation. An applicant must, however, in the application for the grant of representation, give an undertaking to deliver an account of the administration of the estate if so required. Moreover, there is a declaration in the statutory form of application, which is attested to on oath, that there *are* Manx assets. In practice, it may be possible to persuade the court to make a grant in such a case if circumstances justify it.

(c) There is no active supervision of personal representatives, apart, in the case of banks, companies or professionals, from their usual regulation. The court has jurisdiction, however, to hear applications from aggrieved parties (especially beneficiaries, creditors and other personal representatives), and a wide discretion as to what remedy to order. Beneficiaries of the residue of an estate are entitled to an account of the administration, may raise questions and objections and apply to the court for relief.

(d) Objection to steps made in the administration of an estate may be made by beneficiaries or creditors whose interests are harmed by the actions of the personal representatives, or by other personal representatives. In marked contrast to trusts, beneficiaries have no proprietary interest in assets comprised within the estate. They have only a right to have the estate duly administered and to take action to force the personal representatives to make amends for any breach of their duty (*devastavit*). Other personal representatives may also raise questions and objections and apply to the court for relief.

(e) The personal representatives pass assets to those entitled, after liabilities of the deceased and expenses of administration of the estate are ascertained and discharged, by 'assent'. The assent may generally be oral or written, but must be written where it concerns real property. Even where the beneficiaries are the same persons as the personal representatives, and whether for themselves or in trust, there must be an assent. In the case of chattels, there need be no formal assent and an assent may be inferred from the conduct of the parties. There may be additional formalities depending upon the nature of the assets (registration of transfers of shares or land, etc.). Subject to contrary intention expressed in the will, in the case gifts of specific assets, the expense of transferring or delivering assets is borne by beneficiaries. Otherwise it is borne by the personal representatives.

(f) Creditors of the estate will generally receive payment from the personal representatives, provided the estate is solvent. If it is not, the creditors may not be paid in full. There is a statutory order for the payment of unsecured debts. If the executors pay debts of an inferior status with notice of superior ones, and there are insufficient funds to meet the former, they will incur personal liability to discharge those superior debts *in full*.

(g) Where there is a valid will, but no express appointment of executors is made, executors may nevertheless be appointed 'according to the tenor', i.e., it may be inferred from the wording of the will that certain persons were intended to administer the estate. If this is not the case, beneficiaries under the will, beneficiaries who would have taken had the deceased died intestate or creditors may apply to the court for letters of administration with the will annexed. The grant of representation verifies the efficacy of the will as a testamentary document and confers authority on the grantees to administer the estate.

Where the deceased died intestate, a grant of letters of administration may be applied for on notice to all persons beneficially entitled in relation to the estate. Express provision is made allowing creditors of the deceased or of a beneficiary to make such an application.

14. Domicile/Nationality

(a) In the *above*, it has been assumed that Manx law governs the devolution of the estate. As a matter of Manx private international law, however, the law of a deceased's domicile (*lex domicilii*) at death governs devolution of his movables and the law of the location (*lex situs*) governs devolution of immovables. Manx law will, where the result of the reference to foreign law is a reference back to Manx law (*renvoi*), accept the reference and apply Manx law. These rules include the required capacity of an individual making a will ('testamentary capacity'), the form in which, and procedure by which, it must be made ('formal validity') and the provisions that are permissible ('essential validity'). The position is set out in detail in Section B below.

Special rules apply to entitlement to grants of representation where the deceased died domiciled outside the Island. In such cases, a grant will be made to the person entrusted with the administration of the estate by the court of the deceased's own domicile or, if none, to the person beneficially entitled to the estate in the jurisdiction of the deceased's domicile. Otherwise, the court may make the grant to such person as it directs or to the person named as executor in any will in the English language. If the Manx estate is comprised wholly of immovable property, a grant limited to such property may be made to the person who would have been entitled had the deceased died domiciled in the Island. It is common for non-Manx resident persons entitled to apply for grants of representation to appoint attorneys to apply for the grant for their use and benefit.

(b) The court will generally not issue a grant of representation where there are no assets in the Isle of Man (*see* 13(b) *above*). The position is not entirely clear, however, and it may be possible to persuade the court to make a grant in appropriate circumstances.

SECTION B – APPLICABLE LAW/PROCEDURE WHERE FOREIGN ELEMENT/S ARE INVOLVED

1. Jurisdiction

(a) Jurisdiction is claimed by the Manx court for administration of assets located in the Isle of Man at the date of death and, probably, foreign movables brought into the Island before any person has obtained title to them under the laws of another jurisdiction and reduced them into possession. Detailed laws determine what assets are located where. Beneficial ownership of assets is located where the asset is located.

(b) All assets owned by the deceased in the Isle of Man require a Manx grant of representation. The devolution of the estate is affected by domicile if the asset concerned is movable (*see* 14(a) *above*), but not the requirement for a grant of representation.

(c) The Common Law Division (Testamentary Jurisdiction) of the High Court of Justice of the Isle of Man deals with all non-contentious business (including applying for grants of representation and lodging caveats). In practice, dealing with an ordinary application is largely a ministerial function. The Chancery Division hears contentious proceedings.

2. Applicable Law

As a rule, the governing law for the administration of an estate depends upon the jurisdiction by whose authority the personal representatives collect the assets. Therefore, the *lex situs* governs devolution of immovables and the *lex domicilii* of the deceased at death governs the devolution of movables (*see* 14(a) *above*).

Additional rules govern whether or not a will is formally valid in cases involving a foreign element (*see* 10 *below*).

International Succession

3. Foreign Succession/Inheritance Orders

(a) Foreign orders or grants (including those obtained in any jurisdiction in the United Kingdom or the Commonwealth) are not recognized in the Isle of Man.

(b) While a foreign order will not be given effect in the Isle of Man, the court has a wide discretion (especially in cases of intestacy) as to the appointment of personal representatives. It may make a grant of representation to a person charged in the jurisdiction of the deceased's domicile (*see* 14(a) *above*).

(c) Since foreign orders are not recognized, application must be made to the court in the same manner as applies to Manx estates lacking non-Manx involvement. The original will will probably have been deposited in another court if a foreign order has been made in respect of it. In that case, a copy of the will and the order, both certified by the court (together with a translation supported by affidavit by a person qualified to give the translation), will be required with the application. An affidavit of law will probably also be required, in particular for an estate of a non-Manx domiciliary not comprising solely immovable Manx assets.

4. Two or More Succession or Probate Orders

Foreign orders are not recognized under Manx law, but may allow a person named in one to make an application to a Manx court for a grant of representation in the Isle of Man.

If there is a will appointing executors who are applying for a grant of probate in the Isle of Man, that will normally be conclusive (although the court retains discretion). If there are no executors appointed who are willing and able to act, the court will make a grant of representation whomever it thinks most fit. If the deceased dies domiciled in the Isle of Man, where it exercises its discretion, the court will naturally lean in favour of Manx personal representatives. Conversely, if the deceased is not domiciled in the Isle of Man at death, personal representatives entrusted with the administration of the estate in the country of the deceased's final domicile (or their attorneys or persons nominated by them) may be preferred. The location of the assets comprised in the estate will also be a factor.

5. Assets

The Manx courts will not make orders directly in relation to assets outside the Isle of Man at the deceased's death and which have not at least been brought into the Island after death while still in the nature deceased's assets.

6. Expert Evidence

(a) If a will has already been proved in the courts of the deceased's domicile, it will not normally be necessary for expert evidence to be obtained to confirm its formal

338

validity under that law. Otherwise, where the law of another jurisdiction affects a decision of the Manx court (for example, whether a will possesses essentially validity or is not formally valid where it has not been admitted in the jurisdiction of the testator's domicile), it is a matter of fact in Manx courts. Evidence may be adduced.

(b) The Manx court may accept evidence of foreign law, where it is required, in the form of an affidavit given by a person having necessary knowledge or experience (as set out in the affidavit) or a certificate by, or act before, a notary in the relevant jurisdiction. A personal appearance will only be required where the matter is contentious and not all the parties accept the evidence. Even then, it may be that the witness can not be compelled to appear (although, tactically, it may be preferable for him to do so and may result in exclusion of the evidence if he does not).

7. Unity of Succession

The Isle of Man is a schismatic jurisdiction, and will apply the *lex domicilii* (*see* 14(a) *above*) to movables (including that of a unitary jurisdiction) where the deceased died domiciled outside the Isle of Man. Manx law will accept *renvoi* where the *lex domicilii* refers the issue of succession to movables or immovables to the laws of the Isle of Man, and apply domestic Manx law to such assets as a result.

8. Formalities

See 10 *below*.

9. Legislation

The *1961 Hague Convention on the Conflict of Laws Relating to the Form of Testamentary Dispositions* extends to the Isle of Man. *The International Wills Convention* (to give it its full title, the '*Convention Providing a Uniform Law on the Form of an International Will*') and the *Convention on the Establishment of a Scheme of Registration of Wills* have also been provided for, but are not in force.

10. Wills

(a) At common law, a will is formally valid so far as it relates to immovable assets if it complies with the laws of the jurisdiction in which they are located; a will made in accordance with the law of the testator's domicile is properly executed so far as it relates to movable assets. Under statute, a will is also formally valid:

1. if its execution conforms with the domestic law of the jurisdiction in which it was executed or in or of which the testator (at the time of death or execution of the will) had his domicile or habitual residence or was a national;

International Succession

2. if executed on a vessel or aircraft, if its execution conforms with the domestic law of the jurisdiction with which the vessel or aircraft was most closely connected;
3. as regards immovable assets, if its execution conforms with the domestic law of the jurisdiction in which the assets are located (reflecting the common law position, above);
4. as regards the revocation of a will valid under 1, 2 or 3, if it conforms with the law governing the validity of the revoked will; and
5. so far as it exercises a power of appointment, if it conforms with the domestic law of the jurisdiction whose law governs the essential validity of the power.

(b) Where the testator can be taken to have intended that the will be construed according to the law of a particular jurisdiction, it will give effect to that. If not, it will be presumed that he intended it to be construed according to the law of his domicile at the date on which he executed it. A change of domicile after execution of the will is deemed not to affect its construction.

(c) The law applicable to the assets concerned governs the rights of heirs and beneficiaries. Hence, the usual rule of *lex domicilii* applies to movables and *lex situs* to immovables. In fact, individuals aggrieved by what they see as insufficient provision for them under a will or the rules of intestacy may apply for provision (*see* 5 *in Section A*) only if the deceased was domiciled in the Isle of Man at his death. Therefore, even if the foreign law refers such issues to Manx law, the Manx provisions will apply only if the deceased was Manx-domiciled.

(d) *Lex situs* governs the capacity of a beneficiary to take a gift of immovable property. The *lex domicilii* of the testator alone would, strictly, govern capacity to inherit movables. In fact the courts take a more relaxed approach to the position and, if more favourable, the *lex domicilii* of the beneficiary governs capacity to take a gift of movable property.

(e) The question as to the law of which jurisdiction governs testamentary capacity is not straightforward. It is thought that the *lex situs* applies to capacity to make a will of immovable property. In the case of movables, the *lex domicilii* at the date of execution of the will applies.

(f) The usual rules apply, of *lex domicilii* (at death) to movables and *lex situs* to immovables, in determining essential or material validity of a will or of individual provisions in it.

(g) Capacity to exercise a testamentary power of appointment over movables is governed by the testator's *lex domicilii* at the date of execution. The *lex situs* governs the position as regards immovables. A will exercising a power of appointment is formally valid if it meets the requirements of 10(a) *above*. By statute, the exercise by will of a power of appointment is also formally valid if the execution of the will conforms with the law governing the essential validity of the instrument creating the power. The same rule applies to interpretation as it does in (b) *above*.

340

Essential validity of the provision exercising the power depends upon the governing law of the instrument creating (not exercising) the testamentary power of appointment itself in relation to movables and the *lex situs* in relation to movables.

(h) As regards movables, the general view is that, at common law, a will may be revoked by an act of revocation if, by the law of his domicile at the date of the act, it would operate to revoke the will. Whether a later will or codicil revokes or amends an earlier one depends upon the *lex domicilii* at death, because the test of whether the will or codicil is valid applies. In relation to immovables, the *lex situs* rule applies. By statute, where a will is formally valid under the statutory provisions referred to in (a) *above*, a will revoking or amending it will be formally valid if it qualifies under the same provisions. The same law as that governing the making of a will governs the law concerning revival.

(i) There is no reserve to any person under Manx laws of succession. Instead, an act applies to allow application to be made by a person for whom inadequate provision has been made (*see* 4 and 5 in Section A). The right to make application depends upon the deceased's dying domiciled in the Isle of Man. The residence or domicile status of the applicant is not relevant.

11. Domicile/Nationality

(a) Specific reference is made above as to the date at which the testator's domicile is relevant (if it is).

(b) The domicile of a beneficiary is largely irrelevant in Manx law. A rare exception is the rule concerning capacity of a beneficiary to inherit movables (*see* 10(d) *above*).

(c) Under Manx law, nationality is irrelevant and an individual can legally have only one domicile. The rules closely follow those under English law.

12. Taxation

There are no estate taxes in the Isle of Man. Income tax can, however, apply to income-producing assets comprised in a deceased's estate. The personal representatives are in principle liable to income tax on the income arising to the estate. Distributed income will be attributed to the beneficiaries receiving income from an estate. Income tax is therefore payable on Manx-source income in all estates and on worldwide income in the hands of beneficiaries resident in the Island. As regards those who are not so resident, only Manx-source income (other than interest from authorized institutions) will generally be taxed. In practice, where the estate is wound up over a short time span, the Assessor of Income Tax will require only details of the persons to whom income has been distributed. There may be a withholding of income tax on Manx-source income, for which the personal representatives will need to account, where the income is paid to non-residents.

Israel

Prepared by: Louis GARB

Address: 14 Zerach Barnet St.
         Jerusalem 95404
         Israel
Tel.:   +972 2 6528093
Fax: +972 2 6519306
Email: lgarb@netvision.net.il
         Also at Tel Aviv

SECTION A – BRIEF SURVEY OF THE LOCAL SYSTEM

1. Type of System

(a) Although codification is becomingly increasingly prevalent, the Israeli system is closer to the common law. In particular, overwhelming emphasis is placed on precedents.

Israeli inheritance law is based on a 1965 statute as amended entitled *The Law of Inheritance*, hereinafter referred to as the Statute.

(b) Israel does not have a federal system.

2. Wills

(a) There are four possible types of will:

 i. A handwritten will.
   This is entirely written by the testator who must date and sign it.
 ii. A last will before witnesses.
   The will is signed at the end thereof by the testator, and such signature is made by the testator in the presence of two or more competent witnesses present at the same time. Such witnesses shall attest and sign the will in the presence of the testator and of each other, and shall confirm in writing on the will itself that the will was signed by the testator in their presence and in the presence of each other. If the will consists of more than one page, each page other than the final page need not be signed by the testator and his witnesses although this is obviously desirable. This is the most common form of will in Israel.

342

iii. Wills signed before an authority.

The will is made by the testator giving verbal instructions before a judge, registrar, member of a religious court as defined in the Statute or a notary. (An Israeli notary is an advocate, as local practitioners are designated, with at least fifteen years experience who applies to perform this additional function. No further qualifications are necessary.) The contents of the will are recorded by the judge, etc. Alternatively the will is presented by the testator in written form without witnesses to the official concerned. The official shall read the will to the testator who shall declare that this is his will and the official shall confirm on the document itself that it has been read to the testator who has made the aforesaid declaration. If the will has been translated then such fact must also be recorded on the document itself.

(b) *i.* A testator may revoke his will in one of the forms provided for making a will, i.e., by formal document, or by destroying same. A testator who has destroyed his will is presumed to have intended to revoke it. A new will, even though it does not expressly revoke an earlier will, is deemed so to revoke it to the extent to which its provisions are inconsistent with those of the earlier will.

ii. As to the effects of marriage, *see* paragraph 6 *below.*

iii. A revoked will can only be revived by a specific new testamentary document subject to the formalities set out in (a) *above.*

iv. Under unusual circumstances, an oral will is allowed in cases where a person believes himself in danger of death. Both subjective and objective elements are required for this belief on the part of the testator. An oral will must be made in front of two witnesses who hear the testator's instructions. Someone must write down the contents of the testator's instructions and also the circumstances under which they were given and this written confirmation has to be signed by the two witnesses and lodged by them with the court as soon as possible after preparation. An oral will is valid for a period of one month only and is then automatically cancelled if the testator is still alive.

3. Intestacy

The term estate is used herein to mean the total net assets of whatsoever nature left by the deceased and being the subject of inheritance.

(a) The Israeli law of intestacy is regulated by the Statute in terms whereof:

– The spouse of the deceased takes the chattels and a passenger car, which in the ordinary course and according to the circumstances belong to the common household. From the remainder of the estate the spouse shall take as follows:
  – if the testator is survived by children or their offspring or parents – one-half;
  – if the testator is survived by siblings or their offspring or the parents of parents – two thirds. If, however, immediately before the testator's death his spouse had been married to him for three years or longer and at that time lived with

him in the dwelling, which is wholly or partly part of the estate, then the spouse shall take the testator's entire share in the said dwelling and two thirds of the remainder of the inheritance;
  - if the testator is not survived by any of the relatives listed above, then the spouse shall inherit the entire inheritance.

- The children of the deceased take precedence over the parents and the parents take precedence over the grandparents.
  - The children of the deceased share equally among themselves and so do the parents among themselves and the grandparents among themselves.
  - If a child of the testator predeceased him and left children, then those children inherit in place of that child, and in the same manner the children of each of the testator's relatives who predeceased him shall inherit. These provisions do not apply when the testator is survived by a spouse and parents or parents' parents, or by any one of these.
  - For the purposes of the aforementioned provisions, there is no difference between a legitimate, illegitimate, adulterine or adopted child. An adopted child, however, shall be deemed to be a descendant of his adoptive parent and not to be a descendant of his natural parents. The issue of an adopted child likewise inherits from the adopter. An adopted child and his issue do not inherit from the relatives of the adopter on intestacy; the adopter inherits from the adopted child as if he were his parent, but the relatives of the adopter do not inherit from the adopted child on intestacy.

- If any person was found to be disqualified, or if he renounced his share in the estate otherwise than in favour of the testator's spouse, children or sibling, then his share shall be added to the other heirs in proportion to their shares.
- If there is no heir as aforesaid, then the State shall inherit on intestacy. Anything which the State inherits under this section shall be used for purposes of education, science, health and social welfare. However, the Minister of Finance may make grants from the assets of the estate or after payment of the estate's debts may make payments either in a lump sum or in recurring amounts:
  - to any person who immediately before the death of the deceased was dependent on the deceased;
  - to any person or association on which the deceased was dependent immediately before his death;
  - to a member of the family of the deceased or of his spouse, who is not an heir on intestacy.

(b) There is no difference in the division of the estate between movables and immovables. (*See*, however, paragraph 14(a)(*ii*) hereunder.) Subject to the exception noted *above*.

4. Freedom of Testation

(a) There are no compulsory shares or minimum percentages for a surviving spouse, common law wife and/or children. However, *see* paragraph 5 *below*.

(b) *i.* An agreement about the inheritance of a person and a waiver of his inheritance, which was made during the lifetime of that person, is void.

   ii. A gift made by a person, which is intended to vest in the donee only upon the donor's death, is not valid, unless it is made by a will in accordance with the provisions of the Statute.

5. Maintenance

If the deceased left a spouse, children or parents who are in need of support, they are entitled to maintenance out of the estate, whether inheritance is intestate or under will.

The right to maintenance shall be as follows:

– in the case of the spouse of the deceased, until remarriage; however, the court may make a lump sum grant to the widow of the deceased who remarries, if under the circumstances of the case and having regard to the rights of the children of the deceased, the court finds it proper to do so;
– in the case of children of the deceased, until age eighteen, and in the case of an invalid child or a mentally sick child, for the duration of his invalidity or mental sickness, or a child who is a retarded person;
– in the case of an adult child of the deceased for whom the court deems it proper under the circumstances to prescribe maintenance, until age twenty-three;
– in the case of parents of the deceased who were dependent on him immediately before his death, as long as they live.

(b) If a spouse was denied the right of maintenance by the deceased immediately before the latter's death, then such spouse is not entitled to maintenance out of the estate.

(c) If a man and a woman, though they are not married to each other, have lived together as husband and wife in a common household, then upon the death of one of them, neither being then married to another person, the survivor is entitled to maintenance out of the estate, as if they had been married to each other.

Maintenance out of the estate includes the cost of training the entitled person in an occupation.

In determining the right to maintenance and its extent, the court shall take into account, *inter alia*:

– the value of the estate;
– what the person entitled to maintenance may receive from the estate as heir on intestacy or as a beneficiary under will;
– the standard of living of the deceased and of the person entitled to maintenance;
– the assets of the person entitled to maintenance;
– the income of the person entitled to maintenance from any source whatsoever, including a child's claim for maintenance from a surviving parent, and including what a spouse is entitled to receive by virtue of the marital relationship. In the

case of the spouse of the deceased, however, the court shall not take into account income from work or occupation, except to the extent that – immediately before the death of the deceased – such income also served to support the family or the spouse.

The application to determine maintenance should be made prior to division of the estate and only in unusual circumstances will the court allow an application for maintenance for a period of up to six months after the division of the estate.

6. Community Property Between Husband and Wife

Under the law applicable to an Israeli marriage, if no antenuptial contract is entered into, the parties are married in partial community of property. The effect of such community is to create a joint estate in respect of assets acquired after the marriage which are then jointly owned on termination of the marriage, i.e., by death, divorce, etc. The surviving spouse is entitled to half thereof, and only the remaining half is subject to the laws of inheritance together with any assets which were owned by the deceased spouse prior to the marriage or inheritances or presents received by the deceased spouse during the marriage.

An antenuptial contract may vary the property relations between husband and wife. Such contract has to follow certain regulations concerning registration.

7. Gifts (*Inter Vivos*)

Gifts are not set off against the inheritance, unless the testator specifically gives expression to this wish in the testamentary document. Gifts, however, may affect the question of maintenance referred to in paragraph 5 *above*.

8. Capacity

(a) Every person of the age of eighteen years or more may make a will unless at the time of making the will he is mentally incapable of appreciating the nature and effect of his act. The burden of proof that he was mentally incapable at the time rests on the person alleging the same.

(b) A competent witness is a person of the age of eighteen years or over who at the time he witnesses a will is not incompetent to give evidence in a court of law.

Any person who attests and signs a will as a witness, or who signs a will in the presence and by direction of a testator, or who writes out the will or any part thereof in his own handwriting, and the person who is the spouse of such person at the time of the execution of the will, shall be disqualified from receiving any benefit from that will. However, this disqualification does not apply in the case of an oral will. Anyone convicted of hiding or destroying a will, or forging same, and anyone who caused or tried to cause the death of the testator, cannot inherit.

(c) There is no restriction as to who may be a beneficiary of an estate provided that in the case of an individual he is alive at the time of the testator's decease or is born within three hundred days from such date.

9. Authority (Court, Notarial or Other)

i. The appointment of an executor is made by a registrar. It is then the duty of the executors duly authorized as aforesaid to implement the terms of the will or, if there is no will, to implement the laws of intestate succession under supervision of the office of the Administrator-General. There is an increasing tendency on the part of the Israeli courts and registrars to not appoint executors even if one has been specified in the will unless there is a real need for such appointment.

ii. Applications for probate of wills or inheritance orders are now made to the Registrar of Inheritances in the area in which the decease took place, who has taken over the function formerly carried out by the courts. Or, if the deceased was not a resident of Israel, the area in which he left assets. (This relates to procedural and not substantive jurisdiction which will be dealt with below.)

iii. Advocates' fees are by advance negotiation and executors' fees would vary from 2 per cent to 4 per cent depending on the complexity of the estate. In the event of dispute between the executor and the heirs or the Administrator-General's office, the question is decided by the Family Court for the area.

The application is in the form of an affidavit signed by an interested party accompanied by an affidavit of a third party (not an heir) who can attest to the correctness of the allegations, a power of attorney in favour of the advocate dealing with the matter and the *original* will if same exists, and payment of the government fee which presently ranges between USD125–250 depending on whether or not the appointment of an executor is sought. Where the will is in a foreign language other than English, however, it is the practice to require a sworn translation into either Hebrew or English. Some registrars may also require a translation of an English will as well.

iv. The application is then advertised in the official government gazette in order to give the appropriate opportunity to anybody who wishes to oppose the application. Should there be no objection then the registrar will grant an order. In the event of any objection the matter will be referred to the Family Court in the district for a court hearing.

10. Invalidity of Will

(a) Grounds of invalidity of a will derive from the provisions of the Inheritance Statute and the common law. They include:

– invalidity by reason of failure to comply with the formalities prescribed in the law;

- invalidity because the testator does not have the necessary *animus testandi* at the time of the execution, i.e., where he never intended the document to operate as a will at all or where he signs the will under a mistaken belief as to its nature, etc.;
- invalidity where the act of testation is not free and voluntary but is procured by fraud, duress or undue influence;
- invalidity where the will is made dependent upon a condition which is not fulfilled; and
- invalidity because the will is revoked.

If it cannot be ascertained from a testamentary provision to whom the testator made the bequest or what he bequeathed, or if its meaning is unintelligible or, if the execution of a testamentary provision is illegal, immoral or impossible, then it is void.

A will which is complete and regular on the face of it is presumed to be valid until its invalidity has been established and the onus is on the person alleging invalidity to prove such allegation. Furthermore, after the lapse of a year from the time that the undue influence, fraud or duress have ceased to affect the testator, if the testator – though able to revoke the will – has not done so, then the defect in question shall no longer make the testamentary provision void or serve as a ground for its amendment.

(b) Invalidity results in the will being void. However, in this regard attention is drawn to a provision of the Statute which provides that if a court is satisfied that a document or the amendment of a document drafted or executed by a person who has died since the drafting or execution thereof, was intended to be his will or an amendment of his will, the court shall have the discretion to accept that document, or that document as amended, even though it does not comply with all the formalities for the execution or amendment or will referred to in the said law. Similarly, the court has the power to correct clerical errors or errors in the description of a person or asset.

11. Simultaneous Death

When two or more persons have died and the sequence of their death cannot be determined, then the rights in the estate of each of them shall be determined in accordance with the following rules:

- if one of the claimants is a certain heir and another a doubtful heir, then the claimant who is a certain heir takes precedence. A certain heir is a person who would inherit whether or not the other party died first. A doubtful heir is someone who would inherit only if the other party died first;
- if the two claimants are doubtful heirs, the claimant who is the spouse or relative of the deceased whose estate is being distributed takes precedence;
- in the absence of a will, the estate shall be distributed between several claimants of the same order of precedence according to the rules of distribution which apply to intestate inheritance.

It is common practice to insert in a will a clause that in the event of simultaneous death with the testator *or* in the event of death within a specified period of the testator's death, the other party will be presumed to have predeceased the testator.

12. Estate Taxes

No estate taxes exist.

13. Administration of Estates

(a) The appointment of an executor/administrator (these terms have become identical in Israeli law) is not an essential. Furthermore, even if an executor is appointed by will, the registrar or court may decide that such appointment is superfluous, especially if the heirs are all majors and do not suffer from any legal disability. In such case the heirs are expected to administer the estate themselves and should they so wish may give a power of attorney to a third party who will then act in terms of the power of attorney, and his relationship will be defined in terms of the power of attorney and not in terms of the inheritance law; i.e., he will not be subject to any of the supervision or restrictions as are found in the Statute unless these are specifically incorporated in the power of attorney.

(b) If an executor is in fact appointed, he has to submit periodic reports to the Administrator-General and answer any queries raised by him. Unless excused by the will, he will have to give some form of security for the due administration.

(c) The Administrator-General's office scrutinizes and queries the report.

(d) Any of the heirs or unpaid creditors may query or object.

(e) After payment of the debts of the estate and due provision for any maintenance or support for which the estate is liable, the surplus is to be divided between the heirs. A beneficiary (a person entitled to a specific bequest whether in money or in kind) shall receive such item prior to the division amongst the heirs who are to receive the balance of the estate according to percentages. Furthermore, if an estate is insufficient to provide for the monetary bequests specified in addition to specific bequests, the person entitled to a monetary bequest is not entitled to ask a beneficiary of a specific bequest to make good any monetary shortfall or to participate in the monetary bequest.

With regard to the balance of the assets after providing for the specific bequests, a unanimous agreement between the heirs shall be binding upon the executor. In the absence of such agreement, the matter is submitted to the Family Court referred to in paragraph 9 *above*. In any event where immovable property is to be sold and not transferred to a specific heir, then, even should there be unanimous agreement between the heirs, such sale is still subject to the approval of the said Family Court albeit that in virtually in all cases this is a mere formality.

International Succession

(f) The heirs or the executor are obliged to publish notice calling for submission of claims within three months of date of publication, unless because of the circumstances they are released from such duty of publication. An executor is obliged to pay a debt of the estate of which he has learned even if the creditor has not filed a claim as a result of the publication.

With regard to the responsibility of heirs in respect of the debts of the estate, an heir would only be responsible for payment from estate assets until such time as the estate has been distributed. After the estate has been distributed the heir is not responsible for debts which were not paid unless it is proved that he knew of them and in that case only to the maximum value of what he received from the estate. If there was no publication for submission of creditors' claims, each heir shall be liable for any unpaid debts to the extent of the value of the entire estate at the time of the distribution. However, an heir who did not know of a debt at the time of the distribution (and the burden of proof is on the heir to prove that he was unaware of the debt) shall only be reliable to the extent of the benefit he received from the estate.

(g) *See* (e) *above.*

14. Domicile/Nationality

(a) *i.* The nationality of the deceased does not affect any of the answers. The domicile of the deceased, which under Israeli law is defined as the place in which is to be found the 'centre' of his life, is an objective test where all relevant factors such as period of time and majority of connecting factors are taken into account; the intention of the person does not matter. Accordingly, answers to paragraphs 3 to 8 *above* may be affected if the deceased was not domiciled in Israel at the time of his death. The relevant court is the family court in the area in which the deceased lived or in which he left property. If all partners agree then the appropriate religious court can have jurisdiction.

ii. It should be noted that assets which pass on inheritance in terms of the law in which they are situate are subject to the inheritance laws of such place. Where a testator makes a will in respect of assets outside of Israel and such asset does not have to devolve only according to the foreign law, the last will of the testator is to be upheld. However, if the foreign law does not allow an alternative, then, as aforesaid, the assets are to be transferred in terms of the foreign law. It should be noted this does not only apply to immovable property. (Also *see* Section B, paragraph 10 *below.*)

(b) If the deceased was domiciled in Israel, the Israeli court would have jurisdiction to grant an order of probate of succession even if the deceased left no assets there. It is submitted, however, by the author, that if the deceased left assets abroad but no assets in Israel, the court could well regard any such application for local probate as an abuse of the process of court, especially should it be shown that the purpose of such local order was merely to circumvent some foreign law which should more properly have jurisdiction. This question still awaits an unequivocal answer by the courts.

Section B – Applicable Law/Procedure Where Foreign Element/s are Involved

1. Jurisdiction

(a) The courts of Israel have jurisdiction over the estate of any person who was domiciled in Israel at the time of his death, or who left property in Israel. The relevant court is the family court in the area in which the deceased lived or in which he left property. If all partners agree then the appropriate religious court can have jurisdiction.

(b) In the light of the aforesaid, it is apparent that the rules for movable and immovable assets do not differ as far as jurisdiction is concerned.

(c) If Israel has jurisdiction, the registrar (and if necessary the court) in the area in which the deceased died or in which he left assets shall have jurisdiction.

2. Applicable Law

The order of succession to a deceased's assets will be determined by the law of the domicile of the deceased irrespective of where those assets are situated. However, the scission principle applies in that if the distribution of the asset is determined by the *lex situs* (the law of the place where such property is situated) such law will be applied by the Israeli registrar or court. Where a testator who had a foreign domicile left assets in Israel, the law of the foreign domicile shall apply to his entire inheritance, including any assets in Israel. However, if the foreign law holds that Israeli law is applicable, then Israel accepts the *renvoi* and Israeli law would be applicable. On the other hand, if the foreign law refers to a different foreign law, i.e., that of a third country, the Israeli court would disregard such referral and would apply the law of the domicile of the deceased. Even if the court would under normal circumstances have recourse to the foreign law, this will not be the case if the foreign law discriminates against anyone by virtue of race, religion, sex or nationality.

3. Foreign Succession/Inheritance Orders

(a) Where a foreign executor wishes to deal with the property of a deceased person in Israel pursuant to a foreign succession or inheritance order, such a foreign executor would need to apply to the appropriate court for issue of a local order of court. There is no provision for recognition of the foreign order or judgment of inheritance or probate. The application is necessitated by the fact that in terms of the law no person may deal with any assets in Israel belonging to a deceased person, whether or not the latter was ordinarily resident in Israel, except under the supervision and authority of the registrar or court of one of the areas of jurisdiction. Broadly speaking such application requires the documents referred to in Section A, paragraph 9(*iii*) above. It should be noted that if the will is not in Hebrew or English it will have to be translated into Hebrew either by way of notarial translation or some other acceptable method under the circumstances. The affidavits referred to, if signed abroad, must be signed either in front of the Israeli Consul or must bear an apostille and must be likewise translated into Hebrew if not in Hebrew or English. Subject to the exception noted in Section 2 *above*.

Accordingly, from the point of view of Israeli assets, no advantage is served by first obtaining a foreign order.

4. Two or More Succession or Probate Orders

Under Israeli law there is no 'unity of administration.' In other words, there is no rule that the deceased's estate must be administered as a whole by one person in one country. Usually, assets in the estate are administered separately in the different countries in which they happened to be located. Even if a person has received authority in a foreign country to act as an executor, he is not entitled to administer in Israel until a local order is obtained. A non-Israeli resident cannot act as executor. Israeli citizenship, however, is not a requirement.

5. Assets

The local court can assume jurisdiction in the cases mentioned in Section A, paragraph 14(b) *above*.

6. Expert Evidence

(a) Where the deceased had a foreign domicile, the registrar will request an expert opinion from a lawyer as to the foreign law. Generally speaking, as Israel is a country with a very varied immigration, there is little difficulty finding local lawyers conversant with most jurisdictions. Should there be no opposition, the registrar will invariably accept the expert opinion.

(b) In the event of opposition, the matter would be referred to the Family Court as aforesaid. This court may very well require the experts to be available for cross-examination on their opinions.

7. Unity of Succession

The principle of unity of succession whereby questions relating to intestacy or wills are governed by one single law is adhered to in Israel. However, Israeli law adheres to the principle of scission by which, if the distribution of assets on the death of the deceased is governed by the law of *situs*, such law will be followed by the Israeli courts.

8. Formalities

The form of a will is valid according to Israeli law if valid in Israel or valid according to the law of the place where it was made or according to the law of the testator's domicile when he made the will or when he died, and – as far as the will relates to immovable property – also according to the law of the place where the property is located.

For the purposes of the application of the foreign law under this section, the capacity required of the testator or of witnesses shall be deemed a matter of form.

9. Legislation

Israel acceded to and ratified the *1961 Hague Convention on the Conflicts of Laws Relating to the Form of Testamentary Dispositions* on 5 October 1970.

10. Wills

(a) The form of a will is valid according to Israeli law if valid in Israel or valid according to the law of the place where it was made or according to the law of the testator's domicile when he made the will or when he died, and – as far as the will relates to immovable property – also according to the law of the place where the property is located. Subject to the exception noted in Section 2 *above*.

(b) *See* paragraph 2 *above*.

(c) When the law of the place where assets are situate contains a provision for a minimum portion of the assets of the deceased prior to testamentary disposition, should the foreign law specifically exclude the application of any other law, Israeli law will also accept that such minimum portion applies. If the foreign law does not specifically exclude any other law then the provisions of the will shall supersede.

(d)–(g) *See* paragraph 2 *above*.

(h) Amendment and revival: *see* sub-paragraph (a) *above*.

(i) As previously stated there is no reserve in Israeli law subject to the rights of the wife to certain assets as outlined in paragraph 3(a) of Section A *above*. With regard to the assets of a person not domiciled in Israel, *see* (c) *above*.

11. Domicile/Nationality

(a) The domicile at the time of death is determining; *see* paragraph 2 *above*. In determining a person's domicile the Israeli court would have regard to all the factors over several years of the deceased's life in order to determine with which jurisdiction the most 'connecting factors' existed.

International Succession

(b) The domicile of the beneficiary is not relevant. However, if the beneficiary is domiciled in a country which is in a state of war with Israel or where there is a probability that he would not receive any inheritance transferred to him or that the very fact that he had such a connection with a person in Israel could expose him to danger, his share would be held in trust by the Administrator-General's office until such time as it became prudent to transfer it to him.

(c) As stated above, the question of domicile is determined by assessing the connecting factors. Israeli law insists on a decision in favour of one jurisdiction.

12. Taxation

As already stated there are no estate taxes.

Italy

Prepared by: Franco SALERNO CARDILLO

Address: Via Glosue Carducci 6
          90141 Palermo
          Italy
Tel.:   +39 91 333074
Fax: +39 91 331982

Reviewed and updated by
Andrew G. PATON
Allen & Overy
Corso Vittorio Emanuele II, 284
00186 Rome
Italy
Tel.:   +39 06 6842 71
Fax: +39 06 6842 7333
E-mail: andrew.paton@allenovery.com

Section A – Brief Survey of the Local System

1. Type of System

(a) The judicial system in force is that of 'civil law'.

(b) In Italy, there is no federal system.

The judicial system which regulates inheritance law is the same and is valid throughout all of Italy.

The principal source of inheritance law as regards the substantive law is *Il Codice Civile* (the Civil Code), in particular the *Libro Secondo* (the Second Book) (Articles 456 to 809) entitled *Delle Successioni* (Succession).

2. Wills

(a) The will is a formal legal instrument which must always be in written form.

The two ordinary forms of will are the holographic will and the will by way of deed; the latter can be either by way of public instrument or secret.

355

The *holographic will* must comply with the following three conditions: it must be wholly in written form, dated and signed by the testator (Articles 601 & 602 of the Civil Code).

The *will by way of public instrument* is a will signed before a notary in the presence of two witnesses (Article 603 of the Civil Code).

The *secret will* (also referred to as the mystic will) is not commonly used. This will involves the most detailed specifications as to form (Articles 604 & 605).

Briefly, the testator must personally give the notary a document, which is already sealed or will be sealed by the notary, whilst declaring that the said document contains his will. The notary records these proceedings on the document comprising the will or on the envelope in which the will is contained or on another envelope which he has prepared and sealed.

Special wills (referred to as 'privileged') are foreseen in order to allow the testator to express his last wishes with a minimum of formalities when he finds himself in certain situations which do not make it possible for him to have recourse to the ordinary forms of wills dealt with above (Articles 609 to 619 of the Civil Code).

The common feature of such wills is that they are only in force for a limited period of time.

In effect, these wills remain valid only for three months after the testator's position is no longer such as to prevent him from making an ordinary form of will.

International wills: under *Law No. 387 of 29 November 1990* in force since 16 November 1991, Italy has acceded to the *1973 Washington Convention on International Wills* which instituted the 'international will'.

Law No. 387 has empowered notaries on Italian territory and, as regards Italians abroad, Italian diplomatic and consular officials.

(b) *i.* A will is an instrument that can always be revoked.

It is not possible to renounce the right to revoke or to modify testamentary dispositions: such a clause would be without effect.

There is an important exception to this principle in the matter of the 'recognition' of illegitimate children (i.e., an admission of paternity) in a will (whatever form this will may take); this recognition is in effect non-revocable and takes effect from the date of the testator's death even if that will had been revoked (Article 256 of the Civil Code).

Revocation can be express (formal) or implied, total or partial.

Formal revocation, total or partial, including by way of modification can be done by way of a new will, whatever its form, or by way of deed to this effect executed in the presence of two witnesses and before a notary.

Implied revocation can be done by way of the following:
– a later will containing dispositions which are incompatible with previous ones;
– the destruction, tearing up or mutilation, total or partial, of a holographic will;
– the withdrawal of a secret will by the testator, unless the sealed document amounts to an holographic will. In contrast, the withdrawal of a

holographic will deposited with a notary does not amount to an implied revocation;
– the alienation of all or part of a legacy;
– the changing of a legacy as to its form and designation, providing that it can be shown that the testator willingly effected this change.

There is a specific form of *revocation* by operation of law in cases where it is known or it becomes suddenly known that the testator had legitimate children or descendants, even if dead, legitimated or adopted, or also where there is recognition of an illegitimate child.

Finally, as regards the *codicil*, case law deems that it amounts to a testamentary disposition having all the characteristics of a will but that, in practice, makes reference to dispositions in a previous will thereby changing the latter or is integrated with a previous will.

Due to this, there is no difference between wills and codicils as regards those subjects being examined.

ii. Legal commentators and case law maintain that, given the silence of the law on this matter, neither marriage or divorce has any direct effect on a person's will.

iii. A will that has already been revoked, whether formally or tacitly, can be revived, whether in its entirety or partially, by the *revocation of a revocation*, which must be carried out in accordance with the stipulations set out *above* as regards formal revocation (i.e., by will or by deed).

Implied revocation of an earlier revocation is, however, not permitted.

The effect of the revocation is to revive the original will *ab initio*.

3. Intestacy

(a) As will be examined further in 9 *below*, devolution upon succession takes place automatically when the estate passes to the heirs, without the need for attestation by any particular authority.

This fundamental principle applies to succession by will as well as succession upon intestacy.

Before examining the order of succession, it may be useful to remember that by virtue of the institution of 'representation' (governed by Articles 467 et seq. of the Civil Code), when the children of the deceased, whether legitimate, legitimated, adopted or illegitimate, or his brothers and sisters, even illegitimate ones according to prevailing legal opinion, do not or decide not to accept their inheritance, it is their legitimate or illegitimate descendants (according to legal opinion, legitimated and adopted descendants also, when the adoption confers the status of a legitimate child) who will take in their place in accordance with their entitlement.

Finally, it should be noted that the share of a person who has renounced his inheritance passes to his co-heirs, as of right and without the need for consent. This is, however, without prejudice to the right of representation and the law dealing with those cases where the deceased's father and mother cannot or do not wish to succeed. If there is only one person within a particular category of successors to renounce the succession and he does so, the succession will pass to those who would inherit if that person were no longer alive (Article 522 of the Civil Code).

The *order of succession* will now be examined.

The persons to whom the succession devolves upon intestacy are as follows: the surviving spouse, legitimate and illegitimate descendants, legitimate ancestors, collateral relations, other relations up to the sixth degree and the state, in accordance with the order and the rules stated below.

Succession of children (Articles 566 to 567 of the Civil Code): The children only take concurrently with the deceased's spouse. In effect, the existence of children, or their descendants who take by way of representation, will exclude the other categories of possible successors.

The rules regarding children will now be set out in further detail.

As regards their father and their mother, legitimate and natural children take in equal measure. Legitimated and adopted children are treated like legitimate children (that is, children born during the marriage).

It should be remembered that legitimation accords an illegitimate child the status of a legitimate child.

Legitimation can occur either by the subsequent marriage of the illegitimate child's parents or by way of a judicial decision.

As regards *adopted* children, in the Italian judicial system there are two forms of adoption:

- deemed 'special' and regulated by *Law No. 184 of 4 May 1983*, which confers upon the adopted child the same status as that of a legitimate child of the adoptive parent; and
- deemed 'ordinary' and regulated by the Civil Code, which confers upon the adopted child certain rights, including the right to succession, in relation to the adoptive parent but which does not recognize any relation as between the other members of the adoptive parent's family. For example, adoptive brothers are not as such deemed to be related to one another.

As regards this second form of adoption, the adoptive parent does not acquire rights of succession to the adopted child's estate.

The rights of succession of *illegitimate children* presuppose that the parental tie was acknowledged by the deceased (even by way of a will whose provisions are limited solely to such 'recognition'), or declared by a Court.

The only difference between illegitimate children and legitimate children is that the latter are able to settle the share of the estate reverting to the illegitimate children by way of a monetary payment or immovables from the estate, such power being referred to as substitution ('commutation'). Where the illegitimate children do not agree to this, the Court will decide the matter, after having considered the personal and patrimonial circumstances involved (Article 537(3) of the Civil Code).

The case is different as regards *illegitimate children* who cannot be 'recognized' (such as 'incestuous children' born to parents in full knowledge of their relation to one another), who have obtained the right to receive maintenance, instruction and education in accordance with the terms of Article 279 of the Civil Code. They have the right to a life annuity equal to the share of the estate they would have received had they been recognized. Upon their request, this annuity can be capitalized into cash or, at the discretion of the legitimate heirs, into hereditary property.

In addition, if the parent made a disposition to them by way of donation or in the will, such children can renounce the gift and demand payment of the life annuity.

Finally, *children yet to be born* can also succeed, according to the law, if they have already been conceived at the time of death of the deceased (Article 462 of the Civil Code). In the absence of evidence to the contrary, a child is deemed conceived at that time if born within the three hundred days following the death of the deceased. Of course, the right to inherit upon intestacy remains subject to the *condicio juris* of the birth.

Succession of spouse (Articles 581 to 585 and 540 of the Civil Code): In addition to the children, the surviving spouse may take concurrently, as regards the legitimate succession, with other categories of successors:

- the surviving spouse will inherit the entire estate only in the absence of legitimate or illegitimate children, ancestors and brothers and sisters of the deceased;
- where there are children (whether legitimate or illegitimate), the surviving spouse is entitled to half of the estate if there is one child and to a third if there is more than one child;
- where there are legitimate ancestors and/or brothers and sisters, even half brothers and sisters, two-thirds of the estate will go to the surviving spouse, the rest going to the others with a quarter of the estate to the ancestors when there are any;
- where the surviving spouse of an illegitimate child dies without children or parents, the whole of the estate reverts to them. If there are parents, the estate is devolved with two-thirds going to the surviving spouse and one-third to the parents.

It should be noted here that illegitimate brothers and sisters are excluded from taking a share of the succession to the extent that, in accordance with the law, they are not actually deemed to be related. However, these persons will take before the state is entitled to do so.

The *putative spouse* (this term designating a spouse who in good faith or because of violence or a fear of exceptional seriousness contracted into a marriage which was then nullified) benefits generally from the same rights as the spouse. The putative spouse remains, however, excluded from the succession when the deceased whose estate is to pass was validly remarried at the time of his death.

The *separated spouse* is treated the same as a non-separated spouse, providing that the separation was not attributed to him by the courts. If deemed to be at fault, the spouse only has the right to a life annuity if, at the time of the death of the deceased, the spouse had the right to maintenance. The life annuity will be proportionate to the estate and the category and number of legitimate heirs, and cannot exceed the amount of maintenance which the spouse was previously receiving.

International Succession

One of the benefits accorded to the spouse which merits particular attention is *the right to reside in the family home and the use of furnishings belonging to the home*, to which right the spouse is entitled even if he takes concurrently with others if the house and/or the furnishings was owned by the deceased or was held in common ownership (Article 540(2) of the Civil Code).

It is important to note that the spouse can legitimately renounce that part of the estate which would be devolved upon him by law but can retain that part of the estate which the deceased devolves upon him by way of legacy.

This last point is important as regards notarial practice. The notary instructed to execute an instrument disposing of the deceased's residence used formerly as the family home should ensure that the surviving spouse who has renounced his right to succession is party to the instrument. This being in order to establish that the spouse, having the right to reside there, has specifically renounced this right, a general renunciation to the succession being insufficient for that purpose.

The above-mentioned rights of residence and the use of the furnishings are conferred upon the spouse, in accordance with the general rules, for the duration of his life and also apply to the putative spouse and the separated spouse who has not been held responsible for the separation by the courts.

The *divorced spouse* is considered a special case.

In effect, the latter no longer has any family ties with the deceased and his family from the moment the decree of divorce takes effect: they can still benefit from certain rights of succession, however.

Article 9bis of the *Law on Divorce* in effect allows the court, after the death of a spouse obliged to make maintenance payments, to confer upon the spouse having benefited from such payments, if they are in need, the right to a periodical payment from the estate. Such payment is quantified on the basis of the maintenance paid previously, the severity of need, the eventual termination of the maintenance, the estate, the number and category of heirs and their financial positions.

The persons who first benefit from succession then are the surviving spouse and the descendants of the deceased. In the absence of such descendants and in concurrence with the surviving spouse, the legitimate ancestors and the brothers and sisters of the deceased, even half brothers and sisters, will take. In their absence, the closest relations, up to the sixth degree, will take without distinction as to lineage.

In the absence of other persons to succeed (including illegitimate brothers and sisters), the succession will devolve upon the state which, on the one hand, acquires it without having to give consent and without being able to renounce it and, on the other, does not meet the liabilities of the estate if they exceed the value of the assets acquired (Article 586 of the Civil Code).

(b) There is no difference between the succession of movables and immovables.

4. Freedom of Testation

(a) In this judicial system, freedom of testation is limited in that certain persons are entitled to a percentage share which the law reserves to them ('reserved share').

This has a quantitative as opposed to a qualitative effect, in the sense that the testator is free to decide which property and rights are to be given to those with a right to a reserved share as long as such property and rights form part of the succession and amount to the value of the share to which these persons are so entitled.

The right to a reserved share is an intangible right.

The protection of those with a right to a reserved share is assured by the law (Article 549 of the Civil Code) which prevents the testator from imposing charges and conditions on the shares to which certain persons are entitled. All limitations deliberately imposed by the testator in order to reduce the value of the share are void and thereby without effect, as would be the case with: 'I give you the reserved share to which you are entitled on the condition that (. . .).' *See* 7(a) *below* as to the 'reduction' of testamentary dispositions or donations made to beneficiaries which encroach upon the rights of those with a compulsory share, with such 'reduction' in favour of the latter.

It is worth mentioning that a testamentary disposition which conflicts with the rights of those with a reserved share is perfectly valid insofar as it does not necessarily have to be reduced.

The persons who are entitled to a reserved share are as follows: the surviving spouse, legitimate, legitimated and adopted children, illegitimate children and legitimate ancestors.

The surviving spouse: In the absence of children, half of the estate of the deceased will devolve upon the surviving spouse.

In addition even if there are others who take concurrently, the right to live in the family home and the use of furnishings belonging to the home will revert to the surviving spouse if the house and/or the furnishings belonged to the deceased or were held in common ownership.

The same rights apply as regards a surviving spouse who is separated without having been at fault.

As regards such a spouse deemed to be at fault, he only has a right to a life annuity if, at the time of the deceased's death, he had been receiving maintenance.

The children: In the absence of a surviving spouse, if the deceased leaves one child, he has the right to half of the estate; if there are several children, each receives an equal share from two-thirds of the estate. If there is also a surviving spouse, in the case of a single child, he takes one-third of the estate as does the surviving spouse; in the case of several children, half the estate is divided between the children in equal shares and the surviving spouse takes one-quarter.

Legitimate children are able to pay out the amount due to illegitimate children in cash or immovables (referred to as substitution or 'commutation').

Legal opinion is divided as to whether illegitimate children who have not been 'recognized' (i.e., in respect of whom paternity has not been acknowledged) belong to the category of those having a right to a reserved share.

There are also children who cannot be recognized, such as *incestuous children*.

International Succession

Such children can be recognized, however, if at the moment of their conception the parents were not aware of the tie between them, or if the marriage from which the relationship arises was annulled.

By way of contrast, *illegitimate children* can always be recognized.

Succession as between the surviving spouse and the children:

- if there is only one child, one-third reverts to the surviving spouse and one-third reverts to the child;
- if there is more than one child, one-quarter reverts to the surviving spouse and half to the children to be divided in equal parts.

In any event, rights to reside in the family home and the use of furnishings belonging to the home are conferred upon the spouse if the home and/or the furnishings belonged to the deceased or were held in community property.

These rights encumber that part of the estate of which the testator may freely dispose and where this is insufficient, the difference is made up out of the compulsory share of the surviving spouse and then that of the children (Article 540 of the Civil Code).

Legitimate ancestors: In the absence of children, the legitimate ancestors have the right to one-third of the estate; if they take in concurrence with the surviving spouse they take one-quarter of the estate and the surviving spouse takes half.

System used to calculate the reserved shares: To determine what part of the estate can be freely disposed of by the testator (referred to as *quota disponibile*) and also that to be subject to the reserved shares (referred to as *quota indisponibile*), the following calculations are used:

- the assets belonging to the deceased on the date of his death (referred to as the *relictum*) are added together and the deceased's liabilities are then subtracted;
- then the value of the property given during the deceased's life as gifts, whether directly or indirectly (the *donatum*), are 'theoretically' added together in accordance with the rules imposed by the *collazione*, the value of such gifts usually being that upon succession.
- with the value of the estate having been arrived at in this way, the share of the estate which the deceased was able to dispose of freely is then determined.

(b) The Italian legal system (Article 458 of the Civil Code) prohibits all agreements by which a person disposes of his own succession (*patti successori istitutivi* – agreements on the conferment of rights on succession), as well as all agreements by which a person alienates his rights upon succession of a living person (*patti successori dispositivi* – agreements on the alienation of rights upon succession) or renounces such rights (*patti successori rinunziativi* – agreements on the renunciation of succession).

It is uncertain whether agreements on succession are considered contrary to public policy and therefore whether they can be upheld in this legal jurisdiction when they originate in a foreign country which allows for them.

Examples of *agreements on succession that are prohibited*:

– sale of future property considered to be part of the succession of a living person;
– a division which includes property belonging to the succession of a living person;
– a provision which disposes of part of a partnership or, more generally, of co-owned property to other partners or co-owners without any consideration having been given (concentration clauses).

5. Maintenance

The Italian legal system provides for particular forms of maintenance in favour of specified persons who will take in the succession.

These beneficiaries are as follows:

– natural children who cannot be 'recognized';
– the surviving spouse who was separated from the deceased when having been deemed by the courts as responsible for the separation;
– the divorced spouse of the deceased.

6. Community Property Between Husband and Wife

(a)–(b) The Italian legal system provides that community of property as between spouses is the presumed legal patrimonial regime applicable as between them.

Moreover the spouses can opt for a regime allowing for the separation of property or for the conventional regime of community.

When spouses are married under the regime of *statutory community of martial property*, the principal effect of the death of one of the spouses is the 'dissolution of the community of property' (Article 191 of the Civil Code).

In fact, this expression is not meant to signify the actual ending of the community of property, because in reality this takes effect with the division of property, but rather the ending of the obligations and effects arising from the legal 'regime' applicable to the spouses' property (for example, the obligations as to the inalienability of shares are terminated).

In particular, because of the dissolution of the community of property, certain property falls within the 'community of residuo' or the deferred community of property (Article 177(1)(b) and (c) and Article 178 of the Civil Code). According to prevailing legal opinion, the effect of the 'community of residuo' is not such that it would render the spouses joint owners of the property and rights mentioned *above*, but rather it gives rise to a right to credit in favour of the spouse who does not have title to the property, equal to half of the value of such property.

In terms of the succession this gives rise to a debt owed by the deceased to the surviving spouse, and therefore a hereditary liability.

The death of one of the spouses also gives rise to the dissolution of the estate (Articles 167 *et seq.* of the Civil Code). When there are children who are minors, the estate subsists until they are no longer minors.

7. Gifts (*Inter Vivos*)

(a) As was seen in the response given at 4 *above*, those with a right to a reserved share can bring proceedings to have legacies or donations reduced if the latter conflict with their entitlement.

However, before asking for the reduction of donations, persons with a right to a reserved share must account for the value of the property given to them by the will. Donations are reduced starting with the most recent and then working back to those made previously. Contemporaneous donations are reduced proportionately.

(b) The person with a right to a reserved share who asks for the reduction of donations (or testamentary dispositions) must first bring into account and add to his reserved share the donations and other hereditary dispositions which have benefited him, except if he has been exempted from having to do so. In addition the person with a right to a reserved share who succeeds by way of representation (*see* 3(a) *above*) must also bring into account dispositions made by his ancestor. The testator can therefore, by means of an *express* exemption, stipulate that dispositions made to the person with a right to a reserved share are deemed to be from that part of the estate of which the testator is free to dispose with only the excess amount to be brought into account as regards the reserved share.

Of course such exemption is not available against the preceding donees.

However, the dispositions received are not brought into account.

8. Capacity

(a) The general rule is that all those who are not deemed incapable by law can make a will: the causes of incapacity therefore are a closed list.

The following persons are deemed incapable (Article 591 of the Civil Code):

- those who have not yet reached their majority (eighteen years of age);
- those declared interdicted from mental illness;
- those who, though not forbidden to make a will, were for some reason, even temporary, incapable of understanding or acting at the time they drew up their will.

In all the above cases of incapacity, any interested person can challenge the will within a five year period from the date the testamentary dispositions were executed.

(b) It should be noted that the presence of witnesses is only required where the will is made by way of public instrument.

As regards *ordinary wills*, their capacity is governed by the rules on witnesses of public instruments. Article 50 of the *Notarial Law No. 89/1913* provides that witnesses must always be of full age, Italian citizens or foreigners resident in Italy who have reached eighteen years of age, have the capacity to act and be disinterested in the instrument. It also sets out those deemed unsuitable as witnesses: the blind, the deaf, the dumb, those who do not know how to or cannot sign their names, the notary's relations, including his spouse, relations or relations by way of marriage, in direct line including all degrees and in collateral line up to and including the third degree, or the spouse of any one of them.

As regards *privileged wills*, because of the exceptional situations in which they are made, it is accepted that the witnesses may be unable to sign the will, though the reason must be given for this, and, where the use of a privileged will can be justified by reason of contagious disease, public disaster or accident, witnesses of only sixteen and above are acceptable.

(c) Generally, the capacity to benefit from a will is one of the requirements of basic legal capacity, that is, someone's capacity to have legal personality.

As regards *persons*, legal capacity is acquired upon birth.

Children who are yet to be born have the capacity to succeed, by way of the law or will, if they were already conceived at the time of the death of the person whose estate is to pass.

However, it is possible for children not yet having been conceived of a specified person alive at the testator's death, to receive by way of a will.

In all cases, the gift remains subject to the *conditio jurus* of the birth, and, as regards the delay, specific rules are provided for its administration (Article 643 of the Civil Code).

As regards certain *legal entities* (associations, foundations and other institutions of a private nature), the acquisition of the inheritance must be subject to the limitation of the liability for the debts of the estate to the amount of the net assets actually received (referred to as *bénéfice d'inventaire*), in accordance with Article 473, Civil Code, as amended by Law No. 192/2000.

The above rules do not apply to *companies*: they are subject to the usual provisions.

Finally there are certain limitations on the capacity of the following *persons having a special relationship with the testator*:

- *guardian and unofficial guardian* (Article 596 of the Civil Code);
- *notary or other judicial official that receives the will, witnesses and interpreters (Article 597 of the Civil Code).*

Dispositions made in their favour in the will, the drawing up of which they have had part, are null and void.

Related third parties (Article 599 of the Civil Code): Nullity, as provided for the above-mentioned persons, is also applicable when the dispositions are made to third parties, such persons being the parents, the descendants and the surviving spouse of such prohibited persons.

International Succession

9. Authority (Court, Notarial or Other)

(a) It is not necessary for a specific authority to attest the devolution upon succession: this takes place automatically, at the time of the passing of the estate to the heirs.

In the Italian legal system, the verification of the capacity as heir is carried out as follows:

- where succession is by law, by way of the certificates issued by the Registry from which the kinship is established and the certificate of death;
- where succession is by will, by examination of the will after its publication.

In matters concerning succession, recourse is frequently made to *actes de notoriété* (officially recorded documents containing statements by a number of persons as to matters of common knowledge).

The immediate entry into effect of the heir's right to succession constitutes a fundamental principle of the Italian system; what is necessary, however, is that the person entitled to inherit accepts the inheritance.

The acceptance of succession can be manifest or implicit, 'unconditional' or subject to a *bénéfice d'inventaire* (a limitation of the heir's liability for the debts of the estate to the amount of the net assets he actually receives); there cannot, however, be any other partial or conditional acceptance, such acceptance being null and void (Articles 470 ff. of the Civil Code).

Acceptance is deemed *manifest* when the person entitled as heir declares his acceptance or assumes his capacity as heir by way of a public instrument or private written statement.

Acceptance is deemed *implicit* when the person entitled as heir carries out an act which necessarily presupposes his willingness to accept, that is, an act which he would not be empowered to do if he was not acting within his capacity as heir. Succession is deemed to be 'unconditional' when the heir is in possession of the estate property and has not drawn up a *bénéfice d'inventaire* within the prescribed timelimit (three months, which can be extended upon judicial authorization) or has not declared his intention to accept succession upon condition of drawing up a *bénéfice d'inventaire* (forty days from the date that the *inventaire* was established – Article 485 of the Civil Code).

Legacies, on the other hand, are acquired without the need for acceptance, without prejudice to the right of renunciation, and with the legatee having to obtain possession of the legacy from the person charged with its custody (Article 649 of the Civil Code).

(b) The *notary* can be involved at various stages of the succession, but his involvement is not related to the attestation of the devolution of the succession.

The *judicial authorities* (the ordinary court and that of first instance) have jurisdiction in relation to any contentious matter as well as wide jurisdiction and powers of control in particular situations and specific phases of the succession in relation to non-contentious matters.

366

This is notably the case where in the course of the administration of estate property, it is necessary to protect the interests of certain persons (those entitled to inherit who have not yet accepted, those who have yet to be born, creditors and legatees, those taking subordinately, etc.).

The authority with jurisdiction as to territory is that of the location where the estate passes to the heirs, i.e., where the deceased was last domiciled (*see also* Section B1(c)).

The authority with jurisdiction as to subject matter (*la matière*) is established by law on a case by case basis.

10. Invalidity of Will

(a) Testamentary defects which can render the will void or voidable (Article 606 of the Civil Code):

– *Defects rendering the will void:*

  – *Defects as to form:*
    – in the case of a holographic will, the absence of the testator's signature or initials;
    – in the case of a will by way of public instrument, the absence of the testator's declarations written up by the notary, or the absence of the signature of one or other; (it should be remembered that a secret will which does not meet certain requirements may have the effect of an holographic will if it has the features of the latter (Article 607 of the Civil Code));
    – in the case of a special will, the absence of a written statement of the testator's declarations or the absence of the testator's signature or that of the person authorized to receive the will.

– *Other defects:*

It should be remembered that there is no specific set of rules to which reference can be made but only a series of norms which explicitly covers certain cases.

The most important of these will now be set out (*see also* Articles 626, 628, 631, 632, 634 and 647 of the Civil Code):

– Joint or reciprocal wills, that is, wills drawn up by two or more persons in the same instrument in favour of a third person or containing reciprocal dispositions (Article 589 of the Civil Code). Such wills are null and void. According to prevailing legal opinion, these wills would be contrary to the prohibition on agreements on succession as well as the principles as to the applicability of personal law and revocability which characterize the will.
– Testamentary dispositions conditional upon the testator receiving some benefit from the beneficiary's will (the said condition referred to as reciprocity) (Article 635 of the Civil Code). As for conditions of reciprocity, a testamentary disposition made on the condition that the testator in turn benefits from the will of that person is null and void.

– Dispositions in which a trustee is replaced outside of the agreed limits (Article 692 of the Civil Code).

– *Defects rendering the will voidable:*

– *Defects as to form*: This results from all defects in form which do not render the will void, this being the case even with the non-observance of some aspect of notarial law resulting in such a document not conforming to the requirements of a public instrument. Another example relative to holographic wills is where the will is not dated.
– *Other defects*: These would relate to the incapacity of the testator when drawing up the will (*see* 8(a) *above*) or a defect as to the exercise of his own free will (mistake, duress, fraud) (Article 624 of the Civil Code).

In these cases, the will is 'absolutely voidable' in the sense that an action to have the will set aside can be brought by any interested person.

(b) It must be noted first of all that defects as to form will affect the will as a whole, whilst other defects only concern a certain disposition thus giving rise to the partial invalidity of the will.

Invalidity will affect the will differently according to whether it is null and void or voidable.

In the first instance, the will has no effect and the defect can be brought to light at any time by any interested person, or even by the judge, of his own motion.

In the second instance, however, the will is in force up until the time it is deemed voidable. As has already been mentioned, an action to set the will aside can be brought by any interested person; it must be taken within five years following the date upon which the testamentary dispositions were executed (Article 606 of the Civil Code).

Nevertheless, the consequences of the invalidity of a will can in their turn be obviated, within certain limits, by way of *voluntary confirmation and execution* of testamentary dispositions (Article 590 of the Civil Code).

The necessary factors to be examined in particular cases are the knowledge of the cause of nullity and the voluntary nature of the confirmation.

11. Simultaneous Death

(a)–(b) When it is not possible to establish which of the two persons died first, the two are deemed to have died at the same time (Article 4 of the Civil Code).

Therefore neither of the two persons will have succeeded to the other.

12. Estate Taxes

(a) Estate taxes were abolished by Law No. 383 of 18 October 2001, which entered into force on 25 October 2001, and which applies to estates in which the deceased died on or after that date.

A registration tax is, however, payable on the transfer of immovable property forming part of a deceased's estate which is situated in Italy, at the rate of 3 per cent of the value of the immovable property. Pursuant to Law No. 342 of 21 November 2000, this registration tax is reduced to a fixed tax of about Euro 130, in the event that the property consists of non-luxury residential property *and* at least one of the beneficiaries acquires his/her first residential property, with respect to that property.

(b) If the deceased was not resident in Italy at the time of death, the Italian tax law applies only to property situated in Italy.

(c) The only remaining tax, the registration tax referred to in (a) *above*, is payable by all the heirs and/or legatees with respect to that real property, in proportion to the value of their respective inheritances or legacies.

Detailed advice on the application of this tax is recommended, on a case by case basis.

13. Administration of Estates

(a) Before examining the administration of the estate, it is necessary to determine whether the person entitled to inherit has accepted the status of heir and therefore whether he has assumed the status of heir or not.

As a general rule, in effect, the power of administration reverts to the heir. It is true that this power can be subject to certain limitations (when an executor is appointed as will be seen in (g) *below*), or to certain judicial controls (e.g., when the heir accepts the position of heir on condition of a *bénéfice d'inventaire*) but in all cases it is necessary that the person entitled to inherit has accepted the status of heir.

The main problems raised by the administration of the estate occur in the intermediate phase between the moment when the estate notionally passes to the heirs and the actual acquisition of the status of heir by way of the 'acceptance of the status of heir'.

Those persons who, *in the period before the 'heir' acquires that status*, can or must administer the estate, whether by way of statutory requirement, judicial appointment or upon appointment by the testator, will now be detailed:

- *The person entitled to inherit* (Article 460 of the Civil Code): the law gives him a range of powers to allow for the preservation of the estate property. He can take possessory actions *en tutelle* in relation to the estate property, even though he has not yet taken material possession, and he can generally act to protect rights, supervise and administer for a temporary period.
- *Administrator in abeyance* (Articles 528 *et seq.* of the Civil Code): when the person entitled to inherit has not yet accepted the status of heir and is not in possession of the estate property, the court (the judge of first instance in the judicial district in which the succession first took effect) can appoint an hereditary administrator, at the request of interested persons or of its own motion.

International Succession

- *Special administration* (Articles 641 *et seq.* of the Civil Code): there are provisions for certain particular dispositions which have to be made if the heir or the legatee 'accept' upon condition. The same provisions apply if the person entitled to inherit is a child yet to be born who has not yet been conceived at the time the estate passes, that is, a child of a specific person who is living at that time. In contrast, when there is a child yet to be born who has already been conceived, the administration reverts to his parents.
- In the event that a testamentary provision sets up a foundation, its recognition may be authorized by the governmental authority (*Prefetto*) of his own motion, in the event of unjustified delay by the person charged with setting it up.
- *Unconditional heir/s*: In this event, there are no particular administrative problems, in that the heir can freely carry out any act, without any limitation.

If *the creditors or the legatees* are concerned for their interests, they should have recourse to the institution of 'the separation of property' (as governed by Articles 512 *et seq.* of the Civil Code), which allows for the separation of the property (movables and immovables) of the deceased from that of the heir, in order to guarantee the payment of creditors and legatees.

(b) With the exception of the unconditional heir and the person entitled to inherit (whether he is in possession of the estate property or not), all other persons who are involved to any extent in the administration of the estate are obliged to render an account of such administration to the creditors and the legatees, who can ask the judicial authorities to fix a term within which that must be done.

(c) As has already been mentioned, the courts have the power to appoint and also power to control, exercised by the issuing of authorizations necessary for the carrying out of administrative acts or the setting of time limits within which certain activities have to be done.

(d) All those who, in accordance with the conditions and limits mentioned above, have administrative powers over the estate, have at the same time the right to represent the estate before the courts.

(e) With the exception of the case in which an executor is appointed, the heir automatically takes all that which belonged to the deceased, without the necessity of actual delivery from anyone or any judicial authority.
  Certain limits arise as regards the material availability of the property in order to protect the interests of the creditors of the estate and the legatees (notably in the context of the procedure and division arising in connection with the heir accepting upon condition of a *bénéfice d'inventaire*). Even in those situations, however, there is no actual 'delivery' of the estate's assets to the heirs because such property is already in their possession.

(f) *The unconditional heir*: The creditors will be paid as and when they come forward. As has already been noted at (a) *above*, they have the possibility to ask for the separation of the property of the deceased from that of the heir, in order to protect their rights.

The conditional heir (with *bénéfice d'inventaire*): here three systems for the payment of hereditary creditors and legatees are envisaged:

- 'individual liquidation' (Article 496 of the Civil Code): After a certain period of time following the acceptance as heir and the drawing up of the *bénéfice d'inventaire*, provided there is no opposition, the heir can choose to pay the creditors as and when they come forward, without prejudice to their rights as to priority.
- liquidation in relation to creditors taking concurrently (Article 498 of the Civil Code): This will take place provided there is no opposition to it but can also be initiated by the heir of his own motion. This kind of liquidation necessitates the involvement of a notary.
- delivery of property to creditors and legatees (Article 507 of the Civil Code): The heir can deliver all the estate property for the satisfaction of the creditors and legatees, within certain limits and following certain procedures.

The hereditary administrator (*curateur*) *in abeyance*: the administrator can deal with the payment of the estate's debts and the legacies, with the prior authority of the judge of first instance. If, however, there is opposition, he must proceed in accordance with the procedures prescribed for the liquidation in relation to creditors taking concurrently. The obligations of the administrator in abeyance are those which attach also to special administrators nominated when there are testamentary dispositions subject to conditions or terms, and in favour of children which are yet to be born.

(g) The doctrine of seisin (*la saisine*) does not exist in Italy.

Generally the division of property is carried out by the heirs themselves.

Division by the testator: the testator can direct the division. That is, the testator can specify that particular dispositions are to be made in forming the portions. The testator can also direct that the division be carried out according to a valuation drawn up by a disinterested third party, who may even be the executor.

Testamentary executor (Article 703 of the Civil Code): The testator has the right to appoint one or more executors in charge of ensuring that his wishes are followed through, whether in relation to the entire will or part of it.

Persons who cannot be appointed to this role are those who do not have full capacity enabling them to take charge (e.g., a minor, a person who is incapable, a person who is barred); however, an heir or a legatee can be appointed.

Generally the executor also has power of administration over the property of the estate, within the limits set down in the terms of his appointment.

To that end, the executor takes possession of the property and carries out all necessary management. Possession extends over one year which can be prolonged by the courts if deemed necessary.

International Succession

But even if the executor is in possession, he must deliver up to the heir who asks and offers adequate guarantees hereditary property which is not necessary for the exercise of his role.

If he must dispose of property, and more generally, carry out administrative acts of an extraordinary nature, he must first obtain judicial authorization.

In the course of exercising his functions, the executor can be the procedural representative in actions relating to the succession.

Once his functions have come to an end, he has to render an account of his management.

14. Domicile/Nationality

(a) As was seen at 9 *above*, the judicial authorities having jurisdiction in matters relating to succession are those at the location where the estate passes to the heirs, that is, where the deceased was last domiciled (*see also* Section B1(c)).

From this, it follows that the domicile of the deceased at the time of his death is an important determinant in the whole process concerning succession.

As regards the effect of the nationality of the deceased, reference should be made to the information set out in Section B.

(b) The jurisdiction of the courts located where the succession takes place is not dependant upon the deceased having hereditary assets at the said location.

The Italian judicial system does not provide that a judicial authority must act to validate a will or to establish the devolution upon succession as the will takes effect automatically and the devolution upon succession occurs automatically by the simple fact that the estate has passed to the heirs.

On the other hand, the courts have jurisdiction as regards the settlement of disputes on the matter (Article 22 of the Code on Civil Procedure).

The Italian judicial system explicitly provides that whoever is in possession of a holographic will must present it to the notary to have it published, as soon as he is aware of the death of the testator.

The publication itself does not confer validity upon the will but simply constitutes one of the acts necessary to give it an official character in respect of its legal existence (e.g., to allow for certain public procedures to be carried out).

SECTION B – APPLICABLE LAW/PROCEDURE WHERE FOREIGN ELEMENTS ARE INVOLVED

The principal legal source to which reference can be made is *Law No. 218 of 31 May 1995* (reform of the Italian system of private international law), in particular Articles 45 to 49.

Until that Law came into force (1 September 1995), this area was governed by Articles 17 to 31 of the preliminary notes to the Civil Code (in particular Articles 23 to 26) abrogated by the new law.

1. Jurisdiction

(a) In matters regarding succession, Italian jurisdiction applies if (Article 50 of *Law 218/95*):
– the deceased was an Italian citizen at the time of his death;
– the deceased was domiciled in Italy at the time of death;
– the largest share of estate property is located in Italy;
– the defendant is domiciled or resident in Italy or he has accepted Italian jurisdiction, except when the proceedings are in relation to immovables located outside of Italy;
– the proceedings are in relation to property within Italy.

Once the judge has confirmed his jurisdiction, he will assess his authority as to the subject matter.

As mentioned in Section A9, jurisdiction is in relation to territory and subject matter.

As regards the first, reference can be made to (c) *below*, and as to the second, jurisdiction extends not only to non-contentious matters (*see* Section A9) but also to contentious matters in cases provided for by the law (Article 22 of the Code of Civil Procedure); for example, jurisdiction extends to actions to claim a share in an estate or concerning the division of an estate or any other matter at issue between the co-heirs up to and including the division of the estate, etc.

(b) No; as regards general matters, succession is governed by the same laws whatever the nature of the property and the legal relationships with the deceased.

(c) Generally, the judicial authority having jurisdiction on the basis of territory is that where the deceased was last domiciled. If the domicile was abroad, the jurisdiction reverts to the judge at the location at which the largest share of hereditary property in Italy is found, or, failing that, at the location at which the heirs are resident (Article 22 of the Code of Civil Procedure).

2. Applicable Law

Succession upon death is regulated by the national law of the deceased (i.e., that of his citizenship) at the time of his death (Article 46 of *Law 218/95*).

The prevailing criterion therefore is that of nationality.

Where the deceased had several nationalities, the laws of that state with which he had the closest ties are applied. If one of his nationalities was Italian, this will prevail. The criterion of domicile, and in the second instance that of residence, is applied only if the deceased is stateless or a 'refugee' (Article 19 of *Law 218/95*).

If the deceased is subject to a jurisdiction in which rules are expressed in the form of several normative systems based on territorial or personal status, the choice of law to be applied is determined on the basis of criteria used within the foreign jurisdiction, and if this is not possible, the normative system having the closest link to the case in hand (Article 19 of *Law 218/95*).

International Succession

Moreover, it should be noted that in the Italian system of private international law, when reference is made to the law of a foreign country, regard is had to the way in which private international law in that state refers back to the laws of other states, and the conditions upon which that reference is made (doctrine of *renvoi*).

By way of derogation from the objective criteria as to the relationship between the law of the state to be applied and an individual whose estate is to pass examined above, such a person can make his estate subject to the law of the state in which he is resident by explicitly declaring such in testamentary form.

It should be emphasized that in line with the principle of the unity of the law regulating succession, the law chosen by the testator will regulate the entire succession. It is important to note, however, that the choice made will not take effect if, at the time of death, the person having made it no longer resides in that state.

Finally it should be noted that the testator's exercise of choice as to the law to be applied will prevent the doctrine of *renvoi* coming into effect.

3. Foreign Succession/Inheritance Orders

(a)–(c) It should first be mentioned that new Italian law of private international law came into force on 31 December 1996.

This legal reform of private international law provides that all foreign decisions and dispositions will be recognized in Italy without having to have recourse to any other procedure, if certain conditions, such as general adherence to the rules as to jurisdiction, procedural regularity and the upholding of essential rights to defence and public policy, are respected. The procedure is considerably simplified by the new law.

The previous body of law (Articles 796 *et seq.* of the Code of Civil Procedure) continues to be applied to proceedings instituted before 31 December 1996. That earlier law provides that all foreign decisions and dispositions must first, to take effect in Italy, be subject to the procedure of *exequatur* which involves verifying that the requirements of the Italian legal system have been adhered to.

As regards *legal instruments drawn up abroad*, the Italian system (Article 106 No. 4 of the *Notarial Law*) necessitates the deposit of foreign deeds with an Italian notary before they can be relied upon in Italy (say for example, to effect registration in land registers).

The notary will draw up documents relating to the deposit of the instrument, in accordance with those rules pertaining to public instruments (including a translation into Italian) and will ensure in due course that the foreign legal instrument is adapted and integrated (e.g., to ensure that requirements as to publication are met, it may be necessary to include data on title registration upon publication of a will which makes mention of legacies, the objects of which are immovable property).

4. Two or More Succession or Probate Orders

As has already been mentioned, in the Italian legal system, it is not necessary to verify devolution upon succession.

As regards the rest, reference can be made to the information given *above*, with regard had to the fact that it is always the nationality of the deceased that prevails.

5. Assets

The local court can decide upon its jurisdiction even in the absence of hereditary property, if the conditions mentioned in 1(a) *above* apply (Article 50 of *Law 218/ 95*).

6. Expert Evidence

The answer is no, in the sense that in the Italian legal system no such evidence is required.

The notary will check the validity of the form of the will with the criteria provided for by the law of the state which applies; there are no general rules relating to the manner in which knowledge of such law is to be established. In practice, the notary will have recourse to all the means at his disposal, including the knowledge which he may already have of such law, documents provided by the parties and certificates issued by the authorities of the state whose law is to apply.

A Court may appoint an expert to give evidence of foreign law or explain the orders made by a foreign court. The expert must attend Court for the purpose of receiving his appointment and delivering his expertise.

7. Unity of Succession

The answer is yes.

As was mentioned in 1(b) of this Section, in the Italian legal system the fundamental principle is the unity of succession, whether in the sense that all the property and the rights relating to the deceased constitute a single entity passing to the heir or in the sense that, following on from the *above*, a single body of law is applied to the succession, no regard being had to the legal nature of the property and/or rights subject to the inheritance (e.g., movables and immovables), and their location.

8. Formalities

Article 48 of *Law 218/95* on the form of wills provides that a will is considered valid as to form, if it satisfies any one of:

i. the law of the State where it was made;
ii. the law of citizenship of the deceased at the time the will was made or at the time of death;
iii. the law where the deceased was domiciled or resident at the time the will was made or at the time of death.

International Succession

This is in application of the principle in the Italian legal system of preference for the validity of a will. Accordingly, the importance of the *1973 Washington Convention on International Wills* (signed and ratified by Italy) and the use of such 'international will' is only relative.

Italy has not ratified the *1961 Hague Convention on the Conflicts of Laws Relating to the Form of Testamentary Dispositions*.

9. Legislation

No. Italy signed the Convention in 1961 but it has never been ratified by Italy. However, the new rules of private international law are similar to the principles contained in the *1961 Hague Convention*.

10. Wills

(a) As regards the form of wills, the new law concerning private international law is derived from very wide criteria (Article 48 of *Law 218/95*). *See 8 above.*

(b) The law does not specifically provide for this; consideration should be given to the law to be applied to the succession generally.

(c) The rights of those who are entitled to a reserved share in the estate are governed by the law governing the succession. Nevertheless, as regards the inheritance of an Italian national – as such regulated by Italian law – the choice of another law by the testator (*see 2 above*) does not affect the rights that Italian law confers upon those entitled to such a reserved share, if those persons are resident in Italy at the time of the deceased's death.

(d) The capacity to inherit is governed by the law which governs the succession. The law (Article 30 of *Law 218/95*) expressly provides that 'special conditions of capacity, prescribed by the law regulating a relationship, is governed by the same law.'

(e) The capacity to make, modify or revoke a will is governed by the law of the testator's nationality at the time of drawing up, modifying or revoking his will (Article 47 of *Law 218/95*).

(f) *See 10(c) above.*

(g) The Italian system allows for a third party to determine who will be a legatee, within certain limits.

Nevertheless, testamentary dispositions that rely upon the complete discretion of a third party for the designation of the heir or the legatee, or for the determination of the hereditary shares or the object or amount of the legacy, are null and void.

(h) Issues relating to the modification, revocation and the revival of a will have already been generally examined in Section A2.

Italian private international law does not make provision for particular rules in this area, with an exception made in relation to the testator's capacity to modify or revoke his will (*see* (e) *above* on this point).

Therefore the law that governs the succession will also govern these matters, subject to the exception mentioned above.

(i) With the exception of that examined in 10(c), as regards the choice of law the testator can apply, the norms that underpin the rights of a person entitled to a compulsory share do not differentiate as between residents and non-residents, nor as between movables and immovables.

11. Domicile/Nationality

(a) This question has been answered as and when the various different cases were being examined.

Reference should be made therefore to the preceding paragraphs.

(b) The answer is no.

(c) On this matter, reference can be made to 2 *above*.

12. Taxation

Estate taxes were abolished in Italy pursuant to *Law No. 383 of 18 October 2001*. *See* Section A12 *above*.

Japan

Prepared by: Yusuke KOMATSU
Attorney at law of Tomotsune & Kimura

Address: Sanno Grand Building
          14-2, Nagatacho 2-Chome,
          Chiyoda-Ku
          Tokyo 100-0014, Japan
Tel.:   81 3 3580 0800
Fax: 81 3 3593 3336
E-mail: y_komatau@tkm.gr.jp

SECTION A – BRIEF SURVEY OF THE LOCAL SYSTEM

1. Type of System

(a) Civil law.

(b) Civil Code of Japan.
Japan is a single country and does not have any federal system.

2. Wills

(a) All wills must be made by means of a holographic, a notarial or a secret document except for special forms (Article 967). The civil code recognizes the following forms of wills:

i. Ordinary Forms
- Holographic will (Article 968). The whole text of this will must be completely handwritten by the testator and must be signed and sealed by him together with the date and his full name. The written text may be held by the testator or any third party;
- Will by notarial deed (Article 969). This is a notarial deed notarized by a notary public containing the final intentions of the testator, signed and sealed by him in the presence of two witnesses;
- The closed or secret will (Article 970). The testator must affix his signature and seal to the document which contains his will and produce the sealed document to a notary. The notary makes a deed of superscription in which he declares that such document was delivered into his custody and that it contains the last will of

the testator. This deed of superscription has to be signed and sealed by the testator, the notary and two or more witnesses.

ii. Special Forms
– Death bed will (Article 976). A person who is in imminent danger of death may make a will in the presence of three or more witnesses by orally declaring its tenor to one of them. The person to whom the oral declaration is made must write it down and read it to the testator and the other witnesses and each witness must, after having acknowledged the writing to be correct, affix the signature and seal thereto. This will is not valid unless within twenty days from the date of will the family court confirms it;
– Will of a person isolated on account of contagious disease (Article 977). A person who is isolated by administrative measures on account of contagious decease may make a written will in the presence of a police officer and one or more witnesses;
– Will of a person on board a ship (Article 978). A person on board a ship may make a written will in the presence of the captain or one of the clerical staff of the ship and at least two witnesses.

These wills of special forms become invalid if the testator survives for six months from the time of becoming able to make a will in compliance with ordinary forms.

(b) *i.* The aforementioned wills may be amended in accordance with the applicable rules. Any insertion, deletion or other alteration in a holographic will is ineffective unless the testator indicates the place thereof, makes an additional entry to the effect that an alteration has been made, specially adds his signature to such entry and also affixes his seal to the place of alternation. A last will can be revoked explicitly or implicitly. An explicit revocation must be done in the form which is required for the will itself or by a special notarial deed. A will can be revoked implicitly by the making of a later will which contains different intentions of the testator from the earlier will.
   ii. Marriage does not automatically revoke or affect the validity of a will made before marriage, provided, however, that the spouse of the testator may claim for his or her legally secured portion (compulsory share) of the legacy.
   iii. For the revival of revoked will the testator must make a new will.

3. Intestacy

(a) There are three classes of successors (heirs) who succeed to all the rights and obligations pertaining to the properties of the deceased as from the time of commencement of the succession (death) in accordance with the order mentioned below. Each former class excludes the latter:

   i. spouse and children;
   ii. spouse and lineal ascendants;
   iii. spouse, brothers and sisters.

International Succession

A child *en ventre sa mere* is deemed to have been already born in respect of succession (Article 886). If a child had died before the commencement of the succession or lost the right of succession due to the incapacity for succession or due to the disinheritance, his children become successors by virtue of succession by representation; provided that this does not apply to those who are not lineal descendents of the deceased (Article 887).

Article 900 provides for the statutory shares of the successors as follows:

(1) in case the spouse and children are successors, the statutory share of the spouse and that of the children are receptively one-half of the legacy;
(2) in case the spouse and lineal ascendants are successors, the statutory share of the spouse is two-thirds, and that of the lineal ascendants is one-third;
(3) in case the spouse and brothers and sisters are successors, the statutory share of the spouse is three-fourths and that of the latter is one-fourth;
(4) in case there are two or more children, or lineal descendants, or brothers and sisters, their respective statutory shares are equal to each other. The statutory share of an illegitimate child is one–half of the statutory share of a legitimate child. An adulterine child is deemed to be a legitimate child of a couple unless and until a family court denies the legitimacy of the child based on a petition filed by the husband.

(b) There is no difference in the division of the estate between movables and immovables.

(c) *i.* Japanese law prohibits mutual wills and contracts on a future succession. However, an exception is made for spouses who are permitted to make dispositions *mortis causa* in favour of each other in a marriage contract.
   ii. A testator may make a disposition of the whole or a part of the property under either a universal or special title; provided, however, that provisions relating to legally secured portions (compulsory shares) should not be contravened (Article 964).

4. Freedom of Testation

(a) There are compulsory shares for the successors other than brothers and sisters (Article 1028). Any successors other than brothers and sisters are entitled to receive, as their legally secured portions, the following sum:
i. In cases all of the successors are lineal ascendants, one-third of the legacy;
ii. In all other cases, one-half of the legacy.

A legally secured portion is calculated on the basis of adding to the value of the legacy at the time of succession the value of any property which had been made gifts within one year prior to the commencement of the succession and deducting there from the total amount of the obligation of the deceased (Article 1029).

5. Maintenance

No maintenance can be claimed from the estate or the successors by husband, wife, minor children, parents or others.

6. Community Property between Husband and Wife

(a)–(b) The Japanese law recognizes matrimonial community property system. According to this regime all the assets of a husband and wife in their possession either at the time of marriage or acquired during their marriage are deemed to be common property except for the assets acquired by one of the spouses before their marriage and the assets acquired under his or her name during the marriage (Article 762). It is very common in Japan that a substantial amount of the betrothal money is given by a bridegroom to a bride before the marriage and the bride must spend the betrothal money for purchasing household furniture and utensils and bring them to their home when the couple starts their marriage life. Those assets are deemed to be acquired at the time of marriage and to be common property of the couple. Both spouses are entitled to all community assets, except for some personal assets which remain private. When the community property is dissolved by the death of one of the spouses, the surviving spouse is entitled to half of the community property. The other half constitutes the estate, to which the surviving spouse may also be (partly) entitled as a successor.

7. Gifts (*Inter Vivos*)

(a) The value of the gifts to successors made within one year prior to the commencement of the succession is set off against their share of the inheritance (Articles 1030 and 1031). This rule also applies to the gifts made before one year if the donor and the donee acted with knowledge that a loss would thereby be caused to the person entitled to a legally secured portion.

(b) A person entitled to a legally secured portion or his successors may demand an abatement of testamentary gifts and of gifts *inter vivos* to the extent necessary for the protection of the legally secured portion.

8. Capacity

(a) A person aged fifteen years or older of sound mind may make a will (Articles 962 and 963).

(b) The following persons may not act as witnesses: minors, persons judged incompetent or quasi-incompetent, presumptive successors, testamentary donees and their spouses and lineal relatives by blood, the spouses of the notary who executes the last will, the relatives thereof and servants thereof (Article 974). They must understand the language used for the will.

(c) In order to inherit a beneficiary must exist at the moment of the death of the deceased. In this respect an unborn child of the deceased is considered to exist (Article 886). Corporations and charitable bodies are entitled to be beneficiaries.

9. Authority (Court, Notarial or Other)

According to the Japanese law, on the death of the deceased the assets and liabilities of the deceased pass directly to the successors (Article 896). Such successors are entitled to the estate simply because they are called to the estate by law or by the last will of the testator. The successors may, however, accept the estate beneficiary, which is an acceptance without liability for debts beyond the assets inherited, or they may renounce the entire estate (Articles 922 and 938). An estate to which minors are entitled as successors has always to be accepted as an estate beneficiary.

A declaration that a successor renounces the estate has to be filed with the family court of the district where the deceased had his last domicile (Article 938). On the death of the deceased, the custodian of a testamentary document must present it to the family court having the jurisdiction over the matter without delay and apply for probate thereof (Article 1004). This probate procedure does not apply to a will made by means of a notarial deed and the legacy is divided and succeeded by successors themselves in accordance with the terms of the will if an executor is not appointed. A testamentary document closed up with a seal may not be opened except in the family court and in the presence of the successors or their representatives.

10. Invalidity of Will

(a) A will made by a minor younger than fifteen years or a mentally disturbed person is invalid. According to Article 891, a disposition of the assets of the deceased in a will to the following persons is voidable:

(1) any person who has been sentenced to punishment for having intentionally caused or attempted to cause the death of the person to be succeeded to, or of any person who has a prior or the same rank with respect to the succession;
(2) any person who, knowing that the person to be succeeded to was killed by homicide, has omitted to give information or to bring a formal charge; excepting, however, cases where such a person has no capacity to discern right and wrong, or when the guilty party is the spouse or a lineal relative by blood of such person;
(3) any person who has, by fraud or duress, prevented the person to be succeeded to from making, revoking or altering a will relating to the succession;
(4) any person who has, by fraud or duress, induced the person to be succeeded to make, revoke or alter a will relating to the succession; and
(5) any person who has forged, altered, destroyed or concealed a will of the person to be succeeded to relating to the succession.

Finally, wills which do not comply with the form requirements for wills mentioned *above* under paragraph 2(a) are void.

11. Simultaneous Death

(a) The persons who died at the same time or on the same day, without it being possible to make sure who died first, are deemed to have died at the same moment. As a consequence they cannot inherit from each other.

(b) The dates of death are determined by the certificates issued by the Family Register based on the registered record of the Family Registration.

12. Estate Taxes

(a) *The Inheritance Tax Law of 1950* provides for inheritance taxes in respect of an estate.

(b) A resident in Japan is liable to pay the inheritance tax on all assets worldwidely acquired while a non-resident in Japan is liable to pay the inheritance tax only on assets situated in Japan.

(c) The aforementioned taxes are in general levied from the successors.

(d) Inheritance tax rates are as follows:

Taxable Amount for Each Heir	Tax Liability
not over	
¥8,000,000	10% of taxable amount
¥16,000,000	15% of taxable amount minus ¥400,000
¥30,000,000	20% of taxable amount minus ¥1,200,000
¥50,000,000	25% of taxable amount minus ¥2,700,000
¥100,000,000	30% of taxable amount minus ¥5,200,000
¥200,000,000	40% of taxable amount minus ¥15,200,000
¥400,000,000	50% of taxable amount minus ¥35,200,000
¥2,000,000,000	60% of taxable amount minus ¥75,200,000
over	
¥2,000,000,000	70% of taxable amount minus ¥275,200,000

The inheritance tax is imposed on the total value of all properties acquired through inheritance or bequest, less liabilities and funeral expenses. Properties are based on current prices or values at the time of acquisition.

13. Administration of Estates

(a) In the event of intestacy the successors jointly administer the estate (Articles 896 and 898). A testator may designate one or more executors by will or commission a third person to designate the same (Article 1006). However, it is not necessary to appoint an executor. An executor who has consented to assume office must without delay prepare an inventory of the legacies and deliver it to the successors (Article 1011). He has the right and duty to manage and administer the legacy and to perform all acts necessary for executing the will into effect (Article 1012) and the successors may not in any way dispose of the legacies or do any act which would obstruct the execution and carrying of the will into effect by the executor (Article 1013). The executor is deemed to be the representative of the successors (Article 1014).

Furthermore, the executor has to assist the successors with the division of the legacies and has the right to determine the division of the legacies if the successors can not reach any agreement to the division. Since the inheritance tax return must be filed with the competent tax authorities within ten months from the date of inheritance (the date of death) and the inheritance tax must be paid at the time of filing. Accordingly the heirs are compelled to reach an agreement as to the division if no executor is appointed in a will. Otherwise the heirs must pay a high overdue interest.

(b) If there is an executor his tasks are to draw up an inventory of the estate and deliver it to the successors and distribute the legacies to successors in accordance with the intentions of the deceased indicated in the will.

(c) No external supervision is needed, unless there are successors who are incapable of disposing of their property (e.g., minors, person under tutelage). In the latter case a guardian must be appointed for each incapable successor by the Family Court.

(d) Any successor and a court appointed guardian for an incapable successor has the right to query and object to the execution of a will by the executor. If any executor neglects his duties or if there exists any other reasonable cause, any person interested in the execution of the will may apply to the Family Court for the removal of the executor (Article 1019).

(e) The successors are entitled to the assets of the estate as of the moment of death of the deceased. After the partition each of them is solely entitled to the assets which were apportioned to him. The transfer upon partition has to take place in accordance with the general rules of transfer of property, which entails in general, movable goods by handing over, immovable goods by registration with the Registry of Immovable Properties.

(f) The creditors are usually paid by the successors or the executor (if such power was granted to him in will) before the partition. However, a claim of a creditor may also be apportioned to one of the successors, who in that case is obliged to pay the claim.

(g) As explained the successors always distribute the estate themselves in accordance with their legal shares. The successors may, at any time, effect the partition of the estate by their agreement except for the case where partition of the estates is forbidden by the will.

14. Domicile/Nationality

(a) Nationality and habitual residence are only relevant in respect of the applicable law (*see* Section B).

(b) The family court grants an order of probate if the deceased was domiciled and/ or executed a will in Japan but had no assets in Japan.

SECTION B – APPLICABLE LAW/PROCEDURE WHERE FOREIGN ELEMENT/S ARE INVOLVED

1. Jurisdiction

(a) Article 883 of the Civil Code provides that succession commences at the permanent resident (domicile) of the deceased. The family court of the district in which the deceased had the permanent residence has jurisdiction over claims between successors, claims of creditors on the estate, or other legal claims concerning the last will of the deceased. When the deceased was domiciled outside Japan a Japanese court has jurisdiction when movable and/or immovable asset(s) of the estate is (are) located in Japan or when the defendant has his residence there.

(b) There are not any different rules for movable and immovable assets.

(c) The family court of the district where the deceased had a permanent address or where the assets are located has jurisdiction.

2. Applicable Law

The Law on the Choice of Laws (Horei) of 1898 as amended applies to the succession and the will.

Article 26 of this Law provides that the succession shall be governed by the law of the home country (nationality) of the deceased. Article 27 of the Law provides that the formation and effect of a will shall be governed by the law of the home country of the testator at the time of its formation and the revocation of a will shall be governed by the law of the home country of the testator current at the time of its revocation.

In case the deceased or testator had two or more nationalities, the law of the country in which he had the place of permanent residence (domicile) among those countries, or if such country does not exist, the law of the country to which he was most closely related, applies, provided that, one of those nationalities is Japanese, the Japanese law applies (Article 28).

International Succession

If the deceased or testator has the nationality of a country whose various districts are subject to different laws, the law specified by the rule of the country, or if such rule does not exist, the law of the district to which he was most closely related, is the law to apply (Article 28).

Although Japan is not a party to the *1989 Hague Convention on the Law Applicable to Succession*, Japan ratified the *Hague Convention on the Conflicts of Laws Relating to the Form of Testamentary Dispositions* and promulgated the *Law on the Choice of Laws Applicable to the Form of Will in 1964*. Under Article 2 of this Law, a will is valid if its form conforms to any of the following laws:

– the law of the place where the will was made (*lex loci actus*);
– the law of the country of which the testator is a national at the time of formation of the will or at the time of death;
– the law of the place in which the testator had the permanent residence or domicile at the time of formation of the will or at the time of death;
– as regards the will concerning immovables, the law of the place where the immovables exist (*lex situs*).

Article 2 also applies to the form of a will effected by two or more persons in one and the same document (Article 4) although Article 975 of the Civil Code of Japan prohibits such a will made by two or more persons by one and the same document. Article 5 of the Law provides that the restrictions to the form of will by personal qualifications, such as age or nationality shall be deemed to belong to the scope of form and that the same shall apply to the qualifications of the witnesses who are necessary for making the will effective and valid.

3. Foreign Succession/Inheritance Orders

(a) Foreign court orders are not directly enforceable in Japan. A local execution order must be obtained for execution of a foreign court order in respect of local movable and immovable assets (Article 24 of *Civil Execution Law*).

(b) A local execution order must be obtained to give effect to a foreign court order as regards property registration office, bank or any other person in possession of the assets of the deceased. The local execution order is obtained for a foreign court order by filing a petition for the execution order with a court having jurisdiction over the defendant or the assets to be executed.

(c) The foreign successor or executor must file a certified court order with a local court which authorized him to collect or own Japanese assets of the estate.

4. Two or More Succession or Probate Orders

Foreign probate orders given prior to the application before a local court for an order of succession are not taken into account. The Japanese court will always apply its own rules of private international law.

5. Assets

The local court can assume jurisdiction in the absence of assets. *See supra* Section B2.

6. Expert Evidence

(a) The local court has sole discretion to require a foreign lawyer to explain and give evidence regarding the applicable foreign law, but there is no necessity.

(b) Proof of foreign law may be given by way of an affidavit. An appearance in court is not necessary.

7. Unity of Succession

In principle, unity of succession is accepted in Japan. The applicable law governs the whole of the estate wherever the assets are located.

8. Formalities

A will executed in a foreign country must be produced to the family court for probate thereof and for the commencement of succession in Japan.

9. Legislation

The *Hague Convention on the Conflicts of Laws Relating to the Form of Testamentary Dispositions* is applicable. *See supra* Section B2.

10. Wills

(a) In Japan, the applicable law for the execution of wills is determined by the rules as explained in Section B2.

(b) The applicable law for construction and interpretation is determined by the conflict of law rules as discussed in Section B2.

(c) The applicable law for rights of successors is determined by the conflict of law rules as discussed in Section B2.

(d) The applicable law for the capacity to inherit is also determined by the conflict of law rules as explained in Section B2.

International Succession

(e) The applicable law for the capacity to make a will is also determined by the conflict of law rules as discussed in Section B2.

(f)–(i) The applicable law is determined by the conflict of law rules as explained in Section B2.

11. Domicile/Nationality

(a) *See supra* Section B2.

(b) The domicile of the beneficiaries is not relevant.

(c) *See supra* Section B2.

12. Taxation

See supra Section A12.

Jersey

Prepared by: Tony FULTON
Probate Manager
Carey Olsen

Address: 47 Esplanade,
St. Helier,
Jersey JE1 0BD
Tel.: +44 (0) 1534 822280 (Direct Dial)
+44 (0) 1534 888900 (Switchboard)
Fax: +44 (0) 1534 887744
Intenet: www.careyolsen.com

SECTION A – BRIEF SURVEY OF THE LOCAL SYSTEM

1. Type of System

(a) Jersey has a mixed legal system of customary law and common law. Jersey derives its succession law from Norman French customary law, i.e., neither civil law nor common law, although the Royal Court of Jersey has in recent years also been influenced by many English common law authorities. There is a dichotomy between movable estate and immovable estate in that movables need to be administered by executors or administrators whereas immovables vest directly in the heirs as at the date of death. Jersey law therefore distinguishes between matters of administration and matters of succession for movables, but not for immovables. Statute law is of increasing importance, particularly *The Wills and Successions (Jersey) Law 1993* and *The Probate (Jersey) Law 1998*, both of which are influenced by common law concepts.

(b) Jersey is not a part of the United Kingdom and is an independent jurisdiction, both for succession purposes and for tax purposes. It is one of the Channel Islands, but Guernsey and the other islands have their own distinct systems of law.

2. Wills

(a) Formal validity as to movables is normally governed by the law of the testator's domicile. So far as Jersey domiciliaries are concerned, the Royal Commissioner's

389

International Succession

Report of 1860 states that a will of movables has to be signed by the testator and where it is holograph, it requires no witnesses, but otherwise there have to be two witnesses to attest its execution; however, it is not necessary (as it is in England) that they should, in presence and in the presence of each other, attest his signature.

Wills may only be made by persons of full age except that (since 1993) married minors may make a valid will. Wills of movables should be in writing, dated or capable of being dated, signed and properly attested. They should normally be dated but this is not an essential requirement if the dating can be established by extrinsic evidence. It is generally accepted (but not without doubt) that witnesses of movables wills should be of full age. The age of majority was lowered from twenty to eighteen by *The Age of Majority (Jersey) Law 1999* which came into force on 1 November 1999. The will should not be witnessed by a beneficiary or by a relative of the testator or beneficiary to the degree of first cousin by blood or marriage. An executor may act as a witness, but care should be taken not to include a gift or a charging clause in favour of a witness which would certainly invalidate the benefit and may well invalidate the whole will, although possibly a holograph will may stand unaffected even if witnessed as there is no requirement for witnesses. Holograph wills of movables are valid without witnesses if they are wholly written by (or can be proved to have been typed by) the testator and signed by him. Two affidavits of handwriting are usually required to establish authenticity as to handwriting. A signed suicide note has been held to be a valid holograph will. The concept of *donationes mortis causa* is accepted but that of a *nuncupative* or verbal will is not.

Wills of Jersey immovables have special requirements and are governed by the *Loi (1851) Sur les Testaments d'Immeubles* (as amended). They have to be read out loud to the testator (unless they are holograph) and a declaration to this effect is included in the attestation clause. One of the witnesses must be a member of the States of Jersey, one of the Law Officers of the Crown or an advocate or solicitor or, if the will is executed outside the Island, the official witness must be a notary public. Mixed wills of Jersey immovables and other estate have to comply with the more onerous essential validity requirements of wills of immovables and therefore it is usual to make a completely separate will for the Jersey immovables. The will should not be witnessed by a beneficiary or a relative of the testator or beneficiary by blood or marriage to the degree of first cousin. The testator must sign or acknowledge his signature in the presence of two witnesses. The witnesses must sign in the presence of each other and of the testator.

Wills concerning non-Jersey immovables are governed by the rules of the *lex situs*.

(b) *i.* Wills can be amended by codicil or the making of a new will at any time. The amendments will be valid if executed in accordance with the *above* rules in relation to movable or immovable estates as appropriate. Any alterations must be made at the time of signature and should be initialled by the testator and both witnesses.

A will may be revoked in full or *pro tanto* by a new will or codicil, inconsistent with the former and this can extend to a document which purports to be a new will or codicil but which is not in itself valid if the intention is clearly found to be there; by wilful destruction; by writing 'cancelled' across the will and initialling it; or by giving instructions to the testator's lawyer to revoke it.

A divorce, a decree of judicial separation or abandoning the deceased spouse without just cause has the effect of revoking the appointment of the surviving spouse as executor or executrix and revokes any legacy, bequest, devise or share of residue given to the divorced spouse.

ii. Marriage does not revoke a will under Jersey law.

iii. A revoked will may be revived by codicil.

3. Intestacy

(a) The succession of movables and immovables where the deceased is survived by a spouse and/or issue is set out in *The Wills and Successions (Jersey) Law 1993*. Otherwise, the heirs at law are ascertained by customary law and they inherit, if more than one, as tenants in common. If there are no heirs, within the degrees permitted by customary law, the estate passes to the Crown.

The devolution differs between immovables and movables in accordance with the details set out in the chart below. References to 'heirs at law' are explained further below. For immovables, no act or document is required to vest the estate in the beneficiaries as this follows automatically on death of an intestate person. For movables, a Grant of Administration is required, placing the legal title of the estate in an administrator on the death of an intestate person.

An illegitimate child (including an adulterine child) is treated like a legitimate child in relation to an inheritance from his or her mother's estate but cannot 'represent' his or her deceased mother to claim from a grandparent's estate, or inherit from a collateral estate at all. A mother may inherit from her illegitimate child but cannot 'represent' such deceased child to inherit from a grandchild. Illegitimacy confers no inheritance rights on a child to its father's estate or vice versa or to collateral estates or by '*représentation*' – *(Illegitimacy (Jersey) Law 1973)*.

As regards household effects, life interests, adoption and foreigners, *see* further *below*.

Table 1. Intestacy of Immovables

Unmarried person or widow/widower – no children.	Heirs at law as tenants in common in equal shares (or half share if half sibling). No preference for paternal or maternal line. *Représentation* to any degree for descendants of deceased sibling, uncle or aunt.
Married man – widow and children.	Widow has usufruct (i.e., life interest) of matrimonial home unless judicially separated or deserted. No dower. Children and widow share all equally as tenants in common.
Married man – widow but no children.	Widow has all immovables.
Married man – children but no widow.	Children have all immovables sharing equally as tenants in common.
Married woman – widower and children.	Widower has usufruct of matrimonial home unless judicially separated or deserted. No *viduité*.
Married woman – widower but no children.	Children and widower share all equally as tenants in common.
Married woman – children but no widower.	Widower has all immovables. Children have all immovables.

Table 2. Intestacy of Movables

Unmarried person or widow/widower – no children.	Heirs at law in equal shares, i.e., brothers and sisters failing whom their issue failing whom father failing whom mother failing whom uncles and aunts etc., failing whom grandfather etc.
Married man – widow and children.	Widow: household effects (as defined); £30,000; half residue. Children: half residue.
Married man – widow but no children.	All to widow who is entitled to administer the estate.
Married man – children but no widow.	All to children.
Married woman – widower and children.	Widower: household effects (as defined); £30,000; half residue. Children: half residue.
Married woman – widower but no children.	All to widower who is entitled to administer the estate.
Married woman – children but no widower.	All to children.

'Heirs at Law' are the following persons in descending order of priority (i.e., if a member exists in a former class he will inherit to the exclusion of the later classes, *but see below re propres*):

(1) children with eldest son as principal heir or if no sons eldest daughter as principal heir;
(2) grandchildren;
(3) great-grandchildren, etc.;
(4) brothers and sisters with eldest brother as principal heir, etc. or (if prede- ceased) their issue, i.e., nephews and nieces of any siblings who predeceased 'representing' (i.e., standing in the shoes of their parent);
(5) father;
(6) mother;
(7) uncles and aunts with their issue, i.e., (first cousins, etc.) representing them if any predeceased;
(8) grandparents;
(9) great uncles and aunts, etc., or (if pre-deceased) their issue, i.e., second cousins;
(10) great-grandparents, etc.

Interpretation:

(1) Ascendants are always excluded by their descendants when the ascendant is the common ancestor of the intestate and the person who excludes him.
(2) If any person in any of the above categories predeceased the intestate their share is taken by their issue *per stirpes*, e.g., if there were no issue and parents pre-deceased and brothers and sisters predeceased without issue and uncles and aunts predeceased leaving issue, then cousins would inherit by *représentation*, a legal fiction which places a claimant to a succession in the place of a de- ceased ancestor of his through whom he claims.
(3) If there are brothers and sisters of the whole blood and also brothers and sisters of the half blood all of them share in the inheritance or in the *représentation* with half blood siblings taking a single share and whole blood siblings taking a double share.
(4) *Propres paternels* (immovables inherited from the paternal side) inherited by closest relatives on the father's side and *propres maternels* (immovables inherited from the maternal side) inherited by the closest relatives on the mother's side. *Représentation* is permitted to the seventh degree but calculated differently for propres. Division is *per stirpes*.

Household effects include articles of household or personal use or ornament nor- mally situate in or around the matrimonial home. The definition excludes articles used wholly or principally for business purposes, money or security for money, motor vehicles and single articles or sets of articles worth over £10,000.

Divorce or a decree of judicial separation or desertion without cause cancels the right to life enjoyment of the matrimonial home or the inheritance of any movable or immovable estate on intestacy.

Adopted children have the same rights as natural legitimate children under the provisions of *The Adoption (Jersey) Law 1961*. Under customary law 'aliens' were incapable of inheriting on intestacy. Since 1973 EEC nationals were able to inherit and *The Wills and Successions (Jersey) Law 1993* provided that the estate, whether movable or immovable, shall devolve without regard to the nationality of the person so dying or any beneficiary or any person through whom a beneficiary claims by *représentation*.

(b) For the difference in the division of the estate between movables and immovables *see* the tables *above*.

4. Freedom of Testation

(a) As regards immovables: subject to *dower* and *viduité* rights, there is complete freedom of testamentary disposition of immovables with the exception that gifts to a trust and *substitutional* gifts (whereby the testator leaves property to one person through the intermediary of another) are prohibited. Life enjoyment (the *usufruit*) of a property can be given over property of which the bare ownership (the *nue propriété*) is given to other beneficiaries. There is no claim to *légitime* for immovables. A widow is entitled to claim her *dower*, i.e., life enjoyment of one-third of her husband's immovables, and a widower is entitled to his *viduité*, i.e., life enjoyment of all of his wife's immovables. The widow is entitled to dower even if there is no issue of the marriage as long as she had not deserted the husband without cause. Dower has to be claimed and it is not lost on re-marriage. Viduité only applies if a child was born of the marriage and is lost if the husband remarries. It is an automatic right which does not have to be claimed.

As regards movables, *légitime* can be claimed against movables only by the surviving spouse and/or issue as shown in the following chart.

Table 3. Légitime

Unmarried persons.	No restriction on powers of disposition.
Married man – wife and children.	Widow can claim the household effects and one-third as *légitime*. Children can claim one-third *légitime*.
Married man – wife but no children.	Widow can claim the household effects and two-thirds as *légitime*.
Widower – children only.	Children can claim two-thirds as *légitime*.
Married woman – husband and children.	Widower can claim the household effects and one-third as *légitime*. Children can claim one-third as *légitime*.
Married woman – husband but no children.	Widower can claim the household effects and two-thirds as *légitime*.
Widow – children only.	Children can claim two-thirds as *légitime*.
Widow or widower – no children.	No restriction on powers of disposition.

N.B. Issue may represent deceased children and claim *légitime* in their place.

A will of movables which ignores *légitime* rights will stand unaffected by them if these are not claimed within a period of a year and a day from the day from the date of the issue of the grant of probate. Therefore, Jersey does not have full 'forced heirship' since the heirs are not forced to claim their *légitime* and if they fail to do so the estate is distributed according to the terms of the will.

The right of action to claim *légitime* belongs to any of the children (or if dead, their issue) or the surviving spouse. If a child or a spouse has been appointed as an executor he or she is not able to claim because an executor swears an oath to uphold the terms of the will. The heir or spouse making the claim cannot benefit from the terms of the will although children or the spouse not making the claim may do so. Once the claim is made the will is 'reduced,' i.e., it takes effect over what remains after *légitime* of two-thirds is deducted. The claimant is treated as if he or she died immediately after the testator and his or her share under the reduced will goes under any default provisions. This can give rise to a resulting partial intestacy and if so the claimant is not prevented from taking his share thereof. Jersey lawyers have long debated the question as to whether a testator's *inter vivos* gifts to a trust may be subject to a *légitime* claim on the basis that the gift to the trust was a fraud against the *légitime*. This question has not yet been resolved.

(b) It is a well-established principle that gifts of movables made by persons to their descendants are deemed to be advances of inheritance (*avance de succession*). The heir who has received an advance can be required to elect either to bring the value of the advance into the estate (*rapport à la masse*) or to keep it but not participate in the distribution of the estate (*rester sur les avances*). The value is taken as that at the time of the advance. This principle has been extended to apply to husband and wife joint bank accounts where the deceased spouse's contribution to the account has been held to accrue by gift to the surviving spouse which is voidable at the suit of his issue. This principle may in future be applied to gifts to trusts but has not yet. The concept of *promissory estoppel* relating to promises of inheritances was recognized under Jersey law in a case which came before the court in 1985. Contracts have in the past been made in relation to immovables whereby a child or wife has established the exact property which he will inherit or over which she will have dower and these will be binding. The concept of partage no longer applies. There is no concept of successor or family settlements except in relation to contracts to regulate dower.

5. Maintenance

Apart from *légitime* rights and survivorship to joint assets, there is no mechanism for maintenance to be claimable by anyone. Common law partners have no specific entitlement although any jointly owned property will pass to them by survivorship.

6. Community Property Between Husband and Wife

(a) Jersey law has no concept of community of property.

(b) Household and personal effects in the matrimonial home are normally regarded as jointly owned and passing to the surviving spouse by survivorship unless there is evidence to the contrary, in which case the definition of household effects contained in the *Wills and Succession (Jersey) Law 1993* is applied for succession purposes. If assets are held jointly but as *tenants in common*, the deceased's share forms part of his free estate rather than passing to the joint owner.

7. Gifts (*Inter Vivos*)

(a) *See above* paragraph 4(b) for the effect of *avances de succession*.

(b) The extent of the limit of the off-set of any avances is that of the presumptive share of the total estate. Above that limit, the heir may elect to keep his avance and not to participate at all in the free estate.

8. Capacity

(a) As to age *see* paragraph 2(a) *above*. An *interdict*, being a person found not to be mentally capable under the provisions of *The Mental Health (Jersey) Law 1969*, may still be capable of making a valid will. The Royal Court of Jersey has tended to follow English precedent in deciding that mental capacity depends on the three certainties of intention, subject and object. The *interdict* is deemed to have sufficient mental capacity if he is judged to have the intention of the testamentary act and the understanding of the nature of their assets and the identification of those whom he may reasonably be expected to make provision for. Persons suffering from delusion or insanity may make a valid will during a lucid period. Curators are appointed to manage the affairs of *interdicts* but Jersey has no concept of 'statutory wills' since the testator has to make the will himself and it cannot be done by another on his behalf.

(b) *See* paragraph 1(a) *above*.

(c) A gift to a minor is held by a court-appointed *tuteur* until he is of age. However, a gift of movables can instead be retained by the personal representatives until he is able to give a valid receipt. Alternatively, the will may give a direction to pay the parent or guardian, who can then give the executor a valid discharge. As regards immovables, it is considered that the beneficiaries must be alive at the testator's death. As regards movables, absolutely entitled beneficiaries must be alive then but a gift may be made in trust for unborn beneficiaries so long as it lasts no more than one hundred years. In each case unborn children (*en ventre sa mère*) qualify as persons in being as at the date of death of the testator. If the beneficiary predeceases, the gift fails unless there are substitutional provisions. Gifts to charities are preserved from failure owing to uncertainty by the operation of the *cy près* doctrine. Gifts to corporate entities are valid. Gifts in wills of Jersey immovable estate to associations fail unless the beneficiary is an incorporated association or qualifies as another type of corporate entity.

9. Authority (Court, Notarial or Other)

Article 19 of *The Probate (Jersey) Law 1998* requires that a Jersey Grant of Probate or Administration be obtained to establish the right to recover or receive any part of the movable estate situate in the Island of any deceased person. Applications are made by personal appearance only at the office of the Judicial Greffe which performs the functions of the Probate Division of the Royal Court of Jersey (the 'Greffe'). If personal application cannot be made, e.g., because of ill health or living abroad, an attorney needs to be appointed under a formal power of attorney to make the personal application for the grant. The personal representative must produce the original will and any codicils thereto (if any), together with a copy of the death certificate and stamps in payment of the probate stamp fees. The personal representative swears which band of value the estate falls into but is not required to provide an inventory or valuation of the assets and liabilities. Anyone wishing to prevent or oppose the issue of a grant may do so by lodging a caveat with the Greffe. The usual reason for lodging a caveat is if it is thought that someone might try to have an invalid will admitted to probate.

Jersey immovable estate passes automatically to the heirs without there being an executor or administrator or a Grant of Probate or Administration. It is therefore not possible to have movables bequests or legacies given out of Jersey immovable estate. On an intestacy, there is no formal legal procedure whatsoever. If there is a will, it is registered at the Public Registry.

10. Invalidity of Will

(a) The will is invalid if it is formally defective by not having been executed properly or witnessed by properly qualified or independent people. It is invalid if the testator lacks testamentary capacity. The onus of proof rests with the plaintiff who is seeking to disprove testamentary capacity.

Forgery, force, fraud, fiction, fear and undue influence are all factors which cause a will to fail. Undue influence is often alleged but can be difficult to prove as influence may be degrading and pernicious and yet not undue influence in the eye of the law unless coercion is proved.

The will should not be witnessed by a beneficiary or by a relative of the testator or beneficiary to the degree of first cousin by blood or marriage. An executor may act as a witness but care should be taken not to include a gift or a charging clause in favour of a witness which would certainly invalidate the benefit and may well invalidate the whole will although possibly a holograph will may stand unaffected even if witnessed as there is no requirement for witnesses. Holograph wills of movables are valid without witnesses if they are wholly written by (or can be proved to have been typed by) the testator and signed by him.

397

(b) A will which is formally invalid is void but may still have the effect of revoking a previous will. In a case which came before the Royal Court in 1999, a document which was not a valid will stated that it revoked previous wills but the revocation was held to be conditional on a new will being made and as this was not the case, the previous will was held to be valid under the doctrine of *dependant relative revocation*. A will which is invalid for non-formal reasons is voidable.

11. Simultaneous Death

(a) *Commorientes* is covered by *The Wills and Succession (Jersey) Law 1993* which provides for what is to happen in the event of two or more persons dying in an accident or in circumstances rendering it uncertain which of them survived the other. Article 9 of the 1993 Law allows any person interested in the estate of one or more of the deceaseds to apply to the Royal Court for an order declaring whether the deceased died simultaneously or the order in which they died. The court may take account of evidence suggesting one survived the other although the onus of proving survivorship or a predecease rests with the party claiming this. If the court eventually makes an order that the persons are deemed to have died simultaneously, then their respective estates are to be distributed as if neither had survived the other. Nothing in this section of the 1993 law prevents a testator from specifying in his or her will what should happen in the event of the simultaneous deaths or death in the same accident of the testator and any beneficiary under such will.

The significance of this is that where a husband and wife die together in an accident, each is deemed to have predeceased the other. Example: if the husband left his estate to his wife but to his brother if she predeceased him and the wife left her estate to her husband but to her sister if he predeceased her, then the husband's estate goes to his brother and the wife's estate to her sister.

(b) If evidence of death cannot be provided, the court will hear additional evidence and make further enquiries. If satisfied that the death of the person to whom the application relates may be presumed to be beyond all reasonable doubt to have occurred on or after a certain date, it may make a declaration to that effect and such order as the circumstances require (*Probate (Jersey) Law 1998*, Article 7).

12. Estate Taxes

(a)–(c). Jersey has no death duties, estate duty, inheritance tax, gift tax, capital gains tax or value added tax. Income tax is chargeable at the rate of 20 per cent and this has been the applicable rate since 1940. Income tax is chargeable in respect of the income of the period of the administration of the estate and is payable by the personal representative who is obliged to submit an income tax return for the estate. By concession of the Comptroller of Income Tax no income tax is payable on income which is due to a beneficiary who is not resident in the Island for tax purposes. *See* paragraph 9 regarding stamp duties payable in relation to Jersey movables and immovables.

13. Administration of Estates

(a) The production of a grant is necessary (with certain exceptions shown below) to establish the right to recover or receive any part of the movable estate situate in the Island of any deceased person. Immovable estate is not administered and passes directly to the heirs, without a grant under the maxim of *le mort saisit le vif sans ministère de justice*. Movable estates are administered by the *executor* nominated in the will or by the *executor dative* if no executor is nominated in the will or if the executor so appointed is unwilling or unable to act. The court has discretion over the appointment of the *executor dative*, but it would usually be the surviving spouse or principal heir. On an intestacy an administrator is appointed. The heirs are not able to administer movable estates as of right. They have to obtain a grant and the person who has the prior right to obtain a grant is a surviving spouse. Otherwise, it is the *principal heir* who is established in the order of priority under customary law of: eldest son, and if no sons, eldest daughter, and if no issue, eldest brother, and if no brothers eldest sister, and if no siblings father, and if no father mother etc., with the principal heir of a deceased principal heir taking their place by *représentation* in preference to the next in line.

The persons so entitled to a grant may appoint a lawyer, trust corporation or other person under a power of attorney to apply for the grant and administer the estate. The grant is issued to the attorney personally and not as the representative of the person so entitled or until the person so entitled makes an application as would be the case under English law. The attorney swears an oath to well and faithfully discharge the duties of the office of executor or to administer, according to law, all of the movable estate of an intestate deceased.

To qualify as a *trust corporation* a company has to be empowered by its Memorandum and Articles of Association to undertake the business of acting as executor and administrator and authorized by the court to apply for grants of probate and administration. Most companies are therefore not able to act as trust corporations, but many Jersey law firms and accountancy firms and banks have their own trust corporations specifically set up to undertake executor and trustee business.

The Greffe may refuse to make a grant in favour of someone he considers to be an unfit or unsuitable person to administer the estate, e.g., a criminal or bankrupt.

If there is a dispute, e.g., over the validity of a will, a limited grant *pendente lite* may be made to the Viscount or some other person (such as a lawyer) who will be able to collect assets and pay debts and expenses pending resolution of the dispute. A *caveat* may be lodged to delay or prevent the issue of a grant.

The Greffe can revoke a grant if all interested parties give consent. An executor or administrator can be removed from office by the Greffe. If he dies, becomes incapacitated in law or bankrupt, or if he wishes to retire, he can be replaced and another person appointed in his place or as an additional person to act. Second or subsequent grants can therefore be made at the Greffe without reference to the court.

(b) No inventory of assets and liabilities is required on application for a grant. It is sufficient to swear the value of the net estate to not exceed the nearest £10,000 above the actual value. Probate stamp fees are payable on the application, but

International Succession

Jersey banks will not release part of the deceased's deposit in order to make funds available to pay the probate stamp fee. To do so would be to commit the offence of 'intermeddling' in the estate (i.e., disposing of assets without having obtained a grant) which is an offence punishable by an unlimited fine or to imprisonment for a term not exceeding twelve months or to both.

(c) Although estate accounts do not have to be submitted to the court as a general rule, there is an exception if an unsatisfied or disappointed beneficiary challenges the actions of the executor or administrator. The court has the power under *The Probate (Jersey) Law 1998*, Article 24, to order the executor or administrator, on the application of any person interested in the movable estate of the deceased, to exhibit on oath in court a true and perfect inventory and account of the movable estate of the deceased person.

(d) It is generally thought that the persons who have rights to query and object to the manner of the administration are the residuary beneficiaries, the heirs at law (if they are entitled to share in the estate) and creditors. Residuary beneficiaries do not have the right to demand that certain assets are appropriated to their share of residue or that the estate is administered in a particular way. They only have a right to a *chose in action* which is a right to have the estate administered properly. Beneficiaries who are due to receive pecuniary legacies or specific bequests can only object to the extent that they fail to receive their proper entitlement.

(e) Jersey immovable estate passes automatically to the heirs as stated *above*. Beneficiaries who are due to receive pecuniary legacies and specific bequests are not strictly entitled to receive their inheritance until a period of a year and a day has expired from the issue of the grant of probate. *Légitime* rights could be claimed within this period, possibly having the effect of abating the gifts. If a *légitime* claim is made, the gifts made in the will are discharged out of the disposable one-third (the *tiers disponible*).

Tangible assets such as jewellery, paintings and motor cars are transferred by delivery. Stocks and shares can be transferred in satisfaction of a specific bequest or by appropriation to a residuary beneficiary's share of residue by completion of a stock transfer form. Otherwise, investments are sold and the beneficiary receives the net proceeds of sale. Cash due to pecuniary legatees and residuary beneficiaries is usually paid by cheque or by telegraphic transfer. They normally have to wait until the expiry of the year and a day period from the issue of the grant of probate and residuary beneficiaries will usually not be paid until the executors are sure that no *légitime* claim or action to avoid the will has been brought and until the beneficiaries have all approved the estate accounts, although interim distributions are often made in suitable cases. There is no statutory basis for paying interest on legacies under Jersey law, even after the 'year and a day' period has expired, but if a beneficiary sued for payment delayed beyond the year and a day and claimed interest the court could award this at its discretion.

The Probate (Jersey) Law 1998, Article 25 gives the power to the court to vary dispositions either under a will or intestacy and to direct how the distribution shall be altered. Such 'Deeds of Variation' have to be made within two years of the date of death and are normally done for tax purposes, e.g., to redirect an inheritance from an individual to a trust. *The Probate (Jersey) Law 1998*, Article 26, provides that a beneficiary can disclaim his or her inheritance by giving notice in writing to the Judicial Greffier and to the executor or administrator.

(f) Creditors are normally paid out of the residuary estate. If a legitimate claim is made, they are paid out of the gross estate before *légitime* is calculated. In an insolvent estate, the priority for a settlement of claims is (1) costs incurred in winding up the estate; (2) funeral expenses and doctor in connection with last illness; (3) outstanding wages, rates, income tax and rent; (4) other creditors.

(g) If there is no will the distribution is made according to the rules of intestacy as shown in paragraph 3 *above*. If there is a will but no executor nominate, willing or able to act, an *executor dative* is appointed (*see* paragraph 13(a) *above*) who distributes the estate in accordance with the terms of the will.

14. Domicile/Nationality

(a) The nationality or domicile of the deceased is irrelevant for Jersey immovable estate which is governed by Jersey law. The devolution of movable estate and in particular rules relating to forced heirship and *légitime* and the identity of intestate heirs is governed by the laws of the deceased's domicile. The age of majority of a beneficiary is governed by the law of the beneficiary's domicile. Claims by foreign tax authorities are unenforceable in the Royal Court of Jersey although death duties and inheritance taxes in the country of the deceased's domicile are an original liability of the personal representative wherever resident. The Jersey personal representative may be held liable for foreign debts wherever situate.

(b) A Jersey grant may be issued if there are no Jersey assets. The oath can be sworn at a nil value if, for example, a Jersey bank holds certificates in safe custody in relation to non-Jersey assets, or a joint bank account may have passed automatically to the survivor but a claim may be made that an accrual to the estate should apply for succession purposes, or the personal representative may seek to obtain standing in order to commence litigation in the Royal Court of Jersey.

Section B – Applicable Law/Procedure Where Foreign Element/s are Involved

1. Jurisdiction

(a) Due to the success of Jersey as a finance centre, an increasing number of foreign estates include Jersey assets which usually fall into one of the following three categories: (1) bank accounts, (2) unit trust holdings, (3) privately owned investment companies. Other type of assets may include jewellery, coin and stamp collections held in safe custody by Jersey banks, bearer bonds, nominee accounts and shares in Jersey registered public companies.

The legal situs of the assets is normally the place where the rights to a *chose in action* can be enforced, i.e., the place of incorporation for shares in a company but the branch office for an account held with a bank. Bearer bonds are situate where the bonds are actually held. Eurobonds held by Euroclear, etc., to the order of a Jersey bank would not themselves be regarded as Jersey assets but rights to them under a nominee or investment management agreement with a Jersey company will be Jersey assets. If a foreign deceased's estate comprises shares in a privately held investment company, e.g., incorporated in British Virgin Islands or Liberia but the share register of a company is held in Jersey where the administration of the company is conducted, then the shares in the company will be a Jersey asset. If the shares in the company are owned by a trust, the asset does not form part of the deceased's estate. It is considered that where an asset is held as bare trustee, i.e., as a nominee the underlying asset will form part of the deceased's estate, e.g., shares in companies registered in nominee names, as well as the right to call for the asset. This may give rise to both Jersey and non-Jersey grants being required. A debt is situate where the creditor is resident unless it is a speciality debt which is situate wherever the speciality may be at the time of death.

A Jersey grant needs to be obtained in order to acquire legal title to administer Jersey situs movables. About 1,500 Jersey grants are obtained each year for estates of non-Jersey domiciliaries. Applications have been made in respect of persons domiciled in about 180 different jurisdictions in recent years.

Jersey law will apply to movable estate wherever situate of a Jersey domiciliary. For the estate of a non-Jersey domiciliary, the Jersey court has jurisdiction as far as the appointment of the personal representative is concerned while the essential validity of a will and the succession rights to the estate will generally be determined by the law of the deceased's domicile.

(b) Jersey immovable estate is governed by Jersey law no matter where the deceased is domiciled. Foreign immovables owned by Jersey domiciliaries are governed by the *lex situs*, i.e., the laws of the jurisdiction where the property is situate, and the operation of *renvoi* may be relevant in this connection. Movables are governed by the law of the jurisdiction of the deceased's domicile as the *lex successionis*. Jersey is therefore a 'schismatic' jurisdiction which has separate laws for movables and immovables (in common with all of the jurisdictions of the British Isles) and is also a 'dichotomous' jurisdiction in that movables are administered while immovables are not administered (in common with Scotland and Guernsey but unlike England and Wales, Ireland and the Isle of Man).

(c) The Royal Court of Jersey has jurisdiction and contentious matters are dealt with by the court. The Judicial Greffe performs the functions of the Royal Court of Jersey Probate Division and deals with applications for Grants of Probate and Administration, the lodging of caveats and the appointment and removal of personal representatives in non-contentious situations.

2. Applicable Law

Immovables are dealt with under the *lex situs* and movables are dealt with under the *lex successionis* (law of the domicile).

3. Foreign Succession/Inheritance Orders

(a) Foreign orders are not recognized in relation to Jersey immovable estate. For the Jersey movable estate of a non-Jersey domiciliary, a foreign Grant of Probate or Administration or Confirmation, Certificate of Inheritance or Succession or notarial copy of a will such as an '*Acte de Notaire*' and/or an affidavit of foreign law will be recognized unless there is a separate Jersey will which governs the Jersey estate or a separate will dealing with the rest of the world outside the country of the deceased's domicile which *inter alia* therefore covers Jersey.

(b) A small estates exemption procedure applies to Jersey assets with a value of under £10,000 held by the estates of non-Jersey domiciliaries. It is not necessary to obtain a Jersey grant, but the Jersey institution which holds the assets will need to satisfy itself that it is releasing the assets to the right person. They will require to see a copy of the death certificate as proof of death. As far as the estates of British Isles' domiciliaries are concerned, they will require a court-sealed and certified copy of the English, Welsh, Scottish, Northern Ireland, Manx or Guernsey Grant of Probate, Administration or Confirmation. Such authenticated copies of documents give proof of entitlement. The institution will accept the instructions of the executor/administrator and will be willing to release bank accounts and to sell or transfer investments, usually without further formality. The institution concerned is fully indemnified in making such distributions under *The Probate (Jersey) Law 1998*, Article 21, in respect of the following jurisdictions: England and Wales, Guernsey, the Isle of Man, Northern Ireland and Scotland. The small estates procedure also applies to other foreign jurisdictions, but in such cases the institution holding the Jersey assets is not indemnified under the law against claims brought against such assets. The institution is therefore entitled to insist on a Jersey grant being obtained before releasing the assets.

(c) In all other cases it is necessary to obtain a Jersey Grant of Probate or Administration in order to collect the Jersey assets. There is no procedure for the resealing of foreign grants in Jersey. A new 'fast-track' procedure for cases of British Isles domicile was introduced by *The Probate (Jersey) Law 1998*. Executors and administrators no longer have to appoint a local attorney executor or administrator to obtain a Jersey grant and collect the Jersey assets in such cases. The Greffe no longer need to 'make enquiries' into the circumstances surrounding the British grant but will accept a court-sealed and certified copy of that document at its face value. The personal representative is able to swear an oath of executor/administrator before his local solicitor in his home town and submit the copy death certificate, oath and certified grant to a Jersey agent, such as a Jersey lawyer, who then obtains a Greffier's certificate of Grant of Probate/Administration which is then submitted to the institution holding the Jersey asset with instructions to collect, transfer or sell it.

If the small estates exemption or fast-track procedures do not apply, then it will be necessary to obtain a Jersey Grant of Probate or Administration to deal with the collection of Jersey assets. Since 2 January 1999 it is no longer necessary to apply the test of domicile to the formal validity of wills if another method of validity applies, as shown in paragraph 8 *below*, and questions of *renvoi* therefore will rarely apply in respect to the issue of Jersey grants. It is necessary to produce a copy of the death certificate, the original will and any codicils thereto unless this has been proved abroad, in which case a copy of the will and the grant must be produced which is duly authenticated by signature and under seal by the official having custody of the same or the equivalent thereof (e.g., notarial will sealed and certified by the notary). Certificates of inheritance and succession, grants of administration and affidavits of foreign law must be produced as appropriate and translations into English of any foreign documents must be obtained. Stamps need to be obtained and produced in payment of the probate stamp fees when making the application for the grant. Since a Jersey grant can only be obtained by personal appearance at the Judicial Greffe, it is standard practice for foreign personal representatives to appoint a Jersey lawyer or trust corporation as their attorney to obtain the Jersey grant and to administer the Jersey estate. A power of attorney and a deed of indemnity is executed to appoint the attorney executor/administrator and to indemnify him against liabilities in foreign jurisdictions. If the foreign domiciliary has made a will specifically dealing with Jersey movable estate or a 'rest of the world' will of estate outside the jurisdiction of domicile which covers Jersey assets, then the original will is proved at the Greffe. Copies of all other wills executed by the deceased covering assets in other jurisdictions have to be produced so as to satisfy the Greffe that there is no conflict between them and to show that the will dealing with Jersey assets has not been revoked by a later will.

4. Two or More Succession or Probate Orders

Jersey immovable estate is governed by Jersey law and does not recognize any foreign order. Jersey movable estate is governed by the procedure shown in paragraph 3 *above* as far as the appointment of executor or administrator or the 'formal validity' of a will is concerned. Any foreign order referring to the 'material validity' of a will or the rights of beneficiaries or *légitime* or forced heirship rights would be a matter for the Jersey executor/administrator to determine in relation to the devolution of the estate and the distribution of the assets to the heirs or beneficiaries. In cases of doubt it would be usual for the matter to be resolved by obtaining an affidavit of foreign law from a lawyer who is an expert in the succession law of the jurisdiction of domicile. If this does not resolve any difficulties, a representation could be made to the Royal Court of Jersey for directions as to how to proceed or, in contentious matters, Jersey lawyers may be appointed to represent the rights of the various interested parties in an action to be heard before the court.

5. Assets

If a Jersey domiciled person owned no assets in Jersey but owned assets in another jurisdiction, a court sealed and certified copy of any Jersey grant could be provided. If no Jersey grant had been obtained, a foreign jurisdiction might rely on an affidavit of Jersey law provided by a Jersey advocate to determine rights to collect assets or to receive an inheritance. If there are no movables requiring a Jersey grant to collect, it is still feasible to obtain a Jersey grant in certain circumstances, as outlined in Section A, paragraph 14(b) *above*. Connecting factors such as residency, nationality or citizenship, only apply if there is a *renvoi* involving, e.g., British nationality and a 'close connection' with Jersey.

6. Expert Evidence

(a) Expert evidence on foreign law is required in cases where it is not readily apparent which person or persons are entitled to apply for a Jersey grant or whether a will is valid or whether it applies to Jersey assets. An affidavit of foreign law is obtained from a lawyer who is an expert in the succession laws of the deceased's jurisdiction of domicile. He is required to state his qualifications and experience, set out the relevant facts of the particular case, confirm the domicile of the deceased and determine which person or persons are entitled to administer the estate. Difficulties can arise, especially with civil and customary law jurisdictions which do not recognize executors and trustees and where a large number of heirs may have entitlements and over the position of minor beneficiaries. There may also be problems of conflicts of laws and the application of *renvoi*. The affidavit of foreign law is most commonly required in cases of intestacy where the foreign lawyer needs to interpret the effect of a certificate of inheritance or succession or where no order has been made. If a number of heirs are entitled, it is the practice to require all of them to appoint an attorney to apply for the Jersey grant rather than allow members of a class of beneficiaries to appoint one of their number as their attorney who in turn appoints a Jersey agent as his attorney because of the application of the doctrine of *delegatus non potest delegare*. An affidavit of foreign law may be dispensed with in certain circumstances such as where the Greffe is familiar with the procedures in the particular foreign jurisdiction, e.g., a German *Erbschein*.

(b) Such evidence is always provided by affidavit. The necessity for an appearance in the Royal Court of Jersey would only arise if there was a conflict of evidence by foreign lawyers which needed to be resolved by questioning them.

7. Unity of Succession

As stated *above*, immovables devolve according to the *lex situs* while movables devolve according to the *lex successionis* and this schismatic approach contrasts with the unitarian treatment applied by most European jurisdictions. Jersey also has a dichotomous divide in that immovables pass directly to the heir, according to the maxim of *le mort saisit le vif sans ministère de justice*, without any executor or administration of the asset, whereas movables are administered with the executor or administrator having to obtain a Grant of Probate or Administration and being responsible for the administration of the estate and thereafter distributing the estate after debts and expenses have been deducted by giving cash and/or assets to the beneficiaries receiving legacies, bequests and shares of residue.

8. Formalities

The Probate (Jersey) Law 1998, Article 29 provides that:

'(1) A will shall be treated as properly executed if, at the time of its execution or at the time of the testator's death, its execution conforms to: –
　　(a) The internal law in force –
　　　　i. In the territory where it was executed,
　　　　ii. In the territory where the testator was domiciled,
　　　　iii. In the territory where the testator was habitually resident, or
　　　　iv. In a state of which the testator was a national;
　　or
　　(b) The law of the Island.
 (2) For the purposes of this Article, the internal law in force in a territory or state is the law which would apply in a case where no question of the law in force in any other territory or state arose.'

9. Legislation

Jersey never ratified the *Hague Convention on the Conflicts of Laws Relating to the Form of Testamentary Dispositions*, but Article 29 above gives approximate effect to it with the additional provision that conformity to the law of the Island also gives formal validity.

10. Wills

In general, the answers to the following questions are that, in cases of conflicts or foreign factors, the law of the situs of the immovable or the law of the deceased's domicile usually provide the deciding factors. However, there may be exceptions and it is recommended that where appropriate an opinion should be obtained from a Jersey advocate.

(a) Jersey law governs the legal requirements for the execution of wills of Jersey immovable estate, the *lex situs* governs foreign immovables and the law of the person's domicile at the time of making the will governs wills of movables.

(b) The *lex domicilii* will govern construction and interpretation of terminology used in the will. A will trust may possibly be governed by another law if so stated but there is no decided case on this.

(c) The law of the deceased's domicile would apply to the legal rights of heirs/beneficiaries.

(d) Capacity to inherit Jersey immovable estate is restricted so that devises to trusts, to unincorporated bodies and 'substitutions' based on third party determination are void. Capacity to inherit foreign immovables depends on the *lex situs*, capacity to inherit movables depends on the deceased's domicile at the date of death.

(e) Capacity to make a valid will of Jersey immovables depends on mental capacity (the three certainties of intention, subject and object) and having attained the age of eighteen (or if under age, being married). The provisions of *The Age of Majority (Jersey) Law 1999* only apply to wills made after 31 October 1999 and not to codicils amending wills made before that date which do not specify the change of age. Capacity to make a valid will of foreign immovables depends on the *lex situs*, capacity to make a will of movables depends on the laws of the deceased's domicile at the time of making the will.

(f) Essential or material validity affects the estate of a Jersey domiciliary in that there is no *légitime* claim for immovables but there is a claim (by spouse and/or issue) which can be made in respect of movables. A legacy to a witness and undue influence would be a matter for formal validity as opposed to essential validity. For gifts which offend against public policy, or which are for illegal or immoral purposes, it is probable that the ancient Roman maxim of *ex turpi causa non actio oritur* would apply to invalidate the gift.

(g) There can be no power of appointment over Jersey immovable estate since there can be no trusts or 'substitutions.' If the subject matter of the power is foreign immovables, this depends on the law of the *lex situs*. In cases of movables it is probably the law governing the instrument, e.g., trust deed creating the power, which is the determining factor, but there is no decided Jersey case on this point.

(h) The law governing amendment, revocation and revival would normally be determined by the *lex situs* for immovables and the *lex successionis* for movables.

(i) There is no *légitime* claim to Jersey immovable estate but a non-resident would be entitled to claim *légitime* to the movable estate of a Jersey domiciliary. The Jersey movable estate of non-Jersey domiciliaries would be subject to claims made according to the laws of the jurisdiction of their domicile relating to *légitime*, reserved portions, or forced heirship as appropriate. *The Trusts (Amendment) (Jersey) Law 1989* protects Jersey trusts set up by persons domiciled outside Jersey against forced heirship claims or claims that the old Jersey maxim of *donner et retiner ne vaut* should apply.

407

International Succession

11. Domicile/Nationality

(a) Formal validity applies if the will is executed according to the relevant laws at the time of either making the will or at the date of death. Succession rights are determined by the deceased's domicile at the date of death for movables. Capacity and revocation are determined as at the time of making the will or the act of revocation.

(b) The domicile of the beneficiary is not relevant to any of the answers in Section B.

(c) Domicile is a person's permanent home, where they intend eventually to spend the remainder of their life. Whilst the physical fact of residence is an indicator of domicile this may be overridden by evidence of an intention to return to another jurisdiction. A domicile of origin is harder to displace than one of choice and unless a domicile of choice is clearly established and maintained, a domicile of origin will revive. Domicile is not the same as residence for tax purposes. Jersey follows English common law on matters of domicile so that presumably no person can be without a domicile or have more than one domicile at the same time. It is common practice for Jersey wills to contain a declaration of domicile since in cases of doubt it is helpful to know the testator's intentions at the time of making the will. Domicile relates to a territory with a particular legal system as opposed to a country in the political sense. Therefore, there is no such thing as 'British' domicile or USA or Canadian or Australian domicile.

The domicile of origin for legitimate children is the domicile of their father at the time of their birth and for illegitimate children, or those whose father had died, is the domicile of their mother at the time of their birth. Domicile of dependency applies to minor children, whose domicile changes in accordance with the domicile changes of the relevant parent. Married women in Jersey used to take for all purposes the domicile of their husband but this was changed for succession purposes only by *The Probate (Jersey) Law 1998*, Article 30, which came into force on 2 January 1999. Article 30(1) provides that for the purposes of a grant in and the distribution of the movable estate of a deceased woman who has at any time been married, the deceased woman's domicile shall be ascertained by reference to the same factors as in the case of any individual capable of having an independent domicile. Article 30(2) provides that for the purposes of a grant in and the distribution of the movable estate of a deceased minor, the deceased minor shall have first become capable of having an independent domicile when (if at all) he attained the age of sixteen years or married under that age. Article 30(1) has important implications for conflicts of law situations where the deceased is a woman who has married in that an independent domicile should normally be inferred.

A domicile of choice is acquired by going to live in a different jurisdiction with the intention of remaining there permanently. If a domicile of choice is lost the domicile of origin is revived. Fiscal domicile is a legal fiction invented to collect tax revenue. It is of particular importance for the Jersey estates of persons who have a domicile/residence connection with any of the jurisdictions of the United Kingdom as the deemed domicile provisions for inheritance tax may give rise to a tax liability even in cases where a different common law domicile applies. Legal domicile is crucial for succession purposes as different heirs may inherit according to which legal domicile applies (e.g., siblings vs. parents) and *légitime* may or may fail to apply.

12. Taxation

Jersey immovable estate is not subject to income tax except insofar as the beneficiary who inherits and then leases the property which he has inherited is liable for Jersey income tax at the rate of 20 per cent on the rental income received which is assessed on a calendar year basis. He is also liable to pay parochial property rates.

Beneficiaries of Jersey movable estates are only liable to Jersey income tax if they are resident in the Island for tax purposes. The executor or administrator of an estate of a Jersey domiciliary has to complete a tax return for the period of administration and any assessments of tax payable are made on him personally. No assessment is made in respect of income to which a nonresident beneficiary is entitled.

For the Jersey movable estates of non-Jersey domiciliaries there is no requirement to complete a tax return for the period of administration unless any of the beneficiaries are resident in the Island.

Jersey has no death duties, estate duty, inheritance tax, gift tax, capital gains tax, or value added tax. There is no other taxation applicable other than the stamp duty mentioned previously.

Liechtenstein

Prepared by: Kanzlei RITTER WOHLWEND WOLFF

Address: Pflugstrasse 10
    FL-9490 Vaduz
    Fürstentum Liechtenstein
Tel.: +423 236 55 33
Fax: +423 236 56 11

With many thanks to Dr. Alfred Mejstrik

SECTION A – BRIEF SURVEY OF THE LOCAL SYSTEM

1. Type of System

(a) Civil Law.

(b) Liechtenstein is a monarchy based upon a democratic basis. The state authority is divided between sovereign and subjects. A speciality of this monarchical constitution is the legislation investitive and the law-referendum by the nation.

2. Wills

(a) Different forms of drafting a will:

1. *Holograph* (§578 of the Liechtenstein General Civil Code) in one's own handwriting: the entire text must be in the testator's own handwriting and the will must also be signed. Adding time, place and date of drafting is advised, but not obligatory.
2. *Allograph* (§579 Liechtenstein General Civil Code) written by a person other than the testator:
   - not written in the testator's own handwriting, but not drafted as a public document; every will not drafted in the testator's own handwriting must be signed by the testator and by three witnesses. The witnesses must be older than eighteen years and must have legal capacity.
   - as a public document: drafted before the Liechtenstein court and deposited there as an original. Certain persons (mentally or physically handicapped persons) must draft their will in such a manner to be valid.

3. *Private oral will* (§§585 *et seq.* Liechtenstein General Civil Code): the testator must in the presence of three valid witnesses independently declare a statement to be his last will. It is advised, but not a requirement, that the witnesses put down the entire procedure in writing. After the death of the testator at least two witnesses must give consistent evidence before the court with regard to the contents of the testamentary disposition. An oral will does not require subsequent written confirmation.
4. *Deed of inheritance* (§602 Liechtenstein General Civil Code): only between spouses and only with regard to three-quarters of the estate (§1253 Liechtenstein General Civil Code).

(b) Alteration, revocation and revival of a revoked will (§§695 *et seq.* Liechtenstein General Civil Code)

   i. Any valid form of will may be used in order to alter or revoke a will. Persons who are protected in a special way can do this by public deed only. This applies both to wills and legacies. A revoked will in general has to be drafted anew, but in such a case, as regarding the construction of any will, the intention of the testator is essential. The court has to find out this intention.
   ii. No, marriage does not automatically revoke or affect a will.
   iii. A revoked will 'survives' only if the testator, by valid later testamentary disposition, revives formerly revoked wills.

3. Intestacy

(a) Intestate succession as regulated by law (acc. §§727 *et seq.* Liechtenstein General Civil Code) follows the so-called system of succession *per stirpes*. The descendant's blood relatives are summed up in different lines ('*stirpes*') as follows:

1. *1st line*: all children (whether legitimate or illegitimate) and their issue;
2. *2nd line*: parents and their issue (i.e., siblings, nephews and nieces of the deceased);
3. *3rd line*: grandparents and their issue (uncles, aunts, cousins of the deceased);
4. *4th line*: great-grandparents, but not their issue.

The members of the 1st line are first in line to inherit. Only if no member of this line has survived the deceased, will the 2nd line inherit, and so on. Within the single lines the degree of relationship regarding the deceased is relevant, e.g., children prevail over grandchildren, parents prevail over siblings, etc., a predeceased heir is substituted by all his or her issue. All of them form one *stirpe*. When one *stirpe* has died out, its share goes to the other *stirpes* or the entire line is cancelled. The share in the inheritance depends on the number of *stirpes* within the line. The deceased's date of death is relevant.

What has to be considered with regard to Liechtenstein intestate succession is that the surviving spouse is entitled to a part of the inheritance together with these lines (parentels). If the 1st line exists the surviving spouse inherits one-third of the entire estate, the 2nd line or the grandparents exist that such part is two-thirds, in any other case everything. The entitled line (parentel) inherits only the remaining part of the estate.

(b) There is no difference between movables and immovables.

4. Freedom of Testation

(a) A compulsory share (§§762 *et seq.* of the Liechtenstein General Civil Code) exists for the spouse, all relatives of the 1st line ('parentel'), parents and grandparents (ancesters only if there are no descendants). No other relatives are entitled to a compulsory share. The compulsory share for the spouse and the 1st line amounts to half of the statutory portion, for other persons entitled to a compulsory share one-third each of the statutory portion, theoretically ascertained according to the *above* rules.

The compulsory share is a purely obligatory claim against the heirs and has to be satisfied by them in money only. The basis for calculation is the actual true value of the estate. The compulsory share becomes statute-barred three years after publication of the will and if necessary can be claimed in court. The spouse, however, is entitled to those objects which are necessary to maintain his or her lifestyle – they are considered part of the compulsory share (the so-called 'large advancement') – including the right to stay in the marital flat.

(b) In general, nobody may dispose of an expected inheritance, especially with regard to third parties. It is however possible to renounce one's interest in an estate or a compulsory portion with regard to the heirs presumptive. This can be done effectively in notarial form only and must be done prior to the decease.

A gift *causa mortis* is a special form of legacy – also only effective if drafted as a notarial deed. It is a contract and thus is binding both for the donor (the future bequeather) and the donee (the future legatee). Only single objects may be transferred this way, not the entire estate. Anticipative partitions of inheritances are possible either as gifts *causa mortis* or donations *inter vivos*. In the case of the former, the donor cannot make a disposition of the object without the donee's consent, even though he remains the owner.

5. Maintenance

A person entitled to a compulsory portion in the estate who has been lawfully debarred from his compulsory portion has to be granted maintenance at the subsistence level.

A widow has the right to receive reasonable maintenance up to the value of the estate as long as she does not get remarried.

6. Community Property Between Husband and Wife

(a) The statutory regime is separation of property. The spouse inherits if there are children of the deceased one-third, with the parents of the deceased or with the grandparents two-thirds of the estate.

If the spouses agreed upon a communal property then one-half of the entire communal property becomes part of the estate, as is the case for special property of the deceased. Succession is then governed by a possible testamentary contract (which has usually been incorporated in the marriage contract).

A communal estate upon death is possible, but this hardly ever occurs.

(b) There are no further consequences of the matrimonial regime.

7. Gifts (*Inter Vivos*)

(a) The general rule (§787 *et seq.* of the Liechtenstein General Civil Code) is that among those entitled to a compulsory portion, advancements are to be made in such a manner that after the death of the deceased each of them has at least received the compulsory portion he or she is entitled to. For that purpose donations received need not be returned, but if necessary compensation payments must be made.

(b) Basically, each person entitled to a compulsory portion must at least get the portion he or she is entitled to.

8. Capacity

(a) Capacity of testator (§566 *et seq.* of the Liechtenstein General Civil Code): infants up to the age of 14 do not have testamentary capacity. Persons under the age of 18 may draft an oral valid will before the court only. The same applies to persons being in the custody of a guardian. Persons older than 18 years of age have full testamentary capacity.

(b) Capacity of witnesses (§591 *et seq.* of the Liechtenstein General Civil Code): persons under the age of eighteen, insane, blind, deaf and dumb people, people who do not understand the language of the testator and close relatives and persons taking under a will, may not act as witnesses.

(c) Capacity of beneficiary (§538 *et seq.* of the Liechtenstein General Civil Code): in general everyone who may acquire property may inherit, unless he or she is unfit due to criminal acts committed against the deceased (this, however, regards serious crimes only) or due to crimes committed against the last will (e.g., embezzlement, destruction or suppression). He or she must outlive the decedent. For an unborn child a guardian is to be appointed.

International Succession

9. Authority (Court, Notarial or Other)

Probate proceedings as such are to be carried out by the Liechtenstein court. The court summons to appear all possible heirs (by will or by law) to give a testimony (*Erbserklärung*). On the basis of the testimony(ies) the judge releases an order (*Einantwortungsurkunde*). (Liechtenstein Civil Code and §1 of the Liechtenstein probate instructions).

10. Invalidity of Will

(a) A distinction is made between formal defects, rendering a will invalid because it was not drafted in the required form, and defects regarding its contents. There can either be unclear of faulty dispositions by the testator or defects influencing the testator's intention at the drafting of the will, e.g., fraud, mistake or undue influence. The latter will in any case render the will voidable. Defective or unclear dispositions by the testator are to be constructed in a manner meeting his provable intention. If this is not possible, they cannot take effect. In the latter case the will remains in effect with regard to all other parts.

(b) Formal invalidity renders the will void.

11. Simultaneous Death

If it cannot be proved that of two or more persons the one survived the other, then it is assumed they died simultaneously. If one inherits from the other it is assumed that the older one died first. (§51 Liechtenstein Company Law). The property of each of these persons must then be passed separately.

12. Inheritance Taxes

(a) These are laid down in the law of taxes payable on estates and donations. In principle, the percentage of the inheritance tax depends on (i) how close the relationship between the decedent and the heir has been and (ii) the amount the single heir really gets in the end. As regards the first criterion, there are six classes of taxation: the percentage of the taxes vary between 0.5 per cent and 18 per cent.

(b) In Liechtenstein the entire estate is subject to taxation, if either the deceased or the heir (the latter only for the portion received) were Liechtenstein residents at the time of inheritance. All Liechtenstein citizens and foreigners domiciled in or having their usual place of residence within Liechtenstein are deemed Liechtenstein residents (in case of legal entities the seat or place of management is relevant).

(c) Each heir has to pay tax on the property gained through the deceased's death.

13. Administration of Estates

(a) Whenever a person dies, estate proceedings are obligatory and in the course thereof the entitled heir expressly has to claim his or her title in the inheritance (§797 *et seq.* of the Liechtenstein Civil Code). Then the probate court formally transfers title to the entire estate to the heir(s) (so-called *Einantwortung*). Until title to the estate is transferred, all assets of the decedent form a legal entity, the so-called 'dormant-estate'. If this dormant estate has to be represented prior to transfer of title to the heirs and if no declarations of inheritance have been given, a curator may be appointed for the estate.

(b) Either the probate court or a commission (*Inventarisierungskommission*) has to list and value the estate. A final accounting with regard to capital movements after the date of death is required only under certain circumstances (if a curator was appointed or in case of minor heirs). A final accounting has to be presented to the court.

(c) *See* (a) and (b) *above.*

(d) Nobody has the right to query and object at this stage of the succession proceedings. They will be referred to civil proceedings by the probate court.

(e) Upon the so-called *Einantwortung* (transfer of title to the estate) the probate court, after finalizing the estate proceedings, transfers the estate to the heir(s). It is expressly forbidden that anyone, even the entitled heir, on his or her own takes possession of estate objects prior to this stage.

(f) If there are heirs, they have to pay for the deceased's debts and the costs of the estate proceedings. If unconditional declarations of inheritance were given, the heirs have to pay everything no matter whether covered by the estate or not, even using their own property. In case of conditional declarations of inheritance these debts and costs have to be satisfied similar to bankruptcy proceedings either totally or in quotas (depending on the class). The difference between these two declarations is as follows:

1. The heirs make an unconditional declaration of inheritance, i.e., they declare to accept the inheritance unconditionally. The disadvantage is that the heirs incur liability for all debts and legacies of the deceased with their own property to an unlimited amount, even if these debts and legacies are higher than the estate. The advantage is that the property of the deceased need not be officially appraised.
2. The heirs make a conditional declaration of inheritance, i.e., they accept the inheritance subject to the condition that they will incur liability for the debts and legacies of the deceased only to the amount of the assets of the estate. In this case an official inventory and appraisal of the estate must be made. The advantages of this method are: 1) protection of the heir against debts going beyond the assets of the estate, 2) facilitating of the division of the estate, as the value of the parts of the estate are determined.

(g) Basically, the distribution of the estate is to be done by the heirs among themselves and freely. Only the inheritance of minors and wards are to be secured in a way provable to the court.

14. Domicile/Nationality

(a) The relevant articles concerning domicile and nationality are Articles 29 and 30 of the Liechtenstein International Private Law.

Legal succession upon death is to be determined in accordance to the law of nationality to which the deceased belonged at the time of his death.

If inheritance proceedings are carried out before the Liechtenstein court, then legal succession upon death will be determined in accordance with Liechtenstein law.

By virtue of a testamentary will or settlement, a foreign testator can provide that his succession is to be determined pursuant to the law of nationality or the place where he had his last usual place of abode.

A Liechtenstein testator resident abroad can provide by virtue of a testamentary will or settlement that his succession is to be determined pursuant to the law of his nationality or place where he had his last usual place abode.

Testamentary capacity exists and the other prerequisites for a valid testamentary will, settlement or disclaimer of succession are fullfilled if the requirements for validity under one of the following laws are complied with:

1. the law of nationality of the deceased at the date when the disposition was made or at the time of his death;
2. the law of the country in which the deceased had his last usual place of abode at the date when the disposition was made or at the time of his death;
3. Liechtenstein law, in so far as the inheritance proceedings are being heard before the Liechtenstein court.

The provisions stated above apply *mutatis mutandis* to the revocation or rescission of the said dispositions.

(b) If there are no assets in Liechtenstein the court would not grant an order of probate or succession.

SECTION B – APPLICABLE LAW/PROCEDURE WHERE FOREIGN ELEMENT/S ARE INVOLVED

1. Jurisdiction

(a) The Liechtenstein court would hold that it had jurisdiction, if the deceased had domicile and assets or no domicile but immovable property in Liechtenstein.

(b) *See* (a) *above.*

(c) As there is only one court in Liechtenstein, this court always acts as the probate court.

2. Applicable Law

See Section A, paragraph 14 *above*. Immovable property is governed by Liechtenstein law.

3. Foreign Succession/Inheritance Orders

(a) Foreign decisions regarding succession and other rights in the estate except for immovables will be recognized as far as they do not violate Liechtenstein laws.

(b) No, *see* (a) *above*.

(c) *See* 1(c) *above*.

4. Two or More Succession or Probate Orders

See Section A, paragraph 14(a) *above*.

5. Assets

See Section A, paragraph 14(b) *above*.

6. Expert Evidence

Not necessary.

7. Unity of Succession

Yes; regarding the exceptions *see* Section A, paragraph 14 *above*.

8. Formalities

The law of the decedent's nationality at the time the will was drafted, alternatively the law of the domicile upon his or her death, is relevant. (Article 30 *International Private Law* as well as Liechtenstein law, if in Liechtenstein).

9. Legislation

The *Hague Convention* is not applicable.

International Succession

10. Wills

See Section B, paragraph 8 *above*. Wills concerning immovable property in Liechtenstein are however governed by Liechtenstein law.

11. Domicile/Nationality

(a) The law of the decedent's nationality at the date of the execution, alternatively on the date of his or her death is applicable (Article 30 *International Private Law*). For the validity of the will either the date of execution or the date of death is relevant.

(b) No.

(c) The jurisdiction the decedent had the closest relations with, is relevant.

12. Taxation

In this respect, the statements given under Section A, paragraph 12(b, c) generally apply. If neither the deceased nor the heirs were domiciled in Liechtenstein, assets in Liechtenstein would not attract Liechtenstein inheritance tax apart from immoveables.

Mexico

Prepared by: Marcos BERKMAN
Berkman y associados, s.c.

Address: San Francisco nos. 2–5 y 6
         Pisos esq. viaducto Miguel Aleman
         Col del Valle
         Mexico, d.f. 03100
Tel.:   +52 555 6870411/5366149/5439705/5439250
Fax: +52 555 6691582
E-mail: Berkman@netservice.com.uk

Section A – Brief Survey of the Local System

1. Type of System

(a) The Civil Law containing the substantive law relating to successions was inspired by the French Napoleonic Civil Code, with important differences that arise in Mexican Law.

(b) The Civil Code for the Federal District applies in the capital of the Republic in federal matters. The issue of succession is local and is regulated by each Civil Code of the 31 states into which the Mexican Republic is divided, besides the Civil Code for the Federal District. However, most of the codes follow the guidelines of the Civil Code for the Federal District in relation to successions, in the respective section.

2. Wills

(a) In Mexico there are different types of wills and all of them must have as an essential element the formality with which they must be executed.
   The Civil Code for the Federal District regulates the following types of wills:

– *Ordinary Wills*

   i. *Public nuncupative wills*, executed before a notary in which the place, year, month, day and time it was executed are recorded. The notary reads the entire will and the testator signs before him.

ii. *Sealed public wills* may be written by the testator or by another person on his request and on common paper. The testator must initial all the pages and sign at the end of the will, but if he does not know how to or cannot do so, another person may initial and sign it for him at his request. This person shall go together with the testator to file the sealed document and in this proceeding the testator shall declare before the notary that such person initialled and signed in his name the document that contains his last will and the latter will sign on the cover with the three witnesses and the notary.

Those who do not know how to or cannot read do not have capacity to make a sealed public will.

The testator may keep the will in his possession or give it to a person he trusts to guard it, or deposit in the judicial archive.

iii. *Simplified public wills* are wills executed before a notary with respect to real estate to be used for housing by the testator. This obligation must be established in the document in which its purchase is established or regularized by the authorities of the Federal District or any agency or entity of the Federation.

The price of the real property or its value must not exceed twenty-five times the general minimum salary in effect for the Federal District, annualized, when regularization by the authorities is not involved.

iv. *Holographic wills*, which are written completely in the handwriting of the testator. Such a will must contain the day, month and year when it is written and must be signed. Foreigners can draw it up in their own language. It is made in duplicate and the testator's fingerprint is impressed on both copies. The original is deposited in the General Notarial Archive and the copy is returned; on top of the envelope the testator may put the following: 'My will is contained inside this envelope', writing the place and date of deposit. The duplicate will contain the following annotation: 'I received the Sealed Document from Mr. . . . , who states it contains the original of his holographic will and this is the duplicate', the person in charge of the office, the testator and witnesses signing on such envelope. It must be deposited in an envelope sealed with sealing wax in the General Notarial Archive, personally by the interested party, and if he is not known to the person in charge of the office, he must present two witnesses who identify him.

– *Special Wills*

i. *Private wills*, which are permitted in the following cases:

- when the testator has a violent, serious illness that prevents him from going to the notary;
- when there is no notary in the town or judge who can act as receiver;
- when there is a notary or judge in the town but it is impossible for him to attend the execution of the will;
- when military personnel or individuals conscripted to the army are in battle or are prisoners of war;
- when it is impossible for the testator to execute a holographic will.

The will is executed before five witnesses in writing or in cases of utmost urgency it can be made before three witnesses, observing the rules for the open public will as to the formalities that must be observed. Regarding military wills, *see* below.

The will only comes into effect if the testator dies of the illness or the danger in which he was found within the month after such cause arose.

ii. *Military wills*: when the testator is military personnel or in the army and makes his provision at the time of entering war action, being wounded on the battlefield, or being made prisoner of war, he may declare his will before two witnesses by word of mouth, or by delivering to them the sealed document that contains his last provision signed in his handwriting.

iii. *A maritime will* is executed in writing on the high seas, in the presence of two witnesses and the ship's captain, who must all sign it; it is made in duplicate and its execution must be mentioned in the navigation log; it only comes into effect if the testator dies on the high seas or within the month following disembarkation in some place where he could have ratified it or executed a new one.

iv. *Wills made in a foreign country* will have effect in Mexico when they have been formulated in accordance with the laws of the country where they were executed.

A will may be executed abroad before the Mexican Secretaries of Legation, Consuls or Vice Consuls, who take the place of notaries public.

(b) Amendment, revocation and revival:

i. The will can be amended at any time with the same formalities observed during the execution; if it is to be revoked, it is enough for a new one to be executed. However, in the special case of recognition of children in the first will, the second will not revoke the recognition. The revoked will may be re-established by a later one.

ii. Marriage does not affect wills executed previously, but in the case of community property, the marriage articles can establish that the property that the spouses already own will not become part of such community property or that only the property the spouses acquire during the marriage will enter the community property or that all the property that the parties contribute will enter. In this latter case, 50 per cent of the goods of the community property belongs to each spouse *pro indiviso* and in his will such party cannot dispose of the 50 per cent that does not belong to him.

iii. The will can always be restored in accordance with the testator's free will.

3. Intestacy

(a) The order of the *ab intestato* succession is the following:

i. Descendants:
  – If only descendants compete, the estate will be shared in equal parts. If children or descendants in the last degree survive, the former will inherit *per capita* and the latter *per stirpes*. The same thing will be observed in relation

to descendants of children predeceased, who are incapable of inheriting, or who have renounced the inheritance. If only descendants of the last degree survive, the inheritance will be divided *per stirpes* and if in any of these categories there are several heirs, the portion that corresponds will be divided by equal parts. The adopted child inherits like a natural child, but there is no right of succession between the adopted child and the parents of the adopting party. Illegitimate children also inherit equally as do children born within 30 days following legal separation.

– If descendants and the spouse compete, it is important to differentiate the form in which the deceased was married to the surviving spouse: (1) in the case of community property, automatically the 50 per cent *pro indiviso* of the goods that form the community property is assigned to the spouse and the other 50 per cent is divided among the descendants; (2) if the surviving spouse does not have any property of his/her own, or the property s/he has does not equal the part that corresponds to that of a son/daughter (for instance, each son/daughter has assets worth 100, and the survivor spouse possesses assets worth 60), s/he will receive the difference to equal the part that corresponds to a son/daughter (that is 40), and so on, making the corresponding mathematical calculation, to determine the amount to cover each son/daughter and spouse.

When the spouse competes with one or more siblings of the testator of the estate, s/he will have two-thirds of the inheritance, and the remaining one-third will be allotted to the sibling or will be divided in equal parts among the siblings.

– If the deceased was not married and has lived with another person as if such were a spouse for five years immediately preceding his death or when they have had children together, and when both have remained unmarried, the concubine or the male living with a concubine will inherit in the same form as the surviving spouse and with the same differentiation when they compete with descendants.

ii. Ascendants: in the absence of descendants and of a spouse or concubine, the father and mother of the deceased will inherit in equal parts; if only one of them exists, s/he will receive the entire inheritance. If they compete with a spouse or concubine, the inheritance is divided into two equal parts and one is applied to the ascendants and the other to the spouse or concubine.

If there are only ascendants in the last degree in a straight line, the inheritance will be divided into equal parts.

If there are ascendants in both lines, the inheritance will be divided into two equal parts and one will be applied to the ascendants of the paternal line and the other to that of the maternal line. The members of each line will divide the part that corresponds to them among themselves and by equal parts.

If the adopting parties compete with ascendants of the adoptee, the adoptee's inheritance will be divided by equal parts among the adopting parties and the ascendants.

If the spouse of the adoptee competes with the adopting parties, two-thirds of the inheritance correspond to the spouse and the other one-third to adopting parties.

Even when the descendants are illegitimate, ascendants have the right to inherit from their recognized descendants.

iii. In the absence of the above, the closest relatives up to the fourth degree will compete.

If there are only siblings by both lines, they will succeed by equal parts.

If siblings compete with half-siblings, the former will inherit a double portion in relation to the latter.

If siblings compete with nieces/nephews, children of siblings or of half-siblings predeceased, who are incapable of inheriting or have renounced the inheritance, the former will inherit *per capita* and the second *per stirpes*.

In the absence of siblings, their children will succeed, the inheritance being divided *per stirpes* and the portion of each stirpes *per capita*.

iv. In the absence of all the above heirs, the public welfare will inherit.

The closest relatives exclude the more distant and if there are relatives in the same degree, they will inherit by equal parts.

The right to claim an inheritance prescribes after ten years.

(b) The only difference is the practical one where the immovable assets cannot be divided. *See* Section B, paragraph 7 *below*.

4. Freedom of Testation

(a) There are no compulsory shares.

(b) *i*. A contract of inheritance (made prior to death) will be null and void.

ii. Partitions: if the author of the inheritance arranges in his will for some heir to be given certain goods, when the inventory has been approved the executor will deliver these goods to him provided they sufficiently guarantee the general expenses and charges of the inheritance in the proportion that corresponds to them.

Advances: within fifteen days following approval of the inventory, executors may propose to the judge a provisional distribution of the proceeds from the inherited property, specifying the part thereof that shall be delivered to the heirs every two months.

Agreements to make a will: the co-heirs can enter into agreements prior to the partition.

5. Maintenance

Maintenance can be claimed from the estate or the heirs by the following individuals:

i. descendants under eighteen years of age or older if they are unable to work;

ii. spouse if s/he does not have sufficient property or is prevented from working, provided s/he lives honestly and does not remarry, unless there is an express provision by the testator to the contrary;

iii. ascendants: if children compete with ascendants, these ascendants will only have the right to maintenance which in no case may exceed the portion of one of the children;

iv. the person with whom the testator lived as if she were the spouse, for five years preceding his death, or with whom he had children and both have remained free from marriage, provided the survivor does not have sufficient property or is prevented from working, observes good behaviour and does not marry;

v. siblings and the other blood relatives up to the fourth degree, if they are incapacitated.

The obligation to pay maintenance charged to the estate will apply provided there is no other relative with closer kinship to the party who owes maintenance payment.

6. Community Property Between Husband and Wife

(a) By virtue of the community property, the spouse only has a right to the estate property that is outside of such community property, when the portion due to him/her does not equal the portion of a child. *See* paragraph 3(a)*i. above.*

(b) If the marriage was contracted under the community property system, the testating spouse may only dispose of 50 per cent of the community property.

In Mexico there are two types of marriage systems; the community property system whereby both spouses own 50 per cent *pro indiviso* of all the property they acquire during their marriage, and the separation of property ownership system in which each party will be the owner of the property that is in his/her name.

In the event of the death of one of the spouses, if the deceased was married under the community property system, 50 per cent of the goods of such community property belongs to the surviving spouse, who may also inherit by legitimate succession the part that corresponds to him/her with the limitations and in the order of heirs established in the law and detailed in paragraph 3(a) *above.*

7. Gifts (*Inter Vivos*)

Donations made *inter vivos* do not affect the donee's right to be considered like any other heir.

8. Capacity

(a) Anyone can testate, except non-emancipated minors under sixteen years of age or those who habitually do not have complete judgment. The civil status of the testator does not matter. In the case of insanity, the individual can testate in a period of lucidity.

(b) Anyone can be a witness except the employees of the notary, those under sixteen years of age, those who do not have complete judgment, the blind, deaf or mute, those who do not understand the testator's language, the heirs, legatees, their descendants, ascendants, spouse or siblings, under pain of nullity of the testamentary provision with respect to that witness or his relatives and those who have been sentenced due to the crime of forgery.

(c) Every inhabitant of the Mexican Republic of any age can receive through a legitimate will or succession, but may lose this capacity for the following reasons:

i. Lack of legal capacity: those not conceived at the time of the deceased's death or those conceived when they are not viable.

ii. By reason of crime: the individual who has committed homicide against the deceased, his parents, children, spouse or siblings, or who is convicted of a crime against these same people, anyone who has been declared adulterer, the co-author of adultery, the parents with respect to a foundling, abandoned, or prostituted child or one whose sexual morality has been attacked, anyone who did not comply with his obligation to provide support or who did not assist the deceased and anyone who uses violence, wilful misconduct or fraud with respect to the deceased affecting his right to execute or modify his will.

iii. Guardians and administrators with respect to the minor they have under their guardianship do not have capacity to acquire by will, nor does the physician who assisted the deceased in his last illness, the spouse, ascendants, descendants and siblings of the doctor, except if they are legitimate heirs, the notary and the witnesses, their spouses, ascendants, descendants or siblings. Religious ministers, churches and religious sects may not be heirs of the ministers of the same religion or of a private person with whom they do not have kinship within the fourth degree.

iv. Lack of international reciprocity: foreigners who, according to the laws of their country, cannot testate or leave their property to Mexicans through intestacy.

v. Those on whom some office has been conferred in the deceased's will and who have resigned the same without just cause or been removed from it due to bad conduct (guardians, administrators, executors, etc.).

9. Authority (Court, Notarial or Other)

The general rule in the case of testatory and legitimate succession, is that the court must intervene to declare the will valid and recognize the executor or heirs. The exception consists in that a testatory succession may be processed extrajudicially before a notary public when a public will or intestacy is involved, when there is no conflict and the heirs are of legal age. When there are minors as heirs, the procedure will always be carried out before a Family Court.

10. Invalidity of Will

(a)–(b) Considering that by effect of law the will is subject to the general rules of the juridical act, it is obvious that the testator's will must be free from defects.

International Succession

There are several instances of juridical inefficacy of wills. To begin with, it should be pointed out that the nullity of the will is the sanction of a structural defect of the document related to its execution, or when the necessary discipline or law contained in it irreparably lacks the authorization of the legal standards and surpasses the limits of private autonomy. As examples of the foregoing, the will that has been executed in the same act by two or more individuals, the will made under the influence of threats against the person of the testator or his property, or against the person or property of his spouse or relatives, or the will obtained via wilful misconduct or fraud.

The forms prescribed for wills are of a substantial nature in the originating legal act; nonobservance thereof results in the nullity of the will.

The general theory of juridical inefficacy distinguishes between absolute and relative nullity. There is, however, great difficulty in making the same distinction in this context to the degree that relative nullity is a sanction of protection and it is to be used for the protected party; for example, the person who suffered vitiated consent. The case is particularly difficult once the testator has died, because of the interests that he tried to safeguard. It has been concluded, nevertheless, that nullity is absolute when the legal and creative norms have not been observed.

There is also a distinction between partial and total nullity. For example, there will be partial nullity when the heir or appointed legatee acts as a witness, in which case the sanction is limited to annulling the provision that benefits such witness.

Lastly, we should make a brief mention of the lack of legal force of the will. In essence, this is not a sanction because the will fully produces its legal effects.

Simply, a will is lacking in force because of the duty of support detailed in paragraph 5 *above*.

i. Due to the presumption of influence contrary to the freedom of the testator, guardians and administrators do not have the capacity to acquire through the will of the minor, unless they were beneficiaries before being named for the office or after the minor comes of legal age, the guardianship accounts having already been approved. The same holds for the physician who assisted the testator during his last illness, etc. Special mention should be made that by constitutional provision, religious ministers, their ascendants, descendants, siblings and spouses, as well as the religious associations to which they belong, are considered without capacity to inherit by will from individuals whom the ministers have addressed or aided spiritually and with whom they do not have kinship within the fourth degree.

ii. Due to the presumption of influence against the will and integrity of the will, the notary and the witnesses who intervened in the will do not have capacity to inherit through it.

iii. In the case of foreign heirs when there is no international reciprocity, the will is invalid.

iv. Disqualification is a relative incapacity to inherit, given that it operates always in relation to a particular succession.

v. There are three specific cases in which the law sanctions the loss of inheritance rights: the guardian, administrator or executor who has refused the office without just cause, or who due to bad conduct has been removed from exercising it by court order.

11. Simultaneous Death

(a) Our legal system contains the presumption of simultaneous death. There is no transfer of rights between two people who are presumed to have died at the same time.

(b) If there is no external evidence, our legal system provides that they are considered to have died at the same time.

12. Estate Taxes

In our legislation there are no taxes that are levied on inheritances or on bequests. However, there is the obligation to pay the duties, taxes and charges corresponding to the conveyance of ownership of property.

13. Administration of Estates

(a) According to Mexican law, the administration function falls upon the executor. It is an *intuitu personae* office, that is, it presupposes both a relationship of trust with the testator or the heirs, and management of interests that are not necessarily his own. From these two concepts is derived the capacity to be an executor: that the individual be in a situation that allows him to perform the office honestly and objectively (those who have been sentenced for crimes against property cannot be executors). The office is determined by the majority interest and not by the number of persons with an interest.

The executor may be special or universal, a distinction based on the extent of the functions. The special executor has the duty of executing specific acts, while the universal executor is in charge of managing the inheritance (liquidating, dividing, delivering the inheritance, etc.). The executorship may also be successive or joint.

The establishment of the executorship originates from a legal act that has the following distinctive aspects:

i. It may be unilateral or collective. In effect, he may be designated by the testator or by a meeting of heirs.
ii. The executor must accept the office, since he is a volunteer, or he may be excused with or without just cause. In this last case, he is sanctioned by depriving him of what the testator would have left to him. Upon accepting, he must give security for his management unless he is an heir and his hereditary portion is sufficient, or the heirs have dispensed him from furnishing security. The amount of the guaranty is determined in relation to the amount and productivity of the inherited property.

427

International Succession

It should be pointed out that in relation to marriages celebrated under the community property system, when one of the spouses has died, the survivor will continue in possession and administration of the community assets, with the intervention of the representative of the estate as long as the partition does not take place, and may be given them at any time such survivor requests, even if the executor or another person has had the assets previously.

(b) Within ten days of having accepted the office of executor, the inventories and appraisals must be made, with notice to the court in order for the heirs to designate an expert appraiser by majority vote; if they do not come to an agreement, the judge will designate him. The executor must present these within sixty days following acceptance.

An exception to the *above* rule is the case of the inventory done by the court actuary or by a notary appointed by the majority of the heirs when they are minors or when the welfare establishments have an interest in the estate as heirs or legatees.

The executor is required to render an account of his executorship each year, as well as of his management, through the court, to the parties with an interest. This management account must be approved by all the heirs and anyone who is in disagreement may initiate a legal trial at his expense.

(c) There is no external supervision on the part of the authorities. The manifestation of any disagreement concerning their rights is left to the interested parties, who may claim against the administrators of the deceased's estate, without affecting the right of the heir or heirs who were not in agreement with the majority appointment of executor to appoint an intervener who supervises the executor. If the minority in disagreement is formed by several heirs, the appointment of an intervener will be made by majority vote, and if no majority is obtained, the appointment will be made by the judge, electing the intervener from among the persons proposed by the minority heirs.

(d) Once the inventory and appraisal have been done, they are added to the file and are displayed in the clerk's office of the court for five days so that the interested parties can examine them. After this term, if no opposition has been filed, the judge will approve them without further procedure. On the other hand, if the parties with an interest oppose the inventory or appraisal, the latter will be processed with a common hearing.

The heirs, legatees, and the surviving spouse are considered to have an interest in the estate.

(e) The partition presupposes determination of the net assets of the inheritance. For this purpose, an inventory of the property must be done, the property must be priced and the debts paid.

The executor is required to draw up the inventory, something that does not require further formalities, unless there are minor heirs or private welfare institutions that have an interest.

Once the inventory has been concluded and approved, the executor has to liquidate the inheritance.

428

The main effects of the partition are the extinction of the community between heirs and the transformation of the right to inherit into concrete ownership of particular goods.

The acceptance of the inheritance is the act whereby the person in whose favour an inheritance has been made by will or *ab intestato* puts on record the resolution to take on the quality of heir. By its nature it is unilateral, voluntary and free.

The immediate consequence of the acceptance is that the effects are produced retroactively to the date of the testator's death. The main effects of the acceptance are, on the one hand, its definitive nature – once made, it is irrevocable – and on the other hand, that it never may produce confusion between the property of the testator and that of the accepting party. This is known as the right of inventory, which is the limitation of the responsibility of the party who accepts up to the value of the inheritance.

Two basic ideas rule the right of inventory. In the first place, the accepting party is not obligated except to the extent of the inherited property. It should be stressed that the heir is also the heir of the debts and not just of the property, but the law authorizes him to exclude his personal property, since separate patrimonies are involved. In the second place, the inheritance is the patrimony of the heir and he is its holder, but it is not confused with his general patrimony.

(f) The executor has to liquidate the inheritance once it has been concluded and the inventories, appraisals and corresponding accounts have been approved. At this point, therefore, the debts of the estate have to be paid.

Accordingly, the executor pays the debts in the following order: first, funeral expenses and the debts that have been caused in the last illness; second, the expenses for strict conservation and management of the inheritance, as well as the support credits which may also be paid before the inventory is drawn up.

If there is insufficient money in the estate to make the payments mentioned in the above cases, the executor will promote the sale of the chattels and even of the real property, with the formalities respectively required.

Lastly, the inherited debts that are due are paid – i.e., those contracted by the author of the estate independently of his last legal provision and for which he is responsible with his property. As regards these debts, the degree of preference of the creditors must be observed.

(g) If the author of the estate did not designate an executor, the establishment of the executorship originates from a collective juridical act such as the meeting of heirs whereat he is designated.

If the deceased did not specify distribution, the assets of the estate will be distributed *pro indiviso* and by equal parts among those who have an interest.

14. Domicile/Nationality

(a) In accordance with the rule of bilateral conflict adopted by the Mexican legal system, the status of individuals is ruled by the law of the place where they have their domicile. Therefore, considering that the answers given to the preceding questions are restricted to the case in which a Mexican court hears an estate proceeding, they are not affected. Nationality is irrelevant.

(b) The local court or authority would give an order of probate or succession if the deceased was domiciled and/or executed a will in the jurisdiction but had no assets there whatsoever, provided that the author of the estate had his domicile in the Mexican Republic.

SECTION B – APPLICABLE LAW/PROCEDURE WHERE FOREIGN ELEMENT/S ARE INVOLVED

1. Jurisdiction

(a) The rule for bilateral conflict adopted by the Mexican legal system is that the legal status of individuals is ruled by the law of the place where their domicile is. If the case of the succession by an individual who had his domicile within a Mexican court's jurisdiction is submitted to that court, based on such domicile circumstance, the Mexican court will maintain that it has jurisdiction.

(b) There are no different rules for movable and immovable assets. The jurisdiction of the mexican Court applies to immovable property as well, if the deceased was domiciled in Mexico.

(c) The competent judge in hereditary proceedings is the one in whose jurisdiction the author of the inheritance had his last domicile. In the absence of this domicile, the court with jurisdiction in the place where the real estate that forms the inheritance is located would be competent, and in the absence of domicile and real estate, the court of the place where the author of the inheritance died.

The judge in whose territory an estate proceeding is established is competent to hear the following actions:

  i. request for probate of a deceased's estate,
 ii. filings against the succession prior to partition and adjudication of the property, and
iii. nullity, rescission and dispossession of the distribution of the assets of the decedent.

2. Applicable Law

In accordance with Section (2) of Article 13 of the Civil Code for the Federal District in matters of common pleas, and for the entire Republic in federal matters, of the United Mexican States, the status of individuals is ruled by the law of the place where they have their domicile. The domicile applicable is that at the date of death. Immovable property situated in Mexico is governed by Mexican law.

The domicile of individuals is, according to Mexican law, the place where they usually reside, and in the absence thereof, the place where the main centre of their business is. In the absence of both these criteria, it is the place where they simply reside, and in its absence, the place where they are found. It is presumed that a person usually resides in a place where he remains for more than six months.

3. Foreign Succession/Inheritance Orders

(a) Mexico would recognize a foreign court decision provided the court that issued it has assumed competency in a form analogous to or compatible with that of Mexican law. However, if competency was assumed with the aim of avoiding a denial of justice, then even if such competency was not compatible with the competency established by the national legislation, such decision will be recognized and executed in Mexico. Furthermore, all judgments, private arbitral decisions and other foreign jurisdictional decisions will be efficacious and will be recognized in Mexico in everything that is not contrary to internal public order and in accordance with Mexican laws, except as ordered by the treaties and conventions to which Mexico is a party.

(b) A resolution that is only going to be recognized, but not executed, in Mexico, that is, that is only going to be used as proof before Mexican courts, approval or further formalities will not be required in order for it to be considered genuine.

However, for those decisions that require execution within Mexico, it is indispensable that they be approved by the Mexican judge and in accordance with Mexican law.

(c) In order for a foreign decision to have the force of execution, the following conditions must be met:

i. that the formalities established in our law in relation to summonses originating abroad have been satisfied;
ii. that the foreign judge or court had competence to hear and judge the matter in accordance with the rules recognized in international law that are compatible with those adopted by Mexican law;
iii. that those interested have been notified or summoned personally with respect to the actions to be executed in order to guarantee the exercise of their defence;
iv. that the action that originated it is not the subject matter of a trial that is pending between the same parties before a Mexican court;
v. that the obligation for compliance whereof action has been taken is not contrary to public order in Mexico; and
vi. that it fulfils the prerequisites to be considered as genuine.

Despite compliance with the above conditions, the court may deny execution if it is proved that decisions are not executed in the country of origin in similar cases.

As for summonses or letters rogatory sent through foreign courts, they must be accompanied by the following documentation:

International Succession

i. an authentic copy of the jurisdictional decision;
ii. an authentic copy of the proof that evidence that the condition of *iii. above* was performed;
iii. the translations into the Spanish language that are necessary for this effect; and
iv. that the executing party has specified an address for services of process in the place where the approving court is.

4. Two or More Succession or Probate Orders

The rule of bilateral conflict that the Mexican legal system adopts in relation to the law applicable to the status of individuals is that the law of the place where the individual has or had his domicile will rule.

5. Assets

Even if there are no assets in the jurisdiction, if the deceased had domicile in it, the court of that domicile is competent.

6. Expert Evidence

(a) Mexican law determines that the form of juridical acts should be ruled by the law of the place where they are granted; and the juridical effects of such acts and contracts should be ruled by the law of the place where they should be executed, unless the parties validly agree on the application of another law.

Consequently, there is no need to present additional evidence if a will has been recognized by a foreign court, if such was granted in that country. It is not necessary either to exhibit further evidences with regard to inheritance law provisions.

(b) Documentary evidence can be exhibited in writing by a legitimate party, directly or through an attorney-in-fact; therefore, personal appearance before the court is not required.

7. Unity of Succession

This principle is definitely accepted in Mexico, since probate hearings are considered as one of the species of 'universal trials'.

8. Formalities

The formalities of a will executed in a foreign country need not be the same as those in Mexico. Mexican law determines that the form of juridical acts is ruled by the law of the place where they are carried out.

432

9. Legislation

The Mexican State has not signed The *Hague Convention* on wills.

10. Wills

(a), (c)–(i) The law of the place where the will is executed governs, as was mentioned *above*.

(b) Construction/interpretation is that of the place where the judge who hears the probate proceeding has jurisdiction.

11. Domicile/Nationality

(a) We have already mentioned that the decedent's domicile is the determining factor in establishing the competence of the judge who is to hear the probate proceeding; on the other hand, the nationality of the decedent is unimportant for this effect. Obviously, the determining domicile is the last one the author of the estate had, that is, the one he had before death.

(b) The domicile of the beneficiary is irrelevant.

(c) We have already mentioned that in the absence of a domicile of the author of the inheritance, the judge of the place where the real estate that forms the inheritance is located is competent to hear the estate proceeding, and in the absence of domicile and real estate, the judge of the place of death. The nationality is irrelevant.

12. Taxation

The law that imposed the inheritance and legacy tax was repealed in Mexico many years ago. Today only the duties, taxes and charges corresponding to the adjudication of goods and the conveyance of ownership are to be charged. The nationality of the deceased/heir is irrelevant.

The Netherlands

prepared by: Prof. Dr. M.H. TEN WOLDE
               Professor Private Law and Private International Law at the State University Groningen and Director of the Institute for International Estate Planning.

Address: State University Groningen
           Faculty of Law
           PO Box 716
           9700 AS Groningen
Tel.:   +31 6 54 323 428
           +31 50 363 5767
Fax: +31 50 363 7334

Section A – Brief Survey of the Local System

1. Type of System

(a) Civil law.

(b) The Kingdom of the Netherlands consists of three countries:

> the Netherlands, the Netherlands Antilles and Aruba. Each of these countries has its own laws. In the field of succession there are major differences in the national legislation of the Netherlands Antilles/Aruba and the Netherlands. This chapter focuses only on the Netherlands legislation as to succession.

In the Netherlands the concept of a registered partnership (*geregistreerd parnerschap*) is known. Such partnership has almost the same legal consequences as marriage and can be entered into by two people (only) of different or same sex. Throughout the entirety of Book 4 of the Civil Code (*Succession*) registered partners are deemed the same as spouses (Article 4:8 paragraph 1). Besides the concept of a registered partnership the marriage has been opened for two people of the same sex (Article 1:30 CC). The following also applies on these same sex marriages.

2. Wills

(a) All wills must be made in written form. The civil code recognizes the following types of wills:

- *Public will* (authenticated will Article 4:94 CC) is a notarial deed containing the final intentions of the testator. Such deed needs to be signed by the testator.
- *Depot will* (Article 4:95 CC). This will must be signed by the testator. In the event that the testator did not write the will himself or he produced the text by mechanical means (for instance by using a computer) and the will consists of more than one page then every page should be numbered and signed by the testator. According to Article 4:95 paragraph 3, such a will has to be given by the testator to a civil law notary who makes a deed of custody, which has to be signed by the testator and the notary. The testator has to declare that the presented document is his last will. The will may be presented to the notary in closed form (secret will).
- *Emergency wills* (Article 4:98 CC). These wills may be drawn up by officers of the army in case of a war or a civil war.
- *Codicil* (Article 4:97 CC). This is an entirely handwritten deed dated and signed by the testator. A notarial deed is not required. By codicil the testator may only appoint an executor, bequeath specific legacies of clothes, certain jewelry and certain furniture, or give directions in respect of his funeral or the use of his entire body or specific parts for medical or transplantation purposes (donor card).

The civil law notary has to notify the Central Register of Last Wills in The Hague that he has executed a public will or a depot will. These wills remain in the custody of the notary and are thus kept secret. Emergency wills are sent to the Central Register of Last Wills in closed form (Article 4:106 CC). Upon the death of a person the notary first makes inquiries at the Central Register in order to establish whether a last will has been executed or registered in the Netherlands.

(b) *i.* The aforementioned wills may be amended in conformity with the applicable rules. A last will can be revoked explicitly or implicitly. An explicit revocation must be done in the form which is required for the will itself or by a special notarial deed (Article 4:111 CC). A will can be revoked implicitly by the making of a later last will which is contrary to the earlier will. A depot will can also be revoked *if* the civil law notary returns such will to the testator. A codicil can be revoked by destroying it.

ii. Marriage does not automatically revoke or affect the validity of a previous will.

iii. For the revival of a revoked will the testator has to make a new will.

3. Intestacy

(a) There are four classes of heirs who are called to the estate (Article 4:10 paragraph 1 CC). Each former class excludes the latter.

i. the surviving spouse (who is not judicially separated) and the children. Illegitimate, adulterine and adopted children share equally;

ii. parents, brothers and sisters of the deceased;

iii. the grandparents of the deceased;

iv. the great-grandparents of the deceased.

435

Each of the persons who are jointly called to the estate have equal shares (Article 4:11 CC). However there is an exception to this rule if there is a half-brother or half-sister who inherits of the deceased. The descendants of a child, brother, sister, grandparent or great-grandparent inherit by substitution (Article 4:10 paragraph 2 CC).

(b) No distinction is made between succession of movables and immovables.

4. Freedom of Testation

(a) In disposing of his property by last will or donations *inter vivos* the testator does not have a free hand. The children of the deceased are entitled to a statutory portion of the value of the estate (*legitieme portie*; Article 4:63 CC). The surviving spouse is not entitled to such portion. The statutory portion of a child amounts to one-half of its intestate portion.

In calculating the statutory portion, the value of the estate at the time of death and any gifts made by the testator during his life are added together. However the gifts are only added if the testator stipulated this in his last will or upon making the donation.

(b) *i.* Dutch law prohibits mutual wills and contracts on a future succession. However an exception is made for spouses who are permitted to make dispositions *mortis causa* in favour of each other in a marriage contract.

   ii. On the estate of a deceased person who leaves a spouse and children behind, the so-called parental partition by law applies (Article 4:13 CC) unless the deceased declared otherwise in a last will. According to this parental division, the surviving spouse gets (by operation of law) the legal title to the property of the estate and has the obligation to pay the debts of the estate. The children, as heirs, get a claim in money on the surviving spouse equalling their intestate portions. However such claim can only be executed if the surviving spouse is declared bankrupt, the surviving spouse dies, or in the events the testator stipulated in his last will. Besides this the children have volitional interests (*wilsrechten*) in four situations (such as the situation in which the surviving spouse wants to marry again). Volitional interests are legal rights, of which the validity or nullity of as legally binding transaction exclusively depends on the entitlement and the actions of a person who was party to such legally binding transaction or of a third party. By executing a volitional right a child will receive property from the estate instead of a monetary claim on the surviving spouse. The rules in respect of the volitional rights are quite complicated and therefore can not be explained in full in the framework of this book.

5. Maintenance

No.

6. Community Property Between Husband and Wife

(a) The statutory matrimonial regime is that of community property. According to this regime all the assets of a husband and wife in their possession either at the time of marriage or acquired during their marriage become common property. Both spouses are entitled to all community assets, except for some very personal assets which remain private. When the community property is dissolved by the death of one of the spouses, the surviving spouse is entitled to half of the community property. The other half constitutes the estate, to which the surviving spouse may also be (partly) entitled as an heir.

(b) *See* a.

7. Gifts (*Inter Vivos*)

(a) Gifts to descendants and other heirs are not set off against the heir's inheritance unless the deceased stipulated this expressly upon making the donation or by stipulating this in his last will.

(b) Where the value of gifts exceeds the value of the share of the heir involved, the surplus is not set off.

8. Capacity

(a) A person aged sixteen years or older (or a younger married person) of sound mind may make a will.

(b) Dutch law does not require any witnesses to be present at the drawing up of a will by notarial deed.

(c) In order to inherit a beneficiary must exist at the moment the *de cujus* dies. In this respect an unborn child of the deceased is considered to exist.

9. Authority (Court, Notarial or Other)

According to Dutch law, on the death of the deceased the assets and liabilities of the deceased pass directly to the heirs (*saisine*). Such heirs are entitled to the estate simply because they are called to the estate by law or by the last will of the testator. The heirs may however accept the estate as beneficiary, which is an acceptance without liability for debts beyond the assets inherited, or they may renounce the entire estate. An estate to which minors are entitled as heirs always has to be accepted as an estate beneficiary.

A declaration that an heir renounces the estate has to be filed with the registry of the district court of the district where the deceased had his last domicile.

International Succession

A probate procedure is not known in the Netherlands. In order to prove that an heir is entitled to the estate a civil law notary issues a certificate of admissibility (if the deceased did not make a last will) or a certificate of execution (where a last will was made). In such certificate the notary declares who is entitled to the estate and for what part. Furthermore the notary makes declarations concerning the personal status of the deceased, the matrimonial regime, the surviving spouse and the descendants, whether there is a last will and whether the testator has appointed an executor. Any heir may request the issuance of a certificate of admissibility or execution. The certificate gives the heirs the authority to collect any debts and assets of the estate.

10. Invalidity of Will

(a) There are numerous reasons a testamentary disposition may be invalid. A will which is entirely or partially contrary to the law or principles of public decency or public order is wholly or partially invalid and void (Article 4:44 CC). Furthermore a will made by a minor younger then sixteen years or a mentally disturbed person is invalid and void (Article 4:55 CC). A will made under duress is voidable (Article 4:43 CC). A condition in a will which is impossible to comply with, is void (Article 4:45 CC). Finally, wills which do not comply with the requirements of form for wills mentioned *above* under 2(a) are invalid and void (Article 4:109 CC). Failure to comply with other requirements of form makes a will voidable (Article 4:109 paragraph 4).

(b) Whether the entire will is affected by the invalidity of a part of it depends on the specific circumstances involved.

11. Simultaneous Death

(a) People dying at the same time or on the same day, without it being possible to make sure who died first, are deemed to have died at the same moment. As a consequence they can not inherit from each other (Article 4:2 CC).

(b) The dates are determined by the death certificates drawn up by the Registrar of births, deaths and marriages.

12. Estate Taxes

(a) *The Inheritance Gift and Transfer Act of 1956* provides for two taxes in respect of an estate:

1. Inheritance tax due on the fair market value of the (part of) the estate acquired from a deceased person who was resident in the Netherlands at the time of his death.

2. Transfer tax due on the fair market value of specific Dutch assets acquired by inheritance from a person who is not resident in the Netherlands.

Whether a person has his residence in the Netherlands depends on the actual circumstances, for instance the duration of the residence and his other ties (family, friends, business) with the country involved. A Dutch citizen who was resident in the Netherlands is considered to remain a resident of the Netherlands for the purposes of inheritance tax for a period of ten years after he left the Dutch territory. A foreigner who was resident in the Netherlands is only deemed to be resident in the Netherlands for one year for this purpose.

(b) Where the deceased was a resident of the Netherlands (or deemed to be resident) his entire estate is subject to Dutch inheritance tax, regardless of his nationality, the residence or the nationality of the heirs or the location of the assets of the estate. If the deceased had his residence outside the Netherlands transfer tax is due on for instance the following assets: a) assets belonging to a domestic enterprise with a permanent establishment in the Netherlands; b) real estate or rights to real property located in the Netherlands.

(c) The aforementioned taxes are in general levied from the heirs.

13. Administration of Estates

(a) In the event of intestacy the heirs jointly administer the estate. Usually the heirs give a power of attorney to one of the heirs or to the civil law notary to commence the administration. An administrator (executor) can only be appointed under a last will. However it is not necessarry to appoint an executor. The task of an executor is to seal the estate, to draw up an inventory of the estate and to carry out the last will. Furthermore the executor has to assist the heirs with the partition of the estate if they make such request. Besides the aforementioned tasks an executor has to administrate the estate, to call in debts, pay debts and to distribute specific legacies. Of course the heirs may give the executor a power of attorney to fulfil other tasks in respect of the administration of the estate.

(b) If there is an executor, one of his tasks is to draw up an inventory of the estate.

(c) No external supervision is needed, unless there are heirs who are incapable of disposing of their property (e.g., minors, persons under tutelage). In the latter case the partition has to be made by notarial deed and the approval for the partition must be sought from the subdistrict court (*Kantonrechter*).

(d) An heir who is prejudiced by the partition to the extent of more than a quarter of his share may nullify the partition but only if this prejudice has been caused by an error in fact on his part. In the event that the share of an heir is Euro 100,000, the partition may only be nullified by him when he was prejudiced by more than Euro 25,000 because he did not know that certain assets of the estate had such large value. Furthermore a partition can be nullified by the general factors which vitiate consent such as threat, deceit, or abuse of circumstances.

(e) The heirs are entitled to the assets of the estate as of the moment of death of the deceased (*saisine*). After the partition each of them is solely entitled to the assets which were apportioned to him. The transfer upon partition has to take place in accordance with the general rules of transfer of property, in general: movable goods by handing over, immovable goods by notarial deed and registration with the Land Registry.

(f) The creditors usually are paid by the heirs or the executor before the partition. However a claim of a creditor may also be apportioned to one of the heirs, who in that case is obliged to pay the claim.

(g) As explained the heirs distribute the estate themselves in such event.

14. Domicile/Nationality

(a) No, nationality and habitual residence are only relevant in respect of the applicable law (*see* Section B).

(b) Not applicable.

SECTION B – APPLICABLE LAW/PROCEDURE WHERE FOREIGN ELEMENT/S ARE INVOLVED

1. Jurisdiction

(a) According to Article 6 sub (f) Civil Procedure Code the court of the district in which the deceased was domiciled or had his habitual residence at the time of his death has jurisdiction over claims concerning an estate of the deceased.

(b) Nationality and domicile of the deceased are only relevant in respect of the applicable law.

(c) The court of the district where the deceased was domiciled or where he had his habitual residence at the time of death.

2. Applicable Law

On 1 October 1996 the Dutch international law of succession was radically amended. The simple, but vague general rules of conflict applicable to the law of succession were replaced on that date by extensive rules from the *Act on the Choice of Law Rules Applicable to Succession* and the *1989 Hague Convention on the Law Applicable to Succession to the Estates of Deceased Persons*. To date, the convention has only been ratified by the Netherlands. The convention has not yet entered into effect, as ratification by the three countries is necessary for this (Article 28). In anticipation of the future entry into force of the convention, the Dutch legislator has already incorporated the rules of the convention into Dutch legislation. *The Act on the Choice of Law Rules Applicable to Succession* and the rules of the *1989 Hague Convention on the Law Applicable to Succession* apply, in principle, solely to estates distributed after 1 October 1996. Estates which were distributed before that specific date are governed by the old general rules (national law of the deceased).

Article 5 of the convention allows for designation of a choice of law where there is a conflict of law for:

(a) the law of the State of which the deceased is a national at the time the choice of law is made;
(b) the law of the State of which the deceased is a national at the time of death;
(c) the law of the State in which the deceased has his habitual place of residence at the time the choice of law is made;
(d) the law of the State in which the deceased has his habitual place of residence at the time of death.

If the deceased has not made a choice of law then the applicable succession law will be determined on the basis of Article 3:

1. Succession is governed by the law of the State in which the deceased was habitually resident at the time of his death, if he was then a national of that State.
2. Succession is also governed by the law of the State in which the deceased was habitually resident at the time of his death if he had been resident there for a period of no less than five years immediately preceding his death. However, in exceptional circumstances, if at the time of his death he was manifestly more closely connected with the State of which he was then a national, the law of that State applies.
3. In other cases, succession is governed by the law of the State of which the deceased was a national at the time of his death, unless at that time the deceased was more closely connected with another State, in which case the law of the latter State applies.

Settlement of deceased's estates is regulated in Article 4 of the *Act on the Choice of Law Rules Applicable to Succession*. This provides that the settlement and division of an estate of a deceased whose last habitual residence was in the Netherlands is governed by Dutch law. Heirs to the estate are still free to declare another law as applicable to the division. The duty and authority of the administrator is also governed by Dutch law in the event the deceased had his last habitual residence in the Netherlands.

3. Foreign Succession/Inheritance Orders

(a) Foreign court orders are not directly enforceable in the Netherlands unless they are based on a treaty. In the field of international succession such treaties only exist between the Netherlands and Belgium and between the Netherlands and Germany.

International Succession

A local execution order has to be obtained (Article 431 Netherlands Civil Procedure Code). The local judge may give any weight he wants to the foreign decision in respect of the entitlement to the estate.

(b) A foreign heir or executor has to obtain a local certificate of admissibility or a certificate of execution from a civil law notary in the Netherlands. A Dutch notary will in principle recognize the powers of a foreign executor. However under certain circumstances (e.g., when statutory portions of heirs would be violated) he shall refuse to issue such certificate.

(c) The foreign heir or executor has to file notarized documents or certified court orders from which it appears that he is authorized to collect the Dutch assets of the estate.

4. Two or More Succession or Probate Orders

Foreign probate orders given previous to the issue of a local certificate of admissibility or execution are not taken into account. The Dutch notary will always apply his own rules of private international law.

5. Assets

Yes, *see* 2.

6. Expert Evidence

(a) The local court may require a foreign lawyer to explain and give evidence regarding the applicable foreign law, but there is no necessity. A local civil law notary does not have the authority to make such demand. However he may refuse to issue the certificate of admissibility or execution where it is not clear why the heirs would be entitled to the estate according to the applicable foreign law.

(b) Proof of foreign law may be given by way of an affidavit. An appearance in court is not necessary.

7. Unity of Succession

According to Article 7 paragraph 1 of the *1989 Hague Convention on the Law Applicable to Succession*, the applicable law governs the whole of the estate of the deceased wherever the assets are located (unity principle). However exceptions are made in Article 15 (when the *lex situs* imposes a special order of inheritance upon particular assets or operations located on its soil) and Article 4. This latter article introduces a coordination rule which applies to situations in which the deceased made no choice of law. In substance, this article provides that, if the law applicable under the convention is that of a non-contracting State, A, and the private international law of A designates the law of another non-contracting State, B, whose private international law also determines its own law as the applicable one, the harmony existing between these two countries should not be frustrated, which means that the law of State B applies for instance to immovable property located in State B. Thus the principle of unity is affected.

8. Formalities

No. A foreign will established in accordance with the formalities of the applicable law according to the *1961 Hague Convention on Wills* is recognized in the Netherlands.

9. Legislation

The *1961 Hague Convention on Wills* is applicable in the Netherlands.

10. Wills

(a) The applicable law determined by the *1961 Hague Convention on Wills*.

(b) The applicable law determined by the conflict of law rules discussed under Section B.2.

(c) The applicable law determined by the conflict of law rules discussed under Section B.2.

(d) Restrictions on the capacity to inherit arising from the personal status of the heir (such as the question of whether an heir must exist at the moment the testator dies) are governed by his national law. Other restrictions (such as whether an heir can inherit from a testator murdered by this heir) on the capacity to inherit are governed by the applicable law determined by the conflict of law rules discussed under Section B.2.

(e) The national law of the testator at the moment of making the last will.

(f) The applicable law determined by the conflict of law rules discussed under Section B.2.

(g) The applicable law determined by the conflict of law rules discussed under Section B.2.

(h) The applicable law determined by the conflict of law rules discussed under Section B.2.

International Succession

(i) Yes, the rules regarding statutory provisions are applicable when the estate is governed by the local succession law.

11. Domicile/Nationality

(a) Both nationality and domicile (habitual residence) are important.

On 1 October 1996 the Dutch international law of succession was radically amended. The simple, but vague general rules of conflict applicable to the law of succession were replaced on that date by extensive rules from the *Act on the Choice of Law Rules Applicable to Succession* and the *1989 Hague Convention on the Law Applicable to Succession to the Estates of Deceased Persons*. To date, the convention has only been ratified by the Netherlands. The convention has not yet entered into effect as ratification by the three countries is necessary for this (Article 28). In anticipation of the future entry into force of the convention, the Dutch legislator has already incorporated the rules of the convention into Dutch legislation. *The Act on the Choice of Law Rules Applicable to Succession* and the rules of the *1989 Hague Convention on the Law Applicable to Succession* apply, in principle, solely to estates distributed after 1 October 1996. Estates which were distributed before that specific date are governed by the old general rules (national law of the deceased).

Article 5 of the convention allows for designation of a choice of law where there is a conflict of law for:

(a) the law of the State of which the deceased is a national at the time the choice of law is made;
(b) the law of the State of which the deceased is a national at the time of death;
(c) the law of the State in which the deceased has his habitual place of residence at the time the choice of law is made;
(d) the law of the State in which the deceased has his habitual place of residence at the time of death.

If the deceased has not made a choice of law then the applicable succession law will be determined on the basis of Article 3:

1. Succession is governed by the law of the State in which the deceased was habitually resident at the time of his death, if he was then a national of that State.
2. Succession is also governed by the law of the State in which the deceased was habitually resident at the time of his death if he had been resident there for a period of no less than five years immediately preceding his death. However, in exceptional circumstances, if at the time of his death he was manifestly more closely connected with the State of which he was then a national, the law of that State applies.
3. In other cases, succession is governed by the law of the State of which the deceased was a national at the time of his death, unless at that time the deceased was more closely connected with another State, in which case the law of the latter State applies.

444

Settlement of deceased estates is regulated in Article 4 of the *Act on the Choice of Law Rules Applicable to Succession*. This provides that the settlement and division of an estate of a deceased whose last habitual residence was in the Netherlands is governed by Dutch law. Heirs to the estate are still free to declare another law as applicable to the division. The duty and authority of the (foreign) administrator is also governed by Dutch law in the event the deceased had his last habitual residence in the Netherlands.

(b) No, the domicile of the beneficiaries is not relevant.

(c) If neither nationality nor domicile (habitual residence) can be determined, the law that has the closest connections with the deceased at the time of his death will be applied.

In case of dual nationality the law of the nation with which the deceased was more closely connected at the time of his death is applied. According to the Explanatory Report on the *1989 Hague Convention on the Law Applicable to Succession* the habitual residence is determined by an equal weighting of a range of elements.

12. Taxation

See infra A.12.

New Zealand

Prepared by: Ian LAWRENCE
Johnston Lawrence, Barristers and Solicitors

Address: Level 6, Wool House
          Cnr. Brandon & Featherston Streets
          Wellington
          New Zealand
Tel.:   +64 4 472 0940
Fax: +64 4 473 4673

SECTION A – BRIEF SURVEY OF THE LOCAL SYSTEM

1. Type of System

(a) Statute and common law.

(b) There is one system and jurisdiction for the whole of New Zealand.

2. Wills

(a) The formal requirements for execution of a will in New Zealand are prescribed by Section 9 of the *Wills Act 1837* (United Kingdom) and Section 1 of the *Wills Amendment Act 1852* (United Kingdom) both of which are in force in New Zealand. These requirements apply to all wills except those of privileged persons in terms of the *Wills Amendment Act 1955* (New Zealand). The formal requirements are as follows:

– The will must be in writing but there is no restriction on the materials which may be used or the language in which it is expressed. It can for example be printed typewritten or even produced by a photocopy process.
– The will must be signed by the testator preferably with his usual signature to avoid having to prove that signature.
– *The Wills Act* also provides that the signature should be at the foot or end of the will.
    In certain circumstances a 'mark' or even a thumb print or initials may be sufficient, but in such cases the attestation clause should state that the testator

446

signed with his mark. The issue of signing at the 'foot or end' of a will has been liberalised to some extent in New Zealand as a result of a lenient interpretation of the *1852 Act*.
- There must be two witnesses to the signature of the testator and those two witnesses must both be present at the same time and affix their own signatures immediately following the signature by the testator. It is not essential for the validity of the will that the testator should actually see the witnesses sign or that the witnesses should have seen the testator in the act of signing and it will be sufficient if the parties could have seen each other sign, had they chosen to look.

There are a number of exceptions to the observance of formalities and briefly these are as follows:

- a person who is a member of the armed services;
- a mariner at sea;
- a prisoner of war who fell within one of the other exemptions immediately before capture or internment.

There may also be situations where a testator in a will refers to another document which is not actually part of the will or instrument being executed. This might include lists of personal articles or account books setting out loans made or repaid. Such a document must normally be in existence when the will is executed and be sufficiently described to identify it.

– *Movables and Immovables*

For a will to operate in relation to immovables it must be made in accordance with the law of the place where those immovables are situated. In the case of movables and a person making a will abroad, the will is valid if it complies with the law of the place of execution of that will *or* of the domicile of the testator at the time of execution *or* of the place where he was domiciled at the time of death (*Wills Amendment Act 1955*).

(b) *i.* A will may be revoked: by subsequent marriage or divorce; by subsequent will or codicil; by writing declaring an intention to revoke the will and itself executed as a will; and by destruction *animo revocandi*, i.e., with an intention to revoke.
   ii. In the case of subsequent marriage or divorce a will is automatically revoked irrespective of the person's intention, but in other cases there must be a requisite mental capacity and intention to revoke. There can be difficulties where for example a testator requests a third party to tear up a will or destroy it but does not do so himself.

3. Intestacy

(a) The order of succession in cases of intestacy is:

International Succession

i. The spouse of the intestate gets the personal chattels, plus NZD90,000.
ii. The spouse of the intestate also gets one-third of the balance of the estate. The other two-thirds goes to the issue of the intestate. Adopted and illegitimate children (subject to proof) inherit on the same basis as legitimate children.
iii. If the intestate left no issue, the spouse gets two-thirds of the balance of the estate. The other one-third goes to the parents (or surviving parent) of the intestate.
iv. If the intestate left no issue and no parents, the balance of the estate goes to the spouse.
v. If the intestate left no spouse, the whole of the estate goes to the issue.
vi. If the intestate left no spouse and no issue, the whole of the estate goes to the intestate's parents (or surviving parent).
vii. If the intestate left no spouse, no issue, and no parents, the whole of the estate goes to the brothers and sisters of the intestate or, if a brother or sister has predeceased the intestate, to his or her issue.

Further provision is made if the intestate left none of the above.

(b) There is no difference in the division between movables and immovables other than in respect of personal chattels which is set out *above*.

4. Freedom of Testation

(a) There is freedom of testation.

(b) *i.* A contract of inheritance (made prior to death) is not part of New Zealand law. A person may make a claim against an estate alleging a 'testamentary promise' under which one person promised to provide some benefit under a will and it then becomes a question of proving the existence and validity of any such testamentary promise.
ii. *Partages*, *anticipes*, *pactes successoraux ou du famille* are not applicable in New Zealand law.

5. Maintenance

A person may make a claim against the estate pursuant to 'family protection' legislation. Such claims are made where a person alleges that the deceased made inadequate provision for a family member. Application must be made to the High Court and there is a relatively wide discretion to alter the terms of the will upon good cause being shown. However, recent decisions tend to move away from intervention, partly due to the complexity of family and *de facto* relationships in the current times.

There are time limits within which an application must be made, but the court may extend the time if the circumstances justify such an extension and if final distribution of the estate assets has not been completed.

6. Community Property Between Husband and Wife

(a)–(b) *The Property (Relationships) Act 1976* came into effect on 1 February 2002, and has an effect where a marriage or *de facto* relationship of three years or more ends because of the death of one party.

The Act Introduces the concept of 'Relationship Property' – basically property of the marriage or relationship – whether jointly owned or by one party – other than property expressly defined as 'Separate' property.

On death, only the surviving spouse or partner is entitled as of right to make an election. This must be made within six months of the date of death.

Option A is for a division of the relationship property, which will result in the revocation of gifts made under the Will. *Option B* is to inherit under the Will.

In certain limited circumstances, a survivor can make a claim for division of relationship property *and* inherit under the Will. Further, in limited circumstances the exercise of the option *may* be set aside.

It is presumed that *all property* owned by the deceased and all property acquired by the Estate after death is relationship property: subject to any agreement to the contrary, and generally any property which a person does not want to be relationship property must be clearly 'ring fenced' as separate.

These provisions are stated in general terms as the legislation is very recent (at the time of writing) and judicial interpretations of the provisions to date are minimal.

It is possible for a deceased person to be domiciled outside New Zealand, but to have either a wife or *de facto* partner resident and/or domiciled in New Zealand. In such cases it seems, a wife/partner could exercise an option to claim under Option A, half the relationship property (which might be a residence in New Zealand, a real estate investment or perhaps movable property generally situated here such as a bank account or equivalent).

Such a claim may, then be competing with a surviving 'wife' or partner resident or domiciled in the same jurisdiction as the deceased.

It is assumed the number of such situations, and the potential for competing claims, will be very few, but careful consideration of the individual circumstances will be required.

7. Gifts (*Inter Vivos*)

(a) If a gift is made after the will is made, then there is a presumption that the testator intended that such gifts should be in substitution for (in whole or in part) the bequest made in the will. If, however, the gift were made prior to the making of the will and the testator does not make any express reference to the gift, then there is a presumption that the gift was intended to stand on its own. If, however, there is no will, it seems that any person entitled under the intestacy who has also received a gift in their lifetime must account for that gift in the calculation of that part of the estate to which the beneficiary is entitled. That presumption can be rebutted if there is sufficient evidence to do so.

(b) There is no limit prescribed.

8. Capacity

(a) The minimum age to make a will is eighteen years but soldiers on actual military service and mariners or seamen at sea can make a will under that age. A person making a will must also have the mental capacity to do so and not be under any undue influence of another.

(b) Generally, any person competent as a witness in other processes may also witness a will. A person who is a beneficiary under a will must not, however, witness it because that disqualifies that person or the person's spouse from entitlement.

Similarly, a person named as a trustee is not regarded as a competent witness of the will.

Notwithstanding the *above*, the court may override the fact of an incompetent witness if the court can be satisfied, for example, that the testator was aware of the entitlement of the interested witness and there was no question of undue influence or pressure by that person.

(c) Because a person under the age of eighteen cannot give a sufficient receipt, a trustee or executor cannot pay a legacy to a person until that person attains eighteen years.

A child may be regarded as living at a specified time if the construction of the will requires such an outcome. Generally a child *en ventre de sa mère* at the time of death of the testator and who is subsequently born alive is entitled to take both pursuant to a will and on an intestacy.

A trustee should not make payment to a beneficiary who does not have the capacity to give a receipt for any property or accept a transfer of it. In such case it would be appropriate to ensure that an appropriate person or persons is/are constituted as trustee to receive and deal with the assets.

9. Authority

A grant of probate of a will or administration of an estate of a deceased person is made by the High Court of New Zealand on the basis of the deceased having left assets in New Zealand. Generally the application for the grant is dealt with by the registrar of the court, but if there are any complicated issues or disputes, the matter may be referred to a judge. A grant by a registrar is referred to as a grant in common form. Where the will must be proved in greater detail or any issues formally resolved, it will be a grant in solemn form. If the assets in an estate are minimal and there is no real property involved, then the holder of an asset, e.g., a bank, may be prepared to release the funds to a trustee on completion of a declaration rather than by production of a grant of probate.

10. Invalidity of Will

(a) Grounds for invalidity of a will include:

   i. where the formal requirements are not met;
  ii. the testator lacks testamentary capacity;
 iii. there has been undue influence;
 iv. in the case of fraud;
  v. where it is shown that the testator lacked knowledge and approval of the contents of the will.

(b) Basically the will is void and a grant of probate will not be possible. If a grant has been made, it can be revoked but in some cases part of a will may be admitted to probate if the provisions in the will are severable. In the case of a bankrupt deceased, some transactions, with leave of the court, may be voidable against the Official Assignee in bankruptcy.

11. Simultaneous Death

(a) New Zealand law does not recognize the expression 'forced heirship'. *The Simultaneous Deaths Act of 1958* sets out the devolution of property in cases of simultaneous deaths.

(b) The legislation provides that where two or more persons have died at the same time or in circumstances which give rise to reasonable doubt as to which of them survived the other or others, the property of each person so dying shall devolve (and if he left a will it shall take effect unless a contrary intention is shown thereby) as if he had survived the other person or persons so dying and had died immediately afterwards.

12. Estate Taxes

There are no longer any death or estate taxes levied in New Zealand.

13. Administration of Estates

(a) If the deceased person left a will then the estate is administered by the person or persons named as executors and trustees under that will.

If there is no will or no executor is appointed under the will or in those cases where an appointed executor is unable or unwilling to act (or is himself deceased), the court can appoint an administrator to administer the estate of the deceased person.

If there is no will, then the heirs entitled by law to succeed to the estate may be able to administer it without a formal appointment by the court. This will depend on the nature and size of the assets in the estate and in individual cases the formal requirements of the organization holding the assets – such as a bank, insurance office, etc.

(b) The executor or administrator is obliged to keep proper accounts and records and to make information available to beneficiaries, including those having life interest and residuary beneficial interests.

The court has the inherent jurisdiction through the Registrar of Probate to require the filing of proper and true accounts by an executor or administrator and may require those accounts to be verified by affidavit.

In the event that no other person applies for a grant of administration or if there is no other person with a prior right to make such an application, then a creditor may apply for a grant.

(c) When New Zealand had a system of estate duties, detailed formal accounts and evidence of assets and liabilities were required to be filed with the Inland Revenue Department. With the abolition of duties there is no longer any requirement to file accounts in this way.

The court retains an inherent jurisdiction to supervise the administration in the event that a person alleges a breach of trust or misappropriation.

(d) *The Administration Act* provides that a person may lodge with the Probate Registrar a caveat against an application before it is granted. The caveat must state the name and address of the person lodging it and will lapse one year after lodgement unless application for administration is made within that time.

The grounds on which an objection may be made to a grant of probate would include:

− the existence of a later will or an overt act revoking the will;
− that the testator had not in fact executed the will;
− that the formal requirements of execution had not been met;
− a lack of testamentary capacity;
− undue influence;
− fraud.

In the case of letters of administration, objections could be lodged as follows:

− claiming that a will exists;
− an assertion that the applicant for the grant of administration lacks capacity or is not entitled to apply in priority to other persons;
− that the person is otherwise disqualified (for example, is a minor, lacks mental capacity).

(e) Personal effects for which there is no system of formal registration of ownership are transferred by way of delivery only. Securities such as shares, company debentures, are transferred pursuant to a transfer form which is signed by the transferor (and may be required to be signed by the transferee) submitted to the company. New Zealand has a system of registration of land titles and land must be transferred first into the name of the executor or administrator and then to the beneficiaries in accordance with a prescribed form at the Land Transfer Office. It will be necessary to produce for the purposes of registration the original grant of probate or letters of administration.

In the case of other assets such as, for example, insurance policies, certain documentation may be required, including production of the probate or letters of administration and proof of age of the deceased as well as the policy document itself.

(f) The executor or administrator must pay the debts of the deceased before proceeding to distribute to beneficiaries.

(g) *Note*: the term 'grant saisine' is not in use in New Zealand.

As previously noted, if no executor is appointed under the will, the court will point an administrator of the deceased estate. That person is then responsible for distribution. In many cases the person appointed as administrator by the court may be a beneficiary or in some cases, a sole beneficiary. In other cases the administrator may be a professional advisor such as a lawyer or accountant.

14. Domicile/Nationality

(a) In order to be valid the will must be executed in accordance with the law of the country where the deceased was domiciled. If the deceased was not domiciled in New Zealand at the time of making a will or at the time of death, then the New Zealand court may decline a grant of probate. A subsequent change of domicile after execution of the will, however, does not revoke or invalidate it insofar as personal estate in New Zealand is concerned.

(b) If the deceased left no assets at all, whether securities, land or personal effects within New Zealand then a court would in all likelihood decline to grant probate or letters of administration.

Section B – Applicable Law/Procedure Where Foreign Element/s are Involved

1. Jurisdiction

(a) If the deceased has left assets within New Zealand, then the High Court of New Zealand would have jurisdiction to grant probate or administration of the will.

In cases where a deceased was domiciled elsewhere, the High Court would grant probate or letters of administration in order to enable assets in New Zealand to be dealt with. That would apply to those assets which were not transferable by delivery but where a system of registration of ownership was in place.

If a deceased person had made a will in New Zealand while domiciled there but had subsequently acquired a foreign domicile, then if assets remained in New Zealand the court would make a grant. If, however, no assets remained in New Zealand, then provided the will complied with the formal requirements of the newly acquired domicile jurisdiction, there would be no point in obtaining a grant in New Zealand. If, however, the only will in existence was that made during a period of New Zealand domicile and such will was not capable of admission to probate in the jurisdiction of the newly acquired domicile, then it seems that a grant might be made in New Zealand and then re-sealed or re-granted in the foreign jurisdiction.

(b) The High Court can make a grant in respect of either movable or immovable assets in New Zealand.

(c) The High Court of New Zealand covers all the country, and the District Courts which are an inferior jurisdiction do not have the authority to make grants of probate or administration.

2. Applicable Law

If the grant of administration has been made in New Zealand, then the law of New Zealand would be the applicable law.

If administration has been granted in an overseas jurisdiction being the domicile of the deceased at the date of death, then if a re-grant or re-sealing of the administration is required in New Zealand it would normally be made upon verification of the grant in the overseas domicile. If it were then necessary to deal with immovable assets or other assets requiring registration of a change of ownership, then the legal personal representative would need to comply with the New Zealand law in respect of any changes of ownership, registration thereof and generally dealing with the assets. However, the law relating to immovable property remains the law of the domicile.

3. Foreign Succession/Inheritance Orders

(a) A grant made in an overseas jurisdiction would generally need to be the subject of a local grant in New Zealand in order that a legal personal representative could deal with assets. If the holding of assets in New Zealand was minimal, then the company or organization responsible for registration of ownership and changes thereof *may* be prepared to accept the production of a foreign grant. In the case of land, however, that would require the re-sealing or re-granting of administration in New Zealand.

(b) Generally it will be necessary to obtain a re-seal or re-grant in New Zealand to enable local assets to be administered and changes of ownership effected.

As outlined in paragraphs 2 and 3(a) *above*, there is a process for obtaining a re-sealing or re-grant of administration in New Zealand in cases where a grant was properly made in an overseas jurisdiction.

(c) In most cases the process of re-sealing or re-granting as previously outlined would be available subject to documentation being properly certified from the foreign or overseas jurisdiction. There may be some instances where a re-seal or re-grant is not appropriate or not available, and in such case it would be necessary for a new application to be made in New Zealand. It is difficult to envisage a situation where a properly certified and verified overseas grant would not be recognized in New Zealand.

4. Two or More Succession or Probate Orders

A New Zealand court would generally acknowledge the grant of probate or letters of administration made by the appropriate authority in the place of domicile of the deceased. If the assets in New Zealand required registration of a change of ownership (whether movable or immovable assets) then the New Zealand court would, upon completion of appropriate verification, grant a re-seal or exemplification of the probate or letters of administration for use in New Zealand.

5. Assets

If there are no assets within the jurisdiction then presumably there would be no requirement or proposal to obtain a grant. If the deceased were domiciled in New Zealand and the personal representatives wished to establish that domicile, then they would be able to obtain a grant of probate or administration in New Zealand.

If, however, the legal personal representatives were resident outside New Zealand and assets were also situate outside New Zealand, then it seems that provided a court in the jurisdiction where assets and/or the legal personal representative were situated were prepared to make a grant, no action in New Zealand would seem necessary or appropriate.

6. Expert Evidence

(a) A New Zealand court would expect to sight a copy of the probate or letters of administration duly endorsed and verified with the seal and signature of an appropriate officer of the court of the country where the original grant was made. This would then be the court of the country in which the deceased was domiciled at the date of death. If, for example, an original grant had been made in country A with a further grant in country B, the New Zealand court would expect to have evidence of the original grant in country A. The New Zealand court would tend to rely upon the verification by the court of the original jurisdiction rather than on the evidence of any foreign lawyer or jurist.

The New Zealand court would require the appointment in New Zealand of a resident person or persons as attorney for the legal personal representatives named in the original will, so that those persons appointed to deal with assets in New Zealand are in a position to do so and have their own signatures on documentation appropriately verified.

(b) If foreign evidence were required, then it may be given orally or by affidavit. An affidavit may be sworn outside New Zealand before a New Zealand diplomatic representative or a notary public whose signature and verification is generally recognized internationally.

7. Unity of Succession

This is not a concept known or understood in New Zealand law.

8. Formalities

So long as a will for which a re-seal or exemplification is sought in New Zealand complies with the requirements of the jurisdiction of the domicile of the deceased, it will be accepted for grant in New Zealand. This pre-supposes the prior grant in another jurisdiction before seeking to have a further grant in New Zealand.

If a person makes a will abroad and purports to dispose of movable estate, it will be valid if it is made in accordance with the law of the place of execution or of the domicile of the testator at the time of execution or of his domicile of origin, or the law of the place where he was domiciled at the time of his death.

Wills of persons (not domiciled in New Zealand) making wills in New Zealand are valid if they are made in accordance with (a) the law of the place where the person is domiciled at the date of death or (b) the law of New Zealand or (c) the law of the place where the person was domiciled at the time the will was made.

9. Legislation

New Zealand is not a party to the *Hague Convention on Wills*.

10. Wills

(a) If the application for the grant of probate or letters of administration is being made in New Zealand as the jurisdiction of domicile, then the laws of New Zealand, as outlined, will prevail. A will made elsewhere in a jurisdiction of domicile but seeking an original grant in New Zealand in respect of immovable property in New Zealand will also need to comply with the law of New Zealand, but if a prior grant has been made in the jurisdiction of domicile, then the re-sealing or exemplification of the grant will be sufficient.

(b) As a general rule, the law of the testator's domicile will be the applicable law and so the construction or interpretation will be made in accordance with the law of the domicile.

If there is a particular interpretation or construction which is applicable within the jurisdiction in which immovable property is situated (e.g., New Zealand) then in relation to that immovable property the local law will apply.

456

(c) There is no law in New Zealand prescribing a minimum share or portion of an estate which must pass to an heir or beneficiary. The law in New Zealand does provide, however, that an heir or beneficiary believing himself entitled to a share, may apply to the High Court for a determination. The legislation is broadly in the categories of 'family protection' and 'testamentary promises'. There is considerable precedent established, but this is being eroded to some extent by the changing nature of family and personal relationships.

In the case of a will made in a jurisdiction recognizing the doctrine of 'minimum portion' and where the claimant established that right, then that right would probably be recognized in New Zealand as an entitlement and the property in New Zealand would be subject to that right.

(d) The legal capacity of a person to inherit will normally be determined by the law of domicile of that person but this may be affected by the law of the jurisdiction in which immovable property is situate. In New Zealand, in the case of a beneficiary lacking capacity, the court may appoint a specific trustee upon application being made, or the trustees/executors of the testator's will may be placed in the position of trustee for a person making capacity.

(e) The capacity of a person to make a will is basically determined by the law of the domicile of the testator at the time of making of the will. A subsequent incapacity of a testator will preclude that person from making a new will or amending an existing will but would not impact upon the validity of an existing will made when there was no lack of capacity.

(f) The validity of a will would be determined according to the law of domicile and a New Zealand court would expect the application for probate or letters of administration to be made in the jurisdiction in which the deceased was domiciled at the date of death. Hence, if a person has made a will outside New Zealand which would not be a valid will if made within New Zealand and has subsequently taken up domicile within New Zealand, it is desirable to make a new will in accordance with the requirements of the domicile, i.e., New Zealand.

If it were argued that a will had been made under duress, then that matter should be placed before the court for a ruling to be made. A bequest made in a will and deemed to be contrary to public policy could also be subject to contestability. It is generally considered inappropriate for a person who is a legatee under a will to be a witness to that will and if that situation were contested then a legatee may not be entitled to the legacy contained in the will.

(g) New Zealand law provides for two categories of powers of appointment: (a) a general power which gives the donee complete freedom to choose the beneficiaries and may in fact therefore amount to a gift of the property to the donee himself, and (b) a special power which restricts the donee in his choice of beneficiaries requiring him to appoint from the group or class named by the testator.

If a will creating a power of appointment is valid, then the creation of that power is also valid. If then the donee of the power is authorized to exercise that power by will, then it will be the validity of the will of the donee which must meet the criteria of the jurisdiction in which the power of appointment is exercised. If the donee of the power lacks capacity (e.g., mental capacity), then the exercise of the power would be in jeopardy. In such case, if there were a 'default' provision then that provision would come into effect or alternatively, an application to the court might be an appropriate solution.

(h) A will can be amended by the valid execution of a codicil which is effectively a means of amending or adding to the provisions of an existing will. The codicil must refer to the existence of the will itself and indeed to any other prior codicil.

In the same way that the validity of the will is determined according to the law of domicile, so the question of amendment, revocation and revival of a foreign will also be determined by such law.

A will may be revoked as follows:

– marriage of the testator after making a will automatically revokes that will;
– partial revocation may take place as a result of dissolution of a marriage;
– providing the testator has capacity to do so, execution of a subsequent will, writing declaring an intention to revoke (with the same formalities required for a will itself) or destruction. In the case of destruction, a will is not revoked by a merely symbolic destruction – for example, writing 'cancelled' on it – and in order to be revoked the will must be destroyed with the intention of revoking it.

A will may be conditionally revoked and if that condition is not fulfilled, the revocation fails and the will remains in effect.

A will can only be revived by the testator re-executing that will with the usual formalities (if the earlier will is still in existence) by execution of a codicil expressing the intention to revive the will.

(i) The expression 'reserve' is not known in New Zealand but the laws relating to non-residents and movable/immovable property are dealt with *above*, particularly in paragraph 10(c).

11. Domicile/Nationality

(a) These matters have been dealt with in previous paragraphs but it is emphasized that under New Zealand law it is domicile rather than nationality which is the determining factor. The question of determining domicile may be the subject of argument, but in the New Zealand context frequently the issue of a principal residence will be a significant, if not determining, factor. Other factors will include the length of time spent in New Zealand in any one year and particularly at the time of making the will and at the time of death, as well as the carrying on of any business or the obtaining of any long-term employment.

(b) New Zealand law does not concern itself with the domicile of the beneficiary.

(c) Generally, a domicile which has existed will be presumed to continue unless there is significant evidence to the contrary and in such case the person seeking to establish a new domicile carries the burden of proof. If the evidence is not convincing a court will rule in favour of an existing domicile.

If a foreign court has granted probate or administration of a will that of itself will be a factor (but not an over-riding factor) that will be taken into account. If a foreign grant has been made and it is necessary to obtain a grant in New Zealand, then the court is likely to accept that the appropriate action in New Zealand is for a re-sealing or exemplification of the overseas probate.

12. Taxation

There are no longer any death duties or estate taxes in New Zealand. There is no capital gains tax as such in New Zealand and assets which pass to a beneficiary pursuant to a will and which are realized by that beneficiary thereafter would not normally be subject to any taxation on the realized gain. If, however, the particular beneficiary were e.g., already dealing in, say, shares or real estate, then the beneficiary *may* be subject to taxation on the realized gain.

Income tax would be payable in respect of income derived by the estate subsequent to the date of death of the testator or on income derived by the beneficiary upon the passing of the income producing asset to that beneficiary. The rates of tax would vary depending upon whether the beneficiary is a New Zealand resident for tax purposes or an overseas resident. In the case of an overseas resident, the withholding tax deducted at source is generally lower than the resident withholding tax, but the rate of deduction will depend upon whether New Zealand has a double taxation agreement with the country in which the beneficiary resides.

Norway

Prepared by: Gøril Asmussen ZIMMER
Wikborg, Rein & Co

Address: P.B. 1513 Vika
          0117 Oslo
          Norway
Tel.:   +47 22 82 75 00
Fax: +47 22 82 75 01

SECTION A – BRIEF SURVEY OF THE LOCAL SYSTEM

1. Type of System

(a) The legal system of Norway is a civil law system.

(b) The law of Norway covers the Kingdom of Norway as such, including the islands of Svalbard, Jan Mayen, Bouvet, Peter I and Dronning Maud Land, unless exceptions are made in the law.

2. Wills

(a) Pursuant to the *Norwegian Inheritance Act of 3 March 1972* No. 5 (*Inheritance Act*), wills must in general be in writing, and the testator must sign the will or confirm his signature in the presence of two witnesses who must be present at the same time and know that the document is his will.

The witnesses must immediately endorse the will in writing in the presence of testator. They should also state, but this is not a requirement, their position and private address, the time and place, and whether the will is in accordance with the testator's wishes. The witnesses might also confirm that the testator was in full possession of his faculties and whether there are other circumstances that may be of importance to the validity of the will.

The *Inheritance Act* also contains rules governing extraordinary forms of wills. In addition to the *above*, an oral or a holographic will may be acknowledged in certain situations. Oral wills are acknowledged if illness or an emergency prevents the execution of a will in accordance with the ordinary rules for drawing up wills. The will must be communicated orally in the presence of two witnesses. The

460

witnesses must as soon as possible record the will in writing, state why the testator was prevented from complying with the ordinary rules for drawing up wills, and endorse the document. A holographic will is acknowledged in the same circumstances, i.e., if it is established in this way due to illness or an emergency. The holographic will must be written by the testator in his own hand and must not be typewritten.

Extraordinary wills will lapse if, within a three-month period, there have been no circumstances preventing the execution of the will in accordance with the ordinary rules for making ordinary wills.

The above are the only forms of will recognized in Norwegian law.

The ordinary rules governing the drawing up of wills in the *Inheritance Act* also apply to gifts to be fulfilled after the donor is deceased or gifts given on the deathbed.

(b) *i.* The testator may at any time revoke a will in its entirety by complying with the ordinary rules for making wills of the Inheritance Act, *see* paragraph 2(a). A will is also considered revoked by the testator if it is destroyed or crossed off in such a way that it is likely that the testator has changed his mind.

A will may also lapse in its entirety due to circumstances arising after the will was drawn up, if it is obvious that the will no longer shall apply.

A revocation of part of a will is usually made by the execution of a codicil in which it is clearly stated that one or more provisions in the main will are cancelled. Revocation in part can also be effected in a more informal manner by the testator, e.g., by deleting one or more provisions in the will and at the same time adding a written certification in the margin that the provision has been deleted by him. If the testator wishes to combine the revocation with a new provision, this will, however, require a codicil to the will which must be executed in accordance with the ordinary rules for drawing up wills in the *Inheritance Act*.

If the testator executes a new will without indicating that a previous will is revoked, the rule of presumption states that the previous will has lapsed. If a codicil includes provisions that clearly conflict with provisions of the main will, the rule of presumption states that the provision of the codicil will take precedence over the will.

ii. No rule of presumption or other rule will apply if a testator marries after he has drawn up a will. However, the surviving spouse may succeed in claiming full or partial revocation if it is obvious from the will and other circumstances that marriage was not foreseen.

If a married person has drawn up a will with his other spouse as beneficiary, the will will in general be considered as revoked in the event of separation or divorce.

The same rule will most likely apply if a testator has his fiancé(e) as beneficiary and the engagement is broken off.

iii. The testator must comply with the same rules as mentioned *above* under *ii.*

3. Intestacy

(a) Intestate succession is governed by the *Inheritance Act*, which has a system of inheritance classes, going from one to three, depending on the position of the family members.

- *Class one*: In inheritance class one is the intestate's issue (heirs of the body). Illegitimate, adulterine and adopted children are considered issue. The issue will receive the deceased's estate in equal shares. If one of the children has predeceased the intestate, his children will succeed to his share in equal shares.
- *Class two*: If the deceased leaves no issue, the estate will go to the deceased's parents who will receive the deceased's estate in equal shares. If one of the parents has predeceased the intestate, his children will succeed to his share in equal shares. If the predeceased parent does not have any issue, the other parent will receive the whole estate.
- *Class three*: If the deceased leaves no such heirs as mentioned in inheritance classes one and two, the estate will go to the deceased's grandparents who will receive the deceased's estate in equal shares. If one of the grandparents has predeceased the intestate, his share will go to his heirs of the body but not beyond the grandchildren of the grandparent, i.e., the cousins of the deceased. If the predeceased grandparent does not have any issue, the other grandparent on the same side of the family will receive his share of the estate. If there are no grandparents or issue of the grandparents on one side of the family, the grandparents on the other side of the family, or their issue, will receive the whole estate.
- *The deceased's surviving spouse*: If the deceased also leaves a surviving spouse, the surviving spouse will, as a minimum, inherit one-quarter of the deceased's estate whereas the remaining three-quarters will be distributed equally between the issue of the deceased. However, the surviving spouse's share of the estate shall not be less than a fixed sum stipulated by the Government (currently NOK 177,500), unless the value of the entire estate of the deceased is less than this amount, in which case the spouse will receive the entire estate.
  If the deceased leaves no issue (class one), one-half of the estate will go to the deceased's parents or their issue (class two), and the other half of the estate will go to the surviving spouse. However, the surviving spouse's share of the estate shall in this case not be less than a fixed sum set by the Government (currently NOK 266,250), unless the value of the entire estate of the deceased is less than this amount, in which the spouse will receive the entire estate.
  If the deceased leaves no such heirs as mentioned under inheritance classes one or two, the entire estate will be left to the surviving spouse.
- *The State*: If the deceased leaves no such heirs as mentioned under inheritance classes one, two or three or a surviving spouse, the entire estate will go to the State.

(b) There is no difference in the division of the estate on intestacy between movables and immovables.

4. Freedom of Testation

(a) The testator is free to dispose of his assets in a will unless he leaves issue, as described in paragraph 3(a). Pursuant to the *Inheritance Act*, two-thirds of the deceased's estate is statutory inheritance to his issue. If the testator leaves issue, he may therefore freely dispose of only one-third of his estate in a will. However, the statutory inheritance to children is limited to an amount of NOK 1,000,000 to each child.

If the testator is married, he cannot dispose of his assets in a way that reduces his spouse's right of inheritance, as described in paragraph 3(a), unless his spouse is notified before the testator's death. There is no requirement that the spouse agree to the will.

(b) Contracts of inheritance are acknowledged in only two forms:

– An heir may contract with the testator (with or without compensation) to renounce his right of inheritance.
– A testator may undertake not to draw up a will, or not to revoke an existing will.

5. Maintenance

There are no specific rules relating to maintenance. However, children raised by the deceased who are not yet been fully provided for at the time of decease, may in certain circumstances claim a sum from the estate, before the inheritance is distributed among the heirs, to cover their subsistence and education if this is considered fair, depending on the circumstances.

Children living at home who have cared for the deceased without receiving reasonable payment, may also in certain circumstances claim a certain share of the deceased's estate before the inheritance is distributed among the heirs.

'Children' also includes illegitimate/adulterine and adopted children.

6. Community of Property Between Husband and Wife

(a) The statutory rule in Norway is absolute community of property between spouses. Spouses may, however, execute a marriage settlement to the effect that a different division of property shall apply between them.

In the event of full community of property, the surviving spouse is entitled to 50 per cent of the total net assets of the spouses. The remaining 50 per cent constitutes the deceased's estate which is to be distributed according to a will or the rules governing succession on intestacy.

(b) If the spouses have executed a marriage settlement providing a different division of their property, this settlement will be decisive for the distribution of the net value of the estate left by the deceased.

If the marriage settlement provides that the spouses shall have separate properties (no community of property), all of the deceased's assets will constitute the estate.

A marriage settlement may also provide that the deceased's assets are subject to full community of property, whereas the surviving spouse's assets shall be his separate property. In that case, the surviving spouse will keep his separate property and have a claim for 50 per cent of the deceased's assets by virtue of the marriage. In that case, only 50 per cent of the deceased's assets will constitute the estate.

7. Gifts (*Inter Vivos*)

(a)–(b) Gifts to an heir prior to the testator/intestate's death will in general not reduce the heir's inheritance unless a contract of inheritance has been made. It should be noted that it is a prerequisite that the gift is not given on the deathbed, as such gifts must be made by way of a will. However, substantial gifts to an heir of the body may reduce the heir's inheritance if it is so decided by the testator/intestate, or if it is proven that this was the intention of the testator/intestate.

8. Capacity

(a) A testator must be eighteen years of age. If a testator is under eighteen years of age, the will must be confirmed by the King in order to be valid.

(b) Individuals witnessing a will must not be under eighteen years of age and must be in possession of their faculties. If a witness or a close relative to the witness has been included in the will as a beneficiary, the part will that contains gifts to the witness or his close relatives will be invalid.

(c) A beneficiary must be alive or conceived (and then born alive) at the time of the intestate's/testator's death.

9. Authority (Court, Notarial or Other)

A certificate of probate from the Probate Court is always the first step, regardless of whether the estate is administered by the heirs or by an administrator. A petition must be filed with the Probate Court, who will inquire whether all formalities have been observed. The certificate of probate is required in order that the heirs or the administrator may be empowered to dispose of the deceased's assets.

10. Invalidity of Will

(a) A number of errors may invalidate a will. The errors may relate both to form and procedure, lack of capacity, deficiencies relating to the declaration of the testator's intent, or defects in content or authority. A testator must also be in possession of his faculties at the time of execution of the will. A will may be declared invalid if it is established that it has been executed under duress, improper influence or certain forms of abuse.

(b) Most defects cause the will to be declared invalid.

11. Simultaneous Death

(a) If two individuals, who are entitled to inherit from one another, have died and it has been impossible to establish whether one predeceased the other, neither of them will succeed to the estate of the other.

(b) The date of death will be based on the facts in each case. There are no provisions regarding presumption of death.

12. Estate Taxes

(a) *The Inheritance Tax Act of 19 June 1964* No. 14 governs the taxation of estates passing on death and *inter vivos* gifts.

(b) If the deceased was a Norwegian resident at the time of death or a Norwegian citizen, the deceased's worldwide estate is subject to Norwegian inheritance tax. *Inter vivos* gifts are subject to Norwegian inheritance tax if the giver was a Norwegian resident or a Norwegian citizen at the time the gift was given. If a deceased Norwegian citizen was resident in another country, the heirs will not have to pay Norwegian inheritance tax if such taxes are applicable in the country where the deceased was a resident.

All real property situated in Norway is subject to Norwegian inheritance tax even if the deceased was neither a resident nor a citizen of Norway.

The *above* rules may be modified by bilateral tax agreements.

(c) Inheritance tax is charged to the heirs on an individual basis by reference to the estate. There are no inheritance taxes charged on the first NOK 100,000 of the net assets the heir has inherited. Children and parents of the deceased will be charged an inheritance tax of 8 per cent on the net assets received from NOK 100,000 up to NOK 400,000. If the value of the net assets received exceeds NOK 400,000, an inheritance tax of 20 per cent is charged on the exceeding amount. For other heirs, an inheritance tax is charged at 10 per cent of the net assets received from NOK 100,000 up to NOK 400,000 and 30 per cent on the amounts exceeding NOK 400,000.

A proposal has recently been made to increase the amount for which no inheritance tax has to be paid from NOK 100,000 to NOK 200,000. This has not yet been adopted by the Parliament.

The deceased's spouse is not obliged to pay inheritance tax.

Inheritance tax on *inter vivos* gifts is only applicable if the receiver is related to the giver as defined in the Act.

13. Administration of Estates

(a) Estates may be administered by the heirs themselves, or by an administrator appointed in the will or appointed by the heirs, or by the Probate Court. The heirs may administer the estate themselves if all heirs agree and it is not prohibited by the will.

It should be observed that certain estates are exempted from administration. A surviving spouse in a marriage subject to full community of property is entitled to take possession of the deceased's property without administration. If the deceased has children with others than his wife, the spouse is only entitled to take possession of the deceased's property without administration if such heirs consent. At the time of death of the surviving spouse, or if the spouse remarries, the total joint estate of the spouses will be subject to administration and distributed between the heirs.

The surviving spouse in a marriage where the spouses have separate estates may also succeed to the deceased's property without administration if this is in accordance with the marriage settlement, or if the deceased's heirs consent.

(b) Reports on the administration of the estate have to be submitted by the heirs or by the administrator to the Probate Court for inheritance and income tax purposes.

(c) All estates are subject to supervision, but the supervision is more detailed in estates handled by the Probate Court.

(d) If the estate is administered by the heirs, they must in principle agree on all transactions. If no agreement is reached, any of the heirs may demand that the Probate Court take over the administration of the estate.

In relation to estates administered by the heirs or by an administrator, all heirs have a right to take part in all decisions. This does, however, not apply to beneficiaries who receive a fixed sum or a specific chattel from the estate. Such beneficiaries have no right to vote in the estate.

(e) The assets are formally transferred to the heirs who themselves administer the estate according to a court order (certificate of probate). It is then left to the heirs to distribute the assets between themselves as they see fit.

In relation to estates handled by an administrator or the Probate Court, assets are transferred to the beneficiaries when the administrator or the Probate Court no longer requires them for the purpose of the administration of the estate.

A transfer deed is required in respect of real property, other assets may be transferred by any normal manner of transfer that applies to each particular asset.

(f) If the estate is handled by the heirs themselves, at least one of the heirs must undertake the responsibility for the deceased's obligations. The heirs are then personally – jointly and severally – liable for payment to the creditors.

If the deceased's heirs do not undertake the responsibility for his obligations, the estate must twice make a notification, with a two-week interval, in the public gazette *Norsk Lysingsblad* and in one of the larger newspapers in the country, requesting the creditors to register their claim with the estate within six weeks of the date of the last publication of the notification.

All creditors having registered a claim will then be paid by the heirs or the administrator.

(g) *See* paragraph 13(a) *above*.

14. Domicile/Nationality

(a) Pursuant to Norwegian law, the law of the deceased's domicile at the time of death is considered to govern the distribution of all assets.

(b) If the deceased was domiciled in Norway, the local court will give an order of probate even if the deceased had no assets in Norway.

SECTION B – APPLICABLE LAW/PROCEDURE WHERE FOREIGN ELEMENT/S ARE INVOLVED

1. Jurisdiction

(a) The local court will hold that it has jurisdiction if the deceased at the time of death was domiciled in Norway.

If the deceased was not domiciled in Norway at the time of death, a Norwegian Probate Court may still be competent according to a resolution by the Ministry of Justice provided that:

– the deceased was a Norwegian citizen; and
– the deceased's assets are not included under probate in the country where the deceased was domiciled at the time of death; and
– the deceased has a natural connection to Norway, e.g., assets or heirs in Norway.

(b) The sole fact that a person who dies abroad leaves assets in Norway does not make Norwegian courts competent. It makes no difference whether such assets are real property or movables.

Norwegian courts may, as mentioned in paragraph 1(a) *above*, be made competent with respect to assets left in Norway, but only if these assets are not included under probate outside Norway.

(c) If local jurisdiction applies, the local court covering the area where the deceased was domiciled has jurisdiction.

2. Applicable Law

The Probate Court will apply the Norwegian rules relating to administration, whereas the rules governing succession are decided according to the place where the deceased was domiciled at the time of death. It makes no difference in this respect whether the assets are movables or and immovables.

3. Foreign Succession/Inheritance Orders

(a) Foreign probate orders are usually acknowledged in Norway. A foreign administrator who can establish his authority to dispose of the assets of the estate according to his home state rules may ask the Norwegian Probate Court for assistance.

(b) In cases where the Norwegian Probate Court does not have jurisdiction, it is not necessary to obtain an order from the local court to give the foreign authority/administrator possession of assets of a deceased and to give effect to a foreign succession. However, it may be wise to ask the Norwegian Probate Court for assistance.

(c) A foreign authority or administrator must file a petition with the Probate Court. No particular formalities concerning documentation of the foreign succession or inheritance order are required, and the petition may just be a letter explaining the circumstances.

4. Two or More Succession or Probate Orders

In the event of there being an application before the court in the local country for an order of succession or inheritance, and a foreign order already exists in one or more foreign countries, the order of the country of the testator's/intestate's domicile prevails.

5. Assets

See paragraph 1(a) *above*.

6. Expert Evidence

(a) If administration of the estate is to be made in Norway pursuant to foreign inheritance law (*cf.* paragraph 2 *above*), it may be necessary to obtain evidence from a foreign lawyer regarding a foreign will or regarding the inheritance law of a foreign State.

(b) Such evidence will normally be accepted by the Probate Court by way of an affidavit. However, if there is a disagreement among the heirs regarding a foreign will or regarding the inheritance law of a foreign State, the Probate Court may request the evidence to be confirmed by the foreign court.

7. Unity of Succession

This is recognized as the basic principle in Norway.

8. Formalities

A will executed outside Norway is acknowledged if it observes the formality requirements of:

- the law of the country where the will was drawn up; or
- the law of the country of which the testator was a citizen at the time when the will was drawn up or at the time of death; or
- the law of the country where the testator was domiciled at the time when the will was drawn up or at the time of death; or
- the law of the country where the property disposed of in the will is located.

9. Legislation

The *1961 Hague Convention on Conflicts of Laws Relating to the Form of Testamentary Dispositions* is applicable.

10. Wills

(a) Validity requirements must be established in accordance with the rules of the countries as mentioned in paragraph 8 *above*. This means that if a person drew up a will with only one witness in a place where two witnesses are required, the will would be valid if he died in a country where only one witness was required.

(b) As a general rule, a will should be interpreted according to the rules of the country where the will was drawn up. However, this may vary, depending on the circumstances.

(c) The law of the country of domicile at the time of death governs the rights of heirs.

(d) The law of the country of domicile at the time of death governs the capacity to inherit.

(e) The law of the country where the will was drawn up governs the capacity to make a will.

(f) The law of the country of domicile at the time of death governs the question of validity.

International Succession

(g) The law of the country of domicile at the time of death governs powers of appointment.

(h) Amendment, revocation or revival is governed by the law of the country where it was made.

(i) This is applicable both for movable and immovable property.

11. Domicile/Nationality

(a) *See* paragraph 10 *above*.

(b) The domicile of the beneficiary is irrelevant.

(c) The Norwegian rules of competence (extended concept of domicile) usually apply. Otherwise, it may be checked whether the deceased had a particular connection in respect of domicile to a particular country.

12. Taxation

See Section A, paragraph 12 *above*.

Panama

Prepared by: David J. AROSEMENA S. and Guillermo ZURITA
Arosemena Noriega & Contreras

Address: Edificio Banco Do Brasil
Calle Elvira Méndez, No. 10
Panama City
Panama
Tel.: +507 265 3411/213 0300
Fax: +507 264 4569/263 8539/223 2133
E-mail: darosemena@cwpanama.net
URL: http://www.anorco.com

Section A – Brief Survey of the Local System

1. Type of System

(a) Panama has a civil law system.

(b) The Constitution of Panama, enacted in 1972, and amended in 1978, 1983, 1993 and 1994, provides for a centralized republican, democratic, unitary and representative system of government.

Procedural matters such as the enforcement of foreign judgments or 'exequatur', are regulated by the Judicial Code, which applies in all the national territory. As there is a unitary form of government, there are no regional laws.

Everything in connection with the transfer of a deceased person's property is regulated by established guidelines in the Civil Code and the Code of the Family, and the corresponding procedures in connection with property transfer are outlined in the Judicial Code. As we have a unitary form of government, there are no regional laws.

2. Wills

Our Civil Code defines a will as the act whereby a person makes arrangements for the distribution of his/her property or part thereof after his/her demise. The testator may dispose of his/her property as an inheritance or bequest. In case of doubt, even though the testator has not used the expression heir/heiress, if his/her will is clear on this concept, the disposition shall be valid as if it had been done pursuant to

471

general title or inheritance. A joint will is not valid, as two or more joint persons cannot testate in the same instrument, whether this done for their mutual benefit or for the benefit of a third party. The last will and testament is a very personal act; its redaction cannot be left neither in whole or in part to the discretion of a third party nor be done through an agent.

(a) The last will and testament may be common or special. The common last will and testament may be hand-written, open or closed. The special last will and testament may be a sailor's will, a military will, or a will drawn up in a foreign country. Compliance with the full formalities that are inherent to each last will and testament is essential for its execution and validity.

  i. A will is known as *holographic* when the testator writes it in its entirety by himself/herself; it can only be executed by persons of legal age. In order for this type of will to be valid, it must be written in the proper handwriting of the testator (it cannot be written by another person) and signed by him, indicating the year, the month and day that it was drawn up. After the demise the hand-written last will and testament must be submitted to the Circuit Judge of the last known domicile of the testator, or to the Circuit Judge of the place where the testator passed away, within five years, beginning as of the date of the demise.
 ii. A *nuncupative will*, also known as an *open* will, must be executed before a notary public and three qualified witnesses who understand the testator and at least one of whom can read and write. The testator will indicate that this is his last will to the notary and the witnesses. The place, year, month, day and hour of drawing up of the document must be detailed in the instrument. Upon termination of the act, it must be read so that the testator may confirm that he is in agreement with it, and if the testator so agrees, it must be signed forthwith by the testator and the witnesses. The notary will always state for the record that to his knowledge the testator has the required legal capacity to execute the last will and testament.
      In locations where a notary cannot be available, the open will may be executed before five witnesses who meet the legal qualifications. Should the testator be ill and in danger of imminent death, the testator may execute the last will and testament before five qualified witnesses without the need of a notary. A last will and testament so executed shall be rendered invalid if two months have lapsed as of the date that the danger or epidemic has ceased to exist. In the event that the testator should pass away before the said term, it shall furthermore become invalid if it is not registered as a public deed before a competent judge within three months after the demise, whether it was drawn up in writing or orally.
iii. A *mystic will* is a closed last will and testament that may be hand-written by the testator, or by another person on his/her petition, indicating the place, day, month and year when it was written. The closed form of the ordinary last will and testament is intended to hold secret its provisions until after the demise of the testator. Illiterates, including the deaf-mute, cannot use this kind of last will. The testator appears with the closed last will and testament, or closes and seals it in the presence of the notary and three qualified witnesses, stating that the

sealed document being filed contains his last will and testament, indicating whether it is hand-written and signed and countersigned by him/her or written by some other person and signed by him/her at the foot of every page, or if due to the fact that he cannot sign, someone else has done it for him/her at his/her request. On the cover of the last will and testament, the notary issues the corresponding minutes of execution, attesting that it has been executed and that all the corresponding formalities have been observed, that the testator is known to him or duly identified, and that to the knowledge of the notary the testator has the required legal capacity to execute such last will and testament.

iv. A *sailor's will* is the special last will and testament executed during a maritime voyage made by those aboard, in the manner of a closed or open last will and testament. If it is a war ship, the respective commander authorizes the last will and testament. On merchant vessels, the captain or his appointees with the aid of two qualified witnesses authorize the last will and testament.

v. *Military last will and testament*: During wartime, military personnel in action, volunteers, prisoners and other individuals, army employees, or those accompanying them, may execute their special last will and testament before an officer or commander. This right is available to individuals of an army force present in a foreign country and to members of the national police. Should the testator be ill or hurt, the last will and testament can be executed before the physician who is taking care of the testator. Should the testator be assigned to a post, the last will and testament can be executed before the official in charge. In all cases, it shall always be necessary to have two qualified witnesses present. At any moment close to a war action a military last will and testament may be executed verbally before two witnesses. But this last will and testament shall become invalid if the testator survives the situation in which he made his/her last will and testament, or if it is not formalized by the witnesses before the judge advocate.

vi. Panamanians can testate *outside the national territory*, subject to the laws of the country where they may be found. In addition they may testate on the high seas during a cruise in a foreign vessel, subject to the laws of the nation under which the vessel is registered. Holographic wills can also be made, even in countries where laws do not acknowledge such last will and testament. Joint wills will not be valid in Panama even if they are authorized by the laws of the country where they were drawn up. An open or closed last will and testament can be executed in a foreign country before the diplomat or consular representative of Panama in that place. In these cases such agent shall act as a notary, and all the formalities established by law will be respectively complied with. The domicile of the witnesses is irrelevant.

(b) i. All the testamentary provisions are essentially revocable, even though the testator might have indicated in the testament his resolution to never revoke them. The last valid declaration of the will of the testator prevails over previous wills. The derogatory clauses to future testamentary provisions and those in which the testator orders that revocation of the last will and testament shall not be valid, are deemed not to have been included if the testator fails to have obeyed certain forms.

All provisions in documents that are found in the domicile of the testator or elsewhere after his/her demise, pertaining to the institution of heirs, testamentary gifts or bequests, will become void should those documents fail to meet the above-mentioned requirements of the hand-written last will and testament.

The last will and testament in which the formalities established by law have not been complied with, is void. That is the reason why the will cannot be revoked in whole or in part except pursuant to the necessary formalities. Panamanian legislation does not admit codicils.

ii. Wills executed before marriage maintain their validity. However, the obligation to insure support to certain relatives shall be charged to the estate of the testator.

iii. The last will and testament as an act of disposition of all assets or part thereof by the testator after his/her demise, can be revoked by the last manifestation of his/her will, and therefore it is established that all testamentary provisions are essentially revocable upon compliance with the necessary formalities. Consequently, the law revokes the foregoing last will and testament by the perfected last one, if the testator does not express in the latter that the former is to subsist in whole or in part. Nonetheless, the previous last will and testament recovers its force if the testator revokes the last one afterwards, and expressly declares it to be his/her will that the first one be valid.

3. Intestacy

Succession is the transfer of the rights, assets and liabilities that form part of the inheritance of a deceased person to a surviving person, in accordance with the law and/or the testator's will.

An heir is an inheritor pursuant to general title, and a legatee is a beneficiary pursuant to a specific title.

The succession is called intestate, when the law designates the heirs. In these cases the order of succession is determined by family ties. Consequently, the closest relative inherits to the exclusion of the remote relative, save where a right of representation exists.

No difference exists between real estate and other type of assets that constitute the totality of the inheritance.

(a) The surviving spouse, sons and daughters of the deceased have a right to a proportional part of the estate. There is no difference between legitimate, adopted and illegitimate children.

The order of succession is established by law for blood-related heirs and is as follows: direct descendants; parents in the event the deceased had no children.

The order of succession in intestate proceedings is as follows:

i. The testate succession corresponds, in the first place, to the direct line in descendant parentage. The children and their descendants, including adopted children and their descendants, are the successors in equal shares to the parents and other ascendant relatives without distinction.

ii. If the deceased person does not have any children or descendants, the estate will be inherited by his/her ascendant relatives, excluding collateral relatives. If both parents exist, then the estate would be divided between spouse, the mother and the father in equal parts. If only the mother or the father of the deceased exists, then the surviving spouse will receive half of the estate.

iii. In the absence of descendant or ascendant relatives in direct line, the collateral relatives will inherit as follows: If there is a surviving spouse, not legally separated or divorced by final order, the spouse will inherit one-third with one-third going to collateral relations on the parental side and the remaining third to the maternal side.

iv. In the absence of relatives entitled to inherit pursuant to the aforementioned rules, the municipality of the last domicile of the deceased will inherit the estate.

(b) There is no distinction between the succession of movables and immovables.

4. Freedom of Testation

Every competent person may dispose by means of a last will and testament of his/her assets, as long as he/she allows for an allowance for maintenance and food support of the children entitled thereto by law, until they become of legal age and for life should they be handicapped children, and for his/her parents, spouse and handicapped children as long as they need such support. These are the only people entitled to maintenance.

An inheritance agreement or any other juridical act subscribed before the demise of a person lacks binding force. Only the provisions that comply with the formalities or requirements of the last will and testament have juridical or compulsory effect.

In connection with a family, only allowances or provisions can be established for maintenance or food support in favour of *bona fide* dependents lacking sufficient resources for their sustenance.

5. Maintenance

It has already been expressed that in this country the freedom to testate is limited only by legal provisions for food and maintenance support in favour of dependents who lack resources for their sustenance. If the testator or deceased person had made no provision, his/her dependants may claim the corresponding allowances from the estate.

6. Community Property Between Husband and Wife

(a) Couples married prior to 1995 have absolute separation of personal property. Couples married after 1995 who have not entered into a prenuptial agreement with a clause for separation of personal property are subject to a joint property system, in which each spouse will be entitled to 50 per cent of the joint property. The spouses can also opt for the system of participation in profits and in this case, in the event of the demise of one of the spouses the surviving spouse is entitled to at least one-fourth of the estate of the deceased spouse.

(b) In connection with the common property of spouses, for the disposition of assets, the consent of each spouse is required. This consent can be expressed in a separate document. Joint wills, however, are not valid.

7. Gifts (*Inter Vivos*)

Gifts to heirs prior to the death become part of the property of the heir. Therefore, these gifts are not withdrawn from the heir's inheritance.

8. Capacity

(a) Persons who are twelve years of age or older, of either sex, are qualified to testate is they are found to be mentally competent. The last will and testament made before becoming mentally ill is valid.

(b) The persons designated as heirs or beneficiaries cannot act as witnesses for last will and testaments executed before a notary. Spouses or relatives of the testator are not allowed as witnesses to wills.

(c) Every natural or juridical person has the qualification to succeed or to receive a succession, including minors and unborn children.

9. Authority (Court Notarial or Other)

An order of succession is only granted through Circuit Courts following a petition filed by a lawyer or law firm. Notary publics and other authorities cannot issue orders regarding succession.

10. Invalidity of Will

Last will and testaments are annulled whenever the formalities provided by law are not complied with. Particularly, the last will and testament drawn up due to violence, lie or fraud is to be annulled. Whoever prevents a person from freely executing his last will and testament will lose his inheritance right, without prejudice to the criminal responsibility in which he has incurred. The will will be void and not voidable.

11. Simultaneous Death

(a) In case of simultaneous death, the person who considers that one of the deceased died before or after another must prove that allegation. If there is no evidence of the order of the deaths, there is a presumption that all died at the same time and, therefore, there is no succession between them. Therefore, there is no presumption that a younger person survives an older, etc.

(b) The date of death may be determined by all legal means, e.g., experts, etc.

12. Estate Taxes

As of the year 1995, the inheritance tax was eliminated.

13. Administration of Estates

(a) When the testator has left a will, all of the inheritance will be administered by the person whom the testator appointed as testamentary executor, and in absence thereof by the heirs. In intestate successions, the estate is managed by the heirs as they begin to show up. If there are two or more heirs and they do not reach an agreement as to the administration of the assets jointly or by one of them or by a third party, the judge will appoint an administrator until an order is given or the distribution is carried out. By petition of any of the heirs, the administrator appointed by the judge must guarantee his administration to the judge's satisfaction. By petition of any of the heirs, the administrator who is found negligent or to have mishandled the administration of the assets may be removed from his position.

The court orders the executor to pay the creditors with the resources from the inherited assets.

(b) No estate reports have to be submitted.

(c) There is no external supervision by the authorities.

(d) Heirs and creditors have the right to query and object.

(e) Usually, the heirs have possession of the assets and the court recognizes the right of property of said assets. If assets are not in possession of the heirs, then the court orders the delivery of the assets to the lawful heirs by whoever is in actual possession of the assets.

(f) The court orders the executor of the will to pay creditors of the estate.

14. Domicile/Nationality

(a) The above answers are subject to the condition that Panamanian law applies. If the nationality or the domicile of the deceased was relevant in order to determine the applicable legislation, the preceding rules would not be used in cases where the deceased was not Panamanian or was not domiciled in Panama. In practice, both nationality and domicile are irrelevant and the above answers will not be affected.

(b) In the event of a dispute, the local court would have jurisdiction even if there were no assets, provided that the deceased had his domicile in Panama when he died.

SECTION B – APPLICABLE LAW/PROCEDURE WHERE FOREIGN ELEMENT/S ARE INVOLVED

1. Jurisdiction

(a) The local court has jurisdiction if the deceased had his domicile in Panama at the date of his death. However, in the case of a person with domicile in various countries, the judicial claims may be initiated in a Panamanian court having jurisdiction in the specific place where the majority of the assets in Panama are situated.

(b) The Panamanian courts must necessarily deal with cases relating to immovable assets if they are situated in Panama. They also deal with movable assets that may be in Panama, and there are no different rules for these types of assets. Panamanian courts do not handle cases relating to real property located in another country.

(c) The local court having jurisdiction is the Civil Circuit Court in the place where the deceased had his/her domicile. If the deceased did not have domicile in Panama the court where the immovable property is located would have jurisdiction.

2. Applicable Law

The applicable law as to capacity is the law of nationality; the applicable law as to the form of the will is the *locus regit actum*.
   In Panama there is no specific provision or rule to determine the applicable law. The law for succession should be the law of domicile at date of death. In the event of a clash between domicile and nationality, the law of domicile would apply. *Lex situs* applies to immovable property.

3. Foreign Succession/Inheritance Orders

(a) Provided that the local requirements for the recognition and enforcement of the foreign judgments are met, the foreign order may be enforced or recognized in respect of local assets.

(b) It is necessary to obtain a local court order to give effect to a foreign order.

(c) In order to obtain the enforcement of a foreign judgment, it is necessary to attach to the request a true copy of the foreign judgment. Furthermore, the plaintiff must prove:

- that the judgment has been issued as a consequence of the enforcement of a personal cause of action;
- that the judgment has not been issued in default;
- that the judgment is characterized as *res judicata* or final judgment by the law applicable to the court which issued the judgment;
- that the defendant was duly notified personally of the process and was granted the right of defence;
- that the foreign judgment is not contrary to public policy.

4. Two or More Succession or Probate Orders

A foreign court order is not valid in Panama unless it is recognized by a local court.

In the event of two simultaneous judgments or orders where the one issued abroad had already been recognized by a local court, the interested party could allege that the matter had already been resolved. If the foreign court order or judgment has not been recognized yet, it has no legal standing in Panama and, therefore, could not prevent a local court dealing with the matter. In the event that the deceased is Panamanian or if the deceased was domiciled in Panama, the judgment rendered by a local court shall prevail. Also any judgment regarding a testamentary succession shall prevail over any judgment concerning an intestate succession.

5. Assets

The principal connecting factor in order to establish jurisdiction is the last domicile of the deceased. If there are no assets in the jurisdiction but the deceased was domiciled in Panama, our courts would still have jurisdiction.

6. Expert Evidence

(a) Depending on the case, it might be necessary to request the opinion of a foreign lawyer. However, there are other possible means of bringing evidence as to the foreign law, such as by way of a report issued by the authorities about the content and interpretation of its own law or certified copies of the legal text itself.

(b) An affidavit in connection with information on foreign law would be valid in Panama. It would not be necessary to have the foreign lawyers present in Panama.

7. Unity of Succession

Unity of succession is accepted in Panama.

International Succession

8. Formalities

The formalities of foreign wills need not be the same as those in Panama. As a general rule, the principle of *locus regit actum* applies.

9. Legislation

The *1991 Hague Convention on the Conflicts of Laws Relating to the Form of Testamentary Dispositions* is not applicable.

10. Wills

In case of conflicts or foreign factors the following laws govern:

(a) Legal requirements for execution of wills: the law of the country where the will is executed.

(b) Construction/Interpretations: Panamanian law if the assets are situated in Panama.

(c) Rights of heirs/beneficiaries: Panamanian law if the deceased was Panamanian.

(d) Capacity to inherit: the law of nationality (i.e., citizenship).

(e) Capacity to make a will: the law of nationality of the deceased.

(f) Essential or material validity of will: the law of the country where the will is executed.

(g) Not applicable.

(h) With respect to the formal rules, *locus regit actum*; with respect to the material rules, Panamanian law if the assets are situated in Panama.

(i) No rules regarding reserve to a non-resident would apply.

11. Domicile/Nationality

The *above* answers were predicated upon the basis that Panamanian law applied. If the nationality or the domicile of the deceased was relevant in order to determine the applicable legislation, the proceeding rules would not be used in cases where the deceased was not Panamanian or was not domiciled in Panama.

If a person has several domiciles in different places, the court will have to determine which one is the principal or the last domicile. In connection with nationality, apparently the nationality normally used by the person will prevail.

The domicile of the beneficiary is not relevant for the purpose of establishing jurisdiction.

12. Taxation

Residence is not a relevant factor regarding taxation.

Poland

Prepared by: Monika PINAKIEWICZ, advocate*

Address: 46/48 Ogrodowa Str.
          00-876 Warsaw
          Poland
Tel.:   +48 22 652 35 68
Fax: +48 22 842 30 41
E-mail: monika.pinakiewicz@poczta.neostrada.pl

Section A – Brief Survey of the Local System

1. Type of System

(a) Civil law.

(b) Poland does not have a federal system. The Polish Civil Code applies across The Republic of Poland.

2. Wills

(a) Polish inheritance law recognizes several forms of a will:

(1) Ordinary wills

i.   Holographic will

> This is a written will drawn up entirely by hand and signed and dated by the testator. If any part of a will is typed or written by another person at the testator's direction or if the will is not signed by the testator, then such a will is absolutely invalid. The absence of a date does not, however, result in the invalidity of a will if there is no doubt as to either the testator's capacity to make the will, the contents of the will or the sequence of several wills. In the event of any doubt as to the will's date, evidence may be heard to ascertain the date of the will.

---

* The author wishes to acknowledge the assistance of Andrzej Siemiątkowski of Allen & Overy Poland Sp. z o.o. in the preparation of this chapter and especially Section B.

482

ii. Notarial will

Notarial deeds comprising a will are drawn up by a notary. Upon the reading of the will, the notary must make sure that the testator understands the contents and meaning of the notarial deed and that the deed is consistent with the testator's intent. The deed is then signed and the original copy of the deed is kept on file at the notary's office.

iii. Allographic will

The testator may declare his last will orally in the presence of an official of the local borough and at least two witnesses. The testator's declaration is drawn up in the form of a record with an indication of the date on which the record was drawn up. The record is then read to the testator in the presence of the witnesses and signed by the testator, the official and the witnesses.

The testator may not limit himself to reading out a written draft will drawn up by another person and merely confirming it as his last will. However, the testator may read out a draft will prepared by himself. All the activities relating to drawing up the will, i.e., the making of the testator's declaration, the making of the record and the reading and signing of the record must take place in the presence of the official.

This form of will may not be made by persons who are mute or deaf.

(2) Special wills

Special wills have two characteristic features: *i.* they can only be made in the event of certain special circumstances which make it impossible, or at least difficult for the testator to draw up an ordinary will; and *ii.* their force in law is limited in time.

i. Oral will

This is an oral declaration of the testator made in the presence of at least two witnesses with a precise indication of which property items are given to whom in the event of death. The oral will may relate to movable and to immovable items as well.

For such a will to be valid, its contents must be confirmed in either of the following ways:

– One of the witnesses or a third party records the testator's declaration before the lapse of one year of the date on which the declaration was made, with an indication of the place and date of the testator's oral declaration and the place and date of the record. That record is signed by the testator and at least two witnesses, or alternatively by at least three witnesses (Article 952 paragraph 2 of the Civil Code). The testator's declaration may be drawn up in the above manner either during the testator's lifetime or after his death but in any event, it must be drawn up within one year of the date on which the testator orally declared his last will.

If the testator's declaration was recorded during the testator's lifetime, the testator and at least two witnesses in whose presence the testator declared his will must sign the record. If the testator's declaration was recorded after the testator's death, the record is signed by all of the witnesses (which must be at least three) in whose presence the declaration was made.

If the contents of an oral will have not been confirmed in the above manner, then:

– They may be confirmed, within six months of the date of the testator's death (i.e., the date the inheritance was opened), by consistent testimonies of three witnesses before the court. If the testimony of one of the witnesses cannot be heard, then the court may consider the other two witnesses' testimonies as sufficient, provided they are consistent.

For this six-month time limit to be maintained, it is sufficient that before the end of six months from the testator's death, the court is presented with a letter stating that the testator had left an oral will which has so far been confirmed. The hearing of the witnesses evidence by the court may then take place even after the lapse of the time limit.

The Civil Code allows an oral will only:

– if there are grounds for concern that the testator will die soon;
     Concern that the testator will soon die may only exist objectively. There-fore, according to life experience and medical knowledge, the testator's health condition at the time of drawing up the testator's will (e.g., in relation to old age or a chronic illness) should justify the concern for his imminent death.
– if, due to special circumstances, it is impossible or substantially difficult to make an ordinary will.

Such circumstances may exist for example where there is, at the time of making the will a flood, communications interruption or epidemic, or as a result of the testator's personal reasons, e.g., age, illness, lack of ability to write or read.

ii. A will on a Polish sea vessel or aircraft

Being aboard a Polish vessel or aircraft (including a military aircraft and ves-sel), even with no threat of disaster, allows for the making of a will in a special form. The testator declares his will before the captain (or his deputy) and in the presence of two witnesses. The captain records the testator's will indicating the date on which it was made, reads out the text to the testator in the presence of the witnesses, whereupon the text of the will is signed by the testator, the captain and the witnesses.

iii. Military will

This may be made only in a time of mobilization, war or detention in captivity. Despite the existence of those circumstances, this type of will may be made in one of the forms described *above*.

All special wills lose their validity after a lapse of six months from the cessation of the circumstances for which they were made unless the testator dies before the lapse of that time frame. It is necessary to have a full form of a special will, as a simplified form of a special will does not guarantee that the actual intention of the testator will be fully respected.

(b) *i.* A will may be revoked at any time, either in its entirety or in respect of any of its individual provisions.
    A will may be revoked by:

- Making a new will. The form in which the revoked will was made does not have to be kept. The contents of the new will may be limited only to the revocation of the previous will or it may include new provisions concerning the testator's inheritance.
    If the testator drew up a new will without revoking the previous will, only those provisions of the previous will which cannot be reconciled with the contents of the new will be revoked by the later will. If the new will does not contradict the contents of the previous will, it is assumed that there are two wills, and that the previous will was not revoked.
- Destroying a will (e.g., tearing up or burning the will) or depriving it of the properties which make it valid (e.g., deleting or tearing out the signature) results in revocation of the will only if accompanied by the testator's intent to revoke the will. For the destruction of a will to be considered as consistent with the testator's intention, the will must be personally destroyed by the testator.
- Making changes indicating an intention to revoke individual provisions of a will (e.g., deleting one provision by the testator) results in a revocation of that one provision only, whereas the action of striking out the entire will and writing the word 'revoked' would result in a revocation of the whole will.

If the testator drew up several wills having exactly the same contents, carrying the same date or various dates, then several equally effective wills exist. When one such will is revoked, the others remain valid.
ii. Marriage of the testator does not have any impact on the contents of the testator's will. A will which was drawn up before marriage is still valid.
iii. Polish law permits a testator to revoke the revocation of a will. However, the law lacks a provision stating whether in the event of revoking a prior revocation the original will is revived. In that situation the testator's intention must be ascertained to resolve the uncertainty. If it follows from the testator's

declaration that his intention was to revive an original (revoked) will, then the will remains in force.

iv. Polish inheritance law does not make a distinction between a will in which only a heir is appointed and a codicil which contains other provisions other than the appointment of a heir. (i.e., in effect there is no concept of codicil in Polish Law.) The will is the only accepted legal document in Polish law in the event of death while any dispositions of property in the event of death are effective only when they were incorporated in a valid will.

In practice, property objects donated by the testator to several persons may almost exhaust the whole inheritance. A problem which then arises is whether those persons are heirs or merely legatees. It is assumed that the persons are considered as heirs appointed to inherit the entire inheritance and their respective shares in the inheritance are determined as a ratio of the value of individual objects to the value of the inheritance. As heirs, the persons are also consequently responsible for any inheritance debts.

3. Intestacy

In the event of a death where the deceased does not leave a will (i.e., intestate death), the Civil Code provides statutory succession for the following relatives of the intestate: spouse, descendants (children, grandchildren, grand grandchildren, etc., with no limitation by the degree of kinship) parents, siblings, and siblings' descendants.

All children inherit from an intestate parent irrespective of whether they were born to married or unmarried parents, and irrespective of whether the child was born of an adulterous relationship.

A *nasciturus*, i.e., a child already conceived at the time of the testator's death, has a legal capacity to inherit provided that the child is born alive.

Full adoption leads to equal rights for the child. In the case of partial adoption, however, the child will not inherit from other relatives of the deceased.

In the event of an intestate death, the surviving spouse inherits by virtue of the law if at the time of the death he/she was married to the deceased. Planned changes to Polish law introducing the concept of separation, provide that a married but separated spouse will be deprived of his/her capacity to inherit.

(a) Order of succession

(1) By virtue of the law, the intestate's children and spouse inherit first in equal parts, with the part of the spouse not to be less than one-quarter of the entire estate. It must be noted here that as a rule, spouses are subject to a community property of husband and wife where they have equal shares. If one of the spouses dies, one-half of the existing community property is included in the inheritance. The surviving spouse has one-half of the community property and a respective part of the inheritance which constitutes the other half of the community property.

The intestate's children receive the entire inheritance if:
– at the time of his death, the deceased was not married; or
– the marriage was annulled after the intestate's death; or

– under a decision of the court, the intestate's spouse is excluded from the inheritance following a successful application to the court for divorce on the basis of the fault of the intestate's spouse.

Children inherit in equal parts. If one of the children did not live to see the opening of the inheritance, that child's part passes to his children (the intestate's grandchildren) in equal parts.

(2) In the absence of any descendants, the intestate's spouse, parents and siblings are automatically appointed to inherit by operation of the law. The share of the spouse who inherits concurrently with the intestate's parents, or siblings, or parents and siblings amounts to one-half of the inheritance.

The share of the inheritance of each parent who inherits concurrently with the intestate's siblings amounts to one-fourth of that part which passes jointly to the parents and siblings. The remaining part is inherited by the siblings in equal parts.

If one of the parents did not live to benefit from the operation of the intestacy rules then, that part which would have gone to him/her passes in one-half to the other parent and in one-half to the intestate's siblings.

If in addition to the spouse only the parents or only the siblings are to inherit, they inherit in equal parts what is due to the parents and siblings jointly.

If any of the intestate's siblings do not live to benefit from the operation of the laws of intestacy, the part of the inheritance which would have gone to him/her passes to his descendants. In the absence of any descendants of the deceased, parents, siblings or the siblings' descendants, the entire inheritance falls to the deceased spouse. In the absence of the deceased descendants and spouse, the whole inheritance falls to the deceased parents, siblings and the siblings' descendants. In the absence of the deceased spouse and relatives appointed to inherit by virtue of the law, the inheritance falls to the State Treasury.

(b) It makes no difference whether the inheritance is movable or immovable property but if the inheritance comprises a farm, the order of succession is more complex and completely different. The order of succession for farm land will not be discussed here.

4. Freedom of Testation

(a) According to a customary principle of Polish law, the testator subject to time 'legitim', may freely dispose of his property despite the lack of an explicit provision in this regard in the Civil Code. The testator may appoint any person as heir (the only requirement is that a beneficiary who is a natural person must be alive and a beneficiary who is a legal entity must exist at the time of the testator's death) and may freely dispose of all or a part of his property in his will.

In the event that the testator appoints a person outside the circle of his nearest relatives to inherit the whole of his property, the interests of the nearest relatives are protected by the concept of *legitim*.

The testator's descendants, spouse and siblings are entitled to a *legitim* if they would have been appointed to inherit by virtue of the law in the event of an intestate death. If those persons are permanently unable to work or if the eligible descendants are minors, they are entitled to two-thirds of the share in the testator's property which would have fallen to them in the case of statutory inheritance, and in other cases, to one-half of such shares. Persons entitled to a *legitim* may claim from the successor only the payment of the cash amount equivalent to the value of the *legitim*.

(b) *i.* Polish law generally prohibits the entering into agreements for the inheritance of a person who is still alive. The one exception to this rule relates to an agreement for renunciation of succession between a prospective testator and a statutory heir. A person who has renounced succession may still inherit if appointed to inherit by virtue of a will.

An agreement for the renunciation of succession must be executed in the form of a notarial deed, otherwise it will be null and void. The renunciation of succession also includes the descendants of the person who has renounced succession. A statutory heir who has renounced succession is treated as if he had not lived until the opening of an inheritance and he does not acquire the right to a *legitim*.

The law provides for a possibility to revoke the renunciation of succession. This may take place by a notarized agreement and whose parties include the person who has renounced succession and the prospective testator.

ii. This concept does not exist under the *Polish Inheritance Law*.

5. Maintenance

The testator's grandparents may demand maintenance from the testator if: (i) they do not inherit; (ii) live in penury; (iii) cannot obtain any means of maintenance from other persons; and (iv) if the testator's heir is not one of the persons required to provide maintenance to the testator's grandparents.

6. Community Property Between Husband and Wife

Spouses are subject to the statutory rule of community property of husband and wife. This means that any objects acquired in the course of marriage by either spouse are a part of the spouses' community property which, under Article 42 and Article 43.1 of the Family and Guardianship Code, is shared in one-half by the surviving spouse, while the other half is allocated to the deceased spouse's property.

In addition to his/her share in the community property, a spouse may also have his/her own separate property (e.g., property acquired by the spouse prior to marriage, property acquired by a spouse as a beneficiary under a will or property surrogated to either of the aforementioned) which forms an inheritance together with the spouse's share in the community property. However, if the spouses are not subject to statutory joint property, meaning that at the time of opening an inheritance they had separate properties, the inheritance left by the deceased spouse is exclusively his/her property and the surviving spouse therefore does not have any participation in community property which does not exist.

The proportions, in which each spouse is entitled to participate in the community property can be different. Namely, each of the spouses may demand that their shares in their community property be determined by taking into account the extent to which each of them contributed to that property. This demand may be made by the surviving spouse to the heirs of the deceased spouse. However, it should be noted that the reason for such demand must be properly evidenced and that demand is successful only if the deceased spouse generally squandered the community property during their life.

According to Polish law, in the case of statutory succession, the testator's spouse is a privileged heir. The privileged position manifests itself in the first and second groups of statutory heirs (*see* 3 *above*) in the size of the share (in the first group not less than one-quarter and in the second group, one-half of the entire inheritance). Moreover, the testator's spouse as statutory heir is entitled *ex lege* to objects of household equipment which are included in the inheritance and which, during the testator's lifetime, were used by the testator's spouse together with the testator or exclusively on his/her own (Article 939.1 of the Civil Code). In two cases, inheriting spouse is not entitled to any objects of household equipment by virtue of the law:

(1) when the spouse inherits by law jointly with the testator's descendants who lived with the testator at the time of his death; and
(2) if the spouses' cohabitation ceased during the testator's lifetime, meaning that there occurred an actual separation of the spouses, usually involving separate residence of the spouses.

7. Gifts (*Inter Vivos*)

(a) According to Polish law, *inter vivos* gifts prior to death will have an impact in two situations:

– upon distribution of the inheritance; and
– upon calculation of the value of a *legitim*.

The inclusion of *inter vivos* gifts in calculating the value of the legitim and the distribution of the inheritance depends on the will of the testator who may exempt a specific number of gifts from obligatory inclusion or alternatively may impose such an obligation. Such an exemption may have already been made in a contract of donation or in a will. The obligation to take into account gifts in distributing the inheritance and calculating the legitim occurs in the event of distribution of the inheritance between descendants or between descendants and spouses inheriting under the rules of statutory succession. If the testator's spouse inherits concurrently e.g., with the testator's siblings, the obligation to take account of an *inter vivos* gift by the testator does not exist. However, the testator may not oblige other statutory heirs (parents, siblings, siblings' children and the spouse inheriting together with relatives other than descendants) to take account of an *inter vivos* gift in distribution of the inheritance.

International Succession

The regulations governing the inclusion of gifts in an inheritance are applied in proportion to the testator's expenses incurred for raising and providing general and vocational education to a descendant if such expenses are in excess of an average measure which is customary for a given community.

(1) Limit of set-off

In the event the testator has not expressed his clear will, all *inter vivos* gifts are subject to inclusion in the distribution of the inheritance, except petty gifts which are customarily given in certain relationships, e.g., on the occasion of a holiday, wedding, etc. Whether a gift was a petty one or not depends among other things on the financial standing of the testator and heir.

If the value of a gift which is subject to inclusion exceeds the value of the inheritance, the heir is not required to return the resulting surplus. In this case, neither the gift nor the heir required to include the gift is taken into account upon the distribution of the inheritance.

The inclusion is carried out in such a manner that the value of gifts which are subject to inclusion is added to the inheritance or to that part of the inheritance which is subject to distribution among the heirs who are mutually required to perform the inclusion, whereupon each of those heirs' inheritance is determined and enlarged by the value of the gifts which are subject to inclusion. The value of a gift is determined according to its condition at the moment the gift is given and at its price as of the moment of distribution of the inheritance.

(2) Determination of a legitim

When determining a *legitim*, *inter vivos* gifts made by the testator are included in the inheritance, with the exception of:

– petty gifts which are customarily given in certain relationships; and
– gifts given more than ten years before opening the inheritance to persons who are neither heirs nor are entitled to a *legitim*.

The value of a gift is determined according to its condition at the moment the gift was given and at its price as of the moment of establishment of the *legitim*.

8. Capacity

(a) According to Polish law, persons who are eighteen years of age or above or who have married prior to reaching that age and who are not incapacitated have the capacity to make a will i.e., capacity of testation. The testator must have the capacity of testation at the time of making his will. His loss of the capacity of testation at a time does not have any influence on the validity of a will which was made before.

A person who has the capacity of testation may draw up any type of will, both ordinary and special.

490

(b) The inheritance law distinguishes between two kinds of incapacity to be a witness:

– absolute incapacity, or the inability to act as a witness for any type of will; and
– relative incapacity involving the inability to be a witness upon the making of a will by specific persons or upon the making of certain dispositions.

(1) Absolute incapacity

The following persons may not be witnesses to a will:

– persons without full capacity to perform acts in law (e.g., minors, incapacitated persons for whom a temporary adviser was established in the course of incapacitation proceedings);
– persons who are blind, deaf or mute;
– persons unable to read or write;
– persons unable to speak the language in which the testator is making his will; and
– persons convicted for false testimony by a valid court judgement.

(2) Relative incapacity

A person to whom a benefit is provided in a will may not be a witness for that will. Additionally, such a person's spouse, relatives or relations by affinity (of the first and second degree) or persons remaining in an adoptive relationship with that person also may not act as witnesses.

If one of the above-mentioned persons witnesses a will, only the provisions of the will which provide a benefit to that person, his spouse, relatives or relations by affinity (of the first and second degree) or a person remaining in an adoptive relationship with that person are invalid. However, if it follows from the contents of the will or from the circumstances that the testator would not have made such a will without the invalid provision, the entire will is invalid.

The above provision precludes the possibility for a natural person who is a representative of a legal entity for which a benefit was provided in a will to act as a witness.

(c) Both natural persons living at the time of opening an inheritance and legal entities existing at that time may be heirs. Additionally, a child already conceived at the time of opening an inheritance (*nasciturus*) may be a heir if born alive. In turn, a foundation appointed by a testator in his will may be a heir if it is entered in the foundations register within two years of the date on which the will is announced.

9. Authority (Court, Notarial or Other)

According to Polish law, the heir acquires an inheritance *ipso iure* (i.e., by the operation of law). The opening of the inheritance takes place upon the death of the deceased person. The acquisition of the inheritance is confirmed by the court on all occasions upon the request of the person who has a legal interest in such confirmation. The circle of persons concerned includes most of all heirs, those entitled to a *legitim*, legatees and the testator's and heir's creditors. The confirmation of acquisition of an inheritance may not occur before the lapse of six months of the date the inheritance is opened unless all known heirs have already submitted their statements confirming their acceptance or rejection of the inheritance.

In the course of probate proceedings the court investigates who is a heir and in particular calls for submission of the will. If the will is submitted, the court will proceed with opening and announcing the will.

Following the probate proceedings, the court issues a decision naming the testator and all of the heirs and their respective shares. The decision of the court will state the names of the beneficiaries of the entire estate but will not specifically state which beneficiary is entitled to a particular section of the estate, unless the inheritance includes a farm in which case the decision separately names the beneficiaries who have inherited the farm.

If the person who has obtained a confirmation of acquisition of an inheritance is not a heir or if that person's share in the inheritance is other than the share confirmed, such a person may apply to the court for the reversal or alteration of the court's original decision. An application for instituting such proceedings may be submitted by each of the persons concerned.

10. Invalidity of Will

(a) A will may be invalid due to:

   i. a lack of capacity of testation;
  ii. its form;
 iii. defects of a declaration of will; and/or
  iv. its contents.

Under Polish law an invalid will may only be held to be void. Expanding on the above, a will may be invalid because:

   i. A will may be drawn up and revoked only by a person who has a full capacity to perform acts in law. Wills may neither be drawn up nor revoked by a representative. A will drawn up by a person who does not have the capacity of testation is invalid. It may not be validated by the testator (e.g., by way of confirmation) after he has acquired the capacity of testation;
  ii. Polish inheritance law precisely defines the form in which a will may be drawn up (*see* point *i.*). Any failure to preserve the due form results in the invalidity of the will. Conversion into a valid form is allowed to a certain extent in respect of allographic wills. A will considered invalid due to formal deficiencies may be deemed a valid oral will;
 iii. A will is invalid if it was drawn up:

- in a condition precluding a conscious or free decision and expression of intent;
- under the influence of a mistake justifying the supposition that if the testator had not acted under the influence of the mistake, he would not have drawn up a will of such contents; or
- under a threat.

The Civil Code stipulates that the invalidity of a will for the *above* reasons may not be claimed after the lapse of three years from the day on which the person having a legal interest learned of the reason for invalidity, and in any case after the lapse of ten years of the date the inheritance was opened. Thus there is an exception to the fact that all wills which have a defect of declaration are invalid and therefore void.

iv. A will, as with any legal act, is invalid if it is inconsistent with the law, the principles of public order (and more specifically those of social existence) or if it is aimed at circumventing the law. Inconsistency with the law occurs most often when there is a violation of provisions of the inheritance law such as the prohibition on the appointment of a heir subject to a condition or a time limit, the prohibition on substitution of an heir on trust, i.e., the heir's obligation to keep the inheritance acquired and to leave it in case of death to another person appointed in the will, or the prohibition on execution of a joint will.

11. Simultaneous Death

A natural person acquires an inheritance if such a person is alive at the time the inheritance is opened (with the exception of an already conceived child). Therefore, according to Polish law, a person who died before the testator or simultaneously with him may not be an heir. This is why a death certificate issued by a medical doctor must specify not only the date but also the hour of death. Article 32 of the Civil Code may be of assistance in resolving this issue, as it contains a presumption described as the simultaneous death presumption, according to which, if several persons have lost their lives as a result of a common danger, it is presumed that all the persons have died simultaneously. Persons who died simultaneously may not inherit from one another. This applies both to the deceased person's intestate and testate heirs.

12. Estate Taxes

The issue of taxation on inheritance is regulated by the *Law of 28 July 1983 (as amended) on the Tax on Inheritance and Gifts*. Tax is payable on assets both in Poland and abroad. However in the case of assets abroad, tax is payable in Poland only when at the time of opening an inheritance, the heir was a Polish citizen or was permanently residing in Poland.

Tax is not payable on inherited movable property located in Poland if on the day of acquisition neither the heir nor the testator were Polish citizens and were neither residing nor domiciled in Poland.

International Succession

Tax is due on the value of acquired assets and property rights less any debts and burdens (the net value of the estate) determined according to the condition of the assets and property rights on the day of acquisition and at market prices as of the date on which the tax liability arises. If the heir or legatee has been burdened with a legacy or order, the value of the resulting burden is charged to the inheritance.

Debts and burdens also include the expenses of the testator's last illness if such expenses have not been covered during the testator's lifetime. This also includes the costs of the testator's funeral, the costs of probate proceedings, the remuneration of the will's executor, the payments towards a legitim and any other costs.

The tax rate is determined depending on the tax group in which the testator is included and there are three tax groups. Inclusion in a tax group is made according to the personal relationship between the heir and the testator. The rates of tax are not fixed but vary according to the amount allowed tax free but are approximately 7 per cent, 12 per cent and 20 per cent.

13. Administration of Estates

Although the testator may appoint an executor of his will, this is not very popular practice in Poland.

A will may be executed by any natural person, e.g., one of the heirs, a legatee or a third party. The only requirement is that such a person must have the full capacity to perform acts in law.

If the testator who appointed an executor of his will failed to precisely specify the executor's rights and duties, the executor of the will must administer the estate, pay off any inheritance debts, execute the testator's legacies and orders and subsequently hand the estate over to the heirs in accordance with the testator's intent and the provisions of the Civil Code. An executor may dispose of the estate on his own within the limits of proper management. The executor may sue and be sued in respect of matters resulting from the administration of the estate. He may also sue in respect of matters relating to rights comprised in the estate and be sued in matters concerning inheritance debts.

The executor is not required to submit any reports on his activity unless directly requested by the successor(s). If the executor neglects his duties or is not able to perform them (e.g., due to illness), he may be dismissed from his function.

A similar function to that of executor of a will is performed by a 'curator of the estate' appointed by the court to administer the estate under the court's supervision until the testator's heirs call for their inheritance. However, this function, similarly to the function of executor, is not often exercised.

Generally, the concept of an administration of an estate (as occurs in English law) is not known to Polish law.

Under Polish law there are only two situations in which the concept of administration (understood as management over the estate) emerges:

(1) if the estate is not in the possession of any successor then the court should administer the estate through the so-called 'curator of the estate';
(2) if the testator appoints an executor of his will.

Therefore:

(a) The estates are administrated either by the curator of the estate or by the executor of the will as well as by heir/heirs or by the third person who has the estate in possession but holds this possession without any legal grounds. The court appoints the curator of the estate and the testator appoints the executor of a will;

(b) The curator of the estate must submit its reports to the relevant court. The executor of a will on demand by successor(s) should prepare the reports and deliver to them;

(c) The court supervises the curator of the estate and may remove him. The court does not have any control over the executor of a will but he can be dismissed by the court from his function if he neglects his duties or is not able to perform them, e.g., due to illness at the request of any successor or the executor of a will himself;

(d) The only possible objectors to the activities of the administrator are the relevant court, successor, third parties having an interest, e.g., legitim;

(e) There is no special procedure, the estate is handed over under general law;

(f) The curator of the estate cannot repay the estate debt. The executor of a will may repay the debtors; and

(g) If the possession of the estate has not been taken over by successor and it is in the possession of the third party, the successor has a claim against that third party to distribute the estate to the successor.

14. Domicile/Nationality

The significance of nationality and domicile is discussed in Section B.

In brief, a Polish court will confirm the acquisition of an inheritance even if the estate does comprise any assets as the court generally does not inspect any elements of the estate.

SECTION B – APPLICABLE LAW/PROCEDURE WHERE FOREIGN ELEMENT/S ARE INVOLVED

Poland is a party to a number of bilateral international agreements which lay down different rules for the selection of law and court jurisdiction. The section below does not take into account any changes arising from those agreements.

1. Jurisdiction

A Polish court would be competent to deal with a succession if:

International Succession

(a) the deceased held the Polish citizenship upon his death; or

(b) the testator held no citizenship and resided in Poland at the time of his death.

If a Polish citizen died in Poland, the Polish courts have an exclusive jurisdiction.

It would seem from the *above* principles that an application for probate proceedings in respect of a deceased foreigner (holding a citizenship other than Polish) should be rejected even when the testator's last place of domicile was in Poland, his entire movable property was located in Poland or when the testator's heirs were exclusively Polish citizens. To eliminate any negative jurisdiction conflicts, the Supreme Court decided that when an heir cannot obtain a confirmation of his rights before a court of the foreign country, a Polish court shall be competent.

If an inheritance includes any real estate located in Poland, Polish courts have an exclusive jurisdiction. When the real estate is located abroad, the jurisdiction of Polish courts is excluded.

In the case of movable property, whether located in Poland or abroad, Polish courts shall be competent, providing that the requirements described in point 1(a) or 1(b) above are met.

2. Applicable Law

According to the *Polish International Private Law of 12 November 1965* the Polish court will apply the law of the country whose citizen the testator is upon the testator's death as the substantive law.

In the event the testator held no citizenship, the court will apply the law of the testator's place of residence, and if the testator had no place of residence, then Polish law shall be applied. Where a Polish citizen holds more than one citizenship, Polish law is applied, and where the testator held several foreign citizenships, the law of the country with whose citizenship the testator had the closest affinity will be applied.

The validity of a will and other acts in law in case of death is generally determined by the law of the country whose citizen the testator was at the moment such acts were made but in relation to the form it is sufficient if the form of the country, in which such acts had been made, was observed.

As far as the form of a will is concerned, Poland is a party to the *Hague Convention of 5 October 1961* which is concerned with the form of testamentary dispositions. The provisions of the *Hague Convention* have been effective in Poland since 2 November 1969. Poland made a reservation that it will not apply those provisions of the convention which according to Polish inheritance law are not of inheritance-related nature (e.g., adoption).

3. Foreign Succession/Inheritance Orders

(a) In Poland, foreign court judgments, depending on their character, must be recognized in an appropriate manner or confirmed in order to be enforceable. However, this only applies to movable property located in Poland and does not apply to real estate located in Poland.

(b) For a foreign decision to be recognized or confirmed as enforceable (*exequatur*) an appropriate application must be filed to a district court. Polish courts do not examine the grounds of foreign decisions. Following a decision of a Polish court and the payment of applicable taxes (confirmed by a relevant confirmation from the tax office), the documents may be presented to the applicable authorities and persons in whose holding or custody an inheritance remains in order to transfer the inheritance to the heir.

However, the acquisition of land in Poland by foreigners, including acquisition by way of succession, is in addition regulated by the *Act on Acquisition of Land by Foreigners of 24 March 1920 (as amended)*.

Two situations may be distinguished, depending on the status of the successor/ heir:

- In the event the acquiring person is entitled to statutory succession (e.g., a successor according to the laws of intestacy), the *Act on Acquisition of Land by Foreigners* does not apply and land may be acquired freely.

   The fact of being a statutory successor is established on the basis of the national law of the deceased person and if the national law of the deceased person does not allow statutory succession, then statutory succession is established in accordance with Polish Law.

- In the event the acquiring person is entitled to succession by will and at the same time is not a statutory successor, then such a person has to apply for a permission of the Minister of Interior, within one year from opening the succession. The permission is granted by the Minister of Interior with the consent of the Minister of Defence and in case of agricultural land with consent of the Minister of Agriculture. If the permission is not obtained, the land is acquired by statutory successors.

   Succession of farms in Poland are regulated differently and due to its complex nature, this is not described here.

(c) The Polish Code of Civil Procedure makes a distinction between foreign judgments on civil matters not requiring compulsory execution and the foreign judgments which can be enforced through compulsory execution (enforceable judgments). Judgments regarding succession fall within the category of judgments not requiring compulsory execution.

These judgments are recognized by the Polish court by way of declaration of the recognition of foreign judgment. Under reciprocal arrangements with foreign countries, a previous foreign judgment will be recognized and enforced by Polish courts by way of declaration if:

- the judgment is enforceable and final in the country in which it has been issued;
- the matter does not fall within the exclusive jurisdiction of the Polish courts or the courts of another country pursuant to Polish law or an international treaty;
- a party to the judgment has not been denied the opportunity to defend itself or, if it lacks capacity to be a party, to have appropriate legal representation;
- the matter has not been finally resolved by a Polish court or if the matter has not been submitted to a competent Polish court before the judgment of the foreign court is issued;

– the judgment does not contradict basic principles of public policy in Poland; and
– in a case where the foreign court purported to apply Polish law, Polish law was properly applied or where Polish law should have been applied but was not, the foreign law actually applied does not differ significantly from the Polish law.

4. Two or More Succession or Probate Orders

This may arise where there are two probate proceedings pending – one before the Polish courts and one before the foreign courts. Polish rules of procedure provide for the following method of resolution of conflicts between proceedings pending before a foreign court and the decision of such a court and proceedings pending before a Polish court and its decision:

(a) if the decision of the Polish court became final before the foreign judgment had been passed, then the foreign judgment may not be recognized but if the judgment of the foreign court is recognized before the decision of the Polish court has become final then the proceedings before the Polish court shall be discontinued;

(b) if a case is brought before a Polish court when the judgment of the foreign court has become final and one of the parties invokes the final foreign judgment the court may stay the proceedings and set a time limit for the interested party to apply for recognition of the foreign judgment;

(c) if a decision of the foreign court is taken when the case has been already brought before the Polish court then the foreign decision may not be recognized and the matter shall be decided by the Polish court.

5. Assets

Polish courts generally do not examine the contents of estates so there are no issues arising from the examination of assets. There are two main exceptions to this. The first is when there is real estate which is located abroad. In this case the Polish courts have no jurisdiction to decide who shall be heir. The second case is where the inheritance involves farm land. The Polish courts will, on confirmation, specify who is to inherit the farm land.

6. Expert Evidence

(a) *Oral evidence*

Foreign law (substantive or procedural) is not treated as a fact that needs to be proved. If a case includes circumstances revealing a foreign element, the court examines the conflict of laws and based on the *Polish International Private Law* (Polish conflict rules) determines the relevant law. If the foreign law applies, the court applies it *ex officio*. The court may request the Minister of Justice to provide the text of the foreign law and for an explanation of the foreign court practice. The court may also seek expert opinion as to the contents of the foreign law and foreign court practice. However, the courts generally make such a request to the Minister of Justice as opposed to seeking expert opinion.

Poland joined the *European Convention on Information on Foreign Law* prepared in London on 7 June 1968. According to that Convention, states are obliged to inform other states of their legal regulations, thereby facilitating the work of the courts required to apply foreign law.

(b) *Written Evidence*

A written affidavit from an expert witness may be sufficient if it raises no doubts but the court may summon an expert to ask him questions on the basis of its own decision or at the request of one of the parties.

7. Unity of Succession

Polish law applies the rule of unity of succession.

8. Formalities

Under *Polish International Private Law*, the validity of a will and other legal actions related to succession shall be decided under the law of the country of the testator's domicile as at the day of taking such legal actions. However legal actions shall be effective provided the form set out in the law of the country where the actions are taken is observed. This rule has been modified by the *1961 Hague Convention* (*see* 2 and 9).

9. Legislation

Since 1969 Poland has been a member to the *Hague Convention of 5 October 1961 on the Conflicts of Laws Relating to the Form of Testamentary Dispositions.*

10. Wills

(a) The legal requirements for the execution of a will are those listed in Article 1 of the *Hague Convention* (i.e., in most cases the law of the jurisdiction in which the will was drawn up will apply as to these formalities);

(b) The rules of construction/interpretation of the will are those of the law of the country of the testator's citizenship as at the date of the execution of his will;

(c) The rules relating to the rights of heirs and beneficiaries would be dependant upon the law of the country of the testator's citizenship as at the date of his death;

International Succession

(d) The capacity to inherit is dependant upon the law of the country of the heir(s) in question;

(e) The capacity to make a will is dependant substantially on the law of the country of the testator's citizenship as at the date of execution of the will. However the choice of the form of testamentary disposition due to age, citizenship or other personal issues like illness, mental deficiency or limited capacity of concluding Poland legal transactions shall be decided pursuant to the law referred to in Article 1 of the *Hague Convention*;

(f) Essential or material validity of wills or a particular bequest is dependant upon the law of the country of the testator's citizenship as at the date of execution of his will;

(g) Powers of appointment are dependant upon the law of the country of the testator's citizenship as at the date of the execution of his will;

(h) Amendment, revocation and revival of a will is dependant on the law of the country of the testator's citizenship as at the date of the execution of his will;

(i) The applicability of laws regarding reserve to a non-resident in respect of movable/immovable property is dependant on the law of the country of the testator's citizenship as at the date of his death.

11. Domicile/Nationality

(a) Under the principles of *Polish Private International Law*, the Polish court will apply the law of the country of the testator's citizenship upon the execution of his will as the substantive law;

(b) The domicile of the beneficiary under the will is not relevant and has no impact on the validity, interpretation and enforcement of any will subject to restrictions in relation to acquisition of farm land and real property as mentioned in paragraph 3;

(c) The impact of citizenship is further discussed at point 2 *above*.
   If the domicile is unclear, the domicile is determined in each case by the following factors:

– any facts which may suggest that a given place is that of principal residence; and
– intention to stay in a given place permanently.

12. Taxation

The estate taxes are, subject to any international agreements regarding the avoidance of double taxation, the same for residents and non-residents.

Portugal

Prepared by: Notaria Benvinda A. FERREIRA da SILVA

Address: 5 Cartorio Notarial do Porto
         Rua das Carmelitas, 26
         4050 Porto
         Portugal
Tel.:   +351 22 2083871
Fax: +351 22 2082938

SECTION A – BRIEF SURVEY OF THE LOCAL SYSTEM

1. Type of System

(a) Civil Law.

(b) No. Portugal is juridically unitary. The Civil Code is in force over all of Portuguese territory (i.e., continental territory as well as the autonomous regions).

2. Wills

(a) There are ordinary forms of will and special forms of will.

Ordinary forms of will:

- *by way of public instrument* (Article 225 of the Civil Code): this will is drawn up by the notary, as dictated by the testator, in his register;
- *secret* (Article 2206 of the Civil Code): this will is drawn up and signed by the testator or drawn up by another person at the testator's request. The will is signed by the latter and is approved by the notary.

Special forms of will:

- *Military and related wills*: these are for use by military personnel or civilians at the service of the military, whether in battle or in barracks, within as well as outside of the country, where communications have been severed and there is no notary available, or if they are taken prisoner of war.

501

International Succession

Article 2210 of the Civil Code provides that military wills can be by way of public instrument if they are drawn up by the commanding officer in the presence of two witnesses.

They can also be secret if they are drawn up by a soldier, or the like, and presented to the commanding officer in the presence of two witnesses.

Military wills must be deposited with the military authorities for perusal by a notary who comes from the domicile or the last domicile of the testator.

- *Wills made at sea*: these are for use by persons aboard a warship or a merchant vessel at sea. They are drawn up in the presence of the commanding officer and according to those rules applying to military wills (Article 2214 of the Civil Code).
- *Wills on board aircraft* (Article 2219 of the Civil Code): these are for use by persons aboard an airplane and follow those rules applying to military wills and wills made at sea.
- *Wills in times of public emergency* (Article 2220 of the Civil Code): these can be drawn up in the presence of a notary or a priest following those rules applying to public or secret military wills.

International wills: The *1973 Washington Convention on International Wills* was ratified by Portugal by the *Approving Law 252/75 of 23 May 1975* and entered into force on 9 February 1978.

Portuguese law does not allow for the holographic will or the joint will.

The testator on his deathbed can summon the presence of a notary, in order to draw up a will by way of public instrument or to obtain approval of a secret will. The notary cannot refuse to attend no matter the day or time.

(b) *i*. A will can only be modified by another will.

The right to revoke a will is one which cannot be renounced and can be carried out expressly or tacitly.

Express revocation is undertaken by way of another will or by public instrument.

The will is deemed *revoked tacitly* when there exists another later will incompatible with the former.

The law, however, provides that when there are two incompatible wills, both dated the same, contradictory provisions in those wills are deemed not to have been written (Article 2213 of the Civil Code).

Revocation, express or tacit, takes effect even if the will revoking a former will is itself revoked. However, a previous will takes effect or is revived if the testator, at the time he revokes the later will, expressly declares that he wishes to revive the provisions of the previous will (Article 2135 of the Civil Code).

If the secret will is found torn up, it is deemed to have been revoked, except if it can be proven that this was not carried out by the testator or that the latter would not have wished to revoke the will or that if he had lost his mental faculties at that time.

ii. No, unless the provisions of the will encroach upon the compulsory share of the estate which will pass to the spouse.

iii. As regards a subsequent will, the testator can revive a previous will which had been revoked if he expressly declares this to be his intention.

However, if the revoked will includes a 'legitimation' (or the recognition of a child born or conceived out of marriage), that legitimation will continue to subsist even if expressly revoked, in accordance with the principle that legitimation is an irrevocable act (Article 1858 of the Civil Code).

3. Intestacy

(a) Succession is deemed either legal or negotiable and within the first category, either legitimate or compulsory and within the second category, either contractual or testamentary.

If the deceased has not validly and effectively disposed of all or part of his estate, his rightful heirs will take upon succession (Article 2131 of the Civil Code).

Legitimate or rightful succession (*succession légitime*) then takes effect in the absence of the deceased's intentions whereas compulsory succession, as regards entitlement to compulsory shares, takes effect despite his intentions.

As regards *legitimate succession* (i.e., *upon intestacy*), the *order of succession* is set out in Article 2133 of the Civil Code.

In accordance with that provision, the order of succession is as follows:

– the surviving spouse;
– the surviving spouse and descendants;
– the surviving spouse and ancestors;
– brothers and sisters and their descendants including illegitimate and adulterine children;
– other collateral relations up to the fourth degree;
– the state.

The spouse ranks in the first class of heirs in the absence of children. In the event that there are children, the surviving spouse ranks with them in the second class.

If the deceased leaves a spouse and descendants, they will take concurrently. If there are no descendants but there are ancestors, the spouse takes concurrently with them. If there are no descendants or ancestors, the spouse is the sole heir.

The heirs in each of the classes are preferred to those in the class which follows (Article 2134 of the Civil Code) except for when the right of representation is given effect.

Within each of the classes themselves, the heirs most closely related to the deceased are preferred to those who are more distantly related (Article 2135 of the Civil Code).

If heirs of a class entitled to the estate cannot or do not wish to take, heirs in the class immediately following take. If only one or some of the heirs in a class do not wish to take, that part of the estate will go to the others in the same class, without prejudice to the right of representation, which allows the descendants of such an heir (or legatee) to take if the latter refused or was unable to accept his inheritance (Article 2039 of the Civil Code).

International Succession

As to the order of succession more generally, *the heirs entitled to a compulsory share* take first, as a function of their entitlement to such a share of the estate (the compulsory shares being that part of the estate of which the testator cannot freely dispose because it is 'reserved', legally and compulsorily, for heirs so entitled).

Heirs entitled to a compulsory share are as follows:

– the surviving spouse and the descendants; or
– the surviving spouse and the ancestors.

The descendants will exclude the ancestors. That is, if the deceased has left descendants, the ancestors will not be heirs. The surviving spouse takes concurrently with the ancestors if there are no descendants and is the sole heir entitled to a compulsory share if the deceased has left no descendants or ancestors.

Following on from those entitled to a compulsory share, *the contractual heirs* will take in those cases in which they are allowed to do so by law (donations upon marriage and between spouses).

In third place *the testamentary heirs* will take, that is those who were specified in the will.

Finally *the legitimate heirs* will take, that is, those whom the law designates as successors to the deceased upon intestacy.

(b) No, there is no difference between the succession of immovables and that of movables. There is unity of succession.

4. Freedom of Testation

(a) Portuguese law does provide for a part of an estate which cannot be disposed of freely by the testator if there are heirs who would be legally entitled to it (i.e., surviving spouse, descendants, ancestors).

The compulsory share of the surviving spouse, if he does not take concurrently with descendants or ancestors, is equal to one-half the estate.

That part of the estate subject to compulsory shares for *the surviving spouse and children* taking concurrently is equal to two-thirds of the estate.

If the deceased has not left a spouse, the share to which *the children* are entitled is equal to one-half of the estate if there is one and two-thirds if there are two or more (Article 2159 of the Civil Code).

If the deceased has not left a spouse or descendants, that part of the estate to which *the ancestors* are entitled will amount to one-half if those taking are either the mother or father, and to one-third if those taking are ancestors of the second degree or more.

Descendants of the second degree and those who follow have the right to the share that would have gone to their ascendant (Article 2160 of the Civil Code).

The division of the estate between the spouse and children in this instance is done by way of 'capitation', that is, divided into parts in accordance with the number of the heirs. The surviving spouse, however, cannot not receive less than one-quarter of the estate (Article 2139 of the Civil Code).

Therefore, if the deceased has left a spouse and two children, each has a right to one-third. If he has left a spouse and four children, the spouse is entitled to 1/4 of the estate and the children to three-quarters.

There is no difference as between *legitimate and illegitimate descendants*. Non-discrimination between children born in and out of wedlock is a principle enshrined in the constitution.

Adopted children acquire the status of children and have the same rights as blood children.

Children who have not been fully adopted (*adopté de forme simple*) are not entitled to a compulsory share of the estate. They have only the status of legitimate heirs and will take only if the deceased has not left a spouse, descendants or ancestors.

Brothers and sisters are never entitled to a compulsory share of the estate. They are only legitimate heirs and can be disinherited by will.

In contrast to that part of the estate subject to compulsory shares, *the disposable share* (*quotité disponible*) is that share of the estate of which the testator can freely dispose to the benefit of any persons.

(b) *i.* Agreements on the succession of a living person are, in principle, illegal according to Portuguese law.

All agreements are deemed null and void if they renounce the inheritance of a living person or make over one's own inheritance or that of a third person presently alive.

ii. Notwithstanding this prohibition in principle on agreements on the succession of a living person, there are certain contracts which can be entered into by living persons which will have an effect upon death.

The law permits the appointment of trustees in relation to donations (Article 902 of the Civil Code). The donation will be for the benefit of others after the donee dies.

In a contract for a perpetual annuity (Article 1231 of the Civil Code), there is a right that can be passed on, successively, to those who follow.

As regards a contract for a life annuity, the second beneficiary will receive the annuity once the first has died.

Article 1719 of the Civil Code allows for persons who are engaged to stipulate in their marriage contract that the division of their property will be carried out in accordance with those rules on the community of property between spouses, should they have common descendants and the cause of the dissolution of the marriage is death.

The law also allows for advance division (referred to as *partage anticipé* and *donation-partage*). In effect Article 2029 of the Civil Code deals with a contract by which a person, with the consent of the others who will take, makes a donation (whether subject to life interests or not) of all or part of his property to the presumptive heirs entitled to compulsory shares. If the donees pay or promise to pay the value which attaches proportionally to the property donated to the others who will take, such contract does not amount to an agreement on the succession of a living person and is therefore valid.

Such advance division is done by way of deed.

5. Maintenance

Since 1978 the law provides that the surviving spouse is entitled to a compulsory share of the estate. Despite this, the rule on *apanage* in relation to the surviving spouse is still in force (Article 2018 of the Civil Code). This rule provides that upon the death of one of the spouses, the surviving spouse has the right to maintenance out of the revenue realized from the property left by the deceased.

The surviving spouse has the right to be considered first, when the property is being divided, in relation to the right to live in the family home and the right to make use of the movables (Article 2013 of the Civil Code).

There is also protection for the person who was living as husband or wife with the deceased.

The law provides, for the benefit of a person who, at the time of death of the person whose property is to pass, was unmarried or judicially separated or was a common law spouse, in conditions analogous to those who are married, the right to maintenance from the estate of the deceased.

6. Community Property Between Husband and Wife

(a) Under the regimes of community of property or after-acquired property between spouses, half of the marital property belongs to the surviving spouse. The other half forms part of the deceased's estate.

Article 1719 allows spouses to stipulate in their marriage contract that if the marriage is dissolved by the death of one of them and they share common descendants, the division of property will be in accordance with the rules of the community of property, independent from the stipulated marital regime.

(b) Each spouse can plan to dispose of, upon his death, his own property and his half share in community property in favour of those who will be entitled to a compulsory share, without prejudice to what is provided for by law.

In order to dispose of specific community property, the testator must obtain the consent of his spouse, which must be officially recorded, for example, in the will that contains this disposition.

Except for a stipulation to the contrary, the property which is given by a fiancé(e) in a contract of marriage is considered to be that of the recipient, independent from that of the marital regime (Article 1759 of the Civil Code).

7. Gifts (*Inter Vivos*)

(a) Portuguese law relies upon the institution of *colação*, which provides for restitution to be made to the estate by descendants (and only these heirs) in order that the principle of equality between the heirs is respected (Article 2014).

Restitution can, however, be dispensed of by the donor by way of deed of gift or later in a deed or will.

Gifts that exceed that part of the estate of which the testator can freely dispose, however, are always subject to reduction (Article 2168).

Reduction always begins with the testamentary dispositions.

If these are not sufficient, then recourse is had to donations. Of these, recourse is first had to the last donation and then, should that not be sufficient, to those which precede it.

(b) Only the descendants are obliged to make restitution. It is not required by the descendant's spouse if the latter is the donee.

Restitution applies to all that the deceased spent for which he was not reimbursed, for the benefit of the descendants.

Expenses incurred in relation to marriage, maintenance, the starting up and establishment of descendants, which accord with the custom, social status and financial standing of the deceased, are not subject to restitution.

8. Capacity

(a) Everyone except those who are deemed incapable by law is able to make a will (Article 2188 of the Civil Code).

Those who cannot make a will:

- *minors who are unemancipated*: In principle the minimum age for making a will is eighteen. However, it is possible to make a will before this if the minor is emancipated. Now emancipation is only conferred upon marriage, the minimum age of marriage being sixteen years of age.
- *persons suffering from mental disorders*: Such persons are barred from making a will. In addition those who are suffering from *accidental incapacity*, though not having been barred, cannot make a will. The latter refers to a person, who at the time of making his will, finds himself unable to understand the meaning of his declaration or who is unable to exercise his free will, even if only provisionally (Article 2199 of the Civil Code).

Relative incapacity: The testator is also prevented from making a will benefiting certain persons, as such wills are nullified.

A will cannot be made in favour of the testator's guardian, trustee or the legal administrator of his property, unless these persons are descendants, ancestors or collateral relations, up to the third degree.

The testator cannot make a will in favour of a doctor or nurse who cares for him, or of a priest who provides him spiritual assistance, if the will is made while the testator is ill and then dies from that illness.

It is also forbidden to make a will in favour of a person with whom the testator committed adultery, unless the marriage had already broken down or the spouses were judicially separated or separated from each other for more than six years before the time the estate passes to the heirs or unless the disposition is made to ensure for the maintenance of the beneficiary.

A disposition made to a notary having drawn up the will, or having approved a secret will, to a person having written up the will, to witnesses having attested to the will, or to other persons having been involved with the execution of the will or its approval is also forbidden.

As regards marital status, each of the spouses is able, after the death of one of them, to dispose of his own property and half of that held in community, without prejudice to those reductions laid down by the law in favour of heirs entitled to a compulsory share.

The disposition of a specific object forming part of the community property between spouses necessitates the consent of the other spouse. This consent must be given by way of notarially recorded instrument or must be contained in the will in which such disposition is made (Article 1685 of the Civil Code).

(b) The following persons cannot be witnesses:

– those who have lost their powers of reasoning;
– unemancipated minors (*see above*);
– persons unable to understand Portuguese;
– the deaf, dumb and blind;
– those officials working at the notary's office;
– the spouse, relations or those directly related by way of marriage, or collateral relations up to the second degree of the notary, the testator or the beneficiaries;
– a husband and wife at the same time;
– those who are unable to sign; and
– those who will or may receive some benefit deriving from the estate by way of the will.

(c) The state, as well as all natural persons, born or conceived at the moment the estate passes to the heirs, who are not excluded by law, have the capacity to inherit and have legal, testamentary and contractual capacity.

Others having the capacity to inherit are the following:

– those who are not yet conceived but who will be issue of a specific person who is alive at the time the estate passes to the heirs; and
– legal entities and companies.

Those who do not have the capacity to inherit because they are deemed unfit or unworthy to do so are as follows:

– a person convicted of wilful homicide or of being an accomplice to such, even if death did not actually result, of the person whose estate is to pass, his spouse, descendant, ascendant, adoptive parent or adopted child;
– a person convicted of bringing false or malicious accusations against the persons set out directly *above*, in relation to a crime for which the sentence is more than two years imprisonment;
– a person who, either by fraud or duress, made a testator revoke or modify a will or prevented him from doing so;
– a person who, by fraudulent means, removed, hid, tore or falsified a will, whether before or after the death of the person whose estate is to pass.

9. Authority (Court, Notarial or Other)

The devolution of the estate is certified by a deed or by a judicial inventory.

10. Invalidity of Will

(a)–(b) All contractual declarations, including those relating to transfers, which are legally required to comply with certain formalities are invalid should they not comply with such formalities (Article 220).

A will is a legal instrument which necessitates recourse to certain formalities. A will which is not in the legally prescribed form is null and void (*see*, however, Section B8 *below*).

In general terms, Portuguese law requires that every will should contain the following:

– the elaboration of a basic text;
– the expression of the testator's wishes in a manner which is clear and complete.

There are also specific formalities to be complied with as regards wills by way of public instrument, secret wills (Article 2204 of the Civil Code), special wills and international wills (*see 2 above*).

Moreover, those wills which are contrary to Portuguese law, public order or public decency will be deemed to be invalid.

The failure to obtain the necessary consents (for example, so that one spouse can dispose of common property if he has married under the regime of community property or, even if married under the regime of the separation of property, if he wishes to dispose of the family residence) will render the will null and void.

The invalidity of a will is, however, different from the invalidity of contracts in general. It is subject to a regime which is similar to that of setting aside (*annulation*). Only those who would take if the will or disposition is invalidated can apply to have the will set aside.

It is also possible for a person who would benefit should a disposition be deemed nullified to obtain confirmation of such nullity (Article 2309 of the Civil Code). This is an exception therefore to the rule that only those transfers which can be set aside can be confirmed.

The law provides that testamentary dispositions arising by mistake, fraud or duress are voidable (*annulable*) (Article 2201 of the Civil Code).

A will containing false representations is also voidable, once it is discovered that though apparently for the benefit of the person specified, it is actually for the benefit of another (Article 2200 of the Civil Code).

11. Simultaneous Death

(a) In such cases, the persons deceased do not inherit from one another. There is no transmission of inheritance or legacies as between them.

(b) Proof of the time of death is obtained by all possible means.

The predecease of the 'deceased', as regards the heir or the legatee, must be proven by the heirs of the latter.

If no proof is offered, the law presumes simultaneous death. The person whose estate is to pass and his heirs will be deemed to have died at the same time so that no dispositions will take effect as between them.

12. Estate Taxes

(a) All transfer of property, whether *inter vivos* or *mortis causa*, are subject to inheritance tax and transfer tax.

The regime is that of progressive taxes and depends upon the tie of kinship between the deceased and the heir or the legatee.

Inheritance tax for the *surviving spouse and the children* under the age of eighteen or incapacitated as heirs is from 0 to 33 per cent.

For *other descendants* it is from 4 to 36 per cent.

For the *ancestors or brothers and sisters* it is from 10 to 49 per cent.

For *others* who take it is from 30 to 76 per cent.

(b) All movables and immovables located on Portuguese territory are taxable.

In principle, no tax is due on *property located abroad*, even if owned by Portuguese or foreigners domiciled in Portugal, in order to prevent double taxation.

For *property located in Portugal* there are a number of exceptions and exemptions, which benefit legal persons and entities.

(c) Each heir is taxed as opposed to the estate.

Certain heirs benefit from deductions and reductions.

13. Administration of Estates

(a) Up until its division and distribution, the estate is administered by, the *cabeça de casal* (*tête de couple*), a person resembling the 'head of family' yet somewhat different. (Since the reform in 1977 of the Civil Code, the 'head of family' is no longer recognized in Portugal. This used to refer to the husband.)

In accordance with the law, the function of *tête de couple* is conferred upon persons in the following order:

– the surviving spouse;
– the testamentary executor;
– the relations who are legal heirs and most closely related;
– the testamentary heirs.

If the entire estate has been distributed by way of legacies, the person who will act as *tête de couple* is the legatee who has benefited most; should there be more than one in this instance, preference is given to the oldest.

If the spouse, heir or legatee is incapacitated, their respective legal representatives will exercise these functions (Article 2082 of the Civil Code).

However, these rules are not mandatory.

Those who are interested can, should they all be in agreement (as can the Public Ministry, if a statement of assets and debts is drawn up), decide that the administration of the estate and the function of the person acting as the *tête de couple* revert to another person.

(b) Even if the law does not specifically require the administrator to draw up such report, he does have to provide an annual written statement of administration (Article 2238 of the Civil Code).

One of the heirs or the spouse has the right to demand that the *tête de couple* distributes to all those entitled up to half of their respective entitlements unless these assets are necessary for the payment of administration charges (Article 2092 of the Civil Code).

(c) There is no external control over the administration.

(d) It is the *tête de couple*.

(e) Before the division, the administrator of the estate presents a report on the administration on an annual basis and should there be any outstanding balance in credit, after having deducted the amount necessary to cover the next year's expenses, this is distributed to those interested, according to their respective rights.

The handing over of the assets to the heirs culminates with the act of division (*partage*).

(f) The *tête de couple* only meets those expenses arising from the funeral as well as administration costs, without prejudice to the fact that the testator can empower the testamentary executor to deal with the legacies and other charges of the estate whilst he is also acting as *tête de couple*. This is provided that a judicial inventory has not been carried out (Article 2327 of the Civil Code).

The payment of the other debts of the estate must be met by all the heirs.

After division, the heirs are only liable for charges proportionate to their respective shares in the inheritance.

(g) The estate of the deceased is distributed by way of division (*partage*).

The powers as regards the inheritance can only be exercised jointly, by all the heirs, or against them (Article 2091 of the Civil Code).

Nevertheless, if there are several heirs, one of them can request property in the hands of a third party without that latter being able to object on the grounds that the property does not belong entirely to that heir (Article 2078 of the Civil Code).

It is heirs between themselves that divide the property. The testamentary executor is only empowered to do those things which the testator has allowed him to do within the limits of the law (Article 2325 of the Civil Code). If the testator does not specify the executor's powers then, (in accordance with Article 2326 of the Civil Code), the latter can do the following:

International Succession

- deal with the testator's funeral, pay the costs and the priests, in accordance with the provisions set out in the will and, if nothing was specified, in accordance with the customs of the testator's country;
- to supervise the execution of the testamentary dispositions and uphold them, if necessary, in law;
- to exercise the function of *tête de couple* in accordance with the provisions of Article 2080(1)(b) of the Civil Code. (It is he who will exercise the function of *tête de couple*, in the absence of the spouse.)

The division having been carried out, each heir is deemed, from the moment the estate passed, the sole heir of that property which he inherits, without prejudice to what is provided for by law as regards the income of the estate.

14. Domicile/Nationality

(a) In accordance with Portuguese law, the succession is governed by the personal law of the person whose estate is to pass, (the personal law being that of his nationality) at the moment of his death. This law will serve to define the powers of the administrator of the estate as well as that of the testamentary executor.

The law of nationality at the time of declaration (that is, at the time of the execution of the will) also governs the interpretation of the respective clauses and dispositions, unless there are explicit or implicit references to another law (Article 64 of the Civil Code).

However, Portuguese law respects the principle of *renvoi*. If the law of a nationality refers to the legislation of another and the latter is deemed to have jurisdiction, it will be the law of the latter which is applied. If the law of the nationality refers to that of Portugal, it is this law which will be applied.

(b) The court of the location at which the estate passes has jurisdiction over the inventory and the declaration and authorization of the heirs.

However, if the estate passes abroad, the following are deemed competent:

- the court of the location of the immovables; or
- the court of the domicile of the deceased if the latter has not left any immovables in Portugal.

Article 348 of the Civil Code provides that a person invoking foreign law must prove the existence and content of such. The court, however, if it has jurisdiction, must seek *ex officio* to find such proof.

The court of the domicile of the deceased can in this manner apply foreign law.

SECTION B – APPLICABLE LAW/PROCEDURE WHERE FOREIGN ELEMENT/S ARE INVOLVED

1. Jurisdiction

(a) A Portuguese Court will have jurisdiction over an inheritance if:

512

– the last domicile of the deceased was in Portugal;
– the deceased left immovables in Portugal;
– the inheritance law to be applied is that of Portugal.

(b) The Portuguese rule of private international law is that of the unity of succession. The devolution of the entire estate is done in accordance with the same rules, that of the law of the nationality of deceased. Nevertheless according to Article 17(1) of the Civil Code, if the private international law designated as the Portuguese conflicts of law rule refers back to the law of another which deems itself competent, then it is the national law of the latter which must be applied.

(c) The court with jurisdiction as regards inheritance is that of first instance in the domicile of the deceased at the time of his death. If his domicile is outside of Portugal, it is the court of first instance of the location of the immovables or, failing this, that of the location of the greater part of movables. The court which carried out the inventory upon the death of one spouse will be that which has jurisdiction for that of the other upon death, unless the marital regime was the separation of property.

2. Applicable Law

The court will apply that law which regulates the succession in accordance with Portuguese private international law. On this basis, in principle, the law to be applied is that of the nationality of the deceased (*see* Section A14).

By virtue of Article 348 of the Civil Code, the court is to establish *ex officio* the foreign law to be applied in the particular case before it. In effect, the court has to do so when the parties have not invoked such law and such law is to apply in accordance with Portuguese private international law.

When it is not possible to determine the content of the foreign law that is applicable, however, the court will apply Portuguese law. Furthermore the court will accept renvoi for Portuguese law.

3. Foreign Succession/Inheritance Orders

(a) A foreign judgement must in principle be revised and ratified by the Portuguese court having jurisdiction if it is to be enforceable in Portugal.

(b) It is, in principle, the law of nationality which will determine the transfer of the assets.

The heirs can confirm their rights of inheritance by way of a *declaration of the heirs* or by way of *an authorization of the heirs* in the form of deed and in which a declaration is made, having been attested to by three persons whom the notary considers to be trustworthy or the *tête de couple*, as to the identity of the heirs of the deceased and there being no other persons who could, in accordance with the law, take concurrently with them or have priority over them as to the inheritance.

A declaration of the heirs can be carried out by way of a judicial inventory.

An authorization of the heirs, whether notarial or judicial, gives them a title enabling them to obtain funds held by the deceased at banks and to make entries in land and commercial registers in relation to the property subject to the inheritance.

If title has been established abroad, in a foreign language, this must be translated so that it can be produced to the Registries and the tax officials, in order that taxes be settled.

(c) Foreign documents are valid in Portugal as long as they conform to the law of the location at which they were issued.

4. Two or More Succession or Probate Orders

It is the law of the nationality which determines the devolution of succession, but Portuguese law respects the principle of *renvoi*.

Even if Portuguese law is that to be applied, the devolution of succession can be recorded by a foreign deed which is in accordance with the formalities of the law of the location at which it was issued.

5. Assets

See above.

6. Expert Evidence

No. However, in order that a Portuguese notary draw up an 'authorization of heirs' for a deceased person who was a foreign national, that is, in order for him to be able to declare who the heirs are, he must ask the local consulate of the country of which the deceased was a national for a document confirming the legal order of the succession according to the national law of the deceased or that of his testamentary capacity.

7. Unity of Succession

Yes.

8. Formalities

No, the wills are valid as regards formalities if they conform to the law of the location in which they were drawn up. More generally, *locus regit actum*, or the law of the nationality of the person whose estate will pass, or the law relating to conflicts of law could apply.

But if the law of the nationality of the testator requires a certain formality, the absence of which would result in its nullity, even if such formality only applies abroad, it will also be required in Portugal.

A will made by a Portuguese national living abroad in accordance with that national law does not take effect in Portugal unless it observes an 'official formality'.

Legal opinion is divided as to what such official formality implies. Some consider that a will in a written form would meet that requirement whilst others maintain that a will not only has to be in writing but must also be executed or approved by a notary or some other official of equivalent standing.

9. Legislation

The *1961 Hague Convention on the Conflicts of Laws Relating to the Form of Testamentary Dispositions* has not been ratified, the instrument of ratification never having been deposited or published in the Official Journal, and is therefore not in force in Portugal.

However, the *Decree of 327/77 of 10 August 1977* approved the process of recognition of the certificates to which the Convention refers in relation to the administration of international inheritances.

The *Decree 3/82 of 19 January 1982* approved ratification of the *1972 Basle Convention* on the establishment of a system for the registration of wills.

10. Wills

(a) *See* 8. It is the principle of *locus regit actum* that determines the validity of a will as regards its form. Nevertheless, the admissibility of joint wills or agreements on succession is governed by the law of nationality.

(b) The interpretation of testamentary clauses and dispositions is governed by the law of nationality except if there are explicit or implicit references made to other laws (Article 54 of the Civil Code).

(c) It is the law of nationality which governs all inheritance rights.

(d) It is governed by the personal law (i.e., the law of nationality) of the person whose estate is to pass.

(e) It is the law of nationality at the time of the execution of the will. A person who acquires another nationality after having made the will retains the power of revocation in accordance with the terms of the law that first applied.

(f) As regards the interpretation of a will, the law of the nationality of the testator at the time he draws up his will is that which will apply, unless reference is made explicitly or implicitly to another law. As regards the capacity to make or modify a will or have recourse to special forms of will (if the testator is a minor), the law to be applied is that of the nationality of the testator at the time he signs the will.

International Succession

(g) It is the law of succession that regulates these powers.

(h) *See* (e) *above.*

(i) It is the law of nationality which applies to the protection of that part of the estate which may be subject to compulsory shares.

11. Domicile/Nationality

(a) The law relating to the capacity to make a will and the interpretation of its clauses is that of the nationality of the testator at the time the will is drawn up (*see* 10(e)). The law relating to formalities is that of the location the will is executed.

(b) No.

(c) The law of inheritance is that of nationality. The personal law of a stateless person is that of his habitual domicile or, if he is a minor (under the age of eighteen) or a person lacking the capacity to make a will, that of his legal domicile.

   In the absence of an habitual domicile, it is the occasional domicile which applies and, if this cannot be established, it is the location at which the deceased is found.

12. Taxation

No, there is no difference.

Scotland

Prepared by: Michael MILLER, Advocate

Address: Advocates Library
Parliament House
Edinburgh
EH1 1RF
Scotland
United Kingdom
Tel.: +44 131 226 5071
Fax: +44 131 225 3642
E-mail: Mjmiller1@hotmail.com

Section A – Brief Survey of The Local System

1. Type of System

(a) The legal system of Scotland is a hybrid of common law and some general principles seen in a Civilian system which is derived from Roman law.

(b) When the kingdoms of England and Scotland united into the United Kingdom of Great Britain by the *Act of Union in 1707* the separate law of Scotland was preserved. In 1998 the Scotland Act c.46 established devolution and a Scottish Parliament to deal with certain domestic matters while other matters were reserved for the UK Parliament. This chapter deals with the separate law of succession in Scotland which is governed primarily by the common law, the *Succession (Scotland) Act 1964* and the *Requirements of Writing (Scotland) Act 1995*.

2. Wills

(a) *The Requirements of Writing (Scotland) Act 1995 c.7* changed the law significantly in relation to the authentication (formerly called probativity but now self-proving status) and formalities required for wills. Self-proving status means that the will is presumed to have been validly executed because it appears to be. It proves its authenticity and the rights and obligations within it. The will may be reduced in the Court of Session but strong proof is needed. Section 1(2)c stipulates that a

517

written document is required for the making of any will, testamentary trust disposition and settlement or codicil. Section 2(1) stipulates that subscription alone is required for the will to be formally valid. Wills do not need to be signed on every page unless self-proving status is required.

Section 3 sets out certain presumptions as to the testator's subscription and its date and place. If the testamentary document consists of more than one sheet the testator's subscription is not presumed unless every sheet bears to have his or her signature. Only one witness is required and the testing clause or equivalent ought to state the name and address of the witness. A testator can not be a witness. By Section 3(4)c a document will not be presumed to have been subscribed by its granter where a witness did not know the testator, was not of full age namely sixteen since the *Age of Capacity (Scotland) Act 1991 c.50* or was mentally incapable of acting as a witness. Under the *1991 Act* all children male or female have testamentary capacity from the age of twelve. By Section 3(7) the job of the witness is to see the testator sign the document or to be the person to whom the testator acknowledges his subscription. There is now no distinction between holograph and typewritten wills and the status of privileged wills has been abolished.

Section 9 provides for subscription on behalf of a testator who is blind or unable to write. The term notary has been replaced by 'relevant person' as defined. The concepts of death bed and secret wills do not apply in Scotland. Donations *mortis causa* are recognized and there are three requirements namely: the gift must be made in contemplation of death; the object must be delivered to the donee or equivalent to show *animus donandi* (the intention to gift); and the donor must have manifested an intention to make an immediate gift to rebut the presumption against donation. The object forms part of the deceased's estate at the date of death as the deceased may change his or her mind at any time before death.

(b) *i.* The same rules on authentication and validity apply to codicils as to wills.

   ii. Marriage or divorce will not affect the terms of a prior will but the surviving spouse may claim the rights of *jus relictae* (widow) or *jus relicti* (widower) which are called legal rights and which are indefeasible rights to movable property. These rights may be excluded by express discharge or by agreement in an ante-nuptial marriage contract. Where a spouse and children (whose legal right is called *legitim*) survive, the movable estate after payment of debts is divided into three parts and the spouse is entitled to one-third; the children are entitled to one-third and the remaining one-third, termed the free estate, is bequeathed as instructed by the testator. Where a spouse survives with no children or children survive and not the spouse, the movable estate is divided into two parts and the second half (the free estate) is bequeathed as instructed.

   iii. A testamentary document may be expressly revoked by physical destruction with that intention or by a clause of revocation in a subsequent testamentary deed. Implied revocation may apply in whole or part if there are inconsistent provisions in a subsequent deed. Provided the will has not been physically destroyed the original deed may be revived if the provisions are revoked by a further deed and the terms of the original will are not affected.

3. Intestacy

(a) Intestate succession is governed by the *Succession (Scotland) Act 1964*. After the payment of the deceased's debts and any other liabilities and charges on the estate there are three sets of rules to be considered before the final division.

i. Prior Rights

(a) The housing right under Section 8 applies to a surviving spouse who is entitled to the deceased's interest in any one house owned or tenanted by the deceased at the time of his or her death. The surviving spouse must have been ordinarily resident in the house at the death and there is a maximum benefit of £130,000. Further there is a right to the furniture and plenishings of the house up to a value of £22,000 subject to certain heirlooms.

(b) There is a monetary right under Section 9 where the surviving spouse is entitled to £35,000 if the intestate is survived by children and £58,000 if there are no children.

ii. Legal Rights

From Section 10(2) legal rights are exigible from any movable estate remaining after the satisfaction of the prior rights under Sections 8 and 9. The legal rights of a spouse are referred to *above* at paragraph 2(b)(ii). The children share a *legitim* fund and there are rules on its division *per capita* (equally among issue) or *per stirpes* (degree of surviving issue).

iii. Succession to the Free Legal Estate

Section 2 sets out the order as follows and the succession of a prior class excludes any subsequent class:

– children (an adopted child is treated as a natural-born child of the adoptive parents);
– half to parent(s) and half to brothers and sisters;
– brothers and sisters only;
– parent(s) only;
– spouse only;
– uncles and aunts;
– grandparents;
– brothers or sisters of any of his or her grandparents;
– ancestors of the intestate by generation without distinction between paternal and maternal lines. The Crown takes as *ultimus haeres* where no other entitled person survives by Section 7.

(b) As stated in paragraph 2(b)*ii*. the legal rights of the surviving spouse (*jus relictae* or *jus relicti*) and children (*legitim*) are exigible only from the deceased's movable estate. This distinction between movables and immovables (heritable property) is also required to calculate the surviving spouse's prior rights under Sections 8 and 9. The law maintains the distinction to calculate liabilities between movables and immovables. Accordingly the assimilation of movables and immovables which is sought in Section 1 of the *1964 Act* is only seen in the division of the free legal estate.

4. Freedom of Testation

(a) The main restriction on testamentary freedom is the existence of the legal rights of a spouse and descendants mentioned in paragraph 2(b)*ii*. Apart from paragraph 4(b)*ii*. below there is no distinction relating to illegitimate, including adulterine, children who have full rights of succession or adopted children who are treated as children of the adopter(s) and have no rights in the succession of their natural parents. There are other restrictions on accumulating income with capital for excessive periods and the courts have power to strike down testamentary provisions which are contrary to public policy.

(b) *i.* Inheritance contracts made before death are not enforceable.

   ii. There are no concepts of partition, anticipation, successor or family settlements but by Section 37(1)(a) the *1964 Act* does not apply to any title, coat of arms, honour or dignity transmissible on death which are governed by the older rules of primogeniture and preference of the male line. Adopted and illegitimate children are excluded from this succession.

5. Maintenance

The surviving spouse's prior rights may be supplemented by aliment. See the *Family Law (Scotland) Act 1985* Section 1(4) and Section 37(1)(c) of the *1964 Act*. The rule provides that 'A person who is owed an obligation of aliment may claim aliment from the executor of a deceased person or from any person enriched by the succession to the estate of a deceased person.' Accordingly children are covered by this provision.

6. Community Property Between Husband and Wife

(a)–(b) Two factors determine whether the property comprised in a special destination, which is a disposition of a particular property, usually immovables but may be movables, to a particular named person in a deed dealing with title on the death of the owner, forms part of the deceased's estate namely, whether there is power to revoke the destination and whether revocation occurred. Heritable property is often bought by husband and wife equally with a special destination in the title to the surviving spouse as successor to the other spouse's one-half *pro indiviso* share. Section 30 of the *1964 Act* means that the special destination will be recognized unless a testamentary disposition specifically refers to it and there is a declared intention to evacuate it. The provision must be reconsidered if there is a divorce as the destination will remain until it is evacuated.

7. Gifts (*Inter Vivos*)

(a) Unless there is an advance towards the legal right of *legitim* which is made clear by the deceased that the sum is to come out of the estate, gifts are not set off against the heir's inheritance but may be considered for inheritance tax calculations.

(b) No limit applies.

8. Capacity

(a) As mentioned *above* testamentary capacity applies from the age of twelve. Marital status is not a factor. The Courts will look at all the circumstances to ascertain whether an ill testator has mental capacity and it is a matter of degree after proof.

(b) *See* paragraph 2(a). Witnesses must be over sixteen years of age and not be mentally incapable of acting as a witness. It is irrelevant if the witness is a beneficiary under the deed.

(c) There is the *conditio si testator sine liberis decesserit* which presumes that the testator would not intend to omit from succession his or her own children. It applied originally to make provision for a posthumous child of the testator but the scope has been extended to include children born after the date of execution of the will and the effect is that the subsequent birth of any children may revoke the will and the estate may fall into intestacy. The presumption is rebuttable if the testator intended to exclude the child and the onus is on the child to challenge the will. There are complex interactions to consider before invoking this procedure.

There is also the *conditio si institutus sine liberis decesserit* which provides that if no express bequest has been made for the children of a predeceasing beneficiary, the testator would not have intended to overlook the beneficiary's predecease and would have intended for the beneficiary's children to take the legacy. There are a number of complications involved with this doctrine.

9. Authority (Court, Notarial or Other)

The procedure for an order of succession is through the Commissary Courts by Confirmation which constitutes title to all movable and immovable estate in Scotland and provides title to certain assets in England and Wales.

10. Invalidity of Will

(a) There is a distinction between authenticity and formal and essential validity. Fraud, duress and coercion will invalidate a will.

(b) The will is void if there is no capacity due to insanity or age. A challenge on the ground of total incapacity of the testator is based on averments that the testator did not have the necessary intent. The will is voidable if the challenge is based on facility and circumvention (namely pressure); and undue influence where the vulnerability of the testator allows the trust placed in a beneficiary to be abused. A challenge on this ground is based on the testator having a disponing mind (intent) but it is affected by the will of another such that it is not the testator's own mind (intent). There are a number of factors which require to be considered as to whether prescription applies to such a claim including whether the claim is against the property or a trustee as defined for the purposes of the *Prescription and Limitation (Scotland) Act 1973* as amended.

11. Simultaneous Death

Section 31 of the *1964 Act* provides a presumption of survivorship based on age. The younger is presumed to have survived the elder for all purposes of succession. There is an exception to this presumption for the purposes of the testamentary provision where the younger person died intestate and the older one left a testamentary disposition in favour of the younger one whom failing a third party. Where they are husband and wife there is a presumption that neither survived the other irrespective of age.

12. Estate Taxes

(a) The *Inheritance Tax Act 1984* governs the taxation of estates and *inter vivos* gifts within a number of years of the donor's death.

(b) Domicile is defined for the purposes of the *Inheritance Tax Act*.

(c) The value of the estate is the first factor but the executor pays the tax.

13. Administration of Estates

(a) The executor not the heirs administers the estate. If there is a will the executor-nominate is named. On intestacy the person with the beneficial interest in the deceased's estate will be found entitled to the office of executor-dative.

(b) An inventory of the estate is drawn up and this is presented to the court by the executor so that Confirmation may be granted. An oath or affirmation to an inventory is made.

(c) The commissary court process is primarily to give title to the executor to administer the deceased's estate. The executor is still under a duty to lodge an account with the commissary court and the Capital Taxes Office to show his or her intromissions with the deceased's estate.

(d) There are different rules depending on the objection or challenge to the executor. The executor ought ideally to be over eighteen years of age. A beneficiary may bring an action of accounting against the executor to obtain his or her entitlement. Under the *Trusts (Scotland) Act 1921* as amended any person having an interest in the trust estate may petition the appropriate court for the appointment of a new executor-dative who has been struck down by illness. There are provisions which allow a curator *bonis* to be appointed to an *incapax* executor.

A judicial factor may be appointed where there is no one eligible and willing to be confirmed as executor or where the executor has been removed from office.

(e)–(f) Only after the deceased's debts, funeral expenses and inheritance tax are paid may the executor distribute the assets to the beneficiaries.

(g) As mentioned *above* an executor-dative is appointed by the court.

14. Domicile/Nationality

(a) All testamentary writings must accompany the Inventory for Confirmation. The validity of a testamentary writing is determined by the law of domicile. The law of domicile will determine the testamentary capacity and the validity of testamentary dispositions *seen* in paragraph 2(a) *above*.

(b) The Scots law of domicile presupposes that there is one operative domicile. Whether there are assets in Scotland is not a factor in determining domicile which is habitual residence at the time of death and intention but there must be assets within the jurisdiction before Confirmation may be granted. If Scottish domicile is found there is the further question which Sheriffdom gives local domicile. The Inventory has appropriate spaces for estate in England and Wales and estate held abroad although Confirmation may not be granted for all this estate.

SECTION B – APPLICABLE LAW/PROCEDURE WHERE FOREIGN ELEMENT/S ARE INVOLVED

1. Jurisdiction

(a) Local domicile at the date of death is the primary factor in holding there is jurisdiction.

(b) Succession to movables is governed by the law of the domicile of the deceased whereas succession to immovables is governed by the *lex situs* of the property.

(c) If the deceased died domiciled in a particular Sheriffdom it will have jurisdiction. Which court in the Sheriffdom has jurisdiction will be ascertained by the last ordinary residence. If the deceased had no fixed or known domicile except that it was in Scotland the commissary court in Edinburgh has jurisdiction.

International Succession

2. Applicable law

The local court will apply the law of the domicile at the date of death subject to certain exceptions some of which may be seen in the following paragraphs. The *lex situs* governs immovable property.

3. Foreign Succession/Inheritance Orders

(a) Where a deceased died domiciled in a country other than Scotland the commissary court in Edinburgh has jurisdiction and Confirmation may only be granted to estate in Scotland. The *lex fori* determines all questions relating to the administration of assets recovered by a grant of administration. The *lex domicilii* determines succession to the movable estate.

(b) Confirmation is required.

(c) Where there is a grant of probate the original grant with the will or an exemplification (official copy of a document under the seal of the issuing court or office) must be produced. The document must be authenticated and an office copy is not sufficient. If there is no foreign probate but the will is kept in the custody of a notary, a notarial copy is required under the hand and seal of the notary and the notary's signature must be authenticated and an opinion from someone other than the notary must be produced stating that the notarial copy is entitled to the same faith and credit as the original will. If a notary does not retain custody of the will there must be produced the original will and an opinion from a person versant in the law of the foreign domicile stating the validity of the will and who is entitled to administer the estate.

4. Two or More Succession or Probate Orders

Domicile will prevail and the *lex situs* prevails over immovable property.

5. Assets

See paragraph 1 *above*. Domicile rules and location for *lex situs*.

6. Expert evidence

(a) *See* paragraph 3 *above*.

(b) The opinion may be in the form of an opinion, affidavit or notarial certificate according to the forms in use in the country to which it relates.

524

7. Unity of succession

See paragraph 10 *below*.

8. Formalities

The *lex fori*, Scotland, states that the *lex domicilii* applies so those rules must be followed.

9. Legislation

The *Wills Act 1963* which applies in Scotland and the *1964* Act followed the *1961 Hague Convention on the Conflict of Laws Relating to the Form of Testamentary Dispositions*.

10. Wills

(a) A will is properly executed if its execution conforms to the internal law regulating execution.

(b) As mentioned in paragraph 3(a) administration, which means all steps of procedure in completion of title and all the duties of the executor up to the point of division, is governed by the *lex fori*. This includes obtaining Confirmation, payment of Inheritance Tax, collection of assets and payment of debts. Distribution of the estate is governed by the *lex domicilii*. Classification between administration and distribution is governed by the *lex fori*.

(c) Rights of beneficiaries are determined by the law of the last domicile of the deceased for movables and *lex situs* for immovables.

(d) Capacity to grant a discharge to the executor may be determined by the law of the domicile of the beneficiary or the *lex situs* for immovable property.

(e) Capacity to make a will is determined by the law of the deceased's last domicile but the domicile at the time of making the will may be considered.

(f) Same as (c) *above*.

(g) The court may look not to the law of last domicile but to the law which the testator has chosen as being the system of law he or she most had in mind when framing the will.

(h) Amendment, revocation and revival may be referred to the law of the testator's domicile at the date of revocation; not at the date of death.

International Succession

(i) For immovable property the *lex situs* at the date of the survivorship of the reserve may be considered not the date of death of the testator. For movable property the same date may be taken but the law of domicile would apply.

11. Domicile/Nationality

(a) Domicile at the time of death mostly rules.

(b) *See* paragraph 10(d).

(c) Where a question arises such that it cannot be definitely averred in which country the deceased was domiciled an averment of alternative domicile may be made in the application for Confirmation.

12. Taxation

The taxation attaches to the value of the estate and is paid by the executor and there would be no difference in the taxation treatment of a non-resident heir and a local heir.

South Africa

Prepared by: J.R. FLAX (updated by A. VAYANOS)
Sonnenberg Hoffman Galombik

Address: Norwich on St. George's
        9 St George's Mall
        Cape Town 8001
        P. O. B. 2293 Cape Town 8000
        South Africa
Tel.:   +27 21 410 2500
Fax: +27 21 410 2555

SECTION A – BRIEF SURVEY OF THE LOCAL SYSTEM

1. Type of System

(a) Common law supplemented by statute.

(b) Uniform system.

2. Wills

(a) The form of wills is specified in the *Wills Act No. 7 of 1953* (as amended). No will shall be valid unless:

- the will is signed at the end thereof by the testator or by some other person in his presence and by his direction; and
- such signature is made by the testator or by such other person or is acknowledged by the testator and, if made by such other person, also by such other person, in the presence of two or more competent witnesses present at the same time; and
- such witnesses attest and sign the will in the presence of the testator and of each other and, if the will is signed by such other person, in the presence also of such other person; and
- if the will consists of more than one page, each page, other than the page on which it ends, is also so signed by the testator or by such other person anywhere on the page; and

– if the will is signed by the testator by the making of a mark or by some other person in the presence and by the direction of the testator, a commissioner of oaths certifies that he has satisfied himself as to the identity of the testator, and each page of the will, excluding the page on which his certificate appears, is also signed, anywhere on the page by the commissioner oaths who so certifies.

'Sign' in terms of the *Wills Act* includes the making of initials and, only in the case of a testator, the making of a mark.

In terms of the *Wills Act* if a Court is satisfied that a document is intended to be a will, it will order that it be accepted as valid despite non-compliance with the formalities. This is discussed further under 10 *below*. Wills may be amended by codicil or by amendment of the will itself, but subject to a number of formalities. Codicils are subject to the same formalities in relation to form and execution as are wills.

(b) *i.* A will may be revoked in a number of ways including by its destruction with the necessary intention to revoke or by a later document which itself complies with the same formalities as a will.

ii. Marriage does not automatically revoke a will. However, in terms of Section 2B of the *Wills Act* if any person dies within three months after his marriage was dissolved by a divorce or annulment by a competent court and that person executed a will before the date of such dissolution, that will shall be implemented in the same manner as it would have been implemented if his previous spouse had died before the date of the dissolution concerned, unless it appears from the will that the testator intended to benefit his previous spouse notwithstanding the dissolution of his marriage.

iii. A will which has been revoked may be revived by a properly executed testamentary document clearly indicating an intention to revive that will.

3. Intestacy

(a) The South African law of intestacy is regulated by the *Intestate Succession Act* 81 of 1987 (as amended) in terms whereof:

– If the deceased is survived by a spouse but not by a descendant such spouse shall inherit the intestate estate.
– If the deceased is survived by a descendant but not by a spouse, such descendant shall inherit the intestate estate. Subject to the succession rights of the surviving spouse as set out directly *above*, intestate succession among descendants is *per stirpes* and by representation. Descendants mean children and further issue *ad infinitum* of the deceased i.e., grandchildren, great-grandchildren and so on. Succession *per stirpes* and by representation means that the intestate estate is divided into as many equal portions as there are children of the deceased who survive him and children who have predeceased him leaving descendants who survive him.

Illegitimate and adulterine children are treated equally the same as legitimate children. Each child who survives him takes one share while the share attributed to a deceased child is distributed equally among his children. If one such pre-deceased child has died leaving descendants, his descendants take his share *per stirpes* by representation.

– If the deceased is survived by a spouse as well as a descendant, such spouse shall inherit a child's share of the intestate estate or so much of the intestate estate as does not exceed in value an amount fixed from time to time by the Minister of Justice by notice in the Government Gazette (presently R125,000), whichever is the greater, and such descendant shall inherit the residue (if any) of the intestate estate. A child's portion in relation to the intestate estate of the deceased, shall be calculated by dividing the monetary value of the estate by a number equal to the number of children of the deceased who have either survived him or have died before him but are survived by their descendants, plus one.

– If the deceased is not survived by a spouse or descendant but is survived by both his parents, his parents shall inherit the intestate estate in equal shares, or if he is survived by one of his parents, the surviving parent shall inherit one-half of the intestate estate and the descendants of the deceased parent the other half and if there are no such descendants who have survived the deceased, the surviving parent shall inherit the intestate estate.

– If the deceased is not survived by his spouse or descendant or parent but is survived by: (a) descendants of his deceased mother who are related to the deceased through her only, as well as by descendants of his deceased father who are related to the deceased through him only; or (b) descendants of his deceased parents who are related to the deceased through both such parents; or (c) any of the descendants mentioned *above*, the intestate estate shall be divided into two equal shares and the descendants related to the deceased through the deceased mother shall inherit one-half of the estate and the descendants related to the deceased through the deceased father shall inherit the other half of the estate.

– If the deceased is not survived by a spouse or descendant or parent but is survived only by descendants of one of the deceased parents of the deceased who are related to the deceased through such parent alone, such descendants shall inherit the intestate estate.

– If the deceased is not survived by a spouse, descendant, parent or a descendant of a parent, the other blood relation or blood relations of the deceased who are related to him nearest in degree shall inherit the intestate estate in equal shares.

– Where there are no blood relations to inherit, the intestate estate shall pass to the State.

For the purposes of the aforementioned provisions, an adopted child shall be deemed to be a descendant of his adoptive parent or parents and not to be a descendant of his natural parent or parents, except in the case of a natural parent who is also the adoptive parent of that child or was, at the time of the adoption, married to the adoptive parent of that child.

(b) There is no difference in the division of the estate between movables and immovables, provided that South African law applies.

International Succession

4. Freedom of Testation

(a) No, however:

– a child who is not self-supporting will have a claim for maintenance against the estate of the deceased;
– a surviving spouse will have a claim against the estate of his or her deceased spouse under the *Maintenance of Surviving Spouses Act No. 27 of 1990* for the provision of his or her reasonable maintenance needs until his or her death or remarriage insofar as he or she is not able to provide therefor from his or her own means and earnings.

(b) *i.* A contract of inheritance/*pactum successorium*, with very limited exception, is considered invalid by reason of being against public policy, i.e., *contra bonos mores*.
ii. No, except for family settlements. South Africa is very familiar with the concept of trusts.

5. Maintenance

As referred to in 4 *above*, a surviving spouse and a child will in certain circumstances have a claim against the estate of a deceased for maintenance. The capacity of the claimant in such circumstances is that of a creditor and not of an heir or legatee.

6. Community Property Between Husband and Wife

(a) The answer to this depends upon the matrimonial regime applicable to the marriage.
(b) In terms of the *Matrimonial Property Act 88 of 1984*, if no antenuptial contract is entered into, the parties are married in community of property, the effect of which is to create a joint estate. If the marriage is in community of property, besides certain damages, generally speaking, one-half of the entire nett joint estate will devolve in accordance with the provisions of the deceased spouse's will or intestate succession.

Generally in South Africa in order to avoid adverse implications of a marriage in community of property, the parties prior to their marriage enter into an antenuptial contract excluding community of property either with or without the operation of a system known as the accrual system. If the marriage is out of community of property without accrual, each party retains full legal title to his or her own assets. If the marriage is out of community of property with accrual, then on the termination of the marriage by death or divorce, a compensatory claim will arise in favour of the spouse (or his or her estate), whose estate has shown less growth during the marriage against the other spouse (or his or her estate), regard being had to the particular terms of the relevant contract.

7. Gifts (*Inter Vivos*)

(a) South African law recognizes the concept of collation. Collation applies in both testamentary and intestate succession. Collation is the duty incumbent on descendants who wish to share as heirs in the estate of an ascendant either by will or *ab intestato*, of accounting to the estate for certain gifts or advances received from their ascendant during his lifetime. Thus where a child, grandchild or remoter descendant who is liable to collate has received money or property from his parent, grandparent or remoter ascendant during his lifetime, e.g., as portion of his inheritance or as a marriage settlement or to start him in business, he is obliged, in the absence of an indication to the contrary (usually in the will of the deceased), to bring into collation what he has received, or its value, for the purpose of calculating how the inheritance is to be divided among the heirs

(b) There is no limit as such. An heir who does not wish to collate may renounce his inheritance.

8. Capacity

(a) Section 4 of the *Wills Act* provides that every person of the age of sixteen years or ever may make a will unless at the time of making the will he is mentally incapable of appreciating the nature and effect of his act and the burden of proof that he was mentally incapable at the time rests on the person alleging the same.

(b) Section 1 of the *Wills Act* defines a 'competent witness' as a person of the age of fourteen years or over who at the time he witnesses a will is not incompetent to give evidence in a court of law.
   In terms of Section 4A of the *Wills Act*, any person who attests and signs a will as a witness, or who signs a will in the presence and by direction of a testator, or who writes out the will or any part thereof in his own handwriting, and the person who is the spouse of such person at the time of the execution of the will, shall be disqualified from receiving any benefit from that will. Notwithstanding these provisions, however, a court may declare a person or his spouse to be competent to receive a benefit from a will if the court is satisfied that the person or his spouse did not defraud or unduly influence the testator in the execution of the will. Furthermore a person or his spouse who in terms of the law relating to intestate succession would have been entitled to inherit from the testator if that testator had died intestate shall not thus be disqualified to receive a benefit from that will, provided that the value of the benefit which the person concerned or his spouse receives, shall not exceed the value of the share to which that person or his spouse would have been entitled in terms of the law relating to intestate succession. A person or his spouse who attested and signed a will as a witness shall not be thus disqualified from receiving a benefit from that will if the will concerned has been attested and signed by at least two other competent witnesses who will not receive any benefit from the will concerned. The nomination in a will of a person as an executor, trustee or guardian shall for the *above* purposes be regarded as a benefit to be received by such person from that will.

(c) The general rule is that any person (natural or juristic) may be a beneficiary of an estate. However, there are special statutory provisions applicable to persons with limited legal capacity, i.e., an inheritance devolving on a minor beneficiary must be paid to the Guardians' Fund (although a provision is usually inserted into a will to provide to the contrary). Furthermore 'unworthy persons' or persons who, for example, unlawfully caused the death of the testator, may not be entitled to inherit. Illegitimate children may inherit from any person including their parents. In terms of Section 2D of the *Wills Act*, any benefit allocated to the children of a person, or to the members of a class of persons, mentioned in the will shall vest in the children of that person or those members of the class of persons who are alive at the time of the devolution of the benefit or who have already been conceived at that time and who are later born alive.

9. Authority (Court, Notarial or Other)

The administration of an estate in South Africa does not involve the granting of an order of succession. Letters of executorship which authorize executors to act are issued by the Master of the High Court on application in due form and it is then the duty of the executors duly authorized as aforesaid to implement the terms of the will or, if there is no will, to implement the laws of intestate succession under supervision of the office of the Master of the High Court. The authority of the executors is accordingly derived in terms of letters of executorship issued as aforesaid having regard to the terms of the will and the provisions of the *Administration of Estates Act 66 of 1965*.

10. Invalidity of Will

(a) Grounds of invalidity of a will derive from the provisions of the *Wills Act* and in terms of the common law and include invalidity by reason of failure to comply with the formalities prescribed in the *Wills Act*, invalidity because the testator does not have the necessary *animus testandi* at the time of execution, i.e., where he never intended the document to operate as a will at all etc., invalidity where there has been fraud, duress or undue influence, invalidity where the will is made dependent upon a condition which condition is not fulfilled and invalidity because the will is revoked. A will which appears regular on the face of it will be presumed to be valid until it is shown to be otherwise and the person alleging invalidity bears the onus of proving such allegation.

(b) Invalidity results in the will being void. However, in this regard attention is drawn to the provisions of Section 2(3) of the *Wills Act* which provides that if a court is satisfied that a document or the amendment of a document drafted or executed by a person who has died since the drafting or execution thereof, was intended to be his will or an amendment of his will, the court shall order the Master to accept that document, or that document as amended, for the purposes of the *Administration of Estates Act*, as a will, although it does not comply with all the formalities for the execution or amendment of wills.

11. Simultaneous Death

(a) No particular rules apply in the case of simultaneous death of beneficiaries. A beneficiary must survive a deceased in order to inherit, unless the provisions of the will, for example, specify that the benefit should nevertheless be paid to such beneficiary's estate.

(b) There is no method other than the application of factual evidence for the purposes of determining the order of death of beneficiaries. Unless there is clear evidence to the contrary, the South African courts are likely to find that the relevant persons died simultaneously. Therefore it is common practice to insert in a will a clause that in the event of simultaneous death with the testator or in the event of death within a specified period after the testator's death the relevant beneficiary will be presumed to have predeceased the testator.

12. Estate Taxes

(a) Estate taxes exist in the form of estate duty which is payable at a flat rate (presently 20 per cent) subject to a basic exemption (presently R1.5 million) and that in respect of property accruing to a surviving spouse. Furthermore, capital gains tax was introduced in South Africa in 2001 and in terms of the legislation the death of a person is deemed to be a disposal for capital gains tax purposes. As with estate duty exemptions are available, for example, in respect of assets which pass to a surviving spouse.

(b) Estate duty is levied on the assets and deemed assets worldwide of a deceased person who dies ordinarily resident in South Africa. This is however subject to a special exemption in respect of assets situated outside of South Africa acquired before the deceased became ordinarily resident in South Africa for the first time or acquired by way of inheritance from a person who was ordinarily resident abroad at the date of his death, or as a donation from a person ordinarily resident abroad at the date of the donation. Depending on the states involved double taxation treaties should also provide some relief.

(c) Estate duty is payable out of the assets of the estate of a deceased person although there are instances where the executor may recoup the estate duty from certain persons.

13. Administration of Estates

(a) The *Administration of Estates Act* provides that no person shall liquidate or distribute the estate of any deceased person except under letters of executorship granted or signed and sealed under the Act. As such, a foreign executor may not proceed to deal with any part of the administration of the estate of a deceased person without being properly authorized to act by the Master. Generally, letters of executorship are granted to persons nominated as such under the will of the deceased. If the deceased died intestate or failed to appoint executors in terms of his will, the Master of the High Court appoints the executors in terms of and subject to the provisions of the *Administration of Estates Act*. In such circumstances an order of preference is prescribed in terms of the *Administration of Estates Act*.

(b) The executors are required in terms of the *Administration of Estates Act* to administer the estate under the supervision of the Master of the High Court and which process specifically involves a full account of the assets and liabilities of the deceased at the date of his death and of the distribution to the heirs thereto, described as a Liquidation and Distribution account.

(c) The administration process is very specifically regulated in terms of the *Administration of Estates Act* and is, as mentioned, supervised by the Master of the High Court. The Liquidation and Distribution Account lies open for public inspection for a period of twenty-one days.

(d) Any person interested in the estate may at any time before the expiry of the period allowed for inspection, lodge an objection to the Account (together with reasons), with the Master of the High Court.

(e) The Executor is responsible for the distribution of the assets in the estate to the heirs and legatees in accordance with the terms of the will or in accordance with the laws of intestate succession. The manner of transfer of the assets will depend upon the type of asset involved but the cost of such transfer will ordinarily be borne by the estate.

(f) The creditors whose claims have been admitted by the executor will be paid by the executor out of estate funds.

(g) If the testator did not appoint an executor, the Master of the High Court will appoint one who will follow the procedures set out in the *Administration of Estates Act* and will be responsible for the liquidation and distribution of the estate.

14. Domicile/Nationality

(a) The general basis of jurisdiction is the presence in South Africa of property belonging to a deceased person wherever such person may have been domiciled or resident. In respect of the estate of a deceased person, or any portion thereof, jurisdiction lies:

– in the case of a deceased person who was, at the date of his death, ordinarily resident within the area of jurisdiction of a High Court, with the Master appointed in respect of that area; and

– in the case of a deceased person who was not at that date so resident, with the Master to whom application is made to grant letters of executorship and to sign and seal any such letters already granted in respect of the estate concerned.

Thus once jurisdiction has been established in South Africa by the presence of property then it is place of death not nationality that determines the jurisdiction within South Africa applicable to the administration of the estate. In the case of estate duty, however, ordinary residence of the deceased is significant, location of the assets is significant and the terms and provisions of applicable Double Tax treaties are likewise significant.

No act performed by a Master in the *bona fide* belief that he has jurisdiction shall be invalid merely on the ground that it should have been performed by another Master. Only one Master will exercise jurisdiction in respect of a particular estate.

(b) The *Administration of Estates Act* applies to the estate of any person who died on or after 2 October 1967 leaving property or a document purporting to be a will within South Africa. If a deceased person died while resident within a particular jurisdiction, the Master of the High Court of that jurisdiction would be prepared to authorize a qualifying applicant to act whether or not there were assets situated within that jurisdiction presumably, however, on the basis that the deceased owned property of one type or another within South Africa. However, the formalities implemented might vary depending on the quantum of the assets within such jurisdiction as the *Administration of Estates Act* provides for a simplified procedure where the aggregate of all assets within South Africa to be dealt with do not exceed a specified value or in certain instances where there is only movable property in South Africa.

SECTION B – APPLICABLE LAW/PROCEDURE WHERE FOREIGN ELEMENT/S ARE INVOLVED

1. Jurisdiction

(a) *Generally*
– Whether a South African court has jurisdiction is generally accepted to be dependent on a two-fold enquiry, namely, whether there are sufficient links between the dispute/matter and the territory, which links are known as jurisdictional connecting factors or *rationes jurisdictiones* and which include domicile, residence, commission of a delict, creation of a contract, breach of contract, submission and the situation of property, and, secondly, the notion that jurisdictional rules should ensure that the court is in a position to give a meaningful judgment (known as the doctrine of effectiveness). In other words, if the court has no control over the personal property of the defendant, it cannot guarantee the plaintiff anything more than a theoretical proposition in his favour. Thus the court will search for the appropriate *ratio juristictionis* and then ask whether it can give an effective judgment.

International Succession

Specifically
– Under the law of administration of deceased estates, a deceased estate may not be dealt with or liquidated until an executor has been appointed by a Master of the High Court of South Africa as it is only a person acting under the supervision and authority of a Master who may deal with estate assets. Thus even if a person has received authority in a foreign country to act as an executor, he is not entitled to administer a deceased estate in South Africa until a Master has given authority, either by issuing letters of executorship or by signing and sealing letters previously issued elsewhere. The basis of the Master's jurisdiction (and hence the South African courts' jurisdiction) would be the presence, in South Africa, of property belonging to the deceased and it is considered irrelevant whether the deceased was domiciled or resident within South Africa.

(b) There are different rules for movable and immovable assets, depending on the matter to be decided by the court. An executor is not required to collect and administer property of the deceased situated outside of South Africa. The local court will have jurisdiction in respect of movables situated within South Africa and those movables which come into the possession of the executor, which were situated outside of South Africa. For a local court to have jurisdiction over immovable property, such property must be situated in South Africa.

(c) Once it has been established that the South African courts have jurisdiction, it is necessary to identify which local court in particular will have jurisdiction. The *Administration of Estates Act* seeks to settle potential conflicts between the jurisdictions of the Masters within South Africa. If the deceased was, prior to his death, ordinarily resident within a particular court's area of jurisdiction, the Master attached to that court is competent to appoint an executor. If the deceased was not, however, ordinarily resident within a Master's area of jurisdiction, then the Master to whom application was made for letters of executorship will have jurisdiction.

2. Applicable Law

Which law the court applies depends upon the characterization of the legal claim or question to be decided. The order of intestate succession to a deceased's movables will be determined by his *lex ultimi domicilii* (the law of the domicile of the deceased at the time of his death), irrespective of where those movables are situated. As far as immovable property is concerned, however, the *scission* principle applies in that the distribution of immovables is generally determined by the *lex situs* (the law of the place where the immovable property is situated).

3. Foreign succession/Inheritance Orders

Caveat: South African law is not familiar with the concepts of orders of succession or inheritance as the South African courts are not required to grant such orders in order to enable an executor or administrator to distribute the assets of the deceased's estate. Instead, letters of executorship which authorize executors to act are issued by the Master of the High Court.

In light of the caveat raised above, it is unclear whether to treat a foreign succession or inheritance order as the equivalent of South African letters of executorship or whether to treat such orders as foreign judgments *per se*. The questions raised in this section are accordingly dealt with in terms of both of these scenarios.

(a) *Foreign succession/inheritance order – equivalent of South African letters of executorship*
Where a foreign executor wishes to deal with the property of a deceased person in South Africa pursuant to a foreign succession or inheritance order, such a foreign executor would need to apply to the appropriate Master of the High Court for issue of letters of executorship. The aforesaid application is necessitated by the fact that in terms of the law no person may deal with any assets in South Africa belonging to a deceased person, whether or not the latter died ordinarily resident in South Africa, except under the supervision and authority of a Master of the High Court. The process of applying to the appropriate Master for issue of letters of executorship is facilitated by the provisions of the *Administration of Estates Act* which provides that the letters of executorship issued in certain states need only be signed and sealed by the local Master, before the foreign executor can administer the deceased's South African estate. The relevant states are currently Lesotho, Botswana, British Columbia, British Guiana, Channel Islands, Eire, Kenya, New South Wales, New Zealand, Zambia, Malawi, Zimbabwe, Namibia, Swaziland, Tanzania, the United Kingdom, Victoria. Once the letters of executorship have been so signed and sealed, the provisions of South African law will govern the administration of a deceased's South African estate.

Foreign succession/inheritance order – equivalent of foreign judgment
In view of the fact that the *Administration of Estates Act* makes provision for a specific procedure whereby a foreign executor is empowered to deal with a deceased estate in South Africa, it may be that there is no scope or application in this area of law for the rules governing recognition and enforcement of foreign judgments. A court faced with the prospect of being asked to enforce a foreign succession or inheritance order may simply refer the matter to the relevant Master for the issue or signing and sealing of letters of executorship. There may, however, be circumstances when it is not feasible to have new letters of executorship issued or existing ones signed and sealed, in which event it may be necessary to approach the relevant local court and bring an application to have the foreign order enforced.

In terms of South African law, the following four conditions need to be fulfilled before a foreign judgment will be recognized and enforced:

– The foreign court which pronounced the order or judgment must have had international jurisdiction or competence to decide the matter. The general rule of international competence is that the *forum rei sitae* will be internationally competent in respect of both movable and immovable property.
– The foreign court judgment rendered must be final and conclusive and must not have become superannuated.

International Succession

– The recognition and enforcement of the foreign order or judgment must not be against public policy (including the observance of the rules of natural justice), that the judgment or order was not obtained fraudulently and that the order or judgment does not involve the enforcement of a foreign penal or revenue law.
– The enforcement of the order or judgment must not be precluded by the provisions of the *Protection of Businesses Act of 1978* (as amended). The ambit of this legislation is extremely wide since most foreign judgments touch 'ownership to any matter or material', only rarely will a judgment be able to be enforced without the permission of the Minister.

(b) From the *above* it is apparent that in order to give effect to a foreign succession or inheritance order, it is necessary to apply for letters of executorship or have the foreign letters of executorship signed and sealed by a local Master or, to the extent that the foreign succession or inheritance order is regarded as a foreign judgment, to have such foreign judgment recognized and enforced by the South African courts.

(c) *Foreign succession/inheritance order – equivalent of letters of executorship*
A foreign executor wishing to deal with assets of a deceased's estate in South Africa is required to apply to the Master of the High Court for the issue of letters of executorship which entails such person furnishing the Master with a death notice, the will (if there is one), a document known as the Acceptance of Trust, a bond of security should the Master require such security, and an inventory of the assets of the deceased's estate.

Where signing and sealing is competent and is sought, the following documents must be lodged with the Master:

– authenticated letters of executorship (original or copy) granted in the state concerned;
– duly certified and authenticated copy of the will (if any) of the deceased;
– an inventory of all property known to belong to the deceased within South Africa;
– where the person applying is not resident in South Africa, an authenticated document choosing *domicilium citandi et executandi* within South Africa;
– if this has not already been lodged, a death notice. The Master may require an authenticated death certificate as well;
– in certain instances, the Master may also require the executor to furnish security.

Foreign succession/inheritance orders – equivalent of foreign judgment
As far as the recognition and enforcement of foreign judgments is concerned, South African courts regard foreign judgments as not being directly enforceable but as constituting a cause of action that will be enforced by the courts. Thus a foreign judgment may be enforced by an ordinary action.

4. Two or More Succession or Probate Orders

Caveat: South African law is not familiar with the concepts of orders of succession or inheritance as the South African courts are not required to grant such orders in order to enable an executor or administrator to distribute the assets of the deceased estate. Instead, letters of executorship which authorize executors to act are issued by the Master of the High Court.

In South African law there is no 'unity of administration', in other words, there is no rule that the estate must be administered as a whole by one person in one country. Usually, assets in the estate are administered separately in the different countries in which they happen to be located. Even if a person has received authority in a foreign country to act as an executor, he is not entitled to administer an estate in South Africa until a Master here has given authority.

From a practical point of view this is not an issue in South Africa as the Master does not have any opposition to different executors being appointed in respect of each state in which the deceased held assets. The Master has no opposition to a foreign executor collecting and distributing assets situate in another country. As far as the Master is concerned, each group of assets situated in a different country is treated as a separate deceased estate.

5. Assets

The basis of the Master's jurisdiction to issue letters of executorship seems to be the presence in South Africa of property belonging to the deceased. It would appear that the authority to administer a deceased estate can apply only to assets situated in South Africa and assets situated in a foreign country which have, in fact, come into possession of the South African executor in his capacity as such.

6. Expert Evidence

(a) With the enactment of the *Law of Evidence Amendment Act 45 of 1988*, it is now no longer necessary to prove foreign law in every case as where the foreign law 'can be ascertained readily and with sufficient certainty', judicial notice can be taken of the foreign law.

Where the will is in a foreign language, however, a sworn translation thereof by a sworn translator appointed by the South African courts is required.

Where the *above* Act is not applicable, the only way in which foreign law may be proved is by expert evidence.

(b) One of the most frequent forms of evidence of foreign law accepted in the past is on affidavit or by way of a certificate from a practitioner in the foreign country. Such affidavit or certificate evidence is, of course, not subject to cross-examination and therefore cannot be rigorously tested and thus although in principle an affidavit or certificate evidence of foreign law should not be acceptable, considerations of convenience and cost, coupled with long local practice, suggest that it will continue to be admitted, at least where its admission is not opposed.

International Succession

7. Unity of Succession

The principle of unity of succession whereby questions relating to intestacy or wills are governed by one single law is not adhered to in South Africa. Instead, South African law adheres to the principle of *scission* by which the distribution of movables on the death of the deceased in most instances is governed by the law of his domicile, whilst the distribution of immovables is generally governed by the law of the *situs*.

8. Formalities

Section 3*bis* of the *Wills Act* deals with wills executed in accordance with the internal law of other states but does not apply in respect of wills made by a person who died before 4 December 1970 or made by a South African citizen in a form other than in writing.

Common Law Rules:
In respect of movables, there is authority to the effect that a will is formally valid if it complies with either the *lex loci actus* (the law of the country where it was executed), with the *lex domicilii* at the time of execution of the will or the *lex ultimi domicilii*.

In respect of immovable property, a will is formally valid if it complies with the requirements either of the *lex loci actus* or the *lex situs*.

*Section 3*bis *of the* Wills Act:
In terms of Section 3*bis* of the *Wills Act*, a will shall not be invalid merely by reason of the form thereof, if such form complies with the internal law of the state or territory:

1. in which the will was executed;
2. in which the testator was, at the time of the execution of the will or at the time of his death, domiciled or habitually resident; or
3. of which the testator was, at the time of the execution of the will or at the time of his death, a citizen.

Furthermore, a will shall, so far as immovable property is disposed of therein, not be invalid merely by reason of the form thereof, if such form complies with the internal law of the state or territory in which that property is situated.

9. Legislation

South Africa acceded to and ratified the *1961 Hague Convention on the Conflicts of Laws Relating to the Form of Testamentary Dispositions* on 5 October 1970 with certain reservations.

540

10. Wills

(a) The provisions of Section 3*bis*(2) of the *Wills Act* should be noted:

> 'Any requirement of the internal law of any other state or territory in terms of which a testator of a particular age or nationality or having any other personal qualification is to observe special formalities in the execution of a will, or a witness to a will is to possess certain qualifications, shall be construed as a requirement relating to form only.'

From the *above* it is apparent that any legal requirements are regarded as formal requirements and thus provided that the form of the will complies with the internal law of the state or territory adumbrated in 8 *above*, the will in question will be regarded as valid.

(b) In respect of movables, the testator should be entitled expressly to choose a law to construe the terms used in the will. In the absence of any manifest intention, the law applicable should be that which it can be assumed the testator had in mind when writing the will. This would normally be the law of his domicile at the time of execution because it can be presumed that the testator is familiar with those rules.

In respect of immovables, the choice lies between the *lex situs* and the *lex domicilii* at the time the will was made. Where interpretation by the *lex domicilii* would lead to the creation of rights in immovable property unknown or unlawful under the *lex situs*, then it will readily be held that the *lex situs* has been impliedly chosen.

(c) As was indicated in Section (a) *above*, there are no compulsory shares or minimum percentages for heirs or beneficiaries. However, the general rule is that the *lex ultimi domicilii* of the testator determines this in respect of movables and *lex situs* in respect of immovables.

(d) The law with regard to movables on this question is rudimentary and confusing. The generally accepted rule is that capacity to take under a will is governed by the *lex domicilii* of the testator at the time of making his will. The academic writers submit that in principle the testator's *lex domicilii* should apply where the beneficiary's capacity to inherit movables is closely tied to the making of the will (e.g., rules barring witnesses from receiving a benefit). On the other hand, where the capacity relates to a quality personal to the beneficiary (e.g., lack of age) his own domiciliary law at the date the will was executed should apply. In respect of immovables, the *lex situs* will apply.

(e) With regard to movables, the *lex domicilii* prevails but it is unclear whether it is the *lex ultimi domicilii* or the *lex domicilii* at the time of making the will but appears to be the latter. In the case of immovables, the *lex situs* applies.

International Succession

(f) With regard to movable property, the *lex domicilii* of the testator at the time of death is the governing law. With regard to wills (or bequests) of immovable property, the *lex situs* governs.

(g) In terms of South African law, except in very limited circumstances, a testator cannot in terms of his will give another person the power to determine how his estate is to be distributed after the death of the testator. This may then be a matter of essential or material validity which has been discussed in (f) *above*. However, Section 3*bis* of the *Wills Act* provides that a will shall so far as therein a power concerned by any instrument is exercised or a duty imposed by any instrument is performed, not be invalid merely by reason of the form thereof, if such form complies with the internal law of the state or territory in which such instrument was executed.

(h) Amendment and revival:

There does not appear to be any case or statute law in South Africa dealing with either of these two issues but it is likely that the *lex domicilii* will govern in respect of movables and the *lex situs* in respect of *immovables*.

(i) Revocation:
Section 3*bis*(1)(d) of the *Wills Act* provides for a later will revoking an earlier will. The revocation will be formally valid if it complies with any of the potential testing laws (as identified in 8 *above*) for the later will.

Aside from the statutory provisions, however, there is no Roman Dutch authority on questions of revocation. With regard to movables, it has been suggested that a distinction should be drawn between revocation by the *voluntas* of the testator and revocation *ipso jure*. In the former case, if the testator intended to revoke his will, he would regulate his act by the law which governed him at the time, in other words, the *lex domicilli* at the date of revocation. In the case of revocation *ipso jure* which might depend on events such as marriage, the birth of a child or the granting of a divorce, the same rule shall apply, in other words, the domiciliary law at the date of revocation. In the case of immovables, the *lex situs* applies. However both in respect of movables and immovables the issue may, for example, be one of matrimonial property rather than a testamentary issue with different rules therefore applying.

(j) It is assumed that the concept of 'reserve' is the self-same concept being referred to in Section (a). As indicated in 4(a), there is no concept of reserve in South African law.

11. Domicile/Nationality

(a) It is apparent from the discussion in 10 *above* that it is generally the domicile which determines any of the *above* answers and this domicile may be at the time of death or at the time of making the will, depending on which aspects of the will are being examined.

(b) It is apparent from the discussion in 10 *above* that the domicile of the beneficiary may be relevant, but very rarely.

(c) It is the *lex fori* which determines where a person is domiciled regardless of what the *lex causae* might be. South African law of domicile is founded on the principle that each person should have one and only one domicile at any time.

12. Taxation

The estate taxes which are levied in South Africa are levied in terms of the *Estate Duty Act 45 of 1955* which applies to 'any person' and there are no domiciliary, residential or geographical limitations in respect of the persons whose estates fall within the net of the Act. The very wide scope of the Act is, however, mitigated by the fact that an estate, to be taxable, must consist of 'property' as defined in the Act and the Act seeks to exclude from the definition of property, *inter alia*, any right in immovable property and movable property situated outside South Africa if the deceased was not ordinarily resident in South Africa at the time of his death. Furthermore, the Act allows for the deduction from estate duty assessed of any foreign death duties payable on property situated outside South Africa. There may, furthermore, be relief from double taxation agreements. Also, as mentioned *above*, capital gains tax may also be payable and there are important differences between the exposure of residents and non-residents to capital gains tax.

Spain

Prepared by: Isabel ESCUDERO
BROSA, Abogados y Economistas
Addresses:

Barcelona
Avenida Diagonal, 598
08021 – Barcelona (Spain)
Tel.: (34) 93 240 41 51
Fax: (34) 93 202 29 97

Madrid
Paseo General Martinez Campos, 19
29010 – Madrid (Spain)
Tel.: (34) 91 593 42 44
Fax: (34) 91 593 04 55

Bilbao
Gran Via, 44
48011 – Bilbao (Spain)
Tel.: (34) 94 423 03 36
Fax: (34) 94 423 93 82

Sevilla
Avenida Republica Argentina, 20
41011 – Sevilla (Spain)
Tel.: (34) 95 428 60 99
Fax: (34) 95 427 93 55

SECTION A – BRIEF SURVEY OF THE LOCAL SYSTEM

1. Type of System

(a) Spanish law constitutes a system referred to as civil law and therefore shares the characteristics of Roman law and codification.

(b) Spain is not a federal political entity, but its structure is quite similar. To be precise, the Constitution of 1978 establishes a central state and seventeen autonomous communities. However, regarding inheritance law, there are only six 'foral'

544

territories which have special civil laws and the rest is governed by the Spanish Civil Code. The regions which have their own regime of successions are Catalonia, Aragon, Navarre, the Basque country, the Balearic Islands and Galicia.

For the applicable general law, the Civil Code; for Aragon, the *Compendium of Civil Law* of 21 May 1985, *Succession Law* of 24 February 1999 and *Marital Regime and Widow's Pension Law* of 23 February 2003, which will be in force 23 April 2003; for the Balearic Islands, the *Compendium of Civil Law of Balearic Islands* rewritten 6 September 1990; for Catalonia, the *Code of Succession of Catalonia*, of 30 December 1991 and *Compendium of Civil Law*, as revised 30 September 1993; for Navarre, the *Compendium of Civil Law of Navarre* of 1 March 1973 and Foral Law of 1 April 1987 and for the Basque country, the *Law of Foral Civil Law of the Basque country* of 1 July 1992, revised 26 November 1999.

2. Wills

(a) Forms of wills: In accordance with the Civil Code, there are two forms of wills: general and special.

The general forms of wills are:

(1) The *open will*, which is the most usual form in Spain. It is a recorded document which contains the testator's intentions as declared in the presence of a notary. There is no need for witnesses, except in the following special cases: when the testator cannot sign, he is blind or illiterate or upon testator's or notary's request (Article 697 of the Civil Code).
(2) The *secret will*, in relation to which the testator does not disclose his intentions, only the contents of the envelope when handing it to the notary, in accordance with the formalities set out in Article 707 of the Civil Code. However, this form of will is rarely used in Spain.
(3) The *holographic will* which is written by the testator without the presence of a notary. However, it is mandatory that this testament is in writing and signed by the testator himself and contains the full date. The holographic testament can only be granted by a person who is of full age. Furthermore, the testator must validate those words which have been crossed out, corrected or added between the lines by way of his signature. The Spanish civil law also permits foreigners to make a holographic will in their own language (Article 688 of the Civil Code). During the five years after the testator's death, it is mandatory to carry out certain formalities for the verification of the will in order to obtain its legal validity, i.e., to register the holographic will by a notary and afterwards to obtain its judicial confirmation, as provided for in Articles 689 to 693.

The special forms of wills are those which the military will make in times of war (the naval will) and those drawn up in a foreign country. These forms of wills are rarely used in practice and in all these cases some kind of probate is required to ensure that the testator's intentions are taken down properly (Articles 716 to 736 of the Civil Code).

Finally, there are the *imminent death will* which is made by the testator before five suitable witnesses and without the presence of a notary (Article 700 of the

Civil Code) and the *epidemic case will*, which is made by the testator without the presence of a notary and before three witnesses over the age of sixteen (Article 701 of the Civil Code). In both cases, these wills become ineffective two months later, if the risk of death or the epidemic have passed.

Regarding the special regional civil laws, the following should be noted:

Aragon: The will can be drawn up before a chaplain, when the presence of a notary is not possible. The formalities of recording and confirmation are mandatory. Likewise, the spouses can make a joint will. This joint will can be revoked by both spouses or by one of the spouses with respect to his/her provisions, strictly.

Catalonia: A will can be made in the presence of a priest. The codicils and testamentary accounts are recognized, but these documents only complete a previous will. Consequently, their legal effects are limited.

Navarre: A will can also be made in the presence of a priest, and the codicils and testamentary accounts are recognized with the same limited effects. There is also the will of confraternity, made by two or more persons who do not have to be related. This will can take any form allowed with the exception of that of a holographic will. Its revocation is subject to special rules.

Basque country: There is a special will (*hil – buruko*) which is made in the presence of three witnesses when the testator is in risk of dying. This will becomes ineffective two months later, if the risk of dying has passed. Likewise, if the testator dies during these two months, and this will is not authenticated within three months after his death, it will become ineffective. Spouses can also make a joint will of confraternity, which requires the presence of a notary, and is subject to limitation as to its revocability.

(b) Amendment, revocation or revival: The wills can always be rectified, revoked or renewed only by making a subsequent will, replacing the previous one.

   i. The concept of a codicil is not recognized as a general rule in Spain, except in some regional regimes of succession. In addition, the testator by virtue of a codicil can never revoke or appoint an heir or disinherit him. It can only complete or reduce a previous will. A codicil must comply with the same rules for the wills, including the holographic will conditions. If not, it is ineffective.

   ii. The marriage does not revoke a previous will. It only has an effect insofar as the spouse has the right, as widower or widow, to a usufruct in the legal conditions provided for in the general Civil Code or special regional laws. However, the ordinary practice consists of making a will after the marriage.

   iii. A will can be revived provided that the testator revokes the subsequent will and expressly states the intention that the first is valid again and it has full legal effect. If this is not, the subsequent will always revoke the previous one. When succession occurs, the last will is the only valid one. (Article 739 of the Civil Code).

3. Intestacy

(a) Order of succession: intestacy happens when a person dies without a will; the will does not deal with all the testator's property (and in such a case intestacy relates only to that property that the testator has not disposed of) the condition regarding the appointment of an heir is invalid or the heir cannot inherit, because he has previously died or he does not accept the inheritance (Article 912 of the Civil Code).

The order of succession is practically the same in all the succession regimes in Spain (Civil Code and regional laws), because they incorporate the order of succession of Roman law. The order of succession is the following (Articles 930 to 958):

1. the deceased's children and their descendants;
2. in the absence of children and their descendants, the ascendants;
3. in the absence of descendants and ascendants, the widower/widow;
4. in the absence of the mentioned *above*, the estate will be ceded to the collateral relatives up to the fourth degree, firstly sisters and brothers, *per capita*, then the children of sisters and brothers *per stirpes*;
5. finally, in the absence of the collateral relatives to the fourth degree, the estate will be ceded to the state.

In the cases 1 and 2 the surviving spouse receives his/her compulsory share as usufruct.

When those to inherit are the descendants, ascendants or the surviving spouse, a notary can appoint them as heirs upon intestacy by notarial deed, in accordance with the Notarial rules. If the estate descends to the collateral relatives and state, only the judge has jurisdiction to appoint them as heirs in intestacy and with the official inspection of the prosecutor (Articles 977 to 1000 of the Code of Civil Procedure of 1881).

(b) Difference in the division of the estate between movables and inmovables: As a general rule, there is no difference. However, it should be noted that in the regional civil laws of Aragon, Navarre, Biscay in the Basque country and Aran Valley in Catalonia there are special systems regarding immovables which come from a specific family branch. In this case, the relatives included in the line from which this estate comes from, are the only ones that can inherit.

4. Freedom of Testation

(a) Regarding the Civil Code, there are legitimate portions or compulsory shares which descend to certain family members (Articles 806 to 847 of the Civil Code) and their beneficiaries are referred to as legitimate inheritors. These relatives are the descendants, and in their absence, the ascendants and a surviving spouse who is not legally separated from the deceased. Brothers and sisters are not legitimate inheritors, i.e., a single person, who has three brothers and sisters, but has no children, parents and grandparents, can legally make a will appointing as heir one brother or sister and set aside the rest.

International Succession

Where there are children, the part of the estate subject to compulsory share is two-thirds. One-third is given in equal shares to the children. The testator can dispose of an other third in favour of the descendants he/she prefers (improvement compulsory share). Thus, the testator can only freely dispose of one-third of the estate, which can be given to anyone the testator chooses.

The compulsory share to which ascendants are entitled is half of the estate (Article 809 of the Civil Code) unless the surviving spouse participates in the succession. In this case, the estate is reduced to one-third.

The surviving spouse is always entitled to receive the usufruct of the compulsory share, never the property. If the spouse coincides in the succession with the children, he/she is entitled to one-third of the state; with ascendants, one-half of the estate and two-thirds of the estate if there are neither descendants nor ascendants (Articles 834 to 840 of the Civil Code).

All the descendants (whether legitimate, illegitimate, including adulterine children or adopted children) have equal rights to receive the property of the compulsory share by succession (Article 39.2 of the Constitution of 1978).

In relation to special regimes of civil law, there are specific systems, as follows:

Aragon: Only the descendants are entitled to a compulsory share. The marriage confers the usufruct over all the property of the spouse predeceased.

Catalonia: The part of the estate subject to compulsory share is one-fourth of the estate, which is held by the children and their descendants, or in their absence, by the father or the mother. In accordance with Article 352 of the *Succession Law* of Catalonia, the legitimate inheritors are matrimonial, non-matrimonial and adopted children by equal parts. Likewise, the legitimate portion is a net one-fourth of the estate (Article 355 of the *Succession Law* of Catalonia). In other words, a net outright transfer of the estate, not a usufruct. The surviving spouse is only entitled to one-fourth of the estate ('marital quarter') provided that, at the moment of the spouses's death, he/she has no financial resources (Article 380 of the Successions Code of Catalonia).

Navarre: The law establishes the right to the absolute freedom of testation. The compulsory share is purely formal and with no patrimonial contents. The usufruct of the surviving spouse relates to all the deceased's property at the time of his/her death.

Basque country: the children and the descendants are entitled to compulsory shares of the estate, which amount to four-fifths and, in their absence, the parents and other ascendants are entitled to a compulsory share amounting to one-half of the estate. Within each of the groups, the testator can freely choose and divide the property in equal or unequal shares. The surviving spouse gets one-half of the usufruct over all the estate if he/she coincides with the descendents or ascendants. In the absence of these, he/she takes two-thirds of the usufruct over the estate.

(b) The Spanish Civil Code is opposed to contractual inheritance. However, the regional regimes recognize a wide range of contracts on succession. Usually, these contracts are made on the occasion of the marriage. The contracts of succession are not revocable, in principle, which is the main difference in relation to the wills. Finally, it should be noted that people make no use of them in practice.

5. Maintenance

In Spanish law there is no specific provision to this effect, because maintenance is related to the concept of family solidarity, not to inheritance and consequently. It constitutes a situation governed by family law (Articles 142 to 153 of the Civil Code or Articles 259 to 272 of the Family Code of Catalonia).

However, some provisions arising from a succession situation should be noted. For example, in connection with the dissolution of the matrimonial community of joint-assets, Article 1.408 of the Civil Code establishes that the expenses related to the upkeep of the spouses or, if this should be the case, that of the surviving spouse and the children, will be charged upon the mass of the community property during the division of the estate between the heirs. However, a deduction will be made in the property given to them for that part which exceeds what they will have received by way of receipts and revenue. Likewise, in Navarre there is a similar provision (*Law 89* of the Compendium of Civil Law).

In Aragon, in relation to the dissolution of the marital community property and the adjudging of the inheritance is carried out in the meantime, the surviving spouse is held to its administration and can charge his/her living expenses and that of those living in the spouse's household to it (Article 53 of the Compendium of Civil Law).

In Catalonia there is the mourning year in favour of the surviving spouse. During a year after the death, the widow/widower will have the right to live in the marital house, to keep the household goods, as well as charge his/her living expenses to the deceased's estate, provided that he/she has not the usufruct in the estate or he/she does not enjoy the right of *tenuta* (the right to receipts and revenues), in accordance with Article 11 of the Compendium of the Civil Law of Catalonia as revised 30 September 1993. Likewise, in the Basque Country, upon dissolution resulting from the death of one of the spouses and provided that there are no descendants, the surviving spouse who had gone to the country estate of the deceased will have the right to live there (for as long as the survivor remains unmarried) for a year and one day (Article 58 of *Foral Civil Law*).

Finally, it should be noted that the alimony in favour of a divorced or separated person is not extinguished automatically by virtue of the death of the debtor. However, the heirs can claim the suppression or the reduction of the alimony to the limit of their compulsory shares (Article 101.2 of the Civil Code). Likewise, in Catalonia the heirs can claim the reduction or the suppression of the alimony if the estate is not sufficient to pay it (Article 86.2 of the Family Code of Catalonia).

6. Community Property Between Husband and Wife

In Spain there are different legal conditions, depending on regional regimes of civil law. As a general rule, the marital status is founded on the freedom of contract and the spouses can establish a marital contract (*capitulaciones matrimoniales*) before marriage or afterwards. The marital regime can always be modified, without prejudice to third parties.

(a) Civil Code: In the absence of a marital contract, the auxiliary legal regime is that of joint-assets acquired after marriage (*sociedad de gananciales*), by virtue of which the spouses are owners of half of the income or profits during the marriage. Consequently, after the death, the surviving spouse has the right to one-half of the community property of the deceased and the other half is distributed as inheritance.

(b) In Aragon there exists the 'marital consortium', and in Navarre the 'community of after-acquired property', which are quite similar to joint-assets regime of the Civil Code mentioned *above*.

(c) In Catalonia and the Balearic Islands, there is no community of property ('separated property regime'), unless the spouses make a marital contract establishing otherwise.

(d) In Basque country: the community is universal, by way of half shares for each the husband and the wife, all movables or immovables whatever the origin, belonging to one or other spouse. Each of the spouses has the exclusive right to administer the property that they had owned. The administration of after-acquired property is done jointly by both spouses. Both of the spouses must consent to the selling of property.
    The division of the community property is peculiar: if there are common children, the income is consolidated and a hereditary community is established between the surviving spouse and the heirs of the deceased while the division and assignment of the estate property is carried out. If the spouses have no common children, the community property is dissolved and liquidated by a similar way as joint-assets regime.

7. Gifts (*Inter Vivos*)

In accordance with Spanish law, a person is free to make gifts *inter vivos*. Regarding the legal effects, the following should be noted:

(a) If there are heirs with a right of compulsory share, the gifts are subject to an obligation of the donee to add the value of the gift to the inheritance in order to determine the assets of the estate and to assess the value of the compulsory shares of the estate.
(b) If the value of the gifts exceeds the share which the donor could have made over to the beneficiary, the gift is reduced in order not to affect the compulsory share of the other heirs, in accordance with the principle that no one can give or receive by way of donation more than they could have given or received by will.

8. Capacity

(a) Minors up to fourteen years old and those who are not of sound mind for a long or short period, are unable to make a will (Article 663 of the Civil Code). Furthermore, a person must be of full age in order to make a holographic will. If a person is not of sound mind as established in a judgment but he has not been deprived of the right to make a will by the judge, he can make a testament, provided that he is examined previously by two doctors appointed by the notary (Article 665 of the Civil Code).

Marital status has no effect on the capacity to make a will. However, the spouses married in accordance with joint-assets regime cannot dispose of half of after-acquired property by will (Article 1379 of the Civil Code).

(b) As mentioned in 2 *above*, the usual forms of wills in Spain, are the *open will* and the *holographic will*, in which the witnesses are not required. In the *open will* witnesses are required only when the testator cannot sign, he is blind or illiterate or upon testator's or notary's request (Article 697 of the Civil Code).

When the witnesses are required in special cases, their capacity is governed by Article 681 of the Civil Code that provides that those who are not allowed to be witnesses are the following persons: minors, except for a will made during an epidemic, when being over the age of sixteen; those totally blind and deaf or mute; those unable to understand the language of the testator; those who are not of sound mind; the spouse or relative up to the fourth degree of consanguinity or up to the second degree of affinity of the legalizing notary and his employees.

In addition, those who are not able to be witnesses in an *open will* are the heirs and legatees, as well as the spouses or relatives up to the fourth degree of consanguinity or up to the second degree of affinity (Article 682 of the Civil Code).

(c) All natural persons and legal entities (companies, corporations, associations, etc.) can benefit from a will, except:

- abortive persons living less than twenty-four hours and associations or corporations which are banned (Article 745 of the Civil Code);
- the priest who confessed the deceased during his final illness, priest's relatives up to the fourth degree, as well as his church, town hall, community or institute (Article 752 of the Civil Code);
- the guardian of the testator when the will is made prior to the ending of the period of guardianship, unless the guardian is an ascendant, descendant, a brother or sister or the spouse of the testator (Article 753 of the Civil Code);
- the notary having drawn up the will and the witnesses, as well as their spouses, relatives or relatives by way of marriage up to and including the fourth degree (Article 754 of the Civil Code);
- the persons who are deemed unworthy as provided in Article 756 of the Civil Code, such as:
  - the parents who have abandoned, prostituted or corrupted their children;
  - those who are convicted of attempting to kill the testator, his/her spouse; his/her ascendants or descendants;

- those who have accused the testator of committing a serious crime and this accusation has been proved false;
- the heirs of full age who know the violent death of the testator and do not report the facts to the judge, unless the judge has proceeded *ex officio* previously;
- those who force the deceased to make or revoke a will by menaces, fraud or duress;
- or those who obstruct the testator from making or revoking a will, as well as replacing, hiding or modifying a subsequent will, by menaces, fraud or duress.

However, the legal conditions regarding unworthiness will become ineffective if the testator knew them at the time of making his will or, if having been aware of them subsequently, he pardons by official document (Article 757 of the Civil Code).

9. Authority (Court, Notarial or Other)

As mentioned in Section 3 about Intestacy, the order of succession regarding the descendants, the ascendants or the surviving spouse, is granted by a notary, in accordance with the Notarial Rules. In the case of succession of the collateral relatives and state, the judge is the only one who can grant the order, with the official inspection of the prosecutor (Articles 977 to 1000 of the Code of Civil Procedure of 1881).

With respect to the descent, it should be noted that it is not automatic and depends on the steps taken by the heirs, which are the following:

(a) the first step is to establish the succession, by way of a will or by a notary public or a judge, as mentioned *above*;
(b) the following step is to accept the inheritance. With the acceptance, the beneficiaries become heirs;
(c) the last step is to divide the property of the estate. The division can be judicial (if there is a disagreement between the heirs); or can be undertaken by a testamentary executor; or by agreement of the heirs.

10. Invalidity of Will

(a) The usual legal conditions for invalidity are the following:

- defects in formalities;
- lack of capacity of the testator (i.e., he is not of sound mind);
- duress, fraud, menace or misrepresentation;
- wrongful omission in a will of an heir-at-law or heir whatsoever;
- disinheritance without a right and fair cause.

(b) The testament will be established as void in case of defects of formalities, lack of capacity, duress, fraud, menace, misrepresentation, intentional omission of a legitimate inheritor and disinheritance without a right and fair cause. However, a will will not be considered null and void if the compulsory shares have been damaged by a wrongful omission, without prejudice to the omitted heir recovering his damaged compulsory share, by reducing a portion of the inheritance.

Finally, it should be noted the principle of *favor testamenti*, by virtue of which there is a reluctance to consider a will as void. Thus, instead of nullifying an illegal disposition in the will, the Civil Code deems that it had not been written. For example, Article 792 provides that 'impossible conditions or those contrary to the law or to public morality will be considered not written'. Article 715 also establishes the opportunity of amending the legal defects by relying on another kind of will. Thus, the 'secret will' will be considered null and void due to defects in formalities, but it will be valid, provided that it complies with the legal conditions of the holographic wills.

11. Simultaneous Death

(a) Article 33 of the Civil Code provides that in the absence of evidences, the presumption applied is that a simultaneous death has occurred. Consequently, there will be no transmission of rights between the deceased.

(b) Unlike Roman law, the Spanish law applies a simultaneous death presumption, unless evidence can demonstrate otherwise. In accordance with Spanish law, there are no limited evidences. However, in this case the most proper evidence should be a forensic certificate.

12. Estate Taxes

(a) There is inheritance tax and local tax on increased value of real estate.

However, in the Basque country and Navarre the inheritance tax does not apply in the cases related to succession of descendants, ascendants or spouses. In Cantabria an inheritance tax does not apply at all.

(b) The inheritance tax applies to all kind of movable estate, independently of the place or country they are. In relation to immovable estate, the tax inheritance and the tax of increased value of real estate only applies to the real estate located in Spain.

(c) The liability for such tax is an obligation attaching to the heir or legatee having their principal residence in Spain. The basis of the assessment tax is the net value of the property inherited (gross value of the property minus encumbrances and inheritance debts, i.e., last illness and funeral expenses).

13. Administration of Estates

(a) The administration of the estate is up to the testamentary executor appointed by the testator; in his absence, to the heirs unanimously and in case of disagreement between the heirs, to the judicial authority.

(b) A report is not compulsory if the inheritance is accepted without conditions. However, if there is a conditional acceptance on inheritance without liability beyond the assets given (*a beneficio de inventario*), it is mandatory to submit an inventory to the notary.

(c), (e) & (g) There is no external supervision. The distribution of an estate is carried out following the testator's dispositions to this effect and if this is not the case, by the executor appointed by the testator. However, if these two cases do not apply, the distribution of the estate is carried out by the heirs unanimously and in case of disagreement, by the judge, the division and distribution of the estate taking place by virtue of a civil process.

If the heirs agree (which is the most usual case) the division and distribution of the estate is carried out unanimously, in accordance with joint-ownership rules applied by analogy (392 to 406 of the Civil Code).

In the regional regimes, there are several legal concepts related to trust on succession or testamentary execution or a simple procedure of partition, i.e., in Aragon there is a 'Hereditary trustee', in Catalonia an 'Appointment by trustee', an 'Heir or legatee of trust' and a 'Testamentary executor' or in Basque country a 'Will by Commissioner', etc.

(d) The heirs, legatees and any beneficiary of the inheritance have the right to query and object in relation to the distribution of the estate. In the absence of special rules, the administration of the estate by the heirs is governed by joint-ownership rules, by virtue of which any heir can carry out due acts (acts which cannot prejudice the estate). However, in case of detrimental acts (i.e., to mortgage or to pledge) the heirs must agree and proceed unanimously.

On the other hand, when an estate is subject to administration, the testamentary executor has the hereditary representation before a Court.

(f) There are no specific rules relating to those who are obligated to pay the creditors of the estate. However, there are rules that preserve creditors' rights, which are the following:

While the property is not divided, the creditors can object to the distribution as long as their credits are paid or secured (Article 1082 of the Civil Code).

Once the division is carried out, the creditors can claim the payment of their credits from any heir (Article 1084 of the Civil Code), even exceeding the value of the property descended (responsibility deemed *ultra vires*), unless the inheritance has been accepted subject to an inventory. In such a case, the creditors can only claim against inheritance assets.

14. Domicile/Nationality

(a) In relation to international succession Article 9, paragraphs 1 and 8 of the Civil Code provides the following:

9.1 'The personal law of an individual is established by his nationality, which will determine his capacity, status, family rights and obligations and succession'.

9.8 'The succession is governed by the national law of the deceased at the time of his death, whatever the kind of property and the country in which it is located. However, the testamentary dispositions and the agreement on succession that have been dictated in accordance with the national law of the testator will remain valid even if the succession is governed by another law, although the part of the estate which is subject to compulsory shares, will be subject to the latter. The rights established by law in favour of the surviving spouse will be ruled by the same law which governs the effects of the marriage, though those compulsory shares of the estate in favour of the descendants will remain safeguarded.'

To sum up, the succession is governed by the national law of the individual at the time of his death, whatever the type of property and the country where the property is located (principle of unity ruled by the national law).

Regarding the division of the estate, in connection with international succession, Article 786 of the new *Civil Procedure Law 1/2000* provides the following: 'If the testator made a different procedure in order to carry out the inventory, liquidation and division of the estate, this procedure will remain valid, provided that the compulsory shares are safeguarded'. This new legal provision allows the testator's autonomy in relation to the division of the estate, provided that the compulsory shares are not affected.

With respect to simultaneous death, the national law of the deceased will apply, in accordance with Article 9.8 of the Civil Code mentioned *above* and it would be reasonable to find compatible solutions or presumptions. However, in case of conflict or discordant solutions, the legal opinion in Spain considers that it should be necessary to decide in accordance with the presumptions established by *lex fori*.

Finally it should be noted that Article 12.2 of the Civil Code admits *renvoi de retour*. In practice, the problems arise when a foreign law does not follow the principle of unity of the succession, but a split system, depending on the kind of property (domicile law in case of movables and *rei sitae* law in case of real estate). Consequently, only if both rules consider the Spanish law as applicable, there will be no conflict. The Sentence of the High Court of Malaga of 18 December 1996 establishes that Article 12.2 of the Spanish Civil Code permits the remission to the Spanish material law provided that the English law permits so. Thus, if an English citizen domiciled in Spain leaves immovable property in Spain and movable property in France, the Supreme Court of Spain establishes that the law which governs his succession is the English one (Sentence of 21 May 1999). However, if an English citizen leaves real estate located in Spain and this is the real estate, the Spanish law would apply, in accordance with the Sentence of the Supreme Court of Spain issued on 23 September 2002.

(b) A Spanish court has jurisdiction if the deceased was domiciled in Spain at the time of his death, disregarding the location of the assets. The place where the deceased made his will has no effect in connection with a Spanish court jurisdiction.

International Succession

1. Jurisdiction

(a) The Spanish courts have jurisdiction regarding succession when the deceased has his last domicile in Spain or his real estate is located in Spain (Article 22.3 of the Judicial Power Law of 1 July 1985).

(b) The succession is ruled by the national law of the individual at the time of his death, whatever the kind of property and the country where the property is located (principle of unity ruled by the national law). However and despite the principle of unity of the succession, the Spanish Supreme Court establishes an exception in relation to the succession of British citizens and it applies *renvoi de retour* when the only property of the deceased is real estate located in Spain.

(c) In connection with succession, the court of the last domicile of the deceased has jurisdiction (Article 52.4 of the Civil Procedure Code 1/2000). Regarding intestacy procedure related to descendants, ascendants or surviving spouse, the notary of the last domicile of the deceased has jurisdiction (Article 979 of the Civil Procedure Code of 1881).

2. Applicable Law

In relation to international succession Article 9, paragraphs 1 and 8 of the Civil Code provides the following:

> 9.1 'The personal law of an individual is established by his nationality, which will determine his capacity, status, family rights and obligations and succession' (*see* also Section A para. 14(a) *above*).

> 9.8 'The succession is governed by the national law of the deceased at the time of his death, whatever the kind of property and the country in which it is located. However, the testamentary dispositions and the agreement on succession that have been dictated in accordance with the national law of the testator will remain valid even if the succession is governed by another law, although the part of the estate which is subject to compulsory shares, will be subject to the latter. The rights established by law in favour of the surviving spouse will be ruled by the same law which governs the effects of the marriage, though those compulsory shares of the estate in favour of the descendants will remain safeguarded.'

3. Foreign Succession/Inheritance Orders

(a) A foreign judgement could be enforced or recognized, disregarding the kind of property. To this effect, it is first necessary to take into account the legal requirements established in Articles 951, 952, 953 and 954 of the Civil Procedure Code of 1881, as follows:

Article 951: 'A foreign judgement is enforceable in Spain according to the international conventions applying to the case.'

Articles 952 and 953: 'If an international convention does not apply, reciprocity is essential to enforce a foreign judgement. Without it, a foreign judgement will not be enforceable in Spain.'

Article 954: 'Where a foreign judgement does not fulfil any of the requirements mentioned in the preceding Articles, it will be enforceable if it complies with the following conditions: 1) The judgement must be issued as consequence of an action *in personam*; 2) It must not be issued by default; 3) The obligation involving the judgment must be licit in Spain; 4) The judgement must fulfil the requirements regarding authentication which are applicable in the country where it is issued as well as the conditions required in Spain in order for this judgement to be considered as authentic.'

In connection with intestacy, the prevailing legal opinion of the Supreme Court is reluctant to require an exequatur, because it is not a real jurisdictional proceeding. In this case, the legal conditions will be grounded on the same requirements of the public record (*documento publico*).

(b) There is no specific procedure for taking possession of the property, except that of the validation of the status of heir and the official recognition of the owner of such property. As mentioned in the preceding paragraph, a public record is not a jurisdictional document. Consequently, the notarial documents related to the adjudging of an inheritance, which have been drawn up in foreign countries and in accordance with their national law, have full effect in Spain, provided that they are dully legalized or apostilled in accordance with the *Hague Convention 1961*, and duly translated by a sworn translator, unless they are written in Spanish (i.e., South American countries).

However, if the matter in question is a judgement, it will be mandatory to enforce it in accordance with the legal requirements established in Articles 951, 952, 953 and 954 of the Civil Procedure Code of 1881, as mentioned in the preceding paragraph (a). It should be noted that Council Regulation (EC) Number 44/2001 of 22 December 2000, does not apply regarding succession matters.

Banks and property registration offices will require that the beneficiaries give proof of the payment of inheritance taxes, and in order to obtain the registration of the inheritance it will be necessary to comply with Article 36 of the Regulation of Mortgages which provides the following:

'the documents handed over or delivered by a public office of a foreign country can be registered if they fulfil the conditions required by the rules of private international law, insofar as they contain the legislation and other necessary formalities for their authentication in Spain. The fulfilment of the formalities of another state, as well as the legal capacity which is necessary regarding this act, can be legalised (among other means) by a certificate or report of the notary or the Spanish Consul, or else by a diplomat, consul or official of the country whose legal system would be applicable'.

Consequently, to this effect the rule of *auctor regit actum* should be taken into account, which requires that each state must establish its competence for public documentation, as well as the external formalities of such documents and guarantees of their authenticity.

(c) *See* the two preceding paragraphs (a) and (b).

4. Two or More Succession or Probate Orders

In a case where there is an application before either the court or the relevant authority in the local country for an order of succession or inheritance and a foreign order already exists in one or more foreign countries, what is the order of preference, or which prevails: domicile (as well as its relevant weight), citizenship, nationality or location of assets (movable or immovable).

As mentioned in this Section, the law that governs succession is that of the nationality of the deceased at the time of his death, disregarding the kind of property and the country in which it is located. In addition, the Spanish courts have jurisdiction regarding succession when the deceased has had his last domicile in Spain or his real estate is located in Spain (Article 22.3 of the Judicial Power Law of 1 July 1985). Consequently, if a Spanish court considers that it has jurisdiction, the enforcement of a foreign judgment related to the same matter would be dismissed.

However and in connection with which order of succession or inheritance prevails, it should be taken into account that Spain has signed bilateral international conventions with Germany (1870), United States (1902), Argentina (1870), France (1862), Greece (1919), Holland (1871), Japan (1911), United Kingdom and Ireland (1886), Portugal (1870), and Brazil, among others. It is also necessary to note that in succession matters, Council Regulation (EC) Number 44/2001 of 22 December 2000, does not apply. Thus, it will be necessary to verify previously if an international convention applies, it being the most usual in these cases that the first application will prevail in relation to the latter. If no international convention applies or, if applying, does not provide in this specific matter, the foreign order of succession or inheritance will not be recognized or enforced if a Spanish court considers it to have jurisdiction.

5. Assets

If there are no assets whatsoever in the jurisdiction but some other connecting factors, e.g., domicile, citizenship, residence, could the local court assume jurisdiction?

As stated throughout this Section, a Spanish court has jurisdiction regarding succession when the deceased has his last domicile in Spain, independently of the kind of property and its location.

6. Expert Evidence

(a) In principle, there is no necessity for a foreign lawyer to give evidence, unless a judicial authority, a notary or a property registration office requires so. Regarding this matter, it should be noted that Article 12.6 of the Civil Code provides the following: 'Those who claim to rely upon foreign law must prove its contents and its validity by the system of probation allowed by Spanish law. However, in order to proceed to its application, the court can use any kind of enquiry deemed necessary'.

(b) As stated in the preceding paragraph, the court can use any kind of enquiry deemed necessary. Consequently, this matter will depend on the judge's criteria in connection with the importance of the case which is discussed and if the court needs some kind of additional clarification. Regarding official documents the rule of *locus regit actum* should be noted and Article 11.1 of the Civil Code (*see* 3(b) *above*).

7. Unity of Succession

Unity of succession is accepted in principle, without prejudice to the exception regarding the inheritances of British citizens only in connection with real estate located in Spain. With respect to this matter, the decided cases of the Supreme Court and High Courts in Spain incline to the applicability of the Spanish law in those cases which the nationality of the deceased refers back to that of his domicile or that of the location of the real estate, if the connecting elements relate to Spain. However, the matter is controversial and it is extremely difficult to give a final opinion.

8. Formalities

No formalities are required. As mentioned throughout this Questionnaire, the formalities of a will are ruled by the law by virtue of which it is made (Article 11.1 of Civil Code). On the other hand, the applicable law in connection with the contents of a testament, will be the national law of the testator (Articles 9.1 and 9.8 of the Civil Code).

9. Legislation

Spain ratified the *Hague Convention on the Conflicts of Laws Relating to the Form of Testamentary Disposition* on 16 March 1988.

10. Wills

In case of conflicts of foreign factors, which law governs:

(a)–(b) Regarding the formalities, the rule of *locus regit actum* applies (Article 11 of the Civil Code). On the other hand, a will drawn up in accordance with the law which rules its contents will be valid and effective. In this connection, Article 9.1 and 9.8 of the Civil Code provide that the law which governs the contents of a will is the national law of the testator.

It should be noted that, despite the formalities of a joint-will being fulfilled, it may not be valid in Spain, despite Article 4 of the *Hague Convention on the Conflicts of Laws Relating to the Form of Testamentary*. In short, if this joint-will is made by Spanish individuals, it will have no effect in Spain because it infringes Article 733 of the Civil Code, even if it is valid in accordance with the rules of the country in which it was drawn up (*lex loci celebrationis*). However, this is a matter quite controversial, because there are other legal opinions which establish the validity of the joint-will dictated by Spanish individuals in accordance with *lex loci celebrationis*, by virtue of Articles 1, 4 and 6 of the *Hague Convention on the Conflicts of Laws Relating to the Form of Testamentary*. In addition, it should be noted that a joint-will is valid in some regional regimes in Spain (i.e., Aragon). Consequently, this legal situation would prevent referring to the exception of public policy.

(c) The wills must be accommodated to the system of compulsory shares established by the national law of the testator, as mentioned *above* in Section A number 14 and Section B number 2. However, if a will does not fulfil this system of minimum portions, it does not become null and void but inefficient. In this case, the beneficiary of the compulsory share can complete his right by reducing the portion of the heir.

(d) Regarding the expression capacity to inherit, two different legal situations should be distinguished:

– Capacity as referred to ability of the individual to claim an inheritance, as well as to acquire property by virtue of succession, is governed by the national law of the beneficiary (Article 9.1 of the Civil Code).
– Capacity as referred to essential requirements of validity of the will referred to certain individuals or legal entities who cannot inherit (i.e., a priest who confessed the deceased *in articulo morte*, banned corporations, etc.), is governed by the national law of the deceased at the time of his death (Article 9.8 of the Civil Code).

(e) It is determined by the national law of the deceased at the time he makes the will, disregarding the place in which he makes it (Article 9.1 of the Civil Code).

(f) It is also determined by the national law of the deceased at the time he makes the will, disregarding the place in which he makes it (Articles 9.1, 664 – 'the will dictated before derangement is valid' – and transitional provision number 2 of the Civil Code, as well as Sentence of the Supreme Court of 22 February 1960). However, if the will must be legally effective in Spain, the inability set out by the national law of the deceased in such moment would be disregarded, provided that this inability infringes public policy in Spain (Article 12.3 of the Civil Code).

(g) Powers of appointment, i.e., where a person in his will nominates someone else who, in his own will, shall have the power to specify the ultimate recipient of the asset which is the subject matter of the original will.

Spanish law does not allow for that legal situation, because a will is an extremely personal act. In short, Article 670 of the Civil Code provides that 'a will is an extremely personal act. A third person cannot be empowered in order to do so. Either a third person can specify the persistence of the appointment of an heir or legatee or choose the portions to be descended when an heir or legatee are named.' However, in some regional regimes in Spain the powers of appointment are legal, as mentioned in Section A, number 13(c), (e), (g).

On the other hand and within the context of the conflict of laws, the legal opinion feels inclined to consider this matter as essential and not concerning the formalities of a will. Consequently, the national law of the deceased at the time of the death would prevail under the *locus regit actum* rule.

(h) The applicable law would be that governing the formal requirements of the subsequent will (Article 11.1 of the Civil Code, *locus regit actum*). In this connection and as mentioned in Section A, number 2, in accordance with Spanish legal system, the wills can be rectified, revoked or renewed only by making a subsequent will, replacing the previous one.

(i) For example, in connection with a matter related to someone resident in France who left a minimum portion to his children which included some real estate located in Spain, the decided cases of the Supreme Court of Spain must be taken into account, as mentioned in Section A, number 14, because the estate is located in two different countries (France and Spain). Consequently, the succession would be governed by the national law of the deceased, in accordance with Article 9.8 of the Spanish Civil Code, which provides that the succession is governed by the national law of the deceased at the time of his death, whatever the kind of property and the country in which it is located. Likewise, the Spanish Courts could have jurisdiction with respect to this succession, in accordance with Article 22.3 of the *Spanish Judicial Power Law* which provides the following: 'The Spanish courts have jurisdiction regarding succession when the deceased has his last domicile in Spain or his real estate is located in Spain.'

11. Domicile/Nationality

(a) As mentioned throughout this Questionnaire, the national law of the deceased at the time of his death governs almost the whole inheritance, except regarding the formalities of the will and the capacity of the beneficiary.

International Succession

With respect to domicile and as stated previously in Section B, number 1, the Spanish courts have jurisdiction regarding succession when the deceased has his last domicile in Spain or his real estate is located in Spain.

(b) The domicile of the beneficiary is not relevant to any of the answers in Section B.

(c) Certainly, this is a controversial matter, particularly with regard to court's jurisdiction. However, it should be taken into account that Spanish law resolves this conflict by virtue of Articles 9.9 and 9.10 of the Civil Code, which considers equivalent 'domicile' to 'principal residence'.

12. Taxation

As mentioned previously (Section A, number 12), the liability for inheritance tax attaches to the heir or the legatee having their principal residence in Spain. Thus, the residence or non-residence of the deceased is absolutely irrelevant.

An heir or legatee having their principal residence in Spain must pay tax inheritance, independently of the kind of property (movables or immovables) and the place in which they are located (Spain or abroad).

An heir or legatee non-resident in Spain must pay inheritance tax in connection with funds and properties and real estate located in Spain.

An heir or legatee (being residents or not) must pay the local tax on increased value regarding the real estate located in Spain.

Sweden

Prepared by: Advocate Lars BERLIN
Advokatfirman Lars Berlin AB

Address: Östermalmsgatan 33
S-114 26 Stockholm
Sweden
Tel.: +46 8 411 14 98
Fax: +46 8 21 63 50

SECTION A – BRIEF SURVEY OF THE LOCAL SYSTEM

1. Type of System

(a) The legal system of Sweden is a civil law system.

(b) The system in Sweden is not federal.

2. Wills

(a) The usual will shall be in writing witnessed by two witnesses, simultaneously present. They must be aware of the type of document but they do not need to know the content of the will. The witnesses must state that the testator is of sound mind.
   Holographic wills are allowed if they are handwritten by the testator.
   A death bed will is in Sweden called an oral will and is valid if it is dictated in front of two witnesses.
   Both holographic wills and oral wills are not valid if the testator has been able to execute a normal will within a period of three months prior to death.

(b) *i.* Amendments must be done in the same way as the execution of a normal will. Revocations can be made by physically destroying the will or by making a clear statement that the will is no longer valid. No specific formalities are required. A validly executed will revokes a will made previously to the extent that it is inconsistent with the previous will. The parts of the previous will that are not superceded by the later will are valid.
   ii. Marriage does not automatically revoke or in any other way affect wills made prior to marriage. The will must be construed to find the testator's true intentions.

563

iii. Revival of a revoked will must be done in the same way as a normal will. However, if the will has been revoked only by a statement, the revival of a revoked will can be made valid through a new statement. These situations are bound to create uncertainty about the testator's wishes and the testator should be advised to execute a new will.

3. Intestacy

(a) The surviving spouse inherits the estate before the children. However, the spouse inherits the estate with some limitation. Spouses are not allowed to dispose of the inheritance by making a will. This is called 'free disposition right' as distinct from 'full ownership'.

However, a child to the deceased who is not a child of the surviving spouse (out of wedlock) has the right to get his inheritance at the death of the first spouse.

Heirs of the body to both spouses will have to wait for their inheritance until the death of the surviving spouse. Adopted children have the same rights as other children.

If the decedent leaves no heirs of the body, the entire estate will be left to the surviving spouse with a 'free disposition right'. After the death of the surviving spouse, the part of the estate that comes from first decedent, will be distributed to the first decedent's parents.

For example:

A man A has assets worth 700 and his wife B assets worth 300. Total assets are 1,000. They have together 1 child C and B has a child D in a previous marriage.

A dies first:
There is *no will and all assets are community property*.
One starts with a marital distribution in which B receives 500. The remaining 500 B gets with 'free disposition right'. This part is 50 per cent of B's total assets after A's death.
When B dies the total assets are 1,200.
C inherits 600 from A. The remaining 600 from B is divided between C and B with 300 each.
If the total assets were reduced to 600 when B dies, C will inherit 300 from A and 150 from the mother. D will inherit 150 from B.
If A and B had written *a will* stating that the surviving spouse shall inherit everything with 'full ownership', the following situation occurs: C can claim that he shall receive his lawful inheritance which is 50 per cent of his inheritance share.
When B dies, C inherits 300 from A and 450 from B and D inherits 450 from B. If the total assets were reduced to 600 when B dies, C will inherit 150 from A and 225 from B and D will inherit 225 from B.

B dies first:

There is *no will and all assets are community property*.

When B dies the total assets are 1,000 and when A dies the assets are 937.5. A receives 500 through the marital distribution and 250 with 'free disposition right'. D will inherit 250 at once but C will have to wait for his inheritance until A dies.

When A dies, C will inherit everything, 312.5 from B and 625 from A.

If the total assets were reduced to 600 when A dies, C will inherit 200 from B and 400 from A.

If A and B had written *a will* stating that the surviving spouse shall inherit everything with 'full ownership', the following situation occurs: C and D can claim that they shall receive their lawful inheritance which is 50 per cent of their inheritance shares.

D will get his share of 125 when B dies and C will have to wait until A dies. The total assets will be 1,094 when A dies.

When A dies, C will get 273.5 from B and 820.5 from A.

If the total assets were reduced to 600 when A dies, C will inherit 150 from B and 450 from A.

If in the previous example the total assets were 150 when B died first, A would receive 75 in the marital distribution. There is no will and all assets are community property:

D would normally receive 37.5 at once but A is entitled to keep at least 144. In this case A can keep 144 + 3 and D will get 3.

When A dies, C will get 3 from B and 144 from A if the assets were the same.

(b) There is no difference between movables and immovables concerning division of the estate.

4. Freedom of Testation

(a) Children have a lawful inheritance which is 50 per cent of the estate, which is received upon the death of the other spouse (*see* 3(a) *above*).

The surviving spouse always has a right to keep SEK 144,000 – (this is for 1996 and linked in relation to inflation) – together with what the surviving spouse gets in the distribution of the marital property made prior to the estate distribution.

If the testator leaves no surviving spouse or children, he is free to dispose of his assets as he likes.

(b) *i.* A contract of inheritance made prior to death is valid in some cases depending on which parties are involved. A person cannot dispose of his estate in any other way but by a will. A child can renounce his inheritance share but not the lawful inheritance share, unless the child gets equal value in another way. A child under eighteen years of age cannot renounce his inheritance at all.

A contract of inheritance between an heir and a third party made prior to death is not valid. This includes contracts between heirs made prior to death.

5. Maintenance

Maintenance can be claimed by unsupported children and the surviving spouse who were dependent on the decedent for their subsistence, for three months from the day of death regardless of whether or not the maintenance will reduce the other heirs' inheritance shares.

Other heirs who were dependent on the decedent for their subsistence can claim maintenance for three months but what they receive in maintenance will be considered as an advance from their inheritance. The maintenance cannot be larger than their expected inheritance.

6. Community Property Between Husband and Wife

(a) 50 per cent of the total community property does not form part of the estate and is not taken into account in division of the estate between the heirs. This will be transferred to the surviving spouse by the marital distribution which is done before the distribution of the estate. This can be changed by the spouses by a marriage settlement. The percentage can also be different if one of the spouses has received a gift on the condition that the gift shall not be community property in marriage.

(b) The spouses can execute a marriage contract establishing a division of property other than equal shares. The contract can state that specific assets shall be separate property. This contract will effect the amount in the estate left by the decedent.

If there is no community of property, all of the decedent's assets will constitute the estate.

(c) If there is no marriage contract, the assets will be divided 50/50 in the marital distribution in case of divorce or at the time of death of one of the spouses. As long as the spouses are married and alive, there is no community of property.

7. Gifts (*Inter Vivos*)

(a) Gifts to direct heirs are presumed to be inheritance in advance and shall be set off the heirs' inheritance unless something else is said or written or unless contradicted by the circumstances. This is often made clear in a deed of gift or in a will.

Gifts to heirs other than direct heirs shall only be set off against their inheritance if this is said or written and not contradicted by the circumstances.

(b) The value of the gift shall be added to the estate before the heirs' shares are calculated. If the recipient of the gift has received more through the gift than his share of the estate, he is not obligated to pay anything back or compensate the other heirs.

8. Capacity

(a) A person who is eighteen years old can dispose of his estate by a will. A person who is or has been married can also make a will even if he is not eighteen years old.

A person who is sixteen years old can also make a will concerning assets which he has the right to use without the permission of his guardian. This can for example be earnings from work or gifts.

The testator must of course be of sound mind.

(b) None of the following people can be a witness:
- children younger than fifteen years;
- mentally disturbed people;
- beneficiaries of the will;
- husband or wife of the testator;
- parents, grandparents, children, grandchildren, brothers, sisters, parents in law, stepfathers, stepchildren of the testator or a beneficiary.

(c) Everyone who is alive, unborn but conceived and later born to life, or child to such person can be a beneficiary of a will.

9. Authority (Court, Notarial or Other)

All the heirs must receive a copy of the will. After they have received a copy, they must file a protest action in court within six months.

If no protest action is filed, the will comes into force after six months. It is not necessary to wait six months if all heirs accept the will and the acceptance is written on the will. The sentence 'I hereby accept/approve of this will' is written on the will followed by the heir's signature.

Before 1 July 1989, it was necessary to send the will to the court before it came into force.

If the heirs do not accept the will, they must file a protest action in court within six months of service of the will. If they do not do so, the will will be in force. There are no special courts for these matters.

10. Invalidity of Will

(a) Possible grounds for defects in formalities are that witnesses lacked capacity or that a holographic or an oral will was not confirmed or replaced by a normally executed will within three months if the testator had the possibility to do so.

(b) Defects in formalities make the will void.
Dispositions under fraud and duress make the will void.

11. Simultaneous Death

(a)–(b) If an heir is deceased and there is no external evidence that the heir was alive when the intestate died, the estate is distributed as if the heir did not survive the intestate.

If a husband and wife die in an accident simultaneously or in circumstances where it is impossible to determine that one survived the other, the estate is distributed directly to their heirs as if neither spouse survived the other.

12. Estate Taxes

(a) Estate taxes exist in Sweden. A surviving spouse can inherit SEK 280,000 without paying estate tax and a child of the body can inherit SEK 70,000 without paying estate tax.

(b) Estate taxes are due on all assets worldwide as long as the decedent was domiciled in Sweden at the time of death.

(c) The heirs are taxed and not the estate but the liability to estate tax is determined by the decedent's domicile.

13. Administration of Estates

(a) The estate is administrated by the parties of the estate, 'estate owners' or 'partners of the estate', testamentary heirs but not legatees. Each one of the parties of the estate can demand on application to the court that an estate administrator should be appointed. Such an application can also be filed by a creditor. A testator can also appoint an estate administrator in the will.

(b) If an estate administrator is appointed, he shall once a year submit a report to at least one of the parties of the estate. At the same time he shall notify the court and the other parties of the estate that the report has been submitted. All parties are entitled to get a copy of the report on demand. If any of the parties of the estate is under eighteen years old, the report shall also be sent to the Superior Guardian Office at the municipality.

(c) On demand by the court or one of the parties of the estate, a custodian can be appointed by the court to supervise the estate administrator.

(d) The parties of the estate have the right to query and object.

(e) The estate distribution is effected by the parties of the estate including testamentary heirs but not legatees.

(f) Within a month after the estate inventory, an agreement must be made with the creditors. After a month the creditors can claim that the estate shall guarantee the debts which are not due for payment or debts that are unsecured. If the debts are not guaranteed within three months, they are due for immediate payment.

(g) The distribution shall be effected by the parties of the estate. The estate distribution shall be written down and signed by all parties of the estate.

14. Domicile/Nationality

(a) Nationality and domicile do not affect the *above* information as long as the *Swedish Decedents' Estate Code* is applicable. However, according to the *Swedish Inheritance Tax Law*, domicile and citizenship make a difference. *See* Section B12.

(b) As long as the decedent is a Swedish citizen or domiciled in Sweden, a Swedish court will give an order of probate even if the deceased had no assets in Sweden.

SECTION B – APPLICABLE LAW/PROCEDURE WHERE FOREIGN ELEMENT/S ARE INVOLVED

1. Jurisdiction

(a) The local court holds that it has jurisdiction in the following situations:
– Swedish citizens;
– local domicile;
– assets within the jurisdiction.

(b) The same rules apply for movables and immovables.

(c) The local court in which the deceased would have had to answer in civil actions. This is in the district where he was domiciled and if he was not domiciled in Sweden, the District Court in Stockholm will have jurisdiction.

2. Applicable Law

The local court applies *lex situs* to immovable property. The local court applies the *lex patriae* of the heir or testamentary heir at the date of death concerning the following issues:
– the right to receive an inheritance or legacy, and
– maintenance from the estate.

International Succession

The local court applies the *lex patriae* of the testator at the date of writing the will or making the legal act concerning the following issues:

- the capacity to make and revoke a will,
- the validity of a will in respect of dispositions made under fraud and duress, and
- the validity of contracts of inheritance made prior to death.

The local court applies either the *lex patriae, lex loci actus* or *lex domicilii* of the testator at the date of writing the will concerning the validity of a will in respect of the formalities. As long as the will is valid in either of the countries, it is considered valid in Sweden. If the will concerns immovables, it is also valid as long it is valid according to the *lex rei sitae*.

The local court applies the *lex patriae* of the testator at the date of death concerning the validity of the content of a will. If the will concerns immovables, it is also valid as long it is valid according to the *lex rei sitae*.

The local court applies the *lex patriae* of the testator at the date of death concerning the following issues:

- the question of whether gifts to heirs made prior to death should be set off against the heir's inheritance;
- the question of forfeiture of the right to receive a legacy.

A Swedish court will not, however, under any circumstances apply rules which breach Swedish *ordre public*.

In addition to *above-mentioned* rules there is special legislation concerning citizens in the Nordic countries, Sweden, Finland, Denmark, Norway and Iceland, domiciled in any of these countries. According to this legislation the court shall apply the *lex domicili*. If the decedent was domiciled in Sweden for less than five years, an heir or testamentary heir, within six months from the date of death, can request that the *lex patriae* should be applied.

3. Foreign Succession/Inheritance Orders

(a) A foreign order will be enforced or recognized in respect of local assets, both movables and immovables, under the following conditions:

- the foreign order must have its origin in the country where the deceased was a citizen or domiciled;
- the foreign order must not concern assets which have been or should have been under Swedish jurisdiction;
- the foreign order must be final;
- the foreign order must not be contrary to Swedish law in parts concerning local assets.

(b)–(c) In order to give effect to a foreign order an application must be filed in *Svea* Court of Appeal in Stockholm. The opposite party will be given an opportunity to make a statement to the court.

4. Two or More Succession or Probate Orders

The citizenship prevails when two or more orders exist. (*See* the first condition set out at 3(a).)

5. Assets

The local court could assume jurisdiction if there is Swedish citizenship or local domicile. (*See* 1(a).)

6. Expert Evidence

(a) There is no necessity for a foreign lawyer to give evidence regarding a foreign will recognized by a foreign court.

The court can order a party to bring evidence regarding the content of foreign inheritance laws or the interpretation of a will.

(b) Evidence regarding foreign inheritance laws can be given through a written statement without the necessity of appearance in court.

7. Unity of Succession

It does not apply.

8. Formalities

The formalities of a will need not be the same as those of Sweden to be recognized in Sweden as long as it meets the formality requirements according to the laws in the country where the will was executed or the laws of the testator's domicile at the time of execution or death. A will which in some way contradicts or breaches Swedish *ordre public* will not be valid.

9. Legislation

The *1961 Hague Convention on the Conflicts of Laws Relating to the Form of Testamentary Dispositions* is applicable in Sweden.

10. Wills

(a) The local court applies either the *lex patriae, lex loci actus* or *lex domicilii* of the testator at the date of writing the will concerning legal requirements for the execution of wills.

International Succession

If the will concerns immovables, it is also valid as long it is valid according to the *lex rei sitae*.

(b) The law which governs the construction/interpretation, e.g., of terminology used in the will, is not clear according to Swedish law. The court will most probably apply the *lex domicilii* at the date of the execution of the will, especially if the will has been executed with the assistance of a local lawyer. The testator's *lex patriae* at that time and also the *lex patriae* at the time of death will probably be taken into account.

(c) The testator's *lex patriae* at the time of death will govern rights of heirs and minimum portions.

(d) The heirs' capacity to inherit is governed by the heirs' *lex patriae* at the time of death.

(e) The testator's capacity to make a will is governed by the testator's *lex patriae* at the time the testator made the will.

(f) The testator's *lex patriae* at the time the testator made the will governs the essential or material validity of the will or particular questions such as duress and legacies to witnesses.

(g) The testator's *lex patriae* at the time of death will govern powers of appointment, i.e., where a person in his will nominates someone else who, in his own will, shall have the power to specify the ultimate recipient of the asset which is the subject matter of the original will.

(h) *See* 10(a).

(i) The laws regarding reserve do apply to a non-resident in respect of both movable and immovable property.

11. Domicile/Nationality

(a)–(b) *See* the answers *above*.

(c) If nationality is unclear or if the deceased has no nationality, the deceased's domicile will govern. If the deceased has more than one nationality and one of them is Swedish, Swedish nationality will govern. If none of the nationalities are Swedish, the court will try to decide in respect of all relevant circumstances what nationality will be the most natural one. Domicile is an important circumstance.

12. Taxation

There are estate taxes in Sweden with total liability for estate taxes on heirs of a resident Swedish citizen and also for a period of ten years after the resident Swedish citizen has become non-resident. Even heirs of a foreign citizen, who was at his death married to a Swedish citizen who had been resident in Sweden at sometime during the period of ten years prior to death, is liable to Swedish estate tax.

If an heir is not totally liable to estate tax, he can be partially liable to estate tax. This depends on the kind of assets situated in Sweden. Immovables situated in Sweden attract liability to estate tax. Also movables in industry and commerce, cooperative flats and royalties attract liability to estate tax. If the decedent was a Swedish citizen, shares in a Swedish company attract partial liability to estate tax.

The heirs are divided into three classes. In class I are the closest relatives, in class III, municipalities, charity organizations and other similar organizations and in class II all other heirs.

In class I the tax is 10 per cent for up to SEK 300,000, 20 per cent for between 300,000–600,000 and 30 per cent for above 600,000.

In class II the tax is 10 per cent for up to SEK 70,000, 20 per cent for between 70,000–140,000 and 30 per cent for above 140,000.

In class III the tax is 10 per cent for up to SEK 90,000, 20 per cent for between 90,000–170,000 and 30 per cent for above 170,000.

Before the tax is calculated, heirs have the right to deduct an amount which is free of estate tax. A surviving spouse, a man or a woman who lived together with the deceased and with whom the heir had a child, has the right to deduct SEK 280,000.

A child of the body and their children have the right to deduct SEK 70,000 and in addition also SEK 10,000 for each year the child has left until eighteen years old.

Heirs in class II and III have the right to deduct SEK 21,000.

Switzerland

Prepared by: Régis LORETAN

Address: Rue Porte Neuve 2
   Case Postale 2233
   1950 Sion 2
   Switzerland
Tel.: 41 27 322 3560
Fax: 41 27 322 3562

Section A – Brief Survey of the Local System

1. Type of System

(a) The juridical system is that of civil law.

(b) Switzerland is a federal state divided into cantons. In accordance with Article 64 of the Swiss Constitution, the central authorities have granted themselves general jurisdiction to legislate in all areas of civil law, whilst reserving for the cantons the power of legislative jurisdiction to deal with specific matters. Therefore, in certain areas, the norms of federal law provide the principles which are then given further precision through cantonal law in order that they can be applied in practice.

An officially or notarially recorded instrument requires that recourse be had to a qualified public official. This does not necessarily have to be an independent notary, as the relevant Swiss legislation provides that the public official may or may not be a notary according to the canton in which the instrument will be executed.

Those cantons which allow for independent notarial practice are the following: Geneva, Vaud, Valais, Neuchâtel, Fribourg, Berne, Bâle-Ville, Uri, Tessin, Argovie, and Jura.

The other cantons either recognize the notary as public servant (Zurich, Schwyz, Thurgovie and Nidwald), mixed notarial practice comprising independent notarial practice and the notary as public servant (Soleure and Grisons) or, finally, public servants or lawyers, to whom official jurisdiction in the remaining cantons is attributed in the place of notaries.

2. Wills

(a) Swiss law recognizes three forms of will, all of which are unilateral instruments in which a declaration is made as to the testator's wishes upon his death, which, in

574

order to be valid, have to comply with a certain formality. The testator must be at least eighteen years of age and have the required mental capacity.

Wills must be held, whether in their original form or as copies, by the public official by whom they were executed. Therefore, an holographic will can be deposited with a public official, who ensures its safekeeping. It seems that only the canton of Valais requires that a declaration be made at its central cantonal authority of all testamentary dispositions deposited with a Valaisian public official. The Swiss authority dealing with wills, a body empowered by the Swiss Federation of Notaries, is a private body to which recourse can be had by all public officials, or private persons, in order to facilitate the search for such document. The fact that recourse to this institution is not mandatory renders the result of such a search uncertain.

An *holographic will* is one in which the text, the date and signature are entirely in the testator's own hand. In accordance with Article 505 of the Civil Code, the date is to be comprised of the year, the month and the day when the will was drawn up. If the indication as to the date is incorrect, the holographic will is voidable only if it is impossible to establish the required temporal data in any other manner and if the date is necessary to determine the capacity of the testator, the priority of several dispositions upon succession or any other question relating to the validity of the will (Article 520(a) of the Civil Code). This type of will is similar to the secret will under French law in the sense that the testator is able to keep it in a secret location. The signature is that of the testator enabling him to be identified.

A *will by way of public instrument* is one executed by a person having the requisite authority according to cantonal law, in the presence of two witnesses (Article 499 of the Civil Code). The testator indicates his intentions to a public official who transcribes them and then gives the testator the document to read (Article 500 of the Civil Code). As soon as the instrument is dated and signed by the testator, he makes a declaration in the presence of the witnesses to the effect that he has read the will which contains his final wishes; the witnesses, who attest to the testator's declaration and also certify as to his capacity to make a will, do not in this case have to know of the terms of the will or attend upon its signature by the testator. If the testator does not read or sign his will himself, the public official reads it out in the presence of the testator and the witnesses. The witnesses then attest that they had the will read to them in the presence of the public official and the testator, with the latter having declared that the instrument contained his last wishes, and certify as to the testator's capacity to make a will (Article 502 of the Civil Code). In every case, the public official will himself date and sign the will (Article 500 of the Civil Code).

The *oral will* is one which can only be used in special circumstances, in particular, in situations involving imminent death, the interception of communications, epidemic or war, which prevent the testator having recourse to the other forms of will (Article 506 of the Civil Code). The testator must declare his last wishes in the presence of two witnesses simultaneously, the latter whom he then entrusts with drawing up an instrument. Immediately after the witnesses have had the testator's last wishes made known to them, one of them retranscribes them, with a view to delivering them to the judicial authority having jurisdiction, or has them transcribed by the said authority, with indication given as to the place, the date and the circumstances in which the will was received. The two witnesses then sign the document (Article 507 of the Civil Code). The oral will becomes invalid fourteen days from the date that the testator regained the ability to use other forms of will (Article 508 of the Civil Code).

(b) *i.* The testator can revoke or modify his will at any time. In order to do this, he can use any of the forms mentioned *above*, and each form, inasmuch as the conditions as to its validity are complied with, can be used to revoke or modify a will that was executed in another form (Article 509 of the Civil Code). Revocation can be total or partial.

A later will, referred to as a codicil in other jurisdictions, that does not expressly revoke any previous wills serves to replace past dispositions inasmuch as they are definitely not only complementary clauses (Article 512 of the Civil Code). In other words, in principle the later will revokes a previous will unless the later clauses plainly appear to be complementary to earlier clauses.

By physically destroying the will, the testator revokes it. If the will is destroyed by accident or an act of a third person and it is no longer possible to reestablish exactly or completely the content of the will, it is deemed no longer valid (Article 510 of the Civil Code).

Finally a legacy of specific property can not only be revoked by will but is no longer deemed effective if it is incompatible with an act by which the testator alienated the property that was the object of the legacy (Article 511 of the Civil Code).

ii. The marriage of the testator does not revoke a will made prior to the marriage. However, by marrying, the testator does affect that part of his estate which is capable of free disposition to the extent that his spouse will be entitled to a compulsory share of his estate; this entitlement could give rise to the spouse requiring the reduction of those testamentary dispositions which encroach upon it.

Finally it is useful to note that Article 154 of the Civil Code provides that: 'divorced spouses are no longer each other's heir and lose all benefits resulting from testamentary dispositions made before the divorce'; this being the case, divorce results then in the automatic revocation of the testamentary dispositions as between the spouses.

iii. If a later will (and therefore, in principle, that which has revoked an earlier will) is simply revoked, the previous will is not revived unless there is an express clause to the contrary.

3. Intestacy

(a) The *surviving spouse* is always heir. He has the right to half of the estate if the deceased has left direct descendants, to three-quarters if the deceased has left no direct descendants but only his parents and their descendants and to the whole estate in other cases (Article 462 of the Civil Code).

The *blood-related heirs* (*héritiers de sang*) take in the succession upon intestacy by category (*la parentèle*), within which the heir the most closely related by degree, or his descendants by way of representation, excludes an heir who is more distantly related by degree. Since 1 January 1978, the date of the entry of new legislation on descent, reference has been made to blood-related heirs as there is no longer any difference between legitimate and illegitimate children. It is likewise with adopted children, who were included as blood-related heirs as from 1 April 1973.

A category comprises a person's descendants of all degrees, including the person himself as long as he is not the deceased. In the order of succession, those in a previous category of relations exclude those in the following category.

Within any one of the categories, an heir's descendants will take by way of representation should the heir predecease the testator. A descendant's descendants may then take likewise by way of representation and so on and so forth (a concept referred to as *la souche*).

The *order of succession* is established by law for the blood-related heirs and is as follows:

- the category of the direct descendants;
- the category of the father and mother and their descendants succeeding by way of lineage; and
- the category of each of the grandparents and their descendants succeeding by way of lineage and sub-lineage.

'Lineage' implies in the second category above a division of the estate by ancestor. In this regard, the third category subdivides in the lineage of the paternal and maternal grandparents, each of these lineages then subdividing into sub-lineages of the paternal grandfather and paternal grandmother and that of the maternal grandfather and maternal grandmother.

More specifically, without prejudice to the entitlement of the surviving spouse as examined *above*, the succession will devolve to the blood-related heirs in the following manner:

- *The children of the deceased* form the first category and the estate will be divided between them according to their number. If a child has predeceased, he will be 'represented' as regards his inheritance by his descendants (who make up the *souche* of the heir). The descendants exclude the heirs of another category from taking.
- Those in the second category in the order of succession are *the father and the mother and their descendants*, where the succession is divided by lineage. Therefore in the absence of descendants of the deceased, the father and the mother of the deceased inherit; if one of the parents has predeceased, his descendants take by way of representation. In the absence of heirs from one lineage, the entire estate devolves to those of the other lineage (Article 458 of the Civil Code).
- The third category in the order of succession is comprised of *the grandparents and their descendants*, each of whom take by lineage, which itself subdivides further into sub-lineages. In the event of the predecease of a grandparent of one of the sub-lineages who did not leave descendants, his share will devolve upon

the other heirs of the same lineage. In the absence of heirs of one of the lineages of the grandparents, the succession will revert to those of the other lineage (Article 459 of the Civil Code).

– The grandparents and their descendants are the last category of heirs who can take upon intestacy. In their absence, succession devolves upon *the canton in which the deceased was last domiciled* or to *the local authority designated by that canton's legislation* (Articles 460 and 466 of the Civil Code).

(b) There is no distinction to be drawn between the succession of movables and immovables. Nonetheless, if part of the succession is comprised of an agricultural holding, the law allows for an heir who wishes to manage it and appears able to do so to be accorded a special privilege as to its inheritance. In this case, the heir is able to take all immovables forming part of the agricultural holding and all movables used for its exploitation (Article 619 of the Civil Code which refers back to Articles 11 to 24 of the *Federal Law on Rural Landholdings*).

4. Freedom of Testation

(a) The intention on the part of state legislators to protect certain heirs is manifested in Article 471 of the Civil Code which provides for part of the estate to be subject to compulsory shares (*la réserve héréditaire*). This part of the estate is designed to guarantee that certain privileged heirs receive a minimum share from the estate reconstituted in its entirety. Before that part of the estate subject to compulsory shares is calculated, it is helpful to know which part of the estate devolves to the heirs upon intestacy.

The shares upon intestacy (*part héréditaire*):

– *The surviving spouse* has the right to the entire estate unless he takes concurrently with the descendants, in which case he takes half of the estate, or unless he takes concurrently with the deceased's parents and their descendants, in which case he takes three-quarters of the estate.
– That part of the estate which will devolve to the *first category* (*the children of the deceased and their descendants*) upon intestacy if there is a surviving spouse is half to be divided in equal shares between the children. In the absence of a surviving spouse, the children receive the entire estate.
– That part of the estate which will devolve to the *second category* (*the father and the mother and their descendants*) in the event there is a surviving spouse and no living members of the first category is a quarter of the estate.
– The entire estate will devolve to the *third category* (*the grandparents and their descendants*) provided that there is no surviving spouse nor any relations in the two *above* categories.

The compulsory shares (*part réservataire or légitime*):

– For *a descendant*, no matter to which degree, the compulsory share is equal to three-quarters of his share upon intestacy.

- For *the father or the mother*, it is equal to half of his or her right to succession upon intestacy.
- For *the surviving spouse*, it is equal to half of his right to succession upon intestacy.

No other relations are entitled to a compulsory share.

That part of the estate which is not subject to compulsory shares is referred to as the 'disposable portion' (*la quotité disponible*), which the testator can leave to whomever he chooses.

(b) *i.* Article 636 of the Civil Code allows for agreements on the succession of a living person. Those which are valid are contracts executed by the heir with co-heirs or third persons, insofar as the person whose estate is subject to the agreement gives his consent. The agreement must be in written form though otherwise there is no particular form to be followed. Once the agreement is made, however, it is irrevocable. By way of the agreement, the person who is to take part of the succession from another obtains only a personal right to receive the latter's share.

   ii. Swiss law recognizes agreements on succession (*pactes successoraux*). They can be used to confer or to take away rights. The person who is to dispose of his estate upon death (i.e., the person relinquishing his rights) must be of full age (Article 468 of the Civil Code). The other contracting party must have the requisite legal capacity in accordance with the ordinary rules.

The agreement on succession is a bilateral instrument, not taking effect until death, which is executed in one of the forms used for the will by way of public instrument. The contracting parties make their declarations of intent simultaneously in the presence of a public official. If the contracting parties sign the instrument, they do so in the presence of witnesses, otherwise the instrument is read to them in the presence of the witnesses, the latter attesting to compliance with the required formalities relating to the will by way of public instrument.

The agreement on succession for the conferment of rights is that by which one of the parties appoints the other heir or legatee (Article 494 of the Civil Code). This agreement can be concluded with or without consideration. It can be reciprocal, e.g., when two spouses agree that the surviving spouse will take that part of the estate of which the testator is free to dispose.

The agreement on succession for the renunciation of rights is that by which an heir renounces, for consideration or not, all or some of his rights in the succession of the other contracting party. The person renouncing loses his status of heir and his renunciation is also, except where it is stipulated to the contrary, binding on his descendants (Article 495 of the Civil Code). The person renouncing may have done so in favour of an appointed heir. If the latter does not take his inheritance, then the renunciation does not come into existence. Likewise, if the renunciation is made in general terms in favour of co-heirs, it will only apply to co-heirs of the same category and will not benefit heirs more distantly related if the beneficiaries of the renunciation do not take advantage of the renunciation (Article 496 of the Civil Code).

Unless there is a stipulation to the contrary, the agreement is binding on the descendants of the person renouncing (Article 495(3) of the Civil Code).

Advance division of property (*partage anticipé*) only exists in terms of a certain kind of advance (*avancement d'hoirie*). This comprises a donation from a living person to one or several of his heirs. As it is an instrument concluded between living persons, it must comply with the rules as to formalities applying to the type of property being donated (that is, an ordinary officially or notarially recorded instrument for immovables, a physical transfer of property for movables, written assignment for debts due, etc. (Article 242 of the Code on Obligations)).

This type of agreement is distinct from that of a donation to be fixed at the time of death of the donor, the latter having to comply with the rules as to formalities for testamentary dispositions (Article 245(2) of the Code on Obligations).

5. Maintenance

The law provides that heirs having lived in a household with the deceased at the time of his death can receive from the estate their expenses for one month if these were previously met by the deceased (Article 606 of the Civil Code).

Article 612(a) of the Civil Code does not provide for a right of maintenance in favour of *the surviving spouse*, but does give him the right to retain the family residence and the furniture belonging to it, inasmuch as such property forms part of the succession; this benefit will then be deducted from his part of the inheritance. Should the circumstances require it, the surviving spouse, indeed even the other heirs, can ask that the right of ownership of the family residence and the furniture belonging to it be converted to a life interest in it, that is, into a right of occupation. This power cannot be exercised over property used for the deceased's business if such property is necessary for the continuation of that business by a descendant.

The law provides that *children* who have not been fully raised at the time of the deceased's death or who are disabled can deduct certain equitable expenses at the time the estate is divided to ensure equity in relation to those children who have been fully raised or educated. They can, therefore, have deducted from the estate, in an equitable measure, their future education expenses (for children who have not yet been fully raised) and rehabilitation expenses (for children who are disabled) (Article 631(2) of the Civil Code).

A person can, by way of an officially or notarially recorded instrument or by will, set up a 'family foundation', where property is to be used exclusively for the payment of expenses relating to the education, setting up and assistance of family members (whether direct or collateral relations) or for similar objectives (Article 335 of the Civil Code). The property is then meant for the assistance of the beneficiaries in specific situations and not for their general upkeep. As it is a foundation, it is a legal entity subject to the same provisions as other foundations, except for the fact that it does not have to be registered with the Commerce Registry (*Registre du Commerce*) (Article 52(2) of the Civil Code) and is not subject to the control of the supervisory authorities (Article 87(1) of the Civil Code).

6. Community Property Between Husband and Wife

(a) By way of marriage contract, spouses can agree to change the division of community property. This modification of the marital regime of community property in favour of one of the spouses cannot, however, encroach upon the right of certain heirs to a compulsory share.

Within the framework of the usual legal regime of the *division of after-acquired property*, the principle applied is that the spouses will each take half of such property. By way of marriage contract executed in the usual officially or notarially recorded form (Article 184 of the Civil Code), the spouses can agree to another method of division. The agreement cannot, however, affect the compulsory shares which should accrue to heirs not common to them both and such heirs' descendants. In other words, only the compulsory shares of the latter are so protected, e.g., in relation to children of the first marriage of one of the spouses, whereas the children common to both spouses do not benefit from such protection (Articles 215 and 216 of the Civil Code).

Within the framework of the regime of *community of property*, an agreement modifying the principle of division by half must be by way of the usual officially or notarially recorded instrument (Article 184 of the Civil Code). Such a modification in the division of such property cannot encroach upon the right of the descendants, whether common or not, to a compulsory share (Article 241 of the Civil Code).

Within the framework of the regime of *separate property* (in principle executed by way of the usual officially or notarially recorded instrument), neither spouse can be advantaged from the point of view of the succession.

(b) The benefit arising from the matrimonial regime of after-acquired property and that of community property, which allows for the surviving spouse either to retain the family residence and the furnishings belonging to it or to occupy such residence and have the use of such furnishings for the rest of his life, will be deducted from the property to revert to him by way of the marital regime.

7. Gifts (*Inter Vivos*)

(a) Refunding (*le rapport*) involves the restitution in kind or the bringing into account of the gifts made *inter vivos* which were received by the lawful heirs by way of an advance. The value of such gifts is taken as at the date the succession passes to the heirs (*see* 4(b)*ii. above*). All gifts, that is, transfers without consideration, in favour of the descendants, having the nature of an endowment, are presumed to be subject to refunding. The institution allows for the entire estate to be reconstituted such that all the heirs are treated in the same way as between themselves. Gifts which are not in the nature of an advance to lawful heirs, that is, those not in the nature of an endowment to the descendants or that are not in favour of such heirs, are not subject to refunding unless the donor has stipulated otherwise. The donor can expressly exempt a beneficiary who would in principle have to apply refunding to gifts received from having to do so. Refunding in relation to the succession is governed by Articles 626 to 632 of the Civil Code.

If a gift is not subject to refunding, it is subject to set-off (*la réduction*). This institution is aimed at ensuring that the compulsory shares are fully reconstituted. The value of the compulsory shares is calculated on the basis of the estate, which has in theory been reconstituted, and, to the extent that the estate's actual assets do not cover the said shares, the beneficiaries of *inter vivos* gifts will be asked to add to the estate the amount necessary to meet the compulsory shares due (Articles 522 to 533 of the Civil Code).

(b) The Civil Code does not provide for any imperative rules as to refunding, with the donor always having the possibility to exclude, demand or limit the refunding to be applied to the gift. Advances in favour of the lawful heirs, endowments made to descendants as well as those gifts whose value exceeds the share of the estate to which the heir is entitled upon intestacy are presumed to be subject to refunding. The usual expenses in relation to the setting-up of a descendant upon his marriage and to the education and instruction of children are presumed not to be subject to refunding. The heir who has renounced his inheritance is never obliged to apply refunding but he may be obliged, if necessary, to apply set-off.

8. Capacity

(a) The drawing up of a will is an act which is strictly personal, which, therefore, requires the actual presence of the testator, who cannot be either represented or have authorized another in its drawing up.

The principle contained in Article 467 of the Civil Code is such that only persons capable of exercising proper judgment and aged eighteen or over can dispose of property by will.

In order to conclude an agreement on succession, the person who is disposing of his property must be of full age (Article 468 of the Civil Code). The other contracting party must have the requisite legal capacity; a child who is capable of discernment and is to receive property without incurring any obligations is able to accept it.

As from 1 January 1996, a person of full age is deemed to be eighteen rather than twenty. The text of Article 468 of the Civil Code, however, has not been amended although that provision covers a situation similar to that addressed by Article 467 of the Civil Code.

(b) Persons who are no longer able to exercise their legal rights, who have been deprived of their civic rights by way of a criminal conviction (which provision was repealed in 1971 but whose effects may subsist for convictions prior to that date), who cannot read or write, and who are the descendants, ancestors, brothers and sisters of the testator, as well as their spouses and the spouse of the testator himself, cannot act as witnesses.

If the witnesses, as well as their descendants, ancestors, brothers and sisters or spouses, benefit from a testamentary gift, only the provision relating to that gift is voidable with the rest of the will retaining its validity (Article 503 of the Civil Code).

(c) The person who is to take in the succession cannot take unless he is already alive and, as regards a child who has already been conceived, if he is born alive (Article 544 of the Civil Code); the testator can, by way of a clause relating to the appointment of trustees, make over specific property or a share of the estate to a person yet to be born (a legal person) or conceived at the time the estate passes to the heirs. In this case, the lawful heirs take subject to the testamentary settlement (Article 545 of the Civil Code).

Furthermore, persons cannot take any part of the estate if they, intentionally and unlawfully, killed or attempted to kill the deceased, permanently incapacitated the deceased such that he was unable to write a will, convinced the deceased, maliciously or by duress, to make or to revoke a testamentary disposition or interfered with the will. Such persons are deemed to have predeceased and their inheritance is taken by their descendants by way of representation (Articles 540 to 542 of the Civil Code).

There is also incapacity as regards those who witness a will (*see* 8(b) *above*) as well as regards a person who has been disinherited. Disinheriting an heir allows the testator to withhold the compulsory share of the estate otherwise due to the former. Disinheriting an heir must be formally authorized by the deceased in a testamentary disposition for reasons which are specified. Such reasons must relate to a grave injury having been inflicted on the deceased or his close family and friends or to a grave omission as to the duties imposed by the law for the benefit of the deceased or his family.

The law also allows for the possibility of disinheriting a descendant who is insolvent, whose assets will go to his creditors. In this case the disinheritance can only apply as regards up to half of that part of the estate subject to compulsory shares, upon condition that this half is assigned to the insolvent heir's children who have been or are to be born.

9. Authority (Court, Notarial or Other)

Once the death has been confirmed, a certificate of heirship or an officially recorded document as to the death will be drawn up. The authority empowered to draw up this document may be different according to each of the cantons. In some cantons, this will be a judge whereas in others it will be a notary. This document will state the heirs, as well as legatees, to whom estate property is to be handed over.

10. Invalidity of Will

(a) A testamentary disposition may be wholly or partially, that is, absolutely or relatively, void.

As regards those dispositions which are *absolutely void*, there are three different manifestations. In the first instance there are instruments which are deemed non-existent, that is, they have the appearance of a will but are lacking some fundamental characteristic, say in the case of a draft, a document drawn up under duress, that which is incomprehensible or that which is a forgery. In the second instance, there are testamentary dispositions which have lapsed, notably say as regards a will which was revoked by a later will, a spouse losing his status as heir through divorce, an heir being unfit to inherit, etc. As to the third, there are dispositions which are automatically invalid, which involve the disposition of property which is not that of the testator (e.g., property which is subject to a trust in favour of a third party) to an heir, etc. In all these cases, those who are interested in the matter can take action to ensure that these dispositions do not take effect.

As regards those dispositions which are *voidable*, these are dispositions drawn up by a person not having the capacity to dispose of his property at that time, such as a minor or a person who is incapable of exercising proper judgment, those which are not the expression of the testator's free will, that is, upon the manipulation of the testator such that he made a particular disposition because he was deceived or threatened (nevertheless, these dispositions are deemed to be effective if the testator has not revoked them one year following the discovery of the deception or the withdrawal of duress or menaces against him), and those which contain illicit or immoral provisions. Voidability is also applicable as to defects relating to the formalities of a will (especially as regards holographic wills as *seen* in 2(a) *above*).

(b) The instruments and dispositions which are *absolutely void* result in the invalidity of the will itself and can be brought up any time by any interested person.

Those instruments and dispositions which are *voidable* can only be opposed by the heirs and legatees concerned within a timelimit of one year from the date of which they became aware of the disposition and the grounds for its invalidity. Such action must be taken at the latest ten years from the time which the estate passed to the heirs by way of the will (Articles 521 and 557 of the Civil Code) or thirty years as against a person who has acted in bad faith if the dispositions are invalid because of their illegality or immorality or because the testator lacked capacity. The voidability can always be invoked by way of an exception procedure.

11. Simultaneous Death

(a)–(b) Article 32(2) of the Civil Code provides that when several persons die and it is not possible to establish if one survived another, their deaths are presumed to have occurred at the same time. Consequently, in accordance with Article 542 of the Civil Code, the presumptive heir or legatee who has not survived cannot take from another.

12. Estate Taxes

(a) Each canton applies its own legislation as regards fiscal matters so that it is impossible to provide an exhaustive treatment of it here. By way of example, in Valais there are no taxes on inheritances between spouses or parents and their children, whereas in Geneva the tax applied can be up to 6 per cent, or 11 per cent if there were no children from the marriage.

Only the canton of Schwytz does not have any taxes on inheritances or donations.

In a very cursory and general manner, it seems that inheritance taxes applying as between the different cantons vary between 10 to 23.1 per cent for brothers and sisters, 15 to 27.3 per cent for aunts and uncles and 20 to 27.3 per cent for great uncles, great aunts, nephews, nieces, great nephews and great nieces.

Taxes on inheritances of persons who are more distantly related or unrelated vary between 25 to 54.6 per cent.

Certain cantons tax the lawful shares passing upon intestacy as well as those received by way of inheritance.

(b) It is also difficult to address this question as regards the whole of Switzerland given that each canton has jurisdiction over fiscal matters relating to succession. Those immovables which are located abroad are not taken into account when determining the assets to be subject to inheritance tax. In contrast, they are taken into account when determining the liabilities of the estate. Sometimes the liabilities are apportioned in a proportionate manner, say when there are international agreements to that effect.

Immovables owned by a deceased person who was a foreign national and domiciled abroad are subject to the inheritance tax of the location at which they are found.

It would seem that jurisdiction over fiscal matters relating to succession is, for all Swiss cantons, linked to the domicile of the deceased as regards movables and to location as regards immovables.

In each canton there are organizations and bodies which are exempt from inheritance taxes. Foreign charitable bodies can also be exonerated in certain cases, in line with reciprocal agreements and practices.

(c) The legislation of each canton serves to establish who is subject to taxes. In principle all the heirs (*l'hoirie*) are jointly responsible for the payment of all taxes, which will be calculated in accordance with what is received by each heir and legatee. In effect, the rate of tax may be different according to whether that part of the estate is to be received by an heir who is directly related or by a legatee who is unrelated to the deceased. Therefore, for the benefit of the tax authorities, the amount due on those parts of the estate received by each beneficiary and the total amount is determined. The beneficiary owes the tax and the estate as a whole is jointly liable.

13. Administration of Estates

(a) In principle the estate is administered by the body of heirs (*l'hoirie*) formed by the sole heirs, who must act in unanimity.

However, and notably when an heir is absent for a prolonged period of time if the measure is to protect his interests, when there is uncertainty as to the persons who are heirs or when not all the heirs of the deceased are known, an authority, which is so designated by each canton's legislation, requires the 'administration *ex officio*' (*l'administration d'office*) (Articles 554 f. of the Civil Code) of the estate, in order that it be protected. If a testamentary executor was appointed by the testator, he will be entrusted with the administration *ex officio*.

The person who is entitled to inherit can reject the inheritance. Instead of rejecting it, however, he can ask that he take the inheritance only upon condition that the rules relating to a *bénéfice d'inventaire* (i.e., limitation of the heir's liability for the debts of the estate to the amount of net assets he actually receives) are applied (Articles 580 ff. of the Civil Code). A request made by one of the heirs will apply as regards the others. This procedure consists in the drawing up of an inventory of all the assets and the liabilities of the deceased by the appropriate authority. After this has been completed, and therefore the estate's exact state of affairs been made known, the heir still has the option to reject the inheritance outright, to accept the inheritance unconditionally, to ask for the division of the estate as between the heirs by an official, or to accept upon condition of the *bénéfice d'inventaire*. In the latter case, the inheritance, with those debts recorded in the *inventaire*, will pass to the heir. All inheritances that devolve to a canton or a *commune* are subject to an inventory according to these rules.

In addition to the case mentioned *above* (where the heir requires it after the completion of the procedure involving the *bénéfice d'inventaire*), the succession can still be subject to division as between the heirs by an official (*liquidation officielle*) (Articles 593 ff. of the Civil Code) whether because an heir requests it be done immediately (unless one of the heirs has accepted the inheritance unconditionally), because the creditors, having expressed persuasive reasons as to their doubts of being repaid, request it, because the legatees, for like reasons, request it, or finally when an insolvent heir rejects the inheritance in order that it should remain beyond the reach of his creditors (Article 578(2) of the Civil Code). The official liquidator deals with the day to day matters concerning the deceased, the fulfilment of his obligations, the recovery of debts, the settlement of the legacies, the undertaking of the necessary procedures and the realization of the property; it should be noted, however, that immovables cannot be sold unless by way of public auction, unless the heirs unanimously authorise the sale on the open market.

Finally the testator may have appointed a testamentary executor in his last wishes. As such, the testamentary executor has, unless the testator has provided to the contrary, the same powers as the official liquidator of the succession. Notably he is entrusted with ensuring that the deceased's last wishes are respected,' and with managing the succession, settling the legacies and dividing the estate. He is, subsidiarily, also jointly responsible for the payment of the inheritance tax. He is completely independent as regards the heirs and can, therefore, act freely in carrying out the testamentary dispositions. In particular, he can alienate movables, as well as sell immovables on the open market should this be appropriate in connection with the division of the estate, and undertake the necessary procedures. In short, he is able to do all that is useful or necessary for the division of the estate. The heirs, moreover, are unable to revoke his mandate.

If a testamentary executor has not been appointed by the testator, the heirs can designate a 'common representative', who can only act within the limits of the mandate having been conferred upon him, whether for a particular purpose or for the whole of the succession. This then involves a standard private contract being concluded between the heirs and their representative.

(b) In principle, a report does not have to be drawn up if the heirs themselves administer the succession, with all the decisions having to be made unanimously. In contrast, if a representative has been appointed, he will provide a report which is then subject to the control of either the heirs (e.g., when a testamentary executor has been appointed) or the relevant authority (*bénéfice d'inventaire*, official division, administration *ex officio*).

Therefore if the succession is administered by the heirs, a report on their administration need not be drawn up. If the succession is administered by an *ad hoc* or mandatory administrator, he must report either to the heirs if they appointed him or to the authority having designated him as the administrator of the succession, e.g., within the context of judicial proceedings.

(c) Except for measures taken in connection with the administration *ex officio*, the *bénéfice d'inventaire* or the official division of the estate that are carried out under the direction of the public authorities, the latter do not intervene *ex officio* in the supervision of the management of the succession.

(d) The body of heirs, which does not have a specific mandate, cannot institute proceedings unless the heirs are unanimous. In particular, all judicial proceedings taken by them or brought against them must be in the name of the body of heirs which comprises all the designated heirs who are then all jointly involved in such proceedings. If the body of heirs appoints an agent, such appointment must be unanimous, and the latter will only be able to act within the limits of the mandate conferred upon him. As was already mentioned *above*, the testamentary executor or the official liquidator has the power to represent the succession in all matters and, as regards legal proceedings, he can plead in his own name when litigating against inheritance by third parties.

(e) The succession takes effect upon the death of the deceased (Article 537 of the Civil Code). From that instant, the estate passes in its entirety to all the heirs who, even without knowing it, are its joint owners (Article 560 of the Civil Code). They can then freely and unanimously agree upon methods by which to dispose of the assets (Article 602 of the Civil Code). However, as regards third parties, it is necessary that the composition of the body of heirs is established by way of a 'certificate of heirship' in order that the heirs can obtain the delivery up of the assets (notably in relation to banks, for accounts to be put at their disposal). The heirs will also acquire the deceased's debts, for which they are jointly responsible (Article 603 of the Civil Code). The legatees only have the right to bring an action as against the heirs to obtain the delivery up of their legacies (Article 562 of the Civil Code). It should be noted that the succession is definitively acquired by all the heirs except for those who expressly reject it within a period of three months after having been made aware of their status. The succession is deemed to be rejected, however, if the insolvency of the deceased was well-known or officially recorded (Article 566 of the Civil Code).

(f) The creditors are paid out of the property of the estate. Unless the creditors have agreed to a division or to a novation (*délégation*) of their debts (i.e., a species of novation), the heirs are personally and jointly liable for the debts of the deceased and of the estate (Article 603 of the Civil Code). This responsibility extends over all their property for five years after the estate has been divided (Article 639 of the Civil Code). In order to avoid any disagreement, knowledge as to the extent of liabilities is helpful and as any heir can request that all debts be paid off or guaranteed before any property has been divided (Article 610 of the Civil Code), it is advisable to draw up an inventory. This inventory is in principle a requirement of fiscal legislation (Articles 154 ff. of the *Federal Law on Direct Federal Tax*), except if the circumstances are such that it can be presumed that the deceased left no assets.

The rights of the deceased's creditors take precedence over those of the legatees (Article 564 of the Civil Code). It is useful to remember that the creditors have the power to request an official division of the property if they have serious grounds for fearing they will not be paid. This request must be made within three months following the death of the deceased or the passing of the estate to the heirs if, at their request, they are not paid off or do not obtain any sureties (Article 594 of the Civil Code).

Moreover, if the succession is officially administered or managed by a testamentary executor or is subject to an inventory or an official division, those intervening in this regard will be responsible for the payment of debts from the property of the estate (*see* 13(a) *above*).

(g) The division of the estate is dealt with by the heirs acting unanimously. They can, by way of joint decision, vary the testamentary or lawful dispositions. However, they cannot refuse to deliver up a legacy without the agreement of the beneficiary. The principle is such that, unless there is provision to the contrary, the heirs have equal rights over the property to be divided (e.g., each of 4 heirs would have the right to one-quarter of the house). The heirs will make up as many portions as there are heirs, so that each will receive his legal part. Once the portions have been made up and distributed or an agreement as to the division and distribution of the estate has been signed by all the heirs, the succession will be deemed to have been completed. If the division is concluded by way of an agreement, the written form is deemed sufficient, though as regards immovables, the written form is deemed necessary (Article 634 of the Civil Code). The division can be partial or complete.

A minor who is not acting under parental authority or a person of full age deemed incapable is represented in the succession and in the agreement on division by a guardian designated by the relevant authority.

In the event of disagreement, each of the heirs can request the intervention of the competent authority, as designated by cantonal law, to direct that adequate measures be taken.

Reference should be made also to the information set out in 13(a) *above* as to the powers of the testamentary executor.

14. Domicile/Nationality

The above information applies only in relation to domestic law. Their provisions are firstly applicable to the succession in its entirety of persons last domiciled in

Switzerland, no matter what their nationality. For immovables that are located abroad, Switzerland renounces its jurisdiction if the state in which an immovable is located claims exclusive jurisdiction. It is realistically accepted that it would be of little use to have decisions made in Switzerland if they are not to be recognized abroad (Article 86 *LDIP*, the latter referring to the *Federal Law of Private International Law*).

In matters concerning succession by way of will, Swiss law allows for a clause in which the deceased requests that the law of his nationality be applied (*professio juris*). In this case, the succession of a foreign national who was last domiciled in Switzerland will be governed in its entirety by the law chosen, for movables as well as immovables, even if such law does not recognize compulsory shares in relation to the estate. In effect, case law provides that the choice of a body of law to be applied to a succession which does not provide for compulsory shares of the estate for certain heirs is not contrary to the international public policy of Switzerland. The law of nationality which is chosen will only apply if, at the time of his death, the testator had not lost that nationality or become a Swiss national (Article 90 *LDIP*). The question as to whether *professio juris* can be established on the basis of an interpretation of the will appears not yet to have been resolved. Therefore the foreign national who wishes to rely on the law of his nationality should act cautiously by making this intention clear in a will.

As regards the recognition of the validity of wills, Swiss private international law refers directly to the *1961 Hague Convention on the Conflicts of Laws Relating to the Form of Testamentary Dispositions*, with it having been made clear that this agreement also applies, by way of analogy, to other forms of instrument executory upon death. This means that a foreign national could draw up his will in Switzerland in accordance with the form prescribed by the law of the state of which he is a national (Article 1(b) of the *1961 Hague Convention*).

(b) The authority having jurisdiction in matters relating to succession is that of the last domicile of the deceased, wherever his assets are located (Article 538 of the Civil Code).

SECTION B – APPLICABLE LAW/PROCEDURE WHERE FOREIGN ELEMENT/S ARE INVOLVED

Preamble: The material provided below does not make reference to specific bilateral conventions and agreements as between Switzerland and other states but is limited to general principles based on the rules of the *Federal Law of Private International Law* (to be referred to as *LDIP*).

1. Jurisdiction

(a) The *LDIP* sets out the following principle: the Swiss judicial or administrative authorities have the power to take the necessary measures for the regulation of the entire succession and to deal with litigation on succession if the deceased, whatever his nationality, had his last domicile in Switzerland; for reasons of effectiveness, Switzerland renounces its jurisdiction over immovables that are located abroad if the state in which they are so located claims such jurisdiction exclusively.

Switzerland recognizes itself as having jurisdiction over movables and immovables located in Switzerland that belong to a foreign national who is domiciled abroad at the time of his death to the extent that the rules as to the private international law of the state in which the deceased was last domiciled refers back (*renvoi*) to the Swiss authority or if that foreign authority does not concern itself with this property (Article 88 *LDIP*).

The Swiss authority also deems itself having jurisdiction to regulate the succession of a Swiss national domiciled abroad at the time of his death if the foreign authorities do not concern themselves with it. Finally, the Swiss authorities always have jurisdiction when a Swiss national last domiciled abroad makes, either by way of a will or an agreement on succession, the whole or part of his estate located in Switzerland subject to Swiss jurisdiction or law. Of course account is still had of the exclusive jurisdiction that may be claimed by the state in which immovables are located (Article 87 *LDIP*).

(b) The jurisdiction as to the regulation of succession is in principle the same for movables and immovables, the only difference resulting from a claim by the state in which immovables are located as to exclusive jurisdiction.

(c) The legislation of each of the cantons determines the authority having jurisdiction *ratione materiae*. The authority having jurisdiction based on location (Articles 86 to 88 *LDIP*), for the whole of the succession, is:
– that of the last domicile of the deceased, if the latter had his domicile in Switzerland at the time of his death;
– that of the location at which property is found in Switzerland belonging to a person having been domiciled abroad and not dealt with by the foreign authority. If property is located in several different areas in Switzerland, the Swiss authority to whom the matter is first referred will have jurisdiction;
– that of the Swiss canton from which the deceased originated when the foreign authority does not regulate the succession, as well as when a Swiss national has made, by way of will, his succession subject to the jurisdiction of the Swiss authorities.

2. Applicable Law

The succession of a person whose last domicile was in Switzerland is subject to Swiss law. However, if the foreign national, by way of will, has made his succession subject to the laws of the state of which he was a national (*professio juris*), this provision will apply, except if, at the time of his death, he had lost that nationality or taken Swiss nationality (Article 90 *LDIP*).

In contrast, if the deceased person had his last domicile abroad, his succession will be subject to the legislation designated by the private international law of the state in which he was last domiciled. However, if a Swiss national had, by way of will, made his succession subject to the law of Switzerland, that law will be applicable. Finally, Swiss legislation is also applicable to the succession of a Swiss national domiciled abroad if that succession is not dealt with by the authorities of the state in which he was domiciled, except if, by way of will, the deceased expressly asked for the law of his domicile to be applied, in which case the Swiss authority will have jurisdiction but will apply the law of his last domicile (Article 91 *LDIP*).

3. Foreign Succession/Inheritance Orders

(a) Article 96 of the *LDIP* provides that not only judicial decisions, but also measures or documents relating to a succession passing to heirs abroad, are to be recognized in Switzerland, inasmuch as they were rendered, taken or drawn up in the state of the last domicile of the deceased or in the state whose law was chosen by the deceased to apply to the succession or if they are recognized in such state, or, in relation to immovables, rendered, taken or drawn up in the state in which they are located or recognized in such state. In relation to an immovable located in a state which claims to have exclusive jurisdiction, only those decisions, measures or documents emanating from that state will be recognized.

Recognition of foreign judicial decisions is subject to an enquiry whose rules are set out in the *LDIP*, as well as in international agreements. Public instruments from abroad should have an apostille in accordance with the provisions of the *1961 Hague Convention on the Conflicts of Laws Relating to the Form of Testamentary Dispositions* or be legalized (by those officials representing Switzerland in the state from which the document emanates).

(b) In addition to the *above*, the delivery of property depends upon the validity of the titles presented. Such titles must emanate from or be recognized by the foreign authorities having jurisdiction in accordance with Article 96 of the *LDIP*. If such is the case, they will be recognized in Switzerland. Foreign decisions which are recognized will be deemed executory by way of the *exequatar* procedure. Public instruments (e.g., those executed by a notary) will be recognized if they have an apostille, the latter doing away with the need for 'legalization' of foreign public instruments (e.g., for France), or if duly 'legalized' (e.g., for Brazil). In principle, a certificate of heirship drawn up by the foreign authorities having jurisdiction, which has an apostille or is legalized, along with a certificate as to foreign law, will allow the body of heirs to take possession of property, such as that held by banks as well as specific items of property, and will also enable them to register the devolution of the immovables in the Land Register.

In order for a particular beneficiary to obtain his property in Switzerland, the certificate of heirship must be accompanied by an agreement as to division (whether total or partial) which is valid in accordance with the foreign law applicable and recognized in Switzerland in accordance with the rules set out in (a) *above*.

(c) As it relates to a judicial decision, the procedure for its recognition is governed by Articles 25 ff. of the *LDIP*. The Swiss court having jurisdiction is that of the canton where the foreign decision was first made known. That court should determine if the foreign judgment is definitive, rendered by those foreign authorities having jurisdiction (as regards matters relating to succession in accordance with Article 96 of the *LDIP*) and conforms to Swiss public policy. If these conditions are met, the Swiss court will recognize the decision and, at the request of the applicant, it will be deemed executory.

Public instruments which have an apostille or are legalized must emanate from a ministerial officer having territorial jurisdiction in accordance with Article 96 of the *LDIP*, with such made clear either in the instrument itself or by having all documents or certificates as to foreign law with an apostille or legalized. If these rules are respected, no other formalities are required to obtain their recognition or execution.

4. Two or More Succession or Probate Orders

The law applicable to the succession governs all that relating to the status of the heirs and division and, therefore, determines who is to take (Article 92 *LDIP*). Article 96 of the *LDIP* provides that not only judicial decisions, but also measures or documents relating to a succession passing to heirs abroad, are to be recognised, inasmuch as they were rendered, taken or drawn up in the state of the last domicile of the deceased or in the state whose law was chosen by the deceased to apply to the succession or if they are recognized in such state, or, in relation to immovables, rendered, taken or drawn up in the state in which they are located or recognized in such state. In relation to an immovable located in a state which claims to have exclusive jurisdiction, only those decisions, measures or documents emanating from that state will be recognized (*see* 2 *above* as to the applicable law).

5. Assets

The principal criterion upon which the jurisdiction of the Swiss authority is based is that of domicile. The subsidiary criteria have been set out in 1 *above*.

6. Expert Evidence

(a) No, Swiss legislation prescribes in Article 16 *LDIP* that foreign law is established automatically but to this end, the parties can be called upon to assist in having it established in relation to inheritance. This being the case, a certificate of foreign law is not necessary, but is preferable in order that the effects of certain testamentary dispositions can be determined, in particular those relating to the powers of the testamentary executor, the respective shares of the estate and all other practical effects deriving from the application of such legislation.

(b) The proof of the content of foreign law, if it is to be provided by one of the parties, does not have to be in any particular form; likewise an affidavit does not have to be validated or approved by any judicial authority.

7. Unity of Succession

Yes, in domestic law as well as international law.

8. Formalities

See the final paragraph of Section A14(a) *above*.

9. Legislation

Switzerland ratified the *1961 Hague Convention on the Conflicts of Laws Relating to the Form of Testamentary Dispositions* on 8 June 1971 and it entered into force on 17 October 1971.

10. Wills

(a) The *LDIP* provides that if the *1961 Hague Convention on the Conflicts of Laws Relating to the Form of Testamentary Dispositions* does not apply directly to the will in question, it will apply by way of analogy. The principle of *locus regit actum* is therefore subsidiary. In contrast, as regards agreements on succession and other forms of reciprocal dispositions upon death, the principle of *locus regit actum* is first applied. However, if the person making over his property subjects the succession to the law of the state of which he is national, the latter will be applied instead and in place of the law of the state in which he is domiciled. Finally, if two persons dispose of property in a reciprocal manner, those dispositions must be in accordance with the law of the state in which each is domiciled or the law of the state of which both are nationals and which is chosen by both (Article 95 *LDIP*). The intention of the legislator is to uphold, insofar as he can, the validity of the will.

(b) As foreign law is established automatically, the terminology used in the will must be in accordance with the law applicable to it, and, therefore, the interpretation of the testamentary dispositions will be carried out in accordance with that law.

(c) The law to be applied regulates all of the succession and therefore applies to the status of the various beneficiaries, such as appointed heirs, those entitled to a compulsory share or legatees (Article 92 *LDIP*). Swiss law, inasmuch as it is the *lex fori*, will not apply.

(d) Again in accordance with Article 92(1) of the *LDIP*, it is the law applicable to the succession which will determine who will take as heir.

(e) Given the tenor of Article 5 of the *1961 Hague Convention on the Conflicts of Laws Relating to the Form of Testamentary Dispositions*, the *LDIP* provides that a person can make a will if at that moment he has the requisite capacity by virtue of the law of the state which is his domicile or that of his habitual residence, or by virtue of the law of one of the states of which he is national.

(f) *See* (a) *above.*

(g) Such a disposition, even if allowed for by the law applicable to the succession, would be unlikely to be executory in Switzerland as such. In effect, domestic jurisprudence deems, on the one hand, that such a disposition would be null and void as a matter of law and, on the other, that such a disposition would offend those rules applying to the acquisition of property and deems that the Swiss law applicable to immovables would override the foreign law applying to succession.

(h) All testamentary dispositions can be revoked or modified in accordance with those rules applying to the form of the will (Article 2 of the *1961 Hague Convention on the Conflicts of Laws Relating to the Form of Testamentary Dispositions* and Article 93 *LDIP*).

(i) Yes, with the exception of the provisions of Article 86(2) of the *LDIP* where a foreign state claims exclusive jurisdiction over immovables which are located on its territory and thereby applies its own legislation.

11. Domicile/Nationality

(a) The answer to this question has been addressed in the course of elaboration of answers to previous questions. In particular, *see* Section A14(a) *above.*

(b) No.

(c) The concept of domicile is not standardized in private international law. The *LDIP* provides that a person has their domicile in the state in which they reside with the intention to settle there. No one can have several domiciles and the judge should determine the one which corresponds to the legal definition. If a person does not have a domicile anywhere, the habitual residence will prevail (Article 20 *LDIP*).

A person's nationality is determined in accordance with the law of the state in relation to which nationality is being put in question.

12. Taxation

There does not seem to be any difference as regards taxation in connection with the domicile of the deceased or the heirs. In order to avoid the imposition of dual taxation, notably for immovables, numerous bilateral conventions have been entered into. As fiscal matters relating to succession are under the jurisdiction of the cantons, it is not possible to give more specific details in the context of this chapter (*see* Section A12(b) *above*).

Taiwan

Prepared by: Nigel N. T. LI, Sophia YEH and Josephine PENG
Lee & Li, Attorneys at Law

Address: 7th Fl., 201 Tun-Hua N. Road,
Taipei, Taiwan 105
Republic of China
Tel.:   886 2 27153300
Fax: 886 2 27133966

Section A – Brief Survey of the Local System

1. Type of System

(a) The Republic of China (ROC) adopts the civil law system.

(b) The ROC has a national judiciary, with no separate state court system.

2. Wills

(a) There are several forms of wills:

(1) Holograph Will
To make a holograph will, the testator must write the entire text of the will and sign and date it in person. In the case of any insertion, deletion or alteration of words, the testator must state in the will the place where the insertion, deletion or alteration is made and the number of words thus affected, and sign his/her name there below. A holograph will is the simplest, most convenient and economical form. However, its simplicity may be the source of disputes between heirs and other parties concerned as to the genuineness of a will.

(2) Notarial Will
To make a notarial will, at least two witnesses are required. The testator must orally state his/her testamentary wishes to the public notary who shall write down such oral statements. The written statements shall be read over and explained by the public notary, and confirmed by the testator and then signed by the public notary, the testator and two witnesses. The document must also be dated.

International Succession

If a notarial will is to be made in a foreign country, the function of the public notary must be performed by the ROC consul or the ROC Representative Office in that foreign country. Otherwise, such a will would not be deemed a valid notarial will under the ROC law. In a debatable ruling, a 1982 ROC Supreme Court judgment held that a notary public of a foreign country may not replace a ROC public notary in making a notarial will in any foreign country.

(3) Sealed Will

To make a sealed will, the testator shall first write the will (or have another person write it), sign the will, have it securely enveloped and then sign his/her name across the seams of the envelope. The testator shall then, in the presence of at least two witnesses, deliver the enveloped will to the public notary and declare that it is his/her will, and, if the will is written by any other party, indicate the name and domicile of such other party. The public notary shall write on the envelope the date on which the will is brought and the declaration of the testator, and sign thereon together with the testator and two witnesses.

The sealed will is thus enveloped with a certain formality, so as to keep it secret and prevent it from being forged. Therefore, if the process of sealing the will has defects so as to render it invalid, but the making of the will being enveloped is in compliance with the formality of making a holograph will, the will shall have the effect of a holograph will.

(4) Dictated Will

A dictated will requires the testator to designate at least three witnesses and make oral statements of his/her testamentary wishes. Such oral statements must be written down, read over and explained by one of the witnesses and confirmed by the testator, and the testator and all the witnesses must sign their names on the will.

(5) Oral Will

An oral will shall be made only when the testator is in imminent danger of death, or in other exceptional circumstances which cause the testator to be unable to make a valid will in any of the *above-mentioned* forms. Such special circumstances call for a more simple and convenient format. The testator has two options available in making an oral will:

i. The testator must designate at least two witnesses and state orally his/her testamentary wishes, which shall be set down in writing by one of the witnesses, dated and signed by all the witnesses.
ii. The oral statement can be tape-recorded, in the presence of two witnesses. First, the testator must orally state his/her name, testamentary wishes and the date of making the will, and then all the witnesses must state their names and their assertion that the will is genuine. The witnesses must securely envelope the recorded tape at the time of testament. The envelope must bear the date of the will and the witnesses must sign their names across the seams of the envelope.

Due to the simplicity of making an oral will, the will's authenticity or the testator's true intention may be challenged. Therefore, the law provides that an oral will shall become invalid after three months from the date the testator is able to make a will in another form. Furthermore, one of the witnesses of the will, or any other interested person, within three months of the death of the testator must present the oral will to the family council (*see* 5 *below* for detailed description) for confirmation of its genuineness. If any objection is made to the family council's decision concerning the authenticity of the will, the objector may apply to the court for judgment.

(b) *i.* The testator may, at any time, revoke or cancel the will:

- by stating his/her intention to revoke or cancel the will in any of the forms required for making a will;
- by stating in the will his/her intention to annul it;
- by intentionally destroying the will;
- by making a new will, such that the former will shall be deemed to be revoked insofar as the provisions are in conflict; or
- by acting in conflict with the contents of the will, which shall be deemed revoked to the extent that the provisions conflict.

Alternatively, codicils may be executed in the same way as a will of the formats of wills is complied with.

ii. Marriage does not revoke or in any other way affect wills made prior to marriage.
iii. Revival of a revoked will may be accomplished by simply making a new will with the same terms as the revoked will.

3. Intestacy

(a) In the case of an intestacy, the estate is vested directly in the heirs and only statutory heirs are recognized. The surviving spouse, together with those persons listed below, shall be heirs in the following order of precedence:

(1) lineal descendants by blood. Children, grandchildren and great-grandchildren fall into this category. An adopted child, a child born out of wedlock or an adulterine child who has been acknowledged or maintained by the natural father, as well as a child *en ventre sa mere* (an unborn child, provided that he/she is subsequently born alive) are deemed legitimate and also fall into this category;
(2) parents;
(3) siblings;
(4) grandparents.

The following are the statutory succession of the spouse and the other heirs:

(1) if the spouse inherits along with lineal descendants, the succession share of each heir shall be equal;

597

(2) if the spouse inherits along with the parents or siblings of the decedent, his/her succession share shall be one-half and that of all other heirs combined shall be one-half;

(3) if the spouse inherits along with the grandparents, his/her succession share shall be two-thirds and that of the grandparents shall be one-third;

(4) if there are no other heirs, the succession share of the sole heir shall be the entire estate.

(b) For the purpose of dividing the estate, there is no difference between movables and immovables.

4. Freedom of Testation

(a) The testator may freely dispose of his/her property in a will to the extent that such disposition does not contravene the provisions in regard to compulsory shares. Compulsory shares are certain shares of the estate statutorily reserved to the heirs, which shall be determined as follows:

(1) one-half of the heir's succession share if he/she is one of the deceased's lineal descendants, parents or spouse; or

(2) one-third of the heir's succession share if he/she is one of the deceased's siblings or grandparents.

The amount of each compulsory share shall be calculated by deducting the amount of the deceased's debts from the estate of the succession. If the heir cannot receive the full amount of his/her compulsory share from the estate because of the legacy made by the testator, the insufficient amount shall be deducted from the legacy.

(b) *i*. The concept of 'contract of inheritance' does not exist in the ROC. A testator must state clearly his/her wishes in the form of a will. Hence a contract entered into by the heirs prior to the deceased's death shall be deemed null and void.

ii. The concepts of partition, anticipation, successor or family settlement exist, as explained below:

– a testator may freely dispose of his/her property during his/her lifetime. However, in calculating the amount of the succession share or the compulsory share of the heirs, any property given to an heir as a gift by the deceased before his/her death for the heir's marriage, setting up of a separate home, or engaging in business, shall be deemed part of the deceased's estate, unless the deceased has specifically expressed otherwise at the time of making the gift;

– the estate may be partitioned with the unanimous consent of the heirs after the estate tax payable is paid in full, provided that the will does not prohibit otherwise;

– successor (legatee) or family settlements may also be arranged as long as such arrangement does not contravene the provisions in regard to compulsory shares.

5. Maintenance

A person who received maintenance from the deceased continuously during the latter's lifetime shall be assigned a certain portion of the deceased's property by the family council, taking into consideration the extent of maintenance he/she used to receive and other relations.

The family council shall be composed of five members and selected from amongst the relatives of the deceased in the following order:

(1) lineal ascendants by blood;
(2) collateral ascendants by blood within the third degree of relationship; and
(3) relatives by blood of equal rank within the fourth degree of relationship.

Among the *above-mentioned* persons, the person nearest, in degree of relationship, to the deceased comes first; and among those of the same degree of relationship, the person living in the same household as the deceased comes first, or the person senior in age comes first in the absence of relative living in the same household. Moreover, a member of the family council as determined by the order specified *above* who cannot or has difficulty to be present at the meeting should be substituted by the relative next in line. Nevertheless, guardians, minors and interdicted persons cannot act as members of a family council.

In the event where there are no such relatives as provided in the preceding paragraphs, or where such relatives do not constitute the statutory number, the court may, on the application of the person who has the right to convene such a meeting, designate person(s) from amongst other relatives to be member(s) of the family council.

Where a meeting of the family council is to be held in accordance with the provisions, it shall be convened by an interested person. In the event that it is impossible or there is a difficulty in convening a meeting of family council, the interested person shall apply to the court for disposition of affairs that should be managed by the family council in accordance with law. The same rule applies where holding of such meeting fails or no resolution is adopted though a meeting of family council is convened.

A family council may not hold a session without at least three members present and may not pass a resolution without the consent of the majority of those present.

6. Community Property Between Husband and Wife

The amendments to Matrimonial Property Regimes took effect on 26 June 2002. According to the amendments, there are the following kinds of matrimonial property regimes:

International Succession

(a) Statutory regime:

The old statutory regime 'union property regime' was abolished. The properties of a married couple, under the new laws, are divided into premarital and post marital properties of which the husband and wife retain his/her respective ownership as well as the right to manage, use and collect revenue from his and her own properties. (Under the 'union property regime', to the contrary, the husband had the right to manage the 'union property', and to use and collect revenue from the properties owned by his wife.) Except for household expenses which should be shared by a married couple according to their financial condition, housework devotion or other events, a couple may negotiate a certain amount of money for his or her spouse's free dispensing.

Upon the end of the statutory regime (e.g., divorce or death of a spouse), the remainder of post marital properties after deducting obligations or debts incurred during the marriage shall be equally distributed between the husband and wife (or the surviving spouse.) The *above* post marital properties exclude 1) the properties obtained by inheritance or without consideration or 2) *solatium*. To prevent a spouse from reducing his or her post marital properties, the other spouse may take the following actions:

(1) if a gratuitous act done to the post marital properties by a spouse during the marriage is likely to be prejudicial to the rights of the other spouse, except for the gifts made for the fulfillment of a moral obligation, he or she may apply with the Court for cancellation of such an act; if a non-gratuitous act is done knowing at the time of the act that it is likely to be prejudicial to the rights of the other spouse, he or she may apply with the Court for cancellation of such an act, provided that the party who profited from such an act also knew of the circumstances upon the receipt of the benefits;

(2) if a spouse, with the intention to reduce the distribution of the difference of the properties, disposes post marital properties within five years before the end of the statutory regime, the other spouse may add the disposed portion to the remaining post marital properties. The disposed portion excludes gifts made for the fulfillment of a moral obligation.

(b) Contractual regime:

The types of contractual matrimonial property regimes remain the same; namely, the community of property regime and the separation of property regime. However, there are a few changes to the *above* regimes under the amendments:

(1) The community of property regime:

All properties and incomes of a married couple, except the 'exclusive properties' such as properties that are exclusively intended for the personal use of either spouse, constitute common property to be owned by them in common. Hence, the common property should be managed jointly by both husband and wife unless there is an agreement that specifies otherwise. For the obligations or debts incurred during the marriage, the fulfillment thereof should be made from the sources of the common property and the exclusive properties of each spouse.

Upon the end of the community of property regime, the husband and wife can take back the properties as agreed in a contract at the beginning of this regime unless there is an agreement that specifies otherwise. As for the common properties obtained during the marriage, the husband and wife can each take back one-half unless there is an agreement that specifies otherwise.

(2) The separation of property regime:

Under this regime, the husband and wife each retain the ownership and the rights to manage, use and collect revenue from his and her own properties. He or she is also responsible for his or her own obligations or debts incurred during the marriage. If a spouse uses his or her properties to fulfill the other's obligations or debit, he or she may have the right to claim such reimbursement.

7. Gifts (*Inter Vivos*)

(a) Any property given to an heir as a gift by the deceased before his/her death cannot be offset against the heir's inheritance, unless the gift is given to the heir due to the heir's getting married, setting up of a separate home, or engaging in business. Under these circumstances, the value of the gift shall be included as part of the deceased's estate of succession, unless the deceased has specifically expressed otherwise at the time of making the gift.

(b) The value of such a gift shall, at the time of the partition of inheritance, be deducted from the successional portion of the heir concerned.

8. Capacity

(a) Any person aged sixteen or over (except an interdicted person) may freely make a will.

(b) The following persons may not act as a witness to a will:

(1) a minor;
(2) a person under interdiction (an interdit);
(3) an heir; his/her spouse, or lineal descendant or ascendant;
(4) a legatee, his/her spouse, or lineal descendant or ascendant; or
(5) a person who is an assistant to, or employed by, or living with, the notary public who signs the testament.

(c) Generally, a beneficiary can be either a natural person or a juristic person. Nevertheless, the following two conditions must be met:

(1) The beneficiary has the right to the inheritance. The beneficiary's right to the inheritance will be forfeited due to any of the following events:
   i. Where he/she has been found guilty of a criminal offense for having intentionally caused or attempted the death of the deceased or of a person entitled to inherit;

    ii. Where he/she has, by fraud or duress, induced the deceased to make, withdraw or alter a will relating to the inheritance;

    iii. Where he/she has, by fraud or by duress, prevented the deceased from making, withdrawing or altering a will relating to the inheritance;

    iv. Where he/she has forged, altered, concealed or destroyed the deceased's will relating to the inheritance; or

    v. Where he/she has seriously ill-treated or insulted the deceased and has been declared unworthy to inherit by the deceased.

In the events of *ii.*, *iii.* and *iv. above*, if the offender has been forgiven by the deceased, his/her right to inherit would not be deemed forfeited.

(2) The beneficiary must be alive at the time of the deceased's death. However, a child *en ventre sa mere* shall be deemed as if he/she was already born with regard to his/her personal rights, provided that he/she was subsequently born alive.

9. Authority (Court, Notarial or Other)

Estate vests directly in the heirs. There is no designated probate division of ROC courts nor any procedure exactly corresponding to probate or grant of administration. In this regard, civil tribunals of ROC courts have probate jurisdiction. If there is a dispute between the heirs or where someone wishes to challenge the will, a civil action may be filed with the district court. An appeal may be initiated with the high court against an unfavourable judgment rendered by the district court; further appeal may be initiated with the Supreme Court against an unfavourable decision rendered by the high court, provided that the subject of the appeal is a claim for property right with a value of more than USD 31,250.

10. Invalidity of Will

(a) A will shall not be deemed valid unless it is made in any of the required forms. An oral will shall become invalid three months from the date the testator is able to make a will in another form. Furthermore, one of the witnesses to the oral will, or any other interested person, within three months of the death of the testator, must present the oral will to the family council for confirmation of its genuineness. If any objection is made to the family council's decision concerning the authenticity of the will, the objector may apply to the court for judgment.

(b) Invalidity results in the will being void.

11. Simultaneous Death

(a) The succession commences with the death of the deceased. An heir must be alive at the time of death of the deceased in order to hold the legitimate right to the inheritance, except where an heir of the first order has died or lost the right to the inheritance before the opening of the succession, his/her lineal descendants shall inherit his/her successional share in his/her place. As such, in the case of a simultaneous death, neither one of the deceased shall become the heir to the other with the exception as stated *above*.

(b) A missing person may be declared dead by the court upon the application of any interested party under the following circumstances:

(1) if he/she had disappeared for more than seven years;
(2) if he/she was over eighty and had disappeared for more than three years; or
(3) if he/she was in peril of his/her life and had subsequently disappeared for more than a year after the end of the peril.

A person who has been declared dead is presumed to be dead at the time specified in the judgment. Furthermore, if several persons have perished in a common disaster and it is not possible to ascertain which of them perished first, they are presumed to have died simultaneously.

12. Estate Taxes

(a) The estate tax is prescribed under the *Estate and Gift Tax Law*.

(b) Article 1 of the ROC *Estate and Gift Tax Law* stipulates that any estate within or outside of the territory of the ROC of a ROC national who frequently domiciled in the ROC shall be subject to the estate tax upon his/her death. Furthermore, for a ROC national who frequently domiciled outside of the ROC and for a non-ROC national, the estate within the ROC upon his/her death shall be subject to the ROC estate tax.

(c) Estate tax is levied on the deceased's whole estate and not on the portion of the estate received by the heir. However, the estate is neither dividable nor transferable until the estate tax is fully paid. Thus all the heirs are jointly liable for payment of the estate tax regardless of whether an individual heir inherits the deceased's whole estate or not.

The estate tax shall be paid by any of the persons listed below in the following sequence:

(1) executor of the will;
(2) heir(s) or legatee(s), in the case where no executor is appointed; or
(3) an administrator elected pursuant to the law, in the case of non-existence of heir(s) or executor of the will. In the event that an administrator is not elected for whatsoever reason within six months immediately following the death of the deceased, the tax office may submit a petition to the court for appointment of an administrator pursuant to the provisions of the Non-litigation Law.

13. Administration of Estates

(a) A testator may, by will, designate an executor or entrust a third person to administer the estate; but a minor or an interdicted person cannot act as an executor. Where the testator did not designate an executor nor a third person to administer the estate, the family council (*see 5 above* for a detailed description) may elect an executor. Where the family council cannot elect such an executor, the executor may be designated by the court upon application by an interested party. These provisions do not apply if the deceased died intestate. Under such circumstances, the administration is in the hands of the heirs. Where there is more than one heir, the estate, as a whole, is owned by all the heirs in common before partition. All heirs shall administer the estate jointly. However, the heirs may elect a person from amongst themselves to manage the estate.

(b) Two reports, as explained below, must be submitted to the government authorities after the death of a person:

(1) Death Registration
An application along with the death certificate of the deceased must be filed with the Household Registrar Office where the deceased domiciled before his/her death for his/her death registration within thirty days of his/her death. The applicant for the death registration must be one of the persons listed below in the following order:
  i. the surviving spouse;
  ii. the relatives;
  iii. the head of household;
  iv. the person who lived with the deceased at the time of death;
  v. the person who handles the matters related to the funeral of the deceased;
  vi. the current administrator of the deceased's house or land; or
vii. an interested party.

(2) Estate Tax Return Report
Regardless of whether estate tax is payable, an estate tax return reporting the property left by the deceased must be submitted by the 'taxpayer' within six months from the date of death to the competent tax office where the household registration of the deceased was located. Written application with stated reason for an extension of three months may be made before the expiration of the original six month period. The tax office may, at its discretion, extend the period in the event of an act of God or other extraordinary circumstances.

The taxpayers, if there is more than one, should file the estate tax return jointly. However, if one of the taxpayers files the estate tax return, the tax return shall be deemed filed on behalf of all the taxpayers. In other words, if one of the heirs files the estate tax return, the other heirs are not required to file the tax return for the same deceased's estate. Furthermore, the heir who files the estate tax return shall submit a 'List of Inheritance' listing all the heirs as well as the supporting identification documents for each of the heirs.

(c) (1) If the application for the death registration is not filed within the prescribed time period, the Household Registrar Office should, upon awareness of such, notify in writing the responsible applicant to file the registration application. If the responsible applicant fails to file the death registration after receipt of the notification, the Household Registrar Office may proceed with the registration at its discretion. In addition, the Household Registrar Office may dispatch an officer to examine and verify household registration related matters.

(2) The Household Registrar Office, upon completion of a death registration, should immediately inform the tax authority in charge in writing of such death registration.

The tax authority in charge, upon awareness of the death or receipt of the death report of the deceased from the Household Registrar Office, should issue and deliver a filing notice enclosed with an estate tax return form to the taxpayer. A reminder should be issued ten days prior to the deadline to remind the taxpayer of the consequences of late filing. The taxpayer is not exempt from the filing obligation even if the tax authority in charge does not issue such notice.

Furthermore, the tax authority in charge should, within two months after receipt of the estate tax return, *i.* examine the return; *ii.* evaluate the estate to determine the amount of tax payable; and *iii.* issue a tax payment notice to the taxpayer for tax payment.

If a taxpayer fails to file the estate tax return within the time limit, or fails to file an extension for the filing of the estate return, the tax authority in charge should proceed with the examination, assess the amount of tax payable accordingly, and notify the taxpayer to make the tax payment within the time limit.

(d) Persons who have an 'interest' in the estate may at any time query or object to the administration of the estate.

(e) A Certificate of Payment of Estate Tax ('Tax Certificate') will be issued by the competent tax office when the estate tax payable is paid in full, while a Certificate of Estate Tax Exemption ('Exemption Certificate') will be issued if there is no estate tax payable after assessment. Furthermore, an application for a Certificate of Consent for Transfer ('Transfer Certificate') may be made if there are special reasons for transferring the ownership of the property before the tax liability is cleared, and guarantee for tax payment can be provided. With respect to the properties that are excluded from the calculation of the value of estate for calculating estate tax, an application may be filed with the competent tax office for a Certificate of Exclusion from Estate ('Exclusion Certificate').

The estate cannot be partitioned, transferred, or sold unless the estate tax payable has been paid in full, or an Exemption Certificate, a Transfer Certificate, or an Exclusion Certificate is obtained from the competent tax office.

The heirs must present the Tax Certificate, Exemption Certificate, Transfer Certificate, or Exclusion Certificate ('the Certificate') to the companies and banks in connection with the estate when requesting for the transfer of company shares or bank deposits.

(f) Since an heir succeeds, from the beginning of the succession, all rights and duties pertaining to the estate of the deceased, the creditors of the deceased should present their claims to the executor, heir, or administrator. The executor, heir, or administrator may make payment out of the estate to such creditors only after the estate tax payable is fully paid. On the other hand, the heir may choose to pay the debt with his/her own property prior to his/her inheritance of the estate.

As heirs are jointly and severally liable for the deceased's debts, to eliminate the risk of repaying the debts from their own property if the estate is insufficient to cover the debts, the heirs may choose to have limited succession to limit the payment of the deceased's debts to the extent of the property acquired by the succession. Under such circumstances, the heirs must, within three months from the time of the death of the deceased, draw up an inventory and submit it to the court. The court shall then give public notice according to the procedure of public summons, calling upon the creditors of the deceased to present their claims within a specified period of time. The heirs shall not, within the specified period of time prescribed by the court, make any payment to any one of the deceased's creditors. Upon the expiration of the specified period of time, the heirs shall make payment out of the deceased's property to those creditors who have presented their claims within the said period of time and to other creditors who are known to the heirs, in proportion to the amounts of their respective claims, but the rights of the preferential creditors must not be prejudiced.

Creditors of the deceased who have failed to present their claims within the specified period of time and are also unknown to the executor, heir, or administrator, may exercise their right to claim only against the remaining portion of the estate.

(g) An estate can be distributed freely amongst the heirs provided that unanimous consent can be reached, unless the will prescribed otherwise.

14. Domicile/Nationality

(a) With respect to the requisites for the establishment and the effect of a will, the law of the country where the testator was a citizen at the time of establishing the will shall apply. Further, in the event of revocating the will, the law of the country where the testator was a citizen at the time of revoking the will shall apply.

(b) The ROC law does not provide for probate proceedings. A will shall be deemed valid if it is made in any of the required forms irrespective of whether any assets exist. The executor may perform his/her duties immediately after the death of the deceased without being probated.

SECTION B – APPLICABLE LAW/PROCEDURE WHERE FOREIGN ELEMENT/S ARE INVOLVED

1. Jurisdiction

(a) All properties of the deceased located in the ROC shall be subject to ROC estate tax, regardless of whether or not the deceased resided in the ROC.

(b) The rules governing movable and immovable assets are the same.

(c) Jurisdiction over an action relating to the right of succession to an estate or partition thereof may be exercised by the court at the place of death of the deceased.

2. Applicable Law

The law of the country where the deceased was a citizen at the time of his/her death shall apply; provided, however, that when a national of the ROC is an heir under the laws of the ROC, he/she may effect succession to the deceased's property which is in the ROC. In the case of the death of a non-ROC national who left property within the ROC and if no one inherits the property under the laws of his/her country, it shall be dealt with according to the laws of the ROC. Taiwanese law applies to immovable property in ROC.

3. Foreign Succession/Inheritance Orders

(a) An estate located in the ROC is prohibited from being disposed or transferred before the heirs pay the estate tax in full. Foreign judgments regarding inheritance are recognized and enforceable in the ROC with respect to the estates in the ROC (both movable and immovable assets), subject to the requirements set forth in 3(c) *below*.

(b) To enforce a foreign judgment, a party must file a separate civil action with a ROC court for recognition of the foreign judgment and declaration that such a foreign judgment is enforceable in the ROC.

(c) A foreign judgment refers to the final decision on a civil case rendered by a judicial authority of a foreign country. A final judgment rendered by a foreign court would be recognized by a ROC court without further review on the merits, unless:

  i. the foreign court, according to the law of ROC, has no jurisdiction over the subject matter of the judgment;
  ii. the losing party is a ROC national and such party did not respond to the litigation; provided, however, that if the notice or order necessary for commencing the litigation had been properly served upon such party within that foreign country, or through judicial assistance in accordance with ROC law, the judgment would still be recognized;
  iii. the foreign judgment contravenes the public order or policy of the ROC; or
  iv. there is no recipical treaty between the ROC and the foreign country.

The conditions for declaring the enforceability of the foreign judgment are the same as those for the recognition thereof. After obtaining this judgment, the claimant may apply for compulsory execution of the foreign judgment if the losing party does not comply with the foreign judgment.

International Succession

4. Two or More Succession or Probate Orders

With respect to succession, the law of the country where the deceased was at the time of his/her death shall apply.

5. Assets

If the deceased had no assets in the ROC but had a domicile in the ROC at the time of his/her death, the ROC court shall exercise its jurisdiction over the matters related to succession and any matters arising out of the deceased's death.

6. Expert Evidence

(a) The law of the country where the testator was at the time of his/her establishment of the will shall apply to the establishment and the effect of a will. Therefore, if there is any dispute over the legality of the will, the court will request the party to provide a foreign attorney's opinion as a supporting document explaining the inheritance laws and regulations of that foreign country.

(b) The ROC courts will usually request that the foreign attorney issue an affidavit.

(c) The affidavit should be notarized by a notary public and then legalized by the ROC Consul or ROC Representative Office in the country where the affidavit is issued. In practice, the ROC courts will not require a foreign attorney to appear in the ROC courts.

7. Unity of Succession

Not applicable.

8. Formalities

The will of a foreigner must be made in accordance with the law of his/her country.

9. Legislation

The *Hague Convention on the Conflicts of Laws Relating to the Form of Testamentary Dispositions* is not applicable.

10. Wills

(a) With respect to the requisites for establishment and the effect of a will, the law of the country where the testator was a citizen at the time of establishing the will shall apply.

(b) *See* 10(a) *above.*

(c) *See* 10(a) *above.*

(d) *See* 10(a) *above.*

(e) *See* 10(a) *above.*

(f) *See* 10(a) *above.*

(g) *See* 10(a) *above.*

(h) *See* 10(a) *above.*

(i) *See* 10(a) *above.*

11. Domicile/Nationality

(a) The will of a foreigner must be made in accordance with the law of the country where the testator was a citizen upon establishing the will. With respect to succession, the law of the country where the deceased was a citizen at the time of his/her death shall govern.

(b) The domicile of the beneficiary is irrelevant to any answers in Section B.

(c) When the law of the country of the party concerned shall apply, but the party concerned is stateless, his/her domicile shall apply. If his/her domicile is unknown, the law of the place of his/her residence shall apply. If the party concerned has several domiciles, the law of the place of his/her domicile which is the closest in relationship shall apply. If the party concerned has a domicile within the ROC, the laws of the ROC shall apply.

12. Taxation

The following are the differences between taxation of a local decedent as opposed to a non-resident deceased:

(1) Scope of Taxable Estate
  i. Property left by the deceased who was a ROC citizen and resided in the ROC constantly shall be subject to estate tax, regardless of whether the location of the property is inside or outside of the ROC.
  ii. Property left by the deceased who was a ROC citizen but did not reside in the ROC constantly or who was a non-ROC citizen shall be subject to the estate tax imposed on the property located within the ROC.

iii. A deceased is regarded as having resided in the ROC constantly if one of the following conditions is met:
    a. the deceased maintains a domicile in the ROC for two years immediately prior to death; or
    b. the deceased maintains a residence in the ROC provided that during the period of two years immediately prior to his/her death, the deceased has stayed in the ROC for over 365 days.

(2) Deductions

The following are the tax deductions from the taxable estate if the deceased was a ROC citizen and resided in the ROC constantly:

i. If the deceased has a living spouse, TWD 4,000,000 shall be deducted;

ii. If the deceased has heirs of lineal descent by blood, TWD 400,000 shall be deducted for each heir. An additional TWD 400,000 shall be deducted for each year before the heirs of the first order reach the age of twenty;

iii. If the deceased has living parents, TWD 1,000,000 shall be deducted for each parent;

iv. A special additional deduction of TWD 5,000,000 is available for each person mentioned in item *i.*, *ii.* and *iii. above* if he/she is seriously handicapped or mentally disabled;

v. If the deceased has heirs who are brothers, sisters or grandparents who were supported by the deceased, TWD 400,000 shall be deducted for each person; and an additional TWD 400,000 shall be deducted for each year before the heirs, who are brothers or sisters, reach the age of twenty;

vi. The entire value of farmland which is for agricultural use and the crops from the land inherited by the heir or the legatee shall be deducted. However, estate tax shall be re-imposed if the farmland has not been used for agricultural purposes for a period of five consecutive years since the date of inheritance and (a) on which agricultural usage has not been resumed within the time limit set by the competent government authorities; or (b) on which agricultural use has ceased after resuming agricultural usage during the time limit set by the competent government authorities. Nonetheless, the farmland is not subject to estate tax if the heir dies, or the farmland is under a compulsory purchase order, or the usage thereof has been changed to non-agricultural purposes according to the regulations.

vii. If estate tax has been levied on the estate inherited by the deceased within the six to nine years prior to the death of the deceased, 80 per cent, 60 per cent, 40 per cent and 20 per cent of the previous tax payment shall be deducted at an annual decreasing rate;

viii. Various taxes, fines and penalties imposed on the deceased before his/her death;

ix. Debts incurred by the deceased before his/her death, which can be proved by reliable evidence;

x. Funeral expenses of TWD 1,000,000; and

xi. Direct expenses necessary for will execution and estate administration.

Items *i.* to *vii. above* are not applicable to non-ROC residents or non-ROC citizens. Items *viii.* to *xi.* are limited to expenses incurred in the territory of the ROC.

(3) Estate Tax Return Reporting

Regardless of whether estate tax is payable, an estate tax return reporting the property left by the deceased shall be submitted within six months of the death of the deceased to the competent tax office where the household registration of the deceased is located. In the case of a non-ROC citizen or a ROC citizen who did not reside in the ROC constantly, an estate tax return reporting the property left in the ROC by the deceased shall be submitted to the tax office where the Central Government is located.

Turkey

Prepared by: YAMANER & YAMANER Law Offices

Office address: Cumhuriyet cad. Gezi Apt. No. 19
                 5th Floor 9–10 Taksim, 80090 Istanbul, Turkey
Tel.:   +90 212 2381065
Fax: +90 212 2380810
E-mail: info@yamaner.com

SECTION A – BRIEF SURVEY OF THE LOCAL SYSTEM

1. Type of System

(a) Civil law.

(b) The Turkish Republic is a unitary and civil law country. Therefore the *Inheritance Law*, which is a part of our Civil Code, applies throughout the country. A new Civil Code draft has also been prepared. The important provisions of this draft will be mentioned *below*.

2. Wills

(a) The Turkish Civil Code recognizes three forms of wills, two of which are standard forms while one of which is referred to as being extraordinary.

Official Form: Under this form of will, the text shall be drawn up with the presence of two witnesses in front of the Court or Notary Public by the Notary Public or Judge, following which the Testator should read and execute the same. The witnesses approve and execute that the testator has read and approved the will. Finally, the Official Functionary shall execute the written document.

Holographic Will: Under this form, the text of the will and date of issue have to be handwritten by the Testator.

Oral Form: Should the testator not have the possibility to draw up the will in one of the forms mentioned *above* due to risk of death, interruption of communication, contagious disease and war, etc., he or she may declare the will to two witnesses. The witnesses shall write and execute this will and apply to the Court at their earliest convenience. The oral will must be written within one month as of the date that the testator's situation becomes normalized.

(b) Cancellation or modification of the will by the testator, may be possible pursuant to the same procedure as the will has been drafted. If there is a difference

612

between the latter will and the former one that contradicts the former one, the former one shall be presumed to be invalid.

   i. a Testator may change or cancel the will anytime he or she so wishes;

   ii. according to Turkish law, marriage does not effect, change or make invalid a will, which was made before the marriage. However, even if the will is drawn up before, the surviving spouse can object to the same up to the amount of his or her 'compulsory share-portion';

   iii. the will, which has been cancelled, shall not have any effect. If, however, a latter will invalidating a former one is cancelled, the former shall come into force automatically.

3. Intestacy

(a) *i.* In Turkish law, as in other continental law systems, the relatives of the testator, as determined by the law, succeed to the inheritance even if there is no will. The beneficiary of a will can succeed if there is more heritage than compulsory share-portion of the legal heirs. According to the *Civil Law*, legal heirs are as follows:

— the heirs of the first order comprise the descendants of the deceased. A descendant who is living when the succession occurs will exclude from the succession those descendants who are related to the deceased through him. If this descendant is no longer living at the same time that the succession takes place, those descendants who are related to the deceased through him will take in his place (succession *per stirpes*) Children will take in equal measures;

— the heirs of the second order comprise the ancestors of the deceased (father and mother) and their descendants (brothers and sisters, nephews and nieces and their children). If the ancestors are alive when succession takes place they alone will succeed in equal measures. If the mother or father is no longer alive when the succession takes place, his/her descendants will take in his/her place in accordance with the provisions applicable to the succession of heirs of the first order. If the deceased parent does not leave any descendants, surviving parent alone will succeed;

— the heirs of the third order comprise the grandparents of the deceased and their descendants (uncles and aunts, cousins, etc.). If the grandparents are alive when the succession occurs, they alone will take in equal shares. If at the time the succession takes place, the grandfather or the grandmother, paternal or maternal, is no longer alive, his/her descendants will take in his/her place. If no such descendants exist, the remaining grandparent alone will succeed and if the latter is deceased as well, his/her descendants will succeed. If at the time of succession the paternal or maternal grandparents are no longer alive and if they leave no descendants, the other grandparents or their descendants will alone succeed. In all instances where descendants take their parent's or grandparent's share, the provisions applicable to the succession of heirs of the first order will also apply.

As regards heirs of the *above* orders, a closer relative will prevent a more distant relative from succeeding. (Turkish Civil Code, Articles 439–442).

ii. If the illegitimate children are duly admitted by the testator or if in a court case it is held that they are the children of the testator, the succession shall be as in the case of the legitimate children.

iii. An adopted child and his or her descendants shall be of the first order heirs of the adopter. On the other hand, the adopter and his or her relatives cannot be the heir of the adopted child.

iv. The surviving spouse will take one-fourth of the inheritance if he or she is with first order of legal heirs, half of the inheritance if he or she is with the second of order legal heirs, three-fourths of inheritance if he or she is with the grandfather's and grandmother's order. If there are no other legal heirs alive when the succession takes place except for the spouse, he or she takes the entire inheritance. The new Draft Civil Code, however, provides that if the grandparents of testator are not alive, the surviving spouse will succeed with the descendants of grandparents (uncles, aunts).

v. Turkey has separation of the properties as its legal regime. Other property regimes may be applicable when duly chosen. In the new Draft Civil Code, 'separation of property' regime is to be changed into a 'unity of property' in respect of properties acquired after marriage. In both regimes, the inheritance portion of the surviving spouse will be amended. Under the new regime, each spouse will take half of the property, acquired by ways other than due to inheritance or donation after marriage and will be the heir of the remaining portion in the ratios mentioned *above*.

vi. If there are no fourth order heirs or surviving spouse, the inheritance will be succeeded by the Government.

vii. Heirs, who commit serious crimes against the testator or his/her relatives or seriously violate his/her family duties, can be debarred from inheriting. Moreover, the heirs who kill or attempt to kill or prevent the testator from drawing up the will or make him/her draw the will up by fraud or threat and the heirs who change the will or keep the will secret, will lose their heir status automatically.

(b) Turkish law does not allow for a distinction to be made between the succession of movables and that of immovables. It should be noted that from the moment of death, the deceased's property passes wholly and immediately to his/her heirs (successors), without the need for official intervention or for any particular form of consent or seisin; this is the case even if the heirs do not realize that the deceased's property has been passed on to them.

4. Freedom of Testation

(a) Freedom of testation is guaranteed by Turkish law. There are, however, certain portions of the members of the deceased's family's inheritance shares that are protected. This is called 'Compulsory Share Portion'. According to the *Civil Law*, the compulsory share portions are as follows:

- half of the inheritance for descendants;
- one-fourth of the inheritance for parents;
- one-eighth of the inheritance for brothers and sisters;
- the surviving spouse will succeed to all of his/her portion if she/he is heir with descendants and with the deceased parents' order and half of his/her portion if he/she is heir with other heirs.

In the new Draft Civil Code, the compulsory share-portions have been decreased to half of their inheritance portion for descendants, one-fourth of their inheritance portion for parents, one-eighth of their inheritance portion for brothers/sisters. For the surviving spouse, the compulsory share-portion is the whole of his/her inheritance portion if she/he is heir with the descendants or parents of testator. In other cases it is reduced to three-fourth of his/her inheritance portion. In the draft, due to this general reduction, an extra compulsory share-portion reduction is not arranged for the wills which are drawn up for appropriating the properties to the public interest.

The age of the testator's children or their being illegitimate (if the illegitimate children are duly admitted by the testator or if in a court case it is held that they are the children of the testator) does not make any difference. Adopted children have the same compulsory share-portion as the other children.

After the succession the descendants whose compulsory share-portions are violated, may bring a court action against the inheriting person to claim his or her compulsory share-portion. Such court action may not be filed if the testator is still alive.

(b) *i.* Inheritance contracts that the testator draws up when he/she is alive, must be drawn up before the judge or notary public in an official form and executed by two witnesses.

Parties can cancel the inheritance contract by a written agreement.

The testator can abolish the contract if the heir or will beneficiary does something, which makes him/her debarred from inheriting.

Should the duties, which have been undertaken in the contract, not be performed by one of the parties, the innocent party can revoke the contract.

Should the appointed heir or will beneficiary of inheritance contract die before the testator, the contract becomes automatically invalid. In this case, if the testator has done the contract for a consideration, he/she is only liable to return what was left from such consideration to the heirs of the beneficiary.

If an 'Inheritance Contract' provides for the passing of the properties to an appointed heir, after the succession takes place, the legal heir can bring an action against said person and claim his/her compulsory share-portion.

ii. Pursuant to Turkish law, it is not possible to provide for a condition in the contract to the effect that the appointed heir or will beneficiary should pass the properties to third parties. However it is possible to provide that, if the appointed heir or will beneficiary has lost his/her status as an heir when the succession takes place, third parties will succeed to the properties instead of him/her and it is also possible to stipulate that the appointed heir or will beneficiary must assign the property to third parties after a certain period of time.

5. Maintenance

Pursuant to Article 585 of the Turkish Civil Code, if the heirs have been living with the deceased, the same life conditions must be ensured for one month after the succession takes place. Heirs who do not live with the testator or a person, who is not an heir but lives with the testator, does not have this right. Apart from this, there is no other special provision in relation to taking care of parents, spouses or children. The compulsory share-portion is deemed to be sufficient for these people.

6. Community Property Between Husband and Wife

(a)–(b) In Turkey, the legal property regime is 'separation of properties' and there is no special provision regarding succession of a co-ownership between spouses. Therefore, there is no exception to the general rule (*see* however 3(a)(v) *above*).

7. Gifts (*Inter Vivos*)

(a) If the deceased donated properties in breach of the *above-mentioned* compulsory share-portion, under certain conditions, the heirs who have compulsory share-portion have the right to claim it back. For taking the properties back, it is not important that these properties were donated to heirs or others. If this donation has been done for the benefit of the other heirs, the amount, which he/she should give back, will be reduced from his/her portion. This type of court case is referred to as a 'reduction case'.

(b) The transactions that are in breach of a compulsory share-portion made by the testator when he/she is alive will be reduced by the *below-mentioned* rules:

- donations, which were done one year before the succession takes place, shall be returned in the amount by which it exceeds the compulsory share-portion;
- the donations, which were done before the *above* period, can be cancelled only if it is proved that deceased has done it in order to debar the heirs from the will;
- the amount claimed can only be that exceeding the compulsory share-portion;
- the expenses, which the deceased made for the descendants in order to establish a business, marriage or release the debt, can be taken back even if it does not breach the compulsory share-portion;
- the right to file a reduction case shall be time-barred one year after the date that the succession takes place and the heirs are aware of this event, and in any case five years after the date of succession.

8. Capacity

(a) A person who is over fifteen years old and has mental capacity may draw up a valid will. One should be over eighteen years old in order to make an Inheritance

Contract. Marital status is not relevant for the capacity to draw up an Inheritance Contract or will.

(b) For official wills, witnesses should be over eighteen years old and have the ability to read and write. The witnesses should not be the beneficiary, the parents or brothers, sisters or their spouse or descendants of the deceased.

(c) A will beneficiary can be either a real person or an entity. Communities, which are not legal entities cannot be will beneficiaries. Age or mental capacity is not relevant. A fetus can be a will beneficiary if she/he lives.

9. Authority (Court, Notarial or Other)

Death is established by way of a certificate drawn up by a registrar or, when a person vanishes, by way of a court judgment allowing for the devolution of his/her assets.

Turkish courts provide for the issuing of an official certificate referred to as the 'Certificate of Inheritance' which includes information as to the identity of the heirs but none as to the size of inheritance. This certificate is issued by the Probate Court and allows third parties to obtain property from the heirs in good faith. It does not, however, carry the weight of final judgment. Any of the heirs of the deceased may apply to the Probate Court to obtain the certificate.

In specific cases, it may be sufficient to present the will by way of public instrument or inheritance contract after the devolution of the deceased's property to establish an heir's status; this may be possible, for example, as regards the land registry index, banks and insurance companies.

10. Invalidity of Will

(a) The validity of the will is effected in the following situations:

- if it is not drawn up in accordance with the required form;
- if the deceased does not have the capacity to draw it up;
- if it is drawn up by the effect of an error, fraud or threat;
- if the will has provisions that are in breach of the law and contrary to public morality.

(b) The will does not become invalid automatically in order to ensure the final intensions of the deceased. A court action for the nullity of the will must be filed within one year starting from the date of the succession and after knowledge of the invalidity reason and in any case five years after the succession takes place. However if the will beneficiary has bad faith, the right to bring court action for the nullity of the will shall expire after thirty years. However, even if the right to claim nullity is time-barred, it can be used as a defense in cases where a claim is brought by the beneficiary.

International Succession

11. Simultaneous Death

(a) Under Turkish law, the deaths of the persons that may be heirs to one another are considered to be simultaneous if the one that has passed away earlier cannot be determined. Persons that have died in the same time cannot be heirs to one another. This principle is called as the 'presumption of simultaneous death'.

12. Estate Taxes

The rates of Inheritance Tax in Turkey are as follows:

for the first 25,000,000,000 TL	1 per cent;
for the following 53,000,000,000 TL	3 per cent;
for the following 107,000,000,000 TL	5 per cent;
for the following 215,000,000,000 TL	7 per cent;
for the part which is over 400,000,000,000 TL	10 per cent.

13. Administration of Estates

(a) Given the fact that in accordance with Turkish law the deceased's property passes immediately and directly at the time of death to the heirs without the intervention of state authorities, there is normally no need for an administrator.

If there are several heirs, the administration of the succession is carried out by all of them. Each joint heir is bound as regards the others to comply with measures, which will allow for an orderly and lawful administration; each heir can also take measures deemed necessary to protect and preserve the property without having to obtain the agreement of the others.

Otherwise each of the joint heirs asks for the division of the property which has devolved, except in special cases.

Should the heirs not reach an agreement as to how the estate be administrated, the court shall appoint an administrator upon the application of any of them. Should the heirs not agree amongst themselves as to the division of the estate, the administration cannot execute the division itself. In this case, the court shall divide the estate upon the application of any of the heirs.

(b) An account of the administration is not necessary for the transfer and the division of the inheritance. The formal registration is necessary in the *above-mentioned* cases, for acceptation of the inheritance by heirs to be written in an account book and for an official liquidation of the estate.

(c) The heirs are competent for the partition of succession and for the administration of estate and there is no state control over it. However, the control is exercised by the court as a condition of the acceptance of the succession by heirs as written in an account book and as a condition of an official liquidation of estate.

618

(d) The heirs, or their legal representatives in cases of incapacity, have such a right, in accordance with the principles laid down by the Turkish Civil Code, as regards the co-ownership of the succession. When a testamentary administrator is appointed, he represents the succession. He can only invoke all rights given to him in connection with the administration of the devolution of the deceased's property at law.

(e) The heirs arc the owners of the property of the deceased as soon as he dies and they take possession directly, though they must establish their rights to the satisfaction of certain third parties. A distinction must be made as regards persons entitled only to a particular legacy, who must obtain their legacy from the heirs.

Heirs can only renounce the succession if they have not previously accepted it, even tacitly. The right of renunciation can only be exercised within a six-week period. This period is extended to six months if the deceased was last domiciled abroad or if the heir himself was residing abroad once the time period had started to run. If the debt of the succession is more than its value; it is considered that the heirs renounced the succession unless the opposite is proved.

(f) In principle the creditors are paid by the heirs, by way of charge upon the property of the deceased which has passed or the heirs' own property if they have accepted the succession. If the creditors had begun proceedings to recover a debt from the deceased whilst the latter had been alive, such proceedings will be suspended until such time as the heirs can be substituted (if they have accepted the succession). The heirs can request that judgment be made against them subject to the limitation of their liabilities. If the heirs renounce the succession, they do not have to pay anything to the creditors. If the heirs require an official liquidation of estate, first the property of the deceased is sold and the creditors are paid and if something is left over, it is shared by the heirs. If there is nothing left over, the heirs are not responsible to the creditors who have also the right on the succession. If the heirs announce that they will accept the succession according to an account book, the creditors who register their credit in an account book that is kept by the court in the period announced, can require from the heirs to fulfil their obligation. If the creditors do not register their debt in the period announced by the court and if there is no culpability, the creditors can only require from the heirs to fulfill their obligation that is limited by the succession. Heirs have joint liability for the debts for five years that begin with the liquidation of the inheritance. The debts become mature after the liquidation of the inheritance, beginning with the maturity. But, after he recognizes the liquidation that determinates which debt belongs to which heirs, he can proceed only against those who are responsible for the debts in accordance with the liquidation conditions pursuant to Article 616 of the Turkish Civil Code.

(g) Until the inheritance has been divided, each of the heirs can dispose of his share in it but is not allowed to dispose of specific property forming part of it. The heirs can only dispose of specific property when acting jointly. Similarly, a debtor cannot settle his account as regards the succession with the repayment of a debt owed only to one of the heirs.

International Succession

Division cannot be carried out as long as the shares of each of the heirs remain uncertain due to the expected birth of an heir.

The obligations relating to the succession must be dealt with first. In order to discharge those obligations, the property, which is to pass, should be converted into cash insofar as this is necessary. The excess remaining after the discharge of such obligations will go to the heirs in accordance with the share each is to take. Writings concerning relations between the deceased, his family or the succession in its entirety remain common property.

If, as often happens, a testamentary administrator has been appointed by the deceased, he is entrusted with the division upon succession as between the heirs if there is more than one heir. He must however, solicit the views of the heirs as to his proposals before dividing the property.

14. Domicile/Nationality

(a) The nationality of the deceased and his domicile are only significant in relation to the application of provisions on the conflict of laws, which will be examined below.

(b) Even given this improbable scenario, where the deceased has no assets, the court would have jurisdiction if the deceased was a Turkish national.

SECTION B – APPLICABLE LAW/PROCEDURE WHERE FOREIGN ELEMENT/S ARE INVOLVED

1. Jurisdiction

(a) The court will deem itself to have jurisdiction if:

- Turkish inheritance law is applicable (even only partially);
- there are assets (movables or immovables) on Turkish territory;
- an international convention confers such jurisdiction (Consular Treaty between Turkey and Germany).

(b) There is no distinction between movable and immovable property for determining the competent court. As shall be explained below, only the application of the law can be changed. However, if there is a conflict in determining the patrimonies of the property because of the inheritance or determining the possession, the competent court is determined by taking into account the location of the immovable as per Article 13 of Turkish Procedural Code.

(c) According to Article 30 of the Turkish Conflict of Law Rules, the court of the place of the last domicile in Turkey shall have jurisdiction in cases regarding inheritance matters. If the last domicile of the deceased is abroad, the court of the place where the estates are located has jurisdiction.

2. Applicable Law

Pursuant to Article 22 of the Turkish Conflict of Law Rules, Turkish Courts apply the national law of the deceased when there is a conflict caused by *Inheritance Law*. The law in force in the domicile of the deceased is applied only if the deceased is a citizen of the country in which he resided. However, the Turkish law is applied in respect of immovable property that is located in Turkey.

The conditions regarding the acquisition and the partition of succession are governed by the law of the country where the succession takes place. The succession without heirs located in Turkey shall be inherited by the State.

3. Foreign Succession/Inheritance Orders

(a) A foreign judicial decision is not usually directly enforceable in Turkey unless a Turkish execution order is obtained (Articles 34, 35, 36, 37, 38, 39, 40, 41 of Turkish Conflict of Law Rules). The recognition of a judicial act in non-contentious proceedings follows the same rules as those applicable to foreign judgments. Proof of entitlement to inheritance from a foreign country does not automatically bind a Turkish court but may be recognized by it (Article 42 of Turkish Conflict of Law Rules).

(b) Turkish Courts cannot recognize *ex parte* judgments. Instead, application must be made to the Turkish court to uphold the decision. Therefore, Turkish courts cannot recognize a determination of heirship obtained as a result of *ex parte* proceedings and heirs will have to apply to the Turkish Court in order to prove a determination of heirship.

(c) For the recognition of a foreign court order, an application must be made to the Turkish Courts as per the procedure provided in Articles 36 and 37 of the Turkish Conflict of Laws Rules (MÖHUK). The following documents should accompany the application: the original and certified translation of the judgment finalized in accordance with the national law of the relevant foreign court, the original and certified translation of a document issued by the relevant authorities of the foreign state declaring that the judgment has been finalized in accordance with that national law.

4. Two or More Succession or Probate Orders

There is no specific rule that regulates a procedure in case there are several demands which are in contradiction with one another. In such cases, the Turkish court considers the foreign court decisions pursuant to the Turkish Conflict of Law Rules mentioned *above*.

If decisions on the same subject of litigation that are given by the courts of the same country are in contradiction with one another, none of them is capable of recognition or execution. In such cases, a new award that removes the contradiction has to be delivered.

If the reason of the contradictory awards is the involvement of different jurisdictions, then the deceased's law will be used as a main law.

5. Assets

Even if there is no property in the place of the Court, which will tender the decision, the Court shall be entitled to judge in accordance with Article 30 of the Conflict of Law Rules if the court is located in the last residence of the deceased. Furthermore, in accordance with Article 27/1, Conflict of Law Rules may be applied to the conflict even if the deceased does not have any property in the country of his nationality.

6. Expert Evidence

(a) In *Turkish Inheritance Law*, documentation proving the inheritance is not a precondition to file a court action. But, pursuant to Article 2/2 Conflict of Law Rules, the judge can seek help from the parties to demonstrate the foreign authoritative law. If the relevant articles in the foreign law cannot be determined, Turkish law will be applied pursuant.

(b) An affidavit with or without judicial confirmation is not excluded as a source of information to be used by the judge as to the contents of foreign law.

7. Unity of Succession

Turkish law admits the unity of succession, whether in domestic law or private international law.

8. Formalities

The law of the foreign country where the will has been drawn up applies to the procedural issues in relation to a will and Turkish courts gives effect to the wills drawn up in accordance with that law.

9. Legislation

The *1961 Hague Convention on the Conflicts of Laws Relating to the Form of Testamentary Dispositions* entered into force in Turkey on 17 January 1983.

10. Wills

(a) The formalities of the will are governed, in accordance with the *1961 Hague Convention in the Conflicts of Laws Relating to the form of Testamentary Dispositions* between the citizens of the states. But the rules of this convention have not been incorporated into Turkish domestic law yet.

(b) As mentioned *above*, the meaning of the interpretation of the testamentary disposition and the meanings of expressions in the text follow the deceased's national law.

(c) The position and the rights of the heir in testamentary dispositions follow the national law of the testator. Disputes concerning the real estate in Turkey follow Turkish law.

(d) The capacity of succeeding follows the national law of the deceased. Turkish law is applicable in respect of real estate located in Turkey.

(e) Testament competency depends on the national law of the testator at the time the testament was made.

(f) The factual and procedural legal sufficiency of the testament depends on the national law of the deceased.

(g) Not applicable.

(h) The replacement, cancellation and validity of the testament follow the deceased's national law or the law of the place where the testament is made.

(i) Turkish Law is applied in respect of the real estate located in Turkey. The deceased's national law is valid for all the other movable and real estates. Agreements to the contrary shall not be of effect.

11. Domicile/Nationality

(a) The deceased's domicile does not have any effect on the answers of the questions mentioned *above* in accordance with the Turkish Conflict of Law Rules.
   As aforementioned, the deceased's domicile and nationality can be important in relation to the form of the testament.

(b) The effects of domicile and nationality are as explained *above*.

(c) In cases when domicile and nationality are uncertain, the last domicile and nationality is taken into account. In Turkish law, only cooperatives can exceptionally have more than one domicile. In such cases, only one of them can be regarded as the domicile.

International Succession

12. Taxation

There are no differences under Turkish law between the taxation of a non-resident deceased/heir as opposed to that of a local deceased/heir.

United States – New York

Prepared by: James Ripley WESTMORELAND
Breed & Associates

Address: 551 5th Avenue, Suite 3500
New York, NY 10017
United States
Tel.:   +1 212 687 6767
Fax: +1 212 687 1197

1. Type of System

In the US there is no federal law regarding wills and inheritance generally. Each of the fifty states has its own laws based on a combination of common law and statutory law. New York State law is based primarily on the English common law with legislative additions and modifications.

Taxation of estates is at both the state and federal level as will be further discussed below.

2. Wills

(a) Each state has its own rules regarding the making of a valid will. In most cases these rules are based on the common law and are, therefore, very similar. The New York State rules are based on the common law and typify the requirements.

To be valid a will must be:

– in writing; and
– signed at the end by the testator who is at least eighteen years old and possessed of sufficient competency, and whose signature was witnessed by at least two witnesses, and who requests and obtains the signatures and addresses of the witnesses (The absence of addresses alone would not, however, invalidate the will).

– *Exceptions to the Formality Rules*

Noncupative (or unwritten wills) are valid in New York State when:

625

– the person making the will is a mariner at sea, or in the armed forces and engaged in armed conflict, or is a person accompanying an armed force engaged in conflict; and
– the provisions of the will are clearly established by at least two witnesses.

In New York State, holographic (or handwritten) wills not executed with formalities are valid when:

– the person making the will is a mariner at sea, or in the armed forces and engaged in armed conflict, or is a person accompanying an armed force engaged in conflict.

These two exceptions to the formal requirements of a will have time limits as regards their validity.

New York State has no provision for death bed wills, however, other states may allow them.

– *Signing Before a Notary, 'Self Proving Wills'*:

Many states, including New York State, allow for a 'self proving' will where the witnesses make and sign an affidavit stating that the will was properly executed and noting the details of such proper execution. The affidavit is signed by the witnesses before a notary public who acknowledges their signatures. (*Note*: a notary public in the US is not the same as a *notaire* in Europe).

(b) *i.* A will and any codicils may be revoked by the testator by:

– creating a new instrument of a later date; or
– physically canceling or destroying the will; or
– revoking the will in writing with the formalities necessary to create a will.

A will may not be partially revoked by destruction.
ii. Marriage will create a right of election for the surviving spouse under which the surviving spouse may elect to take a statutory share based on a complex formula in lieu of the provisions made under the will. Otherwise, marriage does not revoke a will made prior to marriage.
iii. A will may be revived if the later will is shown to have been fraudulently made or made under duress.

Voluntary Revival: Under New York State law, revocation or alteration of a later will will not of itself revive a prior will. A prior will, if properly executed in the first place, may be revived through:

– a codicil, properly executed with the formalities required for a will, which incorporates by reference to the prior will or one or more of its provisions;
– a written document, executed with the formalities required for a will, which declares the revival of a prior will or one or more of its provisions;

- a 'republication' of a prior will by declaring to the original witnesses that the prior will represents the testator's Last Will and Testament and having such witnesses sign and date the prior will at the end of such will;
- a republication of a prior will by having the prior will re-executed with the formalities required for a will.

3. Intestacy

(a) Intestacy is statutory. The common intestate circumstances are as follows:

– *Spouse Survives*:
  - spouse only – spouse inherits all;
  - spouse and issue – spouse takes first US$50,000 and 50 per cent of residue, balance to issue by representation.

The term 'representation' is defined as a disposition of property to persons who take from a deceased ancestor such that the property that passes is divided into as many equal shares as there are:

- surviving children or 'issue' in the nearest generation to the deceased ancestor which contains one or more surviving issue; and
- deceased issue in the same generation who left surviving issue.

Each surviving member in the nearest generation is allocated one share. The remaining shares (from any deceased issue) are combined, the resulting figure is then divided by the number of surviving children of all the deceased issue. The final figure is the share of each surviving child of deceased issue.

For example, a deceased has two living brothers and two deceased brothers in an estate worth US$100. The living brothers each get one share or US$25 each. The deceased brothers had five surviving children among them. The two shares or US$50 allocable to the deceased brothers are divided by five. The surviving children of the deceased brothers receive US$10.

Unless otherwise stated in the will, descendants include:

- adopted children and their children;
- children conceived before but born after death; and
- non-marital children under certain circumstances.

– *No Spouse, No Issue*:

In a situation where there is no spouse or issue, the entire estate devolves upon the surviving parent(s), and where there are no parents, the entire estate devolves upon the issue of the parents by way of representation.

The statute treats relatives of the half blood as though they were relatives of the whole blood.

627

International Succession

(b) As regards intestacy in New York State, a distributee's intestate share will be his statutory share of both immovable and movable items. In order to transfer an interest in real estate, an administrator must be appointed by the court who will have the authority to sign a deed transferring the real estate into the name of the distributee.

4. Freedom of Testation

(a) Other than the spousal right of election, there are no compulsory shares for any inheritance class. There are laws in New York State which try to offer protection from potential unforeseen circumstances, e.g., children born after the execution of a will.

(b) A contract of inheritance would be binding provided it were otherwise binding as regards the laws of contract. Important elements of contract would be whether the persons making the contract had proper capacity and whether there was adequate consideration.

5. Maintenance

Maintenance cannot be claimed from an estate. A spouse has a right of election which may supersede the provisions of a will. In lieu of the will, the spouse may elect to take US$50,000 or one-third of the net estate. The net estate does not include funeral and administration expenses but, under a complex statutory formula, includes all kinds of estate assets, testamentary and non-testamentary.

Maintenance for Minors: There are no provisions under New York State law regarding a child's ability to claim maintenance from an estate.

6. Community Property Between Husband and Wife

New York State is not a community property state. There is statutory law, however, that lists property that becomes vested in the surviving spouse or children under twenty-one (and not the estate). This includes, within certain limits, household items, a car, cash up to an amount of US$15,000 subject, however, to the precedence of the funeral bill, personal property, and animals.

The concept of community property does not exist in the eastern portion of the United States, however, it is the general rule in the Western states, including California.

7. Gifts (*Inter Vivos*)

(a) Gifts are not set off against an inheritance. A gift over US$10,000 to an individual or entity in any one year is subject to federal and state gift taxes which have the same rate structure as estate taxes (*see below*). A married couple may combine their gifts thereby allowing an annual tax free gift to an individual or entity of US$20,000. There is no limit on the number of US$10,000 (US$20,000 per married couple) tax free gifts one may give in a single year, so long as each gift is to a different person or entity.

8. Capacity

(a) The testator must be eighteen years of age and there are no requirements regarding marital status. The general rule regarding a testator's soundness of mind is that the testator, at the time of execution, know in a general way what property he owns, the persons who are the natural objects of his bounty, and what his will provides.

(b) A witness should be someone competent to testify as to the signing of the will and the state of mind of the testator. Otherwise, here are the legal restrictions regarding witnesses:

– a beneficiary may act as a witness to a will, however, unless there are two non-beneficiary witnesses, any disposition or appointment in the will will be void as to that witness. Such beneficiary/witness may still receive an intestate share (if applicable) up to the amount he would have otherwise received under the will;
– an attorney and/or executor may act as a witness to a will. An attorney may also act as executor, however, the attorney must provide a written disclosure to the testator, signed by the testator, in which the testator acknowledges that he understands that the attorney may receive an executor's commission as well as legal fees for services to the estate.

(c) A guardian may need to be appointed if a beneficiary is a child or mentally or physically incapacitated. If a beneficiary's status is the result of some illegal activity, the beneficiary may not take. Otherwise, there are no restrictions regarding the capacity of a beneficiary.
Unborn beneficiaries: Children conceived before but born alive after the death of the testator, will take under the instrument. The same will apply if there is no will.

9. Authority (Court, Notarial or Other)

Letters testamentary are granted by the Surrogate's Court of the county in which jurisdiction is available.
Jurisdiction of the Surrogate's Court: Every Surrogate's Court in New York State has jurisdiction over the estate of a New York State domiciliary. The proper 'venue' of the court is the county of the deceased's domicile at the time of his death. The petition to the Surrogate's Court for letters of administration, or letters testamentary, requires the petitioner (usually the executor under a will or, in an administration proceeding, a close relative) to state specific and detailed information regarding the deceased. This information is made under oath.

International Succession

Generally in the US, domicile is the key to personal jurisdiction and, in this case, jurisdiction over an estate of a deceased. Location of property in the state of domicile will allow *in rem* jurisdiction, which is a limited form of jurisdiction. Place of death may, without other significant contact to the jurisdiction, be of no consequence.

10. Invalidity of Will

(a)–(b) A will may be deemed invalid if the statutory formalities are not followed either on the face of the will (number of witnesses, signature, etc.) or shown not to have been followed (witnesses did not witness signature, testator did not have testamentary capacity). Divorce will make invalid the portions of the will relating to the former spouse. Fraud, duress, and undue influence may be proven by a person objecting to the probate of a will in the Surrogate's Court. Generally, a will is void if the statutory formalities are not followed, otherwise, the will may be selectively voidable by the Surrogate's Court based on facts and other proof.

11. Simultaneous Death

(a)–(b) The general rule in New York State is that if a simultaneous death occurs it is presumed that each survived the other. A will may, however, through a 'common disaster' clause create the presumption as to the survivor.

12. Estate Taxes

(a) Yes, they exist.

(b) Federal tax is based on the worldwide value of the estate at the date of death. The term property includes movables. In addition there are state taxes which are based on the residency of the deceased and the kind of property owned by the decedent in the subject state. New York State, for example, will tax a non-resident's estate on real property located in New York State.

A definition of the assets taxable in the estate is broad. The taxable estate includes jointly held property, the value of an insurance policy, and generally any property over which the deceased had control at the time of his death. The taxable estate is reduced by several different deductions, including costs to administer the estate, funeral costs, state estate taxes paid (for the federal estate tax only), charitable deductions and, the most important, the marital deduction for inheritance going directly to the deceased's spouse. Federal estate taxation is on transition and it would be advisable to check the most recent law before planning an estate.

13. Administration of Estates

(a) The executor (when there is a will) or the administrator (when there is no will) must be appointed by the Surrogate's Court. An heir may petition the court for either position. In the case of intestacy, it is almost always heirs or 'distributees' who receive letters, although a person with an interest in the estate, a creditor for example, may petition for letters.

(b) Reports may be required at various stages of an estate's administration. The original probate petition to the court is a form of report which lists several estate items. The federal and state tax returns report taxable estate assets. An accounting proceeding may be required which will report all estate activity.

(c) The Surrogate's Court generally leaves estate matters in the hands of the attorney or other fiduciaries handling the estate. The court always has the power to intervene and supervise.

(d) Various persons have the right to query and object in the context of the probate or other court proceeding involving an estate. Such persons include relatives or 'distributees', named beneficiaries and executors, creditors, in some cases persons named in prior wills, the Attorney General where charities are involved, and the state tax commission.

(e) Assets are distributed to beneficiaries of the will and distributees of an intestate estate by the duly appointed executor or administrator.

(f) The executor or administrator may pay creditors from estate assets and may be personally liable for such payments in some circumstances.

(g) If a will is submitted for probate without an executor appointed or able to serve, the court may appoint an executor.

It is essential that an executor be appointed to manage an estate. Generally, if no executor is appointed under a will, a relative or creditor may petition the court to become appointed. If no one comes forward, the office of the Public Administrator may petition the court and through this county office, a politically connected lawyer will become executor or administrator.

14. Domicile/Nationality

(a) A will is valid in New York State and the US if it is valid in the jurisdiction in which it was executed. Generally, the main factor regarding jurisdiction for court and taxation issues is domicile at the date of death. Domicile will have an impact on which court has venue or jurisdiction over a matter. 'Domicile' is a question of fact arrived at through a legal analysis of several common sense factors given weight within the context of the deceased's life. There have been many cases in which one state claims the deceased to be domiciled in their state and another state makes the same claim – both seeking the tax benefits of having the estate in their state.

Federal taxation for US citizens applies no matter where they are domiciled. Non-citizens domiciled in the US will be subject to taxation on US assets. State taxes apply to persons domiciled in the state, citizen or non-citizen. A non-resident may be taxed on real estate or other tangible property located in New York State.

(b) A court could allow a deceased's estate to be 'domiciled' in the state, if the factual circumstances merited it.

SECTION B – APPLICABLE LAW/PROCEDURE WHERE FOREIGN ELEMENT/S ARE INVOLVED

1. Jurisdiction

(a) The Surrogate's Court jurisdiction covers all matters relating to a deceased and is broad. Generally jurisdiction is invoked if the deceased was domiciled in the state. Assets in the state provide the Surrogate's Court with 'subject matter jurisdiction', which is called *in rem* jurisdiction.

(b) *In rem* jurisdiction may be based on a movable or immovable object.

(c) The 'venue' of a court is based on a person's county of domicile, however, every Surrogate's Court in the state has jurisdiction over the estate of a New York State domiciliary.

2. Applicable Law

Jurisdiction and venue are based on domicile of the deceased or location of the object in question.

When a deceased is domiciled in a state, that state's laws apply to his estate, i.e., to how persons inherit his property, to taxes, to appointment of executors, etc. If the estate owns property outside of the domicile state, the court in which such property is located may have jurisdiction over the property, but not necessarily the estate.

In order to bring property located outside of deceased's domicile into an estate for distribution to beneficiaries, the executor of an estate may be required to bring a separate proceeding in the state in which the property is located. Often, this separate proceeding, called 'ancillary probate', is necessary when the asset in question is real estate, although there may be cases in which tangible personal property requires a separate proceeding.

As a practical matter, an executor seeking to distribute assets of a deceased located outside of the deceased's domicile needs to follow the rules of that state in order to liquidate or release assets. For real estate, the person signing a new deed to a buyer will need to be someone that the buyer and title company know has transfer authority. The court document from New York State authorizing the executor to act may not be enough for the buyer of Pennsylvania real estate; the buyer and his title company may require a court document from Pennsylvania authorizing this executor to transfer the property. Thus you have ancillary probate. If the property is a bank account in a non-national bank, the institution in the non-domicile jurisdiction may require more than New York State letters of administration before releasing the funds to a New York State executor. In the extreme they would require ancillary letters.

As regards real estate, given a state's interest in real estate located within its borders, the laws applied may go to the validity of the disposition of the property itself. The non-domicile state's jurisdiction will, however, be based on and limited to this property (*in rem* jurisdiction). If there are issues which require application of other laws, unrelated to real estate, then the non-domicile state court will generally apply the laws of the state of the deceased's domicile.

The discussion of which laws apply in such circumstances forms a body of law called 'Conflicts of Law'. When such issues arise, an analysis is made based on several factors and the applicable law is applied accordingly. Conflicts of law issues often arise in cases in which a federal court has jurisdiction over matters involving matters between states.

As regards a disposition of real property, New York State looks to the law of the jurisdiction where the real property is located. The laws of such place shall determine the validity of the disposition under the will (both formally and intrinsically), its interpretation, effect, revocation, alteration and, absent a will, intestate distribution of the property being disposed.

For personal property, the law of deceased's domicile at death will determine.

As regards 'venue', this term applies to which court in a jurisdiction should handle the matter. In New York State every Surrogate's Court has jurisdiction over every New York State deceased's estate. But the proper court to bring any proceeding would be in the county in which the deceased died. This county court would be the proper 'venue'.

3. Foreign Succession/Inheritance Orders

(a) The New York State system will respect the foreign appointed fiduciary who must apply for 'ancillary letters' in order to qualify as an ancillary executor and have authority over assets located in the state. Generally, New York State requires that an original will 'proceeding' take place in the jurisdiction of domicile. As to what defines a proceeding, this would be for the court to determine.

It should be noted that the Surrogate's Court does not have jurisdiction over the estates of non-domiciliaries, unless such non-domiciliary estate leaves property in the state or a has a cause of action in the state. If there is property in the state, it is possible that the Surrogate's Court in the county where the property or action is located would grant original letters. Such court may, however, require a US citizen or institution to act as petitioner.

(b) In order for a New York State institution to release funds, change registration, etc., it may require ancillary letters or original letters and it is unlikely that a non-US foreign order would be accepted.

(c) To obtain ancillary letters, the person seeking same must petition the court in a matter very similar to a person seeking original letters.

International Succession

4. Two or More Succession or Probate Orders

(a) Only the local original or ancillary letters will be accepted, although foreign orders could be relevant from an evidentiary or informational viewpoint.

5. Assets

As noted *above*, the Surrogate's Court in New York State has broad discretion regarding its exercise of jurisdiction over an estate. The exercise of jurisdiction for all US courts is constitutionally based on what are called 'minimum contacts' between the locale in which jurisdiction is sought and the person or entity subject to jurisdiction. Minimum contacts may include intangible concepts such as the existence of a right to a lawsuit or the conducting of business in the jurisdiction in question. Without some kind of minimum contact jurisdiction may not be exercised.

6. Expert Evidence

(a) No, the ancillary probate petition will rely primarily on the foreign order and will require, in most cases, no further evidence.

(b) Should such further evidence be necessary, it may be submitted by way of affidavit.

7. Unity of Succession

(a) The principle does not apply.

8. Formalities

A will valid in the jurisdiction where executed is valid in New York State and the US.

9. Legislation

(a) Not the law in New York State but may be persuasive as authority in cases where New York State law is unclear.

(b) Not the law in New York State but may be persuasive as authority in cases where New York State law is unclear.

10. Wills

(a) A will valid in the jurisdiction where executed is valid in New York State and the US.

New York State has broad rules regarding the validity of wills. A will is valid if it is in writing, signed by the testator in accordance with the local law of:

– New York State; or
– the jurisdiction in which the will was executed, at the time of execution; or
– the jurisdiction in which the testator was domiciled, either at the time of execution or death.

Accordingly, there is considerable room to validate a will, even if the 'intrinsic validity', relating to the substantive law regarding dispositions, is invalid in one of the jurisdictions but not another. New York State also will allow a non-domiciliary's choice of New York State law (as stated in his will) to govern such person's wishes as regards property located in New York State. This could, for example, avoid a forced heirship situation (which may otherwise apply in Spain for example) as regards the New York State property disposed of under the will.

In New York State, validity also turns on the kind of property being disposed of under the will. The law of the land in which real property is located will determine the validity of a disposition of real property. As regards dispositions of personal property, New York State looks to the law of the place the deceased was domiciled at death.

Validity of a will may require a conflicts of law analysis based on the facts of the case.

(b) The New York State court would look to the law of the place where the will was executed regarding construction and interpretation.

(c) Generally, the rights of beneficiaries would be respected unless there was some policy matter that argued against them.

(d) A will valid in the jurisdiction where executed is valid in New York State and the US.

(e) A will valid in the jurisdiction where executed is valid in New York State and the US.

(f) A will valid in the jurisdiction where executed is valid in New York State and the US.

(g) A will valid in the jurisdiction where executed is valid in New York State and the US.

(h) A will valid in the jurisdiction where executed is valid in New York State and the US.

International Succession

(i) A will valid in the jurisdiction where executed is valid in New York State and the US.

11. Domicile/Nationality

(a) The domicile at the time of making the will is not relevant. As long as the will was made in accordance with the laws of the place in which it was made, it will be deemed a valid will in the US.

Domicile at the time of death determines jurisdiction, venue, application of state and federal laws. In situations where a deceased has property and residences all over the world such that domicile is unclear, 'domicile' at time of death would be one of many factors in determining domicile and which laws apply to such person and his estate. If different jurisdictions seek to call this person their own, for tax or other reasons, then whatever courts are involved would weigh all the factors, including where the person resided at time of death, in doing a 'conflicts of law' analysis. Nationality would be an important factor in such an analysis.

(b) Under the laws of New York State and the US generally, a person can leave his estate to anyone he wishes (subject to a right of election for the surviving spouse and the laws of the eight community property states[1]) and the beneficiaries' domicile is not an issue. As discussed *above*, however, the law of the jurisdiction in which real estate is located may have an impact on both the form and substance of the will. Although this factor may have an impact on dispositions of real estate outside the US, it is unlikely that any state's laws would have a substantive impact on a proper disposition of US real estate.

(c) As domicile is such a critical factor, a ruling would necessarily be made. A person can have many residences but only one domicile.

12. Taxation

Both a US resident citizen and US non-resident citizen are subject to the full US estate tax. To avoid double taxation, there are credits available for foreign estate or inheritance taxes paid. As regards state tax, a citizen of one state owning property whether movable or immovable in another state may be subject to estate taxation in that state.

The New York State estate tax law requires non-residents and non-resident aliens to file tax returns on their world wide assets.

---

1. The eight community property states include California, Arizona, New Mexico, Washington, Idaho, Louisiana, Nevada, and Texas. Property acquired during a marriage automatically becomes community property and a deceased's will cannot alienate such property from the survivor. Community property does not include property owned prior to marriage, property that is obtained by gift or inheritance, and property that is agreed between the spouses to be separate property.

As a general rule, a non-resident alien is not subject to federal estate taxation.

New York estate taxes generally 'piggy back' on the federal estate tax by basing the New York estate tax on the amount of the state estate tax deduction on the federal estate tax return. As federal estate taxation is in transition, it would be advisable to check the most recent law before planning an estate.

United States – Pennsylvania

Prepared by: Betty IGDALSKI LAWLER, Esquire

Address: 110 Bala Avenue, Third Floor Bala Cynwyd, PA 19004
Tel.:   610 667 2878
Fax: 610 667 5167

SECTION A – BRIEF SURVEY OF THE LOCAL SYSTEM

1. Type of System

In the United States, there is no federal law governing wills and inheritance. Each state has its own laws. Pennsylvania state law is based on the Probate, Estates and Fiduciaries Code, which can be located in Title 20 of the Pennsylvania Consolidated Statutes. This codification was originally enacted in 1972 and has been amended by a series of acts. There is also precedential case law.

2. Wills

(a) Any person eighteen or more years of age who is of sound mind may make a will. Each will must be in writing and must be signed by the testator at the end thereof, subject to the following exceptions:
(1) any writing after the signature, whether written before or after its execution, shall not invalidate that which precedes the signature;
(2) if a testator is unable to sign his name, he may execute the will by making his mark in front of two witnesses who sign their names to the will in his presence; and
(3) if a testator is unable to sign his name or make a mark, he may declare the will to be valid in front of two witnesses who sign their names to the will in his presence.

A will in Pennsylvania does not need to be witnessed, subject to the *above-mentioned* exceptions. However, when a will is sought to be probated, two witnesses are required who can identify the testator's signature as valid.

Any competent person may be a witness. Any interest the person has in the estate does not disqualify him, but may affect credibility and weight.

An *attested will* may be made self-proved by the acknowledgment thereof by the testator and the affidavits of the witnesses, each made before an officer authorized

638

to administer oaths under the law or made before an attorney at law and certified to such an officer. However, a will signed by mark or by witnesses only cannot be made self-proved.

There are no statutory provisions for *holographic wills* (wills entirely in the handwriting of the testator) in Pennsylvania since subscribing or attesting witnesses are not required in Pennsylvania.

There are no statutory provisions *allowing nuncupative (oral) wills*. However, there is case law indicating that a nuncupative will may be valid as to personal property only if meeting certain prerequisites, including demonstrated intent of the testator to make a will during a last sickness in such extremity as to preclude a written will. A nuncupative will is ineffective as to realty.

There are no other provisions for death bed wills in Pennsylvania.

(b) *i*. A will, or any part thereof, may be amended by a subsequent will and/or by codicil, in writing; by some other writing declaring the same, executed and proved in the manner required of wills; or by being burnt, torn, canceled, obliterated or destroyed, with the intent and for the purpose of revocation, by the testator or by another person in his presence and at his express direction.

   ii. Wills may be modified upon the occurrence of certain circumstances:

   – if the testator is divorced from the bonds of matrimony after making a will, any provision in the will in favour of or relating to the divorced spouse is ineffective unless it appears from the will that the provision was intended to survive the divorce;
   – if the testator marries after making a will, a surviving spouse shall receive the share of the estate to which he would have been entitled had the testator died intestate, unless the will provides him a greater share or unless it appears from the will that the will was made in contemplation of marriage to the surviving spouse;
   – if the testator fails to provide in his will for children born or adopted after making the will, unless it appears from the will that the failure was intentional, such child shall receive out of the testator's property not passing to a surviving spouse, such share as he would have received if the testator had died unmarried and intestate, owning only that portion of his estate not passing to the surviving spouse.

   iii. If, after making a will, the testator executes a later will expressly or by necessary implication, revoking an earlier will, the revocation of the later will shall not revive the earlier will, unless the revocation is in writing and declares the intention of the testator to revive the earlier will, or unless, after such revocation, the earlier will shall be re-executed. Oral republication of itself is ineffective to revive a will.

3. Intestacy

(a) If there is a surviving spouse, intestate succession is statutory in the following order:

International Succession

(1) the surviving spouse inherits the entire estate if there is no surviving issue or parent of the deceased;

(2) if there is no surviving issue but a deceased is survived by parent(s), the first USD 30,000 plus one-half of the balance of the intestate estate goes to the surviving spouse;

(3) if there are surviving issue of the deceased, all of whom are also issue of the surviving spouse, the first USD 30,000 plus one-half of the balance of the intestate estate goes to the surviving spouse;

(4) if there are surviving issue, one or more of whom are not issue of the surviving spouse, one-half of the intestate estate goes to the surviving spouse.

If there is no surviving spouse, or there is a share of the estate to which the surviving spouse is not entitled, then the estate passes in the following order:

(1) to the issue of deceased including illegitimate children;

(2) if no surviving issue, to parent(s);

(3) if no parent(s), then to issue of each of the deceased's parents;

(4) if there is no issue of either the deceased's parents but at least one grandparent survives the deceased, then half to the paternal grandparent(s) or if both are dead, to the children of each of them and the children of the deceased children of each of them, and half to the maternal grandparent(s), or if both are dead, to the children of each of them and the children of the deceased children of each of them. If both the paternal grandparents and the maternal grandparents are dead leaving no child or grandchild to survive the deceased, the half which would have passed to the grandparent(s) or to their children and grandchildren shall be added to the half passing to the grandparent(s) or to their children and grandchildren on the other side;

(5) if no grandparent survives the deceased, then to the uncles and aunts and the children and grandchildren of deceased uncles and aunts of the deceased as provided under law for taking in different degrees;

(6) in default of all persons described *above*, to the Commonwealth of Pennsylvania.

Note: Pennsylvania law does provide for forfeiture of the intestate share of a surviving spouse who wilfully neglected, deserted or refused to support the deceased spouse for one or more years prior to the death of said spouse.

Pennsylvania law also provides for forfeiture of the intestate share of a parent who wilfully neglected or failed to support a minor or dependent child for one or more years prior to the death of said child.

Any person who participates, either as a principal or as an accessory before the fact, in the killing of a person may not in any way benefit from the estate of the victim.

(b) There is no difference in division of the estate between movables and immovables.

4. Freedom of Testation

(a) There are no compulsory shares in Pennsylvania law except that a surviving spouse has a right to an elective share of one-third of the following property:

(1) property passing from the deceased by will or intestacy;
(2) income or use for the remaining life of the spouse of property conveyed by the deceased during the marriage to the extent that the deceased at time of death had the use of the property or an interest in or power to withdraw the income thereof;
(3) property conveyed by the deceased during his lifetime over which he retained a right to revoke said conveyance;
(4) property conveyed by the deceased during the marriage to himself and another with right of survivorship;
(5) survivorship rights conveyed to a beneficiary of certain annuity contracts; and
(6) property conveyed by the deceased during the marriage and within one year of death, i.e., deemed to be in contemplation of death, to the extent that the aggregate amount conveyed to a donor exceeds USD 3,000.

A surviving spouse's election to take or not to take an elective share must be in writing and filed with the clerk of the orphan's court division of the county where the deceased died domiciled. The election must be filed with the clerk before expiration of six months after the deceased's death or before expiration of six months after the date of probate, whichever is later. Under certain terms and conditions, the court may extend the foregoing time limit.

(b) *i.* A contract to die intestate, or to make a will, or not to revoke a will or testamentary provision, or an obligation dischargeable only at or after death, can be established in support of a claim against the estate of a deceased if the following requirement(s) are met:

- provisions of the will of the deceased must state the material provisions of the contract;
- an express reference in a will of the deceased to a contract and extrinsic evidence proving the terms of the contract; or
- a writing signed by the deceased evidencing the contract which is precise, definite and certain, and which is supported by legal consideration.

Oral testimony regarding the existence of a contract is permitted, although it may be viewed with suspicion. However, the execution of a joint will or mutual wills does not create a presumption of a contract not to revoke the will(s).
ii. It is possible for an estate to be distributed in kind. In such case, if there are two or more distributees, one of whom does not wish distribution in kind, either that distributee or the personal representative may request the court to either partition the property, or to direct sale of the property.
iii. If a person dies intestate as to all or any part of his estate, property which he gave in his lifetime to an heir is treated as an advancement against the latters' share of the estate only if declared in a writing by the deceased or acknowledged in writing by the heir to be an advancement. For this purpose, the property so advanced is valued as of the time the heir came into possession or enjoyment of the property or as of the death of the deceased,

whichever first occurs. If the recipient fails to survive the deceased, the property is not taken into account in computing the intestate share to be received by the recipient's issue unless the declaration or acknowledgment so provides.

iv. Family Settlement Agreements are recognized both by case law and statute as an acceptable means of ending the estate administrative process. The Agreement may be recorded with the court as part of the estate proceeding, but acceptance by the court for recording is not construed as court approval of any act of administration nor any act of distribution. The personal representative who distributes property pursuant to a family settlement agreement in lieu of filing an account and having same confirmed by the court, does so at his own risk. Distributions of personal property made pursuant to a family settlement agreement do not bar the rights of claimants who make their claims known to the personal representative within one year after the first complete publication of the grant of letters by the court to the personal representative or thereafter but prior to such distribution. However, if the personal representative makes written demand of a claimant who has not previously given written notice of his claim, and the claimant fails to act, neither the personal representative nor the distributee shall have any further liability. The statute imposes an additional burden on claimants who are claiming against real property conveyed by a personal representative pursuant to a Family Settlement Agreement. Such claimants must file written notice of the claim with the court. Such claim against real property expires at the end of five years after the deceased's death, unless within that time, the personal representative files an accounting or the claimant files a petition to compel an accounting.

5. Maintenance

(a) The estate of a deceased parent of minor children may not be subjected to a child support order for their benefit where neither a pre-existing support order nor a contractual agreement for support exists.

(b) A spouse's obligation to provide support and maintenance for the other spouse terminates with the death of the payor spouse. However, arrearages accumulated under an order of support during payor spouse's lifetime, may be enforced against his estate after death. Likewise, if payor spouse dies before an order is entered but a petition is pending, any maintenance deemed to be owing prior to death can be enforced against the estate.

6. Community Property Between Husband and Wife

(a) The Commonwealth of Pennsylvania is not a community property state.

(b) As is indicated in 4(a) *above* a surviving spouse has the right to an elective share of one-third of certain specified property. In 2(b)*ii. above* is indicated that the law provides for automatic modification when a testator marries after making a will. The effect of this statute is to preserve the intestate share of the surviving spouse without forcing that spouse to elect against the will.

7. Gifts (*Inter Vivos*)

Gifts to an heir prior to death are not set off against the heir's inheritance, with the exception of a written document in which both the deceased and the heir acknowledge the gift to be an advancement (*see* 4(b)*iii. above*).

8. Capacity

(a) Any person eighteen or more years of age who is of sound mind may make a will. Persons under age eighteen are conclusively presumed incapable of making a valid will.

(b) Any competent person may be a witness, including a surviving or purported surviving spouse. Any interest the person has in the estate does not disqualify him as a witness, but may affect credibility and weight.

(c) (1) An otherwise competent testator who is the sole surviving parent of a minor child may appoint a testamentary guardian of the person of such child during his minority or for any shorter period. However, a parent who, for one year or more previous to death, willfully neglected or refused to provide for his child or who deserted the child or willfully failed to perform parental duties, shall not have the right to appoint a testamentary guardian of the person of such child;

(2) A testator who is the parent of a minor child may appoint a testamentary guardian of the real or personal property passing to the minor upon his death when such property:

    i. is devised, bequeathed or appointed to the minor in that person's will or descends from that person to the minor by intestacy;

    ii. is the proceeds of an insurance or annuity contract on the testator's life, unless the owner of the contract has made an *inter vivos* designation of the guardian therefore;

    iii. arises from an *inter vivos* transfer, the major portion of which constituted a gift from the testator, unless the testator has made an *inter vivos* designation of a guardian therefore;

    iv. is a cause of action arising by reason of the testator's death;

    v. is a pension or death benefit from an employer or a society or organization of which the testator was a member; or

    vi. is a tentative trust of which the testator was the settlor.

International Succession

9. Authority (Court, Notarial or Other)

See 3 *hereinabove* on Intestacy and 4(a) on Spouse's right of election. Other than intestacy and spouse's right of election, there is no other mandatory method of succession.

10. Invalidity of Will

(a) A will or any portion thereof, may be held to be invalid on the following grounds:

(1) the testator lacked sufficient testamentary capacity at the moment of execution;
(2) the testator lacked sufficient testamentary intent at the moment of execution to dispose of his assets;
(3) revocation by a later will or codicil;
(4) mistake in execution either by mistake in the identity of the instrument executed, mistake in the inducement for executing the instrument, or mistake as to content of will;
(5) improper execution.

(b) A will is void if:

(1) the testator is a minor;
(2) undue influence was exerted on the testator;
(3) fraud in the inducement voids the entire instrument; fraud in the contents voids only those portions affected by the fraud, unless those portions are so extensive as to destroy the entire testamentary plan;
(4) the signature was forged, pages were substituted, or a prior valid will was fraudulently destroyed.[1]

11. Simultaneous Death

Pennsylvania has adopted the *Uniform Simultaneous Death Act.*
   If there is not sufficient evidence that the persons died other than simultaneously, the property of each person shall be disposed of as if he had survived the other.
   If two or more beneficiaries are designated to take successively by reason of survivorship and there is not sufficient evidence that the beneficiaries died other than simultaneously, the property thus disposed shall be divided into as many equal shares as there are successive beneficiaries.
   Where there is not sufficient evidence that two joint tenants or tenants by the entireties died other than simultaneously, the property so held shall be distributed,

---

1. Fraudulent destruction of a will is a criminal offense in Pennsylvania. *See* Crimes Code, 18 Pa. C.S.A. Section 4103.

one-half as if one had survived, and one-half as if the other had survived. If there are more than two joint tenants, and all of them have so died, the property thus distributed shall be in the proportion that one bears to the whole number of joint tenants.

If both the insured and the beneficiary of a life or accident insurance policy have died, and there is not sufficient evidence that they died other than simultaneously, the proceeds of said policy shall be distributed as if the insured had survived the beneficiary.

None of the *above* provisions applies in the case of wills, living trusts, deeds or contracts of insurance wherein provision has been made for distribution of property different from the statutory provisions.

12. Estate Taxes

Pennsylvania imposes two death taxes.

(1) The *Pennsylvania Inheritance Tax* is imposed on:

i. transfers by will or intestacy of a resident deceased on real and tangible property with a situs in Pennsylvania, on intangible personal property regardless of situs, and on real and tangible personal property with an out-of-state situs if same was under agreement of sale at death of deceased and is not subjected to death tax by the jurisdiction in which it is situated;
ii. all real and tangible personal property of non-resident deceased having its situs in Pennsylvania, including property held in trust; and
iii. transfers exceeding USD 3,000 made within one year of the death of the transferror if made without valuable and adequate consideration.

The tax is a flat rate depending on the relationships of the beneficiary to the deceased:

i. transfer to a spouse or transfer from child under twenty-one years of age to a parent = zero tax;
ii. transfer to grandparent, parent, children, lineal descendants and spouses = 4.5 per cent;
iii. transfer to siblings = 12 per cent;
iv. transfer to collateral beneficiaries (nephews, nieces, aunts, uncles, cousins, friends) = 15 per cent;
v. transfer to charities = tax exempt.

At the election of the person filing the return for a non-resident deceased, the tax can be computed:

i. On the entire estate as if the decedent were a Pennsylvania resident; or
ii. Multiply the amount determined in point *i. above* by a fraction, the numerator of which is the real and tangible personal property and the denominator of

which is all the property in the estate before deductions. Otherwise, the applicable rates are applied against the value of the real and tangible personal property located in Pennsylvania reduced by the indebtedness on the property.

Inheritance tax is due at the date of death and becomes delinquent nine months after the date of death. The tax is imposed on the entire net estate. There is no unified credit as with the federal estate tax. Assets are valued as of the date of death.

(2) In addition to the inheritance tax, Pennsylvania imposes an Estate Tax when the inheritance tax actually paid is less than the maximum credit for state death taxes allowable under the federal estate tax regulations. The estate tax, referred to as a 'slack tax', is imposed to insure that the Pennsylvania tax on inherited property is at least as large as the allowable credit for state death taxes on the federal estate return.

The Pennsylvania Inheritance Tax is paid out of the residuary estate unless there is a contrary intent specified in the will.

The Pennsylvania Estate Tax is apportioned in the same manner as the federal estate tax, i.e., equitably among the recipients of the estate, unless otherwise directed by the testator.

13. Administration of Estates

(a) In Pennsylvania, deceased's estates are administered under the jurisdiction of the Orphan's Court division of the Court of Common Pleas. Each county has a Register of Wills which has jurisdiction over probate of wills and the grant of letters to a personal representative.

If there is no viable executor or personal representative named in the will, or in the case of an intestacy, it is essential that an administrator be appointed. An heir may be the personal representative of the estate, either as executor or as administrator.

(b) The personal representative (either executor or administrator) is responsible to file annual status reports on the progress of the estate administration in the event administration of the estate is not completed within two years of the deceased's death.

However, other 'reporting' type forms include the original Petition for Letters, the Inventory, and the Inheritance Tax Return. If there is no Family Settlement Agreement, a formal accounting to the court is required. Additionally, the personal representative is required by law to provide notice of estate administration to all beneficiaries and intestate heirs within three months of the grant of letters.

(c) The Court always has the power to intervene and supervise estate administration, which intervention and supervision is triggered by (1) the filing of a petition asking for court intervention and/or supervision or (2) failure to comply with required estate administration procedures on time such as the filing of the Inventory, filing or providing beneficiaries with notice, or timely filing of the Inheritance Tax

Return. The requirement that the personal representative file the Status Report and an accounting where there is no Family Settlement Agreement are standardized methods of court supervision.

(d) Once a will has been admitted to probate, any contest must be raised at the distribution level. The contest may be raised by any party in interest.

(e) Assets can be distributed either in kind or as liquid cash by the personal representative. Distribution can be made either pursuant to a Family Settlement Agreement or upon final confirmation by the Court of the account of the personal representative.

(f) A creditor must make his claim within one year of the advertisement of the grant of letters.

(g) Distribution is not effected if the testator did not appoint an executor. The Court will appoint a personal representative.

14. Domicile/Nationality

(a) Nationality of a deceased does not effect probate and estate administration. If the deceased was domiciled in Pennsylvania, or if a non-domiciled deceased had property in Pennsylvania, Pennsylvania Courts have jurisdiction over the estate.

(b) An estate may be raised for a deceased who was domiciled in Pennsylvania but had no assets in Pennsylvania. This may be done in the case when an estate is raised for litigation purposes only, such as to appoint a personal representative to pursue a medical malpractice or wrongful death action.

SECTION B – APPLICABLE LAW/PROCEDURE WHERE FOREIGN ELEMENT/S ARE INVOLVED

1. Jurisdiction

(a) The Orphans' Court, a division of the Court of Common Pleas of Pennsylvania, is the trial court in each county of Pennsylvania. The Orphans' Court has mandatory jurisdiction of the administration and distribution of the real and personal property of deceased's estates. The Register of Wills in each county probates Wills and grants letters testamentary and of administration to personal representatives. The Court, through the Register of Wills, accepts jurisdiction based on the last residence at date of death as well as location of assets within the Commonwealth.

(b) The rules for movable and immovable assets are the same.

International Succession

(c) The venue for deceased's estates is based on the county which was the last residence of the deceased, or, if the deceased was not domiciled in Pennsylvania, then any county in which the deceased's property is located.

2. Applicable Law

The last residence of the deceased is the basis of both jurisdiction and venue. If the deceased was not domiciled in Pennsylvania, jurisdiction and venue are based on the location within Pennsylvania where the deceased's assets are located. If the decedent had no domicile in Pennsylvania, and no property located in Pennsylvania, and service of process is to be made in Pennsylvania upon his personal representative as authorized by law, then letters on the deceased's death may be granted by the Register of Wills of any county in the state.

3. Foreign Succession/Inheritance Orders

(a) Foreign orders are recognized and enforced by the courts of Pennsylvania. However, if the foreign fiduciary wishes to exercise a power with respect to Pennsylvania real estate, the will must be admitted to probate in Pennsylvania as required by law.

(b)–(c) A foreign fiduciary may institute proceedings in Pennsylvania and may exercise all the powers of a local fiduciary, as long as there is no estate administration pending in Pennsylvania. In the event there is an estate administration pending in Pennsylvania, the foreign fiduciary may not exercise any powers unless he is appointed ancillary fiduciary by the Register.

A foreign fiduciary must file with the Register of the county where the power is to be exercised, or the proceeding is instituted, or where the assets are located, an exemplified copy of his/her appointment in the foreign jurisdiction, together with an exemplified copy of the will, if any. The foreign fiduciary must also execute and file an affidavit with the Register of the county where the power is to be exercised or the proceeding is instituted or the property is located, stating that the estate is not indebted to any person in the Commonwealth. The affidavit must also indicate that he/she will not exercise any power not permitted in the appointing jurisdiction. Additionally, upon commencing any proceeding in a Pennsylvania court, the foreign fiduciary must file an exemplified copy of his/her official bond. In the event no bond was posted, the Pennsylvania court may require a bond or may require an additional bond as further security.

If the foreign fiduciary is a personal representative or trustee under the will of a non-resident deceased, he may not exercise any powers within Pennsylvania for one month after the deceased's death.

If a foreign fiduciary exercises a power to sell or mortgage any real estate in Pennsylvania, all taxes due thereon must be paid to the local and state taxing authorities.

Pennsylvania is lenient in granting powers to foreign fiduciaries in dealing with bank accounts in Pennsylvania and in transferring securities of Pennsylvania corporations. The probate code permits a foreign fiduciary to have all the powers of a local fiduciary. He/she need not submit proof of his appointment, the will or post a bond to the local Register. Rather, he/she need only submit same to the financial institution in which the asset is located.

4. Two or More Succession or Probate Orders

Since validity of execution of a will as well as appointment of an administrator in the event of intestacy are governed by where the deceased was domiciled at the time of death, a judgment on administration proceedings by a competent court in the jurisdiction where the deceased was domiciled will generally take precedence. Under Pennsylvania law, judgments obtained in courts of sister states are entitled to full faith and credit under Article 4, Section 1 of the United States Constitution. However, judgments of foreign courts are subject to the principles of comity. In all matters, Pennsylvania courts are permitted to exercise jurisdiction only where there are sufficient contacts with the Commonwealth pursuant to the United States Constitution.

5. Assets

If there are no assets whatsoever in the jurisdiction but some other connecting factors, the local courts may still assume jurisdiction. *See above.* But note that jurisdiction was refused in a Philadelphia case where the non-resident deceased had no assets in Pennsylvania. The Court *sua sponte* ordered the Register to vacate the letters of administration it had previously granted.

6. Expert Evidence

The Pennsylvania statute specifically provides that a will in a foreign language may not be filed for probate or for any other purpose in the office of the Register of Wills unless there is attached to it a translation into English, sworn to be correct. A writing filed in violation of the statute is not deemed to serve as notice to any person.

The Pennsylvania statutes under judicial procedure state that in determining the law of any jurisdiction or governmental unit outside Pennsylvania, the tribunal may consider any relevant material or source, including testimony, whether or not submitted via party or admissible under the rules of evidence. Foreign law may be proved by taking the depositions of lawyers of that state. The depositions can then be introduced into evidence without the need for the foreign lawyer to appear in person. The determination of the tribunal is a question of law subject to review on appeal.

International Succession

7. Unity of Succession

The principle does not apply.

8. Formalities

The validity of a foreign executed will as to personality is determined by the law of testator's domicile at time of death as to validity of execution, validity of disposition and matters of construction. As to real estate, the validity of such matters is determined by the law of the situs of the real estate.

The Pennsylvania Statute specifically recognizes as valid, those foreign wills which are executed in compliance with the law of the jurisdiction where the testator was domiciled either at the time of execution or at the time of death.

9. Legislation

The *Hague Convention on The Conflicts of Laws Relating to the Form of Testamentary Dispositions* has not been adopted in this jurisdiction.

10. Wills

(a) The Pennsylvania probate code provides that a will is validly executed if executed in compliance with Pennsylvania legal requirements, or in compliance with the law of the jurisdiction where the testator was domiciled at the time of execution of the will or at the time of his death.

(b) A will which devises an interest in land is construed in accordance with the law designated in the will. In the absence of such a designation, the will is construed in accordance with the rules of construction that would be applied by the courts of the situs.

Regarding an interest in movables, a will is construed in accordance with the law designated in the will. In the absence of such a designation, the will is construed in accordance with the rules of construction that would be applied by the courts of the state where the testator was domiciled at the time of death.

In general, the meaning of words used in a will depends upon the intentions of the testator. If it is impossible to ascertain the intentions of the testator, the rule of law governs.

(c) Pennsylvania law will give recognition to rights of heirs and beneficiaries as to minimum shares. The only recognized minimum share in Pennsylvania is a surviving spouse's 'forced' or 'elective' share. (*See* 4 in Section A.) The validity of a land devise is determined by the law of the situs. As to movables, the law of the state in which deceased was domiciled at the time of death governs.

(d) A will valid in the jurisdiction where executed or testator was domiciled at the time of death is valid in Pennsylvania.

(e) A will valid in the jurisdiction where executed or testator was domiciled at the time of death is valid in Pennsylvania.

(f) A will valid in the jurisdiction where executed or testator was domiciled at the time of death is valid in Pennsylvania.

(g) A will valid in the jurisdiction where executed or testator was domiciled at the time of death is valid in Pennsylvania.

(h) A will valid in the jurisdiction where executed or testator was domiciled at the time of death is valid in Pennsylvania.

(i) A will valid in the jurisdiction where executed or testator was domiciled at the time of death is valid in Pennsylvania.

11. Domicile/Nationality

(a) In every case, it is the domicile of the testator at the time of death, and not nationality, which is determinative.

(b) Domicile of a beneficiary is not relevant in conflicts of law cases.

(c) If domicile of the deceased is unclear, or the deceased had more than one domicile, the domicile stated in the will, if any, will govern.

12. Taxation

See 12 in Section A.

Venezuela

Prepared by: Dr. Angel Gabriel VISO
Viso, Rodríguez, Cottin, Medina, Ramírez & Asociados

Address: Torre Banvenez
          Pisos 13 y 14
          Avenida Francisco Solano
          Sabana Grande
          Caracas 1050
          Venezuela
Tel.:   +58 212 761 61 82/84/   +58 212 762 20 92/95
          +58 212 763 53 89/   +58 212 762 67 08
Fax: +58 212 762 45 62

SECTION A – BRIEF SURVEY OF THE LOCAL SYSTEM

1. Type of System

(a) In Venezuela, there is a civil law system.

(b) According to Article 4 of Venezuelan Constitution, Venezuela is a federal and decentralized state, 'in the terms established by this Constitution'.

From the practical point of view, matters such as succession are regulated by the National Power. Thus, the same legal system applies for the entire country.

2. Wills

(a) There are two classes of will, the ordinary and the extraordinary. The first is subdivided into open wills and closed wills. Any person wishing to read an open will is able to do so as its content is public. Closed wills are of confidential nature.[1]

There are three kinds of *open will*:

---

1. A new law on Public Registry and Public Notary has been enacted recently. It is cleat that in certain cases the notary has taken over certain attributions that registrars used to have. In other cases it is not so clear. Furthermore, the regulation of the new law has not been implemented yet. It is uncertain when the new law will be implemented. Therefore, there are some uncertainties as how the new wills shall be executed. Section (a) reflects our best interpretation on the matter.

- a will which complies with the general requirements for the execution of documents before a public notary. It is signed before a public notary, in the presence of two witnesses. An original and two copies are delivered;
- a will executed before a public notary and two witnesses but without having to be notarized immediately. However, a subsequent re-execution before the notary is necessary in order to be able to obtain the ordinary effects of a will;
- a will executed before five witnesses, but without the presence of any public notary. The will must be signed by the witnesses. This type of will does not take effect unless:
  1. at least two of the said witnesses acknowledge their signature and the content of the will before a court within six months of the execution of the will; and
  2. the testator also acknowledges his will before a court at the same time as the witnesses do.

Closed wills have to be executed in accordance with the following procedure: the will is written and placed in an envelope which is then closed and sealed in such manner that it cannot be opened without altering the envelope. The will is presented to the public notary by the testator, who declares that it is his will before three witnesses. A statement is written up on the envelope, which must comply with the legal requirements, and is signed by the public notary and the witnesses.

Extraordinary wills may be executed in the following cases:

- *epidemics*: Such a will is executed before the registrar or any court in the presence of two witnesses. It loses its validity three months after the epidemic has ended or after a relocation to an area in which there is no such epidemic, unless the testator dies before the end of the three months. This will must subsequently be registered in order to have its usual effects;
- *voyages at sea*: The testator may prepare such a will whilst traveling on a merchant ship or naval vessel. The will is executed before the captain of the ship (or the officer in his place) and two witnesses. Its validity expires two months after the arrival of the testator at a location at which he could execute an ordinary will, unless he dies before that time;
- *soldiers in combat*: Such a will requires the presence of two witnesses. Its validity expires two months after the period of combat has ended.

Holographic wills are not valid in Venezuela.

(b) *i.* There are three kinds of revocation:
  - *express*: It may be total or partial. The formalities required for the execution of a will must be complied with in order to revoke it;
  - *tacit*: According to leading Venezuelan jurists,[2] a tacit revocation of a will occurs upon:
    1. the execution of a new will whose content is totally or partially contrary to or incompatible with the previous will. Such revocation may be total or partial;

---

2. Francisco López Herrera, *Derecho de Sucesiones*, pages 484–489, Universidad Católica Andrés Bello, Manuales de Derecho, 1994.

2. in certain cases, the destruction of the will;
3. the alienation of an asset made over in a legacy;
4. the transformation by the testator of an asset made over in a legacy.

   – *legal*: If at the time the testator executed his will he did not have or did not know that he had descendants and after his death it becomes known that he did leave descendants, such descendants have the right to request the revocation of the will.
   The codicil must comply with the same requirements as the will.
ii. Marriage does not revoke wills made prior to marriage. Unless there is a legal separation of assets between the spouses, the surviving spouse has the right to a certain share of the inheritance (*see* 4 *below*).
iii. A testator may revoke a previous revocation, thus reviving the revoked will, by executing a new will.

3. Intestacy

(a) The order of succession upon intestacy is as follows:

– the *descendants* (whether illegitimate/adopted or not) succeed their ascendants. The children exclude the other descendants and, as a rule, the closest descendants exclude remoter ones. The descendants exclude all the other possible successors, except the husband or wife;
– in the absence of descendants, the *ascendants* inherit. The closest ascendants exclude the remotest ones. The ascendants exclude all the other possible successors who are more distantly related;
– in the absence of descendants and ascendants, the *brothers and sisters* inherit. The brothers and sisters exclude the other collateral relations;
– in the absence of descendants, ascendants, brothers and sisters, and spouse, *the other collateral relations* inherit, the closest excluding the more remote, up to the sixth degree of consanguinity;[3]
– the *surviving spouse* who is not physically separated and whose assets are not legally separated always inherits from the deceased spouse and is never excluded by any other class of successor. If there are descendants, the surviving spouse has the right to receive a share equal to that received by any child. If the spouse survives with ascendants only, he has the right to half of the inheritance (the other half devolving upon the ascendants). If the spouse survives with the brothers and sisters of the deceased only, the same rule applies. The spouse excludes the other collateral relations.

---

3. The proximity of the family links is determined in the following way: if the persons involved are descendants or ascendants, one counts the number of persons and subtracts one, e.g., between a grandson and his grandfather there are two degrees (the grandson, the father and the grandfather equals three, less one, which is two). If they are collaterals, it is necessary to go from one of the persons to the common ancestor and to the other person following the applicable rules, e.g., between two first cousins, there are four degrees (one of the first cousins, his father or mother, the grandfather, the uncle, the other first cousin equals five, less one, which is four).

(b) In principle, the division should be made in kind, whether the estate is composed of movables or immovables.

4. Freedom of Testation

(a) In Venezuela, the descendants, the ascendants and the surviving spouse (who is not legally separated) are granted the ownership of half of that they would have had upon intestacy (*la legítima*). Nevertheless, the heirs who have been granted such rights do not all inherit: they follow the same order of succession and the same rules of exclusion as previously explained (*see* 3(a) *above*).

(b) *i.* Contracts of inheritance made prior to death are prohibited in Venezuela.

    ii. The ascendant can divide the estate between his children or other descendants by means of a gift or a will.

Although the testator, as a general rule, cannot forbid the division of the estate, he could do so if at least one of the heirs is a minor. In that case, he may prohibit the division until one year after the last minor has come of age. Even in that case, however, the court may allow for division if there are circumstances deemed to require it.

Finally, although there is a principle according to which no one can be forced to retain community property, the heirs may decide to do so for a fixed period of time, which is not to exceed five years. In such a case, the court, for the same reason expressed in the preceding paragraph, may permit the division.

5. Maintenance

The spouse, minor children or parents of the heirs can claim maintenance from the latter and from their respective share of the estate. The estate has no legal personality. The person obliged to provide maintenance is the person indicated by the law to do so. Therefore, the spouse, children, etc., of the heir could claim against him for maintenance with respect to all his assets, but could not deprive the other heirs of their respective portion.

6. Community Property Between Husband and Wife

(a) Before the marriage, the spouses may agree on a special regime for the assets they own or will own after the wedding. If they do not elect a special regime, in principle, the assets they earn or acquire after the marriage will belong to each of them in equal shares. However, there are certain assets listed in the Civil Code which will always belong to one of the spouses (e.g., assets included in a succession).

If a couple who are unmarried live together as husband and wife, there is a presumption that their assets, acquired after their union, are held in common.

(b) Each spouse is heir to the other. However, they lose such right when there is a physical separation and a separation of assets.[4]

7. Gifts (*Inter Vivos*)

(a) Gifts are brought into account in order to calculate the legitimate portions, to verify whether the compulsory shares have been exceeded and, if so, to calculate how the corresponding reduction should be effected. In addition, if an heir who has the right to a legitimate portion wishes to reduce the gifts to third parties by the deceased (made either by way of acts *inter vivos* or *mortis causa*), the gifts received by such third parties shall also be brought into account.

Finally, the gifts can be set off against an heir's inheritance provided that such an heir is the child or descendant of the deceased, and there are other such heirs (*colación de donaciones*). In such a case, there are several alternatives, all of which are meant to ensure that the equality of all the heirs in such conditions is maintained. The person whose inheritance is to pass can exempt the heir from the obligation to set off. However, such relief is limited by the compulsory shares of the other heirs.

(b) *See* 7(a) *above*.

8. Capacity

(a) In principle, the testator must be sixteen years of age.[5] Nevertheless, if the testator, being less than sixteen years old, is married, divorced or a widower, he may execute a will.

Those who lack capacity to execute a will are the following:

– a person who is insane or has been declared incompetent by a court;
– the deaf-and-dumb or those who cannot speak and are incapable of writing;
– a person who cannot read, in relation to the execution to a closed will (*see* 2(a) *above*).

(b) The requirements relating to witnesses of the execution of a will are as follows:

– they must be of full age, know the testator and be able to read and write;
– blind people and the completely deaf or dumb cannot be witnesses;
– people who cannot understand the Spanish language are not allowed to witness a will;

---

4. The separation between husband and wife is an intermediate step, after which there can be either a reconciliation or a divorce. The physical separation (*separación de cuerpos*) suspends the obligation to live together without any effect whatsoever on the economic matrimonial regime. The separation of assets – which is not compulsory – implies the end of the regime of community property.
5. Full age is eighteen.

- the relatives (up to the fourth degree of consanguinity or the second of affinity) of the Registrar who authorizes the instrument, as well as the heirs, legatees or devisees, or their relatives (in the same degrees as *above*), of open wills, are incapable of witnessing the execution of a will;
- persons who are less than twelve years of age, those lacking capacity and 'professional' witnesses cannot be witnesses.

(c) Capacity is the rule and incapacity the exception. A distinction must be made between the capacity of a beneficiary if there is a will or not. In cases of intestacy, there are two main causes of incapacity: the non-existence of the beneficiary and 'indignity'. Indignity arises when:

- the beneficiary has perpetrated or tried to perpetrate a crime or is an accomplice of a crime against the person of whose succession he could be the beneficiary, or against his spouse, descendant, ascendant or brother/sister. The crime must be punishable by a term of imprisonment of more than six months;
- the beneficiary has been declared guilty of adultery with the spouse of the deceased;
- the beneficiary, being a relative of the deceased, has refused to provide assistance to the deceased, despite the fact that he was able to give such assistance.

If there is a will, the same rules apply, except that it is possible to name as beneficiary a person not yet born, provided that the unborn is the child of a person who is alive when the testator dies.

It appears to be possible to name as beneficiaries, companies, foundations, associations, etc., not yet incorporated, provided the testator establishes the rules in order to incorporate such entities.

Apart from that, *in the absence of a will*, the following lack capacity:

- churches, whatever religion, and entities whose rules or the law do not allow for the alienation of real estate;
- priests or ministers of any religion, unless the heir is the spouse, an ascendant, descendant or relation of the testator up to the fourth degree of consanguinity;
- the guardian, who cannot take advantage of the will of his ward if the will was executed before the approval of the guardianship, whether or not the testator dies after such approval. Such rule does not apply if the guardian is an ascendant, descendant, brother, sister or the spouse of the testator;
- in relation to a person having been married more than once, the surviving spouse cannot receive by way of will a portion greater than that left to the least favoured of the children of the previous marriage(s);
- the registrar, or any other public officer, either civil, military, marine or consular who has executed an open will; or the witnesses who have participated in the execution of the will.

Likewise, the person who has written up a closed will cannot take part, unless the testator has given his approval in his own handwriting of such gift or has verbally expressed his approval before the Registrar and the witnesses having executed his will, and either fact has been recorded in the respective instrument.

International Succession

Clauses in a will in favour of one or more of the *afore-mentioned* people are null and void. That is the case even if the beneficiary is a 'straw man'. There is a legal presumption that the father, the mother, the descendants and the spouse of those lacking capacity are 'straw men'.

9. Authority (Court, Notarial or Other)

The ownership of the estate is transmitted directly from the deceased to the heir(s) without the intervention of any court, notary public, etc. Of course, if there is any legal dispute with respect to the succession, the court will intervene.

10. Invalidity of Will

(a) The possible grounds for invalidity are as follows:

– defects in formalities;
– the heir lacking the capacity to receive the inheritance (*see* 8(c) *above*);
– the testator lacking capacity to execute a will (*see* 8(a) *above*);
– the testator lacking capacity when executing the will, having been mistaken on some substantial point, suffered violence (duress) or having been misled by someone.

(b) The general rule is to verify whether the infringement of the law was related to a rule of public policy or proper behaviour (*buenas costumbres*) or not. In the first instance, the will will be void, whilst in the second, it will be voidable. Defects in essential formalities render the will void.

11. Simultaneous Death

(a) In case of simultaneous death, the person who considers that one of the deceased died before or after another must prove that allegation. If there is no evidence of the order of the deaths, there is a presumption that all died at the same time and, therefore, there is no succession between them. Thus, there is no presumption that a younger person survives an older, etc.

(b) The date of death may be determined by all the legal means, e.g., experts, etc.

12. Estate Taxes

(a) There is a national tax upon the transmission of assets, rights etc., *mortis causa*. The tax is imposed upon the net patrimony of the deceased (calculating the value of the assets and then deducting the debts and any legate or charges imposed by the deceased). Each heir or legatee pays a percentage calculated upon his portion of the economic value of the inheritance. The percentage varies depending on two factors: the proximity of the heir with the deceased and the economic importance of the inheritance.[6] For example: the children of the deceased, if the value of his portion of the inheritance is less than 15 tax units,[7] must pay a tax of one per cent. On the contrary, if the heir is not a relative of the heir and the value of his portion of the inheritance is more than 4,000.01 tax units, the percentage shall be 55 per cent.

(b) According to the *Law of Taxes upon Successions, Gifts and other Related Matters* (*Ley de Impuesto sobre Sucesiones, Donaciones y demás Ramos Conexos*), the tax is to be paid on assets situated in the national territory. However, when the law determines whether the assets are to be considered as situated within the national territory, it includes certain extraterritorial situations.

In accordance with the law, the following assets are deemed situated in the national territory:

– shares, obligations and credit instruments issued in Venezuela and those issued outside Venezuela by legal entities incorporated or domiciled in the country;
– shares, obligations and other instruments of credit issued outside Venezuela by foreign legal entities when they are owned by people domiciled in the country;
– rights or shares which correspond to assets situated in Venezuela;
– personal rights or obligations whose legal origin is in Venezuela.

(c) The beneficiaries of the succession are taxed, that is to say, the heirs, the legatees and the devisees.

13. Administration of Estates

(a) The heirs administer the estate in principle. Thus, it is not essential to appoint an administrator.

However, there is nothing that prevents the appointment of an administrator provided that the majority of the heirs approve of such an appointment. If a majority is not formed or if the agreements between the heirs are very detrimental to the common assets, the court may intervene and, if necessary, appoint an administrator.

On the other hand, when the heir lacks the capacity to administer his property (e.g., minor, insane), his parent or guardian will have to administer his assets, including his portion of the inheritance.

The following assets, however, cannot be administered by the parents:

– those assets transmitted to such an heir from an inheritance, legacy or devise upon condition that the parents do not administer such assets. Such rule shall not apply to the assets received by the heir as his legitimate portion;

---

6. It is a progressive tariff.
7. As of today, one simple taxing unit is equivalent to Bs. 19,400.00. The taxing unit is updated each year, in accordance to the inflation.

– those assets transmitted to such an heir from an inheritance, legacy or devise, which were accepted against the will of his parents who hold the *patria potestas*. However, if there was no agreement between them, the administration shall revert to the parent who would have wished to accept the inheritance.

If one of the *above* two cases arises, the court shall appoint an administrator, unless the testator has named one for that purpose.

Furthermore the heir who has accepted the inheritance upon condition that an inventory is drawn up (*heredero bajo beneficio de inventario*)[8] is obliged to administer the estate.

Finally, the testator who designates an heir, legatee or devisee who has no capacity to administer his property may name an administrator for the assets transferred, even if the heir, legatee or devisee is already under the *patria potestas* or has a guardian who represents him and administers the rest of his assets. The testator is authorized by law to exempt the administrator from giving reports.

(b) If there is an administrator, he must report to the heirs. In addition, if the administrator was appointed by the court, he must report to it. Generally, parents of minor children do not have to report on their administration. Nevertheless, if the parents wish to alienate the assets or carry out any act exceeding simple administration, they will have to request the approval of the court.

If a person ceases to be a guardian before the majority of the ward, he must submit a final report to the new guardian, with the intervention of the *protutor*.[9] If the ward has reached his majority, the final report must be submitted to him, but it will only become final once the *protutor* or another person named by the court has examined the report.

The heir who accepted the inheritance upon condition of an inventory must submit a report to the devisees, legatees and creditors.

(c) *See* (a) and (b) *above*.

(d) Depending on the case, it will be the person or the court having to approve the report.

(e) The heirs have the possession that the deceased had over his assets when he died. If the deceased had lost possession of such assets, or the heirs lost it after

---

8. The acceptance of the inheritance upon condition of an inventory implies that there is no confusion between the estate and the assets of the heirs. Additionally, the assets of the inheritance will cover the obligations of the same, but if the obligations are larger than the assets, the heirs will not be forced to pay the debts from their own assets, as would be the case if the inheritance had been accepted unconditionally.

9. The 'protutor' is a person appointed to act on behalf of a person lacking capacity when his interests are in conflict with those of the guardian. He must supervise the conduct of the guardian and inform the court if he thinks that the guardian is endangering the education and interests of the ward. If there is no guardian, he must ask the court to appoint a new guardian to act on behalf of the minor and take the actions which are deemed urgent.

his death, the heirs have the right to take judiciary action in order to recover possession.

(f) As a general rule, the heirs must pay the debts of the inheritance *pro rata* to their share in the estate.

The ordinary effect of the inheritance is that both patrimonies (of the deceased and of the heir) form only one patrimony. Therefore, the heirs are liable not only as regards the assets of their inheritance but also as regards their own assets. The purpose of the acceptance upon condition of an inventory is to separate both patrimonies. In such a case, the heir will only be obliged to pay debts up to the value of the assets. The heir will not be liable for the difference between the debts and the assets.

In principle (there are exceptions), the heir has ten years beginning with the date of the death to accept the inheritance. After the ten years, the statute of limitations applies. The heir has the same period of time in order to accept 'upon the condition that an inventory is drawn up'. However, with respect to the heir who has the physical possession of the inheritance, special rules apply, which very much shorten the time period for that kind of acceptance.

(g) The heirs must distribute the assets among themselves. In such a case they can appoint a person to effect the distribution. If there is no agreement, the heirs can take judicial action in order to effect the distribution, and a distributor shall be designated.

14. Domicile/Nationality

(a) The *above* answers were predicated upon the basis that Venezuelan law applied. If the nationality or the domicile of the deceased was relevant in order to determine the applicable legislation, the preceding rules would not be used in cases where the deceased was not Venezuelan or was not domiciled in Venezuela. For further details, *see* Section B2 *below*.

(b) As it was pointed out at 9 *above*, such an order is not required under Venezuelan law. In theory, the local court (in the event of a dispute) would have jurisdiction even if there were no assets, provided that the deceased had his domicile in Venezuela when he died.

SECTION B – APPLICABLE LAW/PROCEDURE WHERE FOREIGN ELEMENT/S ARE INVOLVED

1. Jurisdiction

(a) In principle, the local court holds that it has jurisdiction if the deceased had his domicile in Venezuela at the date of death; or if there are assets of the estate in Venezuela.

International Succession

(b) The Venezuelan courts must deal with cases relating to immovable assets if they are situated in Venezuela. That is not necessarily the case, however, with respect to movables.

(c) It may be either the local court having jurisdiction in the place where the deceased had his last domicile, or, if there are assets located in Venezuela, the Venezuelan court having jurisdiction in the place where the majority of the assets in Venezuela are situated.

2. Applicable Law

The applicable law may refer to different matters: 1. The applicable law as to capacity is the law of domicile; 2. The applicable law as to the form of the will may be the *locus regit actum*: the law which regulates the content of the will, or the domicile of the testator. Any will executed according to any one of these laws is valid from that point of view; 3. The proper law for succession is the law of domicile at the date of death. If a will is executed abroad and the testator is domiciled in Venezuela when he dies, the will shall be valid from the point of view of its form if executed according to the law of the foreign country. However, from the point of view of the will itself and the distribution of the assets among the heirs, legatees, etc., the applicable law will be the Venezuelan one. Therefore the *legítima* and the other rules affecting the freedom of testation must be respected. Venezuelan law applies to immovable property in Venezuela.

3. Foreign Succession/Inheritance Orders

(a) Provided that the local requirements for the recognition and enforcement of the foreign judgments are met, the foreign order may be enforced or recognized in respect of local assets, excluding immovable property in Venezuela.

(b) It is necessary to obtain a local court order to give effect to a foreign order.

(c) In order to obtain the enforcement of a foreign judgment, it is necessary to attach to the request a copy of the foreign judgment together with the enforcement order of the court. Furthermore, the plaintiff must prove that:
– the foreign court has issued judgment in a matter where the Venezuelan courts did not have exclusive jurisdiction over that matter;
– the foreign court had jurisdiction over the matter, according to the principles of international procedural jurisdiction established in the Civil Procedure Code;
– the judgment is characterized as *res judicata* by the law applicable to the court which issued the judgment;
– the judgment is of a private nature;
– the defendant was duly notified of the process and was granted the right of defense;

- the foreign judgment is not incompatible with a previous judgment characterized as *res judicata*;
- the decision of the foreign court does not refer to a dispute related to real estate situated in Venezuela.
- there is no judiciary proceeding pending before the Venezuelan courts, initiated before the foreign judgment was issued, and referred to the same purpose and having the same parties;
- the foreign judgment is not contrary to public policy;
- the decision of the foreign court does not refer to a dispute related to real estate situated in Venezuela.

The *afore-mentioned* facts must be established by way of an authentic certification issued by the competent authority of the country where the judgment was issued, which must be legalized. Venezuela has approved the *Hague Convention* in order to eliminate the legalization of public foreign documents. Therefore, if the country where the foreign judgment was issued also approved the said convention, only the apostille would be required. If the judgment is written in a language other than Spanish, it must be translated.

After the plaintiff's request, the defendant must be notified; the notification may take some time, e.g., if the defendant lives abroad. The Government Attorney (*Fiscal General de la República*) must also be notified. After these notifications, the defendant has ten days to appear in his defense. The local court must then decide whether it recognizes the foreign judgment or not. However, the Venezuelan Supreme Court has been flexible enough to allow the parties supplementary time in order for them to provide additional evidence. Moreover, the court may decide that additional evidence is to be given, establishing the time period for that purpose.

4. Two or More Successions or Probate Orders

As previously stated (*see* 3(b) directly *above*), a foreign court order is not valid in Venezuela unless it is recognized by a local court. On the other hand, a court order of succession or inheritance is not required under Venezuelan law.

In any event, in accordance with the general rules (*see* 3(c) *above*), a foreign court order or judgment shall not be recognized in Venezuela if there was a proceeding pending before the Venezuelan courts, initiated before the foreign judgment was issued and referred to the same purpose and between the same parties.

If there are two simultaneous judgments or orders, and the one issued abroad had already been recognized by a local court, the interested party could allege that the matter has already been resolved.

If the foreign court order or judgment has not been recognized yet but was issued before the commencement of the proceeding before the Venezuelan courts, the matter is subject to interpretation. One could argue that according to Article 58 of the *International Private Law* Venezuelan jurisdiction is excluded. On the other hand, it is possible to claim that the foreign court order has no legal standing in Venezuela and, therefore, could not prevent a local court from dealing with the matter.

International Succession

5. Assets

As previously explained, one of the connecting factors in order to establish jurisdiction is the last domicile of the deceased (*see* 1 *above*).

6. Expert Evidence

(a) The general principle is that the court without request will apply foreign law. However, for practical reasons, depending on the case, it might be necessary to request the opinion of a foreign lawyer. There are other possible means of bringing evidence as to the foreign law, such as by way of a report issued by the authorities about the content and interpretation of its own law or certified copies of the legal text itself.

(b) The affidavit is not expressly regulated in Venezuelan law. However, a statement of two lawyers is accepted when referred to evidence and information on foreign law. Although if this is contested, there are some grounds upon which it could be argued that its nature is similar to that of a deposition of a witness and, therefore, subject to cross examination if requested by the court or the other party.

7. Unity of Succession

Unity of succession is accepted in principle.

8. Formalities

As previously said (*see* 2 *above*), the applicable law as to the form of the will may be the *locus regit actum*: the law which regulates the content of the will, or the domicile of the testator. Therefore, it is not necessary, that formalities of a will executed in a foreign country are the same as those in the local country for such a will to be recognized or submitted for a succession order.

In the specific area of succession, in order to have legal effects in Venezuela, a will executed in a foreign country must have followed the rules applicable in such country and it must have been executed in an authentic form allowed for by that country. However, the same instrument cannot have been executed by more than one person. Furthermore neither verbal wills nor holographic wills are accepted.[10]

---

10. There could be discussion on this paragraph because the *International Private Law* (which is a newer law) does not refer to this point, whereas the Civil Code (an older law) does. In case there are contradictions between law, there are two rules about how to determine which law prevails. The first one is that the newer law modifies the older one. The second rule is that the special law prevails. In this case, since the Civil Code refers specifically to the will and the International Private law does not refer to it, I believe the rule established in the Civil Code applies.

9. Legislation

The *1961 Hague Convention on the Conflicts of Laws Relating to the Form of Testamentary Dispositions* is not applicable.

10. Wills

(a) The law of the country where the will is executed, the law which regulates the content of the will or the domicile of the testator (*see* 8 *above*).

(b) The last domicile of the deceased.

(c) As for (b).

(d) The law of domicile.

(e) As for (d).

(f) As for (b).

(g) As for (b).

(h) With respect to the formal rules, *see* (a) *above*; with respect to the material rules, *see* (b) *above*.

(i) If the Venezuelan law is applicable because the last domicile of the deceased was in Venezuela, the Venezuelan laws regarding reserve shall apply, no matter the place of residence of the heirs.

11. Domicile/Nationality

(a) *See* 2 *above*.

(b) The domicile of the beneficiary is not relevant.

(c) For International Private Law purposes there is a legal definition of domicile for a physical person: the place where such person has his residence. There is no specific rule with respect to legal entities. Therefore, the general rule of the Civil Code applies: the place where a person has his main affairs and interests. If the domicile is unclear, for instance if the person has several residences, or has affairs or interests in different places, the court will have to determine which one of two or more places is the principal. Regarding nationality, it seems that the nationality normally used by the person will prevail.

12. Taxation

Residence is not a relevant factor regarding taxation.

West Indies

Prepared by: Karen NUNEZ-TESHEIRA
Council of Legal Education
Hugh Wooding Law School

Address: Gordon Street
          St. Augustine
          Trinidad
          West Indies
Tel.:   +1 868 662 5835/8514/5860
Fax: +1 868 662 0927

This chapter deals with the law of English-speaking Caribbean territories and thereby covers the law applicable in the following countries: *Anguilla, Antigua & Barbuda, Barbados, Dominica, Grenada, Guyana, Jamaica, Montserrat, St. Christopher & Nevis, St. Lucia, St. Vincent & the Grenadines, The Bahamas, and Trinidad & Tobago.*

Section A – Brief Survey of The Local System

1. Type of System

(a) The legal system of the *English-speaking Caribbean, save St. Lucia*, is the English common law system.

(b) The legal system of *St. Lucia* is governed by the Civil Code which has introduced elements of the English common law.

2. Wills

(a) In general, a will must be in writing and signed by a testator who is of full age and sound mind. The testator is required to either sign the will or acknowledge his signature previously made, in the presence of two or more competent witnesses, and these witnesses must sign in the presence of each other as well as in the presence of the testator. If the will is witnessed by a beneficiary or the spouse of a beneficiary, the will is valid but the gift to the beneficiary is null and void.

In *Trinidad & Tobago*, with respect to the testator's signature, such signature must be physically placed at the end or foot of the will, failing which the entire will is deemed invalid.

In *all the other jurisdictions save St. Vincent & the Grenadines*, if the signature appears at, after, following, under, beside or opposite to the end of the will, the entire will is deemed valid once the court is satisfied that the testator intended to give effect by such signature to the document signed as his will. However, a will cannot be validated by the signature of witnesses which is inserted later in time after the testator's signature was made or which is underneath or follows the signature in space unless it can be proven that the lines appearing thereunder were written before the signature was made.

In *St. Vincent & the Grenadines* the testator's signature need not appear at the end of the will in order to validate the entire will. The only statutory requirements are that it should appear the testator intended his signature to give effect to this will and that his signature was placed there after the will was written.

With respect to the competency of witnesses to a will, it should be noted that in *St. Lucia*, the witnesses to a non-notarial will are required to be full age, one of whom must also be a justice of the peace.

In *Barbados, St. Vincent & the Grenadines and Trinidad & Tobago* statutory wills may be made. The provisions of the respective mental health legislation of these territories empower the High Court *inter alia* to make an order authorizing a person to execute a will for a mental patient.

With regard to *privileged wills*, such wills are valid in *all the Caribbean territories, save Trinidad & Tobago and Jamaica*. Such a will may be completely oral or completely written, and if written it need not be signed nor witnessed. Privileged wills are available to limited classes of testators, namely soldiers in actual military service and mariners and seamen at sea. These testators need not attain the age of majority in order to validly execute a privileged will. However, there must be evidence that the document or declaration was intended by the testator to be of testamentary character.

Holographic wills are valid only in *Barbados and St. Lucia*. With respect to *Barbados*, a holographic will need not be signed by the testator nor by the witnesses. However, with respect to *St. Lucia*, these wills must be signed by the testator although they need not be witnessed.

Notarial wills are applicable to *St. Lucia* only and are in the form of a notarial document received either before two notaries or one notary and two witnesses. In accordance with the relevant articles of the Civil Code, the testator must sign the will in the presence of the witnesses, or declare that he cannot do so after it has been read to him by one of the notaries in the presence of the other or by the notary in the presence of the witnesses. The witnesses must then sign their names to the will in the presence of the testator and each other. Each witness must be named and described in the will and the place and date of execution must also be stated.

International wills are applicable to *Barbados* only, and are made in compliance with the *1973 Washington Convention on International Wills* which provides for a uniform law in the form of an international will. With respect to formalities, such wills must be written and read to the testator in the presence of two witnesses and executed in the presence of an authorized person who is appointed by the Minister of Legal Affairs. The appointee must be an attorney-at-law and is required to prepare and sign a certificate of verification to the effect that the requisite formalities have been complied with.

(b) *i.* Alterations may be made in a will prior to execution or after execution of the testamentary instrument. In the former case, execution of the alterations is unnecessary and the will takes effect as altered.

Alterations made after execution are only admitted to proof if executed according to the manner prescribed by the relevant statute, namely by re-execution of the entire will in the manner prescribed for the making of a will or by execution of the individual alterations in accordance with the relevant statutory provision of the respective territory.

In *all the Caribbean jurisdictions* considered in this chapter, a will may be revoked by a will, codicil or other attested document evincing an intention to revoke the same.

With the *exception of St. Lucia*, the statute provides that revocation of a will by destruction may be effected by burning, tearing or otherwise destroying the will either by the testator or by someone in his presence and acting by his direction. In *St. Lucia* the statute provides that wills and legacies may be revoked by means of destruction, tearing or erasure of a non-notarial will deliberately effected by the testator or by his order. Further, where the act of destruction of a will is effected by someone other than the testator, there is no statutory requirement that it be done in the testator's presence.

In *St. Lucia* the relevant articles of the Civil Code provide that a will or legacy may also be revoked on the grounds of conspiracy of the legatee in the death of the testator or by reason of grievous injury done to the testator's memory.

ii. As a general rule, *in all the jurisdictions*, marriage automatically revokes a will made by either party to the marriage prior to the marriage. However in *Barbados and Trinidad & Tobago*, where a will is expressed to be made in contemplation of marriage, such will is not revoked by the subsequent marriage of the testator.

In *St. Vincent & the Grenadines* a will made in expectation of marriage is not revoked by the subsequent marriage of the testator if it appears from the will that at the time it was made the testator was expecting to be married to a particular person and intended that a disposition in the will should not be revoked by his marriage to that person.

In *Anguilla, Antigua & Barbuda, Dominica, Montserrat, St. Christopher & Nevis, St. Lucia and Trinidad & Tobago*, a will made prior to the solemnization of a death-bed marriage or marriage in extremis is not revoked by such a marriage.

In *St. Lucia and St. Vincent & the Grenadines*, where, after a testator has made a will, a decree of the court dissolves or annuls that marriage or declares it void, the will, including any disposition made thereunder, takes effect unless it appears from the will that the testator intended any disposition therein to be revoked by the divorce or annulment.

iii. In *all the territories*, republication of a will may be effected either by re-execution of the original will or by making a duly executed codicil to the will containing some reference to the will.

With the *exception of St. Lucia*, the relevant statute provides that the revival or the restoration to effect of a will or codicil which has been revoked can only be effective if there is evidence of intention to revive. The requirement for evidence of such intention may be satisfied by express words referring to the revoked will and indicating the intention to revive same or disposition of the testator's property inconsistent with any other intention or by some other expression which clearly evinces that intention.

In *St. Lucia*, in the absence of statutory provisions governing the method of effecting revival of a revoked testamentary document, the pre-statutory position applies and a will may therefore be revived by implication. Further, unlike the other territories, a former will may be revived by revocation of a later will.

3. Intestacy

(a) Although the persons entitled to inherit the residuary estate of an intestate vary somewhat from jurisdiction to jurisdiction, as a general rule the surviving spouse and issue of the intestate are the primary beneficiaries of the estate. However, because of the sheer volume of material, it is impossible in this chapter to examine the statutory provisions on distribution for the various territories in any detail. Therefore only the general provisions governing distribution upon intestacy of a deceased person's estate in the various Caribbean territories will be considered.

The Bahamas: According to the provisions of the relevant acts, which are based on the pre-1925 English inheritance laws, the surviving husband is as a general rule entitled to the entire personal estate of his wife while the surviving widow is entitled only to a share of one-third with the remainder to the issue or next of kin. If there is no surviving spouse then the children are entitled in equal shares or grand-children or great grand-children sharing *per stirpes*. In the event that the intestate leaves neither spouse nor issue, the intestate's father and mother are entitled in equal shares to the personal estate. If the intestate leaves no spouse, issue or parent, his brothers and sisters are entitled in equal shares to the personal estate.

The residuary realty of the intestate passes to the heir-at-law by virtue of the common law doctrine of descent.

Barbados: According to the statute, if an intestate dies leaving:

- a spouse and no issue or next of kin, the spouse takes the whole estate;
- a spouse and no issue but next of kin, then the spouse shall take two-thirds of the estate, the remainder to be distributed in equal shares among the next-of-kin;
- a spouse and one child, the spouse takes two-thirds and the remainder to the child;

- a spouse and children, the spouse shall take one-third and the remainder to the children;
- neither spouse nor issue, the residuary estate is divided between the mother and father in equal shares if both survive, but if only one survives, the survivor takes the whole estate;
- neither spouse, issue nor parent, the whole estate is divided between the brothers and sisters in equal shares.

Anguilla, Antigua & Barbuda, Dominica, Montserrat and St. Christopher & Nevis: The residuary personal and real estate of an intestate is distributed or held on trust *inter alia* in the following manner:

- if the intestate leaves a husband or wife, the surviving spouse shall take personal chattels absolutely;
- the residuary estate (other than the personal chattels) shall be held:
  - if the intestate leaves no issue, upon trust for the surviving spouse for life;
  - if the intestate leaves issue, upon trust as to one-half for the surviving spouse for life and subject to such life interest, on the statutory trusts for the issue of the intestate and the other half in the statutory trusts for the issue of the intestate;
  - if the intestate leaves no issue or surviving spouse, upon trust for the intestate's mother and father in equal shares, but if one survives, the survivor takes the whole estate upon trust;
  - if the intestate leaves no spouse, issue or parent, upon trust for the intestate's brothers and sisters in equal shares.

Grenada: According to the statute, if the intestate leaves:

- a surviving spouse but no issue, the surviving spouse is entitled to one-half of the intestate's estate and the remainder devolves in order of priority to the persons being next of kin of the intestate;
- a surviving spouse and issue, the surviving spouse is entitled to one-half absolutely and the issue to the remaining half in equal shares;
- issue but no surviving spouse, the issue is entitled to the whole estate in equal shares;
- no surviving spouse or issue, then the father and mother are entitled to the whole estate in equal shares;
- no spouse, issue or parent, the brothers and sisters are entitled to the whole estate in equal shares.

It should also be noted that the statute further provides that the surviving spouse may apply to the court for a variation order so as to increase his share of the intestate's estate. This is provided that he can prove to the satisfaction of the court, on a balance of probabilities, that he contributed whether directly or indirectly to the intestate's estate to such a degree that he should be entitled to more than his statutory share of the intestate's estate.

Guyana: The surviving spouse is entitled to one-third of the intestate's residuary estate and the remainder is distributed in equal parts to the children of the intestate; if any of the children are dead, to their descendants *per stirpes*. In the event that the intestate leaves no children or descendants, then one-half to the surviving spouse, the remainder to those persons being next of kin of the intestate. Such persons include, in order of priority: the mother, father, great-grandmother and great-grandfather of the intestate.

Jamaica: The relevant statute provides that:

- the surviving spouse takes:
  - the personal chattels absolutely;
  - $10,000 or a sum equal to 10 per cent of the net value of the estate;
  - two-thirds of the residuary estate absolutely if there is only one issue;
  - one-half if more than one issue;
  - if no child or other issue, but parent or parents, two-thirds of the residue absolutely.

- if the intestate leaves no surviving spouse, the intestate's residuary estate is held upon statutory trust for the issue of the intestate;
- if the intestate leaves no surviving spouse or issue, the mother and father are entitled in equal shares to the residuary estate absolutely but if only one parent survives, the survivor takes the whole estate absolutely;
- if the intestate leaves no surviving spouse, issue or parent, the intestate's residuary estate is held upon trust for the brothers and sisters in equal shares.

St. Lucia: The persons entitled to the intestate's residuary estate are the spouse capable of inheriting, children and descendants and collateral relations within the stipulated order of priority.

In general, if the deceased leaves:

- a spouse capable of inheriting and issue, the surviving spouse takes one-third and the child/children take the remainder in equal shares;
- no issue but leaves a spouse capable of inheriting and a father and mother or either of them and collateral relations up to nieces or nephews in the first degree inclusive, the surviving spouse takes one-third; the father and mother or the one surviving takes one-third, and the collateral relations *mentioned above* one-third;
- neither spouse capable of inheriting nor issue, the mother and father or the one surviving takes one-half, and the collateral relations as *mentioned above*, the other half.

In order to qualify as a spouse capable of inheriting a surviving wife must abandon all her rights to community of property, that is all property acquired after marriage, which may have existed between the deceased and herself, as well as rights of survivorship accruing to her under her contract of marriage. Similarly, for the husband to succeed to his wife's estate he must first transfer to his deceased wife's estate his share in any community of property which may have existed as well as any rights conferred on him by any marriage contract.

Community of property is placed under the exclusive management of the husband and on the death of either spouse the survivor is entitled to a vested interest in one-half of the assets comprising the property held in community. The remainder is distributed in equal shares amongst the children, if any, of the intestate as next of kin.

A surviving spouse may renounce within the time stipulated his/her right to community property and thus qualify as a spouse capable of inheriting. In such cases the spouse is entitled *inter alia* to:

- one-third and a child/children to the remaining two-thirds in equal shares;
- one-half if the deceased dies leaving no issue; the other half to the father and mother in equal shares or to the one surviving.

Where the surviving spouse elects to retain the property held in community, the heirs of the deceased spouse are entitled to a share in all profits made and income earned from such property.

St. Vincent & the Grenadines: If the intestate leaves:

- a surviving spouse but no issue, then one-half to the surviving spouse, the remainder to the next of kin of the intestate being in order of priority, the mother and father of the intestate, the brothers and sisters of the whole blood;
- a surviving spouse and issue, then one-third to the surviving spouse and the remaining two-thirds to the issue of the intestate;
- issue but no surviving spouse, the issue is entitled to the whole estate in equal shares;
- neither spouse nor issue, the father and mother are entitled to the whole estate in equal shares but if one of them survives, the survivor takes the whole estate;
- no spouse, issue or parent, the brothers and sisters are entitled to the whole estate in equal shares.

Trinidad & Tobago: The persons beneficially entitled to the intestate's estate in order of priority are:

- if there is no lawful issue, the surviving spouse;
- if there is lawful issue, one-third thereof to the surviving spouse and the remainder to the lawful issue of the deceased;
- in the absence of lawful issue and surviving spouse, then to the persons being of kin who would be entitled to the personal estate of the intestate by the law of England at that time. Such persons in order of priority include the father of the intestate who is entitled to the whole estate absolutely and where the father predeceases the intestate, the mother together with brothers and sisters are next entitled to the whole estate in equal shares.

It is to be noted that in *all the jurisdictions save Barbados and Jamaica* a *common-law spouse* has no rights of inheritance upon an intestacy.

In *Barbados* a *spouse* may be excluded from succeeding to the deceased's spouse estate where he is a spouse against whom the deceased obtained a judicial order of separation or where the surviving spouse failed to comply with a decree of restitution of conjugal rights obtained by the deceased or was guilty of desertion which desertion has continued up to the death for three years or more.

In *St. Lucia* spouses married in community who do not renounce their rights with respect thereto obtain a vested interest in half of the property held in community of property and are by such election excluded from succeeding to the intestate's estate.

In *Grenada and St. Vincent & the Grenadines* for the purpose of devolution on intestacy, the surviving spouse is deemed to have predeceased the intestate while a decree of separation is in force and the separation continues and in *Trinidad & Tobago*, judicially separated spouses are not entitled to claims in intestacy with respect to each other.

With the *exception of the Bahamas*, a *child* born out of wedlock to an intestate father has the same rights of inheritance on an intestacy as a legitimate child with effect from the date of commencement of the relevant legislation on the status of children or its equivalent in each of the territories.

In *Barbados, Dominica, Grenada, Guyana, Jamaica, St. Lucia, St. Vincent & the Grenadines, the Bahamas and Trinidad & Tobago* for the purposes of inheritance upon an intestacy, at or after the making of an adoption order on the death intestate of the adoptee, the estate of the deceased devolves in all respects on the adopted child as if that child was born of the adoptee. This rule applies to the estate of an intestate dying after the commencement date of the respective legislation of each jurisdiction.

In *Anguilla, Antigua & Barbuda, Montserrat and St. Christopher & Nevis* an adopted child is entitled only to a share in the estate of his natural parents and not the adoptee parents, whether or not the adoptee parent dies before or after the making of the adoption order. For further information as to whom would be considered a 'child' *see* 4.

(b) With the *exception of the Bahamas*, there is no difference between the devolution of movable and immovable assets in any of the Caribbean territories. In *the Bahamas* an intestate's movable assets devolve on the next of kin in accordance with the prescribed statutory order of priority, while the immovable assets devolve on the heir-at-law in accordance with the common law doctrine of descent.

4. Freedom of Testation

(a) With the *exception of Barbados, Guyana, Jamaica and Trinidad & Tobago*, a testator has complete freedom of testamentary disposition. With respect to these territories, qualifying members of the deceased's family circle have the statutory right to apply to the court for financial provision out of the deceased's estate.

However, the persons entitled to apply to the court for financial provision out of the deceased's estate vary among the jurisdictions.

International Succession

In *Guyana and Jamaica* a person who qualifies as a common law spouse, within the guidelines prescribed by the statute, may apply for reasonable provision out of the deceased's estate. Such entitlement is not limited to maintenance.

With respect to *Barbados*, it is to be noted that a spouse (including a common law or statutory spouse) is not a qualifying member of the deceased's family circle.

In *Barbados, Guyana, Jamaica and Trinidad & Tobago* a son or daughter of the deceased includes one that is legally adopted by the deceased, born out of wedlock to the deceased and *en ventre de sa mère*. There are however distinctions in each territory regarding the definition of a 'child'. In *Barbados* a minor child or a child incapable of maintaining himself by reason of mental or physical disability (until cesser of the disability) may apply for reasonable provision. In cases of intestacy, these classes of persons also qualify as statutory dependents but with respect to the incapable child, he must have been maintained by or living with the deceased person at the date of his death. Further, these classes only qualify as dependents if the laws relating to intestacy do not make provision for them.

In *Guyana* a child of the deceased includes any child of the deceased irrespective of age, mental or physical incapacity as well as any person, not being a child of the deceased, who was treated as a child of the family.

In *Jamaica* a child of the deceased means a child under the age of eighteen years and includes a child of the deceased's husband or wife, as the case may be, who has been accepted as one of the family by the deceased. However, a child either of or over the age of eighteen years may be regarded as a child if under the age of twenty-three years and pursuing academic studies or receiving trade/professional training, or if there are special circumstances which justify the disregard of the age limit.

In Jamaica apart from the deceased's spouse and children, a parent, including a person who stands in *loco parentis* to the deceased and who was maintained, wholly or partly, or legally entitled to such maintenance by the deceased, qualifies as an applicant for financial provision.

In *Guyana* any person who immediately prior to the death of the deceased was either wholly or partially maintained by him may apply for provision.

(b) *i.* As is the position in England, a contract of inheritance may be validly made but the only remedy available to a disappointed beneficiary in the event that he fails to receive the benefit of the gift which the testator contracted to leave to him, is to bring an action against the deceased's estate for damages for breach of contract. Should the estate prove insufficient to meet the disappointed beneficiary's claim, he will have no further remedy against the estate.

ii. Mutual wills are applicable to all the Caribbean territories. In order to establish a mutual will it must be shown that the will of both parties thereto (usually husband and wife) was made pursuant to an agreement by each of them not to revoke his or her respective will. Although such wills are revocable, in the event of the unilateral revocation by one of the parties thereto whilst both are still alive, the aggrieved party may bring an action for breach of contract. In instances where the first-to-die dies with his mutual will unrevoked and he has no knowledge of any revocation by the survivor, his estate may bring an action for breach of trust against the survivor or his personal representative as upon the death of the first to die, the court imposes a trust on the property which is deemed to be the subject matter of the mutual will.

5. Maintenance

See 4 *above.*

6. Community Property Between Husband and Wife

Community of property is applicable only to *St. Lucia* (*See* 3, *St. Lucia*). However, as is the case in England, if community of property is recognized by the matrimonial domicile of the deceased, the indigenous laws of the various Caribbean territories will treat only that part of the deceased's estate which is not part of the community of property, as forming part of the deceased's estate.

7. Gifts (*Inter Vivos*)

(a) Unless expressly stated in the will, a gift made to a beneficiary prior to the death of the deceased will not be set off against the beneficiary's entitlement under the will.

(b) Not applicable.

8. Capacity

(a) Apart from privileged wills, a testator is required to be of full age in order to make a valid will (which is eighteen years in all the territories *except Anguilla* where the age of majority is still twenty-one years). In all the jurisdictions, irrespective of the type of will, a testator is required to be of sound mind at the time of execution of his will. The term 'sound mind' is interpreted in case law to mean that the testator must understand the nature of his assets and the persons who are to be the objects of his bounty. The fact that the testator suffers from insane delusion will not preclude him from making a valid will provided that the delusion remains latent at the time of execution of the will and the delusion bears no connection with the dispositions in the will. A will may also be validly made by a testator who is generally insane, but experiences a lucid interval at the time of execution of the will.

In *Barbados, St. Vincent & the Grenadines and Trinidad & Tobago*, a will may be made for a mental patient by some person so authorized by order of the High Court. Apart from the usual formalities required for making a valid will, such wills must be sealed by the court.

(b) With the exception of *St. Lucia and Guyana*, a child who possesses the requisite competence to give evidence may be a competent witness to the execution of a will.

675

In *St. Lucia* according to the relevant article of the Civil Code the witnesses are required to be of full age (eighteen years). In *Guyana* the relevant statute provides that persons above the age of fourteen years who are competent to give evidence in any court of law are competent and qualified to attest to the execution of a will.

(c) An unborn child (subsequently born alive) may inherit. Apart from in *the Bahamas*, there is no distinction between legitimate and illegitimate children.

9. Authority (Court, Notarial or Other)

In order to obtain legal title to the estate of the deceased, it is first necessary to obtain the relevant grant of representation from the High Court. With respect to common form applications, such applications are made to and granted by the respective Registrar of the High Court of the various territories, save and except in *Guyana* where the grant is issued by the Registrar subject to an order of the Chief Justice, and in *the Bahamas* where the grant is made and issued by the Chief Justice. Where there is contention with respect to the validity of a will, the application is required to be made to the High Court 'in solemn form'.

With the *exception of Trinidad & Tobago*, an executor derives his authority to act from the will and the grant of probate is mere authentication of his authority although the grant will be necessary where the executor is required to prove title. In *Trinidad & Tobago*, statute provides that an executor derives his title from the court. With respect to an administrator (either in cases of intestacy or in cases where no executor is appointed or is unwilling or unable to act), the appointment of the administrator is made by the court in all the jurisdictions.

10. Invalidity of Will

(a)–(b) A will which fails to comply with the relevant statutory formalities of the various territories, as outlined in 2(a) *above*, or which has been executed by a testator who lacks the requisite testamentary capacity shall be deemed void. The presence of coercion, fraud or undue influence at the time of execution will render a will void.

With respect to *Trinidad & Tobago, Jamaica, Barbados and Guyana*, a will which is invalid may nevertheless be used in support of a claim for reasonable provision out of the deceased's estate. *See 4 above.*

11. Simultaneous Death

(a)–(b) *Common law position: Barbados, Guyana and Trinidad & Tobago*:

Where persons who are in immediate succession to each other, whether on a testacy or an intestacy, die in circumstances in which it is uncertain which of them died first and the evidence fails to establish the survivorship of either of them, each would be presumed to have predeceased the other, and the grant of the estate of each of them is made on that basis.

In cases of testacy, however, a testator may by his will make express provision for the disposition of his estate which may effectively exclude the operation of this doctrine.

Statutory position: *Anguilla, Antigua & Barbuda, Dominica, Jamaica, Montserrat, St. Christopher & Nevis, St. Vincent & the Grenadines and the Bahamas*:
In the *above-mentioned* territories, there is a statutory presumption in cases of simultaneous death of persons in immediate succession to each other that the parties have died in order of seniority; that is, the younger is presumed to have survived the other.

However with respect to *Anguilla, Antigua & Barbuda, Dominica, Montserrat, St. Christopher & Nevis and St. Vincent & the Grenadines*, this statutory presumption is excluded in the case of the intestacy, partial or total, of an elder spouse irrespective of whether the younger spouse died testate or intestate.

St. Lucia: In all cases where it is impossible to ascertain the order of survivorship, the presumption of survivorship is determined by the circumstances and in the absence thereof, by, *inter alia*, the following rules:

- where those who perished were under fifteen years of age, the eldest is presumed to have survived;
- if those who perished together were all between the full ages of fifteen and sixty, and of the same sex, the order of nature is followed, according to which the youngest is presumed to survive; and where they were of different sexes, the male is always presumed to have survived.

12. Estate Taxes

To date, in *all of the Caribbean territories*, estate taxes or death duties have either been abolished or as in the case of Guyana and Jamaica have been repealed and replaced by another form of tax. In *Guyana* a process fee based on the value of the deceased's estate is payable prior to the issue of the relevant grant. In *Jamaica*, a transfer fee, which is similar to English inheritance tax, is payable on the real property of the deceased. This tax is payable after the grant has been obtained and is necessary to effect a transfer or conveyance of the deceased's real property to the beneficiary concerned.

13. Administration of Estates

The administration of estates is carried out by personal representatives (executors or administrators) who may be appointed by the deceased's will or by the court.

(a) The powers and duties of executors and administrators with respect to administration of estates include ascertaining and collecting the assets of the deceased, managing the deceased's assets during administration, paying all debts and liabilities of the administration and of the estate and distributing the residue of the estate of the deceased to the person(s) entitled.

(b) The personal representative is required to file an inventory or its equivalent with the application for the relevant grant of representation. This inventory which sets out the value and extent of the deceased's estate is essentially used for the purpose of calculating the attorney-at-law's fees. The value of the estate as stated in the inventory is also recorded in the relevant grant. However with the abolition of estate taxes in all territories except Guyana and Jamaica, the value of the estate as stated in the inventory is no longer used for the purposes of determining tax liability. *See* 12 *above.*

(c) The executor or administrator is not required to give an account of his administration of the deceased's estate unless called upon the court to do so.

(d) Any beneficiary who wishes to challenge the administration of the estate by the personal representative may apply to court to object.

(e) Upon the payment of all debts of the estate, the personal assets of the deceased are distributed to the beneficiaries, usually in an informal manner. However, with respect to real property, a deed of assent duly registered is necessary to effect a transfer from the personal representative to the beneficiary or beneficiaries, of whom he may be one.

(f) The estate creditors are paid out of the residuary estate of the deceased. However with the *exception of Anguilla, Antigua & Barbuda, Dominica, Montserrat and St. Christopher & Nevis*, there is no legal requirement, as in England, to convert the deceased's assets into cash for the purpose of paying the debts of the estate. Assets are only realized where there is insufficient cash available to pay the debts of the estate.

(g) Where no executor is appointed by the testator or the executor appointed is unwilling or unable to act, an administrator is required to be appointed by the court in accordance with a clearly defined order of priority. The grant in such instances is a grant of letters of administration with will annexed.

14. Domicile/Nationality

(a) With respect to the devolution of the immovable property of the deceased, the applicable law is the *lex situs* and devolution of movable property is governed by the law of the deceased's domicile at the date of death.

(b) The courts of the various Caribbean territories are authorized to issue nil grants, that is, grants where the deceased left no assets in the relevant Caribbean territory. Although there are no judicial pronouncements on this matter, the courts in the

Caribbean territories, in practice, adopt the English position and are reluctant to issue such grants, unless necessary for the purposes of bringing or defending an action against the deceased's estate within the relevant Caribbean territory.

SECTION B – APPLICABLE LAW/PROCEDURE WHERE FOREIGN ELEMENT/S ARE INVOLVED

1. Jurisdiction

(a) Before obtaining legal title to the assets of a deceased person, whether movable or immovable, a grant of Probate or Letters of Administration is required. In this regard, the courts of the various Caribbean territories have jurisdiction over the deceased's assets, movable or immovable, which are located within the territory, irrespective of the deceased's domicile at the date of death.

(b) While the law with respect to the devolution of movable and immovable assets may vary among the territories, for the purpose of obtaining a grant of Probate or Letters of Administration, the rules or requirements are the same whether the deceased's assets are movable or immovable.

(c) Applications for grants of Probate or Letters of Administration are made in all cases to the Registry of the High Court of the various Caribbean territories except in the case of *Trinidad & Tobago* where these applications may be made to the Sub-Registry in Tobago, provided the deceased died resident in that island and in *Jamaica*, where the deceased's estate is valued at Jamaican $500,000 or less. In such instances, the application for the grant may be made to the Magistrate's Court in the district in which the deceased died resident.

In *all the territories* where there is contention as to the validity of the deceased's will, a probate action will have to be commenced in the High Court. It is to be noted that in all the territories, there is no division of the High Court, as in England, in which applications for a grant may be made nor is there any division of the High Court in which contentious proceedings are brought.

2. Applicable Law

Please *see* Section A14 *above*.

3. Foreign Succession/Inheritance Orders

(a)–(c) Where a deceased has left assets to be administered within more than one probate jurisdiction, an application may be made to reseal the grant of representation or to obtain an ancillary grant of representation before title can be had in the assets of the deceased.

679

International Succession

Most of the Caribbean territories limit the probate jurisdictions from which resealing applications can be made. While most territories restrict such applications to grants of representation issuing out of Britain, the Commonwealth or colonial grants, some territories such as *the Bahamas and Antigua and Barbuda* allow resealing applications to be made with respect to grants issuing out of the United States of America, and in the case of *Barbados*, any part of the world.

With respect to applications for the resealing of grants of representation, notice of intention to apply for resealing is first published or advertised for a specified period. Once the relevant period has expired, an application *ex parte* to the Registrar of the High Court in the respective territories is made. Among the documents which are filed with this application are a duly certified copy of the grant together with an office copy of the will, if any. Where the application is made by an attorney, a duly registered power of attorney must also be filed. Additionally the domicile of the deceased must be established by affidavit. Where there is a will, an affidavit as to foreign law is not required.

Where the procedure for the resealing of grants cannot be invoked, an application may be made to obtain an ancillary grant of representation.

According to the respective non-contentious probate rules of the various territories, persons entrusted by the court of domicile, persons beneficially entitled by the law of domicile, or persons chosen by the discretionary powers of the court may, depending on the circumstances, apply for and obtain an ancillary grant of the deceased's estate.

With respect to the admissibility to proof of testamentary dispositions made under the will of a deceased who has died domiciled outside the jurisdiction in which an application for an ancillary grant with respect to his estate is made, it will depend on whether the common law or statutory position applies to the respective Caribbean territory. In *Guyana and Jamaica*, in accordance with the common law, a will is valid to pass movable estate if executed in accordance with the laws of the testator's last place of domicile, and in *Guyana, Jamaica and Trinidad & Tobago*, with respect to immovable estate, if executed in accordance with the law of the country where the real property is situated.

In *Trinidad & Tobago*, a will is deemed to have been validly executed with respect to movables where it was executed in accordance with the law of the place where it was made or where it is valid by the law of the place where the testator was domiciled at the time of execution or by the law in force in a Commonwealth territory where the testator was domiciled. Where the testator is not a Commonwealth citizen, the common law position applies.

In *the Bahamas and Eastern Caribbean territories*, a will is treated as properly executed with respect to real and personal property, irrespective of the date of the will, domicile or residence of the testator provided that it is executed in accordance with the domestic law in force in the territory where it was executed, or in the territory where at the time of execution or death the testator was domiciled or had his habitual residence or was a national.

Further, a will is deemed to be properly executed in these territories if executed on board a vessel or aircraft where such execution conforms to the law in force in the territory with which, having regard to its registration and any other relevant circumstances, the vessel or aircraft may have been most closely connected or where it disposes of immovable estate provided its execution conforms to the internal law in force in the territory where the property is situated.

The relevant statutory provision in *Barbados* is effectively the same as that which obtains in the Eastern Caribbean territories.

In all jurisdictions, save Guyana, Jamaica and Trinidad & Tobago, where the will of the deceased has been proved by a court of competent jurisdiction in the deceased's place of domicile, it will be accepted as properly executed without the need to file an affidavit as to foreign law.

However, in *Guyana, Jamaica and Trinidad & Tobago* a notary public certificate/affidavit as to foreign law is necessary to give effect to dispositions of the deceased's personal estate. With respect to the admissibility to proof of dispositions of real estate, the equivalent of an affidavit of due execution is required.

4. Two or More Succession or Probate Orders

By virtue of the probate rules of the various territories a grant of representation may be issued to the person entrusted with the administration of the estate by the court having jurisdiction at the place where the deceased died domiciled. The foreign order by which administration of the estate was conferred upon such person entitles him to apply for a grant within the relevant Caribbean territory.

5. Assets

Please *see* Section A14(b) *above*.

6. Expert Evidence

(a) Where a person has died domiciled outside the jurisdiction of the respective Caribbean territory in which a grant with respect to his estate is sought, an affidavit as to foreign law may have to be filed with the application in order for the will to be admitted to proof and thereby give validity to the testamentary dispositions made thereunder.

The affidavit in such instances is required to be deposed to by an attorney-at-law or some other person suitably qualified to give expert evidence to the effect that the will was executed in accordance with the law of the foreign country concerned. In addition, the affidavit should deal with the applicant's entitlement to administer the deceased's estate.

For purposes of authentication, the affidavit must be sworn to before a person duly authorized to administer oaths in the respective Caribbean territories. These persons include a commissioner of oaths, notary public, a justice of the peace, a consular or diplomatic agent, or a judge of a superior court.

(b) Except in instances where the application for the grant is being made in 'solemn form', an affidavit as to foreign law will suffice and there will be no need for any foreign expert to appear and give evidence in court. However, with respect to probate actions, or solemn form applications, *viva voce* evidence is required unless waived by the court.

7. Unity of Succession

Please *see* Section A14(a).

8. Formalities

In *Guyana, Jamaica and Trinidad & Tobago*, with respect to immovables, a will is deemed to be validly executed in these territories if executed in accordance with the law of the country where the real property is situated. In *Guyana and Jamaica*, insofar as movables are concerned, a will is treated as valid if executed in accordance with the laws of the testator's last place of domicile. However, in *Trinidad & Tobago* with respect to movables, a will executed by a Commonwealth citizen is valid if executed in accordance with, *inter alia*, the law of the place where it was made.

With respect to the *other Caribbean territories*, a will is deemed to be valid if executed in accordance with the provisions of the *Wills Act 1963*, England or its equivalent thereto.

9. Legislation

By virtue of the adoption of English legislation, the *1961 Hague Convention on the Conflicts of Laws on the Form of Testamentary Dispositions* is applicable to *all the Caribbean territories* considered in this chapter save and except *Jamaica, Guyana and Trinidad & Tobago*, where the common law position still applies.

10. Wills

Where conflict of laws arise with respect to wills, the following should be noted:

(a) The legal requirements for the execution of a will vary according to the nature of the asset. Accordingly a disposition of immovables within the particular territory must be valid according to the *lex situs* while the law of the deceased's domicile at death governs movables.

(b) With respect to construction of wills, the courts will give effect to the testator's true meaning, domicile not necessarily being the dominant factor. It should be noted, however, that in the absence of a contrary intention, there is a presumption that the testator intended his will to be construed according to the law of his domicile at the time of execution of the will.

(c) The law governing devolution of assets will also determine the rights of heirs and beneficiaries. Thus, the law of the deceased's domicile at the time of death governs movable assets while the *lex situs* governs immovables.

(d) Similarly, the considerations outlined in (c) *above* apply to capacity to inherit, with capacity to inherit movables depending on the law of the deceased's domicile at death and capacity to inherit immovables on the *lex situs*.

(e) Capacity to make a will of movables is subject to the law of the deceased's domicile; it is submitted that the *lex situs* governs capacity to dispose of immovable assets although no decisive authority on this latter point has been pronounced.

(f) Accordingly, the validity of a will is to be determined by the law which governs the disposition of the particular asset.

(g) The capacity and exercise of a power of appointment which purports to deal with movables depends on the law of the testator's domicile at the time such power was created. Capacity to exercise this power over immovables depends on the *lex situs*.

(h) Revocation, other than by subsequent will, is dealt with according to the law of domicile at the time of revocation. However, the law by which the will was executed applies to amendment, revocation by execution of a subsequent will and revival of wills.

(i) With respect to *Guyana, Jamaica, Trinidad & Tobago and Barbados*, (*see* Section A4), inheritance provisions only apply where the deceased died domiciled within these respective territories.

11. Domicile/Nationality

(a) As a general rule the devolution of an estate is dealt with according to the deceased's domicile at the date of death. With respect to the admissibility of wills, a will may be valid where executed in compliance with the legal requirements of the various territories. However, where capacity to execute a will or capacity to exercise a power under the will or validity of revocation is concerned, domicile at the date of the purported act is relevant.

(b) The domicile of a beneficiary is of no relevance.

(c) In accordance with the respective laws of the various Caribbean territories, a deceased acquires a domicile of origin at birth, which if he is legitimate, is the domicile of the father, and if illegitimate, the domicile of the mother.
    A person may also acquire a domicile of choice when he reaches the age of sixteen years by, *inter alia*, being physically present in the relevant territory and establishing an intention to reside there either permanently or indefinitely.

International Succession

A person may also acquire a domicile of dependency until the age of sixteen years should the domicile of the parent change during that period.

12. Taxation

With the exception of *Jamaica*, a tax in respect of the transfer of the deceased's estate to the respective beneficiaries is not payable. However, in *Jamaica*, the transfer tax which is payable is with respect to the transfers made and, accordingly, it is the domicile of the deceased, rather than that of the beneficiaries, which is relevant.